lonely planet



# Estonia, Latvia & Lithuania

Anna Kaminski, Hugh McNaughtan, Ryan Ver Berkmoes

## PLAN YOUR TRIP



## ON THE ROAD

SARAH COGHILL/LONELY PLANET ©

BARTENDER AT LABIETIS (P223), RĪGA, LATVIA

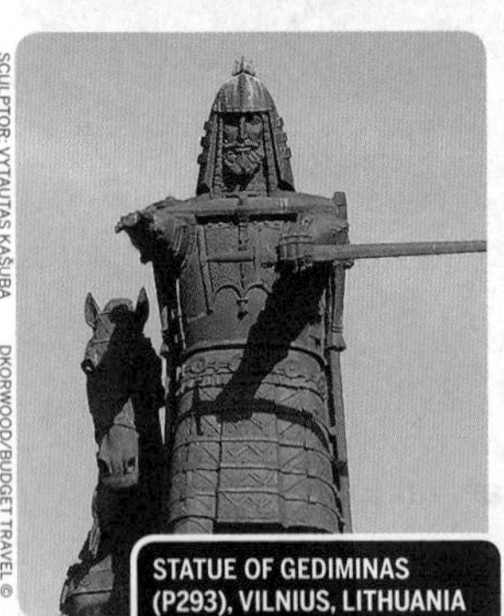

SCULPTOR: VYTAUTAS KAŠUBA DKORWOOD/BUDGET TRAVEL ©

STATUE OF GEDIMINAS (P293), VILNIUS, LITHUANIA

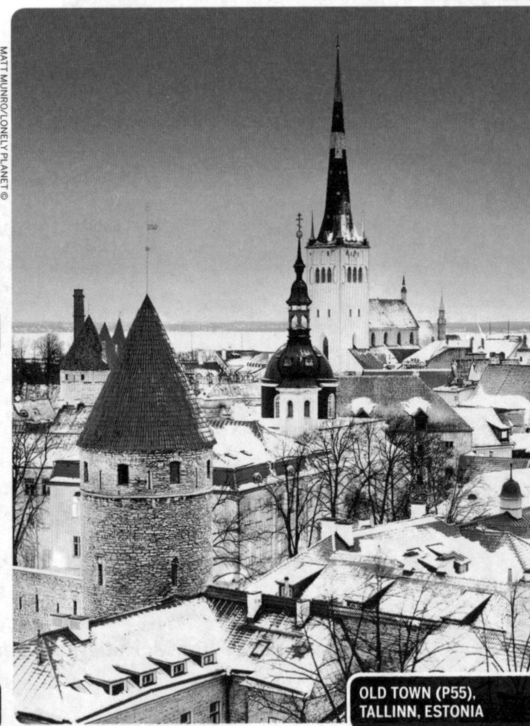

MATT MUNRO/LONELY PLANET ©

OLD TOWN (P55), TALLINN, ESTONIA

# Contents

# Welcome to Estonia, Latvia & Lithuania

*A land of crumbling castles, soaring dunes, enchanting forests and shimmering lakes – a trip to the Baltics proves that fairy tales do come true.*

## Teensy but Diverse

Estonia, Latvia and Lithuania are tiny. Yet in this wonderfully compact space there are three distinct cultures – with different languages, traditions and temperaments. Take, for example, the three unique yet equally compelling capitals: flamboyantly baroque Vilnius, chic art-nouveau Rīga and majestically medieval Tallinn. Or explore their traditional and contemporary art scenes – from the carving of crosses in Lithuania to the latest gallery installations across the Baltics. When it comes to cultural mileage, the Baltic is a fuel-efficient destination.

## Cold War Comrades

For all their differences, the Baltic States suffered the slings and arrows of 20th-century misfortune together. And when the time came, they answered the 'to be or not to be' question hand in hand, singing loudly in the affirmative. Visitors will encounter many heartbreaking and horrifying reminders of the Nazi and Soviet occupations, including numerous war relics, mass-grave memorials and excellent social-history museums. Meantime, distinctive Stalinist architecture and striking socialist-realist art continue to fascinate. And doesn't everyone love a happy ending?

## Super Nature

Endless sandy beaches, a multitude of lakes, large tracts of forest and wildlife-rich wetlands: the Baltic States may be flat, but they don't lack natural appeal. Best of all, the relatively low population density means there's plenty to go around. Many of Europe's large mammals linger in quiet corners, although the wolves, bears, elks and lynx know better than to mug for tourist snapshots. You're more likely to see white storks in their bathtub-sized nests balanced on lamp posts or the odd startled deer scampering along the roadside.

## Magic in the Air

From Tallinn's storybook turrets to the ghostly ruins of Latvia's Ludza Castle, romantic adults and spellbound children will find plenty of intrigue in this ancient and alluring landscape. Folk tales abound of holy lakes, magic springs and the witches and goblins that inhabit the darkest forests and most treacherous bogs. This was the last corner of Europe to be Christianised, and even now, in out-of-the-way places, you may stumble across ribbons tied to trees in sacred groves and coins deposited on mysterious offertory stones. Suspend disbelief and let your imagination take flight.

## Why I Love Estonia, Latvia & Lithuania

By Anna Kaminski, Writer

When I was growing up in the Soviet Union, the Baltics were still part of the Motherland, and they're intertwined in my mind with my own family's experiences: my grandparents; sunbathing on a beach in Pärnu; my mother hiking in Ignalina's forests. As an adult, I came to know the Baltics more intimately and to fully appreciate their centuries-old architecture, the cobbled lanes of the capitals and the detritus of communism, stripped of its former power. Plus, the fizz of *kvass* and the comforting, spud-heavy Baltic cuisine never fail to take me back to my childhood.

**For more about our writers, see p456**

Above: Three Brothers building (p201), Rīga, Latvia

# Estonia, Latvia & Lithuania

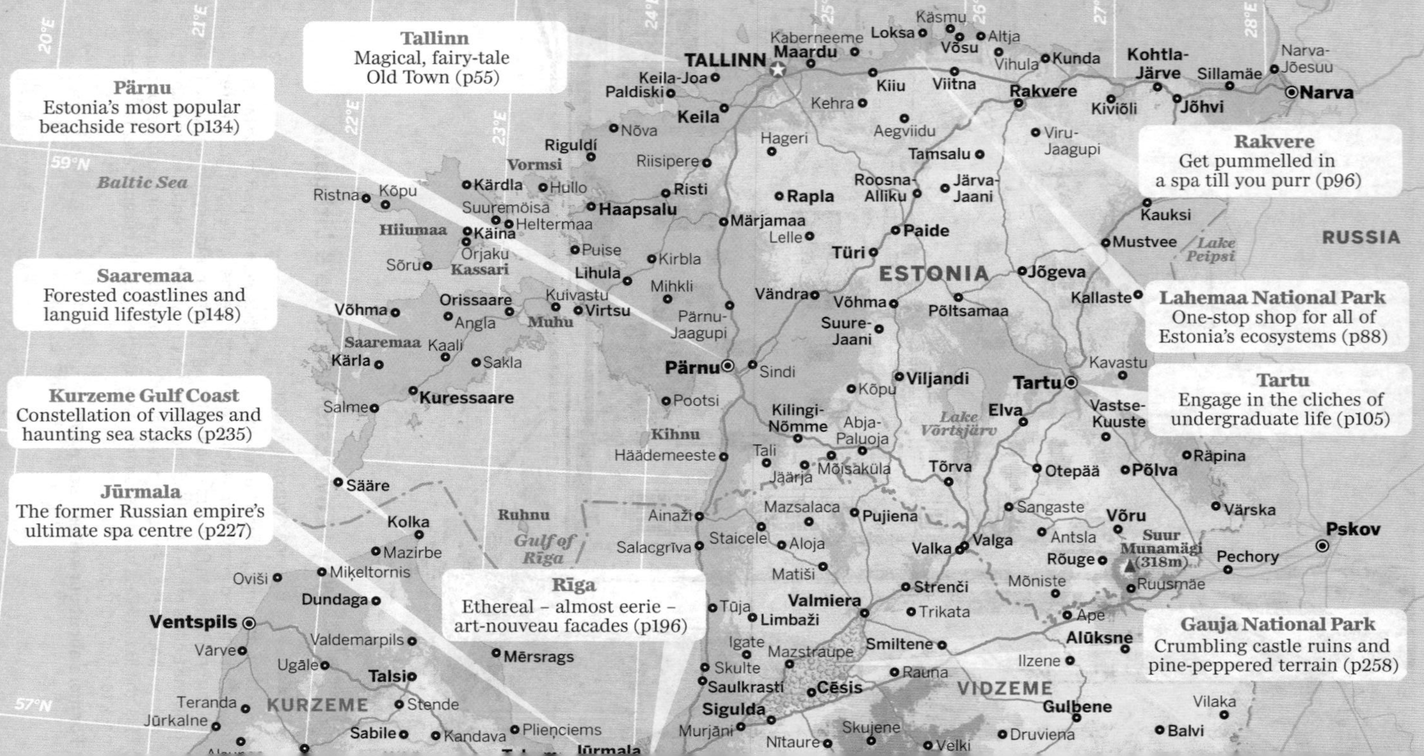

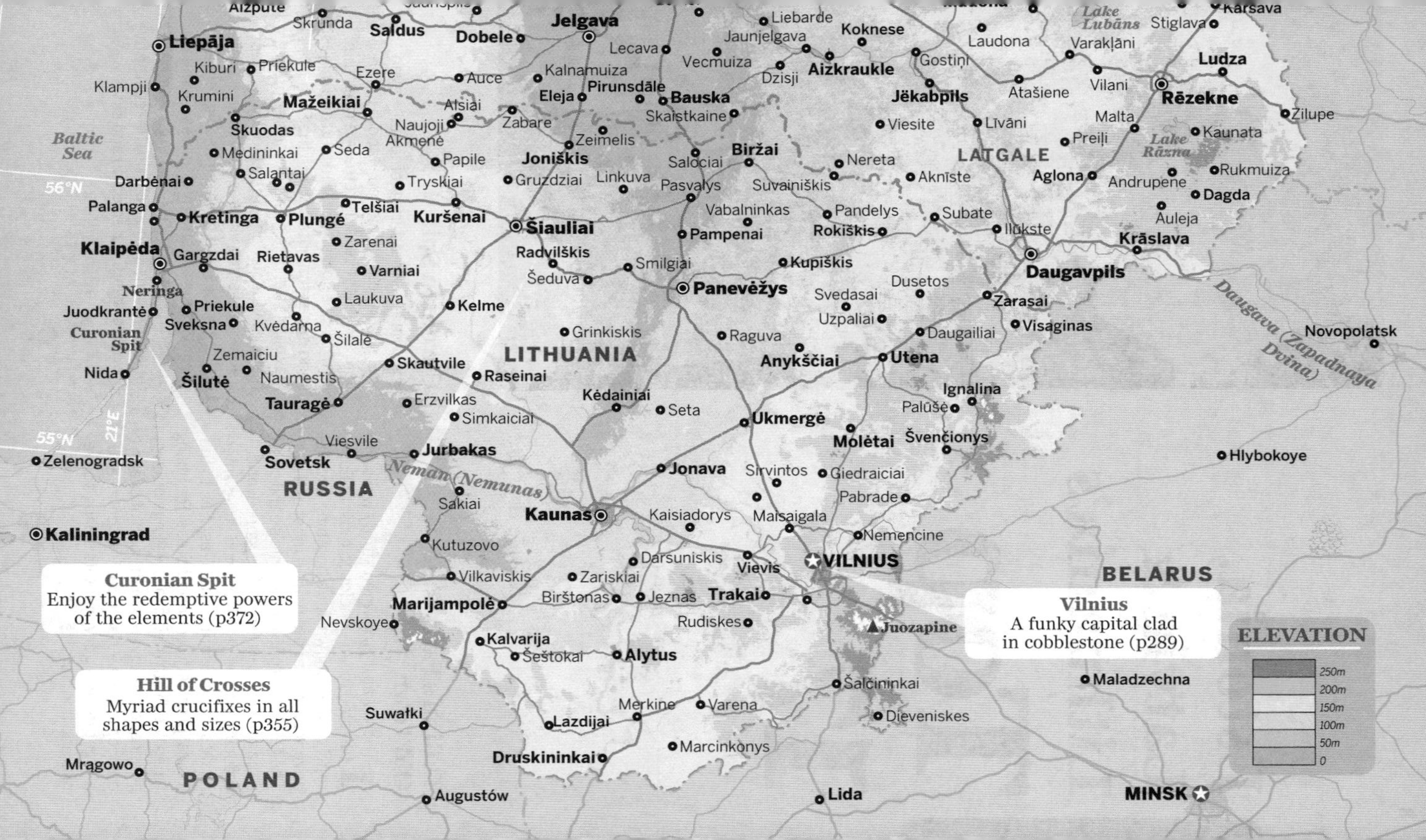
Curonian Spit
Enjoy the redemptive powers of the elements (p372)
Hill of Crosses
Myriad crucifixes in all shapes and sizes (p355)
Vilnius
A funky capital clad in cobblestone (p289)
ELEVATION
250m
200m
150m
100m
50m
0
LITHUANIA
RUSSIA
POLAND
BELARUS
LATGALE
Baltic Sea
56°N
55°N
21°E
Liepāja
Skrunda
Saldus
Dobele
Jelgava
Liebarde
Jaunjelgava
Koknese
Laudona
Lake Lubāns
Stiglava
Kārsava
Kiburi
Priekule
Klampji
Krumini
Ezere
Auce
Kalnamuiza
Lecava
Vecmuiza
Dzisji
Aizkraukle
Gostiņi
Atašiene
Varakļāni
Vilani
Ludza
Rēzekne
Zilupe
Mažeikiai
Alsiai
Naujoji Akmenė
Zabare
Eleja
Pirunsdāle
Bauska
Skaistkaine
Jēkabpils
Viesite
Līvāni
Malta
Preiļi
Lake Rāzna
Kaunata
Rukmuiza
Skuodas
Medininkai
Seda
Papile
Zeimelis
Joniškis
Salociai
Biržai
Nereta
Aknīste
Aglona
Andrupene
Dagda
Darbėnai
Salantai
Tryskiai
Gruzdziai
Linkuva
Pasvalys
Suvainiškis
Palanga
Kretinga
Plungė
Telšiai
Kuršenai
Šiauliai
Vabalninkas
Pandelys
Subate
Auleja
Pampenai
Rokiškis
Ilūkste
Krāslava
Klaipėda
Gargzdai
Rietavas
Zarenai
Varniai
Radviliškis
Šeduva
Smilgiai
Kupiškis
Daugavpils
Neringa
Juodkrantė
Priekule
Sveksna
Laukuva
Kvėdarna
Kelme
Panevėžys
Svedasai
Dusetos
Zarasai
Curonian Spit
Šilalė
Grinkiskis
Uzpaliai
Raguva
Daugailiai
Visaginas
Novopolatsk
Daugava (Zapadnaya Dvina)
Nida
Zemaiciu Naumestis
Šilutė
Skautvile
Raseinai
Anykščiai
Utena
Tauragė
Erzvilkas
Simkaiciai
Kėdainiai
Seta
Ukmergė
Ignalina
Palūšė
Molėtai
Švenčionys
Viesvile
Sovetsk
Jurbakas
Neman (Nemunas)
Sakiai
Jonava
Sirvintos
Giedraiciai
Pabrade
Hlybokoye
Zelenogradsk
Kaunas
Kaisiadorys
Maisiagala
Nemencine
Kalininigrad
Kutuzovo
Darsuniskis
Vievis
VILNIUS
Vilkaviskis
Zariskiai
Birštonas
Jeznas
Trakai
Marijampolė
Nevskoye
Rudiskes
Juozapine
Kalvarija
Šeštokai
Alytus
Šalčininkai
Maladzechna
Suwałki
Merkine
Varena
Lazdijai
Dieveniskes
Marcinkonys
Druskininkai
Mrągowo
Augustów
Lida
MINSK

# Estonia, Latvia & Lithuania's Top 17

## Tallinn's Fairy-Tale Old Town

1 There was a time when sturdy walls and turreted towers enclosed most of Europe's cities, but wartime bombing and the advent of the car put paid to most of them. The Old Town (p55) of Estonia's capital is a magical window into that bygone world, inducing visions of knights and ladies, merchants and peasants – not least due to the locals' proclivity for period dress. Rambling lanes lined with medieval dwellings open onto squares once covered in the filth of everyday commerce – now lined with cafes and altogether less gory markets selling souvenirs and handicrafts.

## Curonian Spit

2 There's something elemental – even slightly old-fashioned – about Lithuania's loveliest seaside retreat: a long, thin strip of pine-forest-covered land and majestic sand dunes that juts out into the Baltic Sea. Maybe it's the pine scent or the sea breezes, the relative isolation, or the picture-perfect traditional fishing villages with their elaborate weathervanes that have enticed writers and dreamers here for many decades. Come to Curonian Spit (p372) to recharge your batteries and renew your faith in the redemptive powers of wind, water, earth and sky.

1

RICHARD CAVALLERI/SHUTTERSTOCK ©

2

YEVGEN BELICH/SHUTTERSTOCK ©

## Vilnius' Baroque Old Town

3 Narrow, centuries-old streets, hidden courtyards, an elaborate confection of baroque churches and terrace bars serving beer – the Lithuanian capital's Old Town (p294) is one of the most welcoming city centres to wander in the Baltics, come day or night. The ancient and the contemporary coexist seamlessly: whether you're looking for that one-of-a-kind boutique, an organic bakery, a cosy bookshop or a quiet spot for a coffee, they're all just part of the discovery, waiting to be made, as you proceed along some as-yet-unexplored cobblestone alleyway.

## Tartu

4 Tartu (p105) is to Estonia what Oxford and Cambridge are to England. Like those towns, it's the presence of a centuries-old university and its attendant student population (with associated high japes and insobriety) that endows it with its special character. There's a museum on nearly every corner of Tartu's elegant streets and, it seems, a grungy bar in every other cellar. When the sun shines, Toomemägi hill is the place to best observe those eternal cliches of undergraduate life: earnest prattling, hopeless romancing and enthusiastic drinking. Top right: *Kissing Students* statue by Mati Karmin, Town Hall Square (p107)

## Castles & Manor Houses

5 A quick glance at a map reveals the Baltics' key position along the ancient trade routes between Western Europe and Russia. Crumbling castle ruins abound throughout the pine-peppered terrain, each a testament to a forgotten kingdom. For centuries, the region was divided into feudal puzzle pieces, and thus you'll find dozens of manor houses dotting the landscape. Spending the night at one of these elegantly restored mansions, such as those in Latvia's atmospheric Gauja Valley (p268), is a truly unforgettable experience. Right: Cēsis Castle (p266), Latvia

7

## Rīga's Art Nouveau Architecture

**6** If you ask any Rīgan where to find the city's world-famous art nouveau architecture (p209), you will always get the same answer: 'Look up!' Over 750 buildings in Latvia's capital – more than any other city in Europe – boast this flamboyant and haunting style of architecture. Spend a breezy afternoon picking out details in the imaginative facades found in profusion across the centre. Spot an ethereal (and almost eerie) melange of screaming demons, enraptured deities, overgrown flora and bizarre geometric patterns.

## Gauja National Park

**7** Dotted with sweet little towns and dramatic fortifications, Latvia's Gauja National Park (p258) entrances all who visit. The tower of Turaida Castle rises majestically over the sinuous river, a glorious reminder of the fairy-tale kingdoms that once ruled the land. And after you've had your history lesson, set off across the pine-covered hills by foot and bike or thread the river valleys aboard canoe or kayak. The old town of Cēsis and the activities centre of Sigulda will keep you on your toes.

## Hill of Crosses

**8** You might ask yourself: 'Where did they ever find a hill in pancake-flat Lithuania?' And then you glimpse it in the distance – more a mound than a mountain – covered in tens of thousand of crosses, each one an expression of hope, faith or tribute to those who've died in conflicts in Lithuania and abroad. The hill (p355) takes on greater significance when you realise that the crosses planted here represent not just religious faith but an affirmation of the country's identity and a pilgrimage site for Lithuanians and non-Lithuanians alike.

9

10

## Saunas & Spas

9 Although the Finns, Turks and Russians may be more famous for their saunas, Baltic folk too love to hop into their birthday suits for a good soak and steam. There are plenty of spa centres around the Baltics – such as the wonderful Aqva (p97) in Rakvere, Estonia – where you can purr like a kitten while being pummelled by experts, but most here prefer to go native (so to speak) and indulge in a traditional sauna experience: getting whipped by dried birch branches while sweating it out in temperatures beyond 60°C. Sounds relaxing…

Top: Aqva Hotel & Spa (p97)

## Foraged Food

10 Cast away your preconceived notions about potatoes and pork tongue – the Baltic table has long since abandoned the Soviet cafeteria feel and turned to local, seasonal and wild ingredients. The locavore movement isn't just up-and-coming: it has arrived with much ado, and its mascots are mushrooms and berries. Mushrooming and berrying aren't simply pastimes in these parts, they're regional obsessions. The damp climate makes places such as Lithuania's Dzūkija National Park (p337) wonderful spots for finding all sorts of nature's bounty.

## Pärnu

**11** Chances are you're not visiting the Baltic with images of endless sandy beaches hovering before your eyes, but Pärnu (p134) offers exactly that. When the quirky notion of sea bathing became fashionable at the dawn of the 20th century, Pärnu became Estonia's most popular seaside resort, a trend that continued throughout its Soviet spell – and it's hardly less so today. Architectural gems of that period combine with relics of the Hanseatic past to create very pleasant streets to explore, with interesting eateries and bars lurking along them.

## Midsummer's Eve

**12** Although church affiliations are widespread, ancient pagan rituals are still deeply woven into the fabric of all three countries. Storks are revered, even-numbered bouquets of flowers are superstitiously rebuffed and the summer solstice (p42) is held in the highest regard. Though the spiritual element of Midsummer's Eve has largely disappeared, family and friends continue to gather in the countryside for a bright night of burning pyres and revelry. While every town and village has a celebration, one great place to see in the solstice is Lithuania's Lake Plateliai. Above: Bonfire in Kuressaare (p152)

## Jūrmala

**13** Jūrmala (p227) was once the most fashionable spa centre and beach resort in all of the former Russian Empire. And while the sanatorium craze has come and gone, this Latvian resort is still an uber-popular place to hit the dazzling white sands by day or right through the endless summer dusk. Find a concert or just lie back on the beach and listen to the silence. Hit nearby Ķemeri National Park for meandering bog walks and deep and dark explorations of the wild countryside.

## Soviet Relics

**14** It's been almost 30 years since the Baltic States ripped the Iron Curtain to shreds, but while these newborn nations have since developed their own unique character, there are still plenty of dour tenements and crumbling coastal watch-towers that remind us of harder times. Many of the other Soviet relics, however, allow visitors to explore the past à la James Bond. One-time secret facilities – such as the Grūtas Park (p333) in Lithuania – offer mirth, melancholy and wonderment for even the slightest of history buffs. Bottom: Statue of Soviet partisans, Grūtas Park (p333)

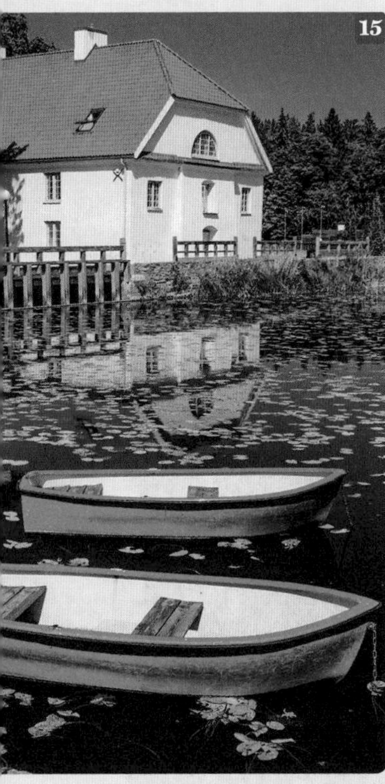
RANDREI/SHUTTERSTOCK ©

A. ALEKSANDRAVICIUS/SHUTTERSTOCK ©

## Lahemaa National Park

**15** Providing a one-stop shop of all of Estonia's major habitats – coast, forests, plains, peat bogs, lakes and rivers – within a very convenient 80km of the capital, Lahemaa (p88) is the slice of rural Estonia that travellers on a tight schedule really shouldn't miss. On top of the natural attractions, there are graceful baroque manors to peruse, pocket-sized villages to visit and country taverns to take refuge in whenever the weather turns and the stomach growls. Cycling its traffic-free roads and trails is the best way to see it. Above: Vihula Manor (p93)

## Kurzeme Coast

**16** While Lithuanians relish dune-fringed Curonian Spit and Estonians have Saaremaa and Hiiumaa, Latvia's Kurzeme (p235) coastline in between is a lonely and contemplative place, with a small constellation of towns betwixt haunting sea stacks and its two stalwart burgs: punky Liepāja in the south and Ventspils further along, with its cream-coloured beaches. Walk for hours on the hard-packed sand with only the wind off the Baltic Sea for company. Things come to a crashing climax in the north at Kolka, where the Baltic Sea meets the Gulf of Rīga.

## Saaremaa

**17** There's something about heading out to an island that lifts a trip out of the ordinary, and while Saaremaa (p148) in Estonia is no tropical paradise, the languid pace of this forested place weaves a magic all its own. The highlight is Kuressaare Castle, the Baltics' best-preserved medieval fortress, looming proudly behind its moat by the harbour. Yet it's the island's windmills, particularly the photogenic quintet at Angla, that provide the iconic Saaremaa image, which you'll see on bottles of beer, vodka and water throughout Estonia. Above: Angla Windmill Hill (p150)

# Need to Know

For more information, see Survival Guide (p415)

### Currency

Euro (€)

### Language

Estonian in Estonia, Latvian in Latvia, Lithuanian in Lithuania. Russian commonly spoken by the older generations; English by the younger ones.

### Visas

Citizens from the EU, Australia, Canada, Japan, New Zealand and the US do not require visas for entry into Estonia, Latvia or Lithuania.

### Money

Multilingual ATMs widely available. Credit cards accepted at most restaurants and hotels.

### Mobile Phones

Prepaid local SIM cards available, though worldwide free roaming deals have rendered them almost obsolete.

### Time

Eastern European Time (GMT/UTC plus two hours)

## When to Go

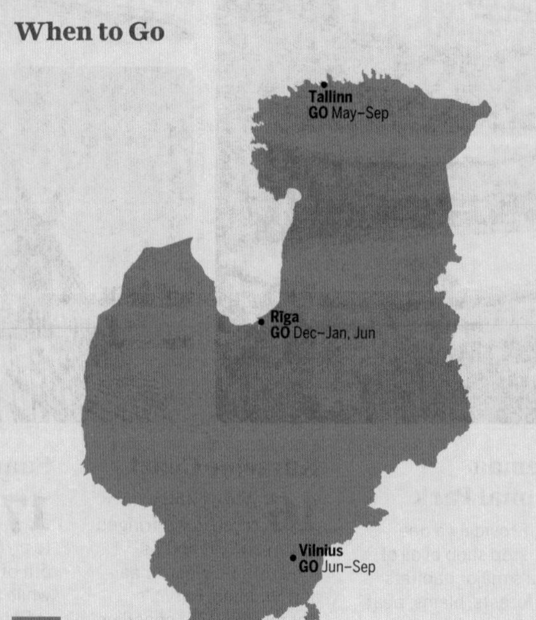


### High Season (Jun–Aug)

- Beds in the capitals get booked out – plan ahead!
- Endless daylight and warm weather encourage alfresco dining.
- Midsummer festivities during the summer solstice are not to be missed.

### Shoulder Season (May & Sep)

- Airfare and accommodation prices drop outside the summer rush.
- Weather is relatively mild; good for hiking and cycling.
- Many attractions reduce their hours of operation.

### Low Season (Oct–Apr)

- Frigid temperatures, limited daylight and snowy landscapes.
- Coastal towns are almost completely shut down.
- Crowds converge on the capitals and ski areas during the holiday season.

## Useful Websites

**Baltic Times** (www.baltictimes.com) English-language newspaper covering all three Baltic countries.

**Visit Estonia** (www.visitestonia.com) Estonia's official tourism site.

**Latvia** (www.latvia.travel) Latvia's official tourism website.

**Lithuanian Travel** (www.lithuania.travel) Lithuania's leading tourism portal.

**Baltic Country Holidays** (www.traveller.lv) Extensive booking network for rural accommodation throughout all three countries.

**Lonely Planet** (www.lonelyplanet.com) Destination information, hotel bookings, traveller forum and more.

## Important Numbers

| | |
|---|---|
| Estonia country code | ☎372 |
| Latvia country code | ☎371 |
| Lithuania country code | ☎370 |
| International access code | ☎00 |
| Emergency | ☎112 |

## Exchange Rates

| | | |
|---|---|---|
| Australia | A$1 | €0.61 |
| Canada | C$1 | €0.68 |
| Japan | ¥100 | €0.84 |
| New Zealand | NZ$1 | €0.57 |
| Russia | 100RUB | €1.41 |
| UK | UK£1 | €1.13 |
| US | US$1 | €0.90 |

For current exchange rates, see www.xe.com.

## Daily Costs

### Budget: Less than €75

- Hostel or guesthouse: €15–40
- Two meals: €15
- Walking around town: free
- Museum entry: €4
- Drinks at a beer garden: €7

### Midrange: €75–130

- Hotel room: €55
- Two meals: €30
- Public transport: €3
- Entry to two top museums: €12
- Drinks at a posh lounge: €16

### Top End: More than €130

- Luxury hotel room: €85
- Two meals: €60
- Taxis: €10
- A day spent at museums: €18
- Bar crawl: €25

## Opening Hours

Hours vary widely depending on the season and the size of the town, but the following are fairly standard:

**Banks** 9am–4pm or 5pm Monday to Friday

**Bars** noon–midnight Sunday to Thursday, until 2am or 3am Friday and Saturday

**Cafes** 9am–10pm

**Post offices** 8am–6pm Monday to Friday, 9am–2pm Saturday

**Restaurants** noon–11pm or midnight

**Shops** 10am–6pm Monday to Friday, 10am–3pm Saturday

**Supermarkets** 8am–10pm

## Arriving in the Region

**Rīga Airport** (p424) Bus 22 (€2, 25 minutes) runs to the city centre, 13km away, at least every 30 minutes. A taxi to the city typically costs €15.

**Tallinn Airport** (p424) Bus 2 or tram 4 will take you to the city centre (€2) in about 20 minutes. A taxi should cost around €10.

**Vilnius Airport** (p424) Bus 1 runs between the airport and the train station; trains run to/from the central station roughly once an hour between 6am and 10pm. Tickets cost €0.70 and the trip takes less than 10 minutes; buy on board or at the train station. A taxi or Bolt ride to the centre, 5km away, will cost €10 to €15.

## Getting Around

Public transport in the Baltic States is extensive, reasonably priced, quick and efficient.

**Car** Useful for travelling at your own pace, or for visiting regions with minimal public transport. Cars can be hired in every town or city. Drive on the right.

**Bus** Estonia, Latvia and Lithuania have extensive domestic networks, covering all the major towns and linking smaller destinations to them.

**Train** Train services are more limited but cheaper than buses; you'll need to change trains to travel between the three countries.

**Air** Each of the three capitals is linked through regular flights.

For much more on **getting around**, see p429

# What's New

With all three countries committing their resources to developing their respective tourism sectors, the Baltics are steadily growing in popularity among foreign visitors. While on one hand the Baltics optimistically look westwards, the shadow of their large and belligerent neighbour to the east continues to hang over them.

## Lithuania's Modern Gastronomy

A wave of contemporary cuisine is sweeping the country, with a new generation of chefs doing exciting things with seasonal and regional produce. In 2018 no fewer than 20 Lithuanian restaurants made it into the prestigious White Guide (https://whiteguide.com/nordic/en). Stellar examples include the following:

**Nineteen18** (p311) Reimagined Baltic cuisine, highly original nonalcoholic beverages.

**Sweet Root** (p312) Locavore tasting menu utilising interesting ingredients such as beetroot leaves and spruce tips.

**Uoksas** (p348) Surprise tasting menu; all dishes change with the seasons.

## New Concert Halls

On the Baltic coast, two striking new concert halls indulge the Latvian love of music. In Liepāja, it's the Great Amber Concert Hall (p246) near the docks, while in Ventspils it's Concert Hall Latvia (p241).

## Rīga's Miera iela

The hip neighbourhood of Miera iela, in Latvia's capital, goes from strength to strength. New pubs and nightlife venues are drawing crowds, as are some of Europe's best craft brewers, like Ziemeļu Enkurs (p224).

## Pärnu River Unchained

With Sindi Dam and other barriers to unrestricted water flow being removed, Atlantic salmon are free once again to follow traditional migratory routes.

Built in 1975 to provide water for Estonia's (now extinct) wool industry, the Sindi Dam was dismantled in stages from 2015 onwards, its removal allowing free passage for 34 species of fish.

LOCAL KNOWLEDGE

### WHAT'S HAPPENING IN THE BALTICS?

*Anna Kaminski, Lonely Planet Writer*

Talk to locals in all three countries, and you immediately encounter a mix of optimism and trepidation. The former is fuelled by economic growth, the Baltics' growing confidence in themselves as distinctive members of the European family, an increasing number of visitors enticed by new festivals, the ever-evolving dining and craft-beer scenes (the latter particularly true of Tallinn and Rīga), and the prospect of closer integration with Western Europe when Rail Baltica is completed in 2026.

However, there is also ever-present uncertainty, given the proximity of the Baltics' large neighbour. The older generations have grim memories of the Soviet occupation, and despite their nations' membership of the EU and NATO, view Russia's renewed assertiveness with concern. Latvia and Lithuania are also facing population loss, with the young and educated departing for greener pastures elsewhere.

## Tallinn's Vegan Delights

Vegans and vegetarians have never been better served in Estonia, especially in Tallinn. A raft of the capital's best new restaurants have separate menus, or are entirely plant-based. Among them:

**Plant** (p77) Imaginative, seasonal vegan dishes.

**Vegan Restoran V** (p76) Atmospheric interior; menu heavy with tofu, jackfruit and chickpea.

**Tchaikovsky** (p78) Franco-Russian classics, vegetarian tasting menu.

## Patarei

Tallinn's notorious neoclassical sea-fort-turned-prison (p65) is open to exploration. The exhibition 'Communism is Prison' explores the dank cells, corridors and execution chamber where so many suffered.

## Rīga Jūrmala Music Festival

This major new festival (p215) draws big names in classical music to Rīga and nearby Jūrmala. It aspires to be a key stop on the European culture circuit.

## Garden of Destiny

This sprawling project (p254) on an island in the Daugava River southeast of Rīga celebrates Latvia as a nation and opened for the centennial in 2018. It boasts vast new gardens and features.

## Wheeled Revolution

The Baltic capitals and major towns have witnessed a 2019 boom in electric scooters. Whether you love or hate them, they're ever-present and easy to find. Local opinion is divided: some have taken to them with gusto, while others see them as a blight. If you're the former, download the relevant apps and off you go!

## Estonia's Female President

With her victory in the October 2016 presidential elections, Kersti Kaljulaid became Estonia's first-ever female head of state.

## Kaliningrad Gets Crafty

Third-wave coffee shops and craft brews have made inroads into the Kaliningrad social scene. Seek out the award-winning GS Coffeeshop (p412) for Russia's best beans and head to Yeltsin (p412) or Krany i Stakany (p412) for an education in Russian craft beer.

Visiting Kaliningrad to partake in the above became easier from July 2019, with free citizens of 53 countries (including much of the EU but *not* the UK, Canada or the US) becoming eligible for free e-visas.

### LISTEN, WATCH & FOLLOW

For inspiration and up-to-date news, visit www.lonelyplanet.com/lithuania/articles, www.lonelyplanet.com/latvia/articles and www.lonelyplanet.com/estonia/articles.

**www.lithuania.travel/en/blogs** Useful resource pulling together Lithuania-themed blogs and articles.

**www.latvia.eu/blog** All things Latvian by an expat blogger.

**https://hiddentallinn.com/blog** Discover Estonia's capital.

**www.storyaboutfood.com** In-depth incursion into Latvian cuisine by Signe Meirane.

**https://bnn-news.com** Topical news from the three Baltic countries.

### FAST FACTS

**Food trend** Contemporary Baltic cuisine: sophisticated use of seasonal ingredients

**Forest cover** Estonia 51%, Latvia 45%, Lithuania 28%

**Population** Estonia 1.3 million, Latvia 1.95 million, Lithuania 2.85 million

## Ban on Single-Use Plastics

The EU resolution banning single-use plastics – straws, bottles, bags, containers – will be implemented in 2021. The Baltics are already moving towards greater sustainability (though the pace differs from country to country), with paper straws and coffee 'keep cups' gaining in popularity.

# If You Like...

## Castles

The Baltic was once a jigsaw puzzle of feudal territories. Its surviving castles, both ruined and restored, signify the region's strategic location, on the edges of competing civilisations.

**Trakai Castle** This fairy-tale-worthy red-brick castle atop a tiny island provides a scenic backdrop for lake paddles. (p320)

**Kuressaare Episcopal Castle** The Baltic's best preserved medieval castle, moat and all. (p152)

**Narva Castle** A chess match writ large, facing off with its Russian counterpart across the river. (p100)

**Cēsis Castle** The moody dark stone towers of the ever-more-restored old castle were founded by Livonian knights in 1214. (p266)

**Rakvere Castle** Pint-sized princesses and knights don costumes, pet farm animals and have a rollicking good time. (p96)

**Bauska Castle** A Latvian two-for-one: a ruined 15th-century castle with an intact 16th-century one grafted on. (p251)

**Livonian Order Castle** This blocky fortress in the Latvian seaside town of Ventspils houses a fascinating museum of local history. (p240)

**Vastseliina Episcopal Castle** In Estonia's extreme southeast, this place of pilgrimage was once one of the country's mightiest fortresses. (p118)

## Beaches

The Baltic summers may be short, but beach bums are handsomely rewarded with endless stretches of flaxen shoreline during the warmer months.

**Nida** Peace and quiet and unrivalled natural beauty amid sand dunes and pine trees. (p377)

**Jūrmala** The Baltic's original posh beachside spa resort still teems with Russian tycoons and their families. (p227)

**Pärnu** Synonymous in Estonia with summertime fun, Pärnu has golden sand aplenty. (p134)

**Tuhkana** Accessed by a forest path on the Estonian island of Saaremaa, Tuhkana offers comparative serenity. (p151)

**Palanga** Get your party on at Lithuania's premier summertime fun-in-the-sun destination. (p384)

**Saulkrasti** A beautiful sandy Latvian beach with surprisingly few bods on it. (p255)

## Museums

There's a lot of history to document here, but many of the region's museums pay tribute to a bevy of quirkier interests in addition to the region's war-torn past.

**Museum of the Occupation of Latvia** Five decades of occupation are brought to life through the personal stories of the survivors. (p207)

**Museum of Devils** Lucifer in all of his many guises lurks in Kaunas' New Town. (p344)

**City Museum** The tale of Tallinn is told across seven different sites, including this 14th-century merchant's house. (p57)

**MO Museum** Cutting-edge contemporary art and photography showcased at Lithuania's first private museum. (p302)

**Lithuanian Art Museum** Occupies multiple locations across the country, including this branch in Vilnius' Radvilos Palace. (p302)

**Estonian National Museum** Architecturally striking and historically insightful, this wonderful cultural institution is in Estonia's spiritual capital, Tartu. (p111)

## Architecture

The architecture in all three of the Baltic's capitals is as wonderful as it

Top: Kumu (p67), Tallinn, Estonia
Bottom: Demonstration at Rakvere Castle (p96), Estonia

is varied, be it baroque flourishes, medieval gables, dazzling art nouveau, Stalinist confections or modern masterpieces.

**Rīga's Art Nouveau Architecture** Overly adorned facades cloak the hundreds of imposing structures that radiate beyond the city's core. (p209)

**Vilnius' Old Town** All steeples, domes and pillars, the capital's wonderfully preserved Old Town revels in the baroque. (p294)

**Tallinn's Old Town** A treasure trove of medieval battlements, dwellings and public buildings. (p55)

**Kumu** Seven storeys of limestone, glass and copper, Tallinn's art museum by architect Pekka Vapaavuori has set a new standard. (p67)

**St Anne's Church** Not Vilnius' most imposing church, but widely regarded to be its most beautiful. (p295)

## Quaint Villages

You want charming farmsteads and whisper-quiet villages? The Baltic's got them in spades, especially as locals trade their bucolic lifestyles for life in the big city.

**Koguva** Trapped in a picturesque time rift, this fishing village offers a window to the past. (p146)

**Dzūkija National Park** The villages that dot this wilderness are among Lithuania's most traditional and beautiful. (p337)

**Kuldīga** The place 'where salmon fly' is frequently used as the backdrop for Latvian period films. (p246)

**Rõuge** Set in a valley punctuated by seven small lakes, Rõuge exemplifies the Estonian rural idyll. (p122)

**Plateliai** A pretty spot right by the lake and the gateway to Žemaitija National Park. (p389)

**Pāvilosta** The sleepy, beachy setting for a particularly active water-sports scene. (p241)

## Wartime Relics

From Soviet strife and Nazi rule to ancient tribal battles and invading medieval forces, the Baltic has seen more than its share of bloodshed.

**Soviet Secret Bunker** Concealed for decades, this high-security bunker is now a tribute to the Cold War. (p265)

**Karosta Prison** This Russian military prison offers visitors the unique opportunity to experience life as a detainee. (p244)

**Cold War Museum** Žemaitija National Park hides one of the great Soviet secrets: an underground nuclear-missile base. (p389)

**Kiek in de Kök** The museum contained within this imposing tower is devoted to Tallinn's fortifications and military history. (p62)

**Sõrve Peninsula** Saaremaa island's lonely extremity contains battle sites, war graves, bunkers and a military museum. (p156)

**Ninth Fort** Part fort, part sombre cathedral, this place remembers some 50,000 dead: Kaunas' Jews, partisans, prisoners of war... (p344)

## National Parks

Estonia, Latvia and Lithuania stole a lead on their fellow Soviet Republics, establishing the first national parks in the USSR in the early 1970s. They've been entrancing visitors ever since.

**Lahemaa National Park** Estonia's 'Land of Bays' is a wonderland of beaches, forests, bogs and rivers. (p88)

**Gauja National Park** This heavily forested Latvian river valley is liberally sprinkled with enchanting castles. (p258)

**Ķemeri National Park** Combine the ruins of a belle époque spa with dark and moody forests and bogs. (p232)

**Aukštaitija National Park** A mysterious landscape of pine forests, lakes and traditional villages, great for camping, walking and water sports. (p328)

**Soomaa National Park** Wander through Estonia's 'Bogland' on well-maintained boardwalks in search of witches, goblins, bears and wolves. (p132)

## Palaces & Manor Houses

When they weren't at war, the Baltic aristocracy traded fortresses for comfortable country piles. Some have been carefully restored, while others lie in ruins.

**Rundāle Palace** Latvia's primo palatial gem is a tribute to the opulence of the Baltic-German elite. (p252)

**Kadriorg Art Museum** Built by Russian Tsar Peter the Great, Tallinn's pretty palace now houses a branch of the Estonian Art Museum. (p65)

**Palace of the Grand Dukes of Lithuania** A painstaking reproduction of the 17th-century seat of power, right in the heart of Vilnius. (p293)

**Muižas of the Gauja** Spend the night at one of the striking *muižas* (manor houses) dotting the Latvian countryside. (p268)

**Palmse Manor** The centrepiece of Estonia's Lahemaa National Park has been fully restored, along with its many outbuildings. (p89)

**Kolga Manor** From aristocratic heights to Soviet apartment block, Kolga is Estonian history in one grand, crumbling picture. (p87)

## Jewish History

Before WWII, large and thriving Jewish communities had been contributing to the rich culture of the Baltics for centuries. After the war, only a shadow of those communities remained.

**Paneriai** A sombre memorial to the 100,000 people – mostly Jews from Vilnius – murdered here by the Nazis in WWII. (p322)

**Žanis Lipke Memorial** An exquisite museum detailing one Rīga family's fight to save Jews from the Nazis in WWII. (p211)

**Rīga Ghetto & Latvian Holocaust Museum** A reconstructed ghetto flat and photos of the Nazis' victims greet you at this challenging museum. (p210)

**Sugihara House** Showcases the life of a Japanese diplomat and the stories of the thousands of Jews he saved during WWII. (p346)

**Tolerance Centre** Vilnius' evocative museum of Jewish history and culture with multimedia expositions and more. (p300)

# Month by Month

**TOP EVENTS**

**Midsummer's Eve**, June

**Song & Dance Festival**, July (every five years)

**Positivus Festival**, July

**Tallinn Black Nights Film Festival**, November

**Christmas**, December

## January

**New Year's celebrations and continued festive cheer warm the hearts of locals as they weather the limited daylight of what already feels like an endless winter.**

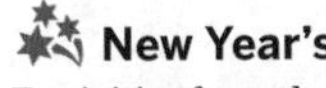

Festivities from the night before continue during this public holiday as locals incorporate pagan practices at family gatherings to ensure a happy and healthy year.

## February

**The cold, dark and icy winter continues, but locals make the most of it as they flock to the countryside for some cross-country skiing.**

### Tartu Ski Marathon

This 63km cross-country race draws about 10,000 competitors to the Estonian countryside; winners complete the course in less than three hours. Participants slide off in sports-mad Otepää. (p127)

### Palanga Smelt Fishing Festival

Held in the Lithuanian seaside resort of Palanga over three days in mid-February, this festival lures hungry fish lovers, who try the city's beloved smelts. There's also the annual 'polar bear' event, at which hardy swimmers frolic in the freezing Baltic waters.

## March

**Locals pull aside the curtains to check the weather outside...yup, it's still winter out there. The main causes for celebration are the Easter holidays, although they sometimes slip into April.**

### Lithuanian Folk Art

The annual St Casimir's Fair (Kaziuko *mugė*), Lithuania's biggest festival of folk arts and crafts, is held at the beginning of March in both Vilnius and Kaunas.

## April

**Frosty nights officially come to an end as the mean temperature stabilises well above zero. Hope of spring has arrived; locals burst forth from their shuttered houses to inhale the fickle spring air.**

### Haapsalu Horror & Fantasy Film Festival

Zombies take over the streets and screens of Haapsalu, on Estonia's west coast. This showcase (www.hoff.ee) of creepy and kooky films is timed to coincide with the April full moon.

### Jazz in Tallinn

Jazz greats from around the world converge on Tallinn, Estonia, in mid-April during the two-week Jazzkaar festival (www.jazzkaar.ee). Musicians play not just at concert halls but on the streets, in squares and parks, and even at the airport.

### Tartu Student Days

Tartu's students let their hair down in this wild

pagan celebration marking the end of term and the dawn of spring in Estonia. A second, smaller version occurs in mid-October.

### Jazz in Kaunas

The annual Kaunas Jazz Festival, held in late April, is arguably Lithuania's most prestigious and popular jazz event. (p345)

## May

**The days are noticeably longer now as weather conditions dramatically improve. Tourist-focused businesses start revving their engines; excitement fills the air in anticipation of a fruitful summer.**

### Old Town Days

Held in Tallinn's cinematic 15th-century streets, this is a week of themed days involving dancing, concerts, costumed performers, sports and plenty of medieval merrymaking.

### New Baltic Dance Festival

This annual festival in early May features contemporary and modern dance, drawing companies from around Lithuania and the world to Vilnius for a week of performances.

### Baltic Ballet

The International Baltic Ballet Festival (www.ballet-festival.lv) in Rīga features stirring performances by Latvian and international companies over three weeks.

## June

**After several fits and bursts of spring sun, the warm weather is finally here to stay. The region-wide Midsummer's Eve festivities herald the peak of the summer season.**

### Trakai Middle Age Festival

A lively tourney in Trakai, Lithuania, that involves competitors dressing up in plate armour and jousting. What's not to love?

### Baltica International Folklore Festival

Alternating between Tallinn (2022), Vilnius (2020) and Rīga (2021) annually, this large festival (www.festivalbaltica.com/en) celebrates Baltic folk traditions, with thousands of performers.

### Rīga Opera Festival

The Latvian National Opera's showcase event (www.opera.lv) takes place over 10 days and includes performances by world-renowned talent.

### Grillfest Good Food Festival

This festival (www.grillfest.ee) sees holidaymakers tucking into grilled food, sushi and everything in between at Estonia's 'summer capital', Pärnu.

### Culture Night

Visual artists and musicians fill the Lithuanian capital of Vilnius with all manner of installations and performances over the course of a single June night (www.kulturosnaktis.lt).

### Baltic Pride

The Baltic's annual gay and lesbian pride festival alternates between each of the three capitals, with Tallinn taking the reins in 2020, Rīga in 2021 and Vilnius in 2022.

### Midsummer's Eve

The region's biggest annual night out is best experienced in the countryside, where huge bonfires flare for all-night revellers.

### International Folk Festival

Held in the town of Nida on Curonian Spit, this annual festival draws folk musicians and dance troupes from various Lithuanian regions and from around Europe. It's held over a weekend in late June.

### Hanseatic Days

The Estonian towns of Viljandi (p131) and Pärnu (p135) celebrate their past as part of the Hansa League of northern trading cities with much medieval merrymaking.

## July

**Summer is in full swing as locals gather on terraces and verandahs during the week to sip mugs of beer alfresco. On the weekends everyone flees the cities for their countryside abodes.**

### Galapagai Rock Music Festival

Lively rock music fest (http://galapagai.lt) in

Lithuania's Ignalina region, getting bigger by the year and attracting bands from Poland, Belarus and beyond, as well as home-grown talent.

### International Festival of Experimental Archaeology

Lively three-day fest (www.kernave.org) in Kernavė, Lithuania, that celebrates Stone Age fire-starting techniques, bronze casting, yarn dyeing, Viking-era smithing and other age-old crafts.

### Christopher Summer Festival

The Christopher Summer Festival (www.kristupofestivaliai.lt) offers two months of classical, jazz and world-music concerts held around the Lithuanian capital of Vilnius throughout July and August.

### Pärnu Film Festival

Coordinated by the city's Museum of New Art, this festival (www.chaplin.ee) showcases documentary films from all over the world. It's held early in the month in the museum and at other venues around Estonia's premier beach resort.

### Klaipėda Sea Festival

This five-day annual festival is held over the third weekend in July and celebrates the Lithuanian seaport's rich nautical heritage.

### Devilstone Music Festival

This rock and metal festival (www.devilstone.net) is held in the central Lithuanian town of Anykščiai in mid-July. Acts perform hard rock, heavy metal, Goth, electronica and speed metal. If you've got the hair, you know where to be.

### Võru Folklore Festival

Mid-July in Võru sees a whir of dancers, singers and musicians decked out in the colourful folk costumes of Estonia and a dozen other nations, celebrating their respective ethnic traditions and cultures.

### Tartu Hanseatic Days

The Estonian city of Tartu goes medieval with three days of costumed peasants, ladies, jesters, knights, crafts demonstrations, markets, family-friendly performances and more during this mid-July festival. (p112)

### Wine Festival

The village of Sabile, Latvia, is famed for its vineyard – the world's most northern open-air grape grower. Your only chance to taste local wine is at this festival.

### Song & Dance Festival

Held separately in each Baltic country every five years, these massive festivals attract people with Baltic roots from all over the world to perform in mammoth choirs or large-scale dance routines that give North Koreans a run for their money.

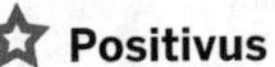

### Positivus

One of Latvia's largest music festivals, Positivus draws big names performing a range of styles, from folk to funk. It's held in a pine forest near the beach close to the Estonian border. (p257)

### Summer Sound

Liepāja holds the title as Latvia's haven for punk and garage bands, so any of its local music festivals is well worth checking out – especially Summer Sound (www.summersound.lv), which draws up to 40,000 people each year.

### Viljandi Folk Music Festival

The Estonian town of Viljandi (www.viljandifolk.ee) is overrun with folk-music aficionados during this hugely popular four-day festival, featuring musicians from Estonia and abroad. More than 100 concerts are held, attended by more than 20,000 people.

### Sigulda Opera Festival

An open-air opera festival (www.opersvetki.lv) that attracts internationally acclaimed singers to the castle ruins of Sigulda, Latvia, for three days at the end of the month.

### Nida Jazz Marathon

Jazz comes to the sand dunes of a Lithuanian Baltic Sea resort during this annual festival (www.nidajazz.lt). Expect several days of concerts – with jam sessions afterwards – at various venues around Curonian Spit in late July and early August.

## August

**Long cloudless afternoons are perfect for the beach and extended holidays from work, as locals savour every drop of golden sun – despite the occasional rainstorm.**

### Rīga City Festival

Rīga all but shuts down for this huge free festival (www.rigassvetki.lv). The parks and waterfront are taken over by scores of activities, from big-name bands to fireworks. Rīgans weep while they sing along with folk songs from their youth.

### Maritime Merriment

Early in the month, Kuressaare (on the Estonian island of Saaremaa) celebrates its marine credentials with its Maritime Festival (www.merepaevad.ee), a weekend of sea-related activities including a regatta, fair, herring-cooking demonstrations, bands and a strong naval presence.

### Film Alfresco

The week-long tARTuFF (www.tartuff.ee) open-air film festival has free screenings of art-house features and documentaries in the atmospheric Town Hall Sq in the heart of Tartu, Estonia. Poetry readings and concerts round out the program.

### Ghost Stories

Held in the grounds of Haapsalu's castle in western Estonia, the White Lady Festival (www.valgedaam.ee) culminates in the appearance of a ghostly apparition in the cathedral window, caused by the reflection of the full moon in the glass.

### Pagan Music

The popular MJR Alternative Music Festival (Mėnuo Juodaragis; www.mjr.lt) celebrates – nominally – Lithuania's pagan roots; it's really just a chance to hear music rarely heard anywhere else. Held over the last weekend in August on an island near the eastern Lithuanian city of Zarasai.

### Birgitta Festival

The atmospheric ruins of Pirita Convent in Tallinn's most popular beach suburb offer an excellent backdrop to classical concerts, ballet, opera, choral works and modern dance (www.filharmoonia.ee/en/birgitta).

### Art by Night

Baltā Nakts (White Night), sponsored by the Contemporary Art Forum, mirrors Paris' night-long showcase of artists and culture around Rīga, Latvia's capital.

### Piens Fest

A hipster's dream festival, Piens Fest (www.piens.nu/fest) feels like an almost accidental gathering of local artists (musical and otherwise) in the Miera iela area of Rīga. Devour fried food, peruse vintage attire and listen to indie beats while sitting on the grass.

### Ezera Skaņas Festival

Surely Latvia's most esoteric musical event (www.ezeraskanas.lv): people take to boats on Kāla Lake at 5am to hear otherworldly music wafting over the water.

### Future Shorts

This Latvian film festival celebrates short films from all over the world. Check out the Facebook page for Future Shorts Latvia.

## September

**The last days of summer quickly turn into the mild beginning of autumn. Rain is more frequent by the end of the month, while leaves turn brilliant colours and tumble off the trees.**

### World Theatre

Sirenos (Sirens) International Theatre Festival is a popular annual drama festival (www.okt.lt) held in Vilnius, Lithuania, from mid-September to mid-October, drawing people from around the world for a robust roster of live theatre.

## October

**Days are noticeably shorter and afternoons on the beach are but a memory now; tourist-focused businesses start shuttering their windows as everyone prepares to hibernate.**

### Gaida Music Festival

One of the highlights of Lithuania's musical calendar is this annual celebration (www.vilniusfestivals.lt/en/gaida) of classical and new music from Central and Eastern Europe. Held in Vilnius.

## November

**Autumn turns to winter as rainy days blend into snowy ones. This is one of the quietest months of the year – summer is long gone, yet winter holiday festivities have yet to begin.**

### Scanorama

Held in Lithuania's four biggest cities (Vilnius, Kaunas, Klaipėda and Šiauliai), this festival (www.scanorama.lt) showcases European films in various formats and genres.

### Mama Jazz

Vilnius' biggest jazz event (www.vilniusmamajazz.lt) is held every November, usually drawing a banner list of top performers from around Europe and the world.

### Tallinn Black Nights Film Festival

Estonia's biggest film festival showcases films from all over the world in the nation's capital over two weeks from mid-November. Subfestivals focus on animated films, children's films and student-made films. (p72)

### Latvian National Day

A whole week of festivities surrounds the anniversary of Latvia's 1918 proclamation of independence on 18 November, including the Rīga Festival of Light.

### Arēna New Music Festival

Showcases contemporary composers and artists working in what might be loosely dubbed the classical tradition; held at venues throughout Rīga, Latvia.

## December

**Yuletide festivities provide the perfect distraction from freezing temperatures as decorations cheer the streets and families gather from all over to celebrate.**

### Christmas in Tartu

Watch the Advent candles being lit while the choirs sing on a fairy-lit Town Hall Sq on the four Sundays leading up to Christmas.

### Christmas Markets

Festive decorations, arts and crafts, traditional foods and entertainment brighten the dark days in the lead-up to Christmas, in each capital's Old Town (and in many other towns around the region).

### New Year's Eve

Enjoy fireworks and revelry on the main squares of Tallinn, Rīga and Vilnius in the countdown to midnight.

# Itineraries

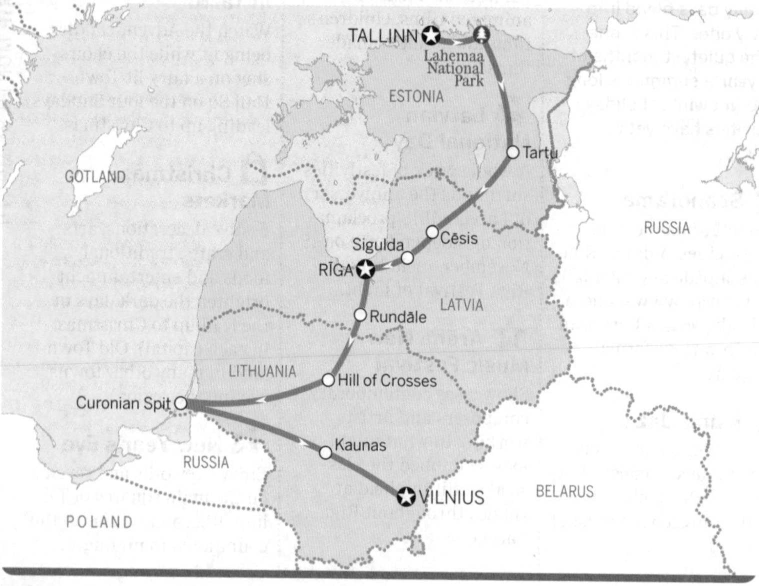

## Best of the Baltic

If you've got limited time but you're keen on seeing the best that each of the Baltic States has to offer, this itinerary captures many of the big-ticket destinations.

Begin your tour in **Tallinn** and roam the magnificent medieval streets of the Estonian capital's Old Town. Delve into the city's treasure trove of gastronomic delights before trekking out to **Lahemaa National Park**. The electric university town of **Tartu** awaits; then skip south into Latvia to take in the crumbling castles of **Cēsis** and **Sigulda** in Gauja National Park. Spend the night at one of the posh manor houses *(muižas)* nearby, then plough through to reach **Rīga**, home to a dizzying array of decorated facades. Next, head south to **Rundāle** to visit the opulent palace – the Baltic's version of Versailles – built by the architect responsible for St Petersburg's Winter Palace. From Rundāle, hop the border into Lithuania and stop for a poignant look at the **Hill of Crosses** in Šiauliai before shooting west to **Curonian Spit**. Spend some time amid the traditional cottages, shifting sand dunes and endless pine forest before a stopover in lively **Kaunas** and ending your trip in flamboyant, baroque **Vilnius**.

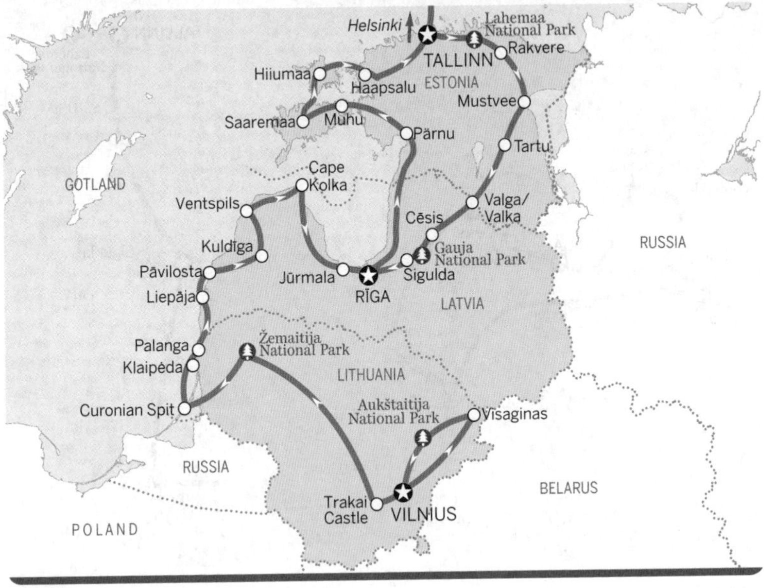

## The Grand Tour

With a month, you can roster in beach time, hiking excursions and visits to the region's little towns – and even fit in a side trip to Helsinki.

Start in Lithuania's beautiful capital **Vilnius**, spending two days wandering the cobblestone streets, checking out Gediminas Hill and taking in the city's historical charms. If nuclear tourism is your bag, do a day trip to **Visaginas** and the Ignalina nuclear power station, then spend a day or two cycling and paddling in **Aukštaitija National Park**. Visit **Trakai Castle** before heading west towards the sea. Stop at **Žemaitija National Park** for a quick lesson in Soviet missile tactics, before relaxing along the dune-filled shores of **Curonian Spit**. Follow the Baltic Sea up through the port city of **Klaipėda** and family-friendly **Palanga** resort to reach the Latvian border.

Over the border is **Liepāja**, famous for its gilded cathedral and hulking Soviet tenements. Weather permitting, head north to surfside **Pāvilosta** before detouring inland to the picturesque village of **Kuldīga**. Continue to the lovely long sands of **Ventspils**, staying overnight before hitting windy and wild **Cape Kolka**. Follow the coast as it snakes past forests and quiet villages to the spa retreat of **Jūrmala** – a hotspot for Russian tycoons and an excellent pit stop. From here **Rīga** is only a short hop.

After two days in the Latvian capital, cross into Estonia to sunbathe in **Pärnu**. Move west to hop between the forested islands of **Muhu**, **Saaremaa** and **Hiiumaa**. Stop for lunch and a castle visit in **Haapsalu** before continuing to **Tallinn**. Allow at least three days to take in the Estonian capital's treasures before ferrying over to **Helsinki** for a night. Back in Estonia, stop overnight in **Lahemaa National Park** before heading through spa-heavy **Rakvere** and **Mustvee**, on the shores of Lake Peipsi, to **Tartu** for a night or two.

Check out the oddball border town of **Valga/Valka**, and stop in the charming Latvian town of **Cēsis** to wander among the fortress ruins. Sample **Gauja National Park**, and in **Sigulda** go bobsledding and bungee jumping. End your Baltic odyssey in Rīga or return to Vilnius.

## 1 WEEK Absolute Latvia

A full week in Latvia offers time to explore a good number of the nation's treasures beyond the attention-stealing capital.

After exploring **Rīga**, visit the forests and imposing castle near **Sigulda** before moving on to the secret Soviet bunker at **Līgatne** and the stone fortress of **Cēsis**. Swing through to **Lake Rāzna** in the peaceful Latgale Lakelands, then stay the night in arty **Daugavpils**. Walk the historic centre and see how the city honours native son Mark Rothko.

Loop back to **Rundāle** to take in the opulence of the palace before blasting on to the coast at **Liepāja**, home to Latvia's garage-band scene, a lively music festival and the strikingly dour Karosta district. Detour inland to **Kuldīga**, one of the country's quaintest towns, then stop overnight in beachy **Ventspils**. Then it's on to **Cape Kolka**, where the Gulf of Rīga meets the Baltic Sea in dramatic fashion.

Follow the coastline through the constellation of lonely seaside villages to **Jūrmala**, the Baltic's most famous resort town, then finish up back in Rīga.

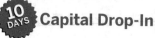

## 10 DAYS Capital Drop-In

Ten days in the Baltic is just the right amount of time to get a feel for each of the region's capitals.

Start in **Vilnius**, Lithuania's capital, exploring the sumptuous baroque architecture amid the curving cobbled streets. Take two or three days to snap photos of Gediminas Hill, savour the dining scene and absorb the rich Jewish history.

Make a side trip to the picturesque castle at **Trakai** before visiting **Rīga**, Latvia's capital and the Baltic's largest city. Haggle for huckleberries at the Central Market and crane your neck to savour the soaring art nouveau architecture. When it comes to day trips, you'll be spoilt for choice. Try cavorting with the Russian elite in **Jūrmala**, Latvia's spa centre; or cranking up the adrenaline in **Sigulda**, with its clutch of adventure sports. Next it's on to Estonia's capital, **Tallinn**, where you'll be treated to a fairy-tale kingdom of medieval architecture, cobbled streets and centuries-old fortifications. Sample the world-class culinary and craft-beer scenes, and finish with a day of cycling around scenic **Lahemaa National Park**.

## 1 WEEK Lithuanian Solo

You can pack a lot into one week in compact Lithuania, but if you've got the time, it's worth stretching this itinerary out to a more relaxed 10 days.

Take at least two days to explore the cathedral, numerous museums and varied dining and nightlife scene of **Vilnius**. Then allow at least half a day to visit nearby **Trakai** to see the fairy-tale island castle. Beach bums and fresh-air fiends should then head to the Baltic coast, visiting the port city of **Klaipėda** with its enchanting historic centre and many bars, before continuing to the sand-and-pine-forest sliver of the Curonian Spit. Base yourself at the enchanting fishing village of **Nida**, ideal for exploring the Spit's giant sand dunes and numerous cycling and hiking trails, and for lazing on white-sand beaches.

Passing back through Klaipėda, it's worth detouring northeast to Šiauliai for half a day to visit the poignant **Hill of Crosses**, before finishing your journey in rough-edged **Kaunas** with its lively nightlife, cobbled medieval streets and vibrant street art.

## 1 WEEK Essential Estonia

If you can drag yourself away from the wonderland that is Tallinn, this itinerary covers a little of everything Estonia has to offer: beaches, countryside, castles, historic towns and quaint villages.

On a week's journey through Estonia, spend at least two days in **Tallinn** to fully explore each crooked nook in the charming medieval core while sampling the spoils of the nation's foodie scene. **Lahemaa National Park** makes for a lovely day trip, while the university town of **Tartu** awaits those looking for cultured city life away from the capital. Swing through **Otepää**, Estonia's self-proclaimed 'winter capital', then switch seasons in **Pärnu**, where sun worshippers come in droves for beach-lazing.

Round off the week on Estonia's western islands. Stop by the time-warped village of **Koguva** on Muhu, then base yourself on Saaremaa at **Kuressaare** – Estonia's prettiest spa town, set around an ancient moated castle. From here explore the island's forested expanse of whooshing windmills, lonely churches and soaring sea cliffs. Finally, take a direct flight back to Tallinn.

Kuldīga (p246), L

# Plan Your Trip
# Road Trips

Whether you plan your itinerary extensively or simply follow the smell of salt and smoked fish up the coastline, you'll find driving in the Baltics a breeze. Roads are generally very good and well-signposted, traffic is slight and drivers reasonably sane. Driving is not only an easy way to explore this region – it's a pleasure.

## Best Trips

### Best Day Trip from Tallinn by Car

Enjoy Estonia's natural beauty and head east early in the morning to watch the forest come to life at Lahemaa National Park. If time permits, swing down to Rakvere to check out the castle before looping back to the capital.

### Best Day Trip from Rīga by Car

If you've got your own wheels, you won't be limited to the most obvious day trips (Gauja National Park, Rundāle, Jūrmala). Go west instead. Consider a stop at Pedvāle to peruse the sculptures at the open-air art museum, then venture on to quaint Kuldīga, a charming village frozen in time.

### Best Day Trip from Vilnius by Car

Most visitors head west to the castle at Trakai, so buck the trend and venture northeast to check out the quiet lakes and hiking paths of Aukštaitija National Park, stopping at Labanoras along the way. You can also swing by the Europos Parkas Sculpture Park on the way back.

## Planning Essentials

### Driving vs Public Transport

To be honest, it's quite possible to explore the Baltics using public transport, which is frequent and all-encompassing. Hire a car here purely for pleasure, convenience and freedom (plus it makes a great travelling suitcase). A car gives you the flexibility to explore the countries' quiet hinterlands, from the towering dunes of Lithuania's Curonian Spit to Estonia's windswept western islands to Latvia's pine-studded inner forests. Take your car off the main roads and stumble upon tiny villages locked away in time, or curious relics from the Soviet era, when the Russians used space-station technology to spy on the West.

Private vehicles far outshine public transport when it comes to convenience. If you're simply travelling between large towns and capitals, we recommend using the bus and train system, which is geared towards commuting professionals and is thus very comfortable. If you plan on exploring the national parks, rural backwaters or the Estonian islands, the limited bus services just aren't up to the job.

If you're travelling with your family or a small group of friends, you'll find the freedom of a car versus the rather high petrol prices a much more amenable equation. However, parking a car can be a hassle in the capital cities, so allow yourself several days to explore them on foot before collecting your hire car and hitting the road.

### When to Go

For fairly obvious reasons, the best time of year to travel with a vehicle is during the warmer months (May to September), which are blissfully free from snow, sleet and any other weather that could have a negative impact on your driving. The warmer months are not, however, completely free of rain – and you'll have to consider booking ahead for ferries to the Estonian islands at busy times in summer (on weekends especially and around midsummer). The summer days are long, which means that driving is relatively safe even in the late evening, though you have to watch out for wildlife at dusk.

### Where to Start & End

You'll be pleased to know that almost all car-hire companies allow you to drive throughout all three Baltic countries (although some will charge a fee for the privilege). However, you'll be hard-pressed to find a service that will allow you to take a vehicle to any countries beyond.

If you hire a car from a smaller local agency, you'll be expected to return the vehicle to the location from which you picked it up. Larger franchise operators will allow you to drop the car off in a different town or even a different Baltic country for an additional fee – making a flight into Tallinn and out of Vilnius entirely possible. If you want to save on the relocation fee and

Swimming at Ginučiai Watermill (p328), Aukštaitija National Park, Lithuania

start and end at the same point, leave from Rīga, complete a figure-eight circuit up into Estonia and down through Lithuania (or vice versa), then return.

# On the Road

## Road Rules

Traffic drives on the right-hand side of the road. Older towns and villages have a proliferation of narrow one-way streets and roundabouts. Blood-alcohol limits are low in all three countries (0.2 in Estonia, 0.4 in Lithuania, 0.5 in Latvia).

Although the Baltic nations have a fairly poor reputation when it comes to road etiquette and collisions, this is mostly unfounded. The main hazards you're likely to encounter are speeding and tailgating. Drivers in the big cities can be aggressive, but you'll find that most are forgiving of wrong turns and lane-changing. You should, however, avoid inner-city driving during the workday rush hour – especially on Friday afternoons in the warmer months, when locals make a beeline to their countryside cottages. Driving in the region's rural parts is rarely a laborious task as populations are sparse. Do, however, be careful of passing vehicles, which tend to speed by unannounced and at surprisingly inopportune moments.

Take extra care on the Tallinn–Tartu highway, known by locals as 'the road of death'. Numerous speed cameras are in effect here, as well as on the Tallinn–Narva highway and throughout Latvia.

## Petrol & Servicing

Although the Baltic countryside can feel desolate and underpopulated, there is a healthy number of service stations in all three countries, and distances between them are not great.

Before taking your vehicle off the lot, make sure to arm yourself with a service phone number for each of the Baltic countries (which your car-rental company should provide anyway), just in case your car should require any attention while on the road. Tyres have been known to get punctures – especially in Latvia, where the road-maintenance infrastructure isn't as solid as it is in Lithuania or Estonia.

Plan Your Trip

# Outdoor Activities

The Baltic countries offer visitors plenty of up-close encounters with Mother Nature at her gentlest: paddling on sparkling lakes, rambling or cycling through pretty forests, and lazing on beaches. Instead of craning your neck at sky-reaching peaks, here you can marvel over accessible nature and superb rural scenery.

## The Great Outdoors

While the flat Baltic countries lack the drama of more mountainous regions, there are places where you're left in no doubt that it's tempestuous nature that's calling the shots – witness the awesome shifting sands of Curonian Spit, or the windswept, desolate Cape Kolka.

There's plenty of breathing space in these countries, too, offering some of the continent's best opportunities to ditch the crowds and simply frolic in the wilderness. Check those population figures and you'll be in little doubt that open space abounds here.

A smorgasbord of active endeavours awaits anyone wanting to delve into the outdoors. You can whet your appetite with berry-picking before feeding on an alfresco meal of brisk, salty air, pristine white-sand beaches and icy-blue Baltic Sea vistas. Want seconds? Try cycling through dense pine and spruce forests; canoeing down a lazy river; or checking out the flora and fauna in a quiet nature reserve. Those craving an adrenaline fix can find some surprising options, too, from bobsledding to bungee jumping. If you still have room for dessert, try baby-gentle downhill or cross-country skiing, or just get hot and sweaty in a traditional rural sauna.

## Best of the Outdoors

### Ultimate Cycling Route

Follow the Baltic coastline from Curonian Spit, up through the Kurzeme Coast, around the Gulf of Rīga and onto the quiet western islands of Estonia.

### Best Authentic Sauna Experience

Try a *pirts*, a traditional Latvian cleanse involving extreme temperatures, a birch-branch beating and jumping into a pond.

### Top Forest Hikes

Lahemaa National Park (Estonia), Gauja National Park (Latvia), Žemaitija National Park (Lithuania).

### Excellent Canoeing Spots

Haanja Nature Park (Estonia), Latgale Lakelands (Latvia), Aukštaitija National Park (Lithuania).

### Must-See Wildlife

Wild boar and elk on Lithuania's Curonian Spit, storks nesting on power poles throughout the Baltic countryside.

### Outdoor Activities Web Resource

**Country Holidays** (www.traveller.lv) Pan-Baltic website offering details on cycling routes, hiking trails and landmarks.

# Cycling

The Baltic offers superb cycling territory. The region's flatness makes tooling around the countryside on a bicycle an option for anyone: casual cyclists can get the hang of things on gentle paved paths, while hard-core fanatics can rack up the kilometres on more challenging multiday treks. Although there's not much along the lines of steep single-track trails, dirt tracks through forests abound, and the varied but always peaceful scenery ensures you'll never tire of the view.

The major cities of the Baltic are also doing their share to increase the usability of bicycles. Urban cycling paths are multiplying each year as bike-share and easy-access rental programs proliferate.

Among the most popular places to cycle in Lithuania are spectacular Curonian Spit, lake-studded Dzūkija and Aukštaitija national parks, around Lake Plateliai and on the forest paths in Labanoras Regional Park.

In Estonia, try the quiet back roads of the islands of Muhu, Saaremaa and Hiiumaa, as well as the bay-fringed, forested confines of Lahemaa National Park.

In Latvia, bicycle is the best way to explore Liepāja, Ventspils, Sigulda and Jūrmala. For a longer adventure, the Latgale Lakelands are ideal, with plenty of paved and unpaved roads leading through beautiful wilderness. The Cape Kolka area is also very popular.

## Plan Your Trip

For DIY planning, check out info-laden www.eurovelo.org. If you want someone to help with planning, a band of dedicated cycling operators offer everything from itinerary-planning services to fully guided treks.

**BaltiCCycle** (www.bicycle.lt)

**City Bike** (www.citybike.ee)

# Spas & Saunas

## Latvia

Latvia's seaside town of Jūrmala is undoubtedly the spa capital of the Baltic. In its heyday it was the holiday centre of the entire Russian Empire – thousands of aristocrats travelled here in droves to slather themselves in curative mud, rinse in sulphur water and enjoy the glorious views of the bay. Today, much of Jūrmala's allure remains, and it's still a popular spot for Russian tycoons to build a holiday home and get massage treatments.

For an authentic cleansing experience, however, you'll have to venture far away from the crowds of Rīga or Jūrmala and head to the countryside, where locals have constructed their own private *pirts* close to the water's edge (pond, river, lake or sea). Several private *pirts* can be booked by travellers, such as the one shared by several hotels in Sigulda; otherwise you'll have to befriend some locals to gain access.

## Estonia

Spa-going is also extremely popular among Estonians, who share their sauna habits with the Finns across the water. You can try a traditional smoke sauna at the Mihkli Farm Museum on Hiiumaa island. Many Estonians refer to Saaremaa island as 'Spa-remaa' for its proliferation of spa resorts, particularly in Kuressaare. You'll find excellent spa spots in Pärnu, Rakvere, Võru and Tallinn as well.

## Lithuania

Lithuania has a less-developed spa and sauna scene than its Baltic brothers, but there are nonetheless a few places to indulge. The two most popular spa destinations are the fabled 19th-century spa town of Druskininkai, on the Nemunas River, and quieter Birštonas; of the two, Druskininkai is the destination of choice for serious spa-seekers. The town, which has been in the healing business for more than 200 years, boasts mineral spas for sipping (with a reputedly recuperative effect on everything from the stomach to the heart), mud baths, a relatively mild climate and miles and miles of surrounding forest, which keeps the air fresh and clean.

Added to that are modern diversions, such as a huge water park, which make the town a perfect respite for the healthy as well as the ailing.

### WORKING UP A SWEAT

Given that it's cold, dark and snowy for many months of the year, it's little surprise that the sauna is an integral part of local culture. Most hotels have one, and some cities have public bathhouses with saunas. But it's those that smoulder silently next to a lake or river, by the sea or deep in the forest that provide the most authentic experience.

There are three main types of sauna in the Baltic:

- In Finnish-style saunas an electric stove keeps the air temperature high (between 70°C and 95°C) and humidity low. These are found in plenty of private homes, most hotels and all spas and water parks etc. Public sauna complexes charge an hourly fee and there are plenty of small private saunas that can be rented by the hour. Some hotels will charge, but others have free facilities for guests, or a free morning or evening sauna included as part of the rate; some hotel suites have a private sauna attached to the bathroom.
- The smoke sauna is the most archaic type, where a fire is lit directly under rocks in the chimney-less building (generally a one-room wooden hut) – heating can take up to five hours. After the fire is put out in the hearth, the heat comes from the warmed rocks. The smoke is let out just before participants enter; the soot-blackened walls are part of the experience. Smoke saunas are rare but have become more popular in recent times.
- The 'Russian sauna', or steam sauna/steam bath, is not as popular in the Baltic region as the Finnish style of sauna, and is found mainly in spas or water parks. In these, the air temperature is medium (about 50°C) and humidity is high.

Locals use a bunch of birch twigs to lightly slap or flick the body, stimulating circulation, irrespective of which sauna type they're sweating in. Some also lather their bodies in various oils and unguents (honey products are popular).

Cooling down is an equally integral part of the experience: most Finnish-style saunas have showers or pools attached, while the more authentic smoke saunas are usually next to a lake or river. In the depths of winter, rolling in snow or cutting out a square metre of ice from a frozen lake in order to take a quick dip is not unheard of.

In public saunas, such as those in spa hotels, a set of rules is usually posted outlining sauna etiquette and what to wear. Swimming costumes are generally required in mixed-gender areas (for men, Speedo-style briefs are the strong preference – some places forbid board shorts), while people tend to go nude in single-sex facilities. Some places provide towels or paper sheets to sit on.

## Hiking

While the Baltic countries lack the craggy grandeur or wild expanses of some of their neighbours, a day or two hiking in one of the forested national parks is rewarding all the same. All that forest (it covers 51% of Estonia, 45% of Latvia and 28% of Lithuania) just begs to be explored, especially if there are beaver dams to spot, berries to pick or tales of resident witches and fairies to hear along the way.

Grab your hiking boots, breathe deeply of the pine-fresh air and hit the trails in the likes of Žemaitija and Aukštaitija National Parks in Lithuania, Gauja National Park in Latvia and Lahemaa National Park in Estonia. Pretty villages and towns that make good bases for exploration include Otepää and Rõuge in Estonia; Valmiera and Cēsis in Latvia; and Nida, Juodkrantė and Ignalina in Lithuania. If ordinary walking doesn't float your boat, make a beeline for Estonia's Soomaa National Park, where you can go on a guided walk through the park's wetlands using special 'bog shoes' that give you access to otherwise hard-to-reach areas.

Above: Water sports on the lagoon, Curonian Spit National Park (p372), Lithuania

Left: Cranes, Matsalu National Park (p146), Estonia

## Water Sports

Having been cooped up for most of the winter, the region comes alive in summer, with locals and visitors taking any opportunity to soak up some vitamin D during the gloriously long days. You're never far from the sea or a lake offering fishing, sailing, windsurfing and swimming. And when the weather doesn't favour outdoor frolicking, there's no shortage of wet and wild water parks (with indoor pools, slides, saunas etc) in big cities and holiday areas – these operators know from experience that a Baltic summer is no guarantee of beach-going weather.

Great Baltic beach spots are Pärnu, Narva-Jõesuu and Saaremaa in Estonia; Jūrmala, Ventspils, Pāvilosta and Liepāja in Latvia; and Palanga, Klaipėda and Nida in Lithuania. More heart-pounding water sports, such as kitesurfing and windsurfing, can be attempted at Pāvilosta in Latvia or on the Curonian Lagoon in Lithuania.

### Canoeing & Rafting

Watching the landscape slide slowly by while paddling down a lazy river is a fabulous way to experience the natural world from a different angle. As the region's rivers are not known for their wild rapids, this is a great place for beginners to hone their skills or for families to entertain the kids. Even if you're usually more into wild than mild, the region's scenic beauty and tranquillity create such a Zen experience you'll quickly forget you haven't hit a single rapid.

In Latvia, the Gauja and Abava Rivers offer uninterrupted routes stretching for several days, and you can join an organised tour or rent gear and run the routes on your own – the best places to start are Sigulda and Cēsis for the Gauja, where you'll find scores of outfitters. The Latgale Lakelands are also excellent. In Lithuania, Aukštaitija National Park, Labanoras Regional Park, Dzūkija National Park, Trakai and Nemunas Loops Regional Park all offer the opportunity for great canoeing; in Aukštaitija and Trakai in particular, you'll find scores of canoes and stand-up paddleboards (SUPs) for hire. Canoes or traditional *haabjas* (Finno-Ugric boats carved from a single log) are a good way to explore Soomaa National Park in southwest Estonia – you can even learn to build your own *haabjas*. Otepää is another good Estonian spot to organise and access canoe trips, as is Haanja Nature Park, plus Matsalu and Vilsandi.

### Fishing

Abundant lakes and miles of rivers and streams provide ample fishing opportunities in all three countries. Visit a regional tourist office for the scoop on the best angling spots and information pertaining to permits.

In the dark depths of the Baltic winter there is no finer experience than dabbling in a touch of ice-fishing with vodka-warmed local fishing folk on the frozen Curonian Lagoon, off the west coast of Lithuania, or at Trakai. The Nemunas Delta Regional Park is another good western Lithuanian fishing spot. In Latvia, the Latgale Lakelands are packed with hundreds of deep-blue lakes offering fishing opportunities galore. In northern Kurzeme, Lake Engure is another favourite angling spot. Huge Lake Peipsi is popular in Estonia.

## Berrying & Mushrooming

The Balts' deep-rooted attachment to the land is reflected in their obsession with berrying and mushrooming – national pastimes in all three countries. Accompanying a local friend into the forest on a summer berrying trip or autumn mushrooming expedition is a wonderful way to appreciate this traditional rural pastime.

If you're keen on picking but lack a local invitation, join an organised tour (locals closely guard the location of their favourite spots, so just asking around probably won't reap any useful information). For info on berrying and mushrooming tours, check out www.atostogoskaime.lt (Lithuania), www.maaturism.ee (Estonia) and www.celotajs.lv (Latvia), and ask at local tourist offices.

Of the more than a thousand types of mushroom found in the region, around 400 are edible and about 100 are poisonous – never eat anything you're not 100% sure about. Unless you're accompanied by a local expert, you're better off heading

### MIDSUMMER MADNESS

In pagan times it was a night of magic and sorcery, when witches ran naked and wild, bewitching flowers and ferns, people and animals. In the agricultural calendar, it marked the end of the spring sowing and the start of the summer harvest. In Soviet times it became a political celebration: a torch of independence was lit in each capital and its flame used to light bonfires throughout the country.

Today Midsummer Day, aka summer solstice or St John's Day, falling on 24 June, is the Balts' biggest party of the year. On this night darkness barely falls – reason alone to celebrate in a part of the world with such short summers and such long, dark winters. In Estonia it is known as Jaanipäev; in Latvia it's Jāņi, Jānu Diena or Līgo; and in Lithuania, Joninės or Rasos (the old pagan name).

Celebrations start on 23 June, particularly in Latvia, where the festival is generally met with the most gusto. Traditionally, people flock to the countryside to celebrate this special night amid lakes and pine forests. Special beers, cheeses and pies are prepared and wreaths are strung together from grasses, while flowers and herbs are hung around the home to bring good luck and keep families safe from evil spirits. Men adorn themselves with crowns made from oak leaves; women wear crowns of flowers.

Come Midsummer's Eve bonfires are lit and the music and drinking begins. No one is allowed to sleep until the sun has sunk and risen again – anyone who does will be cursed with bad luck for the coming year. Traditional folk songs are sung, dances danced and those special beers, cheeses and pies eaten! To ensure good luck, you have to leap back and forth over the bonfire. In Lithuania, clearing a burning wheel of fire as it is rolled down the nearest hill brings you even better fortune. In Estonia, revellers swing on special double-sided Jaanipäev swings, strung from trees in forest clearings or in village squares.

Midsummer's night is a night for lovers. In Estonia the mythical Koit (dawn) and Hämarik (dusk) meet but once a year for an embrace lasting as long as the shortest night of the year. Throughout the Baltic region, lovers seek the mythical fern flower, which blooms only on this night. The dew coating flowers and ferns on midsummer's night is held to be a purifying force, a magical healer and a much sought-after cure for wrinkles – bathe your face in it and you will instantly become more beautiful and more youthful. However, beware the witches of Jaanipäev/Jāni/Joninės, who are known to use it for less enchanting means.

to a market and checking out the freshly picked produce. The crinkle-topped, yellow chanterelle and stubby boletus are among the best. You can also peruse menus for in-season treasures from local forests.

For fungi fanatics, in Lithuania there is Varėna's mushroom festival, held in September every year.

## Birdwatching

Thanks to a key position on north–south migration routes, the Baltic countries are a birder's paradise. Each year hundreds of bird species descend upon the region, attracted by fish-packed wetlands and wide-open spaces relatively devoid of people. White storks arrive by the thousands each spring, nesting on rooftops and telegraph poles throughout the region. Other annual visitors include corncrakes, bitterns, cranes, mute swans, black storks and all types of geese.

### Estonia

In Estonia, some of the best birdwatching in the Baltic is found in Matsalu National Park, where 280 different species (many migratory) can be spotted, and where regular tours are run. Spring migration peaks in April/May, but some species arrive as early as March. Autumn migration begins in July and can last until November. Vilsandi National Park, off Saaremaa, is another prime spot for feathery visitors; the park's headquarters can help arrange birdwatching tours.

### Lithuania

Some 270 of the 330 bird species found in Lithuania frequent the Nemunas Delta Regional Park, making it a must-visit for serious birders. Park authorities can help organise birdwatching expeditions during the peak migratory seasons. The nearby Curonian Spit National Park offers opportunities for spotting up to 200 different species of birds amid dramatic coastal scenery.

### Latvia

In Latvia, keep an eye out for some of Europe's rarest birds in splendid Gauja National Park. With thick forests and numerous wetlands, Ķemeri National Park near Jūrmala is another great birdwatching spot. Trails, boardwalks and spotting towers make it easy to get to the feathered action. Lake Engure, in northern Kurzeme, is a major bird reservation with 186 species (44 endangered) nesting around the lake and its seven islets.

ADRIENNE PITTS/LONELY PLANET ©

Strawberry picking, Saaremaa (p148), Estonia

## Horse Riding

The gentle pace of horseback exploration is definitely in keeping with the yesteryear feel of parts of the Baltic countries. In Estonia, some of the best and most bucolic places to get saddle-sore include Lahemaa National Park, the island of Hiiumaa, and Tika Talu (p149) on Saaremaa – operators here will usually combine rural and coastal rides, and can arrange multiday treks.

In Latvia, head to Plosti, between Kandava and Sabile in the picturesque Abava River Valley; or the well-established Klajumi Stables (p275), outside Krāslava in the Latgale Lakelands. For some four-legged fun in Lithuania, head to Trakai or to the horse museum in the village of Niūronys, outside Anykščiai.

## Skiing

They might not have anything closely resembling a mountain, but Estonia and Latvia haven't let this geographic hurdle hinder their ski-resort efforts. Instead, these countries have become masters at working with what they've got – and that means excelling at cross-country skiing, constructing lifts and runs on the tiniest of hills, and using rooftops and dirt mounds to create vertical drops. At least they've got the climate working for them, with cold temperatures ensuring snow cover for at least four months of the year. Don't expect much in the way of technical terrain or long powder runs, though.

Otepää in southeast Estonia is probably the best of the Baltic winter resorts. It offers limited downhill skiing, myriad cross-country trails, a ski jump and plenty of outlets from which to hire gear. Lively nightlife and a ski-town vibe heighten the appeal. Kicksledding, cross-country skiing and snowshoe excursions are available at Soomaa National Park.

The Gauja Valley is the centre of Latvia's winter-sports scene. Cēsis offers short-but-sweet downhill runs and loads of cross-country trails. Adrenaline junkies disappointed by Sigulda's gentle slopes can get their fix swishing down the town's 1200m-long artificial bobsled run – the five-person contraptions reach speeds of 80km/h!

Lithuania offers downhill skiing on a modest hill at Anykščiai, as well as cross-country skiing amid deep, whispering forests and frozen blue lakes in beautiful Aukštaitija National Park. There's also a huge indoor slope at Druskininkai.

Plan Your Trip

# Family Travel

Relax. The Baltic States present no particular challenges for parents with kids in tow – whether they're beaming babies or tempestuous teens – and there are oodles of opportunities for family fun. Even when the weather puts a dampener on things, there's plenty to see and do.

## Best Regions for Kids

### Estonia

In Pärnu you'll find an endless shallow, sandy, toddler-friendly beach and an excellent water park. Tallinn excels when it comes to good child-focused museums, fairy-tale castles and medieval town centres, while the castle at Rakvere has myriad activities for little ones.

### Latvia

Gauja National Park is an enchanted forest of towering pines, fairy-tale castles, hidden ogres, secreted Soviet bunkers and myriad adventure activities, such as ropes courses, Tarzan swings and canoeing. Jūrmala is a delightful jumble of water parks and a long, sandy beach with shallow water.

### Lithuania

In Vilnius, there's the TV Tower, funicular rides and an excellent toy museum. Along the Baltic coastline, bikes and boats can be rented along the Curonian Spit, plus there are sand dunes to climb. Palanga boasts a beach with shallow water, in-house restaurant entertainers and funfair amusements. In eastern Lithuania, forest exploration, canoeing and swimming in lakes beckon at the Aukštaitija National Park.

## Estonia, Latvia & Lithuania for Kids

While it may have been a little daunting travelling with kids in Estonia, Latvia and Lithuania back when they were Soviet Socialist Republics, nowadays it's a breeze. All three are part of the European Union, so you can expect the same high standards of regulation as you would in Paris or Vienna for everything from baby food to car seats.

The Baltic countries have a fascinating history; this might be of keen interest to most adult visitors, but a visit to a social-history museum can be lost on toddlers and teens alike. Fortunately, there are tons of opportunities for younger travellers to engage with their surroundings in a fun and meaningful manner at various castles, farm complexes, interactive museums and the like. Almost all attractions offer half-price tickets for school-age children and free entry for toddlers.

Throughout the region you'll find tours – particularly day trips from the capital cities – that shuttle visitors to the various attractions of note around the region's major centres. These trips are, in general, not well suited to youngsters. If you have little ones in tow, it's best to tailor-make your own adventure.

Look out for the 👪 icon for family-friendly suggestions throughout this guide.

## Feeding Time

Well-behaved children are welcome at almost all eateries throughout the region, although the more relaxed, family-style restaurants will probably be more enjoyable for parents and children alike. In Latvia, look out for the Lido chain of self-service bistros: they are cheap and cheerful, and little ones can see all the food on offer before they choose something. Child menus are common in Rīga. In Estonia, anything labelled *kõrts* (tavern) is a good bet.

The stodgy, somewhat bland nature of traditional Baltic food will suit the palates of most children. While they might baulk at the pickled herrings and sauerkraut, the myriad local versions of pork, chicken and potatoes should pose no particular challenges.

Favourite standbys such pizza and pasta are ubiquitous, and usually of sufficient quality to please an adult palate as well. In any event, many places have children's menus serving smaller portions. For something a little different but equally as cheap, filling and crowd-pleasing, try a plate of Russian-style *pelmeņi* dumplings.

On the downside, you won't find many high chairs in restaurants, and nappy-changing rooms are virtually unheard of.

## Other Practicalities

Nappies (diapers) and known-brand baby foods, including some organic ones, are widely available in supermarkets in the main towns.

All of the big-name car-rental brands should be able to supply appropriate car seats, but it's best to check what's available and to book in advance. If you've got a good-quality, comfortable, capsule-style baby seat of your own that you're familiar with, you might want to consider bringing it with you, as they can be very handy as portable cots.

# Children Will Love

## Encounters with History

**Tallinn's Old Town, Estonia** (p55) Fairy-tale turrets, medieval streetscapes and waitstaff dressed as peasant wenches and farmboys.

**Turaida Museum Reserve, Latvia** (p261) Explore the castle, watch blacksmiths at work and seek out the kooky sculptures in the song garden.

**Grūtas Park, Lithuania** (p333) A step back into the Soviet era, with the added bonus of vintage play equipment and a mini zoo for the little ones.

**Rakvere Castle, Estonia** (p96) Smaller kids can dress up as princesses and knights and pet farm animals; older kids can can scream their heads off in the torture chamber and watch alchemists blow things up.

**Palace of the Grand Dukes of Lithuania, Lithuania** (p293) Interactive multimedia displays.

**Soviet Secret Bunker, Līgatne, Latvia** (p265) A hidden bunker, called the Pension, stocked with heaps of relics from the Soviet era – truly interesting for all ages.

**Narva Castle, Estonia** (p100) In summer there's a mock-up of a 17th-century town in the castle yard.

**Ludza Craftsmen Centre, Latvia** (p277) Put your kids to work spinning wool, making pottery and sewing.

**House of Crafts, Ventspils, Latvia** (p240) An old-school classroom features craft demonstrations.

**Old Town Days, Estonia** (p72) This summer celebration of Tallinn's long history has a rich program of kids' activities.

## Fun Museums & Galleries

**Science Centre AHHAA, Tartu, Estonia** (p110) Experiential, science-based displays designed to turn your progeny into mad scientists.

**Tērvete Nature Park, Tērvete, Latvia** (p253) A kid's fantasyland populated by whimsical wood-carved figures that almost come alive in the dark shade of ancient fir trees.

**Tartu Toy Museum, Estonia** (p109) Toys to covet, toys to play with, toys to make grown-ups feel nostalgic.

**Lennusadam Seaplane Harbour, Tallinn, Estonia** (p63) Loads of interactive displays, with a real submarine, an ice-breaker and a mine-hunter to explore.

**Narrow-Gauge Railway Museum, Anykščiai, Lithuania** (p361) Take a ride on a manual rail car and a historic train.

**Tallinn Zoo, Estonia** (p68) Lots of big beasts and cute critters to see and learn about.

**Horse Museum, Niūronys, Lithuania** (p361) Check out the historic carts and carriages, take a ride and bake your own black bread.

**Palamuse Museum, Estonia** (p110) Where else will adults encourage kids to grab a slingshot and shoot a stone through a real glass window?

**Nuku, Tallinn, Estonia** (p68) The national puppet museum offers dress-ups, puppets to play with and look at, and regular shows.

**Toy Museum, Lithuania** (p295) A wealth of toys and games from the 12th century onwards will keep the little ones enthralled for hours.

**Ilon's Wonderland, Haapsalu, Estonia** (p143) Child-focused gallery showcasing the work of noted kids' book illustrator Ilon Wikland.

## Activities

**Sigulda, Latvia** (p261) Long established as the go-to spot for adrenaline lovers. Heart-pounding bungee jumps and bobsled tracks are the main attraction, but there are plenty of more subdued options for younger children.

**Nida, Lithuania** (p377) Shifting sand dunes and miles of windswept beaches make it the best place in the Baltics to build the ultimate sandcastle.

**Ventspils, Latvia** (p239) A huge playground (Children's Town), a narrow-gauge railway and loads of fun things to do on the beach.

**Palanga, Lithuania** (p384) A seaside resort lined with kid-friendly amusements: inflatable slides, merry-go-rounds, electric cars etc.

**Pärnu, Estonia** (p134) This historic town is a veritable magnet for families, with its leafy parks, large indoor water park and lovely shallow, sandy beach.

**Witches' Hill, Juodkrantė, Lithuania** (p375) Wander amid fairy-tale wooden carvings and slide down a devil's tongue.

**Otepää, Estonia** (p125) Estonia's self-proclaimed 'winter capital' actually offers a bevy of nature-related activities throughout the year, including an excellent high-ropes course.

**Jūrmala, Latvia** (p228) A particularly family-friendly beach resort.

**Aqua Park, Druskininkai, Lithuania** (p336) There's a fabulous water park for the kids – and spa treatments for parents!

**Nõmme Adventure Park, Estonia** (p68) This leafy adventure park south of Tallinn offers tree-top rope courses, zip lines, trails and more.

# Good to Know

## When to Go

The long days and mild weather make summer the perfect time to travel around the Baltic with children – although the virtual lack of darkness during midsummer can play havoc with children's sleeping schedules. In summertime, outdoor tourist amenities are in full swing: beach towns come alive and myriad rental cottages dot the interior. It is, however, very popular with all types of holidaymakers, so it's crucial that you book accommodation and car rental in advance (remembering to request cribs and car seats if you require them).

## What to Pack

Don't stress too much about the packing, as whatever you forget should easily be found for purchase in any of the capital cities. Whatever the season, a bathing suit is a must, as there are many heated indoor pools to enjoy when it's too miserable to hit the beaches.

Make sure you've got insect repellent handy before you head onto the islands or into the national parks – the mosquitoes are enormous and voracious.

## Accommodation

Most hotels will do their best to help make kids feel at home. Many have family rooms with a double bed for parents and a single or bunks for the kids. Cots are often available, especially in the larger establishments, although it's best to enquire and request one in advance. There might be a small charge for the cot, but in most instances infants can stay in a double room for free.

# Regions at a Glance

At a glance, the Baltic States look like three easily interchangeable slices, neatly stacked on Europe's northeastern frontier. However, though the region's shared history and topography may be the ties that bind, each country is quite different in other respects – language, religion and temperament being the most obvious examples.

The three capitals are a case in point. Estonia's presents itself as a Gothic fairy tale, Lithuania's is full of the thrilling frills of the baroque, while Latvia's is properly kooky, its famous art nouveau buildings embellished with gods, monsters, crazed cats and nature motifs.

Less variations on a theme than separate movements of a symphony, each of the Baltic States can be savoured individually or combined into a magnum opus. And you can play them in any order you like.

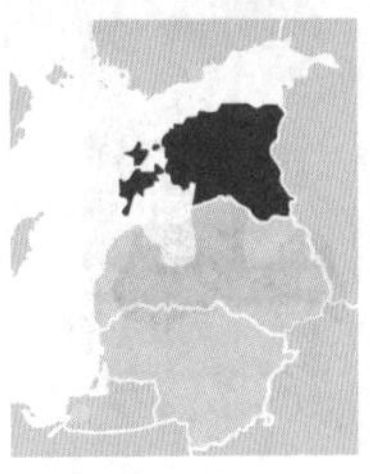

## Estonia

**Historic Towns**
**Castles**
**Nature**

### Hanseatic Heritage

From Tallinn's magnificent medieval Old Town to the genteel lanes and parks of Pärnu and the university precinct of Tartu, Estonia has a wealth of streets that time seemingly forgot.

### Brooding Battlements

There has to be a bright side to being precariously positioned between contending European powers – in Estonia's case, the legacy of a millennium of warfare is a spectacular crop of fortresses scattered throughout the country.

### Forests & Wetlands

Estonia's countryside may be flat and unassuming compared with craggier parts of Europe, but its low population density and extensive forests, bogs and wetlands make it an important habitat for a multitude of mammals large and small, as well as a biannual seasonal influx of feathered visitors.

p50

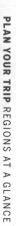

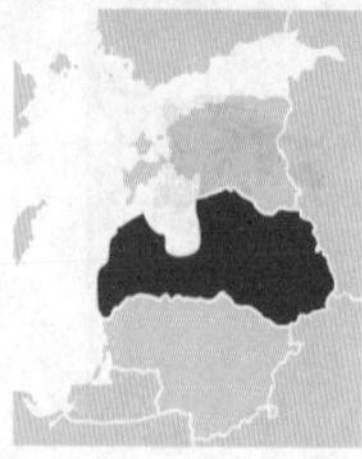

## Latvia

**Architecture**
**Castles**
**Nature**

### Art Nouveau Rīga

No one mastered art nouveau like Rīga's coterie of architects at the turn of the 20th century. They covered the city's myriad facades with screaming goblins, praying goddesses, creeping vines and geometric emblems.

### Noble Remains

Once the feudal playground of German nobles, Latvia is riddled with crumbling reminders of a bygone era. Many of these castles and manor houses have been lovingly restored and transformed into memorable inns – the perfect place to enact your fairy-tale fantasies.

### Scenery & Serenity

Beyond Rīga's clutch of twisting spires and towering housing blocks you'll find miles and miles of quiet forests, intimate lakelands and flaxen, unpeopled shores that beckon the crashing Baltic tides.

p193

## Lithuania

**Nature**
**Architecture**
**Nightlife**

### Untouched Landscapes

The Baltic coast, the dunes of Curonian Spit and the large forests broken up by meadows and lakes: Lithuania's landscape is blissfully unspoiled. Good tourist infrastructure allows you to hike it, bike it or boat it at your own pace.

### Colour & Grandeur

Vilnius' attractive Old Town is filled with Renaissance, baroque and neoclassical architecture. Outside the city, the simple wooden structures of the traditional rural villages will wow you with vivid colours and intricate carvings.

### Vilnius after Dark

Vilnius and Kaunas are home to thousands of students, who haunt their bars and clubs. The centre of Vilnius' action is the Old Town, while in Kaunas it's a choice between Old Town cellar bars and New Town craft beer.

p288

# On the Road

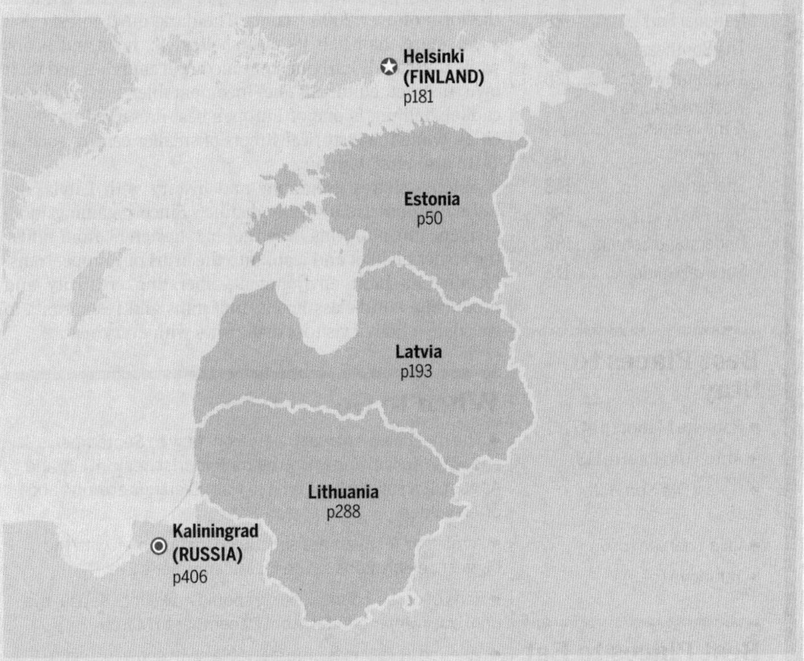

Helsinki (FINLAND) p181

Estonia p50

Latvia p193

Lithuania p288

Kaliningrad (RUSSIA) p406

# Estonia

☎372 / POP 1.3 MILLION

**Includes ➡**



## Best Places to Stay

- ➡ Pädaste Manor (p147)
- ➡ Antonius Hotel (p113)
- ➡ Georg Ots Spa Hotel (p154)
- ➡ Villa Theresa (p97)
- ➡ Tabinoya (p73)

## Best Places to Eat

- ➡ NOA (p79)
- ➡ Kuur (p161)
- ➡ Restaurant Ö (p79)
- ➡ Alexander (p147)
- ➡ Moon (p78)

## Why Go?

'Eesti', as it's known to its people, is a pint-sized gem. Squeezed in between Latvia, Russia and the Gulf of Finland, its sparsely populated territory spills out into the Baltic in the form of over 2000 islands. The dark, quiet forests that cover more than half its face shelter elk, boar and bears, while the islands harbour stout medieval churches and their own distinct cultures. The incomparable, heritage-listed capital, Tallinn, is one of Europe's best-preserved medieval cities, while the historical streets of smaller centres such as Tartu also buzz with life.

Estonia shares geography and history with Latvia and Lithuania, but is culturally distinct. Since regaining independence in 1991, this little republic has crept from under the Soviet blanket and leapt into the arms of Europe, transforming its built environment, liberating creativity and producing world-class hotels, museums and restaurants to welcome a tide of visitors that grows with every year.

## When to Go

➡ The most clement weather is from May to September, and while Tallinn and Pärnu hit their tourist peak in July and August, it's still the best time to visit. Evenings are long and often golden.

➡ Almost all festivals are scheduled for summer, with the biggest celebrations saved for Midsummer's Eve.

➡ Fans of cross-country skiing should make for Otepää, the unofficial winter capital, from December to March.

➡ Yuletide in Tallinn is unforgettable, with snow (usually), bustling markets and a nearly 600-year-old tradition of raising a Christmas tree on the market square.

## TALLINN

POP 434,562

No longer the plaything of greater powers – Danish, Swedish, Polish, German and Soviet – Tallinn is now a proud European capital with an allure all of its own. It's lively yet peaceful, absurdly photogenic and bursting with wonderful sights – ancient churches, medieval streetscapes and noble merchants' houses. Throw in delightful food and vibrant modern culture, and it's no wonder Tallinn seems in danger of being loved to death, especially after a few cruise ships dock. But it's one of those blessed places that seems to cope with all the attention.

Despite the boom of 21st-century development, Tallinn safeguards the fairy-tale charms of its Unesco-listed Old Town – one of Europe's most complete walled cities. Some examples of exuberant post-Soviet development aside, the city clearly realises it's better to be classy than brassy. Hence the blossoming of first-rate restaurants, atmospheric hotels and a well-oiled tourist machine that makes visiting a breeze.

### ESTONIA AT A GLANCE

**Currency** euro (€)

**Language** Estonian

**Capital** Tallinn

**Area** 45,339 sq km

### History

Tallinn's naturally commanding site, on ground overlooking the Gulf of Finland, is thought to have been settled by Finno-Ugric people around 2500 BC. There was probably a proto-Estonian trading settlement here from around the 9th century AD and a wooden stronghold was built on Toompea (*tawm*-pe-ah; the hill dominating Tallinn) in the 11th century. The Danes under King Waldemar II (who conquered northern Estonia in 1219) met tough resistance at Tallinn and were on the verge of retreat when it's said that a red flag with a white cross (the 'Dannebrog') fell from the sky into their bishop's hands. Taking this as a sign of God's support, they went on to win the battle and gain a national flag. The Danes built their own castle on Toompea, and are thought to have given Tallinn its name: *Taani linn,* Estonian for 'Danish town'.

The Livonian Brothers of the Sword, a Germanic order of crusading warrior-monks, took Tallinn from the Danes in 1227 and built the first stone fort on Toompea. German traders arrived from Visby on the Baltic island of Gotland and founded a colony of about 200 people beneath the fortress. In 1238 Tallinn returned to Danish control but in 1285 it joined the German-dominated Hanseatic League as a channel for trade between Novgorod, Pihkva (Russian: Pskov) and the West. Furs, honey, leather and seal fat moved west; salt, cloth, herring and wine went east.

By the mid-14th century, when the Danes sold northern Estonia to the Teutonic Order, Tallinn was a major Hanseatic town with a prime position on the Gulf of Finland trade channel and a population of about 4000. Conflict with the knights and bishop on the hill led the mainly German artisans and merchants in the lower town to build a fortified wall to separate themselves from Toompea. Tallinn prospered regardless and became one of northern Europe's biggest towns. Tallinn's German name, Reval, coexisted with the local name until 1918.

Prosperity faded in the 16th century as the Hanseatic League weakened and Russians, Swedes, Danes, Poles and Lithuanians fought over the Baltic region. Sweden held Tallinn from 1561, withstanding a 29-week siege by Russia's Ivan the Terrible (1570 to 1571) but surrendering to Peter the Great in 1710, when the town was ravaged by plague.

In 1870 a railway was completed from St Petersburg, and Tallinn became a chief port of the Russian Empire. Freed peasants converged on the city from the countryside, increasing the percentage of Estonians in its population from 52% in 1867 to 89% in 1897. By WWI Tallinn had big shipyards and a working class of over 100,000. It was the natural capital of the brief Estonian Republic of 1920–40.

Tallinn suffered badly in WWII, with thousands of buildings destroyed during Soviet bombing in 1944. After the war, under Soviet control, large-scale industry was developed – including the USSR's biggest grain-handling port – and the city expanded, growing to nearly 500,000 from a 1937 level of 175,000. Much of the new population came from Russia and new high-rise suburbs were built on the outskirts to house the workers.

The explosion of Soviet-style settlements in the suburbs meant a loss of cultural life in the centre. By the 1980s, Tallinn's Old

# Estonia Highlights

❶ **Tallinn** (p51) Scouring cobbled lanes for the museums, churches, restaurants and bars of one of Europe's best-preserved medieval cities.

❷ **Lahemaa National Park** (p88) Wandering the forest paths, bog boardwalks, boulder-strewn beaches and manor houses of the country's favourite national park.

❸ **Tartu** (p105) Furthering your education among the museums and student bars of Estonia's second city.

❹ **Saaremaa** (p148) Unwinding among the

windmills, castles, churches, cliffs and spas of Estonia's largest island.

**5** **Muhu** (p146) Hopping over to frozen-in-island-time Koguva village and the bucolic back-country of this green gem.

**6** **Pärnu** (p134) Strolling the golden sands and boulevards of Estonia's 'summer capital'.

**7** **Setomaa** (p118) Touring through the quiet villages, traditional farms and whispering forests of the land of the Setos.

## Tallinn

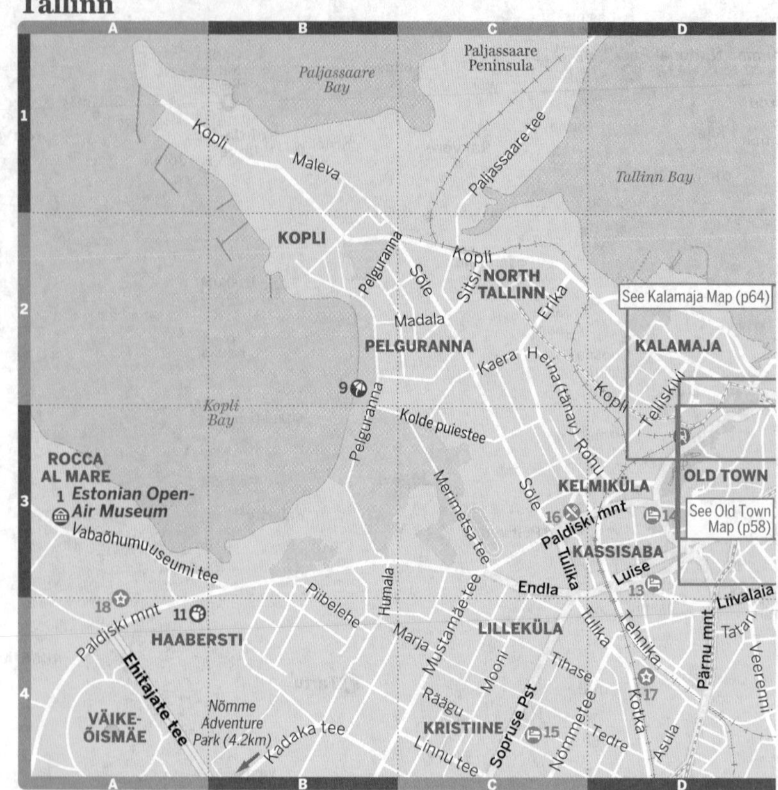


### Tallinn

**Top Sights**
1 Estonian Open-Air Museum ........ A3

**Sights**
2 Film Museum ........ G2
3 Maarjamäe History Centre ........ F2
4 Maarjamäe Palace ........ F2
5 Maarjamäe Stables ........ G2
6 Maarjamäe War Memorial ........ G2
7 Pirita Beach ........ G1
8 Pirita Convent ........ G1
9 Stroomi Beach ........ B2
10 Tallinn Song Festival Grounds ........ F2
11 Tallinn Zoo ........ A4

**Activities, Courses & Tours**
12 Bell-Marine Boat Rental ........ G1

**Sleeping**
13 Kreutzwald Hotel Tallinn ........ D3
14 L'Ermitage ........ D3
15 Valge Villa ........ C4

**Eating**
16 Kolm Sibulat ........ C3

**Entertainment**
17 A Le Coq Arena ........ D4
18 Saku Suurhall ........ A4

Town was run-down, with most people preferring to live in the new housing developments. It began to be renovated late in the decade, with the fight for independence largely playing out on these historic streets.

The 1990s saw Tallinn transformed into a contemporary mid-sized city, with a restored Old Town and a modern business district. Central Tallinn shows a taste for all things new and pleasurable, with IT-driven businesses to the fore and a tech-savvy,

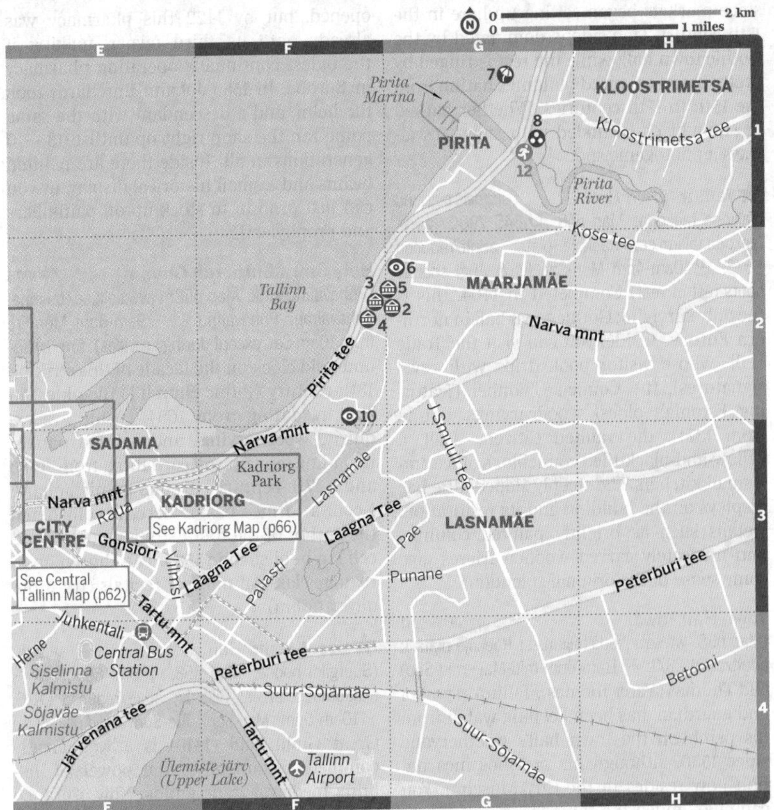


wi-fi-connected populace enjoying increasingly excellent restaurants and life opportunities. However, the outskirts of the city have yet to get the facelift that the centre has received – in these untouristed parts, poverty and unemployment are more evident.

## Sights

### Old Town

The medieval jewel of Estonia, Tallinn's Old Town *(vanalinn)* is without a doubt the country's most photogenic and fascinating locality. Picking your way along the narrow, cobbled streets of its two distinct neighbourhoods, Toompea and the lower town, is like strolling into the 15th century. You'll pass the ornate stone facades of Hanseatic merchants' houses, wander into hidden medieval courtyards, and find footworn stone stairways leading to sweeping views of the red-roofed city. It's staggeringly popular with tourists, but manages to remain largely unspoilt: while most historic buildings have helpful bilingual plaques, pleasingly few have been turned into pizza restaurants.

Of course, being so popular comes with its downsides. In summer as many as six giant cruise ships can descend at a time, disgorging their human cargo in slow-moving, flag-following phalanxes that can bring foot traffic to a complete halt. If you're travelling on such a ship, it's worth noting that Old Town is within walking distance of the harbour; you'll have a much better time if you dodge the organised tours and follow your own path. For everyone else, rest assured that most of the boats steam off again in the afternoon, leaving the streets relatively clear by 5pm.

### Lower Town

**Town Hall Square** SQUARE

(Raekoja plats; Map p58) In Tallinn all roads lead to Raekoja plats, the city's pulsing heart since markets began setting up here in the 11th century. One side is dominated by the Gothic town hall, while the rest is ringed by pretty pastel-coloured buildings dating from the 15th to 17th centuries. Whether bathed in sunlight or sprinkled with snow, it's always a photogenic spot.

**★Tallinn Town Hall** HISTORIC BUILDING
(Tallinna raekoda; Map p58; ☎645 7900; www.raekoda.tallinn.ee; Raekoja plats; adult/reduced €5/3; ⏱10am-4pm Mon-Sat Jul & Aug, shorter hours rest of year) Completed in 1404, this is the only surviving Gothic town hall in northern Europe. Inside, you can visit the Trade Hall (whose visitor book drips with royal signatures), the Council Chamber (featuring Estonia's oldest woodcarvings, dating from 1374), the vaulted Citizens' Hall, a yellow-and-black-tiled councillor's office and a small kitchen. The steeply sloped attic has displays on the building and its restoration. Details such as brightly painted columns and intricately carved wooden friezes give some sense of the original splendour.

**Town Hall Tower** VIEWPOINT
(Map p58; www.raekoda.tallinn.ee; Raekoja plats 1; adult/child €3/1; ⏱11am-6pm mid-May–mid-Sep) Old Thomas (Vana Toomas), Tallinn's symbol and guardian, has been keeping watch from his perch on the town hall's weathervane since 1530, although his previous incarnation now resides in the City Museum. You can enjoy much the same views as Thomas by climbing the 115 steps to the top of the tower. According to legend, this elegant 64m minaret-like structure was modelled on a sketch made by an explorer following his visit to the Orient.

**Town Council Pharmacy** HISTORIC BUILDING
(Raeapteek; Map p58; ☎5887 5701; www.raeapteek.ee; Raekoja plats 11; ⏱10am-6pm Mon-Sat) Nobody's too sure of the exact date it opened, but by 1422 this pharmacy was already onto its third owner, making it the oldest continually operating pharmacy in Europe. In 1583 Johann Burchardt took the helm, and a descendant with the same name ran the shop right up until 1913 – 10 generations in all! Inside there are painted beams and a small historical display, or you can just drop in to stock up on painkillers and prophylactics.

**Holy Spirit Lutheran Church** CHURCH
(Pühavaimu kirik; Map p58; www.eelk.ee/tallinna.puhavaimu; Pühavaimu 2; ⏱9am-6pm Mon-Fri, from 10am Sat, except during services) The blue-and-gold clock on the facade of this striking 13th-century Gothic church is the oldest in Tallinn, dating from 1684. Inside are exquisite woodcarvings and painted panels, including an altarpiece dating from 1483 and a 17th-century baroque pulpit. Johann Koell, a former pastor here, is considered the author of the first Estonian book, a catechism published in 1535. The church hosts regular classical musical recitals (try Mondays at 6pm).

**★Great Guild Hall** MUSEUM
(Suurgildi hoone; Map p58; ☎696 8690; www.ajaloomuuseum.ee; Pikk 17; adult/reduced €8/6; ⏱10am-6pm May-Sep, Tue-Sun Oct-Apr) The Great Guild Hall (1410) is a wonderfully complete testament to the power of Tallinn's medieval trade guilds. Now a branch of the Estonian History Museum, its showpiece exhibition is 'Spirit of Survival: 11,000 Years of Estonian History', illustrating the history and psyche of Estonia through interactive and unusual displays. There's also the old excise chamber, with numismatic relics stretching back to Viking times; the basement, exploring the history of the Guild itself; and sections on Estonian music, language and geography.

## LANGUAGE

| | | |
|---|---|---|
| **Hello** | *Tere* | te-rre |
| **Goodbye** | *Head aega* | head *ae*-gah |
| **Yes** | *Jah* | yah |
| **No** | *Ei* | ay |
| **Thank you** | *Tänan* | *ta*-nahn |
| **You're welcome** | *Palun* | *pah*-lun |
| **Excuse me/I'm sorry** | *Vabandage* | *vah*-bahn-dah-ge |
| **Cheers!** (literally 'to your health') | *Terviseks!* | *ter*-vi-seks |

## TALLINN IN...

### Two Days

Spend your first day exploring **Old Town** (p55). Tackle our **walking tour** (p70) in the morning and then stop for lunch in one of the city's many excellent eateries – **Väike**, (p77), just east of Town Hall Sq, has great menu options. Spend your afternoon exploring one or two of the museums – perhaps the **City Museum** and the branch of the **Estonian History Museum at the Great Guild Hall**. In the evening, dress smart and head to posh Russian restaurant **Tchaikovsky** (p78) for dinner, finishing up in one (or two) Old Town bars.

The following day, do what most tourists don't – step out of Old Town. Head to **Kadriorg** (p65) for a greenery-and-art fix and continue on to **Maarjamäe** (p67) to visit the museums and the war memorial. In the evening, hit the **Rotermann Quarter** (p65) for great food and bars.

### Four Days

Four days is enough to cover the remainder of central Tallinn's highlights, with more nights of eating and partying too. Round out your days with trips to relatively further-flung highlights such as the **Seaplane Harbour** (p63) maritime museum, the **Museum of Occupations** (p63), the **Estonian Open-Air Museum** (p68) and the **TV Tower** (p68).

Allow some time to wander around the super-hip **Telliskivi Creative City** (p65) – a great place to eat and/or enjoy a restorative aperitif – and to explore the blooming **Kalamaja** (p63) neighbourhood, just beyond.

**St Catherine's Church** CHURCH

(Püha Katariina kirik; Map p58; www.hopnerimaja.eu; Vene 14a; €3; ⏲11am-5pm Tue-Sat Jun-Aug) Perhaps Tallinn's oldest building, St Catherine's Monastery was founded by Dominican monks in 1246. In its glory days it had its own brewery and hospital. A mob of angry Lutherans torched the place in 1524 and the monastery languished for the next 400 years until its partial restoration in 1954. Today the part-ruined complex includes the gloomy shell of the church (an atmospheric venue for occasional recitals) and a peaceful cloister lined with carved tombstones.

**St Peter & St Paul's Catholic Cathedral** CATHEDRAL

(Peeter-Pauli Katedraal; Map p58; ☎644 6367; www.katoliku.ee; Vene 18; ⏲9.30am-1pm Sun, 5.30-6.30pm Mon, Tue & Thu-Sat, 7.45-9.30am Wed) Looking like it was beamed in from Spain, this handsome 1844 cathedral was designed by the famed architect Carlo Rossi, who left his mark on the neoclassical shape of St Petersburg. Built where the refectory of its neighbour St Catherine's once stood, it's still one of Tallinn's only Catholic churches, largely serving the Polish and Lithuanian communities (although there's also an English-language mass at 6pm each Saturday). The front courtyard offers some respite from the summertime bustle.

**City Museum** MUSEUM

(Linnamuuseum; Map p58; ☎615 5180; www.linnamuuseum.ee; Vene 17; adult/reduced €6/4; ⏲10am-6pm daily May-Sep, 10am-8pm Tue, to 5pm Wed-Sat, to 4pm Sun Oct-Apr) Tallinn's City Museum is actually split over seven different sites. This location, its main branch, is set in a 14th-century merchant's house and traces the city's development from its earliest days. The displays are engrossing and very well laid out, with plenty of information in English, making the hire of the audio guide quite unnecessary. Displays illuminate Estonian language, everyday life, and artefacts and cultural developments.

**St Nicholas' Orthodox Church** CHURCH

(Püha piiskop Nikolause kirik; Map p58; www.stnicolas.ee; Vene 24; ⏲10am-5pm Mon-Fri, 8am-7pm Sat, 7.30am-3pm Sun) Built in 1827 on the site of an earlier Catholic church appearing in 15th-century records, St Nicholas' was the focal point for the Russian traders that Vene street was named for. It's known for its precious iconostasis (a relic-filled screen that separates nave from sanctuary in Orthodox churches).

**Fat Margaret** MUSEUM

(Paks Margareeta; Map p58; ☎673 3092; www.meremuuseum.ee; Pikk 70; adult/child €6/3; ⏲10am-7pm daily May-Sep, to 6pm Tue-Sun Oct-Apr) Attached to the Great Coast Gate, this

# Old Town

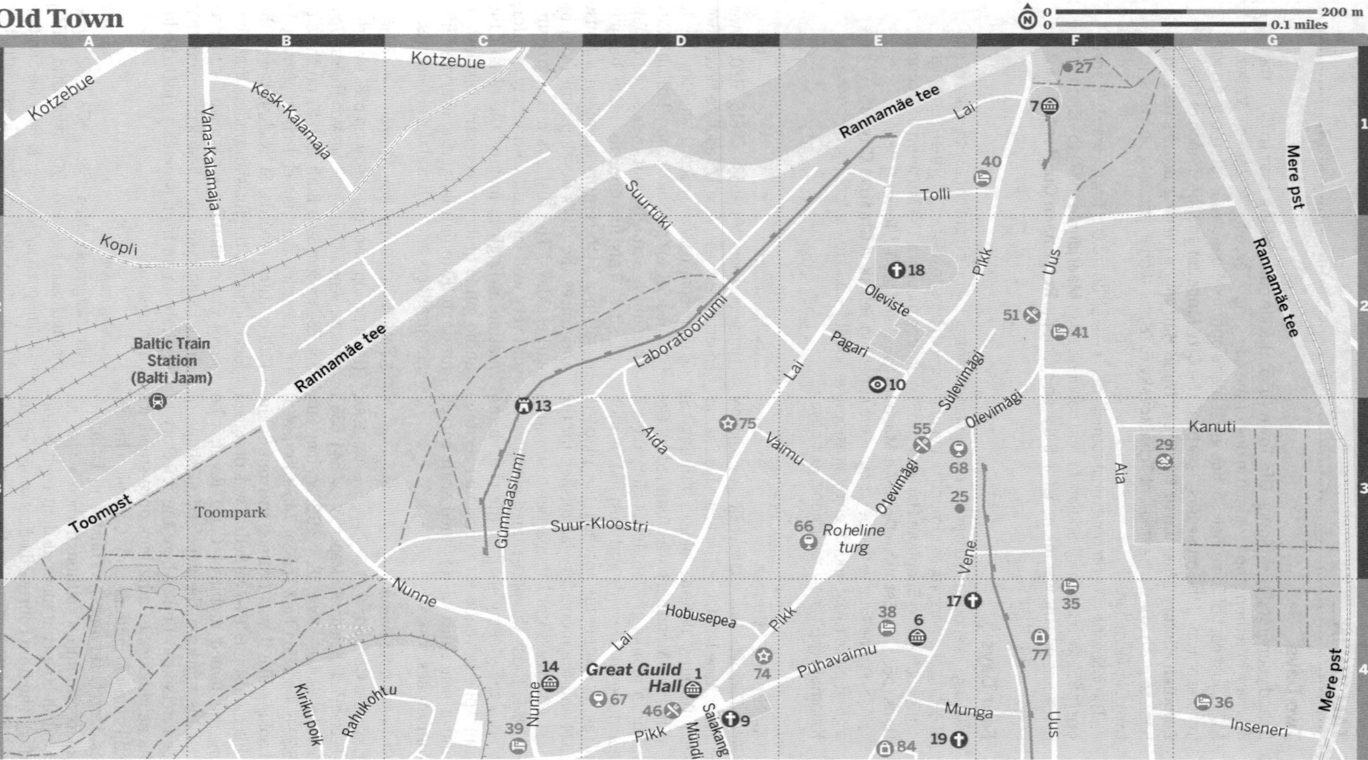
0 200 m
0 0.1 miles
A
B
C
D
E
F
G
1
2
3
4
Kotzebue
Kesk-Kalamaja
Vana-Kalamaja
Kopli
Baltic Train Station (Balti Jaam)
Rannamäe tee
Toompst
Toompark
Suurtüki
Laboratooriumi
Gümnaasiumi
Suur-Kloostri
Nunne
Aida
Lai
Vaimu
Hobusepea
Pikk
Pühavaimu
Great Guild Hall
Saiakang
Mündi
Kiriku poik
Rahukohtu
Tolli
Oleviste
Pagari
Sulevimägi
Olevimägi
Roheline turg
Vene
Munga
Uus
Aia
Kanuti
Inseneri
Mere pst
1
6
7
9
10
13
14
17
18
19
25
27
29
35
36
38
39
40
41
46
51
55
66
67
68
74
75
77
84

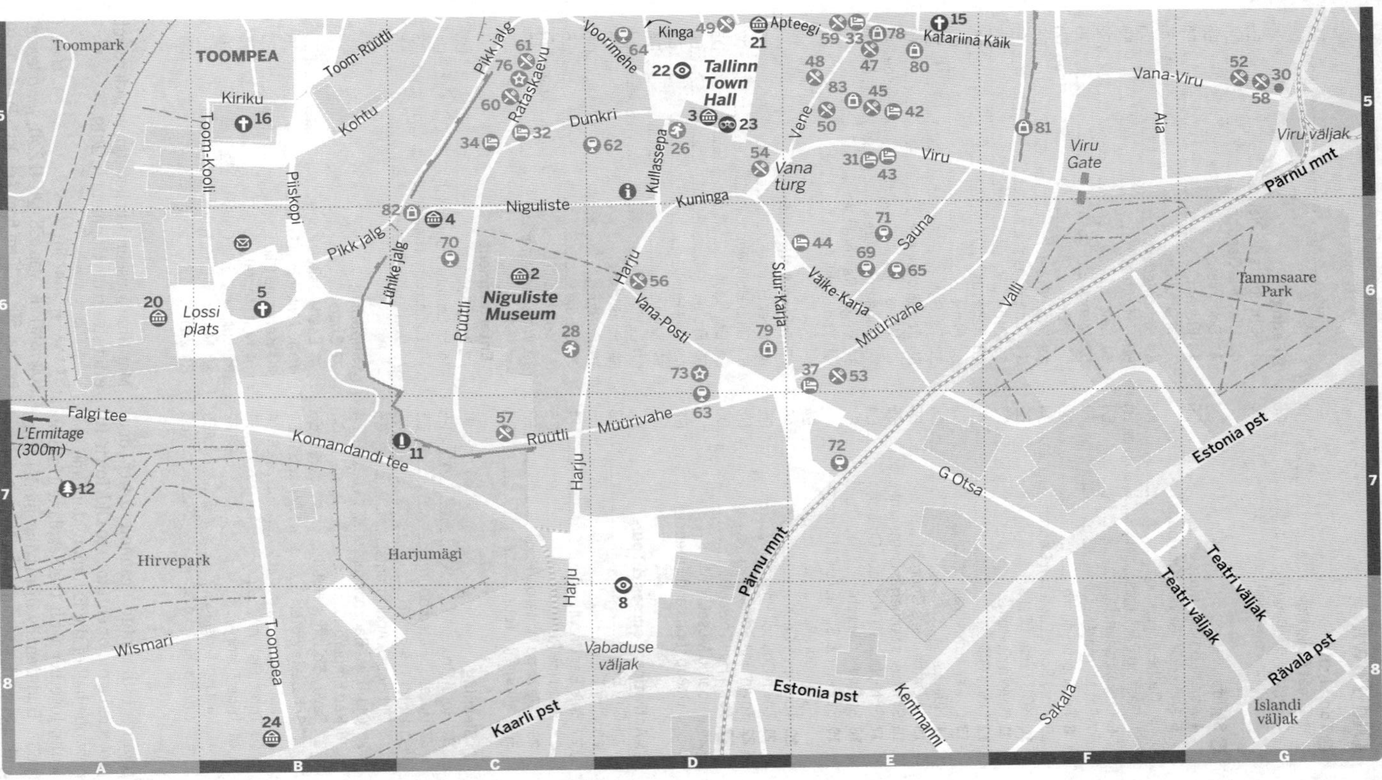

Toompark
TOOMPEA
Toom-Rüütli
Kiriku
Toom-Kooli
Kohtu
Piiskopi
Pikk jalg
Rataskaevu
Voorimehe
Kinga
Apteegi
Tallinn Town Hall
Katariina Käik
Vana-Viru
Dunkri
Kullassepa
Vene
Vana turg
Viru
Aia
Viru Gate
Viru väljak
Pärnu mnt
Niguliste
Kuninga
Pikk jalg
Lühike jalg
Harju
Sauna
Suur-Karja
Väike-Karja
Tammsaare Park
Niguliste Museum
Lossi plats
Rüütli
Vana-Posti
Müürivahe
Valli
Falgi tee
L'Ermitage (300m)
Komandandi tee
Rüütli
Müürivahe
Estonia pst
G Otsa
Harju
Hirvepark
Harjumägi
Harju
Pärnu mnt
Teatri väljak
Teatri väljak
Wismari
Toompea
Vabaduse väljak
Estonia pst
Kentmanni
Sakala
Rävala pst
Islandi väljak
Kaarli pst

## Old Town

**Top Sights**
1 Great Guild Hall ... D4
2 Niguliste Museum ... C6
3 Tallinn Town Hall ... D5

**Sights**
4 Adamson-Eric Museum ... C6
5 Alexander Nevsky Orthodox Cathedral ... B6
Bastion Passages ... (see 11)
6 City Museum ... E4
7 Fat Margaret ... F1
8 Freedom Square ... D8
9 Holy Spirit Lutheran Church ... D4
10 KGB Prison Cells ... E2
11 Kiek in de Kök ... C7
12 Linda Hill ... A7
13 Lower Town Wall ... C3
14 Nuku ... C4
15 St Catherine's Church ... E5
16 St Mary's Lutheran Cathedral ... B5
17 St Nicholas' Orthodox Church ... E4
18 St Olaf's Church ... E2
19 St Peter & St Paul's Catholic Cathedral ... E4
20 Toompea Castle ... A6
21 Town Council Pharmacy ... D5
22 Town Hall Square ... D5
23 Town Hall Tower ... D5
24 Vabamu Museum of Occupations and Freedom ... B8

**Activities, Courses & Tours**
25 City Bike ... E3
26 City Train ... D5
27 Epic Bar Crawl ... F1
28 Harju Ice Rink ... C6
29 Kalev Spa Waterpark ... F3
30 Tallinn City Tour ... G5

**Sleeping**
31 Hotel Cru ... E5
32 Hotel St Petersbourg ... C5
33 Hotel Telegraaf ... E5
34 Old House Apartments ... C5
35 Old Town Backpackers ... F4
36 Red Emperor ... G4
37 Savoy Boutique Hotel ... E6
38 Schlössle Hotel ... E4
39 Tabinoya ... C4
40 Three Sisters ... F1
41 Tribe Theory ... F2
42 Villa Hortensia ... E5
43 Viru Backpackers ... E5
44 Zinc ... E6

**Eating**
45 Chocolats de Pierre ... E5
46 Clayhills Gastropub ... D4
47 Dominic ... E5
48 Elevant ... E5
III Draakon ... (see 23)
49 Kehrwieder ... D5
50 La Bottega ... E5
51 Leib ... F2
52 Manna La Roosa ... G5
MEKK ... (see 37)
53 Must Puudel ... E6
54 Olde Hansa ... D5
55 ORE ... E3
56 Pegasus ... D6
57 Plant ... C7
58 Tai Boh ... G5
59 Tchaikovsky ... E5
Väike ... (see 34)
Vanaema Juures ... (see 76)
60 Vegan Restoran V ... C5
61 Von Krahli Aed ... C5

**Drinking & Nightlife**
62 Beer House ... D5
63 Club Hollywood ... D7
64 DM Baar ... D5
65 Frank ... E6
66 Hell Hunt ... E3
67 Koht ... D4
68 Levist Väljas ... E3
69 Paar Veini ... E6
70 Pôrgu ... C6
71 Studio ... E6
Von Krahli Baar ... (see 76)
72 Whisper Sister ... E7

**Entertainment**
73 Kino Sõprus ... D6
74 St Canute's Guild Hall ... D4
75 Tallinn City Theatre ... D3
76 Von Krahli Teater ... C5

**Shopping**
77 Chado ... F4
78 Eesti Käsitöö Kodu ... E5
79 Ivo Nikkolo ... D6
80 Katariina Gild ... E5
81 Knit Market ... F5
82 Lühikese Jala Galerii ... C6
83 Masters' Courtyard ... E5
84 Zizi ... E4

rotund 16th-century cannon tower once protected a major entrance to Old Town. It's now one half of the Estonian Maritime Museum, together with the Seaplane Harbour (p63). Traditionally displaying model ships and assorted seagoing artefacts from the Maritime Museum's collection, it underwent extensive redevelopment in 2019.

**St Olaf's Church** CHURCH
(Oleviste kirik; Map p58; ☎ 641 2241; www.oleviste.ee; Lai 50; ⏲10am-6pm Apr-Oct) From 1549

until 1625, when its 159m steeple was struck by lightning and burnt down, this (now Baptist) church was one of the tallest buildings in the world. The current spire reaches a still-respectable 124m and you can take a tight, confined, 258-step staircase up the tower (adult/child €3/1) for wonderful views of Toompea and over the lower town's rooftops. Major renovations began in mid-2019, closing the interior to tourists; check before visiting.

**Lower Town Wall** FORTRESS

(Linnamüür; Map p58; ☎644 9867; Laboratooriumi, Kooli & Gümnaasiumi; adult/reduced €2/1.50; ⊙10am-7pm Jun-Aug, shorter hours rest of year) Running along the northwestern border of Old Town, the most photogenic stretch of Tallinn's remaining 1.9km of medieval walls connects nine towers, including the Nunna, Sauna and Kuldjala towers, which can all be entered. Climbing up, you'll see art exhibitions, and displays of arms and armour and the like. Of course, the real attractions are the walls themselves, and the classic red-rooftop views from the top. Outside the walls, the gardens of Towers' Sq are pretty and relaxing.

★ **Niguliste Museum** MUSEUM

(Map p58; ☎631 4330; www.nigulistemuuseum.ekm.ee; Niguliste 3; adult/reduced €6/5; ⊙10am-6pm May-Sep, to 5pm Wed-Sun Oct-Apr) Dating from the 13th century, the imposing St Nicholas' Church (Niguliste kirik) was badly damaged by Soviet bombers in 1944 and a fire in the 1980s, but today stands restored to its Gothic glory. Although deconsecrated, it's a strikingly apt site for the Art Museum of Estonia to display some of its treasures of sacral art – the late-medieval altarpieces, paintings and sculptures you'll see are drawn from all over Estonia, but much of it originally belonged right here, in St Nicholas'.

**Adamson-Eric Museum** MUSEUM

(Map p58; ☎644 5838; www.adamson-eric.ekm.ee; Lühike jalg 3; adult/reduced €5/4; ⊙11am-6pm Tue-Sun May-Sep, Wed-Sun Oct-Apr) Erich Carl Hugo Adamson, a towering figure of 20th-century art in Estonia, is celebrated in this reverent little museum in a historic house with which he actually had no connection. Principally a painter, Adamson's mastery of many creative forms is reflected in a permanent collection of paintings, ceramics, leather- and metalwork and other applied arts. Several temporary exhibitions per year add variety to an already-vast palette. If you're planning on visiting the nearby Niguliste Museum, a combined ticket is €8.

**Freedom Square** SQUARE

(Vabaduse väljak; Map p58) This large paved plaza, once the staging ground for 'spontaneous' displays of Soviet enthusiasm, is now used for summer concerts, skateboarding, impromptu ball games and watching events on the big screen at the southern end. The square sits just outside one of the former town gates, the remains of which are preserved under glass near the northwestern corner. A gigantic glass cross at the square's western end commemorates the Estonian War of Independence.

## Toompea

Lording it over the lower part of Old Town is the ancient hilltop citadel of Toompea. In German times this was the preserve of the feudal nobility, literally looking down on the traders and lesser beings below. It's now almost completely given over to government buildings, churches, embassies and shops selling amber knick-knacks and fridge magnets, and is correspondingly quieter than the teeming streets below.

**St Mary's Lutheran Cathedral** CATHEDRAL

(Tallinna Püha Neitsi Maarja Piiskoplik toomkirik; Map p58; ☎644 4140; www.toomkirik.ee; Toom-Kooli 6; adult/reduced €5/3; ⊙9.30am-5.30pm Jun-Aug, shorter hours rest of year) Tallinn's cathedral (now Lutheran, originally Catholic) was initially built by the Danes by at least 1233, although the current exterior dates mainly from the 15th century, and the tower was completed in 1779. This impressive building was a burial ground for the rich and titled, and the whitewashed walls are decorated with the elaborate coats of arms of Estonia's noble families. Fit view-seekers can climb the tower.

**Alexander Nevsky Orthodox Cathedral** CATHEDRAL

(Map p58; ☎644 3484; www.tallinnanevskikatedraal.eu; Lossi plats 10; ⊙8am-7pm Sun-Fri, to 8pm Sat May-Sep) The positioning of this magnificent, onion-domed Russian Orthodox cathedral (completed in 1900) at the heart of the country's main administrative hub was no accident: many such churches were built in the last part of the 19th century as part of a general wave of Russification in the empire's

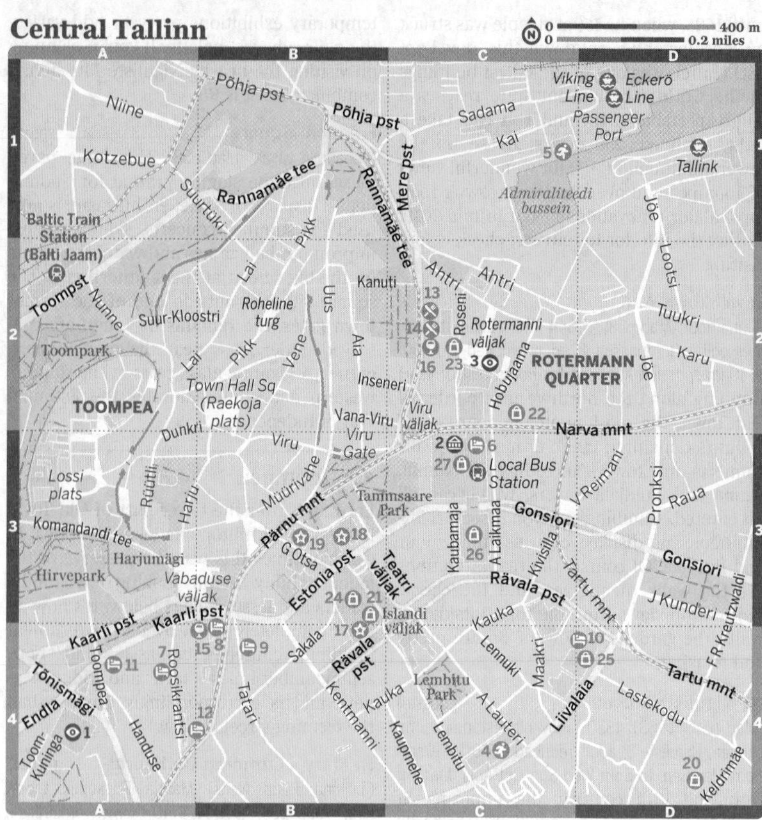


Baltic provinces. Orthodox believers come here in droves, alongside tourists ogling the interior's striking icons and frescoes and snapping its eye-catching profile. Respectful, demurely dressed visitors are welcome, but cameras aren't.

**Toompea Castle** HISTORIC BUILDING

(Map p58; Lossi plats) This Janus-faced pile turns a sugar-pink baroque facade towards Toompea, and a stern 14th-century Livonian visage to the sea and intervening suburbs. Three towers have survived from the Knights of the Sword's hilltop castle, the finest of which is 14th-century Pikk Hermann (Long Hermann – best viewed from the rear). In the 18th century, the fortress was radically updated by Russian empress Catherine the Great, converting it into the pretty-in-pink baroque palace that now houses Estonia's Riigikogu (National Council).

**Linda Hill** PARK

(Lindamägi; Map p58; Falgi tee) Shaded by the 250-year-old linden trees of Lindamäe Park, this small mound near the top of Toompea is named after Linda, wife of Kalev, the heroic first leader of the Estonians. According to legend, Toompea is the burial mound that she built for him. During the Soviet years the statue of the grieving Linda became an unofficial memorial to the victims of Stalin's deportations and executions. Laying flowers here before 1991 was a political act, and a genuinely dangerous one.

**Kiek in de Kök** TOWER

(Map p58; ☎644 6686; www.linnamuuseum.ee; Komandandi tee 2; adult/child €6/4; ⏰9am-6pm May-Sep, to 5pm Tue, Wed & Fri-Sun, to 8pm Thu Oct-Apr) This stout, five-storey cannon tower was one of Tallinn's most formidable defences when built in the 15th century. Its name (amusing to English ears) is Low German for 'peep into the kitchen' – from its heights,

## Central Tallinn

**Sights**
1 Estonian National Library ........ A4
2 Hotel Viru KGB Museum ........ C3
3 Rotermann Quarter ........ C2

**Activities, Courses & Tours**
4 Club 26 ........ C4
5 Sailing.ee ........ C1

**Sleeping**
6 Estoria ........ C3
7 Euphoria ........ A4
8 Hotell Palace ........ B4
9 Monk's Bunk ........ B4
10 Swissôtel Tallinn ........ D4
11 United Backpackers ........ A4
12 Yoga Residence ........ B4

**Eating**
Horisont ........ (see 10)
13 Restaurant Ö ........ C2
14 Sfäär ........ C2

**Drinking & Nightlife**
15 Klubi Teater ........ B4
16 Scotland Yard ........ C2
X-Baar ........ (see 9)

**Entertainment**
17 Artis ........ B4
18 Estonia Concert Hall ........ B3
19 Estonian Drama Theatre ........ B3

**Shopping**
20 Central Market ........ D4
21 Estonian Design House ........ B3
22 Foorum Keskus ........ C2
23 Kalev ........ C2
24 Solaris Centre ........ B3
25 Stockmann Kaubamaja ........ D4
26 Tallinna Kaubamaja ........ C3
27 Viru Keskus ........ C3

voyeurs could reputedly peep *(kiek)* through the wide chimneys of the 15th-century lower town houses into their kitchens *(kök)*. Today it's a branch of the City Museum, focusing mainly on Tallinn's military history and defences, antique arms and armour, and temporary exhibitions.

**Bastion Passages** TUNNEL

(Bastionikäigud; Map p58; ☎644 6686; www.linnamuuseum.ee; Komandandi tee 2; adult/child €8/5; ⏲9am-6pm May-Sep, to 5pm Tue, Wed & Fri-Sun, to 8pm Thu Oct-Apr) Tours exploring the 17th-century Swedish-built tunnels connecting the bastions that ring the town walls depart from the Kiek in de Kök tower. Over the years, they've been used as fallout shelters, homeless refuges and punk rehearsal spaces. Bookings are required, and warm clothes (it's about 10°C, or 50°F, down there) and sensible shoes are recommended. Regular tours finish in the **Carved Stone Museum**, showcasing tablets, statues and other historical lapidary work from Tallinn.

**Vabamu Museum of Occupations and Freedom** MUSEUM

(Okupatsioonide ja vabaduse muuseum Vabamu; Map p58; ☎668 0250; www.vabamu.ee; Toompea 8; adult/child €11/7; ⏲10am-6pm Tue-Sun) The permanent exhibition here, 'Freedom Without Borders', is divided into five sections examining the suffering of Estonians over five decades of occupation by both the Nazis and Soviets, and the processes of recovery and regaining freedom. The photos and artefacts are interesting but it's the enthralling video testimony that leaves the greatest impression – and the joy of a happy ending. The museum maintains the former **KGB prison cells** (Map p58; ☎666 0045; www.vabamu.ee/kgb-prison-cells; Pagari 1, enter from Pikk 59; adult/reduced €5/4; ⏲10am-6pm May-Sep, from 11am Oct-Apr) as a separate historical site (an adult/reduced ticket for both is €14/9).

### Kalamaja

Immediately northwest of Old Town, this enclave of tumbledown wooden houses and decommissioned factories has swiftly transitioned into one of Tallinn's most interesting neighbourhoods. The grim reputation bestowed by its industrial past and the notorious Patarei Prison made this part of town undesirable up until the early 21st century.

Once these were gone, the clapboard houses, tree-lined streets and low costs began to attract people back. Major road projects and the opening of an impressive museum at Lennusadam are only the most visible elements of a revolution started by local hipsters establishing cafes and bars in abandoned warehouses and rickety storefronts.

★ **Seaplane Harbour** MUSEUM

(Lennusadam; Map p64; ☎620 0550; www.meremuuseum.ee; Vesilennuki 6; adult/reduced €15/8; ⏲10am-7pm daily May-Sep, to 6pm

## Kalamaja

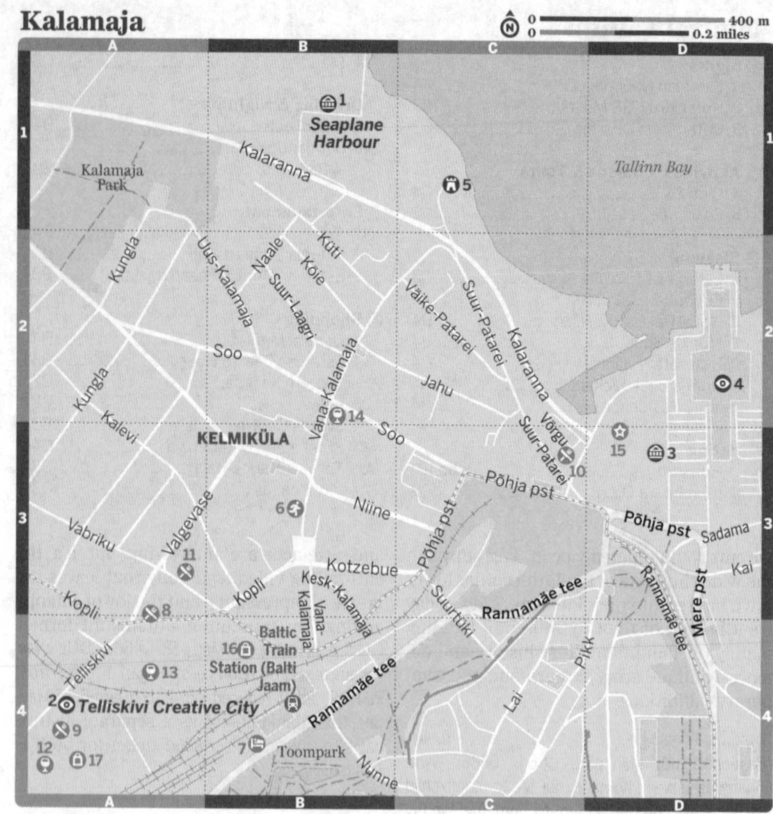


## Kalamaja

**Top Sights**
1 Seaplane Harbour ........ B1
2 Telliskivi Creative City ........ A4

**Sights**
3 Estonian Museum of Contemporary Art ........ D3
4 Linnahall ........ D2
5 Patarei ........ C1

**Activities, Courses & Tours**
6 Kalma Saun ........ B3

**Sleeping**
7 Go Hotel Shnelli ........ B4

**Eating**
8 Boheem ........ A3
9 F-hoone ........ A4
10 Moon ........ C3
11 Siga la Vaca Estonia ........ A3

**Drinking & Nightlife**
12 Pudel ........ A4
13 Sveta Baar ........ A4
14 Tops ........ B2

**Entertainment**
15 Cultural Garden ........ D3

**Shopping**
16 Balti Jaama Turg ........ B4
17 Telliskivi Flea Market ........ A4

Tue-Sun Oct-Apr; P ) When this cavernous, triple-domed building was completed in 1917, its reinforced-concrete shell-frame construction was unique in the world. Resembling a classic Bond-villain lair, the vast space was completely restored and opened to the public in 2012 as a museum celebrating Estonia's rich seafaring heritage.

Highlights include exploring the cramped corridors of a 1930s naval submarine, an elegant collection of ice-yachts, hanging from the ceiling as though in flight, and the many interactive exhibits to try your hand at.

**★Telliskivi Creative City** AREA

(Telliskivi Loomelinnak; Map p64; www.telliskivi.cc; Telliskivi 60a; ) Once literally on the wrong side of the tracks, this set of abandoned factory buildings is now Tallinn's most alternative shopping and entertainment precinct, with cafes, a bike shop, bars selling craft beer, graffiti walls, artist studios, food trucks and pop-up concept stores. But it's not only hipsters who flock to Telliskivi to peruse the fashion and design stores, drink espressos and riffle through the stalls at the weekly flea market – you're just as likely to see families rummaging and sipping.

**Patarei** FORT

(Map p64; 664 5039; www.patareiprison.org; Kalaranna 28; adult/reduced €5/3; 10am-6pm daily Jun-Aug, Tue-Sun May & Sep) A sea fort built in the classicist style in 1840 as part of the defences of the Russian Empire, Patarei was subsequently used as a prison by the Estonian Republic, the Nazis and the Soviets. Peeling, dank and grim, its unrestored halls and cells are home to the unsettling exhibition 'Communism is Prison'. Adorned by explanatory panels, the courtyard walkways, solitary cells, washroom administrative rooms and execution chamber are open to explore.

**Estonian Museum of Contemporary Art** GALLERY

(Eesti kaasaegse kunsti muuseum; Map p64; 514 3778; www.ekkm.ee; Põhja pst 35; noon-7pm Tue-Sun Apr-Dec) FREE Despite its highfalutin name, this grungy old warehouse space is more slapped together than slick. It started as a squat collective in 2006, and exhibitions still tend to be edgier and more oddball than anything you'll find at the more official galleries. For that reason, there are more surprises, but perhaps fewer moments of real artistic success here than at many safer galleries.

## City Centre

**Hotel Viru KGB Museum** MUSEUM

(Map p62; 680 9300; www.viru.ee; Viru väljak 4; tours adult/reduced €11/5.50; daily May-Oct, Tue-Sun Nov-Apr) The Hotel Viru (1972) was not only Estonia's first skyscraper, but literally the only place for tourists to stay in Tallinn at the time. Having all the foreigners in one place made it much easier to keep tabs on them and the locals they had contact with, which is exactly what the KGB did from its 23rd-floor spy base. The hotel offers fascinating, hour-long tours of the facility in various languages.

The timing of English-language tours varies throughout the year – visit the website to check and prebook.

**Rotermann Quarter** AREA

(Rotermanni kvartal; Map p62; www.rotermann.eu) With impressive contemporary architecture wedged between 19th-century brick warehouses, this development has transformed an outmoded (if historically very valuable) factory complex into the city's swankiest shopping and dining precinct. If you're not eating in at one of the many restaurants, an artisanal baker and butcher, together with a well-stocked cheese shop, make it a good place to stock up on supplies.

## Kadriorg

**Kadriorg Park** PARK

(Kadrioru park; Map p66; www.kadriorupark.ee) About 2km east of Old Town, this beautiful park's ample acreage is Tallinn's favourite patch of green. Together with the baroque Kadriorg Palace, its 70 hectares were commissioned by the Russian Tsar Peter the Great for his wife Catherine I soon after his conquest of Estonia (Kadriorg means 'Catherine's Valley' in Estonian).

Nowadays the oak, lilac and horse-chestnut trees give shade to strollers and picnickers, the formal pond and gardens provide a genteel backdrop for romantic promenades and wedding photos, and the children's **playground** (Map p66; Koidula 21a, Kadriorg Park; ) is a favourite free-for-all for the city's youngsters. Stop by the park's **information centre** (Kadrioru pargi infopunkt; Map p66; 601 5783; www.kadriorupark.ee; Weizenbergi 33; 10am-5pm Wed-Sun), housed in a pretty 18th-century cottage near the main entrance, to see a scale model of the palace and its grounds.

From central Tallinn, tram 3 stops right by Kadriorg Park. Buses 1A and 34A (among others) stop at the J Poska stop on Narva mnt, near the foot of the park, while buses 67 and 68 head to the Kumu end.

**★Kadriorg Art Museum** MUSEUM

(Kardrioru kunstimuuseum; Map p66; 606 6400; www.kadriorumuuseum.ekm.ee; Kadriorg

## Kadriorg

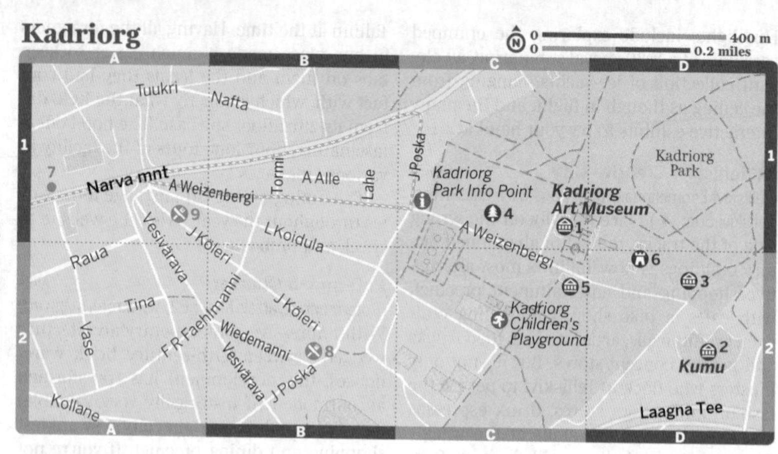


## Kadriorg

**Top Sights**

1 Kadriorg Art Museum ........ C1
2 Kumu ........ D2

**Sights**

3 House of Peter I ........ D2
4 Kadriorg Park ........ C1
5 Mikkel Museum ........ C2
6 Presidential Palace ........ D2

**Activities, Courses & Tours**

7 Tallinn University Summer School ........ A1

**Eating**

8 Mantel ja Korsten ........ B2
9 NOP ........ A1

Palace, Weizenbergi 37; adult/reduced €6.50/4.50; 10am-6pm Tue & Thu-Sun, to 8pm Wed May-Sep, 10am-8pm Wed, to 5pm Thu-Sun Oct-Apr) Kadriorg Palace, a baroque beauty built by Peter the Great between 1718 and 1736, houses a branch of the Art Museum of Estonia devoted to Dutch, German and Italian paintings from the 16th to the 18th centuries, and Russian works from the 18th to early 20th centuries (check out the decorative porcelain with communist imagery upstairs). The pink palace is exactly as frilly and fabulous as it ought to be, and there's a handsome French-style formal garden at the rear.

**Mikkel Museum** GALLERY

(Mikkeli muuseum; Map p66; 606 6400; www.mikkelimuuseum.ekm.ee; Weizenbergi 28; adult/child €6/3.50; 10am-6pm Tue & Thu-Sun, to 8pm Wed; P) This handsome, two-storey weatherboard, the former kitchen for Kadriorg Palace, now displays a small but interesting assortment of paintings, porcelain and sculpture from the museum's benefactor, 20th-century collector Johannes Mikkel. It also hosts occasional temporary exhibitions. Check the website for the four annual Wednesdays when tickets are just €1, or for joint-admission options, such as a combined ticket for the Mikkel and the nearby Kadriorg Art Museum (adult/child €8/6).

**Presidential Palace** PALACE

(Map p66; Weizenbergi 39) Echoing the style of Kadriorg Palace, this grand building was purpose-built in 1938 to serve as the official residence of the Estonian president. It's currently fulfilling that role once more, so isn't open to the public, but you can take as many photos as you like, and peer through the gates at the honour guards out front.

**House of Peter I** MUSEUM

(Peeter I Majamuuseum; Map p66; 601 3136; www.linnamuuseum.ee; Mäekalda 2, Kadriorg Park; adult/reduced €4/3; 10am-6pm Mon, Tue & Thu-Sat, to 7pm Wed, to 5pm Sun May-Sep, 10am-8pm Wed, to 5pm Thu-Sat, to 4pm Sun Oct-Apr) This surprisingly modest cottage was where Peter the Great and Catherine I lived on their early-17th-century visits to Tallinn, while Kadriorg Palace was under construction. A museum since 1806 (and thus Tallinn's oldest), it's filled with portraits, furniture and artefacts that once actually surrounded the Russian royals.

**★Kumu** GALLERY

(Map p66; ☎602 6000; www.kumu.ekm.ee; Weizenbergi 34; adult/reduced €10/8; ⊙10am-6pm Tue, Wed & Fri-Sun, to 8pm Thu) This futuristic, Finnish-designed, seven-storey building is a spectacular structure of limestone, glass and copper that integrates intelligently into the 18th-century landscape. Kumu (the name is short for *kunstimuuseum*, or art museum) contains the country's largest repository of Estonian art as well as 11 or 12 temporary exhibits per year. The permanent exhibition covers 18th-century classics of Estonian art to venerable, intricately painted altarpieces and the work of contemporary Estonian artists such as Adamson-Eric.

**Tallinn Song Festival Grounds** AMPHITHEATRE

(Tallinna lauluväljak; Map p54; ☎611 2102; www.lauluvaljak.ee; Narva mnt 95; ⊙light tower 8am-4pm Mon-Fri) FREE This open-air amphitheatre is the site of Estonia's quinquennial National Song Festival (p72), assorted blockbuster rock concerts and other momentous events. Built in 1959, it's an elegant and curvaceous piece of Soviet-era architecture, with an official capacity of 75,000 people and a stage that fits 15,000. When no events are booked, and by prior reservation, it's possible to climb the 42m Song Grounds Light Tower, where the festival flame is lit. Inside there's a photo display on the song festival's history.

## Maarjamäe

From Kadriorg the coastal road Pirita tee curves northeast alongside Tallinn Bay through Maarjamäe – home to a palace, museums and a war memorial – to Pirita. The coastal path is popular with joggers, cyclists and skaters, offering particularly fine sunset views towards Old Town. From the centre, buses 5 and 34A pass through Maarjamäe while tram 3 goes to Kadriorg.

**Maarjamäe History Centre** MUSEUM

(Ajaloomuuseum; Map p54; ☎696 8630; www.ajaloomuuseum.ee; Pirita tee 56; entire complex adult/reduced €15/8; ⊙10am-6pm daily May-Sep, Tue-Sun Oct-Apr; 👪) This excellent cultural-historical complex, run by the dispersed Estonian History Museum, is anchored by **Maarjamäe Palace** (Maarjamäe loss; ☎696 8600; adult/reduced €8/6), a neo-Gothic 19th-century extravagance built by a wealthy Russian. The palace itself is now a museum; the former **Stables** (Maarjamäe lossi tallihoone; ☎696 8660; adult/reduced €6/4) are a smart exhibition space; the purpose-built **Film Museum** (Filmimuuseum; ☎696 8670; adult/reduced €8/6) has a cinema and exhibits on the process of film-making; and the grounds are a Brobdingnagian reliquary of old Soviet monuments. You can visit everything, or just buy specific tickets (although everything is closely spaced and worthwhile).

**Maarjamäe War Memorial** MEMORIAL

(Kommunismiohvrite Memoriaal; Map p54; Pirita tee 74) Perched on the bluff next to Maarjamäe Palace, this large Soviet-era monument consists of an elegant bowed obelisk set amid a large crumbling concrete plaza. The obelisk was erected in 1960 to commemorate the Soviet troops killed in 1918 – hardly a popular sentiment, as the war was against Estonia and all Estonian monuments to *their* dead were destroyed shortly after the Soviet takeover (many have since been re-erected).

## Pirita

Just past Maarjamäe the Pirita River enters Tallinn Bay and the city's favourite beach begins to unfurl. The area's other claim to fame was as the base for the sailing events of the 1980 Moscow Olympics; international regattas are still held here.

Buses 1A, 8, 34A and 38 all run between the city centre and Pirita.

**Pirita Beach** BEACH

(Pirita Rand; Map p54) Tallinn's largest and most popular beach, Pirita is only 6km from the city. In summer, bronzed sun-lovers fill the sands and hang out in the laid-back cafes nearby. Even when it's bleak and windy there are plenty of wind- and kite-surfers to watch. It's backed by a narrow band of pine forest threaded by a bike track and there are places to buy an ice cream, a drink or lunch.

**Pirita Convent** RUINS

(Pirita klooster; Map p54; www.piritaklooster.ee; Merivälja tee 18; adult/reduced €3/1.50; ⊙10am-6pm Apr-Oct, noon-4pm Nov-Mar) Only the massively high Gothic stone walls remain of Pirita, completed in 1436 as the largest convent in Old Livonia. The rest was destroyed in 1577 by Ivan the Terrible, during the Livonian War. In 1996, Bridgettine sisters were granted the right to return and reactivate the convent, which they oversee from new buildings adjacent to the ruins. Atmospheric concerts are held here in summer – regular visits may not be possible during events such as mid-August's **Birgitta Festival** (www.filharmoonia.ee/en/birgitta; St Bridget's Convent; from €24; ⊙ Aug).

## Kloostrimetsa

Literally 'the convent's forest', this leafy nook spreads out along the north bank of the Pirita River, containing the Botanic Garden and TV Tower. Buses 34A and 38 from the city head here via Pirita Beach (p67).

**Tallinn Botanic Garden** GARDENS

(Tallinna botaanikaaed; ☎606 2679; www.botaanikaaed.ee; Kloostrimetsa tee 52; adult/child €5.50/3; ⊙ gardens 10am-8pm, greenhouses 11am-7pm May-Sep, shorter hours Oct-Apr; P) Set on 1.2 sq km in the Pirita River valley and surrounded by lush conifer woodlands, these delightful gardens boast over 8000 species of plants, scattered between a series of greenhouses and various themed gardens and arboretums. Bring a picnic and make an afternoon of it. Joint admission with the nearby **TV Tower** (Tallinna teletorn; ☎686 3005; www.teletorn.ee; Kloostrimetsa tee 58a; adult/child €13/7; ⊙10am-7pm) is available (adult/reduced €15/8).

## Haabersti

The westernmost district of Tallinn is home to over 43,400 people, although the population only started to intensify following the completion of the Little Flower Hill (Väike-Õismäe) development in the 1970s. This intriguing example of Soviet town planning features a giant oval ring of immense apartment blocks gathered around an ornamental lake. Haabersti includes the seaside subdistrict of Rocca al Mare, home to the Open-Air Museum and Estonia's second-largest shopping mall, the Rocca al Mare Keskus. Buses 42 and 43 head out here from the centre.

**★ Estonian Open-Air Museum** MUSEUM

(Eesti vabaõhumuuseum; Map p54; ☎654 9101; www.evm.ee; Vabaõhumuuseumi tee 12, Rocca al Mare; adult/reduced high season €10/7, low season €8/6; ⊙10am-8pm 23 Apr-28 Sep, to 5pm 29 Sep-22 Apr; P ♿) This sprawling ethnographic and architectural complex comprises 80 historic Estonian buildings, plucked from across the country and resurrected in sections representing the different regions of Estonia. In summer the time-warping effect is highlighted by staff in period costume performing traditional activities among the wooden farmhouses and windmills. Different activities and demonstrations (weaving, blacksmithing and the like) are scheduled and an old wooden tavern, Kolu Kõrts, serves traditional Estonian cuisine.

**Tallinn Zoo** ZOO

(Tallinna loomaaed; Map p54; ☎694 3300; www.tallinnzoo.ee; Paldiski mnt 145, Veskimetsa; adult/

### TALLINN FOR CHILDREN

Tallinn's Old Town, with its evocative medieval streets, picture-book fortifications and ancient houses, is pure eye candy for the under-12 crowd – although those cobblestones can be hard work if yours are still in pushchairs. Tallinners welcome kids almost everywhere; many restaurants have separate children's menus and most larger hotels have play areas and child-minding services.

Children will particularly enjoy the Estonian Open-Air Museum, the zoo, Pirita's beaches, Kalev Spa Waterpark, **Nõmme Adventure Park** (☎5615 9160; www.nommeseikluspark.ee; Külmallika 15a, Nõmme; adult/child €23/8; ⊙10am-8pm Jun & Jul, shorter hours rest of year; ♿) and the seasonal Harju Ice Rink. There's a large playground in Kadriorg Park (p65) and another in Hirvepark, downhill from Toompea.

**Nuku** (Teater muuseum; Map p58; ☎667 9555; www.nuku.ee; Nunne 8; adult/family museum €8/20, child/accompanying adult theatre €11/6; ⊙11am-6pm Tue-Sun; ♿), the state puppet museum, has lots of historic puppets behind glass but plenty to play with too. There's a Cellar of Horrors full of 'evil and scary puppets' (including a vampiric rabbit), a dress-up room, a shadow theatre and windows into the workshops where the puppets are made. Kids and weary adults love **City Train** (Map p58; adult/child €7/5; ⊙11.30am-7pm), a cheery blue little road train that winds a 20-minute circuit through Old Town in summer.

### WHEN BIGGER IS JUST BIGGER

Nothing says 'former Soviet' quite like a brutalist public building, and Tallinn has two that are difficult to miss, both designed by local architect Raine Karp.

**Linnahall** (City Hall; Map p64; www.linnahall.ee; Mere pst 20) Resembling a cross between a nuclear bunker, a WWII sea fort and some inscrutable temple to a vanished god, the Linnahall is in fact a covered concrete arena built for the 1980 Olympics. Originally the Lenin Palace of Culture and Sport, it's an extraordinary structure – rotting, barred, weed-strewn and comprehensively graffitied. Heritage-listed and badly decayed as it is, it's now earmarked for restoration as a concert and convention venue, and has been recently fenced off to keep out the curious.

**Estonian National Library** (Eesti rahvusraamatukogu; Map p62; ☎630 7611; www.nlib.ee; Tõnismägi 2; ⊙10am-8pm Mon-Fri, noon-7pm Sat Sep-Jun, noon-6pm Mon-Fri Jul & Aug) Construction commenced in 1985, but wasn't completed until 1993, making this exemplary Soviet structure ironically one of independent Estonia's first new public buildings. It's clad in the local dolomite limestone and it's well worth popping in to the foyer, if only to check out the pointy red chairs. Frequent exhibitions take place on the upper floors.

reduced May-Sep €9/6, Oct-Apr €6/4; ⊙9am-7pm May-Aug, to 7pm Mar, Apr, Sep & Oct, to 5pm Nov-Feb; P ) Boasting a broad collection of rare goat and sheep species, plus around 350 other varieties of feathered, furry and four-legged friends (including lions, leopards and African elephants), this large, spread-out zoo is gradually upgrading its enclosures into modern, animal-friendly spaces as funds allow. It's the best place to see all of the native species (bears, lynx, owls, eagles) you're unlikely to spot in the wild. There's a new polar-bear enclosure, a children's zoo and a cafe and souvenir shop.

## Activities

Locals attribute all kinds of health benefits to a good old-fashioned sweat and, truth be told, a trip to Estonia just won't be complete until you've paid a visit to the sauna. You won't have to look far – most hotels have one – but Tallinn also has some good public options.

**Club 26** SPA

(Map p62; ☎631 5585; www.club26.ee; Liivalaia 33; pool, gym & sauna single visit €12-15; ⊙7am-10pm) On the top floor of the Radisson Blu Hotel Olümpia, with correspondingly outstanding views, this is one of the most luxurious sauna choices in town. There are two private saunas, each with plunge pool and tiny balcony, that can be booked for up to 10 people (one hour €50 to €80). Food and drink can be ordered to complete the experience.

**Kalma Saun** SPA

(Map p64; ☎627 1811; www.kalmasaun.ee; Vana-Kalamaja 9a; adult €8.50-11, reduced €4; ⊙11am-10pm Mon-Fri, 10am-11pm Sat & Sun) In a grand 1928 building in Kalmaja, Tallinn's oldest public sauna still has the aura of an old-fashioned, Russian-style *banya* (bathhouse). One side, the wood-burning sauna, is set aside for men, while the other, electric-heated and thus slightly cheaper, is for women. Both have plunge pools, benches and refreshments, and private saunas are available (per hour €20; up to six people).

**Kalev Spa Waterpark** SWIMMING

(Map p58; ☎649 3370; www.kalevspa.ee; Aia 18; 3hr visit adult/reduced €16/14; ⊙6.45am-9.30pm Mon-Fri, from 8am Sat & Sun; ) For serious swimmers there's an indoor pool of Olympic proportions, but there are also plenty of other ways to wrinkle your skin here, including water slides, spa pools, saunas and a kids' pool. There's also a gym, a day spa and a 'Sauna Oasis' with Japanese bath, 'Tropical Oasis', Finnish sauna and more.

**Bell-Marine Boat Rental** BOATING

(Map p54; ☎621 2175; www.bellmarine.ee; Kloostri tee 6a; per hour kayak/rowboat €15/19; ⊙10am-10pm Jun-Aug) The Pirita River is an idyllic place for a leisurely paddle, with thick forest edging the water. Bell-Marine rents out rowboats and kayaks from beside the road bridge, close to the convent ruins.

**Harju Ice Rink** ICE SKATING

(Harju tänava uisuplats; Map p58; ☎5624 6739; www.uisuplats.ee; Harju; per hour adult/child €7/5; ⊙10am-10pm Dec-Mar; ) Wrap up warmly to join the locals at Old Town's outdoor ice rink – very popular in the winter months. You'll have earned a *hõõgvein* (mulled or 'glowing' wine) in the warm indoor cafe by the end of your skating session. Skate rental costs €3.



## Tours

The tourist office (p84) and most travel agencies can arrange tours in English or other languages with a private guide; advance booking is required. The free tours leaving from the tourist office are excellent, and should be acknowledged with tips.

**Tallinn Traveller Tours** TOURS
(☎5837 4800; www.traveller.ee) This outfit runs entertaining tours, including a private two-hour Old Town walk departing from outside the tourist office (€15 per person), and a larger free tour (you should tip the engaging guides). There are also ghost tours (€15), bike tours (from €25), a food tour through Kalamaja (€49) and day trips to Lahemaa (€59).

**EstAdventures** TOURS
(☎5308 3731; www.estadventures.ee; from €40; ⊗May-Sep) This upbeat outfit offers themed walking tours of Tallinn ('Tallinn Town and Country', 'View with a Brew'). It also runs free daily tours (two hours, at 1.30pm and 3.30pm) leaving from outside the tourist office.

**City Bike** CYCLING
(Map p58; ☎511 1819; www.citybike.ee; Vene 33; ⊗10am-7pm May-Sep, to 6pm Oct-Apr) This friendly den of cycle-monkeys offers 'Welcome to Tallinn' tours (€21, two hours) from 11am year-round, including Kadriorg and Maarjamäe. 'Other Side' tours (from €21, 2½ hours) take in Kalamaja and **Stroomi Beach** (Map p54; Pelguranna). It also rents bikes (from €7 for the first three hours; €15 per day) and arranges self-guided tours of routes such as Lahemaa to Tartu (from €335).

**Tallinn City Tour** BUS
(Map p58; ☎5301 5623; www.citytour.ee; adult/child 24hr ticket €25/15) City Tour runs red double-decker buses that give quick, easy, hop-on, hop-off access to Tallinn's top sights, accompanied by a recorded audio tour. Tickets are good for 24, 48 or 72 hours. The main stop is on Viru Sq (Mere pst), just outside Old Town, and combo tickets are available that include museum entries, a boat ride or a balloon ride.

## City Walk
## Tallinn's Old Town

**START** FREEDOM SQ
**END** VIRU GATE
**LENGTH** 4KM; THREE HOURS

We've designed this walk as an introduction to Tallinn's meandering medieval streets. Starting at **1 Freedom Square** (p61), take the stairs up into Toompea, noting the stout walls and famous Kiek in de Kök tower on your right, and the Independence monument on your left. Continue to **2 Linda Hill** (p62), from where you can see the remaining medieval elements of **3 Toompea Castle** (p62); backtrack and turn left onto Castle Sq (Lossi plats) for a view of its baroque facade. Directly across the square is onion-domed **4 Alexander Nevsky Orthodox Cathedral** (p61).

Take Toom-Kooli to Toompea's other cathedral, **5 St Mary's** (p61), and cut across Church Sq (Kiriku plats) onto Rahukohtu, where a lane leads to the **6 Patkul lookout** (Patkuli vaateplats), offering terrific views to the sea. Continue winding around the lanes to the **7 Court Square lookout** (Kohtuotsa vaateplats).

Take Kohtu and Piiskopi behind both cathedrals and head through the opening in the wall to the **8 Danish King's Garden**, where artists set up in summer to capture the ageless vista over Tallinn's rooftops. Exit to the left and then take the steps up through the **9 Short Leg Gate Tower**, said to be the most haunted building in Tallinn. Ghostly apparitions have been reported inside this tower, including a crucified monk and a black dog with burning eyes. Turn right and take the long sloping path known as Long Leg (Pikk jalg) through the red-roofed **10 Long Leg Gate Tower** (1380) and into the lower town.

Turn left along Nunne and then veer right onto Väike-Kloostri where you'll come to the best-preserved section of the **11 Lower Town Wall** (p61), linking nine of the 26 remaining towers. Wander through the park to the next small gap in the walls and re-enter onto Aida. At the end of that street, turn left onto Lai, which is lined with 15th-century German merchants' houses; many extend to three or four floors, with

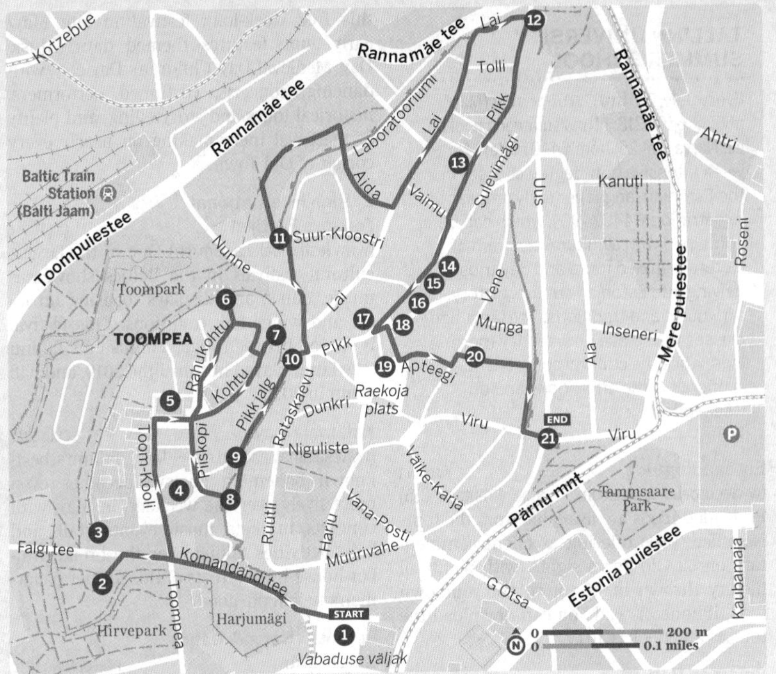


the lower two used as living and reception quarters and the upper ones for storage.

At the very end of Lai, follow the small path to the right alongside the wall to the 12 **Great Coast Gate**, the most impressive of the remaining medieval gates. Note the crest on the outside wall and the crucifix in a niche on the town side.

As you head up Pikk, spare a thought for those who suffered at number 59, the 13 **KGB Prison Cells** (p63). The building's basement windows were bricked up to prevent the sounds being heard by those passing by on the street. Locals joked, with typically black humour, that the building had the best views in Estonia – from here you could see all the way to Siberia.

Further along Pikk are buildings belonging to the town's guilds, associations of traders and artisans, nearly all German-dominated. First up, at number 26, is the 14 **Brotherhood of the Blackheads** (Mustpeade maja). The Blackheads were unmarried young men who took their name not from poor dermatology but from their patron, St Maurice (Mauritius), a legendary African-born Roman soldier whose likeness is found on the building facade (dating from 1597), above an ornate, colourful door. Its neighbour, 15 **St Olaf's Guildhall** (Olevi gildi hoone), was the headquarters for what was probably the first guild in Tallinn, dating from the 13th century. Its membership comprised more humble non-German artisans and traders.

Next up is the 1860-built 16 **St Canute's Guild Hall** (p82), topped with zinc statues of Martin Luther and the guild's patron saint. A little further down the road is the 1410 headquarters of the 17 **Great Guild** (p56), to which the most eminent merchants belonged, and which is now an intriguing museum.

Cross the small square to the left, past the photogenic 18 **Holy Spirit Church** (p56), and take narrow Saiakang ('White Bread Passage' – named after a historic bakery) to 19 **Town Hall Square** (p55). Continue left to Vene (the Estonian word for Russian, named for the Russian merchants who once resided and traded here) and cut through the arch into pretty, cobbled 20 **Katariina Käik**. At the far end, turn right and then left onto Viru, one of Old Town's busiest streets. Finish at the 21 **Viru Gate**, which connects Old Town with the commercial centre of the modern city.

### TALLINN UNIVERSITY SUMMER SCHOOL

Every July, **Tallinn University** (Map p66; ☎640 9218; http://summerschool.tlu.ee; Narva mnt 25; from €440) offers three-week intensive non-degree courses in the Estonian language (early/regular registration €440/490), which can be combined with a cultural program of lectures, guided tours and day trips delving into Estonian culture, history, art, music and traditions. The language classes take place on weekday mornings, while the cultural component is offered in the afternoons and on weekends.

**Euroaudioguide** WALKING
(www.euroaudioguide.com; iPod rental €15) Preloaded iPods are available from the tourist office (p84) offering excellent commentary on 52 Old Town sights, with plenty of history thrown in. If you've got your own iPod, iPhone or iPad you can download the tour as an ebook (€10).

**Reimann Retked** KAYAKING
(☎511 4099; www.retked.ee) Offers sea-kayaking excursions, including a four-hour, 14km paddle out to Aegna Island (from €35 per person). Other interesting possibilities include diving, rafting on the Jägala River, bog-shoeing, snowshoeing and beaver watching.

## Festivals & Events

It seems like there's always something going on in Tallinn in summer, but, aside from Christmas and New Year's, festivals hibernate for winter. For a complete list of Tallinn's festivals, visit www.culture.ee and the events pages of www.visittallinn.ee.

**Jazzkaar** MUSIC
(www.jazzkaar.ee; festival pass €250; ⌚mid-Apr) Jazz greats from around the world converge on Tallinn in mid-April during this excellent 10-day festival, the biggest in the Baltics with more than 90 performances at venues around the city. Tallinn also hosts smaller jazz events in autumn and around Christmas.

**Old Town Days** CULTURAL
(www.vanalinnapaevad.ee; ⌚late May/early Jun; 👪) Kicking off Tallinn's summer each year, this free week-long festival in late May/early June features themed days (Music Day, Medieval Day, Children's Day etc), with dancing, concerts, costumed performers, historical tours and storytelling, and plenty of medieval merrymaking on nearly every corner of Old Town.

**Baltica International Folklore Festival** CULTURAL
(www.festivalbaltica.com/en) One of the largest cultural festivals in the Baltics showcases music, dance and displays focusing on local and wider folk traditions. This festival is shared between Rīga, Vilnius and Tallinn (the latter played host in June 2019, and will again in 2022).

**Kalamaja Days** CULTURAL
(www.kalamajapaevad.ee; ⌚May) Tallinn's best-known bohemian enclave becomes even more lively over the weekend in May, with concerts, markets, music events, stalls and kids' activities taking over the broad, timber-house-lined streets of this former fishermen's neighbourhood.

**Estonian Song & Dance Celebration** PERFORMING ARTS
(www.laulupidu.ee) This is the big one – a tradition stretching back to 1869 and Estonia's foremost cultural celebration. Having celebrated its jubilee in 2019, this immense nationwide gathering convenes in July during the fourth and ninth years of every decade and culminates in a performance of 40,000 singers and dancers at the Tallinn Song Festival Grounds (p67). The youth version slots in during the second and seventh years of each decade.

**Medieval Days** CULTURAL
(☎660 4772; www.folkart.ee; ⌚Jul; 👪) Run by the Estonian Folk Art & Craft Union between Thursday and Sunday of the first full week of July, this happy event brings a parade, carnival and jousting to Old Town, plus a medieval fair to the Town Hall Sq (p55). The kids' area, on Niguliste hill, offers tournaments and plenty of other activities for the young and chivalrous.

**Black Nights Film Festival** FILM
(☎info 5620 8308; https://2019.poff.ee; ⌚Nov) Featuring movies from all over the world, Estonia's biggest film festival brings life to cold winter nights for two weeks from mid-November, attracting over 80,000 attendees and screening more than 250 features and

300 shorts. Subfestivals feature animated, fantasy, student and romance films.

## Sleeping

Tallinn has a good range of accommodation to suit every budget. Most of it clusters in Old Town and its immediate surrounds, where even backpackers might find themselves waking up in a converted merchant's house. Of course, Tallinn is no secret any more, and it can be extremely difficult to find a bed on the weekend in summer.

### Old Town

**Red Emperor** HOSTEL €

(Map p58; ☎615 0035; www.redemperorhostel.com; Aia 10; dm/r from €12/28; @☎) Situated above a wonderfully grungy live-music bar, Red Emperor is Tallinn's premier party hostel for those of a beardy, indie persuasion. Facilities are good, with rooms daubed with 'street art', wooden bunks named for global destinations and plenty of showers, and there are organised activities every day (karaoke, shared dinners etc). Pack heavy-duty earplugs if you're a light sleeper.

**Tribe Theory** HOSTEL €

(Map p58; ☎601 4044; www.tribetheory.com; Uus 26; dm/d from €14/35; ☎) A very 21st-century hostel, with room names like 'inspire' and 'connect', and networking evenings in place of pub crawls, Tribe Theory bills itself as a meeting place for entrepreneurs and digital nomads. Originating in Singapore, it has other sites in Bangalore, Bali and Yangon.

**Old Town Backpackers** HOSTEL €

(Map p58; ☎5351 7266; www.tallinnoldtownbackpackers.com; Uus 14; dm €15; @☎) Enter this baroque house and the whole hostel is laid out before you: a cheery stone-walled room with half a dozen beds that also serves as the kitchen and living room. Given the tightness, late-night partying isn't on the cards, but socialising is inevitable. Books, maps, tea, coffee, board games and a washing machine are all provided.

**★Tabinoya** HOSTEL €€

(Map p58; ☎632 0062; www.tabinoya.com; Nunne 1; dm/s/d €17/37/50; @☎) The Baltic's first Japanese-run hostel occupies the two top floors of a charming old building, with dorms (the four-person one is for females only) and a communal lounge at the top, and spacious private rooms, a kitchen and a sauna below. Bathroom facilities are shared. The vibe's a bit more comfortable and quiet than most of Tallinn's hostels. Book ahead.

**Zinc** HOSTEL €€

(Map p58; ☎5781 0173; www.zinchostel.ee; Väike-Karja 1; s/tw/tr from €35/50/60; ☎) More like a budget guesthouse than a traditional hostel, Zinc doesn't have dorms but its tidy, private rooms, spread over two floors, share bathrooms, a kitchen and TV lounge. Colourful stencils line the halls of the 1914 building, and it's a quiet option in an otherwise noisy neighbourhood.

**Villa Hortensia** APARTMENT €€

(Map p58; ☎641 8083; www.hoov.ee; Masters' Courtyard, Vene 6; s/d from €45/65; ☎) Situated in the sweet, cobbled Masters' Courtyard (p83), Hortensia has four split-level studio apartments with kitchenettes and access to a shared communal lounge, but the two larger apartments are the real treats, with balconies and loads of character. In summer they can get hot, and the downstairs cafe is open until midnight, so pack earplugs if you're an early sleeper.

**Viru Backpackers** HOSTEL €€

(Map p58; ☎644 6050; www.toth.ee; 3rd fl, Viru 5; s/d from €24/38; ❄☎) This small, smartly appointed hostel above one of the main thoroughfares through Old Town offers cosy, brightly painted private rooms, some of which have their own bathrooms. A pancake breakfast is included, and tours and activities can be arranged.

**★Hotel Cru** HOTEL €€€

(Map p58; ☎611 7600; www.cruhotel.eu; Viru 8; s/d/ste €190/240/280; ☎) Behind the pretty powder-blue facade of this boutique hotel you'll find 15 richly furnished rooms scattered along a rabbit warren of corridors. All make sensitive use of original 14th-century features such as timber beams and limestone walls, but the cheapest are a little snug. The attached Restaurant Cru prides itself as one of Tallinn's best (mains €19 to €21). Book online for advance specials and dining and other packages.

**Old House Apartments** APARTMENT €€€

(Map p58; ☎641 1464; www.oldhouseapartments.ee; Rataskaevu 16; apt from €155; P☎) The name 'Old House' does poor justice to this wonderfully refurbished 14th-century merchant's house. It's been split into beautifully

### PRIVATE APARTMENTS & ROOMS

A huge amount of Old Town's housing stock has been developed as tourist apartments, which can prove ideal for travellers who prefer privacy and self-sufficiency on a midrange budget. Agencies manage properties across the city, and while you're less likely to meet other travellers, you'll usually get more space than a hotel room, plus a fully equipped kitchen, a lounge and often a washing machine. Prices drop substantially in the low season, and with longer stays.

furnished apartments (including a spacious two-bedroom unit with traces of a medieval painted ceiling), and there are a further 20-odd units scattered around Old Town. All are in similar buildings, but the quality and facilities vary.

**Three Sisters** BOUTIQUE HOTEL €€€
(Map p58; ☎630 6300; www.threesistershotel.com; Pikk 71; s/d/ste from €189/207/302; ) Offering sumptuous luxury in three adjoining, 14th-century merchant houses in a quiet Old Town location, Three Sisters offers 23 spacious rooms. Each is unique, but all have gorgeous details, including old-fashioned freestanding bathtubs, wooden beams, tiny balconies, blackout blinds and canopy beds. If you've got regal aspirations, the piano suite is the usual choice of visiting royalty.

**Hotel Telegraaf** HOTEL €€€
(Map p58; ☎600 0600; www.telegraafhotel.com; Vene 9; d/ste €225/435; P) This upmarket hotel in a former 19th-century telegraph station delivers style in spades. It boasts a spa, a pretty courtyard, an acclaimed restaurant (mains €28 to €30), swanky modern-art decor and smart, efficient service. 'Superior' rooms, in the older part of the building, have more historical detail but we prefer the marginally cheaper 'executive' rooms for their bigger proportions and sharp decor.

**Savoy Boutique Hotel** HOTEL €€€
(Map p58; ☎680 6688; www.tallinnhotels.ee; Suur-Karja 17/19; s/d €190/203; ) Rooms in cream and caramel tones make this fin-de-siècle hotel an oasis of double-glazed, art deco calm off one of Old Town's busy intersections. Nice boutique touches include fruit on arrival and robes and slippers in every room, but what really sets it apart is the welcoming and attentive staff. Request a room on a higher floor for the rooftop views.

**Hotel St Petersbourg** HOTEL €€€
(Map p58; ☎628 6500; www.hotelstpetersbourg.com; Rataskaevu 7; s/d/ste from €211/225/309; ) Imperial Russia meets contemporary bling in this eclectically furnished hotel, the oldest in Tallinn and one that has sheltered Soviet leader Leonid Brezhnev beneath its roof. The 'lavish imperial style' includes zany light fixtures, faux-fur bedspreads, mirrored chests of drawers, large-scale photographs of ballerinas and a giant Oscar statuette in the foyer. Rates include breakfast and a morning sauna.

**Schlössle Hotel** BOUTIQUE HOTEL €€€
(Map p58; ☎699 7700; www.schlossle-hotels.com; Pühavaimu 13/15; r/ste from €220/585; ) Occupying a 13th-century merchant's house arranged around a central courtyard, this boutique hotel has 23 rooms and an atmospheric, vaulted basement bar. Rooms vary in size and style – the smaller ones have more historic charm while some of the larger ones fall a little short of justifying the price. Little touches such as iPads in the rooms are nice though.

## City Centre

**United Backpackers** HOSTEL €
(Map p62; ☎5685 0415; www.unitedbackpackers.ee; Kaarli pst 11; dm/tw from €16/65; @) Spread over three floors in a nondescript building off a busy road just south of Old Town, this well-kept, friendly wee hostel offers six-, eight- and 12-bed dorms and twin and quad rooms. There's a pleasant and well-patronised common area, a pool table, a bar, board games, and shared laundry, kitchen and bathrooms. A simple breakfast can be had for €5 extra.

**Euphoria** HOSTEL €
(Map p62; ☎5837 3602; www.euphoria.ee; Roosikrantsi 4; dm/r from €11/35; P@) Inspired by Berlin squats and 'alternative communities' in Spain, this hippyish hostel, hidden in an unpromising tower block just south of Old Town, is an entertaining place to stay, with a palpable sense of traveller community. You'll feel especially at home if you like hookah pipes and impromptu late-night jam sessions (pack earplugs if you don't).

**Monk's Bunk** HOSTEL €

(Map p62; ☎636 3924; www.themonksbunk.com; Tatari 1; dm/r from €15/50; @📶) The only monk we can imagine bunking down at Tallinn's self-described 'Number One Party Hostel' is Friar Tuck. There are organised activities every night, including legendary pub crawls aimed at maximum intoxication (Thursday to Sunday nights, €15, with shots at each bar). The facilities are good, with high ceilings, free lockers and underfloor heating in the bathrooms.

**Yoga Residence** APARTMENT €€€

(Map p62; ☎502 1477; www.yogaresidence.eu; Pärnu mnt 32; apt from €100; 📶) The 'Yoga' prefix seems a little strange for a collection of clean-lined new apartments in a solid residential block just south of the centre, until you realise the operators also run yoga, tai chi and meditation sessions. You can expect friendly staff, a basic kitchenette and, joy of joys, a washing machine!

**Hotell Palace** HOTEL €€€

(Map p62; ☎680 6655; www.tallinnhotels.ee; Vabaduse väljak 3; s/d from €147/158; ❄📶🏊) Modern renovations of this architecturally notable 1937 hotel, which has done time as a nationalised Soviet endeavour, have preserved period touches while updating the comfortable, tastefully furnished rooms. Directly across from Freedom Sq, the complex includes an indoor pool, a spa, saunas and a small gym, although they're only free for those staying in 'superior' rooms or suites.

**Swissôtel Tallinn** HOTEL €€€

(Map p62; ☎624 0000; www.swissotel.com; Tornimäe 3; d/ste €195/355; ❄📶🏊) Raising standards across 30 floors at the big end of town, this slick hotel offers 238 elegant rooms, many with superlative views. The bathroom design is ultra-cool (bronze and black tiles, separate freestanding bathtubs and shower stalls) and, if further indulgence is required, there's an in-house spa. Friendly staff, too.

**Estoria** HOTEL €€€

(Map p62; ☎680 9300; www.sokoshotels.ee; Viru väljak 4; s/d from €161/171; P❄📶) The design team at Sokos Hotels has done a great job of eradicating any lingering KGB vibes from this block, connected to the infamous Hotel Viru (p65). Bright orange and green armchairs and gaudy, retro-patterned bedspreads lighten the mood, and each floor has its own little lounge area, set up with a coffee machine, bowls of chocolates and chess sets.

## Kassisaba & Kelmiküla

Immediately west of Old Town, at the base of Toompea hill, these small neighbourhoods have a good crop of modern, midrise, midprice hotels, handy for the train station. Kassisaba is Estonian for 'cat's tail' (referring to the path through the ramparts into Toompea), while Kelmiküla means 'rogues' village' – apt as the area around the train station still retains a little of its roguish feel.

**Go Hotel Shnelli** HOTEL €€

(Map p64; ☎631 0100; www.gohotels.ee; Toompuiestee 37; s/d/f from €87/89/113; P❄📶) Next to Balti Jaam train station (p86), this modern hotel is usefully placed between the nightlife of Kalamaja and the sights of Old Town. The free parking is a godsend, street-facing rooms have extraordinary views of the Toompea skyline, and the family rooms have baths, kitchenettes and sofas. There's also a sauna (for up to five people, first two hours €60).

**L'Ermitage** HOTEL €€€

(Map p54; ☎699 6400; www.lermitagehotel.ee; Toompuiestee 19; d/ste from €120/173; P❄📶) Looking more like a new apartment block than a hermitage, this metal-clad building facing parkland and Old Town walls offers highly styled yet comfortable rooms (ask for a quieter one at the rear). The interior design is contemporary throughout, with white walls splashed with colour. The onsite Restaurant L'Ermitage does very good lunches and dinners (Monday to Saturday, mains €16 to €18).

**Kreutzwald Hotel Tallinn** HOTEL €€€

(Map p54; ☎666 4800; www.kreutzwaldhotel.com; Endla 23; s/d from €111/115; 📶) Scandinavian chic merges with Japanese minimalism at Kreutzwald to create a pleasant place to lay your head, 15 minutes' walk from Old Town. The pricier 'Zen' doubles have spa baths, flat-screen TVs and soothing mood lighting. There's also a health spa (treatments from €29) and Italian restaurant (mains €11 to €16) on-site.

## Kristiine

**Valge Villa** GUESTHOUSE €€

(Map p54; ☎654 2302; www.white-villa.com; Kännu 26/2; s/d/apt without breakfast €49/57/92; P📶) Simple and welcoming, the 'White Villa' sits in a quiet suburb 3km south of the centre; it's a good basic option, particularly if you've got a car. All rooms have fridges and kettles and some have fireplaces, balconies, kitchenettes and bathtubs. It's well connected to Old Town by public transport, and has bikes for rent (€18 per day).

## Eating

Tallinn is a dining gem. Its abundance of casual yet clued-up and innovative restaurants (not to mention its slew of fine diners and taverns aimed at 'medieval' trenchermen) shouldn't be unexpected: it's at a cultural crossroads surrounded by wonderful seafood, fecund farms, forest produce and New Nordic exemplars, so the food really *should* be good. Vegan and vegetarian options have blossomed of late.

### Old Town

**Vegan Restoran V** VEGAN €
(Map p58; 626 9087; www.veganrestoran.ee; Rataskaevu 12; mains €8-13; noon-11pm Sun-Thu, to 11.30pm Fri & Sat) Visiting vegans are spoiled for choice in this wonderful restaurant in a timber-ceilinged, stone-walled setting. In summer the four streetside tables beckon, but the atmospheric interior is where it's at. The food is excellent – expect the likes of tofu-and-spinach-filled pasta with white-wine sauce or jackfruit, chickpea and beetroot balls with potato, onion cream and hummus.

**III Draakon** ESTONIAN €
(Map p58; www.kolmasdraakon.ee; Raekoja plats 1; snacks €1-3.50; 9am-midnight) There's bucketloads of corny atmosphere at this Lilliputian tavern below the town hall, plus super-cheap elk soup, sausages, oven-hot pasties and other snacks designed to accompany beer. The historic setting is unapologetically exploited – expect costumed wenches with a good line in tourist banter, and beer served in ceramic steins.

**Chocolats de Pierre** CAFE €
(Map p58; 641 8061; www.pierre.ee; Vene 6; mains €8-11; 10am-10pm Mon-Thu, from 9am Fri-Sun) Nestled inside the picturesque Masters' Courtyard (p83) and offering respite from Old Town hubbub, this snug, lavishly decorated cafe is renowned for its delectable (but pricey) handmade chocolates. It also sells pastries, hot sandwiches and quiches, making it a great choice for a light breakfast or lunch. There's plenty stronger than hot chocolate on the menu, too.

**Kehrwieder** CAFE €
(Map p58; 524 5645; www.kohvik.ee; Saiakang 1; cakes & sandwiches €3; 8am-11pm Sun-Thu, to 1am Fri & Sat) Unlike many places around Tallinn's Town Hall Sq, this cosy chocolaterie-cafe has an invitingly relaxed ambience. Stretch out on a couch, read by lamplight and bump your head on the arched ceilings. Foodwise, it offers house-made chocolates, pastries and cakes, and pre-prepared wraps and salads. The *hõõgvein* is particularly welcome in frosty weather.

**★Tai Boh** ASIAN €€
(Map p58; 629 9218; www.taiboh.com; Mere pst 1; mains €14-16; 5-11pm Mon-Thu, to 1am Fri & Sat, 2-11pm Sun) This superb pan-Asian eatery adjoining Manna La Roosa feels like a baroque fever dream. Picking a focal point among the opulent kitsch is hard: the chandelier of mannequin arms and feathers, or Barack Obama clad as the Dalai Lama? But the food is no flight of fancy: mainly excellent Thai classics with the odd interloper from Japan, Korea and Malaysia. There's also a separate vegetarian menu.

**★Manna La Roosa** GASTRONOMY €€
(Map p58; 620 0249; www.mannalaroosa.com; Vana-Viru 15; mains €16-19; noon-midnight Mon & Tue, to 1am Wed & Thu, to 3am Fri & Sat, to 10pm Sun) This restaurant-bar is truly a multisensory adventure. Housed in a French-style villa built in 1872 and once used as a pharmacy, its interior is a wacky kaleidoscope of sculptures, absurdist paintings and extravagant furnishings, sourced from around the world by revered Estonian designer Soho Fond. Thankfully the top-notch food, deliciously inventive cocktails and super-cool staff easily justify all the visual excess.

**Must Puudel** CAFE €€
(Map p58; 505 6258; www.facebook.com/mustpuudel; Müürivahe 20; mains €11-14; 9am-11pm Sun-Tue, to 1am Wed, to 2am Thu-Sat) With eclectic retro furniture matched by an equally wide-roaming soundtrack, courtyard seating, excellent coffee, long opening hours and select nights of live music and DJs, the 'Black Poodle' must be Old Town's hippest cafe. It's also charming, welcoming and capable of slinging seriously good cocktails, casual meals or coffee, as the time of day requires.

**Von Krahli Aed** EASTERN EUROPEAN €€
(Map p58; 5859 3839; www.vonkrahl.ee; Rataskaevu 8; mains €13-16; noon-midnight

Mon-Sat, to 11pm Sun; ) You'll find plenty of greenery on your plate at this rustic, plant-filled restaurant (*aed* means 'garden'), beneath the rough beams of a medieval merchant's house. Veggies star here (although all dishes can be ordered with some kind of fleshy embellishment) and there's care taken to offer vegan dishes and gluten-, lactose- and egg-free options.

**Plant** VEGAN €€

(Map p58; 655 0560; www.plantfood.ee; Rüütli 11; mains €10-14; noon-11pm Mon-Sat, to 9pm Sun; ) An excellent example of the flourishing vegetarian and vegan dining scene in Tallinn, Plant is the finished article, from the clean style and hanging greenery of its split-level dining room to its warm, professional staff and the imaginative, delicious vegan dishes issuing from the kitchen. Try the eryngii-mushroom risotto with grilled asparagus, when in season.

**Dominic** EUROPEAN €€

(Map p58; 641 0400; www.restoran.ee; Vene 10; mains €16-19; noon-midnight Mon-Sat, to 9pm Sun; ) With a softly lit, old-fashioned dining room inside a 14th-century house, good French-inspired cooking and a winning wine list, 'Wine Restaurant' Dominic is a firm favourite for romantic dinners *à deux*. Think 45ºC-cooked salmon with potato cream, salmon roe and wild garlic, or girolle risotto with peas, hazelnuts and parmesan, and a cheese plate to finish.

**Väike** ESTONIAN €€

(Map p58; 642 4025; www.rataskaevu16.ee; Rataskaevu 16; mains €10-17; noon-11pm Sun-Thu, to midnight Fri & Sat; ) If you've ever had a hankering for braised elk roast, this warm, stone-walled place can sate it. Although it's hardly tethered to tradition, plenty of Estonian faves fill the menu – fried Baltic herring, fish soup and Estonian cheeses among them. Finish, if possible, with the legendary warm chocolate cake.

Kids are welcome, and can order from their own menu.

**Vanaema Juures** ESTONIAN €€

(Map p58; 626 9080; www.vonkrahl.ee/vanaemajuures; Rataskaevu 10/12; mains €11-16; noon-10pm; ) Food like your grandma used to make, if she was a) Estonian; and b) a really good cook. 'Grandma's Place' was one of Tallinn's most stylish restaurants in the 1930s, and still produces excellent, traditional Estonian fare such as blood sausages with sauerkraut and cowberry jam. Antiques and photographs lend the dining room an antique air.

**Pegasus** EUROPEAN €€

(Map p58; 662 3013; www.restoranpegasus.ee; Harju 1; mains €14-18; noon-11pm Sun-Thu, to midnight Fri & Sat; ) This sleek restaurant occupies three design-driven floors of a Soviet-era building with porthole-style windows and roughcast walls. There's a lightness of touch to the menu, which encompasses sharing plates, soups and inventive mains such as slow-cooked aubergine with peanut cream and smoky tomato foam; the service is lovely, and so is the *leib* (Estonian black bread).

**Elevant** INDIAN €€

(Map p58; 631 3132; www.elevant.ee; Vene 5; mains €17-20; noon-11pm; ) Intriguing aromas arrest visitors as they ascend the wrought-iron staircase to earth-toned dining rooms where diners linger over some of Tallinn's best Indian food. There's a wide selection of vegetarian dishes, some curiosities (four different moose curries and a baby-octopus curry) and an eclectic soundtrack exploring most corners of the globe.

**Clayhills Gastropub** PUB FOOD €€

(Map p58; 641 9312; www.clayhills.ee; Pikk 13; mains €14-18; 10am-midnight Sun-Wed, to 2am Thu-Sat; ) With live music on weekends, comfy couches, a stone-walled upstairs room and sunny summer terrace, Clayhills is a very pleasant place to take a break from a day of wandering through Old Town. It serves up quality grub too: try the rabbit pie, the wild mushroom risotto or the rib-eye with chimichurri.

**La Bottega** TRATTORIA €€

(Map p58; 627 7733; www.labottega.ee; Vene 4; mains €18-20; noon-11pm Mon-Thu, to midnight Fri & Sat, 1-10pm Sun) Ancient wooden beams and stone pillars contrast with a sweeping pine staircase in a high-ceilinged dining room walled with shelves of wine – an atmospheric setting for excellent Italian food with Sardinian sympathies. There's plenty of seafood on the menu, alongside local game meats such as wild boar and mouth-watering homemade pastas.

★**Leib** ESTONIAN €€€

(Map p58; 611 9026; www.leibresto.ee; Uus 31; mains €18-24; noon-3pm & 6-11pm Mon-Fri, noon-11pm Sat, to 9pm Sun) *Leib* (Estonian black bread) is a thing of great beauty and quiet national pride, and you'll find a peerless rendition here: dense, moist, almost fruity in its Christmas-cake complexity. Thickly sliced and served with salt-flaked butter, it's the ideal accompaniment to the delightful New Nordic ('New Estonian'?) food at this garden restaurant in the headquarters of Tallinn's Scottish club (really!).

**Tchaikovsky** RUSSIAN €€€
(Map p58; ☎600 0608; www.telegraafhotel.com; Hotel Telegraaf, Vene 9; mains €28-30; ⏰6-11pm; 📶) Located in a glass-roofed pavilion within the upscale Hotel Telegraaf, Tchaikovsky offers dazzling fine-dining *mise en scène*: armchairs surrounding linen-draped tables, chandeliers, gilt frames and greenery. Service is faultlessly formal, as is the carefully updated menu of Franco-Russian classics, and dinner is accompanied by live chamber music. Order à la carte, or surrender yourself to the six-course degustation (€85; four-course vegetarian variant €60).

**Olde Hansa** ESTONIAN €€€
(Map p58; ☎627 9020; www.oldehansa.ee; Vana turg 1; mains €20-25; ⏰10am-midnight, kitchen closes 11pm; 📶) Period-garbed servers labour beneath large plates of game meats in medieval-themed Olde Hansa, once a Hanseatic merchant's house, now the place to indulge in a gluttonous feast. If it all sounds a bit cheesy, take heart – the chefs have researched historically authentic dishes from Tallinn's medieval glory days. Expect such exotica as boar, elk and bear (all sustainable meats, apparently).

**MEKK** ESTONIAN €€€
(Map p58; ☎680 6688; www.mekk.ee; Savoy Boutique Hotel, Suur-Karja 17; mains €20-22; ⏰noon-11pm Mon-Fri, from 5pm Sat; 📶) The name of the ground-floor restaurant at the Savoy Boutique Hotel (p74) is a contraction of *Moodne Eesti Köök* (modern Estonian cuisine) – defined here as a modern, produce-driven culinary style showcasing the best of what the country has to offer, while borrowing from its Nordic and Slavic neighbours. Expect top-notch produce from Estonia's waters, forests and farms, treated with skill.

**ORE** EUROPEAN €€€
(Map p58; ☎611 7290; Olevimägi 9; mains €17-22, 6-course degustation €53; ⏰noon-11pm Mon-Thu, to midnight Fri & Sat, 1-10pm Sun; 📶🖉) The sleek, arch-vaulted dining room, Scandi-styled furniture and moody lighting set the tone for a refined and pricey dinner. Vegetarians are quite well looked after, with several mains such as pearl barley with chanterelles and roasted zucchini with salted lemon and minted yoghurt among the guinea fowl and beef rib, while the degustation is a skilful exploration of what's in season.

## Kalamaja & Telliskivi

**F-hoone** PUB FOOD €
(Map p64; ☎5322 6855; www.fhoone.ee; Telliskivi 60a; mains €8-10; ⏰kitchen 9am-11pm Mon-Sat, to 9pm Sun; 📶🖉) The trailblazing watering hole of the uberhip Telliskivi complex (p65), the industrial-chic 'Building F' offers a quality menu of pasta, burgers, soups, salads and desserts in an always-lively atmosphere. Wash down your food with a craft beer from the extensive selection and remember to book a table on buzzing weekend evenings. There's a separate vegetarian menu.

**Boheem** CAFE €
(Map p64; ☎631 1928; Kopli 18; pizzas & mains €6-8; ⏰9am-11pm Mon-Fri, from 10am Sat & Sun; 📶) Spilling out from an old clapboard house on one of Kalamaja's main arteries, Boheem is a firm favourite with local bohemians. The cheap and tasty fare includes crêpes, wraps, salads, stews, quiches and pasta dishes, or you can just nurse a coffee or beer and take in the friendly buzz. Next door, there's a pizzeria doing good wood-fired pizzas.

**★Moon** RUSSIAN €€
(Map p64; ☎631 4575; www.restoranmoon.ee; Võrgu 3; mains €15-17; ⏰noon-11pm Mon-Sat, 1-9pm Sun, closed some of Jul; 📶) Quietly but consistently the best restaurant in Kalamaja, Moon (pronounced 'moan'; it means 'poppy') is a gem, combining Russian and broader-European influences to delicious effect. The staff are friendly and switched-on, the decor is cheerily whimsical, and dishes such as *pirozhki* (little stuffed pies) and reputation-transforming chicken Kiev showcase a kitchen as dedicated to pleasure as to experimentation.

**Siga la Vaca Estonia** GRILL €€
(Map p64; ☎5395 7512; Vabriku 6/1; mains €13-16, steaks €24-28; ⏰noon-10pm Tue-Sat; 📶) In an unlikely looking commercial building just north of Telliskivi, 'Follow the Cow' is a super-welcoming Argentinian-style *parilla*

(grill) that will have carnivores watering at the mouth. Starters include Peruvian-style shrimp brochettes with grilled lime and classic *empanadas*, while mains include beer-marinated beef heart, BBQ pork ribs, and superb steaks from Argentina, Uruguay and Australia. Ideal beers and wines have been selected.

**Kolm Sibulat** ASIAN **€€**
(Map p54; ☎664 4055; www.kolmsibulat.eu; Telliskivi 2; mains €15-16; ⏰noon-11pm Tue-Sat; 📶🍃) A judicious hand in the kitchen respectfully reinterprets the cuisines of China, India and Southeast Asia, scattering European staples such as schnitzel and cod cakes amongst the *shimeji* mushrooms, red-curry pastes and kimchi to make sure everyone's happy. A super-friendly operation making great use of a corner-side weatherboard in an up-and-coming area south of Telliskivi, it's really producing the goods.

## City Centre

**Sfäär** EUROPEAN **€€**
(Map p62; ☎5199 5446; Mere pst 6e; mains €13-15; ⏰11.30am-4pm Mon-Sat, 5-10pm Mon-Thu, 5-11pm Fri & Sat, 11.30am-6pm Sun; 📶🍃) Chic Sfäär delivers an inventive menu highlighting great Estonian produce in dishes that gesture east (veggie curry) and west (Arctic char with potato and horseradish). The warehouse-style setting is like something out of a Nordic design catalogue, the cocktail and wine list won't disappoint and there are a couple of vegetarian options that are definitely more than afterthoughts.

★**Restaurant Ö** ESTONIAN **€€€**
(Map p62; ☎661 6150; www.restoran-o.ee; Mere pst 6e; degustation menu €65; ⏰6-11pm Wed-Sat, closed Jul; 📶) Award-winning Ö (pronounced 'er' and named for Estonia's biggest island, Saaremaa) has carved a unique space in Tallinn's culinary world, delivering inventive degustation menus showcasing seasonal Estonian produce. There's a distinct 'New Nordic' influence at play, deploying unusual ingredients such as whey, rye and salted fat, and the understated dining room nicely complements the theatrical but always-delicious cuisine.

**Horisont** EUROPEAN **€€€**
(Map p62; ☎624 3000; www.horisont-restoran.com; Tornimäe 3, 30th fl, Swissôtel; mains €29-31; ⏰6-10pm Tue-Sat; 📶) Combining excellent service, a creative menu, stylish decor and magnificent views over most of the city (except, sadly, Old Town), Horisont offers a wonderful fine-dining experience on the 30th floor of the Swissôtel. Intriguing tidbits and palate-cleansing sorbets are liberally scheduled around dishes such as fried octopus with crispy scallop and coconut-lemongrass risotto with lime gel.

## Kadriorg

**NOP** CAFE **€**
(Map p66; ☎603 2270; www.nop.ee; Köleri 1; mains €8-9; ⏰8am-9pm Mon-Fri, 9am-8pm Sat & Sun; 📶🍃👪) Occupying an old Baltic timber house well off the tourist trail, near Kadriorg Park, NOP (Neighbourhood Organic Place) is the kind of wholesome deli-cafe that's a magnet for yummy mummies, hipsters and itinerant foodies. White walls, wooden floors and a kids' corner provide the *mise en scène*; memorable food such as kimchi latkes and cauliflower-shrimp ceviche provide the drama.

★**Mantel ja Korsten** MEDITERRANEAN **€€**
(Map p66; ☎665 9555; www.mantel-korsten.ee; Poska 19a; mains €14-19; ⏰noon-11pm Tue-Sat; 🅿📶) Tucked away in the leafy, weatherboard-lined streets that merge into the greenery of Kadriorg Park, 'Cloak and Chimney' welcomes guests to a smartly painted green house that's now an ideal space in which to enjoy its artfully prepared Mediterranean dishes. There are one or two inviting vegetarian dishes in each section of a menu heavy on seafood, poultry and seasonal produce.

## Pirita

★**NOA** ESTONIAN **€€€**
(☎508 0589; www.noaresto.ee; Ranna tee 3; mains €19-24; ⏰noon-11pm Mon-Thu, to midnight Fri & Sat, to 10pm Sun; 🅿📶🍃) It's worth the trek out to the far side of Pirita to reach this top-notch waterside restaurant, which consistently backs up its elevated reputation. Housed in a stylish low-slung pavilion with superb views over Tallinn Bay to Old Town, it plays knowledgeably with Asian influences while keeping a focus on the best Estonian and European ingredients and techniques.

## Drinking & Nightlife

Don't worry about Tallinn's reputation as a stag-party paradise: it's easy to avoid the 'British' and 'Irish' pubs in the southeast

### ORGANISED INTOXICATION

If proper inebriation is your benchmark of a good night out, Tallinn has quite a few organised options to help you realise that dream.

The **Epic Bar Crawl** (Map p58; ☎5624 3088; www.freetour.com; €15; ⏰10pm Thu-Sat) leaves from Pikk 72, outside the Bunker Bar, every Thursday, Friday and Saturday at 10pm, for five hours of bibulous indulgence, taking in at least three bars and one club. Led by dedicated drunkards, the tour's price (€15) includes free shots and entry to the club.

Party hostel Monk's Bunk (p75) ups the inebriation level on its **Mad Monk Pub Crawl** with an hour's unlimited beer, cider and shots in its own bar, followed by a free shot in two different bars and club entry. It's priced at €15 and kicks off at 9.30pm, Thursday to Saturday.

corner of Old Town where lager louts congregate (roughly the triangle formed by Viru, Suur-Karja and the city walls). Elsewhere you'll find a diverse selection of bars where it's quite possible to have a quiet, unmolested drink.

##  Old Town

**★Levist Väljas** BAR

(Map p58; ☎504 6048; www.facebook.com/levistvaljas; Olevimägi 12; ⏰5pm-3am Sun-Thu, to 6am Fri & Sat) Inside this much-loved Tallinn cellar bar (usually the last pit stop of the night) you'll find two floors of cheap booze, unabashed music and a refreshingly motley crew of friendly punks, grunge kids and anyone else who strays from the well-trodden tourist path. The discreet entrance to 'Out of Range' is down a flight of stairs.

**DM Baar** BAR

(Depeche Mode Baar; Map p58; ☎644 2350; www.depechemode.ee; Voorimehe 4; ⏰6pm-2am Sun & Tue-Fri, 2pm-3am Sat) If you just can't get enough of Depeche Mode, this is the bar for you. The walls are covered with all manner of memorabilia (including pictures of the actual band partying here) and there's a full list of DM-themed cocktails. And the soundtrack? Do you really need to ask? If you're not a fan, leave in silence.

**Koht** BAR

(Map p58; ☎644 3302; Lai 8; ⏰5pm-3am Sun-Thu, to 6am Fri & Sat; 📶) The abruptly named 'Place' is a haven for beer lovers and social beasts in general. Set back from a thoroughfare in the heart of Old Town, it offers 14 interesting brews on tap, with plenty more in the bottle (which you can take home from the attached bottle shop, open 10am to 10pm daily). The cosy, vaulted cellar-bar, amiably staffed, encourages lingering.

**Whisper Sister** COCKTAIL BAR

(Map p58; ☎5874 7837; Pärnu mnt12; cocktails €10; ⏰7pm-12.30am Sun-Thu, to 2.30am Fri & Sat; 📶) Taking the 'speakeasy' theme seriously, with gorgeous 1930s decor and music to match, Whisper Sister is a contender for the best cocktail bar in Tallinn. The skilled staff behind the marble bar really look after you, and the vibe is unaffectedly friendly (especially after a couple of 'Filthy Martinis').

**Frank** BAR

(Map p58; ☎623 3059; www.frankbistro.ee; Sauna 2; ⏰noon-midnight Sun-Tue, to 1am Fri & Sat; 📶) This bar-bistro is a particular favourite of locals, whether for a schnitzel, a cooked breakfast at dinnertime or just a quiet, well-mixed weeknight drink. An effortlessly stylish environment, welcoming staff and a good wine selection round out a polished package. Next door, Frank Underground concentrates solely on drinking and socialising, from 6pm to 2am Wednesday to Saturday.

**Paar Veini** WINE BAR

(Map p58; ☎660 3036; www.paarveini.ee; Sauna 1; ⏰6pm-midnight Mon & Tue, to 3am Wed & Thu, to 4.30am Fri & Sat; 📶) The name means 'a couple of wines' and that's exactly what locals head here for. The vibe's relaxed and cosy, with comfy sofas, mismatched chairs, good selections on the sound system, candles on the tables and basic nibbles.

**Von Krahli Baar** BAR

(Map p58; ☎626 9090; www.vonkrahl.ee; Rataskaevu 10; ⏰9am-midnight Mon-Sat, to 10pm Sun; 📶) Attached to the independent theatre of the same name, comfortably grungy Von Krahli has courtyard tables and a stone-walled interior that hosts the occasional live band or DJ. It's a great spot for a pre- or post-theatre drink, or an inexpensive meal in an unfussy atmosphere (mains €8 to €11).

**Hell Hunt** PUB
(Map p58; ☎681 8333; www.hellhunt.ee; Pikk 39; ⊙noon-2am; ) Don't let the menacing-sounding name (which actually means 'gentle wolf') put you off – this trusty old trouper has an amiable air, decent food and a huge selection of imported and Estonian beer (some brewed especially for the house). Billing itself as 'the first Estonian pub', it's perennially popular; in summer, drinkers spill onto the little square across the road.

**Põrgu** PUB
(Map p58; ☎644 0232; www.porgu.ee; Rüütli 4; ⊙noon-midnight Mon-Thu, to 2am Fri & Sat; ) While the name may mean 'hell', the descent into this particular underworld is anything but infernal for craft-beer fans. There's a good mix of local and imported varieties, including 14 beers on tap and dozens more by the bottle. The food's good too: borscht, fried chicken livers on toast and plenty of salads and grills.

**Beer House** MICROBREWERY
(Map p58; ☎644 2222; www.beerhouse.ee; Dunkri 5; ⊙noon-midnight; ) This microbrewery offers up the good stuff (seven unfiltered house brews and plenty else besides) in a huge, tavern-like space where, come Friday and Saturday evenings, the traditional Estonian music can rattle the brain into oblivion. For ballast, there's a menu of substantial beer-friendly dishes (mains €13 to €17).

**Studio** CLUB
(Map p58; ☎5599 2557; www.clubstudio.ee; Sauna 1; presale €10; ⊙midnight-6am Fri & Sat) With a renowned sound system threatening tinnitus over two levels (the lower playing more soul and hip-hop; the upper more techno, house and hard beats), Studio is one of Tallinn's premier clubs. Plenty of local DJs want to play there, but international visitors are frequent.

**Club Hollywood** CLUB
(Map p58; ☎5912 4200; www.clubhollywood.ee; Vana-Posti 8; cover varies; ⊙11pm-4am Wed & Thu, to 5am Fri & Sat) A multilevel emporium of mayhem, Hollywood draws the largest crowds and biggest DJ names in Tallinn. Wednesday night is ladies' night (free entry for women), so expect to see loads of guys looking to get lucky. It tends to be the last port of call for the organised pub crawls, so it can get pretty trashy.

## Kalamaja

Tallinn's young and sociable tend to leave the pricey bars of Old Town to the tourists and head to Kalamaja instead. Telliskivi Creative City (p65) is the liveliest nook, but there are cosy local pubs scattered throughout the neighbourhood.

★**Sveta Baar** BAR
(Map p64; ☎5688 9101; www.sveta.ee; Telliskivi 62; entry charged to some events, see website; ⊙5pm-2am Mon & Tue, to 3am Wed & Thu, noon-6am Fri & Sat, 12.30pm-midnight Sun; ) A sprawling, bohemian, charismatic and hugely enjoyable bar-club, Sveta makes great use of a former industrial space in Telliskivi, filling it with colour, potted plants, eclectic furniture and perhaps Tallinn's most alternative crowd. Things spill outdoors in warm weather, and there are frequent DJs and live acts, including plenty from the European underground.

**Pudel** BAR
(Map p64; ☎5866 4496; www.pudel.ee; Telliskivi 60a; ⊙4pm-midnight Tue & Wed, to 2am Thu & Fri, noon-2am Sat, 2pm-midnight Sun) Nothing to do with dogs (the name means 'bottle'), this friendly corner bar in Telliskivi Creative City (p65) is big on craft beer, offering plenty from Estonia and internationally, both on draught and behind glass. The most basic beer snacks imaginable are all there is to eat, but there's a frequent roster of good-time DJs.

**Tops** BAR
(Map p64; ☎5679 6333; Soo 15; ⊙4pm-midnight Tue & Wed, to 1am Thu, to 3am Fri & Sat; ) All you'd want in a chilled-out neighbourhood bar: comfy couches; great beer and cocktails; a stylish, low-ceilinged room arranged around a tiled bar; and a mixed crowd of local misfits. If that's sounding too cosy and sedentary, DJs, comedy nights and open mics are regular affairs.

## City Centre

Options are slim in the City Centre; try around the Rotermann Quarter.

**Klubi Teater** CLUB
(Theatre Club; Map p62; ☎5688 4444; www.klubiteater.ee; Vabaduse Väljak 5; admission €8; ⊙midnight-5am Fri & Sat) Wild cabaret, dancers and live music sometimes complement the DJs at this pulsing club, set in a

### GAY & LESBIAN TALLINN

Tallinn holds the monopoly on visible gay life in Estonia, with a few unobtrusive venues south of Old Town. The main regular celebration is Baltic Pride, which rotates between Tallinn, Rīga and Vilnius every year, usually in June. Tallinn's turn falls in 2020 and 2023.

Long-standing **X-Baar** (Map p62; ☎641 9478; www.facebook.com/xbaar; Tatari 1; ⏲4pm-1am Sun-Thu, to 4am Fri & Sat) is the mainstay of the city's gay and lesbian scene, attracting a mixed crowd of mainly local men and women. It's a relaxed kind of place, with a snug bar and a large dance floor.

1926 building with original details in some rooms, just over the road from Freedom Sq.

**Scotland Yard** BAR

(Map p62; ☎653 5190; www.scotlandyard.ee; Mere pst 6e; ⏲noon-11pm Sun & Mon, to midnight Tue-Thu, to 2am Fri & Sat; 📶) If you appreciate kitsch, themed bars, this is very well done, right down to the prison-cell toilets and staff dressed as English bobbies (although the large fish tank and electric-chair loos are probably less in tune). There's live music many nights, a big menu of all-day pub grub, a small outdoor terrace and clubby leather banquettes.

## ☆ Entertainment

Bills, flyers and newspapers advertise events around the city, or find Tallinn's best English-language listings in *Tallinn in Your Pocket* (free pdf at www.inyourpocket.com). Also check out www.culture.ee, www.concert.ee, www.draamamaa.ee and the ticketing service Piletilevi (www.piletilevi.ee).

### Live Music

Tallinners love live music of all genres, and summer's frequent festivals are augmented, year-round, by plenty of concert venues in and around the city. Touring international acts usually perform at Tallinn Song Festival Grounds (p67), A Le Coq Arena or Saku Suurhall. For major classical concerts, check out what's on at the Estonia Concert Hall. Chamber, organ and smaller-scale concerts are held at various halls and churches around town.

In summer, check out DJs and live acts in art-collective PADA's **Cultural Garden** (Kultuurikatla Aed; Map p64; www.kultuurikatel.ee; Põhja pst 35, entrance at Kalasadama 6; usually free; ⏲10pm-4am when events are scheduled, mid-May–mid-Sep) in Kalamaja.

### Theatre & Dance

Most theatre performances are in Estonian, or occasionally in English or Russian.

**Estonia Concert Hall** LIVE PERFORMANCE

(Eesti Kontserdisaal; Map p62; ☎614 7705; www.concert.ee; Estonia pst 4; ⏲box office 9am-7pm Mon-Fri, or 1hr before performances) The city's biggest classical concerts, and indeed some of Estonia's most significant ceremonies and celebrations, are held in this double-barrelled venue, built in 1913 and reconstructed after WWII bomb damage. It's Tallinn's most prestigious venue, housing both the Estonian National Opera and Ballet (www.opera.ee), and the Estonian National Symphony Orchestra (www.erso.ee).

**Tallinn City Theatre** THEATRE

(Tallinna Linnateater; Map p58; www.linnateater.ee; Lai 23) Originating in Soviet times as the Estonian Youth Theatre, Tallinn's most beloved company performs on seven stages scattered around its main building on Lai (including a summer stage at the rear). The complex actually comprises 16 interconnected medieval houses, but not all host regular performances. Book anything that takes your fancy well in advance, as tickets can be scarce.

**Estonian Drama Theatre** THEATRE

(Eesti Draamateater; Map p62; ☎680 5555; www.draamateater.ee; Pärnu mnt 5; ⏲box office 11am-7pm) This handsome art nouveau–style venue, completed in 1910, became home to Estonia's leading theatre company in 1937. Productions, mainly of classic plays, are in Estonian or English. Productions for children are a regular feature.

**Von Krahli Teater** THEATRE

(Map p58; ☎626 9090; www.vonkrahl.ee; Rataskaevu 10; ⏲box office & bar 9am-midnight) With an attached bar and a reputation for experimental and fringe productions, Von Krahli claims the honour of being the first private theatre established in Estonia following independence from the Soviet Union (in 1992).

**St Canute's Guild Hall** PERFORMING ARTS

(Kanuti Gildi Saal; Map p58; ☎646 4704; www.saal.ee; Pikk 20) Contemporary and classical forms of dance, audio and video installations and cutting-edge theatre productions are just some of the avant-garde entries filling the program at this multi-genre arts space. It occupies a gorgeously facaded craftsmen's guild hall dating to the 13th century.

### Sport

**A Le Coq Arena** FOOTBALL

(Map p54; Asula 4c) About 1.5km southwest of town, this 15,000-seat arena is home to the national squad and Tallinn's football team FC Flora (www.fcflora.ee). It also occasionally hosts concerts and other events.

**Saku Suurhall** BASKETBALL

(Map p54; ☎660 0200; www.sakusuurhall.ee; Paldiski mnt 104b) Basketball ranks as one of Estonia's most passionately watched games, and the big games are held in this 7000-seat arena, the country's largest, 7km west of central Tallinn. Ice hockey, trade shows and concerts are also staged here.

### Cinema

Films are generally shown in their original language, subtitled in Estonian and Russian.

**Artis** CINEMA

(Map p62; ☎box office 663 1380; www.kino.ee; Estonia pst 9; tickets €4.60-8; ⏲box office 10am-15min after last screening begins) On the 3rd floor of the Solaris Centre (p84) – enter from Rävala pst – this art-house cinema shows European, local and independent productions. English-language films are subtitled, usually in Estonian and Russian, but only some foreign-language films get English subtitles.

**Kino Sõprus** CINEMA

(Map p58; ☎box office 644 1919; www.kinosoprus.ee; Vana-Posti 8; tickets adult/reduced €6.50/5; ⏲box office 1hr before scheduled films) Set in a magnificent Soviet-era theatre (be sure to check out the reliefs on the facade), the Kino Sõprus ('friendship cinema') is Estonia's best art-house picture house. It screens films in their original languages, there's bar seating in the screening room itself, and frequent programs (such as 'Brazilian Cinema Week') are curated.

## Shopping

The city's glitziest shopping precinct is the Rotermann Quarter (p65), a clutch of former warehouses now sheltering dozens of small stores selling everything from streetwear to Scandinavian-designed furniture, artisanal cheese, good wines, top-notch bread and dry-aged beef. Telliskivi Creative City (p65) has fewer but more unusual shops, and you'll be tripping over *käsitöö* (handicraft) stores everywhere in Old Town.

### Old Town

★**Masters' Courtyard** ARTS & CRAFTS

(Meistrite Hoov; Map p58; www.hoov.ee; Vene 6; ⏲10am-6pm Thu-Tue, to 10pm Wed) Archetypal of Tallinn's amber-suspended medieval beauty, this cobbled 13th-century courtyard offers rich pickings – a cosy chocolaterie-cafe, a guesthouse, and artisans' stores and workshops selling quality ceramics, glass, jewellery, knitwear, woodwork and candles.

★**Katariina Gild** ARTS & CRAFTS

(St Catherine's Guild; Map p58; www.katariinagild.eu; Katariina Käik, off Vene 12; ⏲11am-6pm Mon-Sat) The stunning medieval lane of Katariina Käik is home to the Katariina Guild, comprising eight artisans' studios where you can happily browse the work of 14 female creators. Look for ceramics, textiles, patchwork quilts, hats, jewellery, stained glass and beautiful leather-bound books. Opening hours can vary among the different studios, but are loosely 11am to 6pm Monday to Saturday.

**Ivo Nikkolo** FASHION & ACCESSORIES

(Map p58; ☎641 9058; www.ivonikkolo.ee; Suur-Karja 14; ⏲10am-7pm Mon-Fri, to 5pm Sat, 11am-4pm Sun) Ivo Nikkolo, one of post-Soviet Estonia's first labels, produces women's fashion that can be floaty and fun, or muted and professional, all made with natural, high-quality fabrics.

**Eesti Käsitöö Kodu** ARTS & CRAFTS

(Estonian Handicraft House; Map p58; ☎644 8873; Vene 12; ⏲10am-6pm Mon-Sat, to 5pm Sun) Associated with the Estonian Folk Art and Craft Union, resurrected in 1992 after its suppression under the Soviets, this is the biggest and best place in Tallinn to shop for Estonian clothes and handiwork. It's all beautifully laid out on floating racks and along the stone walls of this sub-street-level store.

**Lühikese Jala Galerii** ARTS & CRAFTS

(Map p58; ☎631 4720; Lühike jalg 6; ⏲10am-6pm Mon-Fri, to 5pm Sat & Sun) The 'Short Leg Gallery' is full of floaty textiles, jewellery, glass, ceramics and other applied art, all Estonian made. Ask to look at the natural spring-fed waterfall that cascades down the back wall from Toompea above.

### THE MARKET ECONOMY

Whether you're looking for picnic supplies or a knock-off Lenin alarm clock, Tallinn's markets provide fertile hunting grounds and excellent people-watching.

**Balti Jaama Turg** (Baltic Station Market; Map p64; www.astri.ee/bjt; Kopli 1; ⌚9am-7pm Mon-Sat, to 5pm Sun) Behind the Baltic Train Station, where ramshackle stalls and pickpockets once thrived, is this shiny new food and fashion market.

**Telliskivi Flea Market** (Telliskivi Kirbuturg; Map p64; www.kirbuturg24.ee; Telliskivi 60a; ⌚10am-3pm Sat) This is Tallinn's top habitat for vintage bargain-hunters and those looking to lighten their wardrobes. Books, ephemera and other bits and pieces are sold here too.

**Knit Market** (Map p58; Müürivahe; ⌚9am-5pm) Under the Old Town wall just inside the Viru Gate there's a line of stalls selling knitwear (which may or may not be made by the local women behind them). Good for woollen scarves, sweaters, mittens, beanies and socks.

**Central Market** (Keskturg; Map p62; Keldrimäe 9; ⌚7am-5pm) Fruit and vegetables are the main game here but you'll occasionally luck upon a Soviet-era gem in one of the shady shops around the periphery. To get here, take bus 2 or tram 4 to the Keskturg stop.

**Zizi** HOMEWARES
(Map p58; ☎644 1222; www.zizi.ee; Vene 12; ⌚10am-6pm Mon-Sat, to 4pm Sun) Despite the Italianate name, Zizi stocks a range of quality, Estonian-made linen napkins, place mats, tablecloths and cushion covers.

**Chado** TEA
(Map p58; ☎648 4318; www.chado.ee; Uus 11; ⌚noon-6pm Mon-Fri, 11am-4pm Sat & Sun) These passionate provedores specialise in tea in all of its comforting forms, sourcing many of the shop's leaves directly from Asia. Drop by to chat chai with the clued-up staff, or pick up delectable artisanal chocolate.

## Kalamaja

**Estonian Design House** GIFTS & SOUVENIRS
(Eesti Disaini Maja; Map p62; ☎5357 1150; www.estoniandesignhouse.ee; Solaris Centre, Estonia pst 9; ⌚10am-9pm Mon-Sat, to 7pm Sun) A fixture at cutting-edge design fairs, this collective of Estonian designers has a permanent shopfront in the **Solaris** (Solaris Keskus; Map p62; ☎615 5125; www.solaris.ee; Estonia pst 9; ⌚shops 10am-9pm Mon-Sat, to 7pm Sun) shopping centre. Selling the Nordic-with-a-twist work of more than 100 Estonian designers, there's everything from shoes to lamps, furniture and ceramics. Look out for the 'slow fashion' of local designer Reet Aus, who upcycles materials discarded from mass-production processes.

## City Centre

The city centre is where to head for a clutch of shopping malls: **Viru Keskus** (Viru Centre; Map p62; ☎610 1444; www.virukeskus.com; Viru väljak 4/6; ⌚9am-9pm), **Tallinna Kaubamaja** (Map p62; www.kaubamaja.ee; Gonsiori 2; ⌚9am-9pm), **Stockmann Kaubamaja** (Map p62; www.stockmann.ee; Liivalaia 53; ⌚9am-9pm Mon-Sat, from 10am Sun) and **Foorum Keskus** (Forum Centre; Map p62; www.foorumkeskus.ee; Narva mnt 5; ⌚10am-8pm).

**Kalev** FOOD
(Map p62; ☎5452 5829; www.kalev.eu; Roseni 7; ⌚10am-8pm Mon-Sat, 11am-6pm Sun) This local legend has been producing delicious chocolates and other confectioneries since 1806. This Rotermann outlet has a thousand varieties of beautifully presented sugar and cocoa-fat confections to choose from.

## Information

**Tallinn Tourist Information Centre** (☎645 7777; www.visittallinn.ee; Niguliste 2; ⌚9am-7pm Mon-Sat, to 6pm Sun Jun-Aug, shorter hours rest of year; 📶) A very well-stocked and helpful office. Many Old Town walking tours leave from here.

**Toompea Post Office** (Toompea postkontor; ☎661 6616; www.omniva.ee; Lossi plats 4; ⌚10am-5pm Mon-Fri) Small branch in Toompea.

Holders of European Health Insurance Cards (EHIC) are eligible for discounted or free treatment in many cases. Pharmacies, emergency treatment and dental care can be found at the following locations, close to central Tallinn:

**Benu Koduapteek** (☎648 4199; www.benu.ee; Aia 7; ⌚8.30am-8.30pm Mon-Fri, 9am-8pm Sat) One of many well-stocked *apteegid* (pharmacies) in town.

**East-Tallinn Central Hospital** (Ida-Tallinna Keskhaigla; ☎670 7002; www.itk.ee; Ravi 18) Offers a full range of services, including a 24-hour emergency room.

**Tallinn Dental Clinic** (Tallinna Hambapolikliinik; ☎612 1200; www.hambapol.ee; Toompuiestee 4; ⏰8am-8pm Mon-Fri, 9am-3pm Sat, to 2pm Sun) Offers very reasonable treatments.

**Tõnismäe Südameapteek** (☎644 2282; www.sudameapteek.ee; Tõnismägi 5; ⏰24hr) Pharmacy south of Old Town, open 24 hours.

##  Getting There & Away

### AIR

**Tallinn Airport** (Tallinna Lennujaam; Map p54; ☎605 8888; www.tallinn-airport.ee; Tartu mnt 101; 📶) is conveniently located just 4km southeast of the city centre and offers connections with plenty of European, Russian, Turkish and Middle Eastern destinations. A few domestic flights are scheduled to the islands of Saaremaa and Hiiumaa, routes currently handled by Saartelennuliinid (www.saartelennuliinid.ee).

### BOAT

Ferries fan across the Baltic from Tallinn to Helsinki, St Petersburg, Mariehamn and Stockholm.

**Eckerö Line** (Map p62; ☎from outside Finland 358 9 228 8544; www.eckeroline.fi; Passenger Terminal A, Sadama 25-2; adult/child/car from €10/8/19; ⏰ticket office 8.30am-7pm Mon-Fri, 9am-3.30pm Sat & Sun) Two or three daily car ferries between Helsinki and Tallinn (2½ hours).

**Tallink** (Map p62; ☎paid booking line 17 808; www.tallink.com; Terminal D, Lootsi 13) Runs multiple daily services between Tallinn and Helsinki, and an overnight ferry to Stockholm and Tallinn, via the Åland Islands.

**Viking Line** (Map p62; ☎666 3966; www.vikingline.com; Terminal A, Vanasadam; passenger & vehicle from €46) Two daily car ferries between Helsinki and Tallinn (2½ hours).

### BUS

Regional and international buses depart from Tallinn's **Central Bus Station** (Tallinna bussijaam; Map p54; ☎paid helpline 12550; www.bussijaam.ee; Lastekodu 46; ⏰ticket office 7am-8pm), about 2km southeast of Old Town and linked by two tram lines and eight buses. Services depart from here for Latvia, Lithuania, Poland and other European destinations.

The national bus network is extensive, linking Tallinn to pretty much everywhere you might care to go. All services are summarised on the extremely handy Tpilet site (www.tpilet.ee).

The following are some of the main routes:

**Haapsalu** €5 to €9, 1¾ hours, at least hourly

**Kuressaare** €12 to €17, four hours, up to nine daily

**Pärnu** €9 to €11, two hours, up to 11 daily

**Tartu** €8 to €15, 2½ hours, at least every half-hour

**Viljandi** €9.50 to €11, 2½ hours, up to 13 daily

### CAR & MOTORCYCLE

Thanks to an easily navigable network of roads in Estonia, Tallinn is easily reached by car. Crossing into Estonia from Latvia on the Baltica highway is a breeze, as both countries are part of the Schengen Area, so there are no border checks. The main border checkpoint from Russia is at Narva. Car ferries from Helsinki and Stockholm run regular service to Tallinn.

Like accommodation, cars book up quickly in summer, so it pays to reserve ahead. The large international companies are all represented, with desks at Tallinn Airport and usually a city office too. If you haven't booked ahead, enquire at the tourist office about smaller local companies – they're usually cheaper.

Reliable local and international firms include the following:

**Advantec** (☎520 3003; www.advantage.ee; ⏰9am-6pm Mon-Fri, by arrangement Sat & Sun)

**Bulvar** (☎503 0222; www.bulvar.ee)

**Europcar** (☎605 8031; www.europcar.ee)

**Green Motion** (☎5699 5556; www.greenmotion.com; ⏰9am-6pm, collections & returns outside hours by prior arrangement)

**Hertz** (☎605 8923; www.hertz.ee)

**R-Rent** (☎605 8929; www.rrent.ee)

### TALLINN CARD

If you're in Tallinn for more than a fleeting visit, and are keen to see the sights, the **Tallinn Card** (www.tallinncard.ee) is a godsend. You'll pay €26/39/47 for a one-/two-/three-day adult card (children pay €15/20/24) and get free entry to over 40 sights and attractions (including most of the big-ticket ones), unlimited use of public transport and plenty of other discounts on shopping, dining and entertainment. Single tickets to Tallinn's myriad museums, bastions and other diversions are increasingly dear, so you won't need to visit many to start racking up the savings. You can buy the Tallinn Card online, from the Tourist Information Centre, or from many hotels.

### ON THE STREETS

➡ *maantee* – highway (often abbreviated to mnt)

➡ *puiestee* – avenue/boulevard (often abbreviated to pst)

➡ *sild* – bridge

➡ *tänav* – street (usually omitted from maps and addresses)

➡ *tee* – road

➡ *väljak/plats* – square

#### TRAIN

The **Baltic Train Station** (Balti Jaam; Toompuiestee 35) is on the northwestern edge of Old Town; despite the name, it has no direct services to other Baltic states. GoRail (www.gorail.ee) runs a daily service stopping in Narva (€8.10, 2½ hours) en route to St Petersburg and Moscow.

Domestic routes are operated by Elron (www.elron.ee) and include the following destinations:

**Narva** €11, 2¾ hours, four daily
**Rakvere** €5.10, 1½ hours, five daily
**Tartu** €13, two to 2½ hours, 10 daily
**Viljandi** €9.10 to €11, one to 2¼ hours, five daily

## Getting Around

#### TO/FROM THE AIRPORT

From the airport, bus 2 will take you into central Tallinn and then on to the passenger ferry port. Running an average of three times an hour between 6.30am and 11.30pm (slightly shorter hours on weekends), it should get you from the airport to the A Laikmaa stop by Viru Keskus in about 20 minutes, traffic depending. Unless you've had a chance to buy a Tallinn Card (p85) or Ühiskaart (smartcard), you'll buy a single-journey ticket from the driver (€2, exact change required). Simply reverse the process to get back to the airport.

A taxi between the airport and the city centre should cost less than €15. The airport suggests that you use the cabs waiting at the official rank to avoid being scammed (all firms have different rates). Returning to the airport, ask your accommodation provider to book a reputable firm to collect you.

#### TO/FROM THE FERRY TERMINALS

There are three main places where passenger services dock, all less than a 1km walk from Old Town. Most ferries and cruise ships dock at Old City Harbour (Vanasadam). Eckerö Line and Viking Line use **Terminals A & B** (Map p54; Sadama 25/2 & 3) while Tallink uses **Terminal D** (Map p54; Lootsi 13), just across the marina.

Bus 2 runs one to four times every hour between 6.30am and 11.30pm (slightly less frequently on weekends) from the stop by Terminal A, calling at Terminal D, the city centre, Central Bus Station (p85) and airport (p85). If you're heading to the port from the centre, catch the bus from the A Laikmaa stop, out front of the Tallink Hotel. Also from the heart of town, buses 3 and 73 go to the Linnahall stop (on Põhja pst, near the start of Sadama), five minutes' walk from all of the terminals.

A taxi between the city centre and any of the terminals should cost about €5.

#### BICYCLE

Tallinn is very cycle-friendly, despite the cobbles. Distances are minor, bike awareness is high, and there are a number of central outfits hiring decent urban bikes at reasonable rates. Outside Old Town there's a good network of cycle paths (see http://kaart.tallinn.ee) and three guarded 'bicycle parks' operate from 8am to 8pm daily from mid-May to the end of August, at the corner of Harju and Niguliste, on Vabaduse Sq and next to Kadriorg Park's info point (p65).

#### CAR & MOTORCYCLE

Driving in Tallinn is generally relaxed and predictable, although sharing the road with trams and trolleybuses carries complications. On any street where the tram stop is in the centre of the road, cars must stop until the disembarking passengers have cleared the road.

The central city has a complicated system of one-way roads and turning restrictions, which can be frustrating to the newcomer. Surprisingly, you are allowed to drive in much of Old Town – although it's slow going, parking is extremely limited and you can only enter via a few streets. Frankly, it's easier to park your car for the duration of your Tallinn stay and explore the city by foot or on public transport.

#### PUBLIC TRANSPORT

Tallinn has an excellent network of buses, trams and trolleybuses running from around 6am to 11pm or midnight. The major **local bus station** (Map p62; Viru Keskus, Viru väljak 4/6) is beneath the Viru Keskus shopping centre, although some buses terminate their routes on the surrounding streets. All local public transport timetables are online at www.tallinn.ee.

Public transport is free for Tallinn residents, children under seven and adults with children under three. Others need to pay, either buying a paper ticket from the driver (€2 for a single journey, exact change required) or by using the e-ticketing system. Buy a Ühiskaart (a smart card, requiring a €2 deposit that can't be recouped within six months of validation) at an R-Kiosk, post office or the Tallinn City Government customer service desk, add credit, then validate the card at the start of each journey using the orange card-readers. E-ticket fares are €1.10/3/6 for an hour/day/five days.

The Tallinn Card (p85) includes free public transport on all services for the duration of its validity.

Travelling without a valid ticket runs the risk of a €40 fine.

#### TAXI

Taxis are plentiful in Tallinn but each company sets its own fare – there's not too much disparity and prices should be posted prominently. However, if you hail a taxi on the street, there's a chance you'll be overcharged; to save yourself the trouble, order a taxi by phone. Operators speak English and can tell you the car number (licence plate) and estimated arrival time (usually five to 10 minutes). If you're concerned you've been overcharged, ask for a receipt, which the driver is legally obliged to provide.

Throughout Old Town you'll find plenty of bicycle taxis run by pedal power, enthusiasm – and discreet motors for when the going gets tough. You'll generally spot them lingering just inside the town walls on Viru waiting for fares.

Well-established taxi firms include the following:

**Krooni Takso** (☎638 1212; www.kroonitakso.ee; base fare €2.50, per km €0.50-0.55)

**Reval Takso** (☎1207; www.reval-takso.ee; base fare €2.29, per km €0.49)

**Takso24** (☎1224, 640 8927; www.tallinktakso.ee/en/takso24; base fare €2.95, per km €0.60-0.75)

**Tallink Takso** (☎1921, 640 8921; www.tallinktakso.ee; base fare €3.95, per km €0.89-0.99)

**Tulika Takso** (☎612 0000, 1200; www.tulika.ee; ⊙base fare €3.85, per km €0.79-0.89)

# AROUND TALLINN

## Keila-Joa

Flat Estonia isn't known for its waterfalls, and at 6m, **Schloss Fall** (www.schlossfall.com; Meremõisa; castle adult/child €8/5; ⊙castle 10am-6pm; P) in Meremõisa isn't all that high. It's particularly picturesque, however, partly due to its juxtaposition with the little neo-Gothic Keila-Joa Castle, built in 1833 for Count Alexander von Benckendorf. A central, crenellated tower provides a castle-like aspect, but any pretensions to military purpose are purely romantic. Two suspension bridges lead through lush countryside to the top of the horseshoe waterfall where rainbows dance in the spray.

## Padise

The great hulking shell of the burnt-out, 14th-century **Padise Monastery** (Padise klooster) FREE practically insists on exploration.

WORTH A TRIP

### TO THE MANOR REBORN

The Estonian countryside is littered with the once-grand manors of the long-vanished Baltic German and Swedish elite. While most lie in ruin due to either war damage or neglect, an ever-increasing number are finding new lives as boutique hotels and restaurants. Two of the more interesting ones:

**Kolga** (Kolga Mõis; ☎501 0966; www.facebook.com/KolgaSA; Kolga; manor & museum adult/child €4/3; ⊙10am-6pm Tue-Sun Jun-Aug, 9am-4pm Mon-Fri Sep-May; P) In Lahemaa National Park, this photogenically tumbledown, neoclassical manor house dates from 1642, but was largely rebuilt between 1768 and 1820 by the wealthy Stenbock family. Serving as a German military hospital in WWII, and as collective-farm administration and housing during the Soviet period, it's been thoroughly looted and neglected, yet remains stately and impressive. Housed in an outbuilding, the attached museum has collections of Soviet ephemera, artefacts of local rural life and a display on Bronze Age burials at Lake Kahala.

**Põhjaka** (☎526 7795; www.pohjaka.ee; Mäeküla, Paide Parish; mains €15-17; ⊙noon-3pm & 4-8pm Wed-Sun; P Wi-Fi) The refurbished ambience of Põhjaka Manor (founded in 1820) serves as a blank canvas for a wonderful restaurant showcasing fresh Estonian farm produce, where traditional stomach-fillers such as fried Baltic herring with potato salad are taken to the next level of culinary excellence. It's well signposted from the Tallinn–Tartu highway, 90km from central Tallinn (95km from Tartu).

Stairs lead up into the ruins, where you can wander around the masonry and climb to the top of the tower for views stretching for miles over the flat countryside. The former church still has its roof and Gothic windows, and even in its derelict state it's easy to imagine how grand it must once have been.

Nearby, the late-18th-century **Padise Manor** (Padise Mõis; ☎608 7877; www.padisemois.ee; Padise village; s/d from €99/109; P 📶) has an exceptionally beautiful setting, flanked by lawns, tall trees, a stream and a lake. The 20 guest rooms are well appointed, with an antique feel, making this a great choice for a quiet countryside escape. You'll also enjoy the pleasant, formal Restaurant Ramm on-site (mains €19 to €22).

## Kaberneeme

Perched at the tip of a narrow peninsula 40km east of central Tallinn, this sleepy little village would be unremarkable if it wasn't for two things: a long, unpeopled stretch of pine-lined sandy beach, and the pristine waters and islands of the Gulf of Kaberneeme (to the west) and the Gulf of Kolga (east). Although there's a beach right by the marina, you're best to drive southeast along the coast for about 1.5km and look for the designated parking areas within the pine forest.

**Kaberneeme Beach** BEACH
(Kaberneeme Rand) Kaberneeme's peaceful, pine-lined beach runs down the western side of the peninsula. There's decent swimming among the glacial erratics in the shallows, when the weather's warm and calm.

**Aktiivne Puhkus** WATER SPORTS
(☎504 6019; www.aktiivnepuhkus.ee; Kaberneeme marina; ⏱10am-9pm mid-Jun–Aug) Operating out of a shed on the sand near Kaberneeme marina, 'Active Holiday' runs trips to Koipsi, Pedassaar and Rammu – three pretty, forested islands in Kolga Bay. Half-day kayak trips range from €35 to €50, one-hour jet-ski 'safaris' are €190 per person, and skippered boats are €150 per hour.

**OKO** EUROPEAN €€
(☎5300 4440; www.okoresto.ee; Kesk tee 27; mains €14-18; ⏱noon-10pm; 📶) A little sister to Estonia's top-rated restaurant NOA (p79), OKO sits pretty on Haabneeme's popular foreshore, sustaining holidaying families resting between dips and games of beach volleyball with wood-fired pizzas, inventive salads and cocktails. The outdoor seating is glorious on long summer evenings.

### ℹ Getting There & Away

There's no public transport to Kaberneeme. To get here from Tallinn, turn off the main Tallinn–Narva highway (Hwy 1) at Koogi and follow the signs. If you're coming from the east, turn off at Kiiu.

# NORTHERN ESTONIA

Stretching from the capital to the Russian border at Narva, northern Estonia is a place of marked contrasts. Heading east from Tallinn, the natural beauty of Lahemaa, the crowning glory of Estonia's national parks, gives way to an ethnic-Russian enclave that feels distinctly different from anywhere else in the country.

Lahemaa, with its pristine coastline littered with glacial erratics, lush forests harbouring bear and elk, mysterious bogs, decaying manor houses and wood-built villages scattered along clear-running lakes, rivers and inlets, exerts a powerful attraction. But those willing to explore further will find plenty of rewarding sights, including the historic city of Rakvere, the picturesque limestone cliffs around Ontika and the curious spectacle of the seaside city of Sillamäe, a living monument to Stalinist-era architecture. The most striking city of this region is Narva, its doughty 13th-century castle facing off against its historic counterpart, just across the border in Russia.

## Lahemaa National Park

Estonia's largest *rahvuspark* (national park), the 'Land of Bays' is 725 sq km of rural landscape and the perfect retreat from the nearby capital. A microcosm of Estonia's natural charms, the park takes in a stretch of deeply indented coast with several peninsulas and bays, plus 475 sq km of pine-fresh hinterland encompassing forest, lakes, rivers and peat bogs, and areas of historical and cultural interest.

There is an extensive network of forest trails for walkers, cyclists and even neo-knights on horseback. In winter, the park is transformed into a magical wonderland of snowy shores, frozen seas and sparkling black trees.

## Northern Estonia

Loksa, the main town within the park, has a popular sandy beach but is otherwise rather down-at-heel. Võsu, the next largest settlement, is much nicer, with its long sandy beach and summertime bars. It fills up with young revellers in peak season, despite being just a somewhat overgrown village.

### Northern Estonia

**Sights**

1 Oru Park ........ D1
2 Pühtitsa Convent ........ C2
3 Sillamäe Museum ........ D1
4 The Soviet-Era Sillamäe ........ D1
5 Valaste juga ........ C1

**Sleeping**

6 Meresuu Spa & Hotel ........ D1
7 Noorus Spa Hotel ........ D1
8 Saka Manor ........ C1
9 Toila Spa Hotell & Camping Männisalu ........ C1
Valaste Village ........ (see 5)

## Sights

Start your exploration at the national park visitor centre at Palmse Manor.

**Palmse Manor** HISTORIC BUILDING

(Palmse Mõis; ☎5559 9977; www.palmse.ee; Palmse; adult/child €9/7; ⏲10am-6pm Apr-Dec, to 4pm Jan-Mar; P) Fully restored Palmse Manor is the showpiece historic building of Lahemaa National Park, housing the visitor centre in its former stables. The pretty manor house (1720, rebuilt in the 1780s) is now a museum containing period furniture and clothing. Other estate buildings have also been restored and put to new use: the distillery is a hotel, the steward's residence is a guesthouse, the lakeside bathhouse is a summertime restaurant and the farm labourers' quarters became a tavern.

**Sagadi Manor & Forest Museum** HISTORIC BUILDING

(Sagadi Mõis & Metsamuuseum; ☎676 7888; www.sagadi.ee; Sagadi Village; adult/child €4/2; ⏲10am-6pm May-Sep, to 4pm Oct-Apr; P) Completed in 1753, this pretty pink-and-white baroque mansion is surrounded by glorious gardens (which are free to visit), encompassing a lake, numerous modern sculptures, an arboretum and an endless view down a grand avenue of trees. The house ticket includes admission to the neighbouring Forest Museum, whose permanent exhibition, 'The Forest Feeds', tells the story of Estonia's forests and their psychological and physical importance to the country.

**Altja** VILLAGE

First mentioned in 1465, this fishing village has many restored or reconstructed traditional buildings, including fishing sheds on the rocky point and an ancient-looking tavern (actually built in 1976). Altja's Swing Hill (Kiitemägi), complete with a traditional Estonian wooden swing, has long been the focus of Midsummer's Eve festivities, while the 3km circular **Altja Nature & Culture Trail** starts at Swing Hill and takes in net sheds, fishing cottages and the stone field known as the 'open-air museum of stones'.

There are some good beaches between Altja and Mustoja, to the east. A scenic hiking and biking route runs east along the old road from Altja to Vainupea.

# Lahemaa National Park

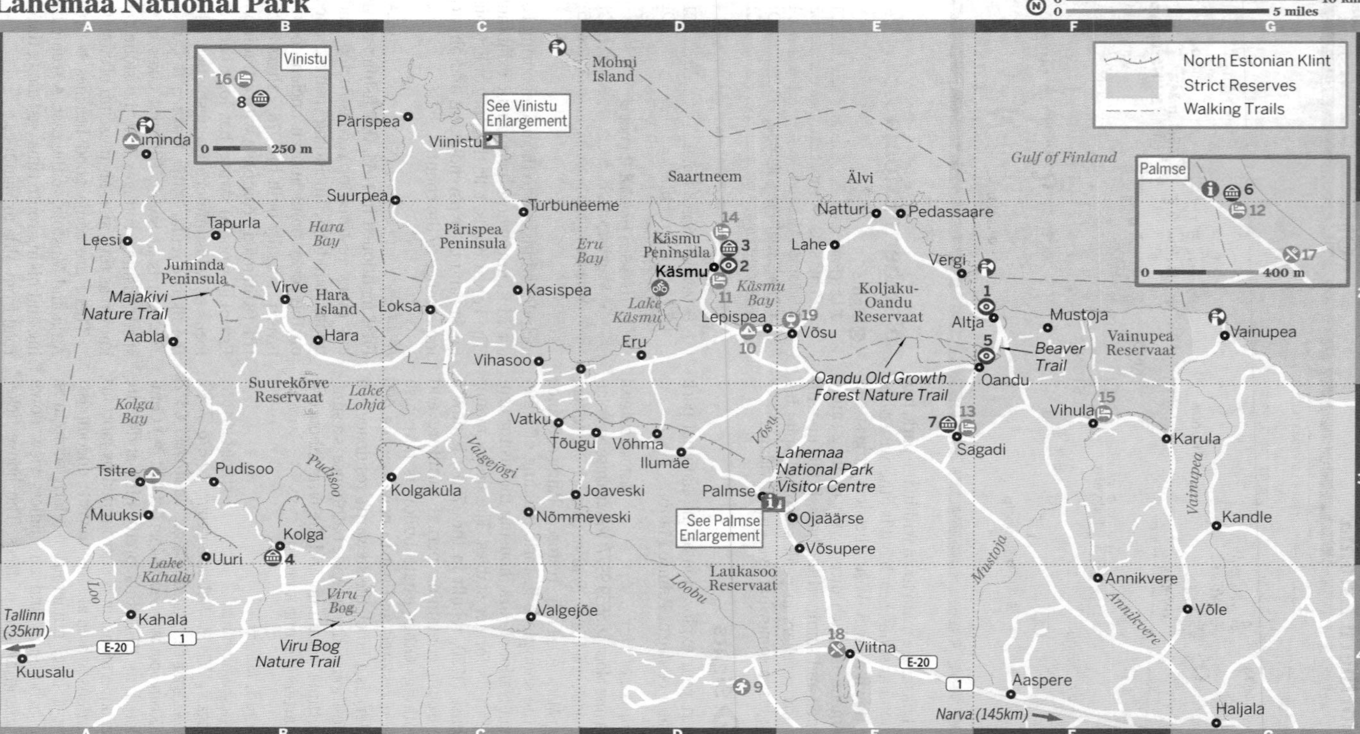

## Lahemaa National Park

**Sights**
1 Altja ........ F2
2 Käsmu ........ D2
3 Käsmu Sea Museum ........ D2
4 Kolga Manor ........ B3
5 Oandu Nature Centre ........ F2
6 Palmse Manor ........ G1
7 Sagadi Manor & Forest Museum ........ E3
8 Viinistu Art Museum ........ B1

**Activities, Courses & Tours**
9 Kuusekännu Riding Farm ........ D4

**Sleeping**
10 Lepispea Caravan & Camping ........ D2
11 Merekalda ........ D2
12 Palmse Guesthouse ........ G2
13 Sagadi Manor ........ E3
Toomarahva Turismitalu ........ (see 1)
14 Uustula Homestay ........ D2
15 Vihula Manor ........ F3
16 Viinistu Art Hotel ........ B1

**Eating**
Altja Kõrts ........ (see 1)
17 Palmse Kõrts ........ G2
Vihula Manor Restaurant ........ (see 15)
Viinistu Restaurant ........ (see 16)
18 Viitna Kõrts ........ E4

**Drinking & Nightlife**
19 O Kõrts ........ E2

**Käsmu** VILLAGE

Known as the 'Captains' Village', from 1884 to 1931 tiny Käsmu was home to a marine school that churned out ship captains. At one stage it was said that every Käsmu family had at least one captain in their midst, and by the 1920s a third of all boats in Estonia were registered to this village. It lies in a stone field boasting the highest concentration of erratic boulders in Estonia.

**Käsmu Sea Museum** MUSEUM

(Käsmu Meremuuseum; ☎529 7135; www.kasmu.ee; Merekooli 1, Käsmu; €3) The former Soviet border-guard barracks at Käsmu now shelters this eclectic museum, displaying artefacts relating to sailing, fishing, smuggling and other marine activities. On the grounds you'll find one of only two wooden lighthouses in the country and a 15m observation tower, manned throughout the Soviet era to prevent defectors from Estonia. The owners of this private museum live on-site, so there are no formal opening hours.

**Viinistu Art Museum** GALLERY

(Kunstimuuseum; ☎5565 1323; www.viinistu.ee; Viinistu harbour; adult/child €4/2; ⏲11am-6pm Wed-Sun; Ⓟ) It's extraordinary that an obscure, remote village near the top of the Pärispea peninsula should be home to one of the country's best galleries, yet Viinistu houses the remarkable private art collection of Jaan Manitski, reputedly one of Estonia's richest men. This ever-expanding assemblage is devoted entirely to Estonian art and pays particularly strong attention to contemporary painting – although you'll also find sculpture, etchings, drawings and some older, more traditional canvases.

## Activities

### Cycling

Lahemaa's shady back roads are perfect for cyclists and many of the park's accommodation providers have bikes to rent (around €10 to €12 per day).

The best off-road route is the 11.6km **Käsmu Cycling Trail**, which is mainly a loop with a couple of lengthy side tracks. Starting at the end of the road in Käsmu, it heads through the forest to the Matsikivi erratic boulder, then continues to the tip of the peninsula, down to Lake Käsmu and pops out back in the village, near the church. You can download a map from the Lahemaa section of www.loodusegakoos.ee.

City Bike (p70) coordinates self-guided tours from Tallinn to the park, continuing to Lake Peipsi and Tartu (from €335 for seven days, including all equipment but not return from Tartu to Tallinn).

### Hiking

Some excellent hikes course through the park's diverse landscapes. Pick up maps and trail information from the Oandu Nature Centre (p96) or visitor centre (p96) at Palmse. The **Oandu Old-Growth Forest Nature Trail** is a 4.7km circular trail, 3km north of Sagadi, that is perhaps the park's most interesting. Note the trees that wild boars and bears have scratched, bark eaten by irascible elk and pines scarred from resin-tapping.

Between Oandu and Altja is the **Beaver Trail** (Koprarada), a beautiful 1km walkway that passes beaver dams on the Altja River, although you're unlikely to see the shy, nocturnal creatures themselves.

## ESTONIAN WILDLIFE

Estonia has 64 recorded species of land mammals; some species that have disappeared elsewhere have survived within the country's extensive forests. The brown bear faced extinction at the turn of the 20th century, but today there are more than 600 in Estonia. The European beaver, which was also hunted to near extinction, was successfully reintroduced in the 1950s and today the population is over 13,000.

While roe deer and wild boar are present in their tens of thousands, numbers are dwindling, which some chalk up to predators – though these animals are hunted and appear on the menu in more expensive restaurants (along with elk and bear). Estonia still has grey wolves (thought to number around 200) and lynx (perhaps 900). Lynx, bears, wolves and beavers are just some of the animals that are hunted each year, although a system of quotas aims to keep numbers stable.

Estonia also has abundant birdlife, with 363 recorded species. Owing to the harsh winters, most birds here are migratory. Although it's found throughout much of the world, the barn swallow has an almost regal status in Estonia and is the 'national bird'; it reappears from its winter retreat in April or May. Another bird with pride of place in Estonia is the stork. While their numbers are declining elsewhere in Europe, white storks are on the increase – you'll often see them perched on the top of lamp posts in large round nests. Black storks, on the other hand, are in decline.

The **Viru Bog Nature Trail** is a 3.5km trail across the Viru Bog, starting at the first kilometre off the road to Loksa (near Kolga), off the Tallinn–Narva highway; look for the insectivorous sundew (Venus flytrap, Charles Darwin's favourite plant).

The 7km **Majakivi Nature Trail** starts on the Loksa–Leesi road, near the charmingly old-fashioned coastal village of Virve, and takes in 7m-high Majakivi (House Boulder); at 584 cu metres, it's Lahemaa's largest erratic boulder.

### Horse Riding

**Kuusekännu Riding Farm** HORSE RIDING
(Kuusekännu Ratsatalu; ☎509 4460; Loobu; riding per hour €25) Just outside the national park, near Viitna, this riding farm arranges riding lessons and trail rides through Lahemaa. Call ahead for bookings.

## Tours

Tallinn Traveller Tours (p70) offers excursions to Lahemaa from Tallinn, at €59 per person. A private tour with the likes of **Estonian Experience** (☎8am-8pm daily 5346 4060; www.nordicexperience.com; 8-person tours per person from €15) ranges from €450 for two people to €620 for four.

## Sleeping

Käsmu, set on a rocky shoreline, has plenty of low-key guesthouses. For rowdier beach action, head to Võsu, a popular summertime hang-out for Estonian students. Guesthouses are scattered throughout the region; the visitor centre in Palmse keeps lists of options. Camping is fantastic in Lahemaa, with lots of free, basic campgrounds administered by RMK (www.loodusegakoos.ee).

**Lepispea Caravan & Camping** CAMPGROUND €
(☎5450 1522; www.lepispea.eu; Lepispea 3, Võsu; sites per person €6, caravan €17, plus per person €2; ⊙May-Sep; P 📶 🐾) In Lepispea, 1km west of Võsu, this campground is spread over a large field fringed by trees and terminating in a little reed-lined beach. Facilities are good, including a sauna (€20 for one hour), kids' playground and decent bikes for hire (per hour/day €2/10). Campers can access mains power for €3.

**Uustula Homestay** GUESTHOUSE €
(☎523 7848; www.uustalu.planet.ee; Neeme tee 78a, Käsmu; sites per person €5, caravan €15, s/d with breakfast €41/62; ⊙May-Sep; P) At the end of the Käsmu road, this complex has simple, cheerful rooms in a white clapboard house by the sea. Campers are welcome to pitch a tent on the shady lawn, although you'll have to pay extra for a shower (€2). Bikes are available to rent at €10 per day, or €3 per hour.

★**Merekalda** APARTMENT €€
(☎323 8451; www.merekalda.ee; Neeme tee 2, Käsmu; d €55, apt from €75; ⊙May-Sep; P 📶) On the southern fringe of Käsmu, this peaceful retreat is set around a lovely large garden right on the bay. Ideally you'll plump for an

apartment with a sea view and terrace, but you'll need to book ahead. Boat and bike hire are available, but breakfast is not.

★**Toomarahva Turismitalu** GUESTHOUSE €€
(☎505 0850; www.toomarahva.ee; Altja Village; sites per person €5, caravan €10, cottage €60, d €90, apt from €120; 📶) This atmospheric farmstead comprises thatch-roofed wooden buildings and a garden full of flowers and sculptures. Sleeping options include two cute rooms with shared bathroom and an apartment that can be rented with either one or two bedrooms. All can be rented for less without breakfast, plus there's a traditional sauna (€30) and bikes (€10 per day) for hire.

**Sagadi Manor** HOTEL €€
(☎676 7888; www.sagadi.ee; Sagadi Village; dm €16, s/d from €60/80; P📶) Waking up within the rarefied confines of Sagadi Manor, with its gracious gardens at your disposal, is a downright lovely experience. There's a tidy 31-bed hostel in the former estate manager's house, while the hotel has fresh and comfortable rooms in the whitewashed former stables, across the lawn. The sauna can be fired up for €20 per hour.

**Viinistu Art Hotel** HOTEL €€
(☎5665 8633; www.viinistu.ee; Viinistu Village; s/d/f with sea view €45/55/80; P📶) Built in an old fish-processing plant, this bright waterfront hotel boasts fresh nautical decor enlivened by hundreds of Estonian artworks. Family rooms are considerably bigger and contain kitchenettes, and the sea-facing rooms with balconies are only slightly more expensive. Just opposite is the associated Viinistu Art Museum.

**Vihula Manor** HOTEL €€
(☎326 4100; www.vihulamanor.com; Vihula; r/ste from €99/179; P📶🏊) As part of its transformation into a spiffy country club and spa, this 50-hectare, 16th-century estate has converted its manor house and several historic outbuildings into guest rooms, eateries and a day spa (treatments from €35). The rooms in the main house, particularly, are slick, elegant places to linger, with tempting bathtubs and quality bedding.

**Palmse Guesthouse** GUESTHOUSE €€
(☎5386 6266; www.palmse.ee; Palmse Manor; s/d/ste €60/90/118; P📶) Housed in Palmse estate's former steward's house (1820), this 16-room guesthouse is a more atmospheric option than Palmse's main hotel. Only the suites have their own bathrooms, though.

## Eating & Drinking

During the summer, you'll find a few traditional places open and catering to tourists, but it's slim pickings in winter. You can load up on provisions in Võsu or Loksa.

**Altja Kõrts** ESTONIAN €€
(☎5341 8513; www.palmse.ee; Altja Village; mains €9-12; ⏰noon-8pm Apr-Sep; P) Set in a thatched, wooden building with a large terrace, this uber-rustic place is run by the same folks behind Palmse Manor. Operating in spring and summer, it serves delicious plates of traditional fare (baked pork with sauerkraut, for instance) at candlelit wooden tables. It's extremely atmospheric and a lot of fun.

**Viinistu Restaurant** EUROPEAN €€
(☎5558 6984; www.viinistu.ee; Viinistu Village; mains €10-13; ⏰noon-7pm; P📶) Part of the complex containing Viinistu Art Hotel and Museum, this smart restaurant-bar specialises in fish from local waters, some of it smoked in-house. Gold sea bream is served with tomato consommé and grilled vegetables, and herring with egg, potato and sour cream. There's an inviting deck, but the sea views are just as good through big picture windows.

**Viitna Kõrts** ESTONIAN €€
(☎520 9156; www.viitna.eu; Viitna; mains €11-13; ⏰11am-11pm Sun-Thu, to midnight Fri & Sat May-Aug, shorter hours rest of year; P📶) A popular pit stop for families travelling between Tallinn and Narva, this reconstruction of a fire-damaged tavern from the early 19th century serves traditional offerings such as honey-roasted pork and herring with potato porridge and cottage cheese. There's also a basic cafe, serving from 7am to 9pm in summer, an outdoor kebab counter, and Estonian handicrafts on sale.

**Palmse Kõrts** ESTONIAN €€
(www.palmse.ee; Palmse Manor; mains €12-14; ⏰11am-10pm Jun-Aug, to 8pm Apr, May, Sep & Oct, 11am-7pm Wed-Sun Nov-Mar; P) Just a short walk south of Palmse Manor, housed in the 1831 farm labourers' quarters, this rustic tavern evokes yesteryear under heavy timber beams with a short, simple menu of traditional Estonian fare. Try the *mulgipuder* (mashed potatoes with barley, bacon and onion) or the crispy carrot cutlets.

1

OLGA_IONINA/SHUTTERSTOCK ©

2

4

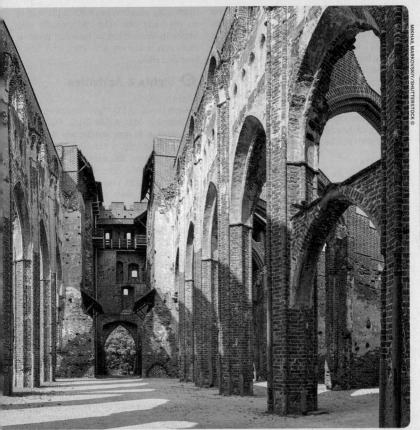

MIKHAIL MARKOVSKIY/SHUTTERSTOCK ©

**. Kuressaare Episcopal Castle (p152), Saaremaa**
Retrace history at Estonia's best-preserved castle.

**. Cathedral ruins (p109), University of Tartu Museum**
Walk among atmospheric ruins dating from the 3th century.

**. House of Peter I (p66), Tallinn**
xplore fascinating artefacts at the former home f Peter the Great and Catherine I.

**. Lahemaa National Park (p88)**
tretch your legs on the peaceful Viru Bog Nature rail (p92) in Estonia's largest national park.

JONATHAN SMITH/LONELY PLANET ©

**Vihula Manor Restaurant** EUROPEAN €€€
(326 4100; www.vihulamanor.com; Vihula Manor; mains €21-24; 6-10pm Sun-Thu, to 11pm Fri & Sat; P) You can dine in the garden or on a balcony, but you'd be missing out on the grand ambience of Vihula Manor's ballroom, with its original parquet floors and art-strewn walls. The food is European-inflected Estonian, including pikeperch with burnt cauliflower and cauliflower cream, elk fillet with celery, garlic and berries, and even *sous vide* bear with mushrooms.

**O Kõrts** PUB
(516 5115; Jõe 3, Võsu; mains €9-10; 11am-11pm Sun-Thu, to 4am Fri & Sat; ) This tavern has a scuffed wooden interior and a broad outdoor terrace, perfect for catching the late-afternoon sun. The menu offers predictable pub fare such as wings, pork, steak and salmon. On Fridays and Saturdays in summer DJs and live musicians keep things going until nearly dawn.

## Information

**Lahemaa National Park Visitor Centre**
(329 5555; www.loodusegakoos.ee; Palmse; 9am-5pm daily mid-May–mid-Sep, Mon-Fri mid-Sep–mid-May) This excellent centre stocks the essential map of Lahemaa (€1.90), as well as information on hiking trails, accommodation and guiding services. It's worth starting your park visit with the free 17-minute film titled *Lahemaa – Nature and Man*.

The **Oandu Nature Centre** (Oandu Looduskeskus; 676 7010; www.loodusegakoos.ee; Oandu; 9am-5pm Mon-Fri, 10am-6pm Sat & Sun mid-May–Aug, shorter hours rest of year; P) is your other port of call.

## Getting There & Around

Lahemaa is best explored by car or bicycle, as there are only limited bus connections within the park. The main bus routes through the park include Rakvere to Sagadi (€2.50, 45 minutes, up to three daily); Palmse (€2.50, 50 minutes, up to five daily); Altja (€2.25, one hour, most days); Võsu (€2.30, one hour, up to five daily); and Käsmu (€2.55, one hour, up to six daily).

# Rakvere

POP 15,264

Roughly halfway between Tallinn and Narva, Rakvere offers a scenically crumbly castle and long old-town streets lined with old timber dwellings. With a giant water park, good hotels and a youthful ambience, it's a thoroughly pleasant place for a pit stop or an overnight stay. The city proudly celebrates its connection to Estonia's most famous son, composer Arvo Pärt, who moved here as a child.

## Sights & Activities

**Rakvere Castle** CASTLE
(Rakvere Linnus; 5333 8160; www.rakverelinnus.ee; Vallikraavi; adult/student €11/9; 10am-6pm daily May-Aug, to 4pm Wed-Sun Mar, Apr, Sep & Oct; ) Originally a Danish stronghold of the 13th century, Rakvere's star attraction is a hulking, atmospheric semi-ruin that now aims to transport visitors back to the days of yore. While much seems aimed towards children (dress-ups and the like), adults may get a kick out of handling the reproduction swords, visiting the 'brothel', trying their hand at archery, perusing artefacts in the 'history room' and trying medieval repasts at the Schenkenberg Tavern (mains €7 to €8).

**Tarvas Statue** MONUMENT
(Kreutzwaldi 1) This massive 7-tonne, 3.5m-high, 7.1m-long statue was completed by local artist Tauno Kangro to commemorate the town's 700th anniversary in 2002. You might be forgiven for thinking that's a lot of bull, but actually it's an aurochs – a large, long-horned wild ox that became extinct in the 17th century. The 1226 Chronicle of Livonia included a description of an ancient wooden castle on Rakvere hill, called Tarvanpea. In Estonian, Tarvanpea means 'the head of an aurochs' – hence the statue.

**Rakvere Oak Grove** FOREST
(Rakvere tammik; Tammetõru tänav) Thought to have been a sacred site to pre-Christian Estonians, this 23-hectare expanse of mature oak and lime forest is a wonderful place for a leafy stroll. On an expanse of lawn near the southern end is **Okaskroon** (Crown of Thorns), a memorial to locals deported to Siberia during the Soviet era. Deeper within the forest there's a small German **military cemetery** marked by triple sets of crosses set between the trees.

**Citizen's House Museum** MUSEUM
(Linnakodaniku majamuuseum; www.svm.ee; Pikk 50; adult/child €2/1.50; 11am-5pm Tue-Sat May-Sep, 10am-4pm Tue-Fri, 11am-3pm Sat Oct-Apr) There are many historic wooden and stone buildings on Pikk street, including this 18th-century home, restored and furnished to reflect Rakvere town life in the early

20th century. Displays include a bourgeois parlour, a cobbler's workshop, a collection of children's toys and a piano that once belonged to Estonian composer Arvo Pärt (who hails from these parts).

**Holy Trinity Church** CHURCH
(Kolmainu kirik; ☎324 3928; www.kolmainu.ee; Pikk 19; ⊙10am-6pm Mon-Sat, to 12.30pm Sun mid-May–Sep) Dating from around 1430, although it's been damaged and repaired several times since, this lovely, whitewashed Lutheran church has a 62m steeple (a 19th-century replacement of an 18th-century original), a carved pulpit with painted panels (1690) and some impressive large canvases. Every year on 16 September it hosts a concert celebrating composer Arvo Pärt's birthday. Between October and mid-May it opens by prior arrangement.

**Church of the Nativity of the Mother of God** CHURCH
(Jumalaema Sündimise kirik; Tallinna 17; ⊙10am-4pm) This cute 19th-century church was originally a two-storey house, bought by Tsar Nicholas I in 1839 to provide a house of worship for Rakvere's Orthodox community. Its gilded onion domes are a landmark for pilgrims come to view the relics of St Sergius, a local priest shot by communists in 1918, and now a martyr of the Russian Orthodox Church.

**Aqva Waterpark & Sauna Centre** SWIMMING
(☎326 0010; www.aqvahotels.ee; Parkali 4; 2½hr pass adult/child from €11/8, incl saunas from €14/10; ⊙9am-10pm Mon-Fri, from 8am Sat & Sun; 👪) Aqva Hotel's pool and sauna complex is one of the best of its kind in the country. Serious swimmers can rack up laps in a 25m covered pool while the kids splash around the wave pool or shoot down the slide. The paddling pool is popular with the under-fives and there's a small outdoor pool and sun terrace.

## Sleeping

★**Villa Theresa** HOTEL €€
(☎322 3699; www.villatheresa.ee; Tammiku 9; s/d €55/65; P❄📶) In a wooded nook on the outskirts of town, this boutique hotel and restaurant offers a winning combination of peace and quiet, comfort, great food and reasonable prices. An antique ambience carries through seamlessly from the old wooden house at the front to the rooms in the modern extension. The restaurant is worth staying in for.

**Art Hotell** HOTEL €€
(☎323 2060; www.arthotell.ee; Lai 18; s/d €42/60; P📶) This idiosyncratic little indie hotel is welcoming and art-strewn – you'd never suspect that at the beginning of the 19th century it was a brothel. Rooms have sloping attic ceilings, frosted-glass bathroom partitions and flat-screen TVs.

**Aqva Hotel & Spa** SPA HOTEL €€€
(☎326 0000; www.aqvahotels.ee; Parkali 4; s/d/ste from €104/124/250; P❄📶🏊) This large, architecturally interesting complex includes a day spa and fabulous indoor water park, making it a predictable hit with families. The water theme is taken to the max here, from the fabulous swirly purple carpet to the aquarium and water wall in the lobby. Standard rooms are on the small size, but they're modern and stylish.

## Eating

**Art Café** CAFE €€
(☎325 1710; www.artcafe.ee; Lai 13; mains €9-11; ⊙11am-10pm Mon-Thu, to 11pm Fri & Sat, to 9pm Sun; 📶) With an inviting rear garden, including a small kids' play area and tables shaded by a broad oak, this cafe serves equally well for lunch, afternoon coffee or evening drinks. Friendly staff ferry out salmon with pesto and fennel, wild-mushroom and rocket risotto, cakes and other treats.

**Berlin Tavern** PUB FOOD €€
(Berliini Trahter; ☎5696 6999; www.berliinitrahter.ee; Lai 15; mains €11-16; ⊙11am-midnight Mon-Thu, to 1am Fri & Sat, to 11pm Sun; 📶) With a flower-trimmed, timber-decked summer terrace that makes ideal use of a plumb spot by Rakvere's Market Sq, this red-brick tavern offers a wide range of drinking snacks alongside salads, soups, dumplings, burgers and honest mains such as pork schnitzel with potatoes and mushroom sauce.

**Villa Theresa** EUROPEAN €€
(☎322 3699; www.villatheresa.ee; Tammiku 9; mains €15-17; ⊙noon-10pm; P📶) If it's a more upmarket, formal ambience you're after, the restaurant at the Villa Theresa hotel is well worth seeking out. The menu offers retro, Frenchified, mainly meaty treats such as duck breast with duchess potatoes and passion-fruit sauce and entrecôte with sweet-potato fries, asparagus and chimichurri.

WORTH A TRIP

## SILLAMÄE

On the highway from Tallinn to Narva (and 27km west of the latter) is Sillamäe, a fascinating relic of Soviet Estonia, and a must for fans of Stalinist neoclassical architecture.

Sillamäe owes its existence to the discovery that oil shale contains small amounts of extractable uranium. Its infamous uranium-processing and nuclear-chemicals factory was quickly built by 5000 Russian political prisoners, while the town itself was built by 3800 Baltic prisoners of war who had previously served in the German army.

An important cog in the USSR's nuclear program, Sillamäe was planned by Leningrad architects and built from scratch in the immediate post-WWII years. Its broad avenues include grand buildings such as a town hall designed to resemble a Lutheran church. In the park opposite there's a wonderful period-piece sculpture of a muscle-bound worker holding aloft an atom.

In the depths of the Cold War, Sillamäe was strictly off limits to visitors, was known by various sinister-sounding code names (Leningrad 1; Moscow 400) and was often omitted from official maps. Yet its importance in the Cold War context meant life for the workers who lived here was generally better than in other parts of the Estonian Soviet Socialist Republic.

Only unfinished uranium was processed at the plant, though the eerily abandoned buildings on the city's western border are testament to Soviet plans to process pure, nuclear reactor–ready uranium. Only the disbanding of the USSR saved Estonia's ecology from this fate. Uranium processing ceased in 1989 and today the radioactive waste is buried under concrete by the sea. Fears of leakage into the Baltic have alarmed environmentalists; EU funding has been channelled towards ensuring the waste is stable and safe, at enormous cost.

These days the privatised Sillamäe plant is the world's main producer of the rare metals niobium and tantalum, which are used in the manufacture of medical and electronic equipment, among other things.

The town itself is the attraction, but while there you can drop by the **Sillamäe Museum** (☎397 2425; www.sillamae-muuseum.ee; Kajaka 17a; adult/student €3/2; ⊙10am-6pm Tue-Fri, to 4pm Sat). Six rooms of exhibitions on Sillamäe, its shale-chemical factory and rural life in Vaivara parish await within this building, erected in the late 1950s in 'retrospective Stalinist' style. There's also an excellent mineral display, and an interesting room set up like a typical1950s Sillamäe flat.

Also worth a visit is the exhibition **The Soviet-Era Sillamäe** (☎397 2425; www.sillamae-muuseum.ee; Kesk tänav 24; €1; ⊙8am-4pm Mon-Fri Jun-Aug, to 5pm Mon-Fri Sep-May). This branch of the city's museum, housed in the Sillamäe Cultural Centre (a former bomb shelter), displays the museum's collection of artefacts from the town's Soviet past: busts, uniforms, flags and large portraits of Lenin and Stalin.

Major domestic destinations served by direct buses to Sillamäe include Tallinn (€8 to €14, 2¾ hours, at least hourly); Rakvere (€5 to €7, two hours, up to nine daily); Narva (€5, 45 minutes, at least hourly); and Tartu (€7 to €12, 2½ hours, up to 10 daily).

## ℹ Information

**Tourist Office** (☎324 2734; www.rakvere.ee; Lai 20; ⊙8am-5pm Mon-Thu, to 4pm Fri year-round, plus 9am-2pm Sat & Sun mid-May–mid-Sep; 📶) Located in the town hall, this friendly centre makes up for limited English with plenty of literature.

## ℹ Getting There & Away

### BUS

The bus station is on the corner of Laada and Vilde, 350m southeast of the tourist office. Major routes, served by multiple operators, include the following:

**Narva** €6 to €10, 2¼ hours, up to 9 daily

**Pärnu** €9 to €11, 3½ hours, three daily

**Tallinn** €4 to €11, 1½ hours, at least hourly

**Tartu** €5 to €13, 2¼ hours, up to eight daily

### TRAIN

Elron has five trains daily to Tallinn (€5.10, 1½ hours) and four to Narva (€5.80, 1½ hours). The train station is on Jaama pst, 1.5km northeast of the tourist office.

## Ontika Nature Reserve

Squeezed between a narrow coastal road and the sea, roughly halfway between Rakvere and Narva, Ontika Nature Reserve protects a section of the limestone escarpment known as the Baltic Klint, where the land falls suddenly into the sea, forming cliffs up to 54m high. The klint extends 1200km, from Sweden to Lake Ladoga in Russia, although 500km of this lies underwater.

The only 'major' settlement on this quiet stretch of coast is Toila, a small spa and beach town to the east of the reserve, where you'll find the delightful Oru Park.

### Sights

**Valaste juga** WATERFALL

At Valaste a viewing platform and metal stair faces Estonia's highest waterfall (varying from 26m to 30m), which, depending on the month, may be a torrent, a mere trickle or photogenically frozen. If you need to stretch your legs, there's a pleasant 1.5km trail through klint forest and along the beach, with boardwalks and information on the geology and biology of the Ontika Landscape Reserve.

**Oru Park** PARK

(Oru Pargi Maastikukaitseala; Toila; 24hr) Oru Park was built around a grand palace in 1899 by Grigory Yeliseyev, at the time one of Russia's richest merchants. In 1935 it became the summer palace of the Estonian president but, sadly, was completely destroyed during the war. Although the building is gone, the surrounding park has been maintained, and is one of Estonia's loveliest places for a summer stroll.

### Sleeping

**Saka Manor** HOTEL €€

(Saka Mõis; 336 4900; www.saka.ee; Saka; sites per person €5, hotel s/d from €66/88, mansion d/ste from €209/253; P) In a peaceful clifftop setting, signposted off the Tallinn–Narva highway just east of Varja, this seaside retreat encompasses a campground, a low-key spa hotel and a restored neo-Renaissance manor house (1864) furnished with English antiques and offering guest rooms and a restaurant (mains €12 to €14). Diversions include tennis, archery, paths through the klint forest to the beach and occasional events.

**Valaste Village** GUESTHOUSE €€

(Valaste Puhkeküla; 332 8200; www.valaste.eu; Kotka; sites per person €5, s/d €30/40, bungalows €75; P) The small, brightly painted guesthouse by Valaste waterfall has a large communal kitchen, well-kept shared bathrooms and a large field for campers. Reception is handled by the cafe, where you can score artery-clogging snacks any time of the day or night.

**Toila Spa Hotell & Camping Männisalu** SPA HOTEL €€

(334 2900; www.toilaspa.ee; Ranna 12, Toila; sites per person €5, cabins from €50, s/d from €60/90; P) Serving both young families and mature holidaymakers, this midrange hotel has a large water park, a spa centre, a children's play area, a gym and two restaurants. Rooms are modest but comfortable, and the camping area among the pines (open May to September) is also a good option, with tent and caravan sites and simple wooden cabins.

### Getting There & Away

There are no direct buses from Tallinn or Narva. If you can get to Jõhvi, bus 105 runs in a circuit from here through Ontika, Kohtla-Järve and Toila several times a day.

## Narva

POP 58,663

Estonia's easternmost city is separated from Ivangorod in Russia by the Narva River and is almost entirely populated by Russian-speakers. It's quite literally a border town: the bridge at the end of the main street is the country's principal link with Russia and no-man's-land protrudes right up to the edge of the town square. Aside from its magnificent castle and baroque Old Town Hall, most of Narva's notable architecture was flattened in WWII. The reconstructed city has a melancholy, downtrodden air, the prosperity evident in other parts of the country visibly lacking. Yet Estonia's third-largest city is an intriguing place for a (brief) visit – you'll find no other place in Estonia quite like it.

### Sights

The little that remains of Narva's war-pummelled Old Town is in the blocks north of the castle. Most impressive is the baroque **Old Town Hall** on Raekoja plats,

WORTH A TRIP

## PÜHTITSA CONVENT

Originally a site of ancient pagan worship, the peaceful hilltop village of Kuremäe, 20km southeast of Jõhvi, is now home to this magnificent Russian Orthodox **convent** (☎337 0715; www.puhtitsa.ee; ⏲7am-7pm; P). Built between 1885 and 1895, its five green onion-domed towers are visible for miles. Murals by the convent gate depict Mary, the Mother of Jesus, to whom the complex is dedicated. The community of nuns works the surrounding land and are self-sufficient; they will give tours to visitors for a small fee. Otherwise you're welcome to enter the gate and visit the church as long as you're dressed modestly.

Local lore has it that in the 16th century, appeared to a shepherd in an oak grove in these parts (conveniently echoing pre-Christian Estonian beliefs in divine beings living in holy groves). An icon of the Dormition of the Mother of God was subsequently found under one of the oaks; it now belongs to the convent, which has become a place of pilgrimage for believers. There is also a revered 'holy spring' here that is said to never freeze.

built between 1668 and 1671. The striking building next to it is the **Narva College of the University of Tartu**. A large modern extension angles out and over the lower part of the building, which is a re-creation of the former baroque stock exchange building that once stood here.

As in Tallinn and Tartu, the Swedes surrounded Old Town with a star-shaped set of bastions and most of the earthen ramparts and some stone retaining walls are still visible. The **Dark Park** *(Pimeaed)* on the Victoria Bastion is a shady spot offering river views, while scattered plaques display a map of the original fortifications, plus a few words on their origin.

**★Narva Castle** CASTLE

(Narva Hermanni Linnus; www.narvamuuseum.ee; Narva Linn; adult/student €8/4; ⏲10am-6pm) Begun by the Danes at the end of the 13th century and strengthened by successive owners including Germans, Swedes and Russians, this castle, along with Russia's matching Ivangorod Fortress across the river, creates an architectural ensemble unique in Europe. The outer walls enclose the large Northern Yard, freely open to the public and containing what must be one of Estonia's last remaining public statues of Lenin. Restored after damage during WWII, bulky Hermann Tower houses the Narva Museum.

**Narva Museum** MUSEUM

(www.narvamuuseum.ee; Narva Linn; adult/child €8/4; ⏲10am-6pm) Narva Museum occupies the Hermann Tower and east wing of the castle. Climb the tower's 51m to a wooden viewing gallery, checking out the exhibits on each level. Most interesting are the before and after pictures of the city's wartime destruction. From mid-May to August the **Northern Yard** is set up like a 17th-century town, complete with an apothecary, blacksmith, potter and lace workshops. Admission is included in the museum ticket.

**Narva Art Gallery** GALLERY

(Narva Kunstigalerii; ☎359 2151; www.narvamuuseum.ee; Vestervalli 21; adult/student €3/1.50; ⏲10am-6pm; P) Spread over three floors of a 19th-century gunpowder storeroom on the Gloria bastion, Narva's art gallery has an interesting collection, including paintings amassed by 19th-century collectors Sergei and Glafira Lavretsov.

**Alexander Church** CHURCH

(Aleksandri kirik; www.eelk.ee/narva; Kiriku 9; ⏲10am-3pm Jun-Aug) Named after the Russian tsar assassinated while it was being built (1881–84), this Lutheran church is the largest religious building in Estonia. It was badly damaged in both of the world wars and the hefty octagonal bell tower was only rebuilt post independence from the USSR. It now serves as Narva's Lutheran cathedral.

**Orthodox Cathedral of the Resurrection** CATHEDRAL

(Voskresensky sobor; Bastrakovi 4) Hidden among dingy apartment blocks northwest of the train station, this 1896 cathedral, built for the workers of the Kreenholm textile factory, has an attractive red-brick exterior and a glittering core. Check out the frescoes inside the dome and the wonderful carved iconostasis.

## Sleeping & Eating

**King Hotel** HOTEL €€
(☎357 2404; www.hotelking.ee; Lavretsovi 9; s/d from €30/40, mains €11-14; P 📶) Within Old Town, not far from the castle, the King offers snug modern rooms in a 17th-century building and a gloomily atmospheric restaurant with a shady terrace. Try the fish *pelmeņi* (dumplings) or lamb stew with aubergine and tomato.

**Antalya Kebab House** TURKISH €
(Puškini 15; mains €5-7; ⏲11.30am-11pm Sun-Thu, to midnight Fri & Sat) Cosy with banquettes and tasselled drapery, the Antalya is the no-frills, satisfying Turkish restaurant every city needs at least one of. Whether it's delicious *lahmacun* (Turkish-style 'pizza'), kebabs *doner* and *shish,* or black-as-death coffee, this humble eatery will sort you out.

**Restoran Rondeel** ESTONIAN €€
(☎359 9250; www.narvamuuseum.ee/est/restoran-rondeel; Peterburi mnt 2; mains €13-14; ⏲11am-8pm) Set inside the Northern Yard of Narva Castle, Rondeel is Narva's best restaurant. Estonian dishes such as local pork, blanketed in mustard sauce, and cold soup with kefir and pickles, are served in a suitably antique – if slightly kitschy – stone-flagged dining room.

## Information

**Tourist Office** (☎359 9137; www.tourism.narva.ee; Peetri plats 3; ⏲10am-5.30pm; 📶) In the centre of town, near the castle.

## Getting There & Away

The train and bus stations are next to each other on Vaksali 2, at the southern end of the main street, Aleksander Puškini.

### BUS

Buses head from here to Rīga and St Petersburg. Domestic routes include the following:

**Narva-Jõesuu** €2, 30 minutes, roughly hourly
**Pärnu** €24, 6½ to 7½ hours via Tallinn, daily
**Sillamäe** €5, 45 minutes, at least hourly
**Tallinn** €13, 3¼ hours, roughly hourly
**Tartu** €7 to €12, 2½ to three hours, nine daily

### TRAIN

Elron runs domestic services to and from Tallinn (€11, 2¾ hours) via Rakvere (€6.80, 1½ hours) four times daily.

# Narva-Jõesuu

POP 2632

About 13km north of Narva, the holiday resort of Narva-Jõesuu (literally 'Narva River mouth') is a pretty but ramshackle town, popular since the 19th century for its long, golden-sand beach backed by pine forests. Impressive early-20th-century wooden houses and villas are scattered around, along with half a dozen hotels and spas – making this a good base for exploring Narva. While it's popular with holidaymakers, especially Russians, the number of once-grand timber villas decaying gently amongst the pines suggests it's yet to regain its full golden-age glory.

**Meresuu Spa & Hotel** SPA HOTEL €€
(☎357 9600; www.meresuu.ee; Aia 48a; s/d/ste from €88/99/176; P 📶 🏊) This shiny 11-storey hotel offers attractive rooms alongside a roll call of extras: sea views, five saunas, indoor and outdoor pools and spas, a gym and wellness centre, a kids' playroom and the requisite restaurant-bar, serving up breakfast buffets and à la carte dining (mains €13 to €15). Spa treatments begin at as little as €9, and packages are available.

**Noorus Spa Hotel** SPA HOTEL €€€
(☎356 7100; www.noorusspahotel.com; L Koidula 19d; s/d/ste from €100/150/225; P @ 📶 🏊) With a name meaning 'youth' it's not clear whether this swanky complex is aiming to attract young people, or those seeking the eternal variety. Rooms are modern and comfortable and the facilities are top-notch, including indoor and outdoor pools, a spa centre with eight different types of sauna, a gym, a restaurant, a bar and even a bowling alley.

## Getting There & Away

Bus 31 runs about hourly to connect Narva with Narva-Jõesuu (€2, 20 minutes). There are also direct services to and from Tallinn (€14, 4¼ hours, three daily), Rakvere (€10, 2¾ hours, two daily) and Sillamäe (€5, one hour, three daily).

# SOUTHERN ESTONIA

One of Estonia's most intriguing regions is also among its least visited. With rolling hills, picturesque lakes and vast woodlands, the south boasts some of Estonia's most attractive countryside. It also contains one of

Estonia's most important cities, the vibrant university centre of Tartu. No matter which direction you head from Tartu, you'll find resplendent natural settings; gateways to outdoor adventure like Otepää and Võru; and quaint towns set on wandering rivers or in picturesque valleys. To the east stretches Lake Peipsi, home to communities of Russian Old Believers, and in the far southeast live the Setos, descendants of Balto-Finnic tribes who settled here in the first millennium.

The southwest is dominated by Pärnu, Estonia's beachside 'summer capital', while lakeside Viljandi has abundant charms, and the bogs of Soomaa are some of the country's most precious enclaves of biodiversity.

# The Southeast

## Lake Peipsi

Straddling the Estonian–Russian border, Lake Peipsi (Chudskoe Ozero in Russian) is the fifth-largest lake in Europe (3555 sq km) – though its maximum depth is only 15m. There are some good, uncrowded beaches to be found on its sandy, 42km-long, northern coast. This area had popular resorts during Soviet times but many of them have been left to crumble and very few new developments have taken their place. Of greater interest are the towns founded by the Old Believers (a schismatic Russian Orthodox sect), the lovely lake shore and bucolic farmland, and a handful of historic sights. Don't forget to pack the mosquito repellent if you're staying by the lake in summer.

Locally caught and smoked fish (trout or salmon) is a speciality of the area – Estonians prize it highly, and some would say it is enough to justify visiting these parts. Look for *suitsukala* (smoked fish) stands scattered all along the main road curving around the lake. For more prosaic needs, there are supermarkets in Mustvee and Kallaste.

### NORTHERN SHORE

On the northeastern corner of the lake, hard up against the Russian border, is **Vasknarva**, an isolated fishing village with fewer than 100 residents and an evocative Orthodox **monastery** that, according to some, once held a KGB radio surveillance centre. The Narva River starts here, draining the lake and forming the border with Russia as it rushes to the Baltic. Also in Vasknarva, the scant ruins of a 1349 Teutonic Order **castle** stand by the shore.

The village of **Alajõe** has the area's main Orthodox church. **Kauksi**, where the main road from the north reaches the lake, has the most beautiful and popular **beach**.

At Kuru, just a couple of kilometres east of Kauksi (off the secondary road from the lake to Iisaku), **Kuru Puhkemajad** (☎529 5088; www.kurupuhkemajad.ee; Ploomi tee 2, Kuru; bungalow/house from €47/127; P) offers rooms in barnlike buildings and wooden cabins – all sharing a communal kitchen and rudimentary bathrooms. The pretty grounds have barbecues and kids' play equipment and you can rent a bike (per hour €2) or motorboat (per hour €100).

### MUSTVEE

With a population of 1358, Mustvee is the largest lakeside town, with a little harbour and a sandy beach. A little further south along the lake a forlorn WWII memorial, **The Grieving Girl** (1973), stands by the shore with her head bowed, 'remembering' the 264 Red Army soldiers buried here in a mass grave. There's also a pretty Old Believers' **church** nearby, dating from 1927.

Operating out of the Kalamestee Maja hotel in Mustvee, **Peipsirent** (☎504 1067; www.peipsirent.eu; Narva 9c, Mustvee) rents out motorboats (10 horsepower per hour/day €30/50, 30 horsepower per hour/day €50/100) and bikes (per day €10). In winter they'll take you out on the lake ice on a snowmobile sledge (per person €10).

### WESTERN SHORE

In the 18th and 19th centuries Russian Old Believers (Starovyery) – a breakaway Orthodox sect who were persecuted for refusing to accept liturgical reforms carried out in 1666 – took refuge on the western shores of the lake. This intriguing community survives in several coastal villages that they founded, the largest of which is **Kallaste**.

A settlement of Old Believers has existed in Kallaste since 1720, when the area was known as Krasniye Gori (Red Mountains) because of the red sandstone cliffs, up to 11m high, that surround the town. Most of its 861 inhabitants are Russian-speaking. It's worth stopping to visit the Old Believers' **cemetery** at the southern end of town, and the sandy **beach** with small **caves**.

**Kolkja** (population 293) is another village of Russian Old Believers, with a dainty,

# Southern Estonia

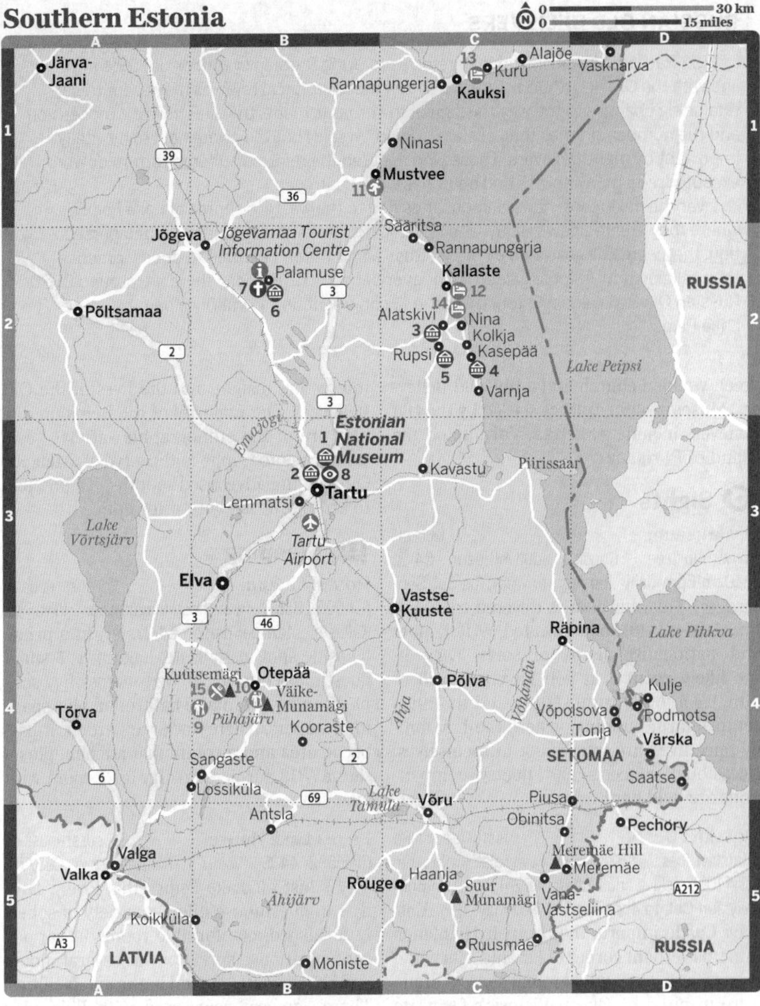


## Southern Estonia

**Top Sights**
1 Estonian National Museum....B3

**Sights**
2 A Le Coq Beer Museum....B3
3 Alatskivi Castle....C2
4 Kolkja Old Believers' Museum....C2
5 Liiv Museum....C2
6 Palamuse Museum....B2
7 St Bartholomew's Lutheran Church....B2
8 Upside Down House....B3

**Activities, Courses & Tours**
9 Kuutsemäe....B4
10 Paap Kõlar's Safari Centre....B4
11 Peipsirent....B1

**Sleeping**
12 Hostel Laguun....C2
13 Kuru Puhkemajad....C1
14 Peipsi Lake House....C2

**Eating**
Fish & Onion Restaurant....(see 4)
Kivi Kõrts....(see 3)
15 Privileeg....B4

### RUSSIAN OLD BELIEVERS

In 1652 Patriarch Nikon introduced reforms to bring Russian Orthodox doctrine into line with the Greek Orthodox Church. Today, these liturgical reforms may seem trivial (including changes to the way the sign of the cross is made, the direction of a procession and the number of times that 'alleluia' should be said) but they were held to be vitally important by many believers. Those who rejected the reforms suffered torture or were executed, and many homes and churches were destroyed.

Over the next few centuries, thousands fled to the western shores of Lake Peipsi, where they erected new villages and worship houses. Although they escaped persecution, they were still governed by tsarist Russia and weren't allowed to openly practise their religion until Estonia gained its independence in 1918. Today there are around 2600 Russian Old Believers in Estonia, living in 11 congregations, primarily along the shore of Lake Peipsi.

green wooden church and a tiny Old Believers' Museum. Other places settled by the Old Believers include **Kasepää**, **Varnja** and the island of **Piirissaar**.

## Sights

**Liiv Museum** MUSEUM
(www.muusa.ee; Rupsi; adult/student €4/3; ⏲10am-6pm daily Jun-Aug, to 4pm Tue-Sat Sep-May; P) This museum is devoted to Juhan Liiv (1864–1913), a celebrated writer, poet and nationalist figure, of sorts. Even in the likely event that you haven't heard of him, it's a lovely rural setting and the 19th-century farm buildings where the Liiv family once lived are interesting in themselves. Occasional concerts and poetry competitions are held here.

**Alatskivi Castle** HISTORIC BUILDING
(Alatskivi loss; ☎528 6598; www.alatskiviloss.ee; Lossi 10, Alatskivi; adult/student €7/4; ⏲10am-6pm daily Jun-Oct, to 4pm Tue-Sun Nov-May; P) Alatskivi Castle imports the Scottish Highlands into this verdant corner of Estonia – its white turrets and stepped baronial-style roofline were inspired by Queen Victoria's favourite abode, Balmoral Castle. In the basement there's a waxworks museum; on the ground floor is an exhibition on the manor; and on the 1st floor are five rooms devoted to Estonian composer Eduard Tubin (1905–82). Outdoors are 130 hectares of publicly accessible parkland filled with oaks, ashes, maples, alders and a linden-lined lane.

**Kolkja Old Believers' Museum** MUSEUM
(☎566 2980; www.vanausulised.weebly.com; Ranna 17, Kolkja; adult/student €3/1; ⏲11am-6pm Wed-Sun May-Sep) Occupying a former school and commune-house, this modest little private museum in Kolkja village provides an interesting insight into the lives of the Old Believers. The majority of the items on display are of the ethnographic variety – costumes, photographs and everyday artefacts. Outside the advertised months, it's possible to arrange a visit with prior notice.

## Sleeping

**Hostel Laguun** GUESTHOUSE €
(☎505 8551; www.hostel-laguun.ee; Liiva 1a, Kallaste; site/r per person €4/17; P) In a prime lakeside spot in Kallaste, Laguun is a small guesthouse offering 10 beds across five simple rooms with shared bathroom, plus space for campers. There's a large garden, a barbecue area and a communal kitchen, plus a sauna (€13 per person). Try for a room with lake views.

**Peipsi Lake House** GUESTHOUSE €€
(☎5592 4435; Võidu 1, Kallaste; s/d €63/70; P 📶) Just off Lake Peipsi, this lovely, family-run guesthouse offers a variety of soberly furnished, comfortable rooms in various configurations, spread over several floors and sharing kitchen and bathroom facilities. There's an expansive yard with kids' play equipment and a barbecue, and a self-contained, two-bedroom apartment next door (from €130 for four).

## Eating

**Kivi Kõrts** ESTONIAN €
(☎506 7605; www.kivikorts.ee; Tartu mnt 2, Alatskivi; mains €8-10; ⏲10am-9pm) Showcasing food from the 'Onion Route', this cosy, dimly lit 'tavern', with its antique-shop-meets-junkyard decor, is built around a really competent kitchen. Definitely seek out freshwater fish from nearby Lake Peipsi, grilled, fried or smoked, and the onion pie.

**Fish & Onion Restaurant** RUSSIAN € (Kala-Sibula Restoran; ☎504 9908; Ranna 1, Kolkja; mains €8-10; ⊙noon-6pm Jul & Aug, shorter hours May, Jun & Sep, by appointment Oct-Mar) This baby-blue weatherboard restaurant, bedecked internally with textiles and sepia photos, offers you the chance to try the Old Believer cuisine, largely based around locally caught fish and onions grown in the villagers' gardens. Fish soup, onion soup, fish stewed or grilled with onions – it's all here.

### Getting There & Around

Getting to and around the lakeside villages is tricky without your own wheels. From Mustvee there are buses to the following destinations:

**Alatskivi** €3 to €4, 1¾ hours with change in Kallaste, several connections daily

**Kallaste** €2 to €4, 30 minutes, up to four daily

**Narva** €6 to €9, two hours, up to six daily

**Tallinn** €13, 3½ to four hours, most changing at Tartu or Rakvere, at least hourly

**Tartu** €5 to €6, one hour, up to nine daily

## Tartu

POP 97,600

Tartu mixes it with Tallinn as Estonia's cultural and intellectual capital. Some also claim it as the spiritual capital, talking about a special Tartu *vaim* (spirit) generated by its historic buildings, and the beauty of its parks and riverfront. The cradle of Estonia's 19th-century national revival, Tartu suffered less Soviet town planning than Tallinn. Its handsome centre is lined with classically designed 18th-century buildings, many now home to bars, galleries, museums and restaurants.

Compact and easily comprehensible, spreading from both banks of the tranquil Emajõgi River, Tartu is Estonia's premier university town. Tartu University, a 17th-century institution where some of the country's greatest intellects have worked, very much sets the tone. Students inject a boisterous vitality into the leafy, historic setting, ensuring a vibrant nightlife for such a small city. And the establishment of the Estonian National Museum here in 2016 has further enhanced Tartu's generous trove of cultural riches.

### History

By around the 6th century there was an Estonian stronghold in Tartu and in 1030 Yaroslav the Wise of Kyiv is said to have founded a fort here called Yuriev. Estonian tribes burnt that down, and control was contested until the Livonian Order (the German 'Brothers of the Sword') became masters of the area in the 13th century. They placed a castle, cathedral and bishop on what henceforth became known as Toomemägi (Cathedral Hill). The surrounding town became known as Dorpat – its German name – until the end of the 19th century.

Throughout the 16th and 17th centuries Dorpat suffered repeated attacks and changes of ownership as Russia, Sweden and Poland-Lithuania fought for control of the Baltic region. Its most peaceful period

### TARTU'S SCULPTURES

Hidden in parks, proudly displayed in squares and skulking in lanes, Tartu's sculptures are often surprising and sometimes plain bizarre. Here are some to look out for:

**Everybody's favourite** The snogging students in front of the town hall.

**Most whimsical** Oscar Wilde and Estonian writer Eduard Vilde, deep in conversation on a park bench in front of Vallikraavi 4. Of course, they never actually met.

**Creepiest** The man-sized naked baby holding hands with the baby-sized naked man on Küüni. It's actually a self-portrait of the artist with his son.

**Most clever** The fountain at the corner of Vanemuise and Struve, which at first glance looks like a tangle of steel tubes with water shooting out the back, but turns into a caricature of famed professor Yuri Lotman (1922–93) when viewed from certain angles.

**Most likely to put you off your chops** The pig standing on a barrel outside the market, with one side already marked up by the butcher. This little piggy went to market; it didn't end well.

**Best 1970s flashback** *Women from the Countryside* in front of the art gallery. The younger woman's flared jeans and obvious lack of a bra would date it to 1978, even if there wasn't a plaque confirming her pedigree.

# Tartu

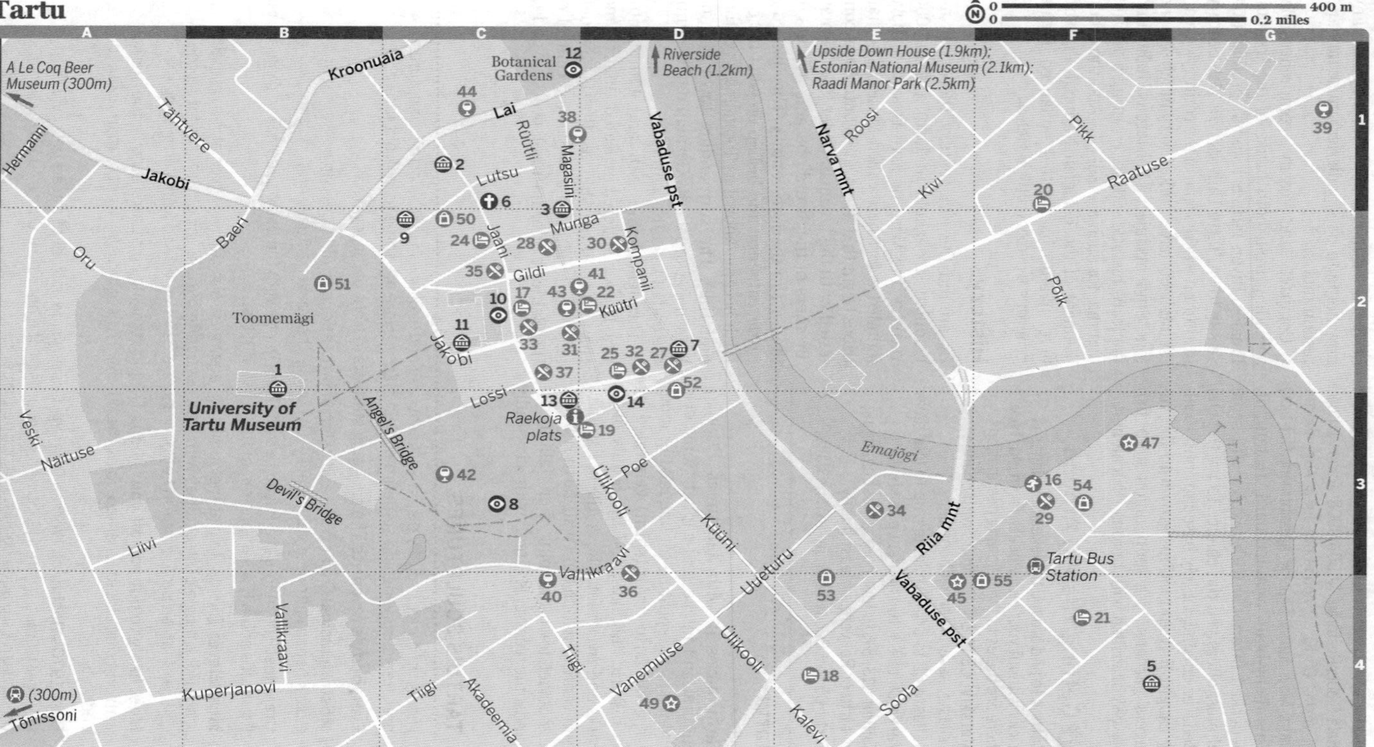
0 400 m
0 0.2 miles
A Le Coq Beer Museum (300m)
Riverside Beach (1.2km)
Upside Down House (1.9km); Estonian National Museum (2.1km); Raadi Manor Park (2.5km)
Botanical Gardens
Toomemägi
University of Tartu Museum
Angel's Bridge
Devil's Bridge
Raekoja plats
Emajõgi
Tartu Bus Station
(300m)
Hermanni
Tähtvere
Kroonuaia
Jakobi
Lai
Rüütli
Magasini
Lutsu
Munga
Jaani
Kompanii
Gildi
Küütri
Lossi
Vabaduse pst
Narva mnt
Roosi
Kivi
Pikk
Raatuse
Põik
Oru
Baeri
Veski
Näituse
Liivi
Vallikraavi
Ülikooli
Poe
Küüni
Uueturu
Riia mnt
Vanemuise
Tiigi
Akadeemia
Kalevi
Soola
Kuperjanovi
Tõnissoni

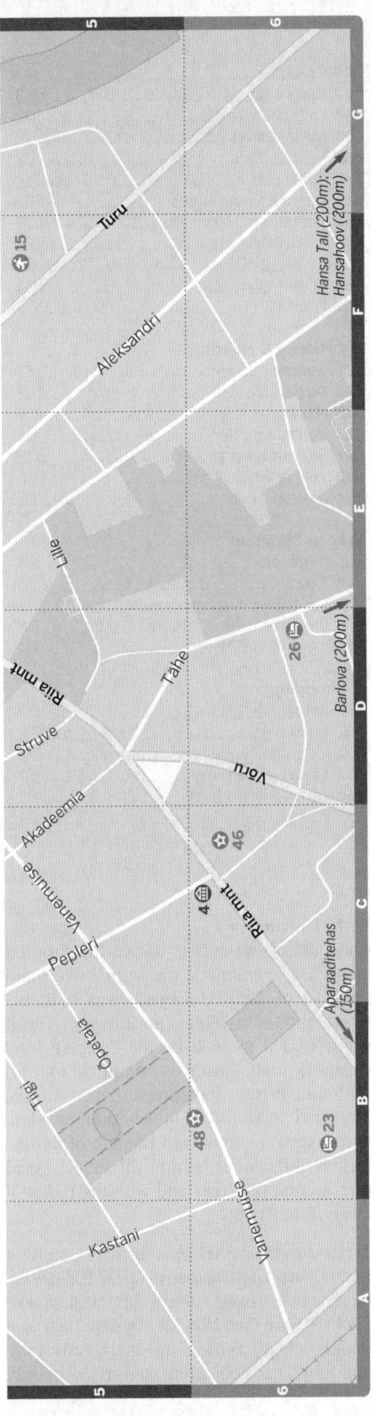


was during the Swedish reign, during which King Gustavus Adolphus founded Tartu University, in 1632 – an event that was to have an enormous impact on the city's future. This peace ended in 1704, during the Great Northern War, when Peter the Great took Tartu for Russia. In 1708 his forces wrecked the town and most of its population was deported to Russia. The fire of 1775 completed the destruction, and much of the town's historic centre, including the town hall, was rebuilt after that date.

In the mid-1800s Tartu became the focus of the Estonian national revival. The first Estonian Song Festival was held here in 1869, and the first Estonian-language newspaper was launched here – both important steps in the national awakening.

The peace treaty that granted independence to Estonia (for the first time in its history) was signed in Tartu between Soviet Russia and Estonia on 2 February 1920. Tartu was severely damaged in 1941 when Soviet forces retreated, blowing up the grand 1784 Kivisild stone bridge over the river, and again in 1944 when they retook it from the Nazis. Both occupying forces committed many atrocities. A monument now stands on the Valga road where the Nazis massacred 12,000 people at Lemmatsi.

The post-Soviet period has largely been one of rebuilding and regrowth, with historic buildings restored, new cultural institutions founded, and an economy recalibrated to welcome a growing influx of visitors.

## Sights

### OLD TOWN

**Tartu Art Museum** GALLERY

(Tartu Kunstimuuseum; ☎5881 7811; www.tartmus.ee; Raekoja plats 18; adult/student €5/4; ⏲11am-6pm Wed & Fri-Sun, to 8pm Thu) If you've been socialising in Tartu's pubs and can't really see straight, don't use this building to anchor your eye. Subsidence caused by the nearby Emajõgi River gives the 1793 structure – former home of an exiled Scot who distinguished himself in the Russian army – a queasy lean of 5.8°, which is more than the Tower of Pisa. It's now an engrossing gallery of Estonian and Baltic art, spread over three levels (tickets are slightly cheaper if you're visiting only one).

**Town Hall Square** SQUARE

(Raekoja plats) Tartu's main square is lined with grand buildings and echoes with the

## Tartu

**Top Sights**
1 University of Tartu Museum ......... B2

**Sights**
2 Citizen's Home Museum ......... C1
3 Estonian Sports and Olympic Museum ......... C2
4 KGB Cells Museum ......... C6
5 Science Centre AHHAA ......... F4
6 St John's Lutheran Church ......... C1
7 Tartu Art Museum ......... D2
8 Tartu Old Observatory ......... C3
9 Tartu Toy Museum ......... C2
10 Tartu University ......... C2
11 Tartu University Art Museum ......... C2
12 Tartu University Botanical Gardens ......... C1
13 Town Hall ......... C3
14 Town Hall Square ......... D3

**Activities, Courses & Tours**
15 Aura Veekeskus ......... F5
16 Pegasus ......... F3

**Sleeping**
17 Antonius Hotel ......... C2
18 Art Hotel Pallas ......... E4
19 Domus Dorpatensis ......... D3
20 Downtown Hostel ......... F1
21 Hotel Tartu ......... F4
22 London Hotell ......... D2
23 Looming ......... B6
24 Tampere Maja ......... C2
25 TerviseksBBB ......... D2
26 Villa Margaretha ......... D6

**Eating**
27 Cafe Truffe ......... D2
28 Crepp ......... C2
29 Dorpat ......... F3
30 La Dolce Vita ......... D2
31 Meat Market ......... C2
32 Pierre's Cafe ......... D2
Polpo ......... (see 22)
Restaurant Antonius ......... (see 17)
33 Restaurant München ......... C2
34 Tartu Market Hall ......... E3
35 University Cafe ......... C2
36 Vilde Ja Vine ......... D4
37 Werner ......... C2

**Drinking & Nightlife**
38 Genialistide Klubi ......... C1
39 Illusion ......... G1
40 Naiiv ......... C4
41 Pühaste Kelder ......... D2
42 Püssirohukelder ......... C3
43 Vein ja Vine ......... C2
44 Zavood ......... C1

**Entertainment**
45 Cinamon ......... E4
46 Ekraan ......... C6
47 Vanemuine Sadamateater ......... F3
48 Vanemuine Small House ......... B6
49 Vanemuine Theatre ......... D4

**Shopping**
50 Antoniuse Gild ......... C2
51 Nukumaja ......... B2
52 Raamatukauplus Krisostomus ......... D2
53 Tartu Kaubamaja ......... E4
54 Tartu Open Market ......... F3
55 Tasku ......... F4

chink of glasses and plates in summer. The centrepiece is the town hall itself, fronted by a statue of students kissing under a spouting umbrella. On the south side of the square, look out for the communist hammer-and-sickle relief that still remains on the facade of No 5.

**Town Hall** HISTORIC BUILDING
(www.tartu.ee; Raekoja plats 1a) Built between 1782 and 1789, this graceful building was designed by German architect JHB Walter, who modelled it on a typical Dutch town hall. The clear focal point of a cobbled square harmoniously lined with classical facades, it's topped by a tower and weather vane, and a clock was added to encourage punctuality in Tartu's students. As well as the council offices, it contains the tourist information centre and a pharmacy.

**Tartu University** UNIVERSITY
(Tartu Ülikool; www.ut.ee; Ülikooli 18) Fronted by six Doric columns, the impressive main building of Tartu University was built between 1803 and 1809. The university itself was founded in 1632 by the Swedish king Gustaf II Adolf (Gustavus Adolphus) to train Lutheran clergy and government officials. Modelled on Uppsala University in Sweden, its principal campus and the site of its historic buildings lies behind this neoclassical pile, among the trees and winding paths of lovely Toomemägi.

**Tartu University Art Museum** MUSEUM
(Tartu Ülikooli kunstimuuseum; ☎737 5384; www.kunstimuuseum.ut.ee; Ülikooli 18; adult/student €6/4; ⏰10am-6pm Mon-Sat May-Sep, 11am-5pm Mon-Fri Oct-Apr) Within the main university building, this collection comprises mainly

19th-century plaster copies of ancient Greek sculptures, plus some mummies and other original artefacts displayed in the **Chamber of Mummies**, painted to look like the interior of an Egyptian tomb. The rest of the collection was evacuated to Russia in 1915 and has never returned. Admission includes entry to the attic **lock-up**, where recalcitrant students were held in solitary confinement, sometimes for weeks – some examples of their 19th-century graffiti remain.

**St John's Lutheran Church** CHURCH
(Jaani kirik; www.jaanikirik.ee; Jaani 5; steeple adult/student €2/1.50; 10am-7pm Jun-Aug, to 6pm Sep-May) Dating to at least 1323, this imposing red-brick church is unique for the rare terracotta sculptures placed in niches around its exterior and interior (look up). Shattered by a Soviet bombing raid in 1944, it long lay derelict, and wasn't fully restored until 2005. Climb the 135 steps of the 30m steeple for a bird's-eye view of Tartu.

**Tartu Toy Museum** MUSEUM
(Tartu mänguasjamuuseum; 746 1777; www.mm.ee; Lutsu 8; adult/student €6/5; 11am-6pm Wed-Sun; ) A big hit with the under-eight crowd (and you won't see too many adults anxious to leave), this is a great place to while away a few rainy hours. Set in one of the best-preserved late-18th-century buildings in the area, this excellent museum showcases dolls, model trains, rocking horses, toy soldiers and tons of other desirables. It's all geared to be nicely interactive, with exhibits in pull-out drawers and a kids' playroom (open 10am to 4pm).

**Citizen's Home Museum** MUSEUM
(Linnakodaniku Muuseum; 736 1545; www.linnamuuseum.tartu.ee; Jaani 16; adult/student €4/2; 11am-5pm Wed-Sat, to 3pm Sun Apr-Sep, 10am-3pm Wed-Sun Oct-Mar) This handsome wooden house, dating to the 1740s and nestled in one of the oldest surviving sections of the city, is furnished to show how a bourgeois family from the 1830s lived. The attention to detail is impressive: whole rooms adhere to the 'Biedermeier style' that was in vogue at the time.

**Tartu University Botanical Gardens** GARDENS
(Tartu Ülikooli botaanikaaed; 737 6180; www.botaanikaaed.ut.ee; Lai 38; greenhouse adult/child €3/2; gardens 7am-7pm Sep-May, to 9pm Jun-Aug, greenhouses 10am-5pm) FREE Founded in 1803, these lush, mature gardens nurture 6500 species, including a large collection of palms and other exotics in the greenhouse. In summer it's often full of local families wandering paths lined with 20th-century sculptures, or grabbing some grass by the ornamental lake.

**Estonian Sports and Olympic Museum** MUSEUM
(Eesti Spordi- ja Olümpiamuuseum; 730 0750; www.spordimuuseum.ee; Rüütli 15; adult/student €6/5; 11am-6pm Wed-Sun) Chronicling more than just Estonian Olympic excellence (although the glittering medal display serves that purpose admirably), this offbeat museum has a real sense of fun. While the photos of puffed-up early-20th-century bodybuilders in posing pouches suggest that they took themselves tremendously seriously, there's no requirement that you should. If you're feeling inspired, take a spin on the exercise bikes, test your strength on the interactive tug-of-war, drive a virtual rally car or change the tyre on a real one.

### TOOMEMÄGI

Rising to the west of the Town Hall, Toomemägi (Cathedral Hill) is the original reason for Tartu's existence, functioning on and off as a stronghold from around the 5th or 6th century. It's now a tranquil park, with walking paths meandering through the trees, university buildings and museums.

The approach from Town Hall Sq is along Lossi, which passes beneath the **Angel's Bridge** (Inglisild), which was built between 1836 and 1838 – follow local superstition and hold your breath and make a wish as you cross it for the first time. A bit further up the hill is **Devil's Bridge** (Kuradisild).

★ **University of Tartu Museum** MUSEUM
(Tartu Ülikool muuseum; 737 5674; www.muuseum.ut.ee; Lossi 25; adult/reduced €6/5; 10am-6pm Tue-Sun May-Sep, 11am-5pm Wed-Sun Oct-Apr) Atop Toomemägi are the ruins of a Gothic cathedral, built in the 13th century by the knights of the Livonian Order after driving the pagan Estonians from this natural defensive formation. It was substantially rebuilt in the 15th century, despoiled during the Reformation in 1525, used as a barn, and partly rebuilt between 1804 and 1809 to house the university library, and is now a museum. Inside there are a range of interesting exhibits chronicling student life.

Start by taking the historic 1920s lift to the top and working your way down.

WORTH A TRIP

## PALAMUSE

This sleepy little town, 35km north of Tartu, is a major drawcard for Estonian tourists due to its role as the setting for Oskar Luts' coming-of-age novel *Kevade* (Spring) and, even more so, as the location for the 1969 movie adaptation of the same. Trotted out every year for a television rerun at Christmas, it's unquestionably the nation's favourite family flick. Even if *Spring* has passed you by, Palamuse makes for a pleasantly rural afternoon trip from Tartu.

The primary sight is the **Palamuse Museum** (☎776 0514; www.palamusemuuseum.ee; Köstri allee 3; admission €4, slingshot €1; ⌚10am-6pm; P), including the rustic schoolhouse where young Luts studied from 1895 to 1899 (the period immortalised in *Kevade*). The subsequent film adaptation was shot here, and the schoolhouse now features displays on all three: the film, the book and the writer.

*Kevade's* primary audience is Estonian, so it's not surprising that English captions are limited. However, it's still fun to potter around the re-created classroom, dorm and teacher's bedroom, and to look at the black-and-white stills of the movie and various stage productions. Best of all, you can hire a slingshot and attempt to re-create a scene in the movie by breaking a window in a neighbouring building. Museum staff assure us that kids have a much better success rate at this than their parents do – and in any case, the window is quickly replaced.

Another star of the movie adaptation of *Kevade*, the lovely, Gothic **St Bartholomew's Lutheran Church** (Püha Bartholomeuse kirik; Köstri allee 4; ⌚9am--5pm) has its roots in the 13th century, although it has been substantially altered over time. Its most interesting feature is a carved wooden pulpit from 1696, festooned with saints and angels.

You can get more information from the nearby **Jõgevamaa Tourist Information Centre** (☎776 8520; www.visitjogeva.com; Köstri allee 1; ⌚10am-5pm Mon-Fri, to 3pm Sat & Sun mid-May–mid-Sep, 10am-5pm Mon-Fri rest of year).

Public transport to Palamuse is limited, with only one bus per day to and from Tartu (one hour).

**Morgenstern Hall** retains the appearance of the historic library and is lined with statues of the Ancient Greek muses. Kids will love the **Cabinet of the Crazy Scientist**, where they take part in some hands-on science themselves. Other highlights include the beautiful **White Hall** and the **Treasury**, which houses eclectic items such as the death mask of Russian poet Aleksandr Pushkin, a 1504 Dürer print, a human hand once used for anatomy lessons and a set of elaborate cheat-sheet scrolls extracted from students in the 1980s.

From May to September the museum ticket also includes entrance to the viewing platform on top of the cathedral tower.

**Tartu Old Observatory** OBSERVATORY
(Tartu Tähetorn; ☎737 6932; www.tahetorn.ut.ee; Uppsala 8; adult/concession €4/3; ⌚10am-6pm Tue-Sun May-Sep, 11am-5pm Tue-Sat Oct-Apr) Built as part of Tartu University in 1810, this intriguing observatory on Toomemägi is a must for fans of astronomy and the history of scientific discovery. The sober, studious-looking facility, topped with a moving observational tower, houses some of the most famous artefacts of 19th-century astronomy, all displayed in perfect order. You can climb the tower, where a huge Zeiss Refractor remains in place; there's a basement exhibition on seismology; and interactive-learning displays await in the Western Hall.

### CITY CENTRE

**Science Centre AHHAA** MUSEUM
(Teaduskeskus AHHAA; ☎745 6789; www.ahhaa.ee; Sadama 1; adult/student €15/11, Planetarium additional €4; ⌚10am-7pm Sun-Thu, to 8pm Fri & Sat; P 👪) This popular centre's interactive exhibits are liable to bring out the mad scientist in kids and adults alike. Allow at least a couple of hours for button pushing, water squirting and knob twiddling, all of it designed to inculcate some scientific principle. Workshops delve into the mysteries of caffeine crystals or cabbage chemistry; the Planetarium runs popular hour-long shows; and upstairs there's a nightmarish assembly of pickled organs and deformed foetuses from Tartu University's collection.

**KGB Cells Museum** MUSEUM

(KGB kongide muuseum; ☎746 1717; www.linnamuuseum.tartu.ee; Riia mnt 15b, enter from Pepleri; adult/student €5/2; ⏲11am-5pm Tue-Sat) This former KGB headquarters and prison, known as the 'Grey House', was donated to Tartu City Museum by the family to which they were returned after the Soviet era. Chilling in parts, the museum has created a highly worthwhile exhibition covering deportations, life in the gulags, the Estonian resistance, and what went on here. Guided tours are €20 extra. Temporary exhibitions visit, and occasional 'Dark Nights' show how terrifying the cells could be.

### KARLOVA & VAKSALI

**Aparaaditehas** AREA

(☎5667 4704; www.aparaaditehas.ee; Kastani 42; ⏲shops generally 11am-7pm Tue-Sat, to 4pm Sun, restaurants generally noon-11pm Mon-Thu, to 1am Fri & Sat, to 6pm Sun) Aparaaditehas (the Widget Factory) is an old 14,000-sq-metre Soviet-era industrial complex where refrigeration equipment and secret submarine parts were made alongside umbrellas and zips that didn't work, to fool the public. Now it's Tartu's hippest dining, drinking, shopping and cultural hub – smaller kin to Tallinn's Telliskivi Creative City. Broad painted stripes evoke its industrial past, while stencils and graffiti adorn its present.

### TÄHTVERE

**A Le Coq Beer Museum** MUSEUM

(☎744 9711; www.alecoq.ee; Laulupeo 15; adult/student €10/3; ⏲tours 2pm Thu, 10am, noon & 2pm Sat; P) Occupying an 1898 tower in Tartu's famous brewery, 10 minutes' walk northwest of the centre, mandatory tours of this museum trace the history of beer since ancient Egypt, before focusing on modern machinery and processes, then dispensing free samples. There's also a gift shop with different brews and plenty of merchandise on sale (10am to 5pm Tuesday to Friday, to 4.30pm Saturday).

### RAADI-KRUUSAMÄE

★**Estonian National Museum** MUSEUM

(Eesti rahva muuseum; ☎736 3000; www.erm.ee; Muuseumi tee 2; adult/student all exhibitions €14/10; ⏲10am-6pm Tue-Sun; P 👪) This immense, low-slung, glass-clad building is arresting – both Estonians and architecture lovers purred when it opened in late 2016. The permanent exhibition 'Encounters' covers national prehistory and history in some detail, paying plenty of attention to the period of Soviet occupations (fittingly – the museum is built over a former Soviet airstrip). Below ground, the wonderful 'Echo of the Urals' exhibition gives an overview of the various peoples making up the Finno-Ugric language family, and there's a hall for its wonderful temporary exhibitions.

The museum is in the grounds of Raadi Manor, which held the original national museum many years ago.

**Raadi Manor Park** PARK

(Raadi Mõisapark; www.erm.ee; Narva mnt 177; ⏲7am-10pm) FREE On the main road heading north out of town stands the sad remains of Raadi Manor, one-time home of the von Liphartide family. It passed to the University of Tartu in the 1920s, but the Soviets took part of the land to build a WWII airfield, attracting bombing that left the once-beautiful baroque-style building a red-brick shell. While the surrounding parks can't match its 18th-century prime, locals still come to stroll around and swim in the lake.

**Upside Down House** HOUSE

(Tagurpidi Maja; ☎5688 1811; www.tagurpidimaja.ee; Roosi 86; adult/reduced €7.50/6; ⏲10am-6pm; P) Looking like something from *The Wizard of Oz*, the Upside Down House is exactly that: a regular house tipped on its head, with everything inside – ceilings, floors, furniture – inverted. It's a bit of harmless fun once you've tired of the more substantial attractions of the nearby Estonian National Museum.

## Activities

**Pegasus** CRUISE

(☎733 7182; www.dorpat.ee; mooring alongside Dorpat Hotel, Soola 6; adult/reduced €9/7; ⏲noon & 2pm Tue-Sun, plus 4pm Sat) The Pegasus can't fly, but it can take up to 74 passengers on an unhurried, 90-minute cruise up and down the river. Basic snacks and drinks are sold on board.

**Riverside Beaches** BEACH

(👪) If the sun's beating down and you can't make it to Pärnu there are a pair of pleasant beaches on opposite banks of the Emajõgi, a little over 1km northwest of the Kroonuaia bridge. You'll also find outdoor exercise equipment, volleyball nets and (hopefully) someone vending snacks and ice cream.

## THE BLUE, BLACK & WHITE

Estonia's tricolour dates back to 1881, when a theology student named Jaan Bergmaan wrote a poem about a beautiful flag flying over Estonia. The only problem, for both Jaan and his countrymen, was that no flag in fact existed. Clearly, something had to be done about this. This was, after all, the time of the national awakening, when the idea of independent nationhood was on the lips of every young dreamer across the country.

In September of that year, at the Union of Estonian Students in Tartu, 20 students and one alumnus gathered to hash out ideas for a flag. All present agreed that the colours must express the character of the nation, reflect the Estonian landscape and connect to the colours of folk costumes. After long discussions, the students came up with blue, black and white. According to one interpretation, blue symbolised hope for Estonia's future; it also represented faithfulness. Black was a reminder of the dark past to which Estonia would not return; it also depicted the country's dark soil. White represented the attainment of enlightenment and education – an aspiration for all Estonians; it also symbolised snow in winter, light nights in summer and the Estonian birch tree.

After the colours were chosen, it took several years before the first flag was made. Three young activist women – Emilie, Paula and Miina Beermann – carried this out by sewing together a large flag made out of silk. In 1884 the students held a procession from Tartu to Otepää, a location far from the eyes of the Russian government. All members of the students' union were there as the flag was raised over the vicarage. Afterwards it was dipped in Pühajärv (a lake considered sacred to Estonians) and locked safely away in the student archive.

Although the inauguration of the flag was a tiny event, word of the flag's existence spread, and soon the combination of colours appeared in unions and choirs, and hung from farmhouses all across Estonia. By the end of the 19th century the blue, black and white was used in parties and at wedding ceremonies. Its first political appearance, however, didn't arrive until 1917, when thousands of Estonians marched in St Petersburg demanding independence. In 1918 Estonia was declared independent and the flag was raised on Pikk Hermann in Tallinn's Old Town. There it remained until the Soviet Union seized power in 1940.

During the occupation the Soviets banned the flag and once again it went underground. For Estonians, keeping the flag on the sly was a small but hopeful symbol of one day regaining nationhood. People hid flags under floorboards or unstitched the stripes and secreted them in bookcases. Those caught with the flag faced severe punishment – including a possible sentence in the Siberian gulags. Needless to say, as the Soviet Union teetered on the brink of collapse, blue, black and white returned to the stage. In February 1989 the flag was raised again on Pikk Hermann. Independence was about to be regained.

**Aura Veekeskus** WATER PARK

(Aura Water Park; ☎730 0280; www.aurakeskus.ee; Turu 10; adult/reduced pool €7/6, water park €9/8; ⏲water park 10am-10pm Mon-Fri, from 9am Sat & Sun, pool 6.30am-10pm Mon-Fri, from 9am Sat & Sun; 👪) Families and lap-swimmers will love this centre, with 50m and 25m indoor pools and a happy, splashy water park with all the trimmings (two slides, water cannon, massage jets, waterfalls, cafe and more).

## Festivals & Events

Tartu regularly dons its shiniest party gear and lets its hair down; check out www.kultuuriaken.tartu.ee for more.

**Tartu Student Days** CARNIVAL

(Tartu Tudengipäevad; www.studentdays.ee; ⏲Apr/May) Catch a glimpse of mass student merriment in early April/late May, when Tartu's young scholars take to the streets to celebrate term's end (and the dawn of spring) with parties, a bespoke-boat race on the river, music and every conceivable diversion. A second, smaller version occurs in autumn.

**Hanseatic Days** CARNIVAL

(Hansapäevad; www.hansapaevad.ee; ⏲Jul; 👪) Tartu's history as an important member of the medieval commercial confederation known as the Hanseatic League is celebrated throughout the city over a mid-July weekend. There are concerts, performances, parades (including a waterborne affair on the Emajõgi) and a fair with more than 400 stalls from Estonia and its neighbours, held in the Town Hall Sq.

**tARTuFF** FILM
(www.tartuff.ee; ⌚Aug) A big outdoor cinema takes over Town Hall Sq for a week in August for this festival of films about love. Screenings are free (it's first come, first served), there's a second screen for documentaries in the Alexander Centre, and the main event is supplemented by poetry readings, concerts and a tARTuFF party in a club.

**Christmas City Tartu** CHRISTMAS
(Jõululinn Tartu; www.joululinntartu.ee; ⌚Dec) Choirs sing as Advent candles are lit in a ceremony in Town Hall Sq at 4pm on each of the four Sundays preceding Christmas. It's a chance to see old Tartu at its most magical: decorated with fairy lights and Christmas trees, and sprinkled with snow.

## Sleeping

### OLD TOWN

**TerviseksBBB** HOSTEL €
(565 5382; top fl, Raekoja plats 10; dm from €15, s/d €22/44; @ 📶) Occupying a historic building in a perfect main-square location, this excellent 'backpacker's bed and breakfast' offers dorms (maximum four beds, no bunks), private rooms, a full kitchen and lots of switched-on info about the happening places in town. With parquet floors and palpable style throughout, it's like staying in your rich mate's cool European pad. Cheers *(terviseks!)* to that.

★**Domus Dorpatensis** APARTMENT €€
(733 1345; www.dorpatensis.ee; Raekoja plats 1; apt for 2 from €70; 📶) Run by a charitable academic foundation, this block of 10 apartments in a mid-18th-century house opposite the town hall offers unbeatable location and value. The units range in size, but all have writing desks and almost all have kitchenettes. The staff are particularly helpful and all profits go towards developing 'responsibility, proactivity and entrepreneurship' in Estonian youth.

**Tampere Maja** GUESTHOUSE €€
(738 6300; www.tamperemaja.ee; Jaani 4; s/d/tr/q €50/80/110/132; P ❄ @ 📶) With strong links to the Finnish city of Tampere (Tartu's sister city), this cosy, central guesthouse features seven warm, light-filled guest rooms in a range of sizes. Breakfast is included, and each room has access to cooking facilities. And it wouldn't be Finnish if it didn't offer an authentic sauna (first hour three to four people €15; open to nonguests).

Bike hire is also an option: €2/10 per hour/day.

**Wilde Guest Apartments** APARTMENT €€
(511 3876; www.wildeapartments.ee; apt from €50; 📶) The people behind the Eduard Vilde Restaurant (p114) also have five beautiful self-contained apartments for rent. Four of them are near the restaurant, either on Vallikraavi or Ülikooli street, with the last one in the striking high-rise tower by the river. All of them have a separate bedroom and a sofa bed in the lounge.

**London Hotell** HOTEL €€
(730 5555; www.londonhotel.ee; Rüütli 9; s/d from €77/88; P @ 📶) The London puts a lot of effort into first impressions – after the glitzy lobby, with its brass trim and water feature, the decor of the rooms at this upmarket hotel is unremarkable. But the location is perfect, and the on-site restaurant, Polpo, produces delights using whatever's in season.

★**Antonius Hotel** HOTEL €€€
(737 0377; www.hotelantonius.ee; Ülikooli 15; d/ste from €171/297; ❄ 📶) Facing the main university building, of which it's a neoclassically styled, early-19th-century contemporary, this first-rate 27-room boutique hotel is loaded with antiques and period features. Breakfast is served in the 18th-century vaulted cellar, which in the evening morphs into top-notch Restaurant Antonius. There's a summer terrace, airport-transfer service and laundry but no on-site parking.

### CITY CENTRE

**Downtown Hostel** HOSTEL €
(5662 0215; www.tartuhostel.ee; Raatuse 22; s/tw with shared bathroom, €20/25; P 📶) This small hostel in a large, featureless block mainly devoted to student accommodation is worth choosing for its cleanliness and quiet neighbourhood, just over the river from central Tartu. There's parking, a basic communal kitchen, and three twin-bed rooms.

**Hotel Tartu** HOTEL €€
(731 4300; www.tartuhotell.ee; Soola 3; s/d €79/92; P ❄ 📶) With roots deep in the Soviet era (it was purpose-built in 1964), it's

no surprise that the Hotel Tartu seems a little dated. But it's undeniably comfortable, and convenient to the bus station, shopping centres, river, urban parkland and the centre of town. And, of course, its 72 rooms have clearly seen changes since the 1960s.

**Art Hotel Pallas** HOTEL €€
(☎730 1200; www.pallas.ee; Riia mnt 4; s/d €60/80; P 📶) The Pallas occupies the site of a former art college and has attempted to channel some of that creativity, especially in the daringly decorated deluxe rooms. All rooms are bright and airy, but request a city-facing room on the 3rd floor, for space and views. Attached Big Ben Pub, offering a menu that 'flirts with British cuisine', is open every night.

### KARLOVA & VAKSALI

**Looming** HOSTEL €
(☎5699 4398; www.loominghostel.ee; Kastani 38; dm €17, d from €32; @ 📶) 🍃 Run by urban greenies with a commitment to recycled materials and sustainable practices, Looming ('creation') offers smart bunk-free dorms and private rooms in a converted art nouveau factory building. Breakfast is only an additional €3, there's an appealing roof terrace for warm weather, and your hosts are mines of information on things to do and see.

**Villa Margaretha** BOUTIQUE HOTEL €€
(☎731 1820; www.margaretha.ee; Tähe 11; s/d/ste from €55/65/90; P 📶) Like something out of a fairy tale, this rambling, creaky, early-20th-century art nouveau house has a sweet little turret and romantic rooms decked out with sleigh beds and artfully draped fabrics (the cheaper rooms in the modern extension at the rear are bland in comparison). It's a little away from the action, but still within walking distance of Old Town.

## Eating

### OLD TOWN

**Werner** CAFE €
(www.werner.ee; Ülikooli 11; baked items €2-5; ⏲7.30am-11pm Mon-Thu, to midnight Fri, 8am-midnight Sat, 9am-9pm Sun; 📶) Upstairs there's a proper restaurant serving proper meals in sober surrounds, but we prefer the cafe downstairs – judging by the buzz, so do the locals. The counter positively groans under a hefty array of quiches and tempting cakes, plus there's a sweet little courtyard at the back.

**Crepp** CRÊPES €
(☎742 2133; www.crepp.ee; Rüütli 16; mains €6-8; ⏲11am-10pm Sun-Thu, to 11pm Fri & Sat) With bentwood chairs, inviting red armchairs, cheery decor and pleasantly efficient service, there's not much to deter you from dropping in here for a crêpe or salad. But perhaps think twice about some of the suggested fillings, such as the galette with blue cheese, ham and pineapple.

**Vilde Ja Vine** EUROPEAN €€
(☎734 3400; www.vilde.ee; Vallikraavi 4; mains €11-15; ⏲11.30am-10pm Mon-Wed, to 11pm Thu, to 1am Fri, 1-11pm Sat; 📶) A spacious, eclectically furnished 1st-floor dining room looking up to the green slopes of Toomemägi is the very pleasant setting for crowd-pleasing fare (such as *paccheri* pasta with lamb and mint ragu) made to match the many pleasant bottles lining the walls. The name references Estonian novelist Eduard Vilde, immortalised in statue form chatting to Oscar Wilde, just outside the restaurant.

**Pierre's Cafe** CAFE €€
(☎730 4680; www.pierre.ee; Raekoja plats 12; mains €8-15; ⏲8am-10pm Mon-Thu, to 11pm Fri, 10am-11pm Sat, to 10pm Sun; 📶) Tallinn's favourite chocmeister has set up on Tartu's main square, offering a refined atmosphere, old-world decor and perfect, melting truffles. It's a prime spot for a coffee and a sugar fix at any time of day, or come back at night to push the boat out properly, with dinner at the attached Pierre Restaurant (mains €15 to €19).

**Polpo** EUROPEAN €€
(☎730 5566; www.polpo.ee; Rüütli 9; mains €19; ⏲noon-11pm Mon-Thu, to midnight Fri & Sat; 📶) In a modern, vaulted space beneath the London Hotell, Polpo isn't the Italian restaurant the name might suggest, but produces some of the best modern European food in town. The smoked sturgeon with salted cucumber, horseradish and dill is a fishy-salty-fresh mouthful of Eastern Europe, while the lamb sirloin with lamb rillettes and pear whisks you west, to France.

**Cafe Truffe** MODERN EUROPEAN €€
(☎742 8840; www.truffe.ee; Raekoja plats 16; mains €13-16; ⏲11am-10pm Sun-Thu, to 1am Fri & Sat; 📶) Truffe calls itself a cafe, and it's certainly happy to fix you up with a good coffee

to brighten up your morning, but with dishes such as beef tenderloin with white asparagus, mushrooms and rosemary butter, it definitely strays confidently into restaurant territory. It also works as a low-key bar, with tables spilling out onto the square in good weather.

**University Cafe** CAFE €€
(Ülikooli Kohvik; ☎518 0866; www.kohvik.ut.ee; Ülikooli 20; mains €11-14; ⌚11.30am-9pm Mon-Wed, to midnight Thu-Sat; 📶) Facing the main building of Tartu University, this venerable institution inhabits a labyrinth of elegantly decorated rooms. It's simultaneously grand and cosy, with serves to sate the most ravenous of scholars. There's a shady summer terrace behind handsome wrought-iron gates.

**Meat Market** GRILL €€
(☎653 3455; www.meatmarket.ee; Küütri 3; mains €9-19; ⌚noon-11pm Mon-Thu, to 1am Fri & Sat, to 10pm Sun; 📶) Grilled meat and cocktails is the simple formula pushed by this slick dude-food joint in the heart of town. A few interlopers like ramen and a 'schnitzel' of taleggio with basil and Korean carrot slip in there, but the real order of business is the unashamedly carnivorous fare: grill-charred wagyu, kebabs of Hiiumaa lamb and the like.

**La Dolce Vita** ITALIAN €€
(☎740 7545; www.ladolcevita.ee; Kompanii 10; pizzas & pastas €8-10, mains €14-19; ⌚11.30am-11pm Mon-Thu, to midnight Fri & Sat, noon-11pm Sun; 📶) Thin-crust pizzas come straight from the wood-burning oven at this cheerful, family-friendly pizzeria and ristorante. While the pizza and pasta are good, if you're happy to pay a little more then mains such as *tagliata* (grilled, sliced beef with rocket and parmesan) and *pollo al limone* (chicken in a creamy lemon sauce) won't disappoint.

**Restaurant München** GERMAN €€
(☎5308 0066; Küütri 2; mains €11-13; ⌚noon-11pm Mon-Thu, to midnight Fri & Sat, to 9pm Sun; 📶) The arched vaults of this semi-subterranean dining room provide an apt setting to eat *obatzda* (a Bavarian dish of several cheeses, melted with butter and spices), sausages with mustard or even, if appetite demands, *schweineshaxe* (roast pork knuckle) with sauerkraut and fried potatoes. The cooking is excellent, and there's plenty of German beer and wine to complement it.

**Restaurant Antonius** EUROPEAN €€€
(☎737 0377; www.hotelantonius.ee; Ülikooli 15; mains €18-22; ⌚noon-11pm Jun-Aug, 6-11pm Sep-May; 📶) A proper, old-school, stiff-linen-and-formal-service fine diner, Restaurant Antonius cocoons its guests in an art-strewn, atrium-lit dining room in the upscale Hotel Antonius. It's expensive, by Tartu standards, but the produce is great, and dishes such as venison with smoked-beetroot cream and marinated kale testify to the skills in the kitchen.

### CITY CENTRE

**Tartu Market Hall** MARKET €
(Tartu Turuhoone; www.tartuturg.ee; Vabaduse pst 1; ⌚7.30am-4pm Mon-Sat, 9am-3pm Sun) Retaining its late-1930s architectural lines yet gleamingly refurbished, Tartu's riverside market hall is great for meat, fruit and veg, smallgoods, pickles, breads, cheeses, fish and other comestibles, many of them uniquely Estonian.

**Dorpat** BUFFET €
(☎733 7180; www.dorpat.ee; Soola 6; buffet €6-8.50; ⌚noon-10pm Mon-Thu, to 11pm Fri & Sat, buffet noon-2pm Mon-Fri; 📶) The restaurant at the Dorpat offers great river views and has a reputable à la carte menu, but it's the weekday lunch buffet that really shines for value. For €6 you'll get a bottomless bowl of your choice of soup and salad, while for €8.50 you get the full bain-marie of meats, vegetables, pastas and other treats too.

### KARLOVA & VAKSALI

**Hansa Tall** ESTONIAN €€
(☎737 1802; www.hansahotell.ee; Turu 27a; mains €10-16; ⌚7am-10pm Mon-Wed, to 11pm Thu, to midnight Fri, 8am-midnight Sat, to 9pm Sun; P 📶) If you want to look at a menu and really know you're in Estonia, head to this super-rustic, barnlike tavern southeast of the centre. You need not try the smoked pig's ears or blood sausage to enjoy the diverse, hearty menu, often-rambunctious live music and even livelier locals.

## Drinking & Nightlife

In summer the bars are quiet, unless they've got outside seating. You'll find most of the non-holidaying students on the designated drinkers' hill behind the town hall. During term, Wednesday is the traditional scholars' party night.

**★Genialistide Klubi** BAR
(www.genklubi.ee; Magasini 5; ⏲noon-3am Mon-Fri, to 4am Sat; 📶) Beloved of Tartu's students, the Genialists' Club is an all-purpose, grungy 'subcultural house' comprising a bar, a cafe, an alternative nightclub, a live-music venue, a cinema and even a specialist Estonian CD store. It's a friendly, unpretentious gem.

**★Vein ja Vine** WINE BAR
(www.veinjavine.ee; Rüütli 8; ⏲5pm-1am Mon-Thu, to 2am Sat; 📶) Serving wine and excellent deli snacks, this little bar attracts a slightly older crowd (postgraduates, perhaps) but still gets jammed and overflows onto the street in summer. The genial owner knows his wines, and is happy to uncork many a bottle to sell by the glass.

**Pühaste Kelder** PUB
(☎775 1313; www.puhastebeer.com; Rüütli 11; ⏲5-11pm Mon, to 1am Tue-Thu, to 2am Fri & Sat; 📶) The outlet pub for Pühaste, one of Estonia's best craft brewers, always has plenty of interesting taps on the go, some of them finished within 24 hours of pouring. The vaulted cellar makes for atmospheric and convivial tasting, and tables are set out on pedestrianised Rüütli street when Tartu's weather allows.

**Barlova** BAR
(☎5682 8117; Tähe 29; ⏲5pm-1am Mon-Thu, to 3am Fri, 7pm-3am Sat; 📶) A lovely, offbeat neighbourhood bar in a weather-beaten clapboard building 2km south of central Tartu, Barlova hosts everything from poetry evenings to art exhibitions and gigs, offers a great range of beers, and spills out onto the pavement in fine weather.

**Naiiv** BAR
(www.naiiv.ee; Vallikraavi 6; ⏲6pm-1am Tue, 8pm-1am Wed, 7pm-2am Thu, 9pm-4am Fri & Sat) Downstairs at Naiiv is cosy and clubbable, with an extensive selection of drinks: ask the clued-up staff for suggestions on good local brews, then find a comfy sofa to sink into or head out to the small rear courtyard. Upstairs, you'll find music, dancing and themed parties.

**Püssirohukelder** PUB
(☎730 3555; www.pyss.ee; Lossi 28; mains €10-15; ⏲noon-10pm Mon & Sun, to 11pm Tue, to 2am Wed-Sat) Set in a vast 18th-century gunpowder cellar built into the Toomemägi hillside, this boisterous pub serves beer-accompanying snacks and meaty meals under a soaring 10m-high vaulted ceiling. There's regular live music and a large beer garden out front.

**Zavood** PUB
(www.zavood.ee; Lai 30; ⏲11am-4am Mon-Fri, from 6pm Sat & Sun) This battered cellar bar attracts an alternative, down-to-earth crowd with its inexpensive drinks and lack of attitude. Underground and emerging acts tend to play here.

**Illusion** CLUB
(☎742 4341; www.illusion.ee; Raatuse 97; admission from €1; ⏲11pm-4am Wed, Fri & Sat) Occupying a grand, gaudily painted Stalin-era movie theatre north of the river (and in which legendary underground parties were held in the 1990s), Illusion has a lavish interior and draws a blinged-up crowd. It closes during university summer holidays.

## ☆ Entertainment

For information on classical performances, see www.concert.ee.

**Vanemuine Theatre** THEATRE
(☎744 0165; www.vanemuine.ee; Vanemuise 6; ⏲box office 10am-6pm Mon-Sat & 1hr before performances) Named after the ancient Estonian song god, this venue hosts an array of theatrical and musical performances, many with English subtitles.

It also puts on shows at its **small stage** (Vanemuise Väike Maja; ☎744 0160; Vanemuise 45a; ⏲box office opens 1 hr before performances) and **Sadamateater** (Harbour Theatre; ☎734 4247; Soola 5; ⏲box office opens 1 hr before performances). The latter has a prime location on the banks of the Emajõgi and tends to stage the most modern, alternative productions.

**Hansahoov** LIVE MUSIC
(☎737 1802; www.hansahoov.ee; Tura 27a) Concerts and theatre productions are regularly staged in the large rustic courtyard of the Hansa Tall tavern.

**Cinamon** CINEMA
(☎5690 6891; www.cinamon.ee; Turu 2; adult/child from €5.50/3) For Hollywood blockbusters, head to the multiplex above the Tasku shopping centre.

**Ekraan** CINEMA
(☎343 380; www.forumcinemas.ee; Riia 14; ⏲1hr before first screening) This smaller cinema complex screens a mix of popular features and more art-house offerings.

## Shopping

The city centre is where to find malls such as **Tartu Kaubamaja** (www.kaubamaja.ee; Riia 1; ⌚9am-9pm) and **Tasku** (www.tasku.ee; Turu 2; ⌚10am-9pm Mon-Sat, to 6pm Sun), and the old-fashioned **Open Market** (Tartu avaturg; www.tartuturg.ee; Soola 10; ⌚7am-5pm Mon-Fri, to 4pm Sat & Sun).

**Antoniuse Gild** ARTS & CRAFTS
(www.loovtartu.ee; Lutsu 3; ⌚9am-6pm Mon-Fri) An array of artisans' studios occupying three old houses set around St Anthony's Courtyard produce ceramics, stained glass, jewellery, textiles, woodcarvings, dolls and other unique treasures. The first recorded mention of St Anthony's Guild, or the Small Guild, was in the 15th century.

**Nukumaja** TOYS
(☎504 1373; www.facebook.com/Nukumaja; Lai 1a; ⌚11am-5pm Thu & Fri, to 3pm Sat) On the side of Toomemägi, next to Tartu's version of the Addams Family house, this sweet, small store sells handmade dolls and toys for the young and young-at-heart.

**Raamatukauplus Krisostomus** BOOKS
(☎744 0010; www.kriso.ee; Raekoja plats 11; ⌚10am-6pm Mon-Fri) On the main square, this excellent bookshop offers plenty of English-language and academic titles (it's on the former site of Tartu University's bookshop).

## Information

**Raekoja Apteek** (☎742 3560; www.apotheka.ee; Raekoja plats 1a; ⌚24hr) Twenty-four-hour pharmacy within the town hall.

**Tartu Tourist Information Centre** (Tartu Külastuskeskus; ☎744 2111; www.visittartu.com; Town Hall, Raekoja plats; ⌚9am-6pm Mon-Fri, 10am-5pm Sat & Sun mid-May–mid-Sep, shorter hours rest of year; 📶) On the ground floor of the town hall.

## Getting There & Away

### AIR

**Tartu Airport** (Ulenurme Airport; ☎605 8888; www.tartu-airport.ee; Lennu tn 44, Reola) is 12km south of the city centre but the only scheduled flights are daily Finnair services to and from Helsinki.

### BUS

Regional and international (p179) buses run by multiple operators depart from **Tartu Bus Station** (Tartu Autobussijaam; Turu 2, enter from Soola; ⌚6am-9pm), next to the Tasku shopping centre.

Major domestic routes:

**Kuressaare** €18 to €22, 5¾ hours, two daily
**Otepää** €2 to €4, one hour, 10 daily
**Pärnu** €9 to €14, 2¾ hours, nine daily
**Tallinn** €8 to €15, 2½ hours, at least every half-hour
**Viljandi** €4 to €6, 1¼ hours, at least hourly

### CAR & MOTORCYCLE

Tartu Airport isn't busy enough to warrant permanent car-hire offices, but cars can be collected and returned there by prior arrangement with the following companies:

**Avis** (☎744 0360; www.avis.ee)
**Budget** (☎528 8824; www.budget.ee)
**City Car** (☎523 9669; www.citycar.ee)
**Europcar** (☎522 2995; www.europcar.ee)
**Hertz** (☎506 9065; www.hertz.ee)

### TRAIN

Tartu's beautifully restored wooden **train station** (☎5854 3844; www.elron.ee; Vaksali 6), built in 1876, is 1.5km southwest of Old Town at the end of Kuperjanovi street. Six express (two-hour) and four regular (2½-hour) services head to Tallinn daily (both €13, buying tickets on board), and there are also four trains a day to Sangaste (€4.30, one hour) and Valga (€5.10, 70 minutes).

## Getting Around

### BICYCLE

Bikes are a very pleasant way to explore compact Tartu, and can be rented from **Kauplas Jalgratas** (☎742 1731; www.kauplusjalgratas.ee; Laulupeo 21; per day €14; ⌚10am-6pm Mon-Fri, to 2pm Sat).

### BUS

Tartu is easily explored on foot but there are also 15 local bus lines. Fares are collected by swiping electronic bus cards (available from R-Kiosk outlets) or contactless bank cards against on-board validators. A one-hour ticket costs €0.83, or €2 if bought from the bus driver in cash. One-day tickets cost €2.11, but you need a minimum of €2.75 credit on your card to buy one.

### CAR

Parking in the city is metered from 8am to 6pm Monday to Friday and through the weekends in July; buy a day ticket from www.parkimine.ee (€5 to €7.50) or pay by the hour at a machine (€0.50 to €1.50).

### TAXI

Local taxi companies include **Takso Üks** (☎742 0000; www.taksod.ee; flagfall €2.80, per km €0.65) and **Tartu Taksopark** (☎730 0200; www.gotaksopark.ee; flagfall €2.95, per km €0.69).

## Setomaa

In the far southeast of Estonia, stretching into Russia, lies the distinct region of Setomaa, where the majority of the world's 15,000-odd Setos live. Culturally it's quite distinct from the rest of Estonia, distinguished by Orthodox Christianity, unique traditional dress, a highly local cuisine and the living Seto language – controversially classified a dialect of Estonian. Add natural beauty and charming farms and villages, and it's a tiny corner of this tiny country well worth exploring.

### Sights & Activities

**★Vastseliina Episcopal Castle** CASTLE

(Vastseliina piiskopilinnus; ☎509 6301; www.vastseliinalinnus.ee; Vana-Vastseliina; museum & castle adult/student €9/7, castle only €3; ⏰10am-6pm daily Jun-Aug, 10am-6pm Wed-Sun Sep, Apr & May, 11am-4pm Tue-Sat Nov-Mar; Ⓟ) Strikingly set on a bluff above the Piusa River in western Setomaa, the photogenic ruins of one of Estonia's greatest medieval strongholds and places of pilgrimage are well worth seeking out. Basic entry allows you to explore the grounds and the walls and three towers that still stand, but a little extra opens access to the medieval theme park and pilgrim house, for activities, re-creations of medieval life and labour, and insights into the pains and pleasures of pilgrimage.

Founded in 1342 by the German Livonian knights on what was the border with Russia, Vastseliina (or Neuhausen, as it was then known) was once the strongest castle in Old Livonia. It prospered from its position on the Pihkva–Rīga trade route and as an important pilgrimage site due to the presence of a miraculous white cross that conveniently materialised in the chapel. The castle was finally destroyed after falling to the Russians in 1700, early in the Great Northern War.

Just outside the castle walls you can visit a small chapel and an old stone building housing a **handicrafts store** and **tavern**, open 10am to 6pm June to Augus and serving 'medieval-inspired' cuisine in a suitably rough-hewn wooden setting.

Vastseliina is also the starting point for a 15km **hiking trail**, which heads across country to the village of Lindora.

Buses head to Vana-Vastseliina from Võru (€2, one hour, four daily) and Obinitsa (€1, 20 minutes, three daily).

**Seto Farm Museum** MUSEUM

(Värska Talumuuseum; ☎505 4673; www.setomuuseum.ee; Pikk 56, Värska; adult/student €5/2; ⏰10am-6pm Tue-Sat, to 4pm Sun & Mon Jun-Aug, 10am-4pm Tue-Sat Sep-May; Ⓟ) Presided over by a wooden carving of the god/king Peko, this museum consists of a 19th-century farmhouse complex, with stables, a granary and the former workshops for metalworking and ceramics. Don't bypass the charming restaurant here or the excellent gift shop – Setomaa's best – selling handmade mittens, socks, hats, dolls, tapestries, books and recordings of traditional Seto music.

**Obinitsa Seto Museum** MUSEUM

(Obinitsa Seto muuseumitarõ; ☎5622 7732; www.setomuuseum.ee; Obinitsa; adult/student €5/2; ⏰10am-6pm Tue-Sat, to 4pm Sun & Mon Jun-Aug, 10am-4pm Tue-Sat Sep-May; Ⓟ) With locally woven textiles in traditional patterns, everyday artefacts from Seto households, presentations on Seto music and folklore, and interesting ethnographic photos, this one-room museum in a log-built cabin provides a window into the Seto world. It's also a good place to pick up tourist brochures.

**Piusa Caves** MINE

(Piusa Koopad; ☎5304 4120; www.piusa.ee; Piusa; adult/student €5/3; ⏰11am-6pm daily Jun-Aug, noon-4pm Mon-Fri, to 5pm Sat & Sun Sep, noon-4pm Sat & Sun Oct-Apr; Ⓟ) Sitting on a band of sandstone nearly 500m thick, Piusa was the site of a major quarry from 1922 to 1966 when it was discovered that the stone contained 99% quartz and was perfect for glass production. The result is a 22km network of cathedral-like hand-hewn caves. Tours into the cave entrance are included in entry to the flash turf-roofed visitor centre.

**Meremäe Hill Lookout** VIEWPOINT

(Meremäe vaatetorn; Kalatsova) In such a flat country, even a modest 204m hill can become a high point. At Meremäe there's a four-storey wooden viewing tower, allowing views over pretty much all of Setomaa on clear days.

### Festivals & Events

**Seto Kingdom Day** CULTURAL

(www.visitsetomaa.ee; ⏰Aug) According to tradition, the Seto god/king Peko sleeps night and day in his cave of sand near Pechory. So on Seto Kingdom Day – the first Saturday in August – the Seto gather somewhere in their district to appoint an *ülemtsootska* (regent).

## THE SETO WAY

Setomaa's native people, the Setos, have a culture that incorporates a mix of Old Estonian and Russian traditions. Like the Estonians they are of Finno-Ugric origin, but the people became Orthodox, not Lutheran, because this part of the country fell under the sway of Russian Novgorod and Pihkva, not the German barons who controlled the rest of Estonia.

The Seto never fully assimilated into Russian culture, and throughout the centuries retained their language, many features of which are actually closer in structure to Old Estonian than the modern Estonian language (Seto is the spelling in the local language; northern Estonians use Setu). The same goes for certain pagan traditions that linger; for instance, leaving food on a relative's grave – this was a common Estonian practice before the German crusaders brought Christianity on the point of a sword.

All of Setomaa was contained within independent Estonia between 1920 and 1940, but the greater part of it is now in Russia. The town of **Pechory** (Petseri in Estonian), 2km across the border in Russia and regarded as the 'capital' of Setomaa, is famed for its fabulous 15th-century **monastery**, considered one of the most breathtaking in Russia.

While a federation of Estonian Seto villages known as the Seto Congress elects a representative Council of Elders every three years, Seto culture looks to be in slow decline. Efforts have been made to teach and preserve the language, and promote customs through organised feasts, but the younger generation is being quickly assimilated into the Estonian mainstream. The impenetrable border with Russia that has split their community since 1991 has further crippled it.

There are 12,600 Seto speakers in Estonia, with only around 3000 of these still residing in Estonian Setomaa. As Setos on the Russian side of the border are entitled to Estonian citizenship based on the pre-USSR border, almost all of the Russian Setos have chosen to move to Estonia. It's estimated that fewer than 200 remain on the Russian side of the border, meaning that many now require a passport to visit the churches and graves of their ancestors.

A closer look at Setomaa reveals its dissimilarity to the rest of Estonia. Notably, Seto villages are structured like castles, with houses facing each other in clusters, often surrounded by a fence. This is in stark contrast to the typical Estonian village, where farmhouses are positioned as far as possible from each other. Here, the Orthodox tradition has fostered a tighter sense of community and sociability.

Aside from the large silver breastplate that is worn on the women's national costume, what sets the Seto apart is their singing style, particularly the female folk singers who improvise new words each time they chant their verses. Seto songs, known as *leelo*, are polyphonic and characterised by solo, spoken verses followed by a refrain chanted by a chorus. There is no musical accompaniment and the overall effect evokes great antiquity.

A cult of Peko, a pagan harvest god, has managed to coexist alongside the Orthodox religion, although the Seto tend to refer to him more as a kingly figure. The 8000-line Seto epic *Pekolanõ* tells the tale of this macho god, the rites of whom are known only to men. The epic dates back to 1927 when the Setos' most celebrated folk singer, Anne Vabarna, was told the plot and spontaneously burst into song, barely pausing to draw breath until she had sung the last (8000th) line.

Information on the region can be found online at www.setomaa.ee and www.visitsetomaa.ee.

With Seto dancing, food, crafts and singing, this colourful event is as fascinating as it is kooky.

**Feast of the Transfiguration** RELIGIOUS
(19 Aug) Every August, hundreds of Setos come to Obinitsa for a procession from the church to the neighbouring cemetery, which has been a place of burial for over 1800 years (long before the Christian invasion). It ends with a communal graveyard picnic featuring lots of apples and honey, and the leaving of food on graves for the departed souls.

### Sleeping & Eating

**Hirvemäe Holiday Park** GUESTHOUSE €€
(Hirvemäe puhkekeskus; 797 6105; Silla 6, Värska; s/d from €33/57; P) Tucked away on a southward-reaching arm of Lake Peipsi,

immediately right after the bridge into Värska, this attractive guesthouse offers both pastel-painted, wood-floored rooms and space to pitch tents. The broad grounds encompass a tiny beach, tennis courts, minigolf, sauna and playground; breakfast is a generous buffet; and the cafe does simple soups, salads and mains.

**Seto Teahouse** SETO €
(Seto Tsäimaja; ☎505 4673; www.setomuuseum.ee; Pikk 56, Värska; mains €5-7; ⏲11am-7pm Tue-Sat, to 5pm Sun & Mon Jun-Aug, 11am-5pm Tue-Sat Sep-May; P 📶) This traditional log cabin makes an unbeatable setting for a Seto home-cooked meal. The hearty fare is nothing fancy – cold Seto soup; fried fish; chicken with apple and onion sauce – but it's an atmospheric delight, especially when warm weather permits lunch on the outdoor terrace overlooking the farm and its 19th-century outbuildings.

**Taarka Tarõ Köögikõnõ** SETO €
(☎5620 3374; www.taarkatare.com; Seto Seltsimaja, Obinitsa; mains €8-9; ⏲10am-8pm May-Sep; P 📶) Set within the low-ceilinged, rough-timbered, colourfully draped space of Obinitsa's Seto community centre, this casual place serves traditional Seto dishes, such as milky, cold soup with tomatoes, gherkins, lettuce and cucumber. You can also buy locally made handicrafts and Seto foods such as *sõir* (a fortified cheese) to take away.

## ℹ Information

The **Setomaa Tourist Information** (☎562 1268; www.visitsetomaa.ee; Pikk 12, Värska; ⏲8.30am-4.30pm Mon-Fri, 10am-2pm Sat) office is in Värska.

## ℹ Getting There & Away

Setomaa is an area that is most profitably explored by car or bike. However, several operators run buses to Värska from Tartu (€4 to €7, 1¾ hours, up to five daily) and Tallinn (€14, 4¼ hours with transfer at Tartu, several daily connections possible). From Võru there are buses to both Obinitsa (€2, 45 minutes, two daily) and Meremäe (€2, one hour, two daily).

# Võru

POP 11,859

Set on Lake Tamula, Võru has a mix of wooden 19th-century buildings (many of which are quite run-down) and some painfully ugly Soviet-era ones. The sandy shoreline is the town's best feature; it's been spruced up with a new promenade and attracts plenty of beachgoers in summer.

Võru was founded in 1784 by special decree from Catherine the Great, though archaeological finds here date back several thousand years. Its most famous resident, however, was neither a tribesman nor a tsarina, but the writer Friedrich Reinhold Kreutzwald (1803–82), known as the father of Estonian literature for his folk epic *Kalevipoeg*.

## 👁 Sights

**Dr F R Kreutzwald Memorial Museum** MUSEUM
(Dr Fr R Kreutzwaldi memoriaalmuuseum; ☎782 1798; www.lauluisa.ee; Kreutzwaldi 31; adult/reduced €3/2; ⏲10am-6pm Wed-Sun Apr-Oct, to 5pm Oct-Mar) Võru's most interesting museum is the house where Dr Kreutzwald, the physician and scholar who compiled Estonia's national epic *Kalevipoeg*, lived and worked as a doctor from 1833 to 1877. Built

### ℹ RUSSIAN BORDER

The official crossing point with Russia in this area is at Koidula, immediately north of Pechory (Estonian: Petseri), but Setomaa is littered with abandoned control points, seemingly unguarded wooden fences and creepy dead ends with lonely plastic signs. One road, from Värska to Saatse, even crosses the zigzagging border into Russian territory for 2km; you're not allowed to stop on this stretch. On any road close to the border you may be inspected, especially if you stop.

Be aware that crossing the border at any unofficial point (even if you have a Russian visa) is illegal and could lead to your arrest. It was in this vicinity that an Estonian security officer was controversially arrested by Russian troops in late 2014 and sentenced to 15 years in prison for spying. Estonia maintains that he was kidnapped from the Estonian side of the border, while Russia insists he was arrested on the Russian side. Just don't take any risks.

in 1793, it's one of the oldest houses in town, with a lovely garden at the rear. Displays cover the doctor's life and career focusing, naturally, on his lasting achievement: the construction of *Kalevipoeg* ('The Son of Kalev', 1861), from his deep research of Estonian folk tales.

**Võru County Museum** MUSEUM
(Võrumaa muuseum; ☎782 4479; www.vorumuuseum.ee; Katariina allee 11; adult/reduced €3/2; ⊙11am-7pm Wed-Sun May-Aug, to 6pm Sep-Apr) Don't be put off by this museum's ugly exterior – its exhibits on regional history and culture from the Stone Age to the present day are definitely worth an idle hour. Captions are in Estonian and Russian, but an English translation booklet is provided. There's also a gallery that displays temporary exhibitions of mainly local art.

**St Catherine's Orthodox Church** CHURCH
(Ekaterina kirik; Lembitu 1a; ⊙4-7pm Sat, 7-11am Sun May-Sep) Like its nearby Lutheran contemporary, Võru's main Orthodox church is dedicated to St Catherine as a nod to the town's founder, Russian Empress Catherine the Great. Completed in 1804, its elegant neoclassical design is topped with distinctly Russian-looking curved steeples. Inside there's a beautiful iconostasis and the remains of Nikolai Bežanitski, a priest killed by the Bolsheviks, who is now honoured as a martyr by the Russian Orthodox Church.

**St Catherine's Lutheran Church** CHURCH
(Katariina kirik; Jüri 9) Dedicated to the early Christian martyr Catherine but named in honour of Tsarina Catherine the Great (whose largesse paid for it), Võru's main Lutheran church was completed in 1793, only nine years after the town was founded. The pyramid over the lintel is a symbol of the Holy Trinity. On the neighbouring square there's a granite monument to 17 locals who lost their lives in the 1994 Estonia ferry disaster (p164).

## Festivals & Events

**Võru Folklore Festival** CULTURAL
(Võru Folkloorifestival; www.vorufolkloor.ee; ⊙Jul) This mid-July festival is the biggest and brightest event on the local calendar – five days full of dancers, singers and musicians decked out in colourful traditional dress.

### SOUTH ESTONIAN LANGUAGES

Visitors may notice a quite different, choppier-sounding language spoken in the southeastern corner of Estonia. Until the end of the 19th century, the Northern and Southern Estonian languages flourished quite independently of each other. Then, in the interests of nationalism, a one-country, one-language policy was adopted, and the dominant Northern Estonian became the country's main language.

Within the Southern Estonian strand there are several distinct language groupings, the largest by far of which is Võro, spoken by around 75,000 native speakers, most of whom live in Võrumaa (Võru County). It's very closely related to Seto, which has an additional 12,500 speakers. Other variants include the Mulgi and Tartu dialects, with 9700 and 4100 speakers respectively.

To learn more about the unique Võro language, contact the Võro Institute (www.wi.ee).

Those that register in advance can sleep on the floor of Võru City Centre School (Vabaduse 12) for just €5 per night – all sleeping material must be brought with you.

## Sleeping & Eating

**Kubija Hotel & Nature Spa** SPA HOTEL €€
(☎786 6000; www.kubija.ee; Männiku 43a; s/d/ste €69/85/135; P 📶 🏊) Tucked away on the forested shores of a lake on Võru's southern fringes, this older hotel may look a little former-Soviet from the outside, but the rooms have been freshened up, and the refurbished spa centre is one of the best in Estonia. Brave locals socialise in the outdoor sauna houses before taking a bracing dip in the lake.

**Spring Cafe** CAFE €€
(☎782 2777; www.springcafe.ee; Petseri 20; mains €11-13; ⊙11.30am-7pm Mon-Sat; P 📶) If you're hankering for something a little less pubby, a little more cafe-bar, this slick lakeside spot should more than satisfy. It has a pretty terrace, a brick-and-timber dining room, and a loungey 2nd floor with big windows. The food's great too, with barbecued pork and chicken a speciality, alongside salads and more typical cafe fare.

## Drinking & Nightlife

**Pubi nr. 17** PUB
(785 8588; www.olle17.ee; Jüri 17; 11am-11pm Mon-Thu, to 2am Fri & Sat, to 9pm Sun; ) This convivial sports pub is a popular meeting place and drinking hole for locals, with a pool table, big-screen TV, back terrace and comprehensive pub-grub menu (mains €10 to €13).

## Shopping

**Karma** ANTIQUES
(503 1612; www.antiques.ee; Koidula 14; 10.30am-3pm Tue-Fri, 10am-2pm Sat) One of Estonia's best antiques stores and a fun place to browse, even if you already have enough WWII helmets, scythes, sleigh bells, Soviet matchbooks and wooden beer steins.

## Information

In the centre of town, the **Võrumaa Tourist Information Centre** (782 1881; www.visitvoru.ee; Jüri 12, entrance on L Koidula; 10am-5pm Mon-Fri, to 3pm Sat & Sun mid-May–mid-Sep, 10am-4pm Mon-Fri rest of year) is good for information not just on Võru, but the surrounding county.

## Getting There & Away

Run by various operators, major services stopping at **Võru Bus Station** (Võru Bussijaam; 782 1018; Vilja 2) include the following:

**Pärnu** at least €10, 3¾ hours plus transfer at Tartu, several connections possible daily

**Rõuge** €1 to €3, 25 minutes, up to 13 daily

**Tallinn** €11 to €16, 3½ to four hours, six direct daily

**Tartu** €3 to €6, 1½ hours, up to 16 daily

**Valga** €4.50, 1½ hours, daily

# Haanja Nature Park

With 169 sq km of thick forests, sparkling lakes and meandering rivers, this protected area south of Võru encompasses some of the most delightful scenery in the country.

The charming village of **Rõuge** sits among rolling hills on the edge of the gently sloping Ööbikuorg (Nightingale Valley), named for the birds that gather here in the spring for the avian version of the songfest. Seven small lakes are strung out along the ancient valley floor, including Estonia's deepest lake, Suurjärv (Great Lake, 38m), in the middle of the village; it's said to have healing properties. Linnamägi, the hill above Linnjärv (Town Lake), was an Estonian stronghold during the 8th to 11th centuries. In the 13th century the ailing travelled from afar to see a healer called Rõugetaja, who lived here. There's a good view across the valley from the hill (accessed from behind the Nightingale Valley Centre).

## Sights

**Luhasoo Nature Reserve** NATURE RESERVE
(Luhasoo maastikukaitseala) Set in untouched swampland straddling the border with Latvia (just outside the boundaries of Haanja Nature Park), this 800-hectare reserve encompasses Estonia's largest integral bog, providing a fascinating glimpse into the country's pre-human past. A well-marked 4.5km trail passes over varied bogs and along a shimmering black lake, with Venus flytraps and water lilies among the foliage. You might spot elk and deer but the most you're likely to see of wolves, bears and lynx is their tracks.

**Suur Munamägi** VIEWPOINT
(www.suurmunamagi.ee; entry via stairs adult/child €4/3, elevator €6; tower 10am-8pm Apr-Aug, to 5pm Sep & Oct, noon-3pm Sat & Sun Nov-Mar; P) Mentioned in the Estonian creation epic *Kalevipoeg*, the modest 318m-high Suur Munamägi ('Great Egg Hill') is the highest peak in the Baltics (although the tree-covered 'summit' is easy to miss if you're not looking sharp). Crack the Great Egg with an ascent of its 29m observation tower, built in 1939 – on a clear day you can see Tartu's TV towers, the onion domes of the Russian town of Pihkva (Pskov) and lush forests stretching out in every direction.

**St Mary's Lutheran Church** CHURCH
(Maarja kirik; Haanja mnt 10, Rõuge; 9am-3pm Thu-Sun Jun-Aug) Rõuge's whitewashed stone church dates from 1730, replacing a 16th-century church destroyed in the Great Northern War. Inside, the focal point is the altar painting *Christ on the Cross* by Rudolf von zur Mülen (1854), framed by a neoclassical relief. Outside there's a monument to the local dead of the 1918–20 independence war, buried in a backyard throughout Soviet times to save it from destruction.

## Sleeping & Eating

If you want to base yourself in the park, Rõuge is your best bet.

**Ööbikuoru Puhkekeskus** CAMPGROUND €
(521 8784; www.visit.ee; Ööbikuoru 5, Rõuge; sites per adult/child €5/2, cabins per person €10-16,

OFF THE BEATEN TRACK

### KARULA NATIONAL PARK

Fairies, ghosts and witches abound in the 123 sq km of wooded hills, small lakes and ancient stone burial mounds that form **Karula National Park** (Karula Rahvuspark; https://loodusegakoos.ee), at least according to local folklore. At its centre is Ähijärv, a beautiful lake ringed with trees and reeds, which has been considered holy since pagan times. The park's lakeside **visitor centre** (782 8350; Ähijärve Village; 10am-6pm daily mid-May–mid-Sep, to 4pm Wed-Fri mid-May–mid-Sep) distributes information and maps for various walking trails, and the long (38km) and short (15km) cycling trails. The Suuremäe campsite is adjacent.

It takes about 90 minutes to loop along the northern end of the lake and through forest and meadows on the blissful 4km-long **Ähijärv Trail**; keep an eye out for woodpeckers and native orchids.

The park is bisected by a partly unsealed road leading from Mõniste village in the south to the town of Antsla in the north.

house €120; P) Set in a lovely spot overlooking Nightingale Valley, this outfit offers lodging in simple wooden cabins, tent sites and self-contained houses (sleeping up to six). Rowboats (per hour €4), canoes (€4) and bikes (€2) are available to rent and there's a sauna heated by an old locomotive (€70 per heating cycle). It's 600m from the main road, signposted as you head south.

**★Ööbikuoru Villa** HOTEL €€
(509 9666; www.oruvilla.ee; Tiida, Rõuge; d/ste €78/148, mains €12-14; P) Spread between two neighbouring buildings overlooking a small lake, this is our top pick in Rõuge for both a bed and a bite. Don't be fooled by the fussy antique-style furniture – the rooms are as comfortable and modern as you could wish for, with lake views and Jacuzzis in the suites. Downstairs, Cafe Andreas serves catfish, pike-perch, duck and other delights.

Boats (€5 per hour) and bikes (€2) are available for hire.

**Rõuge Suurjärve Külalistemaja** GUESTHOUSE €€
(524 3028; www.maremajutus.ee; Metsa 5, Rõuge; d/tr €45/65; P) This cheery, yellow, family-run guesthouse has views over the valley from its pretty garden and 16 inviting, fuss-free rooms (most with private bathroom, some with TV, a few with balcony). Accepting only cash, it also offers a sauna (€50 for three hours), bike rental (€3 per hour) and camping (€3 per person).

## Information

Stock up on maps and information about the park's multifarious hiking and cross-country skiing opportunities from the **Nightingale Valley Centre** (Ööbikuorg Keskus; 785 9245; Rõuge; 10am-6pm mid-May–Aug) in Rõuge or the tourist offices in Võru, Otepää or Tartu. Just off the Rõuge–Haanja road, overlooking the lakes around which Rõuge clusters, the Nightingale Valley Centre also has a handicrafts store, a shop selling locally made food, an experimental 'ancient farm' (built by archaeology students using Iron Age methods), and a 30m-high observation tower offering lovely perspectives over the surrounding country.

## Getting There & Away

There are buses from Võru to Haanja village (€0.80, 25 minutes, up to six daily) and Rõuge (€0.80, 25 minutes, up to nine daily).

# Valga

POP 12,182

Contested between Estonia and Latvia after WWI, Valga was split down the middle at the recommendation of a British mediator. As a result, as you wander around the town centre you'll find yourself passing in and out of Valga and Valka (as the Latvian side is known). Mercifully there are no longer checkpoints (cheers, Schengen!), although you should really carry your passport with you. The local authorities cooperate on important stuff like tourist information and bus services.

Valga is enjoying a slow process of gentrification, but its old wooden houses and parks are still skirted by some grim industrial areas. However, its bloody wartime history makes it an interesting place for a brief stop before moving on. Although there are some large military bunkers and war cemeteries on the Valka side, most items of interest are on the Estonian side of the border.

## Sights

**Valga Museum** MUSEUM
(☎766 8861; www.valgamuuseum.ee; Vabaduse 8; adult/reduced €3/1.50; ⏰11am-6pm Tue-Fri, 10am-3pm Sat) Housed in a handsome art nouveau building that dates to 1911, and has served as both a theatre and a bank, this museum focuses on the local area, with displays on natural history, archaeology, Soviet-era deportations, everyday Soviet life and local hero Alfred Neuland, winner of the gold for weightlifting at the 1920 Olympic Games. Most captions are in Estonian, but there are booklets with English translations. There's also an attached gallery, with modest exhibitions on rotation.

**St John's Lutheran Church** CHURCH
(Jaani kirik; ☎566 16497; Kesk 23; ⏰noon-5pm Wed Jun-Aug, by prior arrangement other times) Built in 1816, St John's in Valga holds the distinction of being the only oval-plan church in Estonia. Its other claim to fame is a rare 19th-century organ, the work of famed German organ-builder Friedrich Ladegast, and still in working order.

**Valga Prison Camp Cemetery** MEMORIAL
(Roheline tänav) An estimated 29,000 Russians died at the Nazi POW camp Stalag-351, which was located in converted stables at Priimetsa on Valga's outskirts. Most died of starvation, cold and disease. Nothing remains of the camp, but a simple, moving monument known as the *Mourning Mother* is located close by. The Soviets took over the camp in 1944 and held German POWs here, 300 of whom are buried among the firs in an official war cemetery nearby.

## Sleeping & Eating

**Metsis** HOTEL €€
(☎766 6050; www.hotellmetsis.com; Kuperjanovi 63; s/d from €55/68, mains €12-14; P ☎) Set on large lawns, this 1912 hotel is Valga's best sleeping option, with 18 pleasant, well-priced rooms, some of which have their own sauna (per hour €20) and Jacuzzi. If you can ignore the hunting trophies staring glassily from the walls, the downstairs restaurant is also very good.

**Voorimehe Pubi** PUB FOOD €
(☎767 9627; www.voorimehepubi.ee; Kuperjanovi 57; mains €7-9; ⏰noon-10pm Mon-Thu, to 3am Fri & Sat, to 9pm Sun; P ☎) On a main road leading east from central Valga, this no-frills, wood-lined pub serves cheap, filling and tasty plates of salmon, schnitzel, pork and the like. DJs spin on the weekend (entry €3 to €5).

## Information

The **Tourist Office** (☎766 1699; www.valgamaa.ee; Kesk 11; ⏰10am-5pm Mon-Fri mid-May–mid-Sep, 10am-4pm Mon-Fri, to 2pm Sat & Sun mid-Sep–mid-May) is on the ground floor of Valga's handsome town hall.

## Getting There & Away

**Valga Bus & Railway Station** (☎512 0295; Jaama pst 10) is a couple of blocks southeast of the town centre.

### BUS

International coaches head here from Russia and Latvia. Major domestic destinations, served by multiple operators:

**Otepää** €3.30, one hour, up to seven daily
**Pärnu** €10, 2½ hours, daily
**Tallinn** €14, four hours, four daily
**Tartu** €6 to €7, 1¾ hours, up to seven daily
**Viljandi** €6.50 to €7.20, 1¾ hours, six daily

### TRAIN

Valga's historic station is the terminus for both the Estonian and Latvian rail systems; you'll have to change trains here if you're heading, say, between Tartu and Rīga (p180). On the Estonian side there are four direct services a day to and from Tartu (€5.10, 70 minutes).

# Sangaste

POP 245

Sangaste is known as the 'Rye Capital of Estonia', which in such a rye-crazy nation is quite an honour. This is largely due to the efforts of the Baltic-German nobleman Friedrich Georg Magnus von Berg (1854–1938), who became known as the 'Rye Count' due to his successful efforts in developing a strain that is now grown throughout the world.

Visiting Sangaste Castle, the 19th-century house that rye built, is the town's highlight.

## Sights

**Sangaste Castle** HISTORIC BUILDING
(Sangaste Loss; ☎529 5911; www.sangasteloss.ee; Lossiküla; adult/student €5/3; ⏰10am-6pm; P) British castle-spotters might experience déjà vu gazing on this majestic red-brick manor house, with its architectural debts to Windsor and Balmoral castles. Completed in 1881 as the home of the 'Rye Count' Friedrich von

Berg, it's regarded as one of the prime examples of Gothic-Revival architecture in the Baltics. History has taken its toll, but visitors can explore the impressive octagonal ballroom and head up a precarious set of stairs to the roof of the tower.

**St Andrew's Lutheran Church** CHURCH
(⏲noon-1.30pm Sun May-Aug) It's thought that the name Sangaste might derive from the Latin phrase *Sanguis Christi* (Blood of Christ), referring to a relic kept in Sangaste's original 13th-century church. The current building dates from 1742, with its baroque gable tower added in 1873. The interior is relatively plain, although it's worth noting the starry sky over the sanctuary and the Calvary scene above the altar, painted in Munich in 1883.

## Eating

**Sangaste Rye House** ESTONIAN €
(Sangaste Rukki Maja; ☎766 9323; www.rukki-maja.ee; Valga mnt 11; mains €8-9; ⏲11am-9pm; P❄📶) This cosy restaurant celebrates Sangaste's 'Rye Capital' status with a menu of southern Estonian cuisine featuring the grain prominently. There's delicious rye bread, of course, plus rye pancakes with smoked salmon, rye-and-cheese-coated schnitzel and plenty of other soups, salads and mains. Upstairs, the 12 tidy, comfortable rooms are very reasonably priced (single/double €39/49).

## Getting There & Away

There's no bus station, but there are daily buses to and from the following destinations:

**Otepää** €2, 30 minutes, five daily
**Tallinn** €11 to €17, 4½ to 5½ hours with transfer in Tartu or Valga, several possible connections daily
**Tartu** €5, 1½ hours, three daily
**Valga** €2.20, 30 minutes, five daily

# Otepää

POP 2124

The small hilltop town of Otepää, 44km south of Tartu, is the centre of a picturesque area of forests, lakes and rivers. The district is beloved by Estonians for its natural beauty and its many possibilities for hiking, biking and swimming in summer, and cross-country skiing in winter. It's often referred to as Estonia's winter capital, and winter weekends here are busy and loads of fun. Some have even dubbed the area (tongue firmly in cheek) the 'Estonian Alps' – a reference not to its peaks but to its excellent Nordic ski trails. The 63km ski marathon kicks off here every February but even in summer you'll see professional athletes and enthusiasts hurtling around on roller skis.

The main part of Otepää is centred on the intersection of the Tartu, Võru and Valga highways, where you'll find the main square, shops and some patchy residential streets.

## Sights

**Pühajärv** LAKE
(Pühajärve) According to legend, 3.5km-long, 8.5m-deep Pühajärv (Holy Lake) was formed from the tears of the mothers who lost their sons in a battle of the *Kalevipoeg* epic. Its five islands are said to be their burial mounds. Pagan associations linger, with major midsummer festivities held here every year. The popular sandy **beach** (Ranna tee) on the northeastern shore has water slides, a swimming pontoon, a cafe and lifeguards in summer.

**Otepää Hill Fort** RUINS
(Otepää Linnamägi) The pretty tree-covered hill south of the church was an ancient Estonian stronghold for around 800 years before it was topped by an episcopal castle in 1224. Known as the 'Bear's Head' *(oti pää)*, it's from this that the town takes its name. Remnants of the fortifications remain on the top along with wonderful views of the surrounding valleys. The castle was largely destroyed in 1396 in a battle between the Bishop of Tartu and the Livonian Order.

**St Mary's Lutheran Church** CHURCH
(Maarja Luteri kirik; ⏲11am-5pm Tue-Sat, 10am-12.30pm Sun Jun-Aug, by appointment Sep-May) Otepää's Gothic hilltop church dates from 1671, although it was largely reconstructed in 1890. Inside there's intricate woodwork, low-hanging chandeliers and an impressive crucifixion scene (1880) above the altar. It was here in 1884 that the Estonian Students' Society consecrated its new blue, black and white flag, which later became the flag of independent Estonia. Bas reliefs flanking the gates and doors celebrate the occasion; they were originally erected in 1934, destroyed during the Soviet era and re-erected in 1989.

**Otepää Winter Sports Museum** MUSEUM
(Otepää talispordimuuseum; ☎766 9500; www.spordimuuseum.ee; Tehvandi Stadium House, Valga mnt 12; adult/reduced €3/2; ⏲11am-5pm Mon-Fri

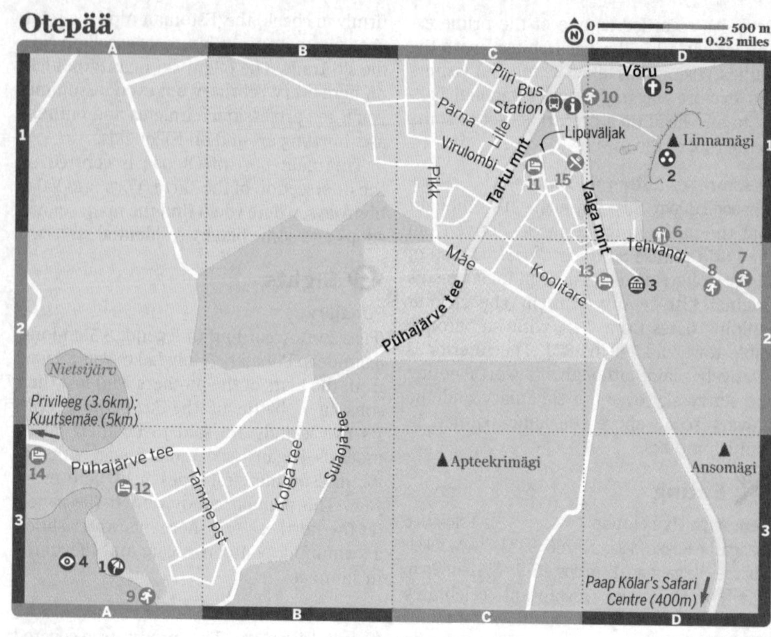


## Otepää

**Sights**

1 Beach ........ A3
2 Otepää Hill Fort ........ D1
3 Otepää Winter Sports Museum ........ D2
4 Pühajärv ........ A3
5 St Mary's Lutheran Church ........ D1

**Activities, Courses & Tours**

6 Fan-Sport ........ D1
7 Otepää Forest Adventure Park ........ D2
8 Tehvandi Sports Centre ........ D2
9 Veesõidukite Laenutus ........ A3
10 VeeTee ........ D1

**Sleeping**

11 Edgari Külalistemaja ........ C1
12 GMP Clubhotel ........ A3
13 Murakas ........ D2
14 Pühajärve Spa & Holiday Resort ........ A3

**Eating**

Edgari Pood ........ (see 11)
Pühajärve Pub ........ (see 14)
Pühajärve Restaurant ........ (see 12)
15 Ugandi Resto ........ C1

& big-event weekends) Big, flash Tehvandi Stadium, used for football and ski events, is a testimony to Otepää's obsession with sport. Within the bowels of the main stand, this two-room museum displays equipment, costumes and medals belonging to some of Estonia's most famous winter athletes.

## Activities

The tourist office has maps and information on hiking, cycling and skiing trails, which range from short and kid-focused to a 20km ordeal. Staff can also provide information on the numerous activities on offer in the region, including horse riding, Frisbee golf, regular golf, snowtubing, sleigh rides and snowmobile safaris.

For cross-country skiing, the closest trails start on the edge of town near Tehvandi Sports Centre. You can also find some good trails near Lake Kääriku.

If you're considering a canoeing or rafting trip, call at least a day or two ahead of time. Operators will pick you up from your hotel, take you to the river and drop you back afterwards.

**Tehvandi Sports Centre** OUTDOORS
(Tehvandi Spordikeskus; ☎766 9500; www.tehvandi.ee; Tehvandi; ski training track per day €6, ski jumping €12, shooting €12) A former training centre for

the Soviet Winter Olympics team, Tehvandi remains a hive of exertion, including Nordic skiing, ski jumping, shooting, cycling, roller skiing and skating. There's a 34m climbing wall and viewing platform attached to the ski-jump tower (entry by lift/stairs €2/3) and you can stay in the centre's turf-covered hobbit hole of a hotel (single/double €50/65).

**Otepää Forest Adventure Park** ADVENTURE SPORTS
(Otepää seikluspark; ☎504 9783; www.seikluspark.ee; Tehvandi 3; ⊙noon-7pm Sat & Sun, with advance booking for at least 6 Mon-Fri; 👪) Explore the treetops on a high-ropes course (adult/child €22/10) or the shrubbery on the kids' adventure trail (must be 80cm to 120cm tall, €5). Alternatively, hurtle all the way to Linnamägi on a zip line (adult/child €8/6) or 20m into the air on the reverse-bungy catapult (€10).

**VeeTee** OUTDOORS
(☎506 0987; www.veetee.ee; Valga põik 2; ⊙11am-7pm Mon-Fri, 10am-8pm Sat, to 6pm Sun) Offers a range of canoeing and rafting trips along the Ahja and Võhandu Rivers, and around the small lakes of the Kooraste River valley (per person €20). It also rents skis and snowboards (from €13) and offers lessons (from €20).

**Toonus Pluss** OUTDOORS
(☎348 1215; www.toonuspluss.ee) Specialises in canoeing trips through the Ahja River valley; tailor-made expeditions can combine canoeing with hiking and mountain biking. It also rents skis and offers instruction.

**Fan-Sport** SNOW SPORTS
(☎507 7537; www.fansport.ee; Valga mnt 4; ⊙10am-7pm Mon-Fri, 9am-9pm Sat, to 5pm Sun) Operating out of the Karupesa Hotel in winter, this outfit rents cross-country skis (three hours/day €7/13), downhill skis (€10/13) and snowboards (€10/13). It can also arrange ski lessons.

**Paap Kõlar's Safari Centre** SNOW SPORTS
(Paap Kõlari Safarikeskus; ☎505 1015; http://safarikeskus.paap.ee; Kaga Farm, Nüpli Village; intro €25, safari per hour €90; ⊙Jan-Mar) Explore the winter wonderland around Otepää in a two-person snowmobile. Intro sessions are available for novices, and advance booking is required.

**Kuutsemäe** SKIING
(☎5647 1197; www.kuutsemae.ee; Arula) In cross-hill country, this resort operates six modest downhill runs – greens, blues and reds ranging from 214m to 476m. It's the area's most developed ski centre, with a tavern, accommodation (twin/triple €59/69) and a skiing and snowboarding school. A day's ski pass in winter is €23 to €26, a one-hour private lesson is €35, and there are summer activities too. It's located 14km west of Otepää at Arula.

**Veesõidukite Laenutus** BOATING
(☎5343 6359; Ranna tee 5; ⊙10am-7pm Jun-Aug) Rents rowboats (€10), canoes (€8), kayaks (€8) and pedalos (€8) from the beach on the northeastern shore of Pühajärv; all prices per hour.

## Festivals & Events

**Tartu Marathon** SPORTS
(☎7421 644; www.tartumaraton.ee; full marathon registration €60; ⊙Feb) Otepää is the starting point for this famous 63km cross-country race to Elva, held every February since 1960 and attracting over 10,000 participants. There are 31km and 16km variants for those without sufficient stamina. The same organisation hosts a range of sporting events (cycling road races, mountain-bike races, running races) in and around Tartu throughout the year.

## Sleeping

Modest hotels and guesthouses are what you'll find here. The low seasons are April to May and September to November; during these months prices are about 10% to 15% cheaper. Higher rates are charged on weekends in high season.

**Murakas** HOTEL €€
(☎731 1410; www.murakas.ee; Valga mnt 23a; s/d/tr €45/49/60; P📶) With only 10 bedrooms, Murakas is more like a large, friendly guesthouse than a hotel. Basic colours, blond wood and striped carpets give the rooms a cheerful freshness, while balconies and drying cabins are very welcome. The sauna room, including a dry sauna, steam room and tubs, is €20/30 for one/two hours.

**Pühajärve Spa & Holiday Resort** RESORT €€
(☎766 5500; www.pyhajarve.com; Pühajärve; s/d/ste from €70/85/135; P@📶🏊) The best thing about this large white complex is its location, set on lawns spreading unhindered to sparkling Lake Pühajärve, but the wonderful glassed-in pool overlooking

the lake comes a close second. Otherwise, there's still a vaguely Soviet vibe about the place and the ample rooms are somewhat spartan. Spa treatments start at €10 for a chair massage.

**Edgari Külalistemaja** GUESTHOUSE €€
(Edgar's Guesthouse; ☎5883 4005; http://edgari.otepäält.ee; Lipuväljak 3; s/d €25/50; 📶) Edgar's occupies the upstairs levels of an attractive brick building, right in the centre of town, with a bakery and tavern below. All rooms have kitchenettes and en suites, but some rooms are tiny and others are larger, with balconies. They're all priced identically, so ask for a bigger one when you're booking.

**GMP Clubhotel** HOTEL €€€
(☎501 0504; www.clubhotel.ee; Tennisevälja 1; studio from €145, ste from €160; P📶) This slick lakeside hotel offers 'apartments' and suites with kitchenettes, funky furniture and comfy beds. There's a luxurious pair of single-sex saunas on the top level, open in the evenings for those who fancy a sunset sweat, and Pühajärve Restaurant is excellent.

## Eating

**Edgari Pood** BAKERY €
(Edgar's Shop; ☎5883 4005; http://edgari.otepäält.ee; Lipuväljak 3; pastries from €1; ⊙8am-6pm Mon-Fri, 9am-3pm Sat) Causing delicious smells to rise through the attached guesthouse above, this bakery does a delightful range of sweet and savoury baking, and sells selected smallgoods and groceries.

**Pühajärve Restaurant** MODERN EUROPEAN €€
(☎799 7000; www.clubhotel.ee; Tennisevälja 1, GMP Clubhotel; mains €14-20; ⊙noon-10pm; P📶) From the 1960s to 1980s this was Otepää's most famous restaurant, but when the Soviet Union went down the gurgler it fell from fashion. The opening of the attached Clubhotel gave Pühajärve a new lease of life and it now serves ambitious dishes such as smoked pork chop with chokeberry-chilli glaze in three upscale rooms or on the summer terrace.

**Ugandi Resto** INTERNATIONAL €€
(☎652 0120; www.ugandiresto.ee; Lipuväljak 26; mains €16-20, pizzas €11-13; ⊙10am-10pm Sun-Thu, to midnight Fri & Sat; 📶) The Ugandi aims to impress, with a circular dining room adorned with geometrically flamboyant wooden fittings, uniformed staff and vaguely 'Scando' furniture. The food pretty much lives up to ambitions, although pizza is probably the most dependable and economical option.

**Pühajärve Pub** PUB FOOD €€
(☎766 5500; www.pyhajarve.com; Pühajärve Spa & Resort; mains €14-20; ⊙11am-11pm Sun-Thu, to 1am Fri & Sat; P📶🖉) The lakeside hotel's casual, all-day pub caters to everyone (kids, carnivores, the health-conscious) with an extensive menu, including eight vegetarian and vegan mains such as wok-fried chanterelles with vegetables and rice. The sunny outdoor terrace is the place to be, but the brick-lined interior, with pool tables and open fire, is not a bad wet-weather option.

**Privileeg** INTERNATIONAL €€
(☎5884 4887; www.privileeg.com; Otepää Golf Course, Mäha; mains €14-17; ⊙10am-11pm; P📶) Defying the adage that restaurants with stunning views never deliver in the kitchen, Privileeg serves delightful fare in a light-washed, glass-walled dining room overlooking the lushly vegetated contours of Otepää's golf course. Hedging its bets somewhat, it offers 'Mediterranean and New Nordic' food, which apparently means plates such as aged duck with carrot pie and berry sauce. Delicious.

## Information

**Otepää Tourist Information Centre** (☎766 1200; www.otepaa.eu; Tartu mnt 1; ⊙10am-5pm Mon-Fri, to 3pm Sat & Sun mid-May–mid-Sep, 10am-5pm Mon-Fri, to 2pm Sat rest of year; 📶) Well-informed staff distribute maps and brochures, and make recommendations for activities, guide services and lodging in the area.

## Getting There & Around

The **bus station** (Tartu mnt 1) is next to the tourist office. Destinations served by multiple companies include the following:

**Narva** €12, 3¼ hours plus transfer at Tartu, two connections per day

**Sangaste** €2, 30 minutes, six daily

**Tallinn** €10 to €15, 3¼ hours plus transfer at Tartu, several connections daily

**Tartu** €4.20, one hour, 10 daily

**Valga** €3.30, one hour, four daily

# The Southwest

The big drawcard of this corner of the country is the beach. Set on a long stretch of sand, Pärnu attracts legions of holidaymakers during the summer. Young partygoers

## Southwestern Estonia

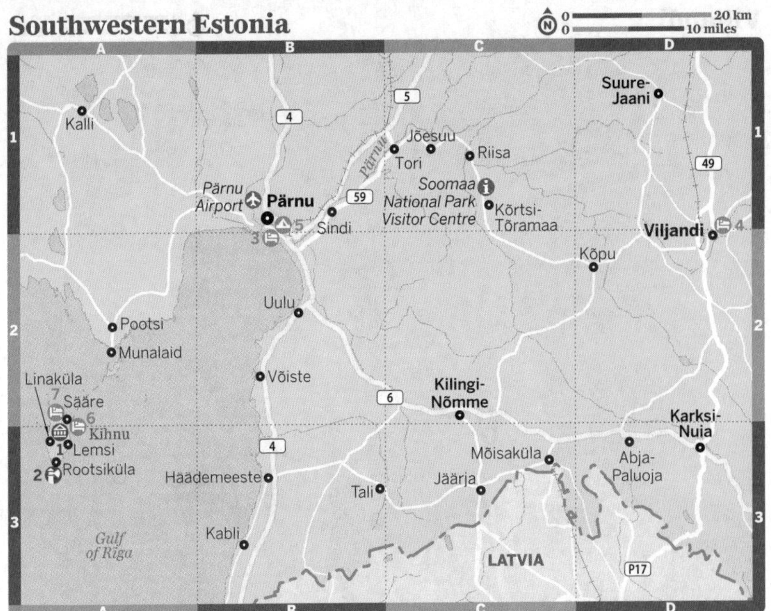


from Tallinn and Tartu head to the sands and nightclubs, just as busloads of elderly out-of-towners arrive seeking spa treatments and mud cures.

East of Pärnu stretches Soomaa National Park, a biodiverse region of meandering meadows and swamps. Viljandi lies just beyond Soomaa; it's a laid-back regional centre and a focus for things folk, especially music.

## Southwestern Estonia

**Sights**

1 Kihnu Museum ... A3
2 Kihnu Tuletorn ... A3
St Nicholas' Orthodox Church ... (see 1)

**Sleeping**

3 Embrace ... B2
4 Endla ... D1
5 Konse Motel & Camping ... B1
6 Rock City Guesthouse ... A3
7 Tolli Tourist Farm ... A2

## Viljandi

POP 17,407

One of Estonia's most charming towns, Viljandi overlooks a picturesque valley with a tranquil lake at its centre. The German Livonian Order, aka the Brothers of the Sword, founded a castle here in the 13th century. The town that grew around it later joined the Hanseatic League, but was the contested property of Swedes, Poles and Russians over the following centuries. It's now a relaxed kind of place, perfect for time-travelling rambles, with some evocative castle ruins, historic buildings and abundant greenery.

If you visit in late July, make sure your accommodation is sorted – the four-day Viljandi Folk Music Festival is the biggest annual music festival in Estonia, and many places are booked out long in advance.

### Sights

**★ Viljandi Teutonic Order Castle** CASTLE

(Viljandi ordulinnus; Lossimäed) FREE Set within a lush park on the natural defensive prominence of Lossimäed, the scant-yet-evocative remains of Viljandi's powerful castle form a picturesque set of ruins with sweeping views over the valley and lake below. Built in 1224 by the German Knights of the Sword on a series of three small hills divided by ravines, it replaced an Estonian hill fort that had stood here since the 9th century. It finally fell into disrepair after the 17th-century Polish-Swedish wars. Only perilously decayed sections of wall and crumbling

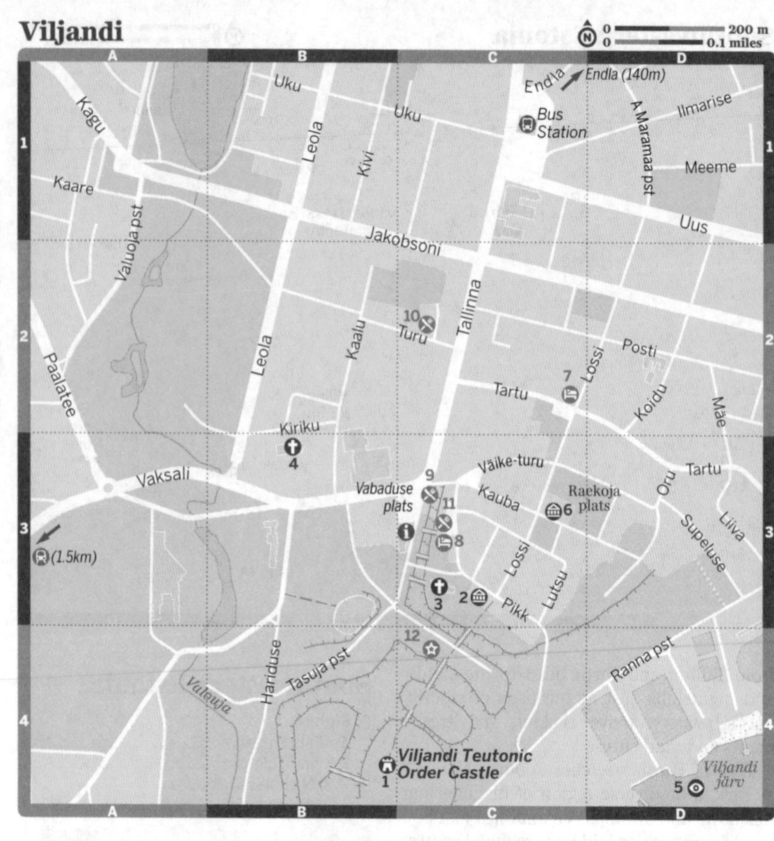


## Viljandi

**Top Sights**
1 Viljandi Teutonic Order Castle ............ B4

**Sights**
2 Kondas Centre ............ C3
3 St John's Lutheran Church ............ C3
4 St Paul's Lutheran Church ............ B3
5 Viljandi järv ............ D4
6 Viljandi Museum ............ C3

**Sleeping**
7 Grand Hotel Viljandi ............ C2
8 Hostel Ingeri ............ C3

**Eating**
Aida ............ (see 12)
9 Fellin ............ C3
10 Suur Vend ............ C2
11 Tegelaste Tuba ............ C3

**Entertainment**
12 Traditional Music Centre ............ C4

foundations remain but you get a sense of the castle's scale, and there are interesting display panels describing its layout. One of the approaches to the fortress is spanned by an elegant 50m suspension footbridge, which was built in 1879 for another set of castle ruins at Tarvastu and was only moved to this site in 1931.

A small cemetery to the rear of the castle park is the final resting place of German soldiers killed here during WWII.

**St John's Lutheran Church** CHURCH
(Jaani Kirik; Pikk 6; 10am-3pm Mon, Wed & Sun, noon-5pm Tue, 1-5pm Thu) This dignified, compellingly picturesque 17th-century church,

with its pale-grey walls and stone altar, has been restored since its Soviet incarnation as a furniture warehouse. It was originally part of a 15th-century Franciscan abbey (hence the stained-glass image of the saint to the right of the altar) and if you look closely you can spot the remains of pre-Reformation frescoes over the arch leading from the porch into the church proper.

**Kondas Centre** GALLERY
(Kondase Keskus; www.kondas.ee; Pikk 8; adult/reduced €3/2; ⏲10am-5pm Wed-Sat Jan-Mar, Wed-Sun Apr & Sep-Dec, 11am-6pm daily May-Aug) Housing vibrantly colourful works by local painter Paul Kondas (1900–85) and other self-taught artists working outside the mainstream, this is Estonia's only gallery dedicated to naïve and outsider art. It's not hard to find – in a marvellously oblique reference to the artist's 1965 work *Strawberry Eaters*, the stalks of all the giant strawberries scattered around town point here. The handsome, red-brick building is the former vicarage of adjacent St John's.

**Viljandi Museum** MUSEUM
(☎433 3316; www.muuseum.viljandimaa.ee; Laidoneri plats 10; adult/reduced €4/2; ⏲11am-6pm May-Aug, 10am-5pm Tue-Sat Sep-Apr) Occupying two floors of a late-18th-century pharmacy on the old market square, this modest museum has displays tracing Viljandi's history from the Stone Age to the mid-20th century. There are folk costumes, stuffed animals, old photos of the city, Viking-era jewellery and a mock-up of what the original castle probably looked like. English translations are limited.

**St Paul's Lutheran Church** CHURCH
(Pauluse kirik; Kiriku 5; ⏲10am-3pm Tue-Fri, to 2pm Sun) Built in 1866 to accommodate Viljandi's growing Lutheran congregation, this visually arresting, Tudor-Gothic-style church has a wooden pulpit and gallery, and a large crucifixion scene above its altar.

**Viljandi järv** LAKE
Accessed by a steep path leading down from Pikk street, the lake is a popular place for a swim on warm summer days. All the usual hallmarks of the Estonian beach are here (volleyball court, cafes, boat rental) and there's a swimming platform just offshore. Come Midsummer's Eve, it's the site of the main celebrations.

## Festivals & Events

**Hanseatic Days** CULTURAL
(http://hansa.viljandi.ee; ⏲Jun) Over a long weekend in early June, Viljandi goes retro, celebrating its past as an important Hanseatic city with food and craft markets, midnight concerts, processions and other public merriment.

**Viljandi Early Music Festival** MUSIC
(Viljandi vanamuusika festival; www.vivamu.ee; ⏲Jul) Archaic instruments and musical forms are showcased in the town's churches and concert halls over a week in mid-July.

★**Viljandi Folk Music Festival** MUSIC
(Viljandi pärimusimuusika festival; www.viljandifolk.ee; festival pass from €65; ⏲Jul) Easily the biggest event on Viljandi's calendar, this hugely popular, four-day music festival is renowned for its friendly, relaxed vibe and impressive international line-up. Estonia's largest music festival, and one of the major folk events on the European calendar, it sees Viljandi's population double in size around the last weekend of July, with over 20,000 attendees at over 100 concerts.

## Sleeping

**Hostel Ingeri** GUESTHOUSE €€
(☎5599 7115; www.hostelingeri.ee; Pikk 2c; s/d from €30/45; P 📶) On one of Viljandi's nicest streets, right among its historical and cultural highlights, this six-room guesthouse offers seriously good value with its bright, comfortable doubles, all with TVs and bathrooms. Plant life and a kitchen for guest use make it a good home-from-home, while the parkside location couldn't be better.

**Grand Hotel Viljandi** HOTEL €€
(☎435 5800; www.ghv.ee; Tartu 11; s/d €79/99; P 📶) In the centre of Viljandi's quiet old town, this moderately chi-chi hotel has 50 art deco–styled rooms with dark-wood trim, satiny chairs, large windows and wildly patterned carpets. There's a pleasant summertime cafe in front, as well as the smart à la carte Restaurant Eve (mains €16 to €18), named for the first upscale hotel in this building, opened in 1938.

**Endla** GUESTHOUSE €€
(Reinup Travel Ltd; ☎5345 7440; www.reinup.ee; Endla 9; s/d €40/50; P @ 📶) There's a vaguely Swiss feel to this little guesthouse, set on a quiet backstreet north of the bus station. The rooms are simple but smartly furnished

and as spick and span as you could ask for. There's an on-site sauna for hire (€13 for the first hour, €7 per hour thereafter).

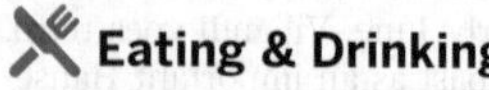

## Eating & Drinking

Dining options in Viljandi are very limited for a town of its size and status, but there are some appealing pubs.

**Suur Vend** PUB FOOD €
(☎433 3644; www.suurvend.ee; Turu 4; mains €7-9; ⏲kitchen 11am-9pm Mon-Sat, to 8pm Sun, bar longer hours; 📶) Friendly service, big portions, a pool table and upbeat options from the jukebox create a cheerful mood at 'Big Brother', a cosy pub with an undeservedly sinister name. There's an outdoor deck, lots of dark wood inside and a reasonably priced menu with plenty of beer-friendly food. Later on, live music and karaoke keep the bonhomie topped up.

**Tegelaste Tuba** PUB FOOD €
(☎433 3944; www.facebook.com/TegelasteTuba; Pikk 2b; mains €7-9; ⏲11am-11pm Sun, Mon, Wed & Thu, to 11.45pm Fri & Sat; 📶🌶👪) The terrace overlooking the park is one of this tavern's drawcards; another is the comfy interior on cold, rainy days. Estonian handicrafts enliven the red-brick walls, and a diverse crowd enjoys the wide-ranging menu of soups, salads and Russian and Estonian comfort food (dumplings and lots of pork and chicken). Note it accepts only cash.

**Fellin** CAFE €€
(☎435 9795; www.kohvikfellin.ee; Kauba 2; mains €12-14; ⏲noon-10pm Tue-Thu, to 11pm Fri & Sat, to 7pm Sun; 🅿📶) 'Local food and live music' is the mantra at this smart cafe-bar near the tourist office, which may be the best of Viljandi's dining options. The menu ranges from light snacks, salads and soups to more substantial meals (duck breast, smoked pork, steamed fish), or you can just call in for a glass of wine.

## ☆ Entertainment

**Traditional Music Centre** LIVE MUSIC
(Pärimusmuusika ait; ☎434 2050; www.folk.ee; Tasuja pst 6; ⏲9am-9pm Mon-Fri, 11am-9pm Sat, to 7pm Sun; 📶) Viljandi's reputation as Estonia's folk-music capital, resting on its annual festival, was cemented with the opening of this modern recital and cultural centre in an old brick storehouse in 2008. It's a place for study and rehearsal, has two state-of-the-art concert halls and houses an upmarket cafe (☎434 2066; www.aidakohvik.ee; mains €13-14; ⏲11am-7pm Sun & Mon, to 9pm Tue-Thu, to 11pm Fri & Sat; 📶) and record store. Call in to find out what's on.

## ℹ Information

The super-helpful **Tourist Information Centre** (☎433 0442; www.visitestonia.com; Vabaduse plats 6; ⏲10am-5pm Mon-Fri year-round, plus 10am-3pm Sat & Sun mid-May–mid-Sep; 📶) offers local maps and information on Viljandi and surrounding areas (including Soomaa National Park) in multiple languages.

## ℹ Getting There & Around

### BICYCLE

**Joosepi Jalgrattapood** (Joseph's Bicycle Shop; ☎434 5757; www.jalgrattad.eu; Kaalu 9; per hour/day €5/12; ⏲9am-6pm Mon-Fri, to 3pm Sat) offers bike hire and service.

### BUS

The **bus station** (bussijaam; www.bussireisid.ee; Ilmarise 1; ⏲7.30am-7pm Mon-Fri, to 5pm Sat, 9am-6pm Sun) is 750m north of the tourist office. Serviced by multiples operators, major destinations include the following:

**Kuressaare** €13 to €15, 4½ hours, two daily
**Pärnu** €6 to €7, 1½ hours, eight daily
**Tallinn** €9.50 to €11, 2½ hours, up to 13 daily
**Tartu** €6 to €7, 1¼ hours, at least hourly
**Valga** €4 to €7, 1½ hours, four daily

### TRAIN

The **train station** (raudteejaam; www.elron.ee; Vaksali 44) is 1.5km southwest of the tourist office. Five trains run daily to and from Tallinn (€9.10 to €11, one to 2¼ hours).

# Soomaa National Park

Embracing Estonia's largest area of swamps, meadows and waterside forests, 390-sq-km Soomaa ('bogland') is well named. It's primarily made up of four bogs – Valgeraba, Öördi, Kikepera and Kuresoo, the peat layer of which measures 7m in places. These ancient wetlands are split by tributaries of the Pärnu River. In March and April, spring flooding creates a 'fifth season' in which waters can rise to 5m, and most Soomaans get around by boat.

A good way to explore the national park and its numerous meandering waterways is by canoe or by *haabja,* a traditional Finno-Ugric single-tree boat, carved from aspen trunks and used for centuries for fishing, hunting, hauling hay and transportation.

## THE FOREST BROTHERS

Today the sleepy marshes and quiet woodlands of Estonia shelter mainly wildlife, but between 1944 and 1956 wild places often now set aside as national parks and nature reserves accommodated the national-liberation movement known as the Metsavennad (or Metsavendlus; Forest Brothers). The Brothers, fierce resisters of the Soviet occupation, were compelled to live an underground existence in the woods, where some remained for years. They knew their terrain well, exploiting it to survive and continue their fight to restore the republic.

The Soviets claimed Estonia in the Molotov-Ribbentrop Pact of 1939 and, after the Germans retreated from a difficult three-year occupation, secured this claim by advancing on Tallinn in 1944. The early resistance, believing this latest occupation would not be recognised in accordance with the British–US Atlantic treaty of 1941 (which states that sovereignty and self-governance should be restored when forcibly removed), rallied support for what some thought would be a new war. As international assistance never arrived, the independence cause remained Estonia's own.

Resistance action began with isolated attacks on Red Army units that claimed the lives of around 3000 soldiers. Tactical expertise and secure intelligence networks resulted in damaging offensives on Soviet targets. At the height of the resistance there were more than 30,000 Forest Brothers and their supporters, including women, the elderly, young people and a network of 'Urban Brothers'. The impact of resistance activity shows in contemporary Soviet records detailing incidents of sabotage on infrastructure such as railways and roads, effective hindrance to initial attempts to make Estonia into a new Soviet state.

In the years that followed, the Metsavennad suffered high casualties, with varied and increasing opposition. The NKVD (Soviet secret police) provided incentives for some locals to infiltrate the resistance. The Soviets coordinated mass deportations of those suspected to be sympathetic to the resistance cause, and some Metsavennad supporters were coerced into acting against the resistance. By 1947 around 15,000 resistance fighters had been arrested or killed. The greatest blow to the Metsavennad came in 1949 with the deportation of 20,000 people – mainly women, children and the elderly – many of whom had provided support and cover for resistance activities.

The movement continued for some years, despite the infinitely greater strength of the Soviet state and the detrimental effect of deportations and collectivisation on sympathetic communities. Some Forest Brothers who were not killed or imprisoned escaped to Scandinavia and Canada.

There are many heroes of the Metsavennad, most of whom came to a violent end. Kalev Arro and Ants Kaljurand (*hirmus*, or 'Ants the Terrible' to the Soviets) were famous for their deft disguises and the humour with which they persistently eluded the Soviets. It was only in 1980 that the final active Forest Brother, Oskar Lillenurm, was found – shot dead in Lääne county.

Much work has been done to compile a history of the movement by recording accounts of local witnesses. Surviving members are regarded as national heroes and are awarded some of the country's highest honours. For more details on the resistance, a good reference is former Estonian prime minister (and historian) Mart Laar's *War in the Woods: Estonia's Struggle for Survival, 1944–1956* (1992).

## Activities & Tours

The 1.8km **Beaver Trail** starts at the Soomaa National Park Visitor Centre and leads past beavers' dams. Another good, easy path is the **Riisa Nature Trail**, a 4.8km loop on a well-maintained boardwalk through the Riisa bog (1.2km of which is wheelchair accessible). Before hitting the paths, especially in winter, it's best to let the centre know what you plan to do, either by email or in person.

**Soomaa.com** OUTDOORS
(☎506 1896; www.soomaa.com) Helping visitors explore Soomaa since 1994, this outfit offers guided and self-guided canoe trips (from €35 per person), bog-shoeing (€110 per person)

and mushroom-picking tours. In winter there's kick-sledding (from €80 per person) and snowshoeing (from €95 per person).

## Sleeping

There are 10 designated sites for free, basic camping in the park, including one near the visitor centre. Each has a longdrop toilet, a fire ring and (usually) firewood, but no running water.

## Information

**Soomaa National Park Visitor Centre** (Soomaa Looduskeskus; 435 7164; www.keskkonnaamet.ee; Kõrtsi-Tõramaa; 9am-5pm Mon-Fri, 10am-6pm Sat & Sun mid-May–Aug, 10am-4pm Mon-Fri rest of year) Information is available from this welcoming, highly professional outfit in Kõrtsi-Tõramaa.

## Getting There & Away

There's a daily bus from Pärnu to Riisa (€2.20, one hour), which is 5km from the visitor centre.

By car, it's easiest to access the park from the Pärnu (western) side, heading through Tori and Jõesuu. Viljandi's actually closer, but the 23km road from the village of Kõpu to the visitor centre is largely unsealed.

# Pärnu

POP 39,728

Local families, hormone-sozzled youths and German, Swedish and Finnish holidaymakers join together in a collective prayer for sunny weather while strolling the beaches, sprawling parks and picturesque historic centre of Pärnu (*pair*-nu), Estonia's premier seaside resort. In these parts, its name is synonymous with fun in the sun; one hyperbolic local described it to us as 'Estonia's Miami', but it's usually called by its slightly more prosaic moniker, the nation's 'summer capital'.

In truth, most of Pärnu is quite docile, with strollable historic streets and expansive parks dotted with turn-of-the-20th-century villas reflecting the town's more fashionable past. Museums, churches, traditional architecture, convivial bars and a decent dining scene all justify a visit. Older visitors from Finland and the former Soviet Union still come here, seeking rest, rejuvenation and Pärnu's vaunted mud treatments.

## History

There was a trading settlement at Pärnu before the German crusaders arrived, but the place entered recorded history in 1234 when the Pärnu River was fixed as the border between the territories of the Ösel-Wiek bishop (west and north) and the Livonian knights (east and south). The town, joined by rivers to Viljandi, Tartu and Lake Peipsi, became the Hanseatic port of Pernau in the 14th century (sinking water levels have since cut this link).

Pernau/Pärnu had a population of German merchants from Lübeck till at least the 18th century. It withstood wars, fires, plagues, and switches between German, Polish, Swedish and Russian rule, and prospered in the 17th century under the Swedes, until trade was devastated by Europe-wide blockades during the Napoleonic wars.

From 1838 it gradually became a popular resort, with mud baths as well as the beach proving a draw. Only the resort area was spared severe damage in 1944 as the Soviets drove out the Nazis, but many parts of Old Town have since been restored.

## Sights

Pärnu straddles both sides of the Pärnu River at the point where it empties into Pärnu Bay. The south bank contains the major attractions, including Old Town and the beach. The main thoroughfare of the historic centre is Rüütli, lined with splendid buildings dating back to the 17th century.

★ **Pärnu Beach** BEACH

Pärnu's long, broad, sandy beach – sprinkled with volleyball courts, pop-up bars, cafes and changing cubicles – is the city's main draw in summer. A curving path stretches along the sand, lined with fountains, park benches and an excellent playground. Early-20th-century buildings are strung along Ranna pst, the avenue that runs parallel to the beach. Across the road, the formal gardens of **Rannapark** are ideal for a summertime picnic.

★ **Museum of New Art** GALLERY

(Uue kunstimuuseum; 443 0772; www.mona.ee; Esplanaadi 10; adult/child €4/2; 9am-9pm Jun-Aug, to 7pm Sep-May; P) Pärnu's former Communist Party headquarters now houses one of Estonia's edgiest cultural spaces, established in 1992 as the country's first museum of contemporary art. Pushing the cultural envelope, it stages an international nude art exhibition every summer, and exhibits over 600 works of contemporary art. Every June it hosts the **Pärnu Film Festival**, a celebration of documentary work founded by filmmaker Mark Soosaar.

**Pärnu Museum** MUSEUM
(☎443 3231; www.parnumuuseum.ee; Aida 3; adult/student €4/2; ⊙11am-6pm Tue-Sun) This museum covers 11,000 years of the Pärnu region's history, from prehistoric relics, right up to a reconstruction of a Soviet-era apartment. Pride of place goes to the 8000-year-old 'Stone-Age Madonna', the oldest sculpture yet found in the Baltics or Scandinavia. Temporary exhibitions are regularly staged, doubling the price of full-access tickets (if you choose to see them).

**St Elizabeth's Lutheran Church** CHURCH
(Eliisabeti kirik; ☎443 1381; www.eliisabet.ee; Nikolai 22; ⊙noon-6pm Tue-Sat, 9am-noon Sun Jun-Aug) Consecrated in 1750, this dignified, rust-coloured Lutheran church was named for Russian Empress Yelizaveta Petrovna, who gifted Pärnu's Lutherans 8000 roubles for its construction. Also giving props to St John the Baptist's mum, its simple interior has low dangling chandeliers, a Gothic-style carved wooden pulpit and a wonderful altarpiece of the Resurrection from Rotterdam (1854).

**St Catherine's Orthodox Church** CHURCH
(Ekatarina Kirik; Vee 8) Built in 1768, this superb baroque church is named after Russian empress Catherine the Great, while also name-checking the early Christian martyr. If it's open, the gilded icons and interior fittings are suitably impressive.

**Tallinn Gate** GATE
(Tallinna Värav; Vana-Tallinna 1) The outline of the 17th-century, star-shaped Swedish ramparts that once surrounded old Pärnu can still be discerned on maps. The one remaining section and its moat, now Vallikäär Park, end at the Tallinn Gate, which once defended the main road to the river-ferry crossing and Tallinn road. There's a scale model of how the town would have looked when the ramparts were intact, just before the gate.

**Town Hall** HISTORIC BUILDING
(Pärnu Raekoda; Nikolai 3) This 1797 neoclassical building now houses the tourist office and a small gallery space. Also note the half-timbered 'Citizen's Residence', dating from 1740, diagonally opposite across Nikolai.

## Activities

**Tervise Paradiis** WATER PARK
(☎445 1666; www.terviseparadiis.ee; Side 14; adult/child 3hr €18/13, 1 day €21/17; ⊙10am-10pm Jun-Aug, from 11am Sep-May; 👪) At the far end of the beach, Estonia's largest water park beckons with pools, slides, tubes and other slippery fun. It's a big family-focused draw, especially when bad weather ruins beach plans. The large resort also offers saunas, spa treatments, fitness facilities and classes, ten-pin bowling and a selection of cafes and restaurants.

**Hedon Spa** SPA
(☎449 9011; www.hedonspa.com; Ranna pst 1; treatments from €30; ⊙9am-7pm Mon-Sat, to 5pm Sun) Built in 1927 to house Pärnu's famous mud baths, this handsome neoclassical building has recently been fully restored and opened as a spa-hotel. All manner of pampering treatments are offered, only some of which involve mud (a 50-minute massage starts at €54). There are two restaurants and a cafe on-site, and soothingly decorated modern rooms (doubles from €93).

## Festivals & Events

Pärnu hosts several major cultural events throughout the warmer months, while the tourist office distributes *Pärnu This Week*, listing weekly happenings around town and also accessible at www.visitparnu.com.

**Grillfest Good Food Festival** FOOD & DRINK
(Hea Toidu Festival; www.grillfest.ee; Vallikäär; ⊙Jun) Over the second weekend in June, more than 50,000 people wend their way around the 350 food vendors in Vallikäär Park, enjoying the best of Estonian and world cuisine. Despite the name, it's not all about barbecued meat: there's a fishing competition, Estonian Food Fair, and plenty of auxiliary attractions.

**Pärnu Hanseatic Days** CULTURAL
(Pärnu Hansapäevad; http://hansa.parnu.ee; Vallikäär; ⊙late Jun) Pärnu goes medieval for a weekend in late June, with a knightly tournament, children's village, market stalls, performances and a poultry and livestock fair. Action centres largely on Vallikäär Park.

**Pärnu Film Festival** FILM
(Pärnu Filmifestival; www.chaplin.ee; ⊙Jun-Jul) This increasingly prestigious international festival of documentary and science film has been a fixture of Pärnu's cultural calendar since 1987. It's held at the Museum of New Art and other venues in town in late June, then heads on the road for two weeks in early July.

## Pärnu

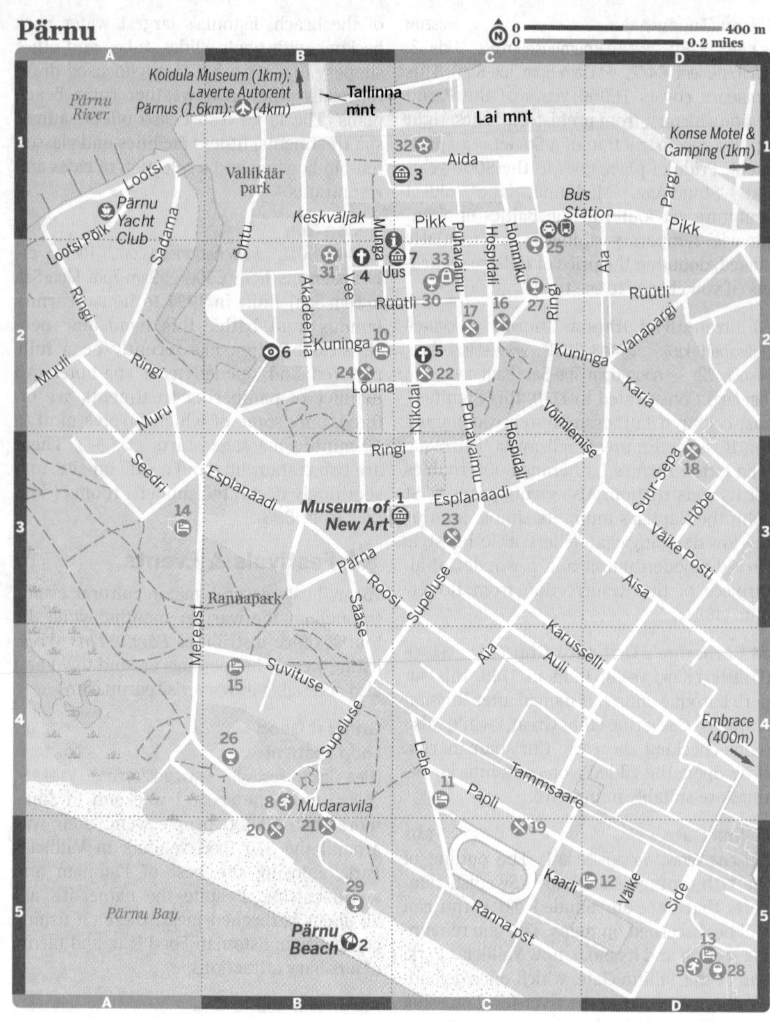


## Sleeping

**Embrace** GUESTHOUSE €€
(☎5887 3404; www.embrace.ee; Pardi 30; d from €60, apt for 4 from €110; P ❄ 📶) Snuggle up in an old wooden house in a quiet suburban street, close to the beach and water park (if a decent walk from central Pärnu). Rooms strike a nice balance between antique and contemporary, and there's a set of four modern self-contained apartments in a neighbouring annex.

**Inge Villa** GUESTHOUSE €€
(☎4438510; Kaarli 20; s/d/ste €56/70/82; P ❄ 📶) Describing itself as a 'Swedish-Estonian villa hotel', this lovely, low-key pre-WWII villa sits invitingly on a quiet, tree-lined street near the beach. Its 11 rooms are simply decorated in muted tones with Nordic minimalism to the fore. The garden, lounge and sauna seal the deal.

**Villa Johanna** B&B €€
(☎443 8370; www.villa-johanna.ee; Suvituse 6; s/d/ste with balcony €50/80/100; P 📶) Decorated with hanging flowerpots and planter boxes, this pretty old-fashioned wooden house offers comfy pine-lined rooms on a quiet street near the beach and extensive parkland. If you're feeling sociable there's an

## Pärnu

**Top Sights**
1 Museum of New Art ... C3
2 Pärnu Beach ... B5

**Sights**
3 Pärnu Museum ... C1
4 St Catherine's Orthodox Church ... B2
5 St Elizabeth's Lutheran Church ... C2
6 Tallinn Gate ... B2
7 Town Hall ... C2

**Activities, Courses & Tours**
8 Hedon Spa ... B4
9 Tervise Paradiis ... D5

**Sleeping**
10 Frost House ... B2
11 Hotell Legend ... C4
12 Inge Villa ... D5
13 Tervise Paradiis ... D5
14 Villa Ammende ... A3
15 Villa Johanna ... B4

**Eating**
16 Lime Lounge ... C2
17 Mahedik ... C2
18 Pärnu Market ... D3
19 Piparmünt ... C5
20 Raimond ... B5
21 Steffani ... B5
22 Steffani ... C2
23 Supelsaksad ... C3
24 Trahter Postipoiss ... B2

**Drinking & Nightlife**
25 Alibi ... C2
26 Pärnu Kuursaal ... B4
27 Puhvet APTEK ... C2
28 Romantic Bar ... D5
29 Sunset ... B5
30 Veerev Õlu ... C2

**Entertainment**
31 Endla Theatre ... B2
32 Pärnu Concert Hall ... C1

**Shopping**
33 Maarja-Magdaleena Gild ... C2

inviting, fire-lit common room and a sauna that fits four at a squeeze. Not much English is spoken.

**Hotell Legend** HOTEL €€
(☎442 5606; www.legend.ee; Lehe 3; s/d/ste from €50/70/90; P Wi-Fi pets) The Tiffany-style lamps, model ships and wooden panelling lend an old-world feel to the lobby, which is quite a contrast to the boxy exterior. Yet inviting, parquet-floored rooms, charming staff and proximity to the beach more than compensate, making this a good midrange option.

**Konse Motel & Camping** CAMPGROUND €€
(☎5343 5092; www.konse.ee; Suur-Jõe 44a; site €17, d with/without bathroom from €70/60; P @ Wi-Fi) About 1km east of central Pärnu, riverside Konse offers camping and a variety of motel rooms with kitchen access. It's not an especially charming spot, but there's a sauna (€15 per hour), and the chance to rent bikes (per day €10) and rowboats (per hour €10). Camping seems less thrifty when you throw in the €5 charge for a shower.

★ **Villa Ammende** HOTEL €€€
(☎447 3888; www.ammende.ee; Mere pst 7; s/d/ste €154/216/436; P A/C Wi-Fi) Built in 1905, the Villa Ammende is an art nouveau masterpiece, and now one of Pärnu's best hotels. Original stylistic touches such as colourful tiles and wrought iron remain on its exterior, while the interior delights with stencilled paintings and carved wood features. Operating as a private home and casino at different times, it was restored in the 1990s as a hotel.

**Frost House** BOUTIQUE HOTEL €€€
(☎5303 0424; www.frosthotel.ee; Kuninga 11; d/ste from €140/210; P Wi-Fi) Little restraint was shown restoring and refurbishing this 1705 house in central Pärnu. An eye-catching profusion of details includes original wooden fittings, chandeliers, metallic bathroom tiles, fur throws, cow-hide poufs and more scatter cushions than any bed could need. It's undeniably luxe, though, with deep, delightful beds, winter fires crackling in the lobby and a restaurant with its own bakery.

**Tervise Paradiis** RESORT €€€
(☎445 1600; www.terviseparadiis.ee; Side 14; s/d/ste from €98/119/172; P A/C Wi-Fi pool) Big (120-odd rooms) and *busy* in summer, this hotel attached to the Tervise Paradiis water park (p135) has slick rooms, all with balconies and most with beach views. Quite apart from the water park, it's a great place for families, with a bowling alley, kids' playroom, a spa, a fitness club, restaurants and a bar. Swedes and Finns love it in summer, so book ahead.

## Eating

**Steffani** PIZZA €
(☎443 1170; www.steffani.ee; Nikolai 24; mains €8-10; ⊙11am-midnight Sun-Thu, to 2am Fri & Sat; 🚸) Steffani is a top choice for thin-crust and pan pizzas, particularly in summer when you can dine alfresco on the big, flower-filled terrace. The menu also stretches to pasta and, oddly, burritos. During summer it also operates out of a **beach branch** (Steffani Suve Pizzarestoran; Ranna pst 1; ⊙11am-midnight Sun-Thu, to 2am Fri & Sat May-Sep; 📶).

**Pärnu Market** MARKET €
(Pärnu Turg; ☎442 6482; www.parnuturg.ee; Suur-Sepa 18; ⊙outdoor market & shops 8am-4pm Mon-Fri, meat & fish Tue-Fri 8am-6pm, to 4pm Sat-Mon, food street 8am-11pm Mon-Fri; 🌿) Pärnu's market is a mash-up of old and new: the 1953-built covered market was refurbished in 2016 and now boasts food outlets and a supermarket. Meanwhile, the traditional business of selling food and clothing continues, in both indoor and outdoor stalls.

**Supelsaksad** CAFE €€
(☎442 2448; www.supelsaksad.ee; Nikolai 32; mains €15-17; ⊙11.30am-9pm Tue-Thu, 11.30am-11pm Fri, 9am-11pm Sat, 9am-9pm Sun; 📶) Looking like it was designed by Barbara Cartland on acid (bright pink and a riot of stripes and prints), this fabulous cafe serves an appealing mix of salads, pastas and meaty mains. If you eat all your greens, make a beeline for the bountiful cake display.

**Piparmünt** MODERN EUROPEAN €€
(☎442 5736; www.kurgovilla.ee; Papli 13; mains €14-16; ⊙noon-9pm Sun-Thu, to 11pm Fri & Sat; P📶) Despite its low-key feel and tucked-away location (it's attached to a small hotel on a side street near the beach), 'Peppermint' is definitely one of Pärnu's better restaurants. The menu changes constantly, but you can expect dishes such as grilled duck breast on pearl barley with bacon, peas and crème de cassis sauce.

**Mahedik** CAFE €€
(☎442 5393; www.mahedik.ee; Pühavaimu 20; breakfast €5-7, mains €14-15; ⊙10am-7pm Sun, 9am-9pm Mon-Thu, 9am-midnight Fri, 10am-midnight Sat; 📶🌿) The name roughly translates as 'organic-ish', and wholesome, largely seasonal food is the focus of this cosy all-day cafe. There are cooked breakfasts such as omelettes with cottage cheese and summer greens, and light mains such as raw salmon slightly marinated in local gin with potato-olive salad and mustard-yoghurt sauce. Out back is a shop selling organic and natural products.

**Lime Lounge** INTERNATIONAL €€
(☎449 2190; www.limelounge.ee; Hommiku 17; mains €15-17; ⊙noon-10pm Mon-Thu, to midnight Fri & Sat; 📶) More adventurous than many places in Pärnu's Old Town, Lime Lounge offers skilfully executed Southeast Asian cooking (the *tom kha gai* is creamy and fragrant, and the seabass with rice-noodle salad gets Vietnamese flavours right) alongside safer European fare. Locals treat it as a cafe-bar as much as a restaurant, lingering over well-chosen wine or cheesecake and coffee.

**Trahter Postipoiss** RUSSIAN €€
(☎446 4864; www.trahterpostipoiss.ee; Vee 12; mains €13-16; ⊙noon-11pm Sun-Thu, to 2am Fri & Sat; 📶) Housed in an 1834 postal building, this rustic tavern has excellent Russian cuisine (ranging from simple to sophisticated), a convivial crowd and imperial portraits watching over the proceedings. The spacious courtyard opens during summer and there's live music on weekends.

**Raimond** EUROPEAN €€€
(☎5556 2686; www.hedonspa.com; Ranna pst 1; mains €23; ⊙6-11pm Sun-Thu, to midnight Fri & Sat; 📶🌿) Named for Estonian composer Raimond Valgre, this is the Hedon Spa & Hotel's night-time fine-diner. At the rear of the complex, opening onto the beach, it offers à la carte choices such as a 'famous' beef tartare incorporating Baltic herring and Estonian pike with tiger prawns, or degustation menus of four and six courses (€49 and €69 respectively). There's also an entire menu for vegans.

## Drinking & Nightlife

**Alibi** BAR
(☎5349 8313; Ringi 1; ⊙5pm-2am Wed & Thu, to 4am Fri & Sat; 📶) A very welcoming little bar in a red-brick building in the old centre, Alibi has a great range of beers and frequent events, including comedy and live music.

**Puhvet APTEK** BAR
(www.aptek.ee; Rüütli 40; ⊙10pm-2am Wed & Thu, to 5am Fri & Sat; 📶) Drop by the old 1930s pharmacy to admire the clever restoration that has turned it into a smooth late-night haunt. Fabulous decor (including original cabinets, vials and bottles) competes for

your attention with cocktails, bar games, DJs and live acts. Expect open-air gigs in summer.

**Veerev Õlu** PUB
(☎442 9848; Uus 3a; ⏲11am-1am Mon-Sat, from 1pm Sun) Named after the Rolling Stones, the 'Rolling Beer' wins the award for the friendliest and cosiest pub by a long shot. It's a tiny, rustic wooden space with good vibes, cheap beer and the occasional live folk-rock band (with compulsory dancing on tables, it would seem). There are a few outdoor tables in summer.

**Pärnu Kuursaal** PUB
(☎5810 0165; www.parnukuursaal.ee; Mere pst 22; mains €8-10; ⏲9pm-4am Fri & Sat; ) This late-19th-century dance hall has been transformed into a spacious countrified beer hall with a large terrace at the back. An older mix of tourists and locals come for the draft beer and the live music, and a menu that takes its meat and beer snacks seriously.

**Romantic Bar** BAR
(☎445 1625; www.terviseparadiis.ee; 8th fl Tervise Paradiis, Side 14; ⏲2pm-midnight) Despite the cheesy name and bland hotel-bar vibe, the superb sea views from this venue make it the perfect setting for a sundowner cocktail or a nightcap, either inside on the white, podlike leather chairs or on the small terrace.

**Sunset** CLUB
(☎444 0429; www.sunset.ee; Ranna pst 3; ⏲11pm-5am Fri & Sat Jun-Aug) Pärnu's biggest and most famous summertime nightclub has an outdoor beach terrace and a sleek multifloor interior with plenty of nooks for when the dance floor gets crowded. Imported DJs and bands keep things cranked until the early hours.

## ☆ Entertainment

In summer, concerts are held at traditional venues such as the concert hall and Kuursaal, as well as in parks such as Vallikäär and Munamäe, the town hall, churches and the grounds of the beautiful Villa Ammende.

**Pärnu Concert Hall** CLASSICAL MUSIC
(Pärnu konserdimaja; ☎445 5810; www.concert.ee; Aida 4; ⏲box office 10am-3pm Mon-Fri & 1hr before performances) This striking riverside glass-and-steel auditorium with first-rate acoustics is considered the best concert venue in Estonia.

**Endla Theatre** THEATRE
(☎442 0667; www.endla.ee; Keskväljak 1; ⏲closed Jun) Pärnu's best theatre stages a wide range of performances (usually in Estonian). It also houses an art gallery, a jazz club and an open-air cafe.

## Shopping

**Maarja-Magdaleena Gild** ARTS & CRAFTS
(☎5887 2790; www.maarjamagdaleenagild.ee; Uus 5; ⏲10am-6pm Mon-Fri, to 3pm Sat) The artisans of the Mary Magdalene Guild sell their wares (leather, glass, paper, weaving, felt, jewellery, pottery) from the main shop downstairs and from their various little studios scattered throughout the building. Established in 2007, the Guild resurrects a 16th-century original, the oldest of Pärnu's known guilds.

## ℹ Information

**Pärnu Tourist Information Centre** (☎447 3000; www.visitparnu.com; Uus 4; ⏲9am-6pm mid-May–mid-Sep, 9am-5pm Mon-Fri, 10am-4pm Sat & Sun mid-Sep–mid-May) Located in the neoclassical town hall, in Old Town.

**Pärnu Central Library** (Pärnu keskraamatu kogu; ☎445 5707; www.pkr.ee; Akadeemia tänav 3; ⏲10am-6pm Mon-Fri, to 3pm Sat Jun-Aug, 10am-7pm Mon-Fri, to 3pm Sat Sep-May) Offers quiet and free wi-fi.

## ℹ Getting There & Away

### AIR

**Pärnu Airport** (Pärnu lennujaam, EPU; ☎447 5000; www.parnu-airport.ee; Lennujaama tee, Eametsa) lies on the northern edge of town, west of the Tallinn road, 5km from the town centre. It's only used by one small airline, **Luftverkehr Friesland-Harle** (LFH, www.lendame.ee), for flights to the islands of Kihnu and Ruhnu, and then only in winter (Thursdays, Fridays and Sundays) when sea travel is impossible. Bus 23 connects the bus station and the airport (€1,15 minutes), or a taxi should cost no more than €8.

### BOAT

From May to October Veeteed runs one to three ferry services per week between Pärnu and Ruhnu Island (adult/child return €20/10, 3¼ hours).

**Pärnu Yacht Club** (Pärnu jahtklubi; ☎447 1750; www.jahtklubi.ee; Lootsi 6) has a marina with a customs point, along with a restaurant and accommodation.

### BUS

Buses stop at the corner of Pikk and Ringi, but the main **bus station ticket office** (Ringi 3; ⏲8am-7.30pm Mon-Fri, to 5pm Sat, 9am-5pm

Sun) is about 100m away, across Ringi (look for the red '*bussijaam*' sign). International coaches head from here to as far afield as St Petersburg. Lux Express (www.ticket.luxexpress.eu) runs to the following destinations:

**Kuressaare** €9 to €16, three hours, three daily

**Tallinn** €9 to €11, two hours, up to 11 per day

**Tartu** €8 to €10, 2¾ hours, up to five per day

**Viljandi** €5 to €7, 1½ hours, up to five per day

Regional bus 321 also runs once a day to Haapsalu (€5.10, 2¼ hours).

### CAR & MOTORCYCLE

**Laverte** (☎5451 2515; www.laverterent.ee; Rõugu 23; ⏰8am-6pm Mon-Fri), a local company, is good for car hire.

## ℹ Getting Around

Pärnu's broad, leafy streets and long beachfront invite cycling in summer. **Tõruke Rattarent** (☎502 8269; www.bicyclerentalparnu.eu; Ranna pst 2; bike per hour/day/week €2.50/10/47; ⏰9am-7pm Jun-Aug) rents bikes from a stand between the beach and the stadium on Ranna pst.

There are local buses but given that all the sights are within walking distance of each other, you probably won't need to bother with them. Travel cards can be bought from kiosks for €2, also the price of an hour's travel, or you can buy the same ticket from the driver for €3.

Taxis line up near the bus station on Ringi. Local companies include **E-Takso** (☎1300; www.etakso.ee; flagfall €2.90, per km €0.96) and **Pärnu Takso** (☎1222; www.parnutakso.ee; flagfall €2.50, per km €0.90).

# Kihnu

POP 487

Kihnu Island, 40km southwest of Pärnu in the Gulf of Rīga, is a living museum of Estonian culture. Many islander women still wear the traditional, homespun, striped *kört* (skirt) nearly every day. There are a handful of sights in the four villages on the 7km-long island, which is fringed with long, quiet beaches along its western coast.

In December 2003 Unesco declared the Kihnu's culture and traditions 'a Masterpiece of the Oral and Intangible Heritage of Humanity'. This honour is a tribute to the rich cultural traditions that are still practised, in song, dance, the celebration of traditional spiritual festivals and the making of handicrafts. Kihnu's language is a distinct dialect of Estonian, with liberal Swedish elements. That the island's customs have remained intact for so many centuries is thanks to its isolation.

## 👁 Sights

### Kihnu Museum — MUSEUM

(☎5818 8094; https://kihnu.kovtp.ee/muuseumist1; Linaküla; adult/child €3/1.50; ⏰10am-5pm May-Aug, 10am-5pm Tue-Sun Sep, 10am-5pm Tue-Fri Oct-Apr; 🅿) You can learn more about Kihnu Jõnn (the locally famous skipper who sailed all the world's oceans) and the island's unique history and culture at this vividly decorated museum in a former schoolhouse in the western village of Linaküla. Workshops such as net-making and doll-making can be prearranged (€25 per person per hour).

### St Nicholas' Orthodox Church — CHURCH

(Nikolaose kirik; Linaküla; ⏰by appointment) The islanders are among the minority of ethnic Estonians who adhere to the Russian Orthodox religion. This pretty little church at the centre of the island dates from 1786, with some mid-19th-century additions. Note the small onion dome crowning the steeple, a sign of its conversion from Lutheranism to Orthodoxy.

### Kihnu Tuletorn — LIGHTHOUSE

(Rootsiküla; adult/child €3/1.50; ⏰10am-6pm daily Jun-Aug, 10am-3pm Sat May & Sep; 🅿) Constructed in parts shipped from England in 1864, this 29m-high lighthouse flashes at passing ships from the southern extremity of Pitkänä peninsula. In summer you can climb to the top to enjoy the views.

## 🛏 Sleeping & Eating

Homestays are popular as they provide an opportunity to interact with locals and experience home cooking. See www.visitestonia.com for options; chances are your hosts won't speak English.

### Rock City Guesthouse — GUESTHOUSE €€

(Rock City Külalistemaja; ☎5626 2181; www.rockcity.ee; Sääre; sites per person €5, d/tr from €30/40, cabin €38; ⏰May-Aug; 🅿📶) Near Kihnu's port, this former Soviet Party lodging offers 45 beds across simple, wood-floored doubles and triples with shared bathroom. There are also three campsites, four double cabins, a sauna house and two four-room houses among the pines. A two-course meal in the 'Rock City Tavern' (open 10am to 6pm) costs €13.

### Tolli Tourist Farm — GUESTHOUSE €€

(☎527 7380; www.kihnukallas.ee; Sääre; sites per person €8, s/d without breakfast from €22/44;

⏲May-Sep; Ⓟ) A working farm in the 19th century, Tolli offers rooms in the main farmhouse, in the barn or in a rustic log cabin, plus sites to pitch your own tent. Other services include a sauna, boating excursions, basic meals, excursions around the island and passage to the mainland in a 10-person fishing boat (€70, irrespective of passenger numbers).

## Information

**Kihnurand Travel Agency** (☎525 5172; www.kihnurand.ee) Arranges day trips and tours.

## Getting There & Away

### AIR

In winter (usually from December or whenever the boats stop), **LFH** (www.lendame.ee) flies to and from Pärnu.

### BOAT

- As long as ice conditions allow (from at least mid-May to the end of October), there are ferries to Kihnu operated by **Veeteed** (☎443 1069; www.veeteed.com) departing from Munalaid, 40km southwest of Pärnu (adult/child/car/bike €4/2/15/1, one hour, two to four daily). Tickets and timetables are available online.
- Buses from Pärnu to Munalaid are timed to meet the ferries.
- On Kihnu, the ferry dock is halfway between the villages of Sääre and Lemsi.

## Getting Around

The best way to get around the island is by bicycle. Various places, including most accommodation providers, hire bikes for around €12 per day.

# WESTERN ESTONIA & THE ISLANDS

One of the Baltic's most alluring regions, the west coast of Estonia encompasses forest-covered islands, verdant countryside and seaside villages slumbering beneath picturesque medieval castles.

Pine forests and juniper groves cover Saaremaa and Hiiumaa, Estonia's largest islands. Quiet roads loop around them, passing unpeopled stretches of coastline broken by historic lighthouses and old wooden windmills – both emblems of the islands. Saaremaa also boasts spa resorts, a magnificent castle and a pretty 'capital' that comes to life during the summer months. It's also the departure point for the wildlife-rich islands of Vilsandi National Park. Muhu and Vormsi are the islands' smaller, quieter cousins.

On the mainland, Haapsalu is an enchanting, partly faded town that was once a resort for 19th-century Russian aristocrats seeking the benefits of its healing mud. The jewel of its Old Town is a 14th-century bishop's castle, today the setting for open-air festivals and summer concerts.

## Haapsalu

POP 9675

Set on a forked peninsula that stretches into Haapsalu Bay, this quaint resort town, 100km from Tallinn, makes a fine stopover en route to the islands. Haapsalu has a handful of museums and galleries, and a few rather modest spa hotels, but the town's biggest attraction is its striking castle. A bit rough around the edges, Haapsalu's Old Town is more rustic than urban, with wooden houses set back from the narrow streets, a slender promenade skirting the bay and plenty of secret spots for watching the sunset.

Those seeking mud or spa treatments might opt for Haapsalu over Pärnu or Kuressaare, though the centres here are a bit more proletarian. Nevertheless, Haapsalu lays claim to superior mud, which is used by health centres throughout Estonia.

### History

Like other Estonian towns, Haapsalu has changed hands many times since its founding. The German Knights of the Sword conquered this region in 1224, and Haapsalu became the bishop's residence, with a fortress and cathedral built soon afterwards. The Danes took control during the Livonian War (around 1559), then the Swedes had their turn in the 17th century, but they lost it to the Russians during the Great Northern War in the 18th century.

The city flourished under the tsars, mostly because of mud. Once the curative properties of its shoreline were discovered in the 19th century, Haapsalu transformed into a spa centre. The Russian composer Tchaikovsky and members of the Russian imperial family visited the city for mud baths. A railway that went all the way to St Petersburg was completed in 1907. In Soviet times, Haapsulu was closed to foreigners.

## Western Estonia & the Islands

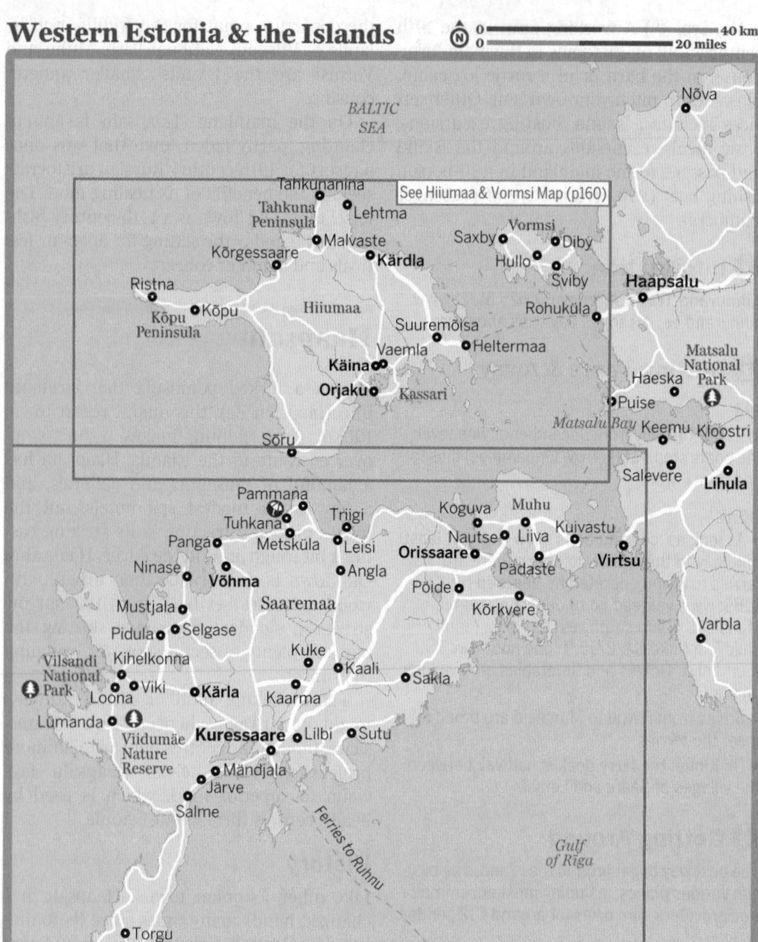


## Sights & Activities

**Haapsalu Episcopal Castle** CASTLE
(Haapsalu piiskopilinnus; www.haapsalulinnus.ee; Lossiplats 3; adult/reduced €12/7; ⌚10am-6pm daily mid-May–mid-Sep, 11am-5pm Wed-Sun mid-Sep–mid-May) Haapsalu's crumbling heart is its bishop's castle, which was western Estonia's centre of command from the 13th to the 16th centuries but now stands in partial, very picturesque ruins. A turreted tower, most of the outer wall and some of the moat still remain. Entry to the grounds is free year-round, but a ticket is required to enter the castle proper, where there's a **museum** devoted to its history, including some creepy tunnels and dramatically displayed medieval weaponry.

Accessed from within the museum is the striking **Dome Church** (properly, St Nicholas' Cathedral), built in a mix of the Romanesque and Gothic styles, with three inner domes. It's the largest such structure in the Baltics and its phenomenal acoustics means concerts are regularly held here. Inside the church, keep your eyes peeled for the ghost of the White Lady.

In summer, the park within the outer walls is used for concerts. There's a wonderful **children's playground** complete with a pirate ship, and a **viewing platform** within one of the towers. You can also try your hand at archery just outside the main gate (€5 for 10 arrows).

**Ilon's Wonderland** GALLERY

(Iloni Imedemaa; ☎5836 2803; Kooli 5; €6; ⏲10am-6pm daily Jun-Aug, 11am-5pm Wed-Sun Sep-May; 👪) Showcasing the works of Estonian-Swedish illustrator Ilon Wikland, who spent her childhood in Haapsalu and is best known for her illustrations for the Pippi Longstocking books, this gallery is fabulously set up for kids, with many artworks hung at their viewing level, plus opportunities to get crafty, play, and watch a film on the eponymous illustrator.

**Haapsalu Kuursaal** HISTORIC BUILDING

(☎5646 2466; www.kuursaal.ee; Promenaadi 1; ⏲noon-10pm May-Sep) This fairy-tale wooden confection, painted pale green and white, sits plumb on the waterfront, surrounded by rose gardens. Stepping into the airy spa hall (1897) is like stepping back into Haapsalu's fin-de-siècle heyday, with a small stage at one end (used for concerts and events) and a summertime restaurant at the other (mains €9 to €11). The ambience trumps the food, but it's certainly worth checking out.

**Town Hall Museum** MUSEUM

(Raekoda muusem; ☎473 7665; www.salm.ee; Kooli 2; adult/reduced €4/3; ⏲10am-6pm daily Jun-Aug, 11am-5pm Wed-Sun Sep-Apr, 11am-5pm daily May) Built in 1775, Haapsalu's former town hall now houses a charming little museum with displays on the history of the resort town, regional history, a re-created pharmacy and the well-preserved mayor's office. Booklets cover gaps in the English-language information offered.

**St John's Lutheran Church** CHURCH

(http://haapsalu.eelk.ee; Kooli 4; ⏲9am-5pm Mon, Fri & Sun) Although it has its roots in the 16th century, the exterior of this whitewashed church owes much to a renovation in 1858. Inside, look out for the sculpted reliefs above the altar (dating from 1630) and the carved pulpit.

**Birdwatching Tower** VIEWPOINT

(Linnuvaatlustorn Tagalahe ääres) Broad, shallow, reedy Haapsalu Bay is a key habitat for migrating waterfowl in Estonia, and is listed as a Ramsar Wetland of International Importance. During their spring and autumn migrations, as many as 20,000 birds descend. If you know your gadwalls from your grebes and fancy a gander at a goosander, head up the birdwatching tower, just seaward of the junction of Jaandi and the southern end of Promenaadi. You may even see circling white-tailed eagles.

**Promenaadi** WATERFRONT

Nineteenth-century Russian toffs, like their counterparts in Victorian England and Paris' belle époque, liked nothing more than a good see-and-be-seen promenade, and the premier strolling route was along the waterfront. Sculptures dating from Haapsalu's fashionable era are scattered along the promenade, including a sundial and a bust commemorating mud-cure pioneer Dr Karl Abraham Hunnius, and the symphony-inscribed **Tchaikovsky Bench** (Tshaikovski pst), erected in 1940.

**Museum of the Estonian Swedes** MUSEUM

(Rannarootsi muuseum; ☎473 7165; www.aiboland.ee; Sadama 32; adult/child €3/2.50; ⏲10am-6pm Tue-Sat, to 4pm Sun & Mon) This quaint museum has relics, photos, old fishing nets and a marvellous tapestry tracing the 1000-year history of Swedes in Estonia, up to their escape back to Sweden on the

## A GHOSTLY VIGIL

Haapsalu's biggest annual event, the **White Lady Festival** (Valge daami päevad; www.valgedaam.ee; ⏲Aug), coincides with the August full moon. The three-day weekend begins with merriment – music, storytelling, and theatre across the town – and culminates with a ghastly apparition. During the full moon every August and February, moonlight at a precise angle creates a ghostly reflection upon a cathedral window. According to legend, the shadow is cast by a young girl who, in the 14th century, was bricked up alive inside the walls.

Back then, the castle was an all-male enclave, and the archbishop got pretty worked up when he heard that a young woman, disguised in monastic vestments, sneaked in to be close to her lover-monk. On the culminating evening, crowds stay out late to see a play recounting the story in the castle grounds (€15 at the door), after which everyone gathers to await the Lady's apparition.

## Haapsalu

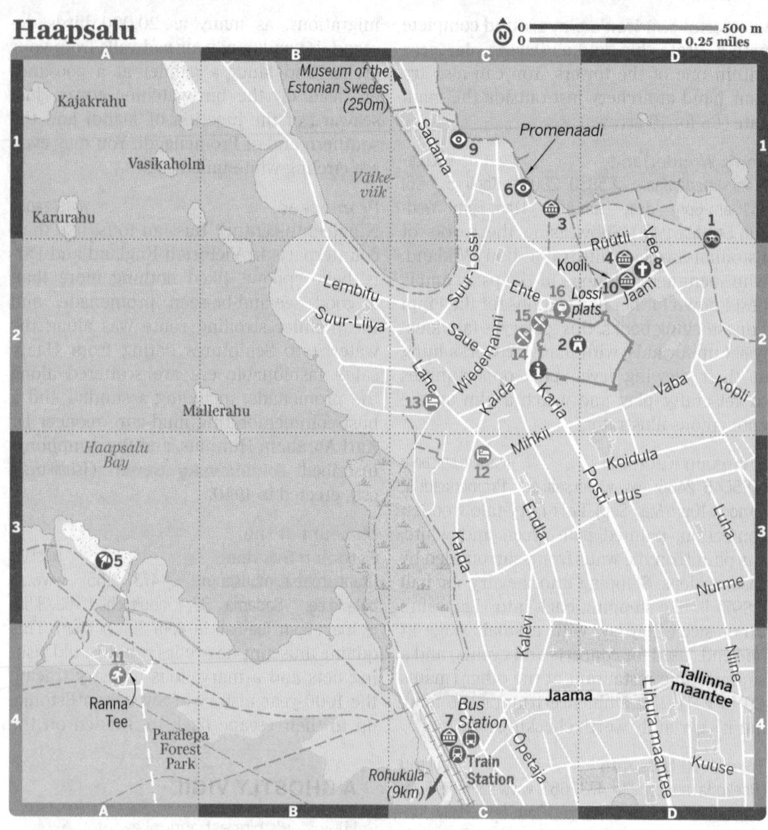


## Haapsalu

**Sights**

1 Birdwatching Tower........D1
2 Haapsalu Episcopal Castle........C2
3 Haapsalu Kuursaal........C1
4 Ilon's Wonderland........D2
5 Paralepa Forest Park........A3
6 Promenaadi........C1
7 Railway & Communication Museum........C4
8 St John's Lutheran Church........D2
9 Tchaikovsky Bench........C1
10 Town Hall Museum........D2

**Activities, Courses & Tours**

11 Fra Mare Thalasso Spa........A4

**Sleeping**

12 Kongo Hotell........C3
13 Lahe Maja........C2

**Eating**

14 Hapsal Dietrich........C2
15 Müüriääre Kohvik........C2

**Drinking & Nightlife**

16 Herman Bistro & Bar........C2

*Triina* in 1944. Antique whistles and other instruments used in Swedish-Estonian music are another feature.

**Railway & Communication Museum** MUSEUM
(Raudtee- ja Sidemuuseum; ☎473 4574; www.salm.ee; Raudtee 2; adult/reduced €4/3; ⊙10am-6pm daily Jun-Aug, 11am-5pm Wed-Sun Sep & May, 11am-5pm Fri-Sun Oct-Apr; P) Haapsalu's attractive former train station, with its wooden-lace ornamentation and grand colonnade, opened in 1907 to transport the Russian nobility to the resort. Designed to keep the royals dry, its 214m-long covered platform

was then said to be the longest in the empire. This boxcar-sized museum records the golden years of train travel, and there are antique locomotives to explore outside. Six times a day in summer, a road train runs between here and Old Town (€5).

**Paralepa Forest Park** BEACH
(☎ rowboat rental 5660 3144; Ranna tee 2; rowboat per hour €8) On the western edge of town, beyond the train station, this shady park has a popular beachfront which, despite being a bit swampy, attracts plenty of sunseekers. There's a 3km and a 5km walking path through the forest, and in summer there's a cafe and a kiosk that rents rowboats. To get to the beach, follow the signs towards Fra Mare Thalasso Spa and keep going.

**Fra Mare Thalasso Spa** SPA
(☎ 472 4600; www.framare.ee; Ranna tee 2; treatments from €22) If you want to experience Haapsalu's reputedly magic mud, this spa hotel offers a variety of treatments for day visitors (massage, baths etc), along with a pool, a sauna and a gym. If you'd like to overnight, rooms are comfortable and up to date, if unremarkable (single/double from €77/104).

## Festivals & Events

Haapsalu has a packed calendar of concerts and festivals, with the action concentrated between June and August.

**Haapsalu Horror & Fantasy Film Festival** FILM
(Haapsalu õudus- ja fantaasiafilmide festival; www.hoff.ee; single ticket/festival pass €5.50/45; ⊙ Apr) Haapsalu is invaded by fans of macabre, blood-splattered and downright creepy films during this four-day festival. The biggest genre-film festival in the Baltics, it's timed to coincide with the April full moon.

**Haapsalu Early Music Festival** MUSIC
(Haapsalu vanamuusika festival; www.haapsalu.ee; Haapsalu Catheral; tickets from €20; ⊙ Jul) Held in late July and making full use of the magnificent acoustics of the Dome Church (Haapsalu Cathedral), this festival celebrates early music and its practitioners from round the world.

**August Blues** MUSIC
(Augustibluus; www.augustibluus.ee; festival pass €65; ⊙ Aug) Over two days in early August, this is Estonia's biggest blues festival. Founded in 1994, it attracts plenty of international acts to add glamour to a rich program of Estonian artists. The grounds of the Episcopal Castle are the main venue, but seven other stages dot Haapsalu. Festival passes are cheaper if preordered online.

## Sleeping

**Lahe Maja** GUESTHOUSE €€
(☎ 516 3023; www.lahemaja.com; Lahe 7; r/cottage/house from €78/140/700; P 📶) The name means 'Bay House' and this very pretty pale-blue wooden house looks like it's escaped from a chocolate box to take its position within manicured lawns overlooking the water. The large main house has four double rooms and a four-person family room, plus there's a separate two-bedroom cottage for rent at the rear.

**Kongo Hotell** HOTEL €€
(☎ 472 4800; www.kongohotel.ee; Kalda 19; s/d/ste from €68/87/150; P 📶) The unassuming exterior gives little indication of Kongo's stylish, Scandi-chic decor – off-white walls, neutral linens and pale wooden floors. Larger rooms are available, with kitchenettes. And the name? A rough drinking den once stood on this spot, known for its brawling. The place was nicknamed 'Kongo' after the African country suffering through civil war at the time.

## Eating & Drinking

**Müüriääre Kohvik** CAFE €
(☎ 473 7527; www.muuriaare.ee; Karja 7; mains €8-10; ⊙ 10am-9pm Sun-Thu, to 10pm Fri & Sat; 📶) With more umlauts in its name than seems reasonable (the name means 'beside the walls'), this gorgeous cafe is clearly the town's favourite, if the crowds are anything to go by. And what's not to love in the warm interior, pretty rear terrace, cabinet full of cakes, and simple menu of fresh, light meals such as salads, pasta and quiche.

**Hapsal Dietrich** CAFE €€
(☎ 509 4549; www.dietrich.ee; Karja 10; mains €11-14; ⊙ 11.30am-8pm Sun-Thu, to 10pm Fri & Sat; 📶) A reboot of a famous, early-20th-century Haapsalu bakery-cafe of the same name, Dietrich is clearly a labour of love, with elements of 1920s and 1930s decor, photos from the old days and a winning way with cakes. The more substantial dishes such as the schnitzel with lingonberry jam or dumplings in duck broth are excellent, too.

WORTH A TRIP

## MATSALU NATIONAL PARK

A twitcher's paradise, **Matsalu** (Matsalu Rahvuspark; www.loodusegakoos.ee) is a prime migration and breeding ground for the Baltic and Europe generally: some 282 bird species have been counted here. Encompassing 486 sq km of wetlands (including 20km-long Matsalu Bay), it was first protected as a reserve in 1957, entered on the Ramsar List of Wetlands of International Importance in 1976, and declared a national park in 2004. Its **headquarters** (472 4236; www.loodusegakoos.ee; Penijõe village; 9am-5pm daily mid-Apr–Sep, Mon-Fri rest of year) are 3km north of the Tallinn–Virtsu road at Penijõe, an early-18th-century manor house near Lihula.

Comprising coastal meadows and woodland, over 50 islands in the Väinameri Sea and the most extensive reed bed in the Baltics, it's home to 49 species of fish, 47 species of mammal and 772 species of vascular plants. But it's the birds people come to see.

Spring migration peaks in April/May, but swans arrive as early as March. Autumn migration begins in July and can last until November. Birdwatching towers, with extensive views of resting sites over various terrain, have been built at **Haeska**, **Keemu**, **Suitsu**, **Penijõe** and **Kloostri**. There are also marked nature trails at Penijõe (3.2km to 7km), Salevere (1.5km) and Suitsu (1km). Bring reliable footwear as the ground is generally boggy, except during summer dry spells.

Next door is a guesthouse with six apartments furnished with the same taste and care (from €85).

**Herman Bistro & Bar** BAR
(473 7131; www.hermanhaapsalu.ee; Karja 1a; mains €7-9; 11am-9pm Sun-Thu, to 2am Fri & Sat; ) With a warm and inviting atmosphere, this brightly painted bar serves sandwiches, hearty meals and cocktails, or you can just slink in for a beer.

## Information

**Haapsalu Tourist Office** (473 3248; www.visithaapsalu.com; Karja 15; 9am-5pm Mon-Fri, 10am-4pm Sat & Sun mid-May–mid-Sep, 11am-5pm Mon-Fri rest of year; ) This friendly, well-staffed office has loads of info about Haapsalu and the surrounding area.

## Getting There & Away

The **bus station** (Raudtee 2) is at the pretty but defunct train station. Major destinations include Tallinn (€5 to €9, 1¾ hours, at least hourly), Tartu (€12, 4¼ hours, daily) and Pärnu (€5.10, 2½ hours, daily). For Hiiumaa, there are two daily buses to Kärdla (€4, 2½ hours) and a daily bus to Käina (€4, 2¼ hours).

Ferries to Hiiumaa and Vormsi leave from Rohuküla, 9km west of Haapsalu.

## Getting Around

You can rent bicycles at **Rattad Vaba Aeg** (521 2796; Karja 22; bikes per hour/day/24hr €2.50/10/16; 10am-6pm Mon-Fri, to 3pm Sat).

Bus 1 runs regularly between Lossi plats, the bus station and Rohuküla (the ferry wharf, 9km west); timetables are posted at Lossi plats and the bus station.

# Muhu

POP 1697

Connected to Saaremaa by a 2.5km causeway, the island of Muhu has the undeserved reputation as the 'doormat' for the bigger island – lots of people passing through on their way from the ferry, but few stopping. In fact, Estonia's third-biggest island offers plenty of excuses to hang around, including bucolic rural landscapes, medieval churches, traditional stone-and-thatch fishing villages, museums, galleries and grand manorial estates.

## Sights & Activities

★**Muhu Museum** MUSEUM
(454 8872; www.muhumuuseum.ee; Koguva; adult/concession €4/3; 9am-6pm mid-May–mid-Sep, 10am-5pm Tue-Sat rest of year; P) Koguva is an exceptionally well preserved, traditional Muhu village, now protected as an open-air museum. One ticket allows you to wander through an old schoolhouse, a house displaying beautiful traditional textiles from the area (including painstakingly detailed folk costumes) and Tooma farmstead, ancestral home of author Juhan Smuul (1922–71), 19th(!) child of a Koguva fisherman. Scattered around are orchards,

wells, moss-covered walls, cellars, a smithy and other perfectly photogenic relics.

**Koguva Kunstitall** GALLERY

(Koguva; ⊙10am-6pm mid-May–mid-Sep) FREE Local craft and artworks adorn the walls and shelves of this meticulously restored thatched longhouse in Koguva.

**Muhu Ostrich Farm** FARM

(Muhu Jaanalinnufarm; www.jaanalind.ee; Nautse; adult/student €4/3; ⊙10am-6pm mid-May–mid-Sep) This working ostrich farm is a decent diversion for families, with opportunities to feed the birds, learn about their habits and buy feather dusters, eggs, and purses and shoes made from ostrich leather. Attached is a mini-menagerie of kangaroos, wallabies, alpacas, emus and ponies (for kids to ride).

**Cycling Routes** CYCLING

(www.muhu.ee/Activities-on-Muhu/) The quiet back roads of Muhu are perfect for two-wheeled exploration, which is a very popular pastime of Estonian holidaymakers. Two cycling routes have been set out: the 53km northern route and the 26km southern route. Both start from the ferry and end at the causeway to Saaremaa, meaning they can be combined into one big loop. Download a map from the website.

## Courses

**Nami Namaste** COOKING

(☎515 2808; www.naminamaste.com; Simisti; 2-night package per person from €295; ⊙May-Sep) Renowned Finnish chef Sikke Sumari offers bespoke cooking classes including meals and accommodation in this tranquil stone farmstead in Simisti, in Muhu's south. Most ingredients are seasonal and local (many are home-grown or foraged), and classes are given in various languages, including English. It's also possible to dine here without taking the class (lunch/dinner €35/52), although numbers are limited.

## Sleeping & Eating

**Vanatoa Turismitalu** GUESTHOUSE €€

(☎5558 7494; www.vanatoa.ee; Koguva; camping per person €5, caravan €15, s/d from €50/58; P 🛜) In the heart of the exquisitely preserved fishing village Koguva, family-run Vanatoa offers 17 comfortably renovated rooms across a listed, thatched longhouse and its outbuildings. Triples have whirlpool baths, and the 'Fyke Shed' is only appropriate for the warmer months. There's also a common area with a pool table, a cafe, a sauna, bike rental and a volleyball court. It's best to book ahead.

★ **Pädaste Manor** HOTEL €€€

(☎454 8800; www.padaste.ee; Pädaste; d/ste from €267/437; ⊙Mar-Oct; P 🛜) If money's no object, here's where to part with it. This manicured bayside estate encompasses the restored manor house (14 rooms and a fine-dining restaurant), a stone carriage house (nine rooms and a spa centre) and a separate stone 'sea house' brasserie. The attention to detail is second to none, from the pop-up TVs to the antique furnishings and Muhu embroidery.

**Kalapoe Kohvik** SEAFOOD €

(☎459 8551; Liiva; mains €8-10; ⊙noon-6pm summer) At the crossroads in Liiva, this humble 'fish cafe', just a simple clapboard shack with outdoor seats for good weather, serves up first-rate fish with basic accompaniments such as cottage cheese, pickles and potato. Call ahead to ensure it's open, or take your chances if you're passing through.

**Alexander** EUROPEAN €€€

(☎454 8800; www.padaste.ee; Pädaste; 3/9 courses €74/131; ⊙1-2.30pm Mar-May & Sep, 7-10.30pm Mar–mid-Oct) Last named Estonia's best restaurant in 2015, Alexander is the culinary centrepiece of the ultra-luxe Pädaste Manor. Offering either a three-course or nine-course *prix fixe* menu, it's a real culinary adventure, focusing on tastes peculiar to Estonia's western islands and the best of what's in season, with nods to 'New Nordic' cuisine and molecular gastronomy.

## Getting There & Away

### BOAT

- Frequent **Praamid** (☎618 1310; www.praamid.ee; adult/child/car €3/1.50/8.40) car ferries make the 27-minute crossing between Virtsu on the mainland and Kuivastu on Muhu.
- Boats depart Virtsu from roughly 5.35am until midnight, with at least one or two sailings per hour up until 10.15pm.
- A 50% surcharge applies to vehicles heading to the island after 1pm on Fridays and departing the island after 1pm on Sundays.
- Up to 70% of each boat's capacity is presold online; the website has a real-time indicator showing what percentage has already been sold. The remaining 30% is kept for drive-up customers and offered on a first-in, first-on basis. You should definitely consider

prebooking at busy times, particularly around weekends in summer.

➡ Tickets purchased online must either be printed out or loaded as an e-ticket on your phone. If you're driving, your licence plate should suffice to show you've paid.

➡ If you miss your prebooked boat, your ticket will be valid for the regular queue on subsequent boats for up to 48 hours.



### BUS

Buses take the ferry from the mainland and continue through to Saaremaa via the causeway, stopping along the main road. Some Kuressaare–Kuivastu services also divert to Koguva and Pädaste on weekdays. Major destinations:

**Kuressaare** €5 to €5.60, one hour, up to 10 daily
**Pärnu** €6 to €11, 2½ hours, three daily
**Tallinn** €12 to €14, three hours, up to seven daily
**Tartu** €13 to €16, five hours, two daily
**Viljandi** €10 to €15, four hours, two daily

# Saaremaa

POP 31,317

To Estonians, Saaremaa (literally 'island land') is synonymous with space, spruce and fresh air – and bottled water, vodka and killer beer. Estonia's largest island (roughly the size of Luxembourg) is still substantially covered in forests of pine, spruce and juniper, while its windmills, lighthouses and tiny villages seem largely unbothered by the passage of time.

Kuressaare, the capital of Saaremaa, is on the south coast (75km from the Muhu ferry terminal) and is a natural base for visitors. It's here among the upmarket hotels that you'll understand where the island got its nickname, 'Spa-remaa'. When the long days arrive, so too do the Finns and Swedes, jostling for beach and sauna space with Estonian urban-escapees.

## History

Saaremaa's earliest coastal settlements (dating from the 4th millennium BC) now lie inland because the land has risen about 15m over the last 5000 years. In the 10th to 13th centuries Saaremaa and Muhu were the most densely populated parts of Estonia. Denmark tried to conquer Saaremaa in the early 13th century; however, in 1227 it was the German Knights of the Sword who subjugated it. The island was then carved up between the knights, who took Muhu and the eastern and northwestern parts of Saaremaa, and the Haapsalu-based bishop of Ösel-Wiek, who made Kuressaare his stronghold.

Saaremaa rebelled against German rule many times between 1236 and 1343, when the knights' castle was destroyed and the Germans were expelled. However, the islander's gains were always short-lived and in 1345 the Germans reconquered the island.

In the 16th century Saaremaa became a Danish possession during the Livonian War, but by 1645 the Swedes had their turn, compliments of the Treaty of Brömsebro. Russia took over in 1710 during the Great Northern War and Saaremaa became part of the Russian province of Livonia, governed from Rīga.

## ℹ Getting There & Away

Most travellers reach Saaremaa by taking the ferry from Virtsu to Muhu and then driving in a personal vehicle or by bus across the 2.5km causeway connecting the islands.

### AIR

**Kuressaare Airport** (Kuressaare Lennujaam; ☎ 453 0313; www.kuressaare-airport.ee; Roomassaare tee 1) is at Roomassaare, 3km southeast of the town centre. Buses 2 and 12 connect it with the bus station at Kuressaare.

Saartelennuliinid (www.saartelennuliinid.ee) flies to/from Tallinn twice daily on weekdays and once on Saturdays and Sundays (return from €52).

### BOAT

Additional to the Muhu ferry, Kihnu Veeteed (www.veeteed.com) runs two boats a day between Sõru on Hiiumaa and Triigi on the north coast of Saaremaa (adult/child/car €3/1.50/8.40, 65 minutes); from mid-September to mid-May there is only one sailing on Tuesdays, Thursdays and Saturdays. Tickets can be purchased at the harbour or prebooked online.

Veeteed also operates twice-weekly passenger-only service from Kuressaare (Roomassaare) to Ruhnu (Ringsu) from May to October (€11 to €17).

Saaremaa is very popular with visiting yachties. The best **marina** (https://sadam.kuressaare.ee; Tori 4) facilities are at Kuressaare. Visit www.sadamaregister.ee for details of this and other harbours on Saaremaa.

### BUS

Buses from the mainland take the Muhu ferry and continue to Saaremaa via the causeway, terminating in Kuressaare. Major routes:

**Muhu Island** €5 to €5.60, one hour, up to 10 daily
**Pärnu** €9 to €16, three hours, three daily
**Tallinn** €12 to €17, four hours, up to nine daily
**Tartu** €18 to €22, 5¾ hours, two daily
**Viljandi** €13 to €15, 4½ hours, two daily

## Getting Around

### BICYCLE

Flat Saaremaa is well suited to exploring by pedal power. Apart from the main highway leading from Muhu to Kuressaare, most of the roads have only light traffic and there are lots of side routes to explore.

Many accommodation providers rent bikes. In Kuressaare, **Bivarix** (455 7118; www.bivarix.ee; Pikk 54; per hour/4hr/day €6/8/15; 10am-6pm Mon-Fri) rents bicycles and touring gear such as trailers for kids or luggage. It can also advise on interesting routes.

### BUS

Local buses putter around the island, but not very frequently. The main terminus is **Kuressaare bus station** (Kuressaare Bussijaam; 453 1661; www.bussipilet.ee; Pihtla tee 2) and there's a route planner online at www.bussipilet.ee.

### ISLAND BREW

Saaremaa has a long history of beer home-brewing and even its factory-produced brew has a great reputation. Tuulik, with its distinctive windmill branding, is the most popular, but don't mention that it's now brewed in Tartu (the popular Saaremaa vodka also has a windmill on its label and it's not distilled here either).

For a classier drop, try Pöide (especially the dark version), which is produced in a microbrewery in the village of the same name. It's available at the pubs in Kuressaare and in craft-beer stockists nationwide.

Beer lovers should be sure to try any homemade beer wherever it's offered. A longtime island tradition, the brew features the traditional malt, yeast and hops, but comes off a bit sour on the palate. It's light and refreshing, best quaffed from a wooden tankard on a warm summer's day.

# Eastern Saaremaa

Apart from the town of Orissaare, which faces Muhu over the channel between the two islands, the eastern end of Saaremaa is sparsely populated and pleasantly rural.

## Sights & Activities

**St Mary's Church** CHURCH
(Pöide) Pöide, 3km south of the main highway, was the Saaremaa headquarters of the German Knights of the Sword and this fortress-church, built in the 13th and 14th centuries, remains an imposing symbol of their power. Pillaged and abandoned in Soviet times and reconsecrated in 1999, it now serves Lutheran, Methodist and Orthodox congregations, and its crumbling exterior is offset by a perfect stained-glass window above the altar.

**Orissaare Oak** LANDMARK
(Kuivastu mnt, Orissaare) Even in a nation where people still leave offerings in sacred groves, Orissaare's most famous landmark is, well, a little weird. Winner of the 2015 *European Tree of the Year* award, this 150-year-old oak stands right in the middle of a football field. The field was laid out around the oak in 1951 and when tractors came to remove the tree, the tree won the battle (although it still bears the scars). Players simply kick around it.

**Maasilinnus** CASTLE
(Maasi) FREE The German knights built this castle, 4km north of Orissaare, during the 14th to 16th centuries and using the forced labour of the conquered locals. It was blown up by the Danes in 1578 to prevent the Swedes from taking it, leaving behind a jumble of stones by a pretty reed-lined shore. Indulge your inner archaeologist by exploring the restored underground chamber.

**Tika Talu** HORSE RIDING
(504 4169; www.tikatalu.ee; Kõrkvere; trail rides per hour €20) Runs trail rides through the coastal plains of eastern Saaremaa, and has an indoor training and dressage facility (€20 per 45 minutes).

# Central Saaremaa

If you're arriving by ferry from Hiiumaa, the first settlement you'll hit is Leisi, a pretty village of old wooden houses, 3.5km from the harbour of Triigi. There are some interesting sights scattered around this section of the north coast, along with plenty of others on either side of the main road heading south to Kuressaare.

## Saaremaa & Muhu

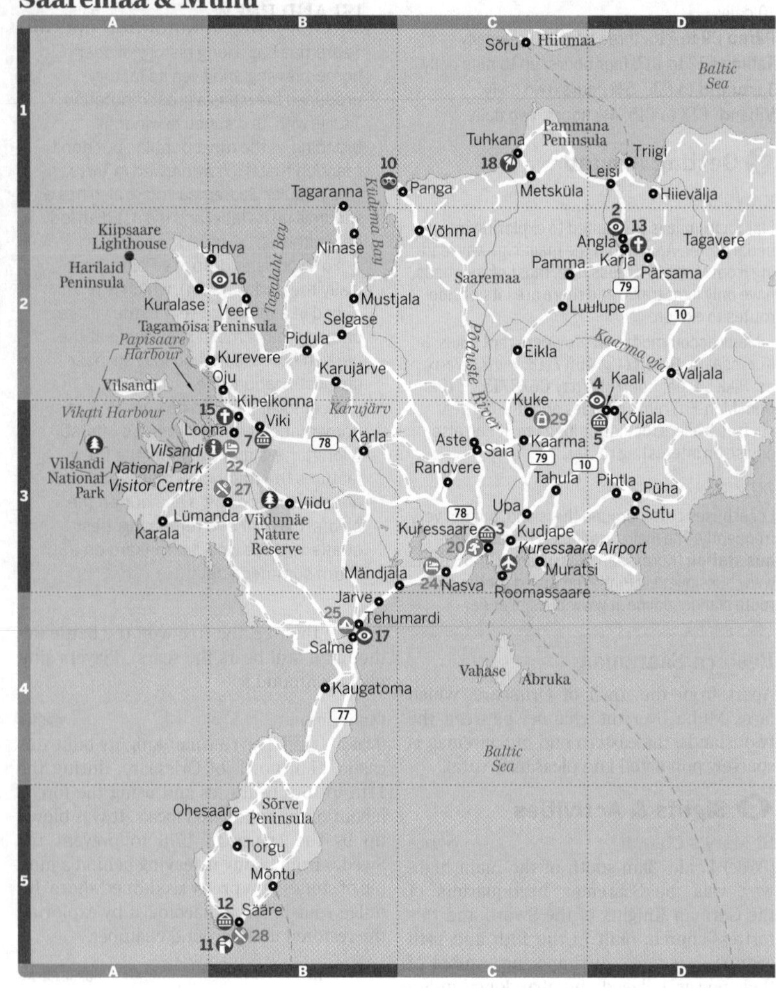


## Sights

**St Catherine's Lutheran Church, Karja** CHURCH
(Karja Katariina kirik; Linnaka village; ⏲10am-5.30pm Mon-Sat, noon-6pm Sun Jun-Aug) The pagan and Christian meet in this fortress-like 14th-century church. Outside there's an interesting panel about pre-Christian symbols with particular reference to some of the 13th- and 14th-century trapezoidal gravestones found here. Inside, oak leaves curl along the top of the columns and there are some interesting symbols painted on the walls.

**Angla Windmill Hill** ARCHITECTURE
(Angla Tuulikumägi; ☎5199 0265; www.anglatuulik.eu; Upa-Leisi; adult/reduced €4/2; ⏲9am-8pm May-Aug, to 5pm Sep-Apr; P 👪) Charge up those camera batteries: this is the site of the largest and most photogenic grouping of wooden windmills on the islands. By the early 16th century there were already nine windmills on this hill. Now there are four small ones, mainly dating from the 19th century, and one large Dutch-style one, built in 1927. There are excellent (free) views from the road, but the modest admission charge allows you to poke around in their innards.

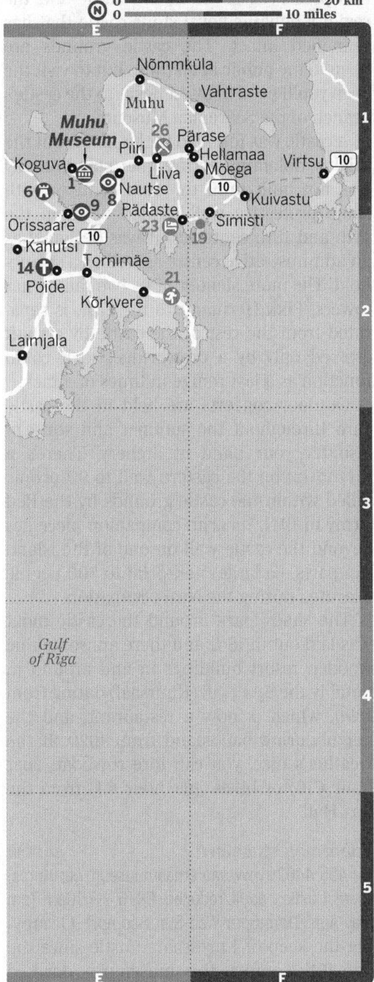


## Saaremaa & Muhu





**Tuhkana** BEACH

Tucked away within pine forest, Tuhkana is one of Saaremaa's best sandy beaches, due in large part to its remoteness. To get here from Leisi, head west for 11km to Metsküla and turn right onto the unsealed road. After about 3km, look for a parking area on your left.

**Panga Pank** VIEWPOINT

Saaremaa's highest cliffs run along the northern coast near Panga for 3km. The highest point (21.3m) was a sacred place where sacrifices were made to the sea god; gifts of flowers, coins, vodka and beer are still sometimes left here. It's a pretty spot, looking down at the treacherous waters below.

**Kaali Crater** LAKE

Estonia has one of the world's highest concentrations of documented meteor craters. At Kaali, 18km north of Kuressaare, is a 100m-wide, 22m-deep, curiously round lake formed by a meteorite at least 4000 years ago. There are a further eight collateral craters in the vicinity, ranging from 12m to 40m in diameter, formed by fragments of the same meteorite. To the pre-Christians, the site was known as the sun's grave, and was used for animal sacrifice.

A tourist village of sorts has sprung up here – there's a small **museum** (www.kaali.kylastuskeskus.ee; adult/child €1.50/1; 9am-7pm), handicrafts stores and a hotel, as well as an old-style tavern offering Estonian fare and locally brewed beer.

## Shopping

**GoodKaarma** GIFTS & SOUVENIRS
(5348 4006; www.goodkaarma.com; Kuke; 10am-6pm Jun-Aug, other times by arrangement) Run by an English-Estonian couple from their farm outside the village of Kaarma, about 15km north of Kuressaare, GoodKaarma makes organic soaps from local ingredients such as juniper, pine and sea-buckthorn berries. If you're interested in getting your hands dirty (or should that be clean), you can book into a 75-minute soap-making workshop (per person €10, minimum five people).

# Kuressaare

POP 13,166

What passes for the big smoke in these parts, Kuressaare has a picturesque town centre with leafy streets and a magnificent castle rising up in its midst, surrounded by a sprawling ring-town of housing and light industry. The town built a reputation as a health centre as early as the 19th century, when the ameliorative properties of its coastal mud were discovered and the first spas opened. Now they're a dime a dozen, ranging from Eastern Bloc sanatoriums to sleek and stylish resorts.

Apart from the castle, the best of Kuressaare's historic buildings are grouped around the central square, Keskväljak. The tourist office is housed in the town hall (1670), a baroque building guarded by a fine pair of stone lions. Directly across the square the Vaekoja pub inhabits a former weigh-house, also from the 17th century.

## Sights

★**Kuressaare Episcopal Castle** CASTLE
(www.saaremaamuuseum.ee) Majestic Kuressaare Castle stands facing the sea at the southern end of the town, on an artificial island defended by stone-faced earth bastions and ringed by a moat. It's the best-preserved castle in the Baltic and the region's only medieval stone castle that has remained intact. The castle grounds are open to the public at all times but to visit the keep you'll need to buy a ticket to the castle's branch of the Saaremaa Museum.

A castle was founded in the 1260s, but the mighty dolomite fortress that stands today was not built until the 14th century, with some protective walls added between the 15th and 18th centuries. It was designed as an administrative centre as well as a stronghold. The more slender of its two tall corner towers, Pikk Hermann to the east, is separated from the rest of the castle by a shaft crossed only by a drawbridge, so it could function as a last refuge in times of attack.

Outdoor concerts are held in the castle yard throughout the summer and you can also try your hand at archery. There's a **memorial** on the eastern wall to 90 people killed within the castle grounds by the Red Army in 1941. Its grim companion piece lies beyond the castle wall on one of the island ramparts – a large **memorial** to 300 people executed during the Nazi occupation.

The shady park around the castle moat was laid out in 1861 and there are some fine wooden resort buildings in and around it, notably the **Spa Hall** (Kuursaal) dating from 1899, which is now a restaurant, and the neighbouring bandstand from 1920. If the weather's nice, you can hire rowboats (per hour €10) or bikes (per hour €4) from the Spa Hall.

**Saaremaa Museum** MUSEUM
(455 4463; www.saaremaamuuseum.ee; Kuressaare Castle; adult/reduced €8/6; 10am-7pm May-Aug, 11am-6pm Wed-Sun Sep-Apr) Occupying the keep of Kuressaare Castle since the late 19th century, this museum is devoted to Saaremaa's nature and history. A large part of the fun is exploring the warren of chambers, halls, passages and stairways, apt to fuel anyone's *Game of Thrones* fantasies. One room near the bishop's chamber looks down to a dungeon where, according to legend, condemned prisoners were dispatched to be devoured by hungry lions (recorded growls reinforce the mental image).

**Suur Töll & Piret** SCULPTURE
Kuressaare's jauntiest statue, created in 2002, features Saaremaa's legendary gigantic hero, Suur (meaning 'the great') Töll and his wife, Piret, carrying a boat laden with fish on their glistening, naked shoulders.

**St Nicholas' Orthodox Church** CHURCH
(Püha Nikolai Kirik; Lossi 8; ⌚10am-2pm Tue-Sat, 9.30am-noon Sun mid-May–mid-Aug) Built by Catherine the Great in 1790, Saaremaa's oldest Orthodox church has twin steeples and an impressive dolomite and wrought-iron gate. A faint image of its name saint has survived on the exterior wall facing the street, while inside there are some lovely icons, including one featuring the church itself.

**Kuressaare Beach** BEACH
(Raiekivi tee 1) Although the best beaches are out of town, this small sandy bay behind Kuressaare Castle fills up with sunbathers, paddlers and volleyball players during the summer.

**St Lawrence's Lutheran Church** CHURCH
(Laurentiuse Kirik; Tallinna 13; ⌚10am-5pm Tue, Wed & Fri, 6-7pm Thu, 11am-2pm Sat Jun-Aug) Although this large, single-naved, dolomite church was rebuilt in its present form in 1836, its prized feature is considerably older: a medieval stone baptismal font rescued from the 14th-century church at Anseküla, destroyed in WWII. Probably from the early 15th century, it's carved with dragon-like creatures. Also worth noting are the grey wooden box pews, low-hanging chandeliers and the fine vaulted roof above the sanctuary painted with an interesting *trompe l'œil* effect.

**Johannes & Joosep Aavik's Memorial Museum** MUSEUM
(Johannes & Joosep Aaviku majamuuseum; www.saaremaamuuseum.ee; Vallimaa 7; adult/reduced €3/2; ⌚11am-4pm Wed-Fri) The Aavik family home is now a small museum dedicated to the life and works of linguist Johannes Aavik (1880–1973), who introduced major reforms to the Estonian language, and his musically talented cousin, Joosep Aavik (1899–1989).

## Activities

**Spa Hotel Rüütli** WATER PARK
(☎454 8100; www.saaremaaspahotels.eu; Pargi 12; adult/reduced €8/5; ⌚7am-9pm; 👪) If the weather means an indoor splash is best, bring the kids to this hotel water park to make use of the pools and 52m slide. Mum and Dad might like to book a spa treatment while they're at it (from €13).

**Saaremaa Golf & Country Club** GOLF
(☎453 3502; www.saaregolf.ee; Merikotka 35; 9/18 holes from €35/60, club hire €40) This 18-hole championship course is immediately west of Kuressaare's town centre.

## Festivals & Events

Kuressaare's dance card is certainly full over the summer. As well as the high-profile festivals, there are regular summer concerts held in the castle grounds and park; find out what's up at the tourist office.

**Saaremaa Opera Festival** MUSIC
(Saaremaa ooperipäevad; www.saaremaaopera.eu; Kuressaare Castle; tickets from €79; ⌚Jul) For a week in late July, about 2000 people pack into the grounds of Kuressaare Castle to watch productions from an international guest company.

**Kuressaare Chamber Music Days** MUSIC
(Kuressaare kammermuusika päevad; www.kammerfest.ee; festival passport €65; ⌚Jul/Aug) Concerts take place all over town during five days in late July/early August, including such evocative venues as the chapter house of Kuressaare's castle.

**Kuressaare Maritime Festival** CULTURAL
(Kuressaare merepaevad; www.merepaevad.ee; Raiekivi Säär; ⌚Aug) Held every August on Raiekivi Säär, the little peninsula behind the castle, this good-natured festival features food stalls, concerts and other performances.

## Sleeping

The tourist office can organise beds in private apartments and farms across the island. Hotel prices are up to 50% cheaper from September through April. Most hotel spa centres are open to nonguests.

**Hotell Mardi** HOTEL €
(☎452 4633; www.hotelmardi.eu; Vallimaa 5a; hostel s/tw €20/30, hotel s/d from €44/67; P 📶) These simple, fuss-free rooms are attached to a college. The hostel rooms have bunk beds and share bathrooms; they're a little institutional, but probably Kuressaare's best cheapies.

**Staadioni Hotell** HOTEL €€
(☎453 3556; www.staadionihotell.ee; Staadioni 4; s/d €44/59; ⌚mid-May–early Sep; P @ 📶) Good-value spacious and bright rooms are available at this pleasant, secluded spot, south of the castle. It's surrounded by parkland and sports facilities. Bikes can be hired here (per day €10) and there's a sauna available.

## Kuressaare

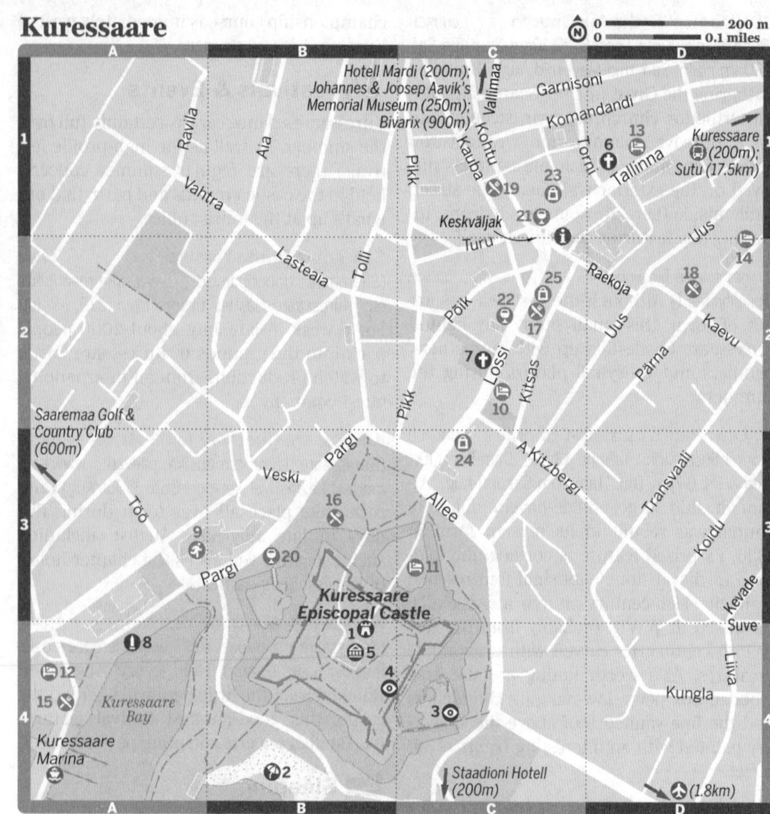


**Karluti Hostel** GUESTHOUSE €€

(☎501 4390; www.karluti.ee; Pärna 23; tw/tr without bathroom €40/50; ⏲Apr-Oct; P 📶) It's hard to imagine this cheerful, 1930s clapboard guesthouse was once home to Soviet naval intelligence. Set among large lawns on a quiet residential street, it's close to the centre, and offers a kitchen for guests to self-cater. There are only a handful of bright, spotless rooms available, so you'll need to book ahead – especially in summer.

★ **Ekesparre** BOUTIQUE HOTEL €€€

(☎453 8778; www.ekesparre.ee; Kuressaare Castle, Lossi 27; r from €175; ⏲Apr-Oct; P 📶) Holding pole position in manicured gardens on the castle grounds, this elegant 10-room hotel has been returned to its 1908, art nouveau glory. Period wallpaper and carpet, Tiffany lamps and a smattering of orchids add to the refined, clubby atmosphere, while the 3rd-floor guests' library is a gem. As you'd expect from the price, it's a polished operator.

★ **Georg Ots Spa Hotel** HOTEL €€€

(Gospa; ☎455 0000; www.gospa.ee; Tori 2; s/d from €133/145, ste €295; P ❄ 📶 🏊) Named after a renowned Estonian opera singer, Gospa has modern rooms with wildly striped carpet, enormous king-sized beds and a warm but minimalist design. Most rooms have balconies, and there's a fitness centre and excellent day spa, including a pool and multiple saunas. Separate freestanding 'residences' are also available, and families are very well catered to. Prices vary widely.

**Arensburg** BOUTIQUE HOTEL €€€

(☎452 4700; www.arensburg.ee; Lossi 15; s/d/ste €115/130/250; P 📶 🏊) Arensburg is almost two hotels in one, with a severe case of old versus new. Our vote goes to the bold and sexy charcoal-and-mustard-painted rooms in the slick 2007 extension (standard rooms in the historic wing are OK but unremarkable). A spa and two restaurants (mains €12) round things out nicely.

## Kuressaare

**Top Sights**
1 Kuressaare Episcopal Castle ........ B4

**Sights**
2 Kuressaare Beach ........ B4
3 Memorial to Victims of the Nazis ........ C4
4 Memorial to Victims of the Red Army ........ B4
5 Saaremaa Museum ........ B4
6 St Lawrence's Lutheran Church ........ D1
7 St Nicholas' Orthodox Church ........ C2
8 Suur Töll & Piret ........ A4

**Activities, Courses & Tours**
9 Spa Hotel Rüütli ........ A3

**Sleeping**
10 Arensburg ........ C2
11 Ekesparre ........ C3
12 Georg Ots Spa Hotel ........ A4
13 Grand Rose Spa Hotel ........ D1
14 Karluti Hostel ........ D2

**Eating**
15 Gospa Restaurant ........ A4
16 Ku Kuu ........ B3
17 Retro ........ C2
18 Saaremaa Veski ........ D2
19 Vanalinna ........ C1

**Drinking & Nightlife**
20 John Bull ........ B3
21 Pub Vaekoda ........ C1
22 Vinoteek Prelude ........ C2

**Shopping**
23 Kuressaare Market ........ C1
24 Lossi Antiik ........ C3
25 Saaremaa Kunstistuudio ........ C2

**Grand Rose Spa Hotel** HOTEL €€€
(666 7000; www.grandrose.ee; Tallinna 15; s/d/ste from €130/135/205; ) Floral and frilly is the theme of this hotel, from the baroque black velvet chairs, chandeliers and water feature in the rose-filled lobby to the rose carpet throughout. Deluxe rooms have a balcony, separate bathtub and shower stall, and over-the-top beds, but feel more crammed than the standard rooms. The spa centre and restaurant (mains €13 to €15) are both very good.

## Eating

**★Retro** CAFE €
(5683 8400; www.kohvikretro.ee; Lossi 5; mains €7-10; noon-9pm Mon-Thu, to midnight Fri & Sat; ) The menu at this stylish little cafe-bar is deceptively simple (mainly burgers, with a few wraps, soups and seafood dishes thrown in), but Retro's kitchen works hard: making its own ciabatta and burger buns, and using top-notch produce. Desserts are delicious, and there's a great selection of Estonian craft beer, perfect for supping on the large terrace out back.

**Vanalinna** CAFE €
(455 3214; www.vanalinna.ee; Kauba 8; cakes & pastries €0.50-3; 7.30am-6pm Mon-Fri, 8am-6pm Sat, to 4pm Sun; ) Attached to a hotel of the same name, this bakery-cafe has an appealing vibe, with its timber-and-stone interior and black-and-white photos hanging from dark-orange walls. The counter has an appealing selection of sandwiches, salads, pastries and ice cream, and there's outdoor seating when the sun shines.

**★Ku Kuu** EUROPEAN €€
(453 9749; www.kuressaarekuursaal.ee; Lossipark 1; mains €14-17; 11am-10pm Mon-Thu, to 11pm Fri-Sun May–mid-Sep; ) Occupying the elegant 1889 Spa Hall from which it takes its name (Ku Kuu is short for Kuressaare Kuursaal), this is Saaremaa's loveliest dining room. The wood panelling and coloured glass provide an atmospheric backdrop for a tasty menu of seafood and island produce that visits various European cuisines. Outdoor dining, immediately opposite the castle, is a summer treat.

The best of each day's catch is usually the best choice, priced by weight.

**Saaremaa Veski** ESTONIAN €€
(Saaremaa Mill; 453 3776; www.saaremaaveski.ee; Pärna 19; mains €14-15; noon-11pm Sun-Thu, to midnight Fri & Sat; ) How often can you say you've dined inside a 19th-century windmill? Without being too touristy, this place keeps quality and ambience at a premium, with plenty of hearty local fare – including wild boar hotpot, beetroot soup and Saaremaa cheeses. Built in 1899, the mill operated until 1941, when the sails were removed to prevent their use for wartime signalling.

**Gospa Restaurant** EUROPEAN €€
(455 0000; www.gospa.ee; Tori 2; mains €15-18; noon-10pm Sun-Thu, to 11pm Fri & Sat; ) Picture windows make the most of the

marina views in the bright and airy dining room of Georg Ots Spa Hotel (p154). The food is light, fresh and creative, making good use of local produce, and there's a separate kids' menu, offering simple treats such as meatball soup and build-your-own pizza.

## Drinking & Nightlife

**Vinoteek Prelude** WINE BAR
(☎453 3407; www.prelude.ee; Lossi 4; ⊙4pm-midnight; 📶) This cosy, dimly lit wine bar in an 18th-century building on Kuressaare's main drag is a great choice for interesting food and wine. Climb the staircase to sofas under the eaves, and choose from a menu of international wines (plenty by the glass), antipasti-style snacks and wine-friendly meals such as wild-boar neck cooked with plums and paprika (mains €18 to €21).

**John Bull** PUB
(☎453 9988; www.johnbull.ee; Lossipark 4; ⊙11.30am-10pm Mon-Thu, to 11pm Fri-Sat; 📶) Despite the name, this pub in the castle park isn't particularly English. In fact, there's more of a Soviet vibe going down: the bar is made from an old Russian bus and there's even a 'red corner' hung with portraits of Lenin. Sit on the deck for great views looking over the moat to the castle.

**Pub Vaekoda** PUB
(☎453 3020; www.vaekoda.ee; Tallinna 3; ⊙noon-11pm Mon-Thu, to 6am Fri & Sat, to 10pm Sun; 📶) The name means 'weigh-house' and this is one of Kuressaare's most significant historic buildings, built in 1663 to measure goods for taxation and commercial purposes. These days it's a relaxed, no-nonsense pub with tables spilling onto the street and serving a robust almost-exclusively meaty menu (mains €12 to €15).

## Shopping

**Lossi Antiik** ANTIQUES
(www.lossiantiik.eu; Lossi 19; ⊙10am-4pm Mon-Fri, 11am-3pm Sat) Just before the castle, this jam-packed little store sells all sorts of antiques, from 19th-century farm tools to Soviet memorabilia. It's a fun place to browse.

**Kuressaare Market** MARKET
(Kuressaare Turg; Tallinna 5; ⊙9am-5pm) This outdoor market has stalls selling all kinds of Saaremaa treats and tat: dolomite canisters, woollen sweaters, wooden handicrafts, smallgoods, honey, strawberries and more, depending on the season.

**Saaremaa Kunstistuudio** ARTS & CRAFTS
(☎453 3748; www.kunstistuudio.ee; Lossi 5; ⊙10am-7pm Mon-Fri, to 6pm Sat, to 4pm Sun) This bright gallery contains a variety of works by Estonian artists, including covetable textiles, ceramics, sculptures and paintings.

## Information

**Kuressaare Tourist Office** (☎453 3120; www.visitsaaremaa.ee; Tallinna 2; ⊙9am-6pm Mon-Fri, 10am-4pm Sat & Sun mid-May–mid-Sep, 9am-5pm Mon-Fri rest of year) Inside the old town hall, it provides maps and guides, lists accommodation and has information on boat trips and island tours.

## Getting There & Around

**Kuressaare Takso** (☎1300, 453 0000; www.kuressaaretakso.ee; day/night flagfall €2.20/2.40, per km €0.80/0.95) is a reliable local taxi firm.

# Southwest Coast

The long stretch of pine-lined sand from Mändjala to Järve, west of Kuressaare, is Saaremaa's main beach resort. The shallow beach curves languidly towards the south, where the 32km Sõrve Peninsula takes over. This beautiful but sparsely populated finger of land comes to a dramatic end at Sääre, with a lighthouse and a narrow sand spit extending out to sea.

The peninsula saw heavy fighting during WWII, and the battle scars remain. Various abandoned bunkers and battlements, and the remnants of the Lõme-Kaimri anti-tank defence lines, can still be seen.

## Sights

**Tehumardi Night Battle Monument** MEMORIAL
(Tehumardi) On the night of 8 October 1944 a gruesome battle took place in the coastal village of Tehumardi between retreating German troops and a Soviet Estonian Rifle Division. The horror defies belief: both armies fought blindly, firing on intuition or finding the enemy by touch. This large Soviet-era monument takes the form of a sword with the stylised reliefs of faces set into it. The Estonian dead lie buried in double graves nearby.

**Sõrve Military Museum** MUSEUM
(Sõrve militaarmuuseum; Sääre; adult/reduced €5/3; ⊙9am-9pm Jun-Aug, 10am-5pm Sep-May)

WORTH A TRIP

## VILSANDI

Vilsandi, west of Kihelkonna, is the largest of 161 islands and islets off Saaremaa's western coast protected as **Vilsandi National Park** (which also includes parts of Saaremaa itself, including the Harilaid Peninsula). The park covers 238 sq km (163 sq km of sea, 75 sq km of land) and is an area of extensive ecological study. The breeding patterns of the common eider and the migration of the barnacle goose have been monitored very closely here. Ringed seals can also be seen in their breeding season and 32 species of orchid thrive in the park.

Vilsandi, 6km long and in places up to 3km wide, is a low, wooded island. The small islets surrounding it are abundant with currant and juniper bushes. Around 250 bird species are observed here, and in spring and autumn there is a remarkable migration of waterfowl: up to 10,000 barnacle geese stop over on Vilsandi in mid-May, and the white-tailed eagle and osprey have even been known to drop by.

**Islander** (☎5667 1555; www.islander.ee; ⊙May-Sep) offers speedboat water taxis to the island (€120 for up to 10 people), as well as diving, waterskiing, tubing and seal-spotting trips.

The **Vilsandi National Park Visitor Centre** (Vilsandi Rahvuspargi Keskus; ☎454 6880; www.loodusegakoos.ee; ⊙10am-6pm daily Jun-Aug, 9am-5pm Mon-Fri Sep-May) is on the grounds of Loona Manor, inland from Vilsandi. Staff can provide information on the park's four basic free campsites and the two private 'tourist farms' offering accommodation and boat transfers. There's also an exposition on the park and its flora and fauna.

Based in former Soviet border-guard barracks, this ramshackle museum showcases military detritus, much of which was scavenged from the surrounding area. Arguably more interesting than the collection itself are the ruins of a massive gun embankment and various other bits of masonry littered around the garden. Included on the same ticket, a nearby cottage is jam-packed with an eclectic array of bugs, butterflies, feathers, skulls, mosses and stuffed critters.

**Sõrve Lighthouse & Visitor Centre** LIGHTHOUSE

(Sõrve Tuletorn; www.sorvekeskus.ee; Sääre; adult/reduced €5/4; ⊙10am-7pm Jun-Aug) The first lighthouse on Sõrve promontory, just a primitive beacon, was built in the 17th century; the current 52m erection dates to 1960. To climb it, it's necessary to buy a ticket to the nearby visitor centre, occupying the old lighthouse-keeper's residence, and presenting displays split over several floors, including a 'nature room', a 'sea room' (devoted to shipwrecks and the rescue service) and a children's playroom.

## Sleeping & Eating

**Tehumardi Camping** CAMPGROUND €

(☎510 5150; www.tehumardi.ee; Tehumardi; campsite per person €7, caravan site for 2 €21, cabins €45; P wi-fi) The best of the campgrounds on the beach stretch, Tehumardi has a leafy site by a little lake. As well as basic four-person wooden cabins there are little hotel-style rooms (with their own bathrooms) and larger houses and bunkrooms for families or groups. Bikes are available for €2 per hour, and laundry is €4 a load.

★**Piibutopsu** APARTMENT €€

(☎520 5300; www.piibutopsu.ee; Ülejõe 19a, Nasva; d/tr/q €65/98/131; P wi-fi) Set on the ample lawn of a private residence down a side street in Nasva (the first little settlement west of Kuressaare), Piibutopsu offers four modern, well-equipped holiday apartments in a custom-built block. The units are grouped around a central lounge with a wood fire, and there's even a mini spa centre on-site. All in all, an excellent option.

**Sääre Paargu** CAFE €€

(☎5550 5555; www.saarepaargu.ee; Sääre; mains €10-13; ⊙10am-10pm mid-May–Aug; wi-fi) Paargu means 'summer house' and this slick little pavilion near the tip of the Sõrve Peninsula only kicks off in the warmer months. Grilled fish, freshly caught locally, is usually the pick of the menu, but there are burgers and grilled chicken too. With a beachside deck and beach-house vibe, it's very popular with visitors to Sõrve Lighthouse.

## Western Saaremaa

Even in summer, it's easy to beat the tourist hordes down this end of the island. The main settlement is sleepy Kihelkonna, which is more an oversized village than a town. It's the gateway to Vilsandi, the most remote of Estonia's national parks.

### Sights

**Mihkli Farm Museum** MUSEUM
(Mihkli Talumuuseum; www.saaremaamuuseum.ee; Viki; adult/reduced €4/3; ⏲10am-6pm daily mid-May–mid-Aug, Wed-Sun early May & mid-Aug–Sep; P) In a pretty setting southeast of Kihelkonna, this early-18th-century farm has been preserved in its entirety, complete with thatched-roof wooden farmhouses, a sauna, a windmill and a traditional village swing. Six generations of one farming family have lived here, and made almost everything you can see.

**Viidumäe Nature Reserve** NATURE RESERVE
(Viidumäe looduskaitseala) Founded in 1957, this reserve covers an area of 26 sq km, with a 26m **observation tower** at Saaremaa's highest point, Raunamägi (a vertigo-inducing 54m). The tower (about 2km along a dirt road north of Viidu) offers panoramic views of the forest and the contours of western Saaremaa, particularly memorable at sunset. There are also three short **nature trails** leaving from the **Viidumäe Nature Centre** (just beyond the tower), highlighting the different habitats of the area.

**St Michael's Lutheran Church** CHURCH
(Mihkli kirik; Kiriku 4, Kihelkonna; ⏲10am-5pm Sat & Sun Jun-Aug) Kihelkonna's tall, austere, early-German church dates from before 1280. It's dark and gloomy inside, partly due to the wooden supports holding up the roof, but it's worth noting the Renaissance *Last Supper* triptych (1591) above the altar and the carved pulpit (1604). The church didn't get its steeple until 1899; before that the bells were rung from the freestanding **belfry** (1638) about 100m away. Once common, the belfry is the only one of its kind remaining in Estonia.

**Tagamõisa Peninsula** NATURAL FEATURE
Much of the beautiful and rarely visited western coast of the Tagamõisa Peninsula is protected as part of Vilsandi National Park, including the Harilaid Peninsula, an important stopover for migratory birds. At its northwestern tip (accessible only on foot) is the striking **Kiipsaare lighthouse**, which due to erosion now sits about 30m out to sea. The erosion has caused the lighthouse to develop a visible lean, although it periodically corrects itself as the constantly mobile sands shift.

### Sleeping & Eating

**Loona Manor** GUESTHOUSE €€
(☎454 6510; www.loonamanor.ee; Loona; s/d €48/69; P 📶) Loona may be a late-18th-century manor house, but it's more homely than palatial, with simple, clean rooms and a quiet atmosphere. There's an unfussy cafe-restaurant (open noon to 10pm May to September, mains €10 to €12), and Vilsandi National Park Visitor Centre is within the grounds.

**Lümanda Söögimaja** ESTONIAN €€
(☎457 6493; www.soogimaja.planet.ee; Lümanda; mains €6-14; ⏲11am-10pm Jun-Aug; P) This rustic restaurant, occupying a schoolhouse once attached to the photogenic church adjacent, just does old-fashioned Saaremaa cuisine. You'll taste dishes that have nourished the islanders for centuries – fish soup, boiled pork with turnips and carrots, and cabbage rolls – with nothing frozen or imported from afar. There's also a shop selling local crafts as you enter.

# Hiiumaa

POP 8482

Hiiumaa, at 989 sq km Estonia's second-biggest island, is a beautiful, bucolic place boasting stunning coasts, forests and farmland. Sustaining a high population of Estonian Swedes, the island has less tourist development than Saaremaa, with considerably fewer options for lodging and dining. There's generally less to do and see than on its larger, southern neighbour, but most visitors are content simply to breathe in the fresh sea air and relax.

Scattered about Hiiumaa you'll find picturesque lighthouses, eerie old Soviet bunkers, empty beaches and a nature reserve with over 100 different bird species. Those seeking a bit more activity can hike, bike, ride horses or indulge in various water sports. And, thanks to the island's microclimate, the weather here is often considerably warmer than on the mainland, only 22km away. For further information about the island, see www.hiiumaa.ee.

### HIIUMAA HANDICRAFTS

Handicraft-hunters will find fertile ground in Hiiumaa, where traditional crafts have been kept alive. One of the best outlets is the museum shop (p164) in Kassari, which carries top-quality woven woollen rugs, among other things. Also worth checking out:

**Heltermaa Crafts House** (Heltermaa Käsitöömaja; ☎515 0319; Heltermaa; ⊙10.30am-7pm Jun-Sep) Everything sold in this craft collective near the ferry in Heltermaa is made on the island.

**Hiiu Wool Factory** (Hiiu villavabrik; ☎463 6121; www.hiiuvill.ee; Vaemla; ⊙9am-6pm Mon-Fri, from 10am Sat year-round, plus 10am-4pm Sun mid-May–Aug) Look for this small mill, which produces traditional woollen garments on 19th century machines, 4km east of Käin.

## Getting There & Away

### AIR

There are two **Transaviabaltika** (http://sll.flights) flights each weekday, and one each Saturday and Sunday between **Kärdla Airport** (Kärdla Lennujaam; ☎463 1381; www.kardla-airport.ee; Hiiessaare) and Tallinn (€21, 30 minutes). The airport is 6km east of the centre of Kärdla, and can be reached on free buses timed to meet all flights.

### BOAT

- Most people arrive in Hiiumaa on the **Praamid Ferries** (www.praamid.ee) service from Rohuküla to Heltermaa (adult/child/car/motorbike €3.40/1.70/10/4.20, 1½ hours, eight to 10 daily).
- The busiest boats are those heading to Hiiumaa on Friday afternoon and returning on Sunday afternoon. A 50% surcharge for vehicles applies after 1pm on these routes.
- Up to 70% of each boat's capacity is presold online; the website has a real-time indicator showing what percentage has already been sold. The remaining 30% is kept for drive-up customers and offered on a first-in, first-on basis. You should consider prebooking at busy times, particularly around weekends in summer.
- Tickets purchased online must either be printed out or loaded as an e-ticket on your phone. If you're driving, your licence plate should suffice to show you've paid.
- If you miss your prebooked boat, your ticket will be valid for the regular queue on subsequent boats for up to 48 hours.
- Ferry services also operate between Hiiumaa and Saaremaa (p148).

### BUS

There are two daily buses between Kärdla and Tallinn (€13, four hours) and one between Käina and Tallinn (€12, 3½ hours), all of which stop in Suuremõisa, Heltermaa, Rohuküla and Haapsalu.

## Getting Around

Paved roads circle Hiiumaa and cover several side routes; the rest are unsealed, and can get very pitted and uneven as they snake through coastal forests. Like many of the quiet nooks of rural Estonia, Hiiumaa is a great place to explore by bike, something you'll see many Estonians doing when the weather smiles. It's compact, almost uniformly flat and none of the roads are particularly busy – unless you happen to hit the rapidly dispersing traffic coming off the ferry.

There are petrol stations at Kärdla, Käina and Emmaste. Many accommodation providers can arrange car or bike hire, as can **Takso Autorent** (☎511 2225; www.carrent-hiiumaa.ee; Kaare 10, Kärdla) in Kärdla, which rents out cars from €25 per day.

Buses, nearly all radiating from Kärdla but some from Käina, get to most places on the island, though are understandably infrequent. Schedules are posted inside the bus station in Kärdla, and online at www.peatus.ee.

## Kärdla

POP 3281

Hiiu County's capital and Hiiumaa's largest town, known from records since the 16th century, flourished around a cloth factory founded in 1829 and destroyed during WWII. It's a green, spacious place of gardens and tree-lined streets, with a sleepy atmosphere and few diversions. Still, it's Hiiumaa's centre for services of all kinds and if you need to stock up on provisions, it has a couple of supermarkets.

The town sits on the edge of the world's 'best-preserved Palaeozoic meteorite crater', not that you'd know it as, despite being 4km in diameter, it's barely visible. It's fair to say that you wouldn't want to have been visiting here 455 million years ago when the impact occurred.

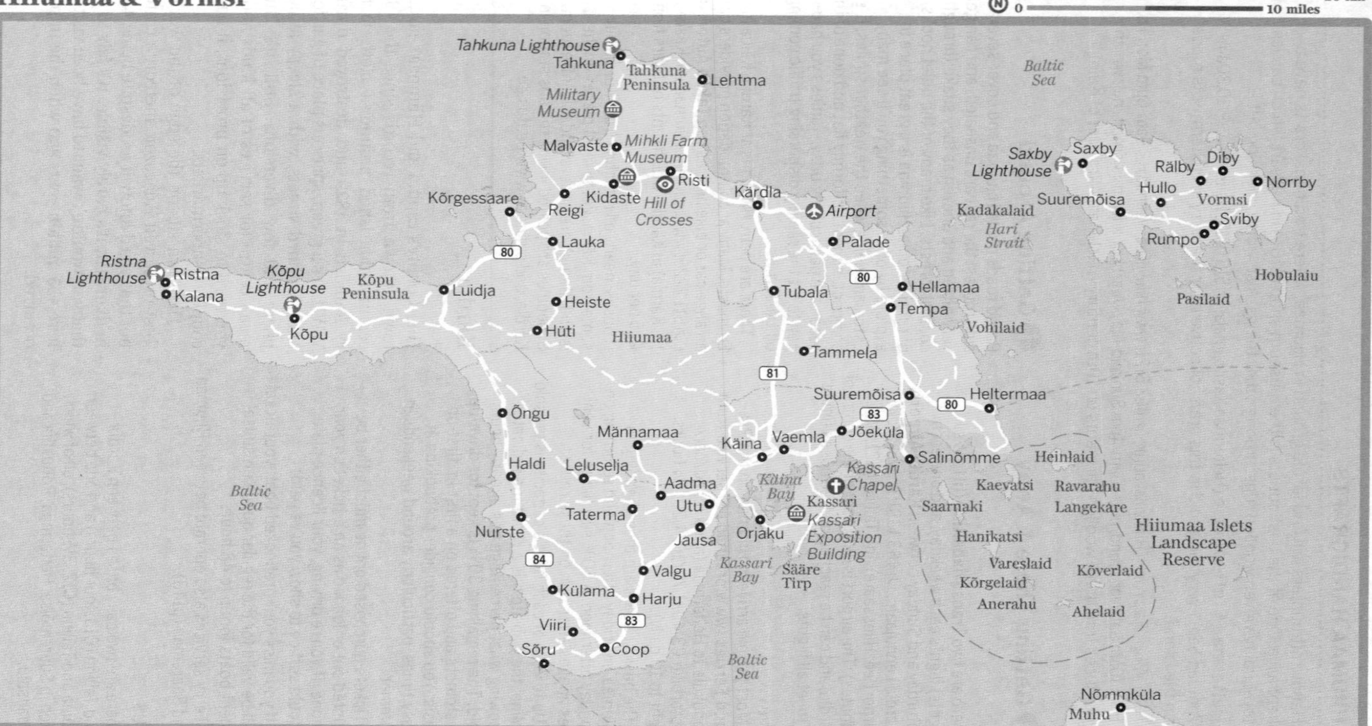
Hiiumaa & Vormsi
0 20 km
0 10 miles
Tahkuna Lighthouse
Tahkuna
Tahkuna Peninsula
Lehtma
Military Museum
Malvaste
Mihkli Farm Museum
Kidaste
Risti
Hill of Crosses
Kõrgessaare
Reigi
Lauka
Kärdla
Airport
Palade
Ristna Lighthouse
Ristna
Kalana
Kõpu Lighthouse
Kõpu
Kõpu Peninsula
Luidja
Heiste
Hüti
Hiiumaa
Tubala
Hellamaa
Tempa
Vohilaid
Tammela
Suuremõisa
Heltermaa
Õngu
Männamaa
Käina
Vaemla
Jõeküla
Salinõmme
Haldi
Leluselja
Aadma
Utu
Taterma
Nurste
Jausa
Orjaku
Käina Bay
Kassari Chapel
Kassari
Kassari Exposition Building
Kassari Bay
Sääre Tirp
Valgu
Külama
Harju
Viiri
Sõru
Coop
Baltic Sea
Baltic Sea
Baltic Sea
Saxby Lighthouse
Saxby
Rälby
Diby
Norrby
Hullo
Vormsi
Suuremõisa
Sviby
Rumpo
Kadakalaid
Hari Strait
Hobulaiu
Pasilaid
Heinlaid
Kaevatsi
Ravarahu
Saarnaki
Langekare
Hanikatsi
Vareslaid
Kõrgelaid
Kõverlaid
Anerahu
Ahelaid
Hiiumaa Islets Landscape Reserve
Nõmmküla
Muhu
80
81
83
84

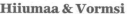

## Sights

**Long House** MUSEUM

(Pikk Maja; ☎463 0291; www.muuseum.hiiumaa.ee; Vabrikuväljak 8; adult/student €4/2.50; ⏱10am-5.30pm daily May-Sep, 10am-4pm Mon-Sat Oct-Apr; P) Built in the 1830s, this handsome, 60m-long timber house once lodged the directors of the Hiiu-Kärdla textile factory, burnt out in WWII. It's now perhaps the best of the four scattered branches of the Hiiumaa Museum, displaying artefacts related to the factory, a reconstructed worker's cottage, work by local artists and a collection of Estonian military- and civil-service medals.

**Kärdla Beach** BEACH

(Lubjaahju) While not spectacular, Kärdla's extremely shallow beach is pleasant enough, with a mixed sand-and-grass shoreline edged by Rannapark. This expanse of lawns and forest was partly built on the site of a Swedish cemetery.

## Sleeping

**Kivijüri Guesthouse** GUESTHOUSE €€

(Kivijüri Külalistemaja; ☎526 9915; www.kivijuri.ee; Kõrgessaare mnt 1; s/d €40/60; P Wi-Fi) This cosy, bright-red country house has only four pleasant rooms, each with TV and bathroom. Breakfast is excellent and there's a backyard patio and lawn to unwind on. The entire house can be rented for €250 per day, with breakfast, and the hospitable, multilingual owners can arrange bike and car rental.

**Padu Hotell** HOTEL €€

(☎463 3037; www.paduhotell.ee; Heltermaa mnt 22; s/d/apt €50/70/80; P Wi-Fi) You may feel like you're sleeping inside a sauna at the Padu, with pine predominating across the walls, floors, ceilings, doors and furniture. All rooms are cosy and decently equipped, (including balconies) but the apartments are quite a bit bigger and some have private saunas (for €10 more). There's also a communal sauna and on-site cafe.

At just €5 extra per person for a one-course evening meal, the half-board option is excellent value.

## Eating & Drinking

★**Kuur** EUROPEAN €€

(☎5689 6333; www.restokuur.ee; Sadama 28; mains €14-16; ⏱11am-11pm Sun-Thu, to 1am Fri & Sat; P Wi-Fi) The name means 'shed', but this delightful harbourside restaurant easily confounds any low expectations that name sets. Smoking its own fish, welcoming guests into an eclectically stylish 'beach shack' dining room-bar, and (most importantly) serving top-notch food alongside judiciously chosen wines, it's a real treat. The spicy seafood soup, a brick-red, piquant fishy broth poured over the local catch, is delicious.

**Linnumäe Puhkekeskus** EUROPEAN €€

(☎521 5931; www.linnumae.ee; Linnumäe küla; mains €11-13; ⏱9am-10pm Sun-Thu, to 11pm Fri & Sat; P Wi-Fi) Technically in Linnumäe, a village blending into the southeastern approach to Kärdla, this restaurant-bar is a cut above the typical roadside joint. Big on BBQ, baby-back ribs, grilled chicken and other meaty favourites, the skilful kitchen also offers pastas, salads and burgers. The interior is cosily fire-lit, or you can lounge outside in fine weather.

**Rannapaargu** CLUB

(☎5666 6800; www.rannapaargu.ee; Lubjaahju 3; ⏱11am-9pm Sun-Thu, to 4am Fri & Sat) This imposing, A-framed wooden establishment overlooking Kärdla Beach is a daytime cafe and night-time club. The food isn't memorable, but on Fridays and Saturdays in summer around 300 people descend to party to DJs and live bands. It doesn't properly kick off until well after midnight.

## Information

**Hiiumaa Tourist Office** (☎504 5393; www.hiiumaa.eu; Hiiu 1; ⏱10am-5pm Mon-Fri, to 3pm Sat & Sun mid-May–mid-Sep, noon-5pm Mon-Fri rest of year), the principal office for the island, is located in the centre of Kärdla.

## Western Hiiumaa

The western half of Hiiumaa is sparsely populated, even for Estonia. Knobbly Tahkuna Peninsula was the scene of a vicious battle between German and Soviet troops during WWII.

The island ends at the narrow Kõpu Peninsula, stretching due west like an index finger pointing straight at Stockholm. If you've been to a few Estonian beaches and refuse to believe that anyone could surf here, be prepared to be proved wrong. At Ristna, where the peninsula protrudes out into the Baltic currents, waves of up to 10m have been seen. It's a dangerous stretch with rips that will do their darnedest to deliver you on the doorstep of Finland, but for experienced surfers it's a blast.

Sõru, where the ferries leave for Saaremaa, is a beautiful spot, with a reed-lined forested shore stretching out in both directions.

## Sights & Activities

**Mihkli Farm Museum** MUSEUM

(Mihkli Talumuuseum; ☎566 66895; www.muuseum.hiiumaa.ee; Malvaste; adult/child €3/2; ⏲11am-6pm Wed-Sat May, Tue-Sun Jun-Aug; P) Hidden away in the forest at Malvaste, 2km north of the Kärdla–Kõrgessaare road, this farm complex, founded by Swedes deported in 1781, is preserved as one of the four components of Hiiumaa Museum. Its original buildings, including a working smoke sauna (€90 for up to 10 people, if booked at least a day ahead), give an authentic taste of basic rural life in Hiiumaa.

**Hiiumaa Military Museum** MUSEUM

(Hiiumaa Militaarmuuseum; www.militaarmuuseum.ee; Tahkuna Village; adult/student €3/1.50; ⏲10am-6pm Tue-Sun mid-May–mid-Sep; P) Despite limited English captions, this small museum in a former Soviet border guard station is quite engrossing, providing insight into the battles fought on this peaceful island in WWII, and its position on the Soviet frontier. There are big items of military hardware to peruse in the yard, while inside there are uniforms, photographs, posters, weapons and medals.

**Tahkuna Lighthouse** LIGHTHOUSE

(Tahkuna Tuletorn; adult/child €2/1; ⏲10am-7pm Tue-Sun May–mid-Sep) Dating from 1874, this 43m lighthouse watches over Tahkuna Peninsula's northwest tip. Beyond the lighthouse stands an eerie **memorial** to the victims of the MS *Estonia* ferry disaster (p164). Facing out to sea, the 12m-tall metal frame encases a cross from the bottom of which a bell with sculpted children's faces is suspended; it only rings when the wind blows with the same force and in the same direction as that fatal night in September 1994, when the *Estonia* went down.

> **LIGHTHOUSE COMBO**
>
> If you're planning on climbing all three of Hiiumaa's lighthouses, a combined ticket is available (adult/student €7/5). Buy it at the first lighthouse you visit.

Between the memorial and the lighthouse is a curious low stone **labyrinth**, a replica of an ancient one found on the island. The idea is that you follow the path between the stones as a form of meditation.

According to Soviet military lore concerning the battle that raged in this vicinity during the Nazi invasion of 1941, the Red Army fought to the bitter end, their last man climbing to the top of the lighthouse and flinging himself off while still firing at the Germans.

On the road leading to the lighthouse you'll see deserted Soviet military installations, including a complete underground bunker that you can wander through; bring a torch (flashlight).

**Kõpu Lighthouse** LIGHTHOUSE

(Kõpu Tuletorn; www.tuletornikohvik.ee; Mägipe; adult/child €3/2; ⏲10am-7pm May–mid-Sep; P) With its pyramid-like base and stout square tower, the inland Kõpu lighthouse is the best-known landmark on Hiiumaa, and supposedly the third oldest in continuous operation anywhere. Built by the Hanseatic League to guide shipping to Tallinn, it was begun in the early 16th century, rebuilt in 1845, and automated in 1963. At 36m high, it can be seen nearly 50km away.

The attached cafe, acceptable for simple meals, shares the same hours as the lighthouse, and concerts are staged on the lawns in summer.

**Ristna Lighthouse** LIGHTHOUSE

(Ristna Tuletorn; Kalana; adult/child €3/2; ⏲10am-7pm Tue-Sun May–mid-Sep; P) Kõpu Peninsula's second lighthouse stands 29.5m high, in all its blazing red glory at the western tip of the peninsula, only 200km from Stockholm. In 1874 it was shipped from Paris, where it was made, together with the lighthouse at Tahkuna. There's a small cafe in the lighthouse-keeper's cottage selling drinks and snacks such as herring with black bread.

**Sõru Museum** MUSEUM

(☎5376 4040; Pärna; adult/child €2/1; ⏲11am-6pm Wed-Sun Jun-Aug, 10am-3pm Mon-Fri mid-Sep–mid-May) Just inland from Sõru *sadam* (port) where the ferry to Saaremaa docks, this little community museum is worth a look. Downstairs you might find art from the village schoolkids or locally made feltwork, while upstairs there's a permanent display containing the usual black-and-white photos of fisherfolk and farmers, interspersed with old nets, shipping charts

WORTH A TRIP

## SUUREMÕISA

Meaning 'great estate', Suuremõisa village is notable for its stately 18th-century **manor house** (Suuremõisa Loss; ☎515 8381; www.suuremoisa-loss.eu; Suuremõisa; adult/student €2/1.50; ⏰10am-5pm daily Jun-Aug, 9am-4pm Mon-Fri Sep-May; P), and nearby Pühalepa Church. Lending its name to the sleepy, surrounding settlement, soberly symmetrical Suuremõisa Manor was built between 1755 and 1760 by Countess Ebba Margaretha Stenbock, over the foundations of earlier structures perhaps dating back to the Livonian Order, which owned this estate in medieval times. While the exterior of the house and its once-landscaped gardens are quite neglected, the interior, largely dating to the early 20th century and including a grand oak staircase and dolomite stone floors, has seen some restoration.

**Pühalepa**, founded by the German Livonian Order in the 13th century, is Hiiumaa's oldest stone church. Completed as a simpler fortress-church in the 14th century, its distinctive Lutheran steeple was added in the 18th century. Close to Heltermaa, where the ferry to the mainland docks, Suuremõisa is definitely only a pit stop, with nowhere to sleep or eat.

and tools. At the very top you can scan the horizon on a heavy-duty set of Soviet border-guard binoculars.

**Hill of Crosses** MEMORIAL

(Ristimägi; P) Northern Hiiumaa had a population of free Swedish farmers until they were forced to leave on the orders of Catherine the Great, with many ending up in the Ukraine on the false promise of a better life. This low forested 'hill' is where the last 1000 Swedes living on Hiiumaa performed their final act of worship before leaving, in 1781. It's become a tradition for first-time visitors to brave the mosquitoes to lay a homemade cross here.

**Surf Paradiis** WATER SPORTS

(☎505 1015; http://surfparadiis.paap.ee; Kalana; adult/child €40/20; ⏰May-Nov) Set on a stretch of beach about 1km down a rutted, sandy road from Ristna (the turn-off is just before you reach the lighthouse), this outfit offers all manner of wet and wild activities. A day pass gets you access to surfing, SUP-ing, kayaking, rowing, snorkelling and other water sports, or you can rent each individually by the hour.

Add-ons include jet skiing, banana-boat rides, fishing, archery and even axe-throwing. There's also accommodation available (double €40) and a beach bar that looks as though it's built from driftwood, but hosts big parties with DJs and makes a mean mojito.

It's a good idea to call ahead, as all activities are weather-dependent, and the place is sometimes booked solidly by groups.

Ristna is a surprisingly demanding surfing spot, so don't attempt to go it alone without first coordinating with the centre, which operates a lifeguard and first aid service.

## Käina

POP 730

Hiiumaa's second-largest settlement is a nondescript kind of place, its most interesting feature being the hulking ruins of St Martin's Church (c 1500), which was set ablaze by a German tracer bullet in 1941. It's inaccessible, yet its austere, roofless bulk begs a photo-stop if passing through.

**Rudolf Tobias House Museum** MUSEUM

(Rudolf Tobiase Majamuuseum; ☎463 2091; www.muuseum.hiiumaa.ee; Hiiu mnt; adult/student €3/2; ⏰11am-5pm Wed-Sat mid-May–Aug; P) On the western edge of Käina, the early-19th-century wood-and-thatch birthplace and childhood home of Rudolf Tobias (1873–1918), Estonia's 'first professional composer', has been preserved in his memory as one of the four components of the dispersed Hiiumaa Museum. There's no English signage but the staff are helpful, and there's a windmill, well and barn asking to be photographed.

**Hotell Liilia** HOTEL €€

(☎463 6146; www.hiiumaale.ee; Hiiu mnt 22; s/d/tr €69/88/107; P 📶) In the lee of Käina's only real landmark, the roofless ruin of 16th-century St Martin's Church, Liilia offers two floors of simple well-kept rooms with pale wooden floors and ceilings. There's also a large restaurant downstairs with a pleasant

## MS ESTONIA: CONSIGNED TO MYSTERY

About 30 nautical miles northwest of Hiiumaa's Tahkuna Peninsula lies the wreck of the ferry *Estonia*, which sank during a storm just after midnight on 28 September 1994, en route from Tallinn to Stockholm. Only 137 people survived the tragedy, which claimed 852 lives in Europe's worst peacetime maritime disaster.

Comparable in scale and impact to the sinking of the *Titanic*, the tragedy remains the subject of contention and conspiracy theory. In 1997 the final report of the Joint Accident Investigation Commission (JAIC), an official inquiry by the Estonian, Swedish and Finnish governments, concluded that the ferry's design was at fault and the crew were probably underskilled in emergency procedures. The report claimed the bow gate was engineered inadequately for rough sailing conditions and that during the storm the visor was torn from the bow, exposing the car deck to tonnes of seawater that sank the *Estonia* completely within one hour. Escape time for the 989 people on board was estimated at only 15 minutes and they were denied access to lifeboats due to the sudden list and sinking of the ferry. For those who did escape, the freezing conditions of the water that night reduced survival time to only minutes.

The integrity of the report was questioned after dissent within the JAIC became public. In 2000 a joint US-German diving expedition and new analysis of the *Estonia*'s recovered visor prompted theories of an explosion on board. Conspiracy theorists claim that the *Estonia* was transporting unregistered munitions cargo, as an illicit trade in weapons was to be curtailed with new export laws about to come into effect. Claims of a cover-up have been bolstered by the alleged disappearance of eight crew members, initially listed as survivors.

Unexplained interference with the wreck, along with the Swedish government's dumping of sand to stabilise it in 2000, further fuelled conspiracy claims and calls for a new inquiry. The governments of Estonia, Finland and Sweden are resolute that the ferry will remain where it sank as a memorial to the dead; the remains of more than 650 people are estimated to be inside.

terrace, open 11am to 6pm Monday to Saturday, and for prebooked breakfast.

## Kassari

POP 260

Covered with mixed woodland, pastures and marshes, and fringed by striking coastal scenery, this 8km-long island is linked to Hiiumaa by two causeways that virtually cut off Käina Bay from the open sea. Protected since 1962, the bay is an important bird reserve, serving as a breeding ground for about 70 different species. You can get a good view of its avian action from the birdwatching tower north of Orjaku. During the hot summer months a large part of the bay dries up and becomes not much more than a muddy field.

### Sights & Activities

**Kassari Exposition Building** MUSEUM

(Kassari Ekpositsioonimaja; ☎5695 1843; www.muuseum.hiiumaa.ee; adult/student €4/2.50; ⏲10am-6pm daily May-Sep, to 5pm Tue-Sat Oct-Apr; P) Located in an old limestone lodge that once formed part of the local manor, and making up one-quarter of the dispersed Hiiumaa Museum, this small exposition showcases artefacts and exhibits on Hiiumaa's history and biodiversity. Among the curiosities: a 1955 Russian-made TV, the jewel-like prism of the 1874 Tahkuna lighthouse and the stuffed body of the wolf that allegedly terrorised the island until its 1971 demise. It also sells excellent handicrafts and special island postal stamps.

**Sääre Tirp** NATURAL FEATURE

Southern Kassari narrows to a promontory with some unusual vegetation and ends in the thin, 3km spit of land known as Sääre Tirp. An end-of-the-world kind of place, it's beautiful for a walk and there's free RMK camping amid the juniper bushes, including fireplaces and toilets, where the road comes to an end.

**Kassari Chapel** CHAPEL

(Kassari kabel; Esiküla; ⏲noon-5pm Thu-Sat mid-Jun–Aug) There's no electricity supply to this pretty, whitewashed, thatch-roofed, Lutheran chapel (1801) at the eastern end of Kassari island, meaning that services are still held in enchanting candlelight. The main distinguishing feature of the sober wood-and-whitewash interior is an unusual pulpit positioned above the altar. It's a good destination for a drive, walk or ride; follow the sign down the dirt road from the easternmost point of the island's sealed road.

**Kassari Ratsamatkad** HORSE RIDING
(☎508 3642, 518 9693; www.kassari.ee; Esiküla; trail ride per hour/day €20/60) Signposted from the main road running down Kassari's eastern flank, Hiiumaa's largest horse farm offers a range of excursions, from short trail rides to day-long treks through forests, marshes, pastureland and unpeopled coastline.

## Sleeping & Eating

**★Dagen Haus** B&B €€
(☎518 2555; www.dagen.ee; Orjaku; d from €95; P 📶) One of Hiiumaa's loveliest options, this restored mid-19th-century granary has rough-hewn walls, timber beams and five stylish bedrooms. The gorgeous communal areas, including a glass-walled terrace overlooking Käina Bay, invite lingering, or you can book one of four separate holiday houses nearby, each sleeping up to five people (€109 to €219). Book well ahead.

**Kassari Puhkekeskus** HOTEL €€
(☎463 6146; www.hiiumaale.ee; Kassari Village; tw/apt €85/100; P ❄ 📶) Abandoned factories are a dime a dozen in Estonia, but cool conversions like this one are scarce. The decor is fresh and modern, and of the 15 rooms even the standards have microwaves and little balconies. Apartments have separate living areas and proper kitchenettes, and open onto a large shared terrace with a spa.

There's a very appealing restaurant and brewhouse attached, rentals can be organised (bikes per hour/day €5/15; rowboat per two hours €20) and there's a sauna for cold weather (first hour €25).

**Vetsi Tall** ESTONIAN €
(☎463 6146; www.hiiumaale.ee; Kassari Village; mains €7-10, sites per person €5, cabins d/tr €40/60, apt €100; ⏲noon-10pm Wed & Thu, to 11pm Fri & Sat, to 9pm Sun Jun-Sep; P 📶) On the western fringe of Kassari Village, this dark and atmospheric tavern (dating from 1843) offers hefty serves of simple food such as herring with cottage cheese and potato. Tiny barrel-shaped wooden cabins are set amid the surrounding apple orchard and camping is also possible, although bathroom facilities are rudimentary. There's also a two-bedroom apartment above the tavern.

**Lest & Lammas Grill** ESTONIAN €€
(☎463 6146; www.hiiumaale.ee; Kassari Village; mains €10-12; ⏲noon-9pm Mon-Sat, to 8pm Sun Jun-Aug, by arrangement autumn and spring; P 📶) The name means 'flounder and sheep' and the emphasis is on the excellent fish and lamb that Hiiumaa is renowned for, alongside curios such as a Kassari herdsman's stew of 'butcher's choice' meat and hemp seeds, and a wholesome chickpea and buckwheat creation. There's also house-cured meats for sale, excellent house-brewed beer, and an inviting, landscaped terrace for warm weather.

Lest & Lammas is part of the Kassari Puhkekeskus holiday complex.

# Vormsi

POP 231

Vormsi, Estonia's fourth-biggest island (93 sq km), rose from the sea around 3000 years ago and continues to rise at a rate of 3mm per year (its highest point is a modest 13m above sea level and is apparently a hiding place for trolls). Except for its voracious mosquitoes, the island has only ever been sparsely inhabited and as a consequence its forests, coastal pastures and wooded meadows have remained relatively undisturbed. Swedes arrived in the 13th century and before WWII they formed the overwhelming majority of the island's then 2500 residents. They fled back to Sweden en masse during WWII and few have returned.

## Sights

The island, 16km from east to west and averaging 6km from north to south, is a good place to tour by bicycle; there is about 10km of paved road. From the ferry it's 1.5km to the village of **Sviby**. The cheerfully named **Hullo**, Vormsi's largest village, lies about 3km west of here. You'll spot ruins of a Russian Orthodox church within an old collective farm, right by the Hullo turn-off. Two kilometres south of here is the much smaller **Rumpo** (these people really do have a way with names!), sitting on an attractive juniper-covered peninsula jutting into Hullo Bay, protected as the Vormsi Landscape Reserve.

Vormsi doesn't have a tourist office, but there are information boards near the ferry wharf.

**Vormsi Landscape Reserve** NATURE RESERVE
(Vormsi Maastikukaitseala; Rumpo) The 3km-long peninsula south of Rumpo, plus the 30 islets in Hullo Bay, are protected as the Vormsi Landscape Reserve. It's a haven for rare lichens and coastal birds, and there's a 6.7km hiking trail running its length, punctuated by three observation towers.

**Vormsi Farm Museum** MUSEUM
(Vormsi Talumuuseum; 530 88320; Sviby; adult/child €2.50/1; 11am-5pm Wed-Sun late May–mid-Sep) Vormsi's Swedish heritage is kept alive in this restored farmstead, also known as Pears Farm. It's a fascinating insight into the ways of a population that fled wartime chaos in 1944, including its distinctive fashion sense (the women wore chunky red socks to advertise their strong legs; nobody wanted a wife who couldn't perform heavy manual work).

**St Olaf's Lutheran Church** CHURCH
(Püha Olavi kirik; Hullo; 10.30am-12.30pm Sun May-Sep) There's a colourful little statue of the saint with his trusty axe in the niche above the door of this squat, whitewashed 14th-century church, just out of Hullo. It has a fine baroque painted pulpit (1660) and medieval ceiling paintings.

**Saxby Lighthouse** LIGHTHOUSE
(Saxby; adult/reduced €2/1; 10am-4pm Wed-Sun Jun-Aug) Built in 1864, this 24m lighthouse is a short walk from Saxby, the island's westernmost settlement. It's especially scenic at sunset.

## Sleeping & Eating

You can find accommodation options online (www.vormsi.ee) or at the tourist office in Haapsalu.

**Rumpo Mäe Puhketalu** B&B €€
(5342 9926; www.rumpomae.ee; Rumpo; d/tr €65/90; Apr-Nov; ) Just a few steps from the lovely reed-fringed coast at Rumpo, this handsome thatched-roof farmhouse has en-suite rooms with an old-style ambience. More basic accommodation is offered in a rustic sauna house (twin €55) and the eight-bed 'small house' (whole house for eight, with breakfast €235), and there's also a field for campers (€18 per person, with breakfast).

**Elle-Malle Külalistemaja** B&B €€
(5647 2854; ellemalle@gmail.com; Hullo; per person €30; P) In a peaceful location between Hullo and St Olaf's Church, this friendly guesthouse has five tidy pine-lined rooms in the main house and a romantic double loft room in a separate wooden cottage (with a private bathroom below). Meals can be arranged (three-course dinner €9) and Elle-Malle (the owner) also sells a small but high-quality selection of local antiques.

**Hullo Kauplus** SUPERMARKET €
(Hullo; 10am-6pm Mon-Thu, to 8pm Fri & Sat, to 5pm Sun; ) Stock up on victuals in Hullo's small general store; there's a post office and internet point attached.

**Krog No. 14** PUB FOOD €€
(514 1418; www.krog.ee; Hullo; mains €11-12; noon-7pm Sun & Mon, to 10pm Tue-Thu, to 3am Fri & Sat Jun-Aug; P) Sitting pretty on the road into Hullo, this red-brick tavern, open in summer, is a delightful place to while away an aimless Vormsi afternoon. The food is simple and delicious: pike cutlets with potato and dill-lemon sauce, wild-boar stew, and other satisfying plates.

## Getting There & Around

Vormsi lies just 3km off the Estonian mainland. **Kihnu Veeteed** (https://new.veeteed.com) plies the 10km route between Rohuküla and Sviby three to five times daily (single ticket per adult/child/car/bike €3.20/1.60/7/1, 45 minutes). There's a 50% surcharge for boats departing Rohuküla after 1pm on Fridays and departing Sviby after 1pm on Sundays. If you're taking a vehicle in the summer, reserve a place in advance online.

Just after the ferry landing, **Sviby Bike Rental** (Sviby Jalgrattalaenutus; 517 8722; 9am-7pm May-Sep) rents bikes for €15 per day, and motor-scooters for €40 per day.

# UNDERSTAND ESTONIA

## Estonia Today

The long, grey days of Soviet rule are well behind Estonia. Today, first-time visitors are astonished by the gusto with which the country has embraced the market economy since regaining independence in 1991. Entrepreneurship is widespread, the economy has diversified considerably, tourism is flourishing, and the dining and cultural landscapes are rich.

It's in the digital sphere that Estonia has excelled, earning it the nickname 'e-Stonia' in the tech world. Various innovations have originated from Estonian software designers, most notably Skype, which allows free voice and video calls to be made over the internet. Estonian citizens can vote, lodge their taxes and affix a digital signature to documents online, and in 2014 Estonia became the first country to offer a virtual 'e-Residency' to nonresidents.

Estonia has been lauded as the outstanding economic success story of the former USSR. It has joined the EU, NATO, Organisation for Economic Co-operation and Development (OECD) and the Eurozone.

Having politically and economically shaken off the Soviet era, Estonia's gaze is very much to the west and the north. Its people view themselves as having more in common (linguistically and culturally) with their Finnish neighbours than they do with Latvia and Lithuania to the south, and see the 'Baltic States' label as a handy geographic reference, but not much more. There's even been talk of further cementing ties with Finland by building a tunnel under the Gulf of Finland to connect the two countries, but the cost of the proposed 50km tunnel, which would be the longest in the world, is likely to be prohibitive.

Meanwhile, if Estonia is increasingly facing west, it's also nervously looking over its shoulder to the Great Bear to the east. The Russian annexation of Crimea and the armed conflict in the Ukraine (widely believed in these parts to have been fomented by the Kremlin) have rattled the nerves of many in this newly independent country. People here are painfully aware of the fleeting nature of the first Estonian independence in the interwar decades. That the current period of statehood has now lasted longer than the first offers only limited reassurance.

Estonia's response to the Ukrainian crisis has been to enthusiastically support sanctions against the Russian Federation and to simultaneously strengthen ties with NATO, with former president Toomas Ilves (2006–16) calling for a permanent base to be stationed on Estonian soil.

Tensions with Russia escalated in 2015 when an Estonian security officer was sentenced by a Russian court to 15 years in prison for spying; the Russians insist that they arrested him on their side of the border while the Estonians (and the EU) claim that he was kidnapped on the Estonian side. Estonia has now declared that it is planning to build a 110km-long, 2.5m-high fence on its land border with Russia (much of the rest of the border is defined by Lake Peipsi and the Narva River).

At the same time, the Estonian government is increasingly aware of the need to improve relations with its own large ethnic Russian minority, a substantial chunk of which have yet to gain Estonian citizenship. While the average Russian living in Estonia has a higher standard of living than the average Russian living in Russia, they still lag behind their Estonian compatriots. A 2015 Amnesty International report noted that Estonia's ethnic minorities, of which Russians are by far the largest, are disproportionately affected by unemployment and poverty.

A drive through some of the crumbling towns of the northeast, where both work and hope are in short supply, gives some clue to the Russian plight. Russian speakers are over-represented in the prison population, HIV infection rates and drug-addiction statistics, and the greater social problems in the Russian community in turn feed the negative stereotypes that some Estonians have about Russians.

While instances of overt hostility based on ethnicity or race are infrequent, they do occasionally occur. The tension, and ultimately violence, that was sparked by the government's decision in 2007 to move a Soviet-era war memorial from the centre of Tallinn demonstrated that fissures remain between the country's ethnic Russians and the rest of the population, and there are regular complaints (from the Russian media, in particular) that Russian-speaking minorities in Estonia are being discriminated against. One strategy from the Estonian side has been to attempt to curb the influence of the Russian media by promoting Russian-language news services from within Estonia.

The delicate situation is now in the hands of Kersti Kaljulaid, elected in 2016 as Estonia's first female head of state.

# History

## Beginnings

Estonia's oldest human settlements date back 10,000 years, with Stone Age tools found near present-day Pärnu. Finno-Ugric tribes from the east (probably around the Urals) came centuries later – most likely around 3500 BC – mingling with Neolithic peoples and settling in present-day Estonia, Finland and Hungary. They took a liking to their homeland and stayed put, spurning the nomadic ways that characterised most other European peoples over the next four millennia.

## The Christian Invasion

By the 9th and 10th centuries AD, Estonians were well aware of the Vikings, who seemed more interested in trade routes to Kyiv (Kiev) and Constantinople (Istanbul) than in conquering their sparsely populated land. The first real threat to their freedom came from Christian invaders from the south.

Following papal calls for a crusade against the northern heathens, Danish troops and German knights invaded Estonia, conquering the southern Estonian fortress of Otepää in 1208. The locals put up a fierce resistance and it took well over 30 years before the whole territory was conquered. By the mid-13th century Estonia was carved up between the Danes in the north and the German Teutonic Order in the south. The Order, hungry to move eastward, was powerfully repelled by Alexander Nevsky of Novgorod on frozen Lake Peipsi (marvellously imagined in Sergei Eisenstein's film *Alexander Nevsky*).

The conquerors settled in at various newly established towns, handing over much power to the bishops. By the end of the 13th century, cathedrals rose over Tallinn and Tartu, around the time that the Cistercian and Dominican religious orders set up monasteries to preach to the locals and (try to) baptise them. Meanwhile, the Estonians continued to rebel.

The most significant uprising began on St George's night (23 April) in 1343. It started in Danish-controlled northern Estonia when Estonians pillaged the Padise Cistercian monastery and killed all of the monks. They subsequently laid siege to Tallinn and the bishop's castle in Haapsalu and called for Swedish assistance to help them finish the job. The Swedes did indeed send naval reinforcements across the gulf, but they came too late and were forced to turn back. Despite Estonian resolve, by 1345 the rebellion was crushed. The Danes, however, decided they'd had enough and sold their part of Estonia to the Livonian Order (a branch of the Teutonic Order).

The first guilds and merchant associations emerged in the 14th century, and many towns – Tallinn, Tartu, Viljandi and Pärnu – prospered as trade members of the Hanseatic League (a medieval trade federation). However, it was mainly German merchants who lived in these towns, while the native Estonians toiled as peasants in the countryside.

Estonians continued practising nature worship and pagan rites for weddings and funerals, though by the 15th century these rites became interlinked with Catholicism, and they began using Christian names. Peasants' rights disappeared during the 15th century, so much so that by the early 16th century most Estonians became serfs (enslaved labourers bought and sold with the land).

The Reformation reached Estonia in the 1520s, with Lutheran preachers representing the initial wave. By the mid-16th century the Estonian church had been reorganised, with places of worship now under Lutheran authority, and monasteries closed down.

## The Livonian War

During the 16th century the greatest threat to Livonia (now northern Latvia and southern Estonia) came from the east. Ivan the Terrible, who crowned himself the first Russian tsar in 1547, had his sights clearly set on westward expansion. Russian troops, led by ferocious Tatar cavalry, attacked in 1558, around the region of Tartu. The fighting was extremely bitter, with the invaders leaving a trail of destruction in their wake. Poland, Denmark and Sweden joined the fray, and intermittent fighting raged throughout the 17th century. Sweden emerged the victor.

Like all wars, this one took a heavy toll on the populace. During the two generations of warfare (roughly 1552 to 1629), half the rural population perished, about three-quarters of all farms were deserted, and disease (such as plague), crop failure and ensuing famine added to the war toll. Except for Tallinn, every castle and fortified centre in the country was ransacked or destroyed – including Viljandi Castle, once among northern Europe's mightiest forts. Some towns were completely obliterated.

## The Swedish Era

Following the war, Estonia entered a period of peace and prosperity under Swedish rule. Although the lot of the Estonian peasantry didn't improve much, cities, boosted by trade, grew and prospered, helping the economy speedily recover from the ravages of war. Under Swedish rule, Estonia was united for the first time in history under a single ruler. This period is regarded as an enlightened episode in the country's long history of foreign oppression.

The Swedish king granted the Baltic-German aristocracy a certain degree of self-government and even generously gave them lands that were deserted during the war. Although the first printed Estonian-language book dates from 1535, the publication of books didn't get under way until the 1630s, when Swedish clergy founded village schools and taught the peasants to read and write. Estonian intellectual life received an enormous boost with the founding of Tartu University in 1632.

By the mid-17th century, however, things were going steadily downhill. An outbreak of plague, and later the Great Famine (1695–97), killed off 80,000 people – almost 20% of the population. Peasants, who for a time enjoyed more freedom of movement, soon lost their gains. The Swedish king, Charles XI (1660–97), wanted to abolish serfdom in Estonian crown manors (peasants enjoyed freedom in Sweden), but the local Baltic-German aristocracy fought bitterly to preserve the legacy of enforced servitude.

## The Great Northern War

Soon Sweden faced serious threats from an anti-Swedish alliance of Poland, Denmark and Russia – countries seeking to regain lands lost in the Livonian War. The Great Northern War began in 1700 and after a few successes (including the defeat of the Russians at Narva), the Swedes began to fold under the assaults on multiple fronts. By 1708 Tartu had been destroyed and all of its survivors shipped to Russia. By 1710 Tallinn capitulated and Sweden had been routed.

### THE SOURCE OF EESTI

In the 1st century AD the Roman historian Tacitus described a people known as the 'Aestii'. In rather crude fashion he depicted them as worshipping goddess statues and chasing wild boars with wooden clubs and iron weaponry. These people were also known as traders of amber. Although Tacitus was describing the forerunners to the Lithuanians and Latvians, the name 'Aestii' was eventually applied specifically to the Estonians, who call themselves Eesti to this day.



## The Enlightenment

Russian domination was bad news for the native Estonian peasants. War (and the 1710 plague) left tens of thousands dead. Swedish reforms were rolled back by Peter I (1682–1725), destroying any hope of freedom for the surviving serfs. Conservative attitudes towards Estonia's lower class didn't change until the Enlightenment, in the late 18th century.

Among those influenced by the Enlightenment was Catherine the Great (1762–96), who curbed the privileges of the elite while instituting quasi-democratic reforms. It wasn't until 1816, however, that Estonia's peasants were finally liberated from serfdom. They also gained surnames, greater freedom of movement and even limited access to self-government. By the second half of the 19th century, the peasants started buying farmsteads from the estates, and earning an income from crops such as potatoes and flax (the latter commanding particularly high prices during the US Civil War, which curtailed American cotton exports to Europe).

## National Awakening

The late 19th century was Estonia's time of national awakening. Led by a new native elite, the country marched towards nationhood. The first Estonian-language newspaper, *Perno Postimees*, appeared in 1857. It was published by Johann Voldemar Jannsen, one of the first to use the term 'Estonians' rather than *maarahvas* (country people). Other influential thinkers included Carl Robert Jakobson, who fought for equal political rights for Estonians and founded *Sakala*, Estonia's first political newspaper.

Numerous Estonian societies formed, and in 1869 the first Song Festival was held. Estonia's rich folklore also emerged from obscurity, particularly with the publication of *Kalevipoeg*, Friedrich Reinhold Kreutzwald's poetic epic that melded together hundreds of Estonian legends and folk tales. Other poems, particularly works by Lydia Koidula, helped shape the national consciousness – one imprinted with the memory of 700 years of slavery.

## Rebellion & WWI

The late 19th century was also a period of rampant industrialisation, marked by the development of an extensive railway network linking Estonia with Russia, and by the establishment of large factories. Socialism and discontent accompanied those grim workplaces, with demonstrations and strikes led by newly formed worker parties. Events in Estonia mimicked those in Russia, and in January 1905, as armed insurrection flared across the border, Estonia's workers joined the fray. Tension mounted until autumn that year, when 20,000 workers went on strike. Tsarist troops responded brutally by killing and wounding 200.

The response of Tsar Nicholas II (1894–1917) provoked the Estonian rebels, who continued to destroy the property of the old guard. Subsequently, thousands of soldiers arrived from Russia, quelling the rebellions; 600 Estonians were executed and hundreds more were sent to Siberia. Trade unions and progressive newspapers and organisations were closed down, and political leaders fled the country.

More radical plans to bring Estonia to heel – such as sending thousands of Russian peasants to colonise the country – were never realised. Instead, Russia's tsar had another priority: WWI. Estonia paid a high price for Russia's involvement – 100,000 men were drafted, 10,000 of whom were killed in action. Many Estonians went off to fight believing that if they helped defeat Germany, Russia would grant them nationhood. Russia had no intention of doing so. But by 1917 the matter was no longer the tsar's to decide. In St Petersburg, Nicholas II was forced to abdicate and the Bolsheviks seized power. As chaos swept across Russia, Estonia seized the initiative and on 24 February 1918 it effectively declared its independence.

## The War of Independence

Would-be independent Estonia faced threats from both Russia and Baltic-German reactionaries. War erupted as the Red Army quickly advanced, overrunning half the country by January 1919. Estonia fought back tenaciously, and with the help of British warships and Finnish, Danish and Swedish troops, it defeated its long-time enemy. In December Russia agreed to a truce and on 2 February 1920 it signed the Tartu Peace Treaty, which renounced forever Russia's rights of sovereignty over Estonian territory. For the first time in its history, Estonia was completely independent.

## Fleeting Independence

In many ways, the independence period was a golden era. The mainly Baltic-German nobility were given a few years to sort their affairs before their manor houses were nationalised and their large estates broken up, with the land redistributed to the Estonian people. It was the first time many peasant farmers were able to own and work their own land.

The economy developed rapidly, with Estonia utilising its natural resources and attracting investment from abroad. Tartu University became a university for Estonians, and the Estonian language became the lingua franca for all aspects of public life, creating new opportunities in professional and academic spheres. Secondary education also improved (per capita the number of students surpassed most European nations) and an enormous book industry arose, with 25,000 titles published between 1918 and 1940 (again surpassing most European nations in books per capita).

On other fronts – notably the political one – independence was not so rosy. Fear of communist subversion (such as the failed 1924 coup d'état supported by the Bolsheviks) drove the government to the right. In 1934 Konstantin Päts, leader of the transitional government, along with Johan Laidoner, commander-in-chief of the Estonian army, violated the constitution and seized power, under the pretext of protecting democracy from extremist factions. Thus began the 'era of silence', a period of authoritarian rule that dogged the fledgling republic until WWII.

## The Soviet Invasion & WWII

Estonia's fate was sealed when Nazi Germany and the USSR negotiated a secret pact in 1939, essentially handing Estonia over to Stalin. The Molotov-Ribbentrop Pact, a nonaggression pact between the USSR and Nazi Germany, secretly divided Eastern Europe into Soviet and German spheres of influence. Estonia fell into the Soviet sphere. At the outbreak of WWII, Estonia declared itself neutral, but Moscow forced it to sign a mutual assistance pact. Thousands of Russian soldiers subsequently arrived, along with military, naval and air bases. Estonia's Communist Party orchestrated a sham rebellion whereby 'the people' demanded to be part of the USSR. President Päts, General Laidoner and other leaders were sacked and sent off to Russian prison camps. A puppet government was installed and on 6 August 1940 the Supreme Soviet accepted Estonia's 'request' to join the USSR.

Deportations and WWII devastated the country. Tens of thousands were conscripted and sent not to fight but to work (and usually die) in labour camps in northern Russia. Thousands of women and children were also sent to gulags.

When Russia fled the German advance, many Estonians welcomed the Nazis as liberators; 55,000 Estonians joined home-defence units and Wehrmacht Ost battalions. The Nazis, however, did not grant statehood to Estonia and viewed it merely as occupied territory of the Soviet Union. Hope was crushed when the Germans began executing communist collaborators (7000 Estonian citizens were shot) and those Estonian Jews who hadn't already fled the country (around 1000). To escape service in the German army (nearly 40,000 were conscripted), thousands fled to Finland and joined the Estonian regiment of the Finnish army.

In early 1944 the Soviet army bombed Tallinn, Narva, Tartu and other cities. Narva's baroque Old Town was almost completely destroyed. The Nazis retreated in September 1944. Fearing the advance of the Red Army, many Estonians also fled and around 70,000 reached the West. By the end of the war one in 10 Estonians lived abroad. All in all, Estonia had lost over 280,000 people in the war (a quarter of its population). In addition to those who emigrated, 30,000 were killed in action and others were executed, sent to gulags or exterminated in concentration camps.

### TALLINN'S CHECHEN HERO

In January 1991 Soviet troops seized strategic buildings in Vilnius and Rīga, and soldiers were ordered to do the same in Tallinn. The commander of the troops at the time, however, disobeyed Moscow's orders, and refused to open fire upon the crowd. He even threatened to turn the artillery under his command against any attempted invasion from Russia. That leader was Dzhokhar Dudayev, who would go on to become the president of Chechnya and lead its independence movement. He was killed by the Russian military in 1995. In Estonia he is fondly remembered for his role in bringing about Estonian independence.

## Back to the USSR

After the war, Estonia was immediately incorporated back into the Soviet Union. This began the grim epoch of Stalinist repression, with many thousands sent to prison camps and 19,000 Estonians executed. Farmers were forced into collectivisation and thousands of immigrants entered the country from other regions of the Soviet Union. Between 1945 and 1989 the percentage of native Estonians fell from 97% of the population to 62%.

Resistance took the form of a large guerrilla movement calling themselves the Metsavennad, or 'Forest Brothers'. Around 14,000 Estonians armed themselves and went into hiding, operating in small groups throughout the country. The guerrillas had little success against the Soviet army, and by 1956 the movement had been effectively destroyed.

Although there were a few optimistic periods during the communist years (notably the 'thaw' under Khrushchev, where Stalin's crimes were officially exposed), it wasn't until the 1980s when Soviet leader Mikhail Gorbachev ushered in an era of *perestroika* (restructuring) and *glasnost* (openness) that real change seemed a possibility.

The dissident movement in Estonia gained momentum and on the 50th anniversary of the 1939 Molotov-Ribbentrop Pact, a major rally took place in Tallinn. Over the next few months, more and more protests were held, with Estonians demanding the restoration of statehood. The Song Festival was one of Estonia's most powerful vehicles for protest. The biggest took place in 1988 when 300,000 Estonians gathered in Tallinn's Song Festival Grounds and brought much international attention to the Baltic plight.

In November 1989 the Estonian Supreme Soviet declared the events of 1940 an act of military aggression and therefore illegal. Disobeying Moscow's orders, Estonia held free elections in 1990 and regained its independence in 1991.

## Independent Estonia Mk 2

In 1992 the first general election under the new constitution took place, with a proliferation of newly formed parties. The Pro Patria (Fatherland) Union won a narrow majority after campaigning under the slogan 'Cleaning House', which meant removing from power those associated with communist rule. Pro Patria's leader, 32-year-old historian Mart Laar, became prime minister.

Laar set to work transforming Estonia into a free-market economy, introducing the Estonian kroon as currency and negotiating the complete withdrawal of Russian troops, a source of particular anxiety for Estonians; the country breathed a collective sigh of relief when the last garrisons departed in 1994. Despite Laar's successes, he was considered a hothead, and in 1994 was dismissed when his government received a vote of no confidence by the Riigikogu (National Council).

Following a referendum in September 2003, approximately 60% of Estonians voted in favour of joining the EU. The following spring, the country officially joined both the EU and NATO. This was followed by membership of the OECD in December 2010 and adoption of the euro in place of the short-lived kroon at the beginning of 2011.

Recurring post-EU-accession themes are the economy, increasing income inequality and strained relations with Russia, particularly over the issue of Estonia's large Russian-speaking minority. In 2016 history was made when Estonia elected its first female head of state, President Kersti Kaljulaid.

### WAGE INEQUALITY & SALMON SANDWICHES

According to Eurostat, in 2008 Estonian men earned an average of 30% more than Estonian women – the largest gender-income gap in the EU. In 2012, in a creatively obscure protest to highlight this gap *(lõhe)*, participating cafes and restaurants on Equal Pay Day sold sandwiches made from salmon (which is also *lõhe* in Estonian) at a 30% surcharge when served with dill (in Estonian *till*, which doubles as a slang word for penis).

# The People

Despite (or perhaps because of) centuries of occupation by Danes, Swedes, Germans and Russians, Estonians have tenaciously held onto their national identity, and are deeply, emotionally connected to their history, folklore and national song tradition. The Estonian Literary Museum in Tartu holds over 1.3 million pages of folk songs, the world's second-largest collection (Ireland has the largest), and Estonia produces films for one of the world's smallest audiences (only Iceland produces for a smaller audience).

According to the popular stereotype, Estonians (particularly Estonian men) are reserved and aloof. Some believe it has much to do with the weather – those long, dark nights breeding endless introspection. This reserve also extends to gross displays of public affection, brash behaviour and intoxication – all frowned upon. This is assuming that there isn't a festival under way, such as Jaanipäev, when friends, family and acquaintances gather in the countryside for drinking, dancing and revelry.

Estonians are known for their strong work ethic, but when they're not toiling in the fields, or putting in long hours at the office, they head to the countryside. Ideal weekends are spent at the family cottage, picking berries or mushrooms, walking through the woods, or sitting with friends soaking up the quiet beauty. Owning a country house with a sauna is one of the national aspirations.

Of Estonia's 1.3 million people, 69% are ethnic Estonians, 25% Russians, 2% Ukrainians, 1% Belarusians and 1% Finns. Ethnic Russians are concentrated in the industrial cities of the northeast, where in some places (such as Narva) they make up a clear majority of the population. Russians also have a sizeable presence in Tallinn (37%). These figures differ markedly from 1934, when native Estonians comprised over 90% of the population. Migration from other parts of the

USSR occurred on a large scale from 1945 to 1955 and, over the next three decades, Estonia had the highest rate of migration of any of the Soviet republics.

One of the most overlooked indigenous ethnic groups in Estonia are the Seto people, who number up to 15,000, split between southeastern Estonia and neighbouring Russia.

According to a 2009 Gallup poll, Estonia was the least-religious country in the world (they've subsequently lost pole position to China), although many consider themselves spiritual, with a nature-based ethos being popular. Since the early 17th century, Estonia's Christians have been predominantly Lutheran, although the Orthodox Church gained a foothold under the Russian Empire and has experienced a resurgence in recent years. Today only a minority of Estonians profess religious beliefs, with 16% identifying as Orthodox and 10% as Lutheran; no other religion can claim over 1% of the population.

Jews arrived in Estonia as early as the 14th century and by the early 1930s the population numbered 4300. Three-quarters escaped before the Nazi occupation; of those that remained, nearly all were killed. Today the Jewish population stands at around 2000, and in 2007 the Jewish community celebrated the opening of its first synagogue since the Holocaust, a striking modern structure at Karu 16, Tallinn.

### CAN I BUY A VOWEL, PLEASE?

Intrigued by the national language? Fancy yourself a linguist? If you're keen to tackle the local lingo, bear in mind that Estonian has 14 cases, no future tense and no articles. And then try wrapping your tongue around the following vowel-hungry words:

- *jäääär* – edge of the ice
- *töööö* – work night (can also be *öötöö*)
- *kuuuurija* – moon researcher
- *kuuüür* – monthly rent

And then give this a go: '*Kuuuurijate töööö jäääärel*', or 'a moon researcher's work night at the edge of the ice'!

## The Arts

Estonia is an undeniably arty place, with its fledgling literature doing ever more to capture a unique national experience, theatre thriving and well patronised, a healthy proportion of locally made films in cinemas and, in summer, a positive explosion of festivals.

### Music

On the international stage, the area in which Estonia has had the greatest artistic impact is in the field of classical music. Estonia's most celebrated composer is Arvo Pärt (b 1935), the intense and reclusive master of hauntingly austere music many have misleadingly termed minimalist. Pärt emigrated to Germany during Soviet rule and his *Misererie Litany, Te Deum* and *Tabula Rasa* are among an internationally acclaimed body of work characterised by dramatic bleakness, piercing majesty and nuanced silence. He's now the world's most performed living classical-music composer.

The main Estonian composers of the 20th century remain popular today. Rudolf Tobias (1873–1918) wrote influential symphonic, choral and concerto works as well as fantasies on folk-song melodies. Mart Saar (1882–1963) studied under Rimsky-Korsakov in St Petersburg (although his music shows none of this influence). His songs and piano suites were among the most performed pieces of music in between-war concerts in Estonia. Eduard Tubin (1905–82) is another great Estonian composer whose body of work includes 10 symphonies. Contemporary composer Erkki-Sven Tüür (b 1959) takes inspiration from nature and the elements, as experienced on his native island of Hiiumaa.

Estonian conductors Tõnu Kaljuste (who won a Grammy in 2014 for a Pärt recording), Anu Tali and Paavo Järvi are hot tickets at concert halls around the world.

Hortus Musicus is Estonia's best-known ensemble, performing mainly medieval and Renaissance music. Rondellus, an ensemble that has played in a number of early-music festivals, performs on medieval-period instruments and isn't afraid of experimentation. Its well-received album *Sabbatum* (2002) is a tribute album of sorts to Black Sabbath – the only difference being the music is played on medieval instruments, and the songs are sung in Latin!

Rock and punk thrives in Estonia with groups such as Vennaskond and the heavy but timelessly Estonian Metsatöll, whose

### KIIKING

From the weird and wacky world of Estonian sport comes *kiiking*. Invented in 1993, it's the kind of extreme sport that, frankly, we're surprised the New Zealanders didn't think of first. *Kiiking* sees competitors stand on a swing and attempt to complete a 360-degree loop around the top bar, with their feet fastened to the swing base and their hands to the swing arms. The inventor of *kiiking*, Ado Kosk, observed that the longer the swing arms, the more difficult it is to complete a 360-degree loop. Kosk then designed swing arms that can gradually extend, for an increased challenge. In competition, the winner is the person who completes a loop with the longest swing arms – the current record stands at a fraction over 7m! If this concept has you scratching your head, go to www.kiiking.ee to get a more visual idea of the whole thing and to find out where you can see it in action (or even give it a try yourself).

song titles and lyrics are rich in archaic Estonian language and imagery. The more approachable Ultima Thule and Smilers are among the country's longest-running and most beloved bands.

The pop- and dance-music scene is also strong in Estonia, exemplified by Estonia's performances in that revered indicator of true art, the Eurovision Song Contest. Tanel Padar won the competition in 2001, making Estonia the first former Soviet republic to achieve this success. The tough-girl band Vanilla Ninja hit the charts throughout Central Europe early in the millennium with various English-language tracks. Stig Rästa of local hitmakers Outloudz teamed up with reality-TV contestant Elina Born to represent Estonia at Eurovision 2015 with *Goodbye to Love*, which subsequently entered the charts in 10 countries.

Eccentric dance diva Kerli Kõiv, better known by her first name alone, has notched up two Billboard US Dance number ones since 2011. Another one to watch is DJ and producer Rauno Roosnurm (aka Mord Fustang), whose remixes have garnered him a following with international clubbers.

See www.estmusic.com for detailed listings and streaming samples of Estonian musicians of all genres.

## Literature

Estonian was considered a mere peasants' language by the country's foreign overlords, rather than one with full literary potential. As a result, the history of written Estonian is little more than 150 years old. Baltic Germans published an Estonian grammar book and a dictionary in 1637, but it wasn't until the national awakening movement of the late 19th century that the publication of Estonian-language books, poetry and newspapers began.

Estonian literature grew from the poems and diaries of a young graduate of Tartu University, Kristjan Jaak Peterson. Also a gifted linguist, he died when he was only 21 years old in 1822. His lines 'Can the language of this land/carried by the song of the wind/not rise up to heaven/and search for its place in eternity?' are engraved in stone in Tartu and his birthday, 14 March, is celebrated as Mother Tongue Day *(emakeelepäev)*.

Until the mid-19th century, Estonian culture was preserved only as an oral folk tradition among peasants. The national epic poem *Son of Kalev (Kalevipoeg)*, written between 1857 and 1861 by Friedrich Reinhold Kreutzwald (1803–82), made use of these rich oral traditions; it was inspired by Finland's *Kalevala*, a similar epic created several decades earlier. Fusing hundreds of Estonian legends and folk tales, *Son of Kalev* relates the adventures of the mythical hero, which ends with his death and his land's conquest by foreigners, but also a promise to restore freedom. The epic played a major role in fostering the national awakening of the 19th century.

Lydia Koidula (1843–86) was the poet of Estonia's national awakening and its first lady of literature. Anton Hansen Tammsaare (1878–1940) is considered the greatest Estonian novelist for *Truth and Justice (Tõde ja Õigus)*, written between 1926 and 1933. A five-volume saga of village and town life, it explores Estonian social, political and philosophical issues.

Eduard Vilde (1865–1933) was an influential early-20th-century novelist and playwright who wrote *Unattainable Wonder* (*Tabamata Ime*, 1912). It was due to be the first play performed at the opening of the

Estonia Theatre in 1913, but was substituted with *Hamlet,* as Vilde's scathing critique of the intelligentsia was deemed too controversial. In most of his novels and plays, Vilde looked with great irony at what he saw as Estonia's mad, blind rush to become part of Europe. For Vilde, self-reliance was the truest form of independence.

Paul-Eerik Rummo (b 1942) is one of Estonia's leading poets and playwrights, dubbed the 'Estonian Dylan Thomas' for his patriotic pieces, which deal with contemporary problems of cultural identity. His contemporary, Mati Unt (1944–2005), played an important role in cementing the place of Estonian intellectuals in the modern world, and wrote, from the 1960s onwards, quite cynical novels (notably *Autumn Ball; Sügisball,* 1979), plays and articles about contemporary life in Estonia.

The novelist Jaan Kross (1920–2007) won great acclaim for his historical novels in which he tackled Soviet-era subjects. His most renowned book, *The Czar's Madman* (*Keisri hull,* 1978), relates the story of a 19th-century Estonian baron who falls in love with a peasant girl and later ends up in prison. It's loosely based on a true story, though the critique of past- and present-day authoritarianism is the crux of the work.

Jaan Kaplinski (b 1941) has had two collections of poetry, *The Same Sea in Us All* and *The Wandering Border,* published in English. His work expresses the feel of Estonian life superbly. Kross and Kaplinski have both been nominated for the Nobel Prize in Literature.

Tõnu Õnnepalu's *Border State* (*Piiri Riik,* 1993, published under the pseudonym Emil Tode) is about a young Estonian man who travels to Europe and becomes a kept boy for an older, rich gentleman. This leads him down a tortuous road of self-discovery. Not a mere confessional, *Border State* is a clever and absorbing critique of modern Estonian values. In popular fiction, Kaur Kender's *Independence Day* (*Iseseisvuspäev,* 1998) tells the misadventures of young and ambitious entrepreneurs in post-Independence Estonia.

The most acclaimed Estonian novel of recent times is *Purge* (*Puhastus,* 2008) by Sofi Oksanen, a harrowing tale weaving together Stalin's purges and modern-day people-trafficking and sex slavery. A bestseller in Estonia and Finland, it's won six major awards and has been published in 36 languages (including English). It was initially created as a play and it's subsequently been made into a feature film and an opera.

## Cinema

The first moving pictures were screened in Tallinn in 1896, and the first cinema opened in 1908. Estonia's cinematic output has not been prolific, but there are a few standouts. It's also worth noting that Estonia produces films for one of the world's smallest audiences – far more per capita than neighbouring Baltic countries. Estonian films capture an impressive 14% of the filmgoing market share.

The nation's most beloved film is Arvo Kruusement's *Spring* (*Kevade,* 1969), an adaptation of Oskar Luts' country saga. Its sequel, *Summer* (*Suvi,* 1976), was also popular, though regarded as inferior. Grigori Kromanov's *Last Relic* (*Viimne Reliikvia,* 1969) was a brave and unabashedly anti-Soviet film that has been screened in 60 countries.

More recently Sulev Keedus' lyrical *Georgica* (1998), about childhood, war, and life on the western islands, and Jaak Kilmi's *Pigs' Revolution* (*Sigade Revolutsioon,* 2004), about an anti-Soviet uprising at a teenagers' summer camp, have made the rounds at international film festivals. Veiko Õunpuu's 2007 film *Autumn Ball* (*Sügisball*), based on the novel by Mati Unt, won awards at seven festivals from Brussels to Bratislava.

In 2014 *Tangerines* (*Mandariinid*), an Estonian-Georgian co-production, became the first Estonian film to be nominated for the Academy Award for Best Foreign Language Film. Set in Georgia, it tells the story of two Estonian farmers who get caught in the crossfires of the war in Abkhazia.

One of Estonia's most popular locally made films is *Names in Marble* (*Nimed Marmortahvlil,* 2002), which tells the story of a group of young classmates and their decision to fight in the War of Independence against the Red Army in 1918–20. It was directed by acclaimed Estonian stage director Elmo Nüganen, and is based on the book of the same name (by Albert Kivikas), banned during Soviet times.

## Theatre

Many of Estonia's theatres were built solely from donations by private citizens, which gives an indication of the role theatre has played in the country's cultural life. This is also evidenced in theatregoing statistics: in 2013 Estonia came third in the EU for theatre attendance in the Eurobarometer survey of cultural participation (behind Sweden and the Netherlands). The results showed that 45% of Estonians attend the theatre at least once a year (the EU average is 28%). Travellers, however, will have trouble tapping into the scene without speaking Estonian.

## Food & Drink

Cuisines from all over the world are represented in cosmopolitan Tallinn, and prices are lower than you'd pay for a similar meal in most European capitals. High-end restaurants tend to be influenced by New Nordic cuisine, a trend emphasising the pure, seasonal flavours of the north.

You'll also find fantastic restaurants in Pärnu, Tartu, Otepää and various manor houses scattered around the countryside and islands.

### Eesti Specialities

Did someone say 'stodge'? Baltic gastronomy has its roots planted firmly in the land, with livestock and game forming the basis of a hearty diet that developed to sustain bodies performing hard rural labour. The Estonian diet relies on *sealiha* (pork), other red meat, *kana* (chicken), *vurst* (sausage) and *kapsa* (cabbage). Potatoes add a generous dose of winter-warming carbs to a national cuisine often dismissed as bland, heavy and lacking in spice. Sour cream is served with everything but coffee, it seems.

*Kala* (fish), most likely *heeringas* (herring), *forell* (trout) or *lõhe* (salmon), appears most often as a smoked or salted starter. Lake Peipsi is a particularly good place for tracking down *suitsukala* (smoked fish); look for roadside stands along the shore road. A more acquired taste is *kilu,* pickled Baltic sprat, often served in sandwiches or as part of a breakfast buffet.

Another favourite is *kama,* a thick milkshake-like drink made from a powdered mixture of boiled, roasted and ground peas, rye, barley and wheat mixed together with buttermilk or *kefir* (fermented milk). It's often served as a dessert, with the addition of berries and sugar.

At Christmas time *verivorst* (blood sausage) is made from fresh blood and wrapped in pig intestine (joy to the world indeed!). Those really in need of a culinary transfusion will find *verivorst, verileib* (blood bread) and *verikäkk* (balls of blood rolled in flour and eggs with bits of pig fat thrown in for taste) available in some traditional Estonian restaurants. *Sült* (jellied meat) is likely to be served as a delicacy as well.

The seasons continue to play a large role in the Estonian diet. When spring arrives, wild leek, rhubarb, fresh sorrel and goat's cheese appear, and the spring lambs are slaughtered. During summer there are fresh vegetables and herbs, along with berries, nuts and mushrooms gathered from the forests – still a popular pastime for many Estonians. Be sure to take advantage of the local *turg* (market) and load up on superbly flavoured strawberries (check you're buying the local stuff, not imports).

Autumn was always the prime hunting season and although many species are now offered some protection through hunting quotas, you'll often see elk, boar, deer and even bear making their way onto menus, year-round. In winter, Estonians turn to hearty roasts, stews, soups and plenty of sauerkraut.

Given the cuisine's rustic origins, it's not surprising that bread is a major staple in the diet, and that Estonians make a pretty good loaf. Rye is by far the top choice. Unlike other ryes you may have eaten, Estonian *leib* is moist, dense and delicious (assuming it's fresh), and usually served as a free accompaniment to every restaurant meal.

#### EATING PRICE RANGES

The following price ranges refer to a standard main course.

**€** less than €10

**€€** €10–20

**€€€** more than €20

### Terviseks!

The traditional Estonian toast of *terviseks* translates as 'your health' (easier to remember if you think 'topsy-turvy sex'). Beer is the favourite tipple in Estonia and the local product is much in evidence. The biggest brands are Saku and A Le Coq, which come in a range of brews. In winter Estonians

## EAT YOUR WORDS

Don't know your *kana* from your *kala*? Your *maasikas* from your *marjad*? Get a head start on the cuisine scene by learning the words that make the dish.

### Useful Phrases

| | | |
|---|---|---|
| **May I have a menu?** | *Kas ma saaksin menüü?* | kas mah *saahk*-sin menüü |
| **I'd like ...** | *Ma sooviksin ...* | ma *saw*-vik-sin ... |
| **The bill, please** | *Palun arve* | *pah*-lun *ahrr*-ve |
| **I'm a vegetarian** | *Ma olen taimetoitlane* | mah *o*-len *tai*-me-toyt-lah-ne |
| **Bon appetit!** | *Head isu!* | head *i*-su |
| **To your health!** (when toasting) | *Terviseks!* | *ter*-vi-seks |
| **breakfast** | *hommikusöök* | *hom*-mi-ku-serrk |
| **lunch** | *lõuna* | *lyu*-na |
| **dinner** | *õhtusöök* | *er*-tu-serrk |

### Food Glossary

| | | |
|---|---|---|
| **berries** | *marjad* | *mahrr*-yahd |
| **cabbage** | *kapsas* | *kahp*-sahs |
| **caviar** | *kaaviar, kalamari* | *kaa*-vi-ah, ka-la-*mah*-rri |
| **cheese** | *juust* | yoost |
| **chicken** | *kana* | *kah*-nah |
| **fish** | *kala* | *kah*-lah |
| **fruit** | *puuviljad* | *poo*-vil-yahd |
| **grilled 'chop'** | *karbonaad* | *kah*-bo-noahd |
| **herring** | *räim, heeringas* | rraim, *heh*-rrin-gahs |
| **meat (red)** | *liha* | *li*-hah |
| **mushrooms** | *seened* | *seh*-ned |
| **pancake** | *pannkook* | *pahn*-kawk |
| **pork** | *sealiha* | *sea*-li-ha |
| **potato** | *kartul* | *kahrr*-tul |
| **rye bread** | *leib* | layb |
| **salmon** | *lõhe* | *ly*-he |
| **sausage** | *vorst* | vorrst |
| **sprats** | *kilud* | *ki*-lud |
| **strawberry** | *maasikas* | *mah*-zikas |
| **vegetables** | *köögivili* | *kerrg*-vi-li |
| **white bread** | *sai* | sai |

drink mulled wine, the antidote to cold nights. Estonia's ties to Russia have led to vodka's enduring popularity.

## Where, When & How

Meals are served in a *restoran* (restaurant) or a *kohvik* (cafe), *pubi* (pub), *kõrts* (inn) or *trahter* (tavern). Nearly every town has a *turg* (market), where you can buy fresh fruit and vegetables, as well as meats and fish.

Estonian eating habits are similar to other parts of northern Europe. Either lunch or dinner may be the biggest meal of the day. Cooked breakfasts aren't always easy to find but many cafes serve pastries and cakes throughout the day. Tipping at top restaurants is fairly commonplace but not essential, with 10% sufficient. For reviews of the country's culinary best, see www.flavoursofestonia.com.

If invited for a meal at an Estonian home you can expect abundant hospitality and generous portions. It's fairly common to bring flowers for the host. Just be sure to give an odd number (even-numbered flowers are reserved for the dead).

# SURVIVAL GUIDE

## Directory A–Z

### ACCOMMODATION

If you like flying by the seat of your pants when you're travelling, you'll find July and August in Estonia very problematic. The best accommodation books up quickly in Tallinn, which is especially busy on most weekends. Book a month ahead anytime from May to September.

High season in Estonia means summer. Prices drop substantially at other times. The exception is Otepää, when there's also a corresponding peak in winter.

### CUSTOMS REGULATIONS

When leaving Estonia, there are no limits on how much alcohol you can carry with you, though you'll have to convince border inspection agents that any large quantities are for personal consumption. When it comes to tobacco, there are heavier restrictions if you're headed to Sweden, Finland or the UK.

If arriving from outside the EU, there are the usual restrictions on what can be brought into the country; see the Tax & Customs Board website (www.emta.ee) for full details, including alcohol and tobacco limits.

### EMBASSIES & CONSULATES

For up-to-date contact details of Estonian diplomatic organisations as well as foreign embassies and consulates in Estonia, check the website of the Ministry of Foreign Affairs (www.vm.ee). The following are in Tallinn.

**SLEEPING PRICE RANGES**

The following price ranges refer to a double room in high (but not necessarily peak) season.

**€** less than €35

**€€** €35–100

**€€€** more than €100

**Australian Consulate** (☎650 9308; https://vm.ee; Marja 9, Mustjõe; ⏰9am-5pm Mon-Fri) Honorary consulate; embassy in Stockholm.

**Canadian Embassy Office** (☎627 3311; www.canada.ee; Toom-Kooli 13; ⏰8.30am-5.30pm Mon-Thu, to 3pm Fri) An office of Canada's Baltic embassy, which is in Rīga.

**Finnish Embassy** (☎610 3200; www.finland.ee; Kohtu 4; ⏰8.30am-noon & 1-4.30pm Mon-Fri)

**French Embassy** (☎616 1600; www.ambafrance-ee.org; Toom-Kuninga 20; ⏰9.30am-1pm & 2.30-5.30pm Mon-Fri)

**German Embassy** (☎627 5300; www.tallinn.diplo.de; Toom-Kuninga 11; ⏰8am-5pm Mon-Thu, to 2pm Fri)

**Irish Embassy** (☎681 1870; www.embassyofireland.ee; Rahukohtu 4-II; ⏰10am-1pm & 2-4pm Mon-Thu)

**Latvian Embassy** (☎627 7850; www.mfa.gov.lv; Tõnismägi 10; ⏰9am-5pm Mon-Fri)

**Lithuanian Embassy** (☎616 4991; http://ee.mfa.lt; Uus 15; ⏰8.30am-noon Mon-Fri plus 1-5.30pm Mon-Thu, to 4pm Fri)

**Netherlands Embassy** (☎680 5500; www.nederlandwereldwijd.nl/landen/estland; Rahukohtu 4-I; ⏰visit by appointment)

**Russian Embassy** (☎646 4170; https://estonia.mid.ru; Pikk 19; ⏰9am-5pm Mon-Fri)

**Russian Consulate, Tartu** (☎740 3024; https://estonia.mid.ru; Ülikooli 1; ⏰9am-4pm Mon, Tue, Thu & Fri)

**Swedish Embassy** (☎640 5600; www.sweden.ee; Pikk 28; ⏰9am-noon Mon-Fri)

**UK Embassy** (☎667 4700; www.ukinestonia.fco.gov.uk; Wismari 6; ⏰10am-3pm Mon-Thu)

**US Embassy** (☎668 8100; https://ee.usembassy.gov; Kentmanni 20; ⏰8.30am-5.30pm Mon-Fri)

### INTERNET ACCESS

Wireless internet access (wi-fi) is ubiquitous in 'E-stonia' (you may find yourself wondering why your own country lags so far behind this tech-savvy place). You'll find literally hundreds of hotspots throughout the country. We're talking on city streets, in hotels, hostels, restaurants, cafes, pubs, shopping centres, ports, petrol stations, even on long-distance buses and in the middle of national parks! Keep your eyes peeled for orange-and-black stickers indicating availability. In most places, connection is free.

If you're not packing a laptop or smartphone, options for getting online are not as numerous as they once were. Some accommodation providers offer a computer for guest use and there are still a few internet cafes in large centres. Public libraries have web-connected computers that can usually be accessed free of charge (you may need photo ID).

### LGBTIQ+ TRAVELLERS

Hand-in-hand with its relaxed attitude to religion, today's Estonia is a fairly tolerant and safe home to its gay and lesbian citizens – certainly much more so than its neighbours. Unfortunately, that ambivalence hasn't translated into a wildly exciting scene (only Tallinn has gay venues).

Homosexuality was decriminalised in 1992 and since 2001 there has been an equal age of consent for everyone. In 2014 Estonia became the first former Soviet republic to pass a law recognising same-sex registered partnerships, coming into effect in 2016.

### MAPS

If you're just going to major cities and national parks, you'll find the maps freely available in tourist offices and park centres more than adequate. If, however, you're planning on driving around and exploring more out-of-the-way places, a good road atlas is worthwhile and easy to find. **Regio** (www.regio.ee) produces a good, easy-to-use road atlas, with enlargements for all major towns and cities. **EO Map** (www.eomap.ee) has fold-out sheet maps for every Estonian county and city, as well as a road atlas.

### MONEY

On 1 January 2011 Estonia joined the eurozone, bidding a very fond farewell to its short-lived kroon. ATMs are plentiful and credit cards are widely accepted.

### PUBLIC HOLIDAYS

**New Year's Day** (Uusaasta) 1 January

**Independence Day** (Iseseisvuspäev; Anniversary of 1918 declaration) 24 February

**Good Friday** (Suur reede) March/April

**Easter Sunday** (Lihavõtted) March/April

**Labour Day** (Kevadpüha) 1 May

**Pentecost** (Nelipühade) Seventh Sunday after Easter (May/June)

**Victory Day** (Võidupüha; commemorating the anniversary of the Battle of Võnnu, 1919) 23 June

**St John's Day** (Jaanipäev, Midsummer's Day) 24 June

**Day of Restoration of Independence** (Taasiseseisvumispäev; marking the country's return to Independence in 1991) 20 August

**Christmas Eve** (Jõululaupäev) 24 December

**Christmas Day** (Jõulupüha) 25 December

**Boxing Day** (Teine jõulupüha) 26 December

Taken together, with a few extra days added for good measure, Victory Day and St John's Day are an excuse for a week-long midsummer break for many Estonians.

**WWOOF-ING**

If you don't mind getting your hands dirty, an economical and enlightening way of travelling around Estonia involves doing some voluntary work as a member of Worldwide Opportunities on Organic Farms (www.wwoof.ee) – also known as 'Willing Workers on Organic Farms'. Membership of this popular, well-established international organisation (which has representatives around the globe) provides you with access to the WWOOF Estonia website, which lists organic farms and other environmentally sound cottage industries throughout the country. In exchange for daily work, the owner will provide food, accommodation and some hands-on experience in organic farming.

### TELEPHONE

There are no area codes in Estonia; if you're calling anywhere within the country, just dial the number as it's listed. All landline phone numbers have seven digits; mobile (cell) numbers have seven or eight digits and begin with 5. Estonia's country code is 372. To make an international call, dial 00 before the country code.

### TOURIST INFORMATION

In addition to the info-laden, elegantly structured, multilingual website of the Estonian Tourist Board (www.visitestonia.com), there are tourist offices in most cities, and many towns and national parks throughout the country. At nearly every one you'll find English-speaking staff and lots of free material.

## Getting There & Away

### AIR

More than 20 airlines have scheduled services to Tallinn year-round, with additional routes and airlines added in summer. The main Baltic services:

**airBaltic** (www.airbaltic.com) Multiple daily flights between Tallinn and Rīga.

**Finnair** (www.finnair.ee) Up to six flights a day between Helsinki and Tallinn, and daily flights between Helsinki and Tartu.

### BUS

The following bus companies all have services between Estonia and the other Baltic States:

**Ecolines** (www.ecolines.net) Major routes: Tallinn–Pärnu–Rīga (seven daily), five of which continue on to Vilnius; Tallinn–St Petersburg (six daily); Tartu–Valga–Rīga (two daily); Vilnius–Rīga–Tartu–Narva–St Petersburg (four daily).

**Lux Express & Simple Express** (www.luxexpress.eu) Major routes: Tallinn–Rīga (up to 13 daily); Tallinn–St Petersburg (up to 10 daily); Rīga–Valmiera–Tartu–Sillamäe–Narva–St Petersburg (four daily).

**Eurolines** (www.eurolines.lt) Two daily Tallinn–Pärnu–Rīga–Panevėžys–Vilnius–Kaunas–Warsaw buses.

### CAR & MOTORCYCLE

The three Baltic countries are all part of the Schengen agreement, so there are no border checks when driving between Estonia and Latvia. There's usually no problem taking hire cars across the border, but you'll need to let the rental company know at the time of hire if you intend to do so; some companies will charge an additional fee.

### TRAIN

Valga is the terminus for both the Estonian and Latvian rail systems, but the train services don't connect up. From Valga, Estonian trains operated by Elron (www.elron.ee) head to Elva, Tartu and Tallinn, while Latvian trains operated by Pasažieru vilciens (www.pv.lv) head to Valmiera, Cēsis, Sigulda and Rīga. There are also direct trains to Tallinn from St Petersburg and Moscow.

## Getting Around

### BICYCLE

- Touring cyclists will find Estonia mercifully flat.
- Cycling around peaceful rural areas is a popular summer pastime in Estonia, and bike hire is offered in all cities, most towns, and many places of accommodation.

### BUS

- The national bus network is extensive, linking all the major cities to each other and the smaller towns to their regional hubs. It can be faster and cheaper than taking trains.
- All services are summarised on the extremely handy T pilet (www.tpilet.ee) site.
- Don't presume that drivers will speak English.
- Concessions are available for children and seniors.

### CAR & MOTORCYCLE

- Estonian roads are generally very good and driving is easy.
- In rural areas, particularly on the islands, some roads are unsealed and without lines indicating lanes, but they're usually kept in good condition.
- Winter poses particular problems for those not used to driving in ice and snow.
- Car hire is offered in all the major cities.

### TRAIN

Train services have been steadily improving in recent years. Domestic routes are run by Elron (www.elron.ee) but it's also possible to travel between Tallinn and Narva on the Russian-bound services run by GoRail (www.gorail.ee).

The major domestic routes:

**Tallinn–Rakvere** Five daily, with four continuing to Narva

**Tallinn–Tartu** Eleven daily

**Tallinn–Viljandi** Five daily

**Tartu–Sangaste–Valga** Four daily

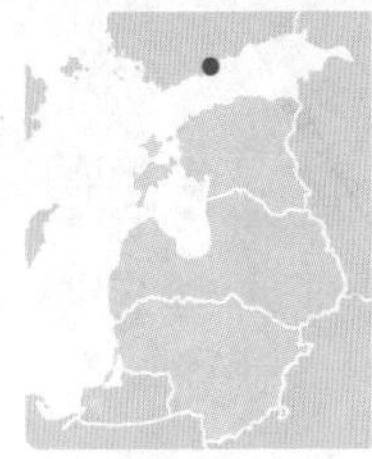

# Helsinki Excursion

☎358 / POP 648,040

**Includes ➡**



## Best Places to Stay

- ➡ Hotelli Helka (p188)
- ➡ GLO Hotel Kluuvi (p188)
- ➡ Hotel Finn (p188)
- ➡ Both (p188)

## Best Places to Eat

- ➡ Restaurant Olo (p189)
- ➡ Kuu (p189)
- ➡ Skiffer (p189)

## Why Go?

At the neck of the Gulf of Finland bottle (for that's how it looks on the map), two capitals – Helsinki and Tallinn – face each other like two old mates. The 90km separating them can be covered in two hours, and an armada of boats is ready to assist you in this not-so-daring and highly enjoyable pursuit.

In every respect as Baltic as the three east-Baltic capitals, Helsinki boasts an exceptionally scenic setting: 70% of its area is an archipelago of little islands. Sea views are never far as you explore this modern, style-forward city, hovering perennially at the top of the world's urban liveability index.

It also offers an interesting historical comparison, for Finland had every chance of repeating the fate of the Baltic States but, unlike them, it repelled the Soviet invasion in 1939, and stayed free. And you can certainly see the difference that made to this prosperous and architecturally rich city.

## When to Go

- ➡ Helsinki has year-round appeal; there's always something going on.
- ➡ The summer kicks off in June, when terraces sprout outside every cafe and bar, and the nights seem to never end.
- ➡ There's a bit of a lull in July when Finns head off to their summer cottages, but in August the capital is repopulated and raring to go.
- ➡ If you feel like seeing the wintry side of town, go in December, when you can ice-skate and absorb the Christmassy atmosphere before temperatures get too extreme.

## Helsinki Highlights

❶ **Helsinki's bars** (p190) Sinking a few sundowners at Maxine, then descending into the nightlife maelstrom.

❷ **Suomenlinna** (p183) Grabbing a picnic and exploring these fortress islands.

❸ **Punavuori** (p190) Browsing the world-famous Design District.

❹ **Museums and Galleries** (p184) Drinking deeply from the city's huge range of cultural institutions; Kiasma is first stop for great contemporary art.

❺ **Cycling** (p192) Exploring Helsinki's great network of cycle paths on a bike from one of 150 City Bike stations.

❻ **Kotiharjun Sauna** (p187) Sweating out any unhealthy habits in this traditional sauna.

❼ **Dining** (p189) Trying traditional Finnish comfort food or experimenting with New Suomi cuisine at Olo.

## Sights

The **Kauppatori** (market square) is the heart of central Helsinki; it's where urban ferries dock, and souvenirs and fresh fish and berries are sold.

Helsinki has more than 50 museums and galleries, including many special-interest museums that will appeal to enthusiasts. For a full list, check the tourist office website (www.myhelsinki.fi) or pick up its free *Museums* booklet.

### ★Suomenlinna FORTRESS

(Sveaborg; www.suomenlinna.fi) Suomenlinna, the 'fortress of Finland', straddles a cluster of car-free islands connected by bridges. This Unesco World Heritage site was originally built by the Swedes, as Sveaborg, in the mid-18th century. Visually striking and historically evocative, it offers at least a day's diversions: several museums, bunkers and fortress walls, and Finland's only remaining WWII submarine. Cafes and picnic spots are plentiful.

Ferries (www.hsl.fi; day ticket €5, 15 minutes, four hourly, fewer in winter) depart from the passenger quay at Kauppatori.

From May to September, **JT-Line** (www.jt-line.fi; adult/child return €8/4) runs a water bus from the Kauppatori, making three stops on Suomenlinna (20 minutes).

At Suomenlinna's main quay, the pink **Rantakasarmi** (Jetty Barracks) building is one of the best preserved of the Russian era. It holds a small exhibition and the helpful, multilingual **tourist office** (029-533-8120; 10am-6pm May-Sep, to 4pm Oct-Apr), which offers downloadable content for your smartphone. **Guided tours** (029-533-8410; adult/child €11/4; in English, 3 daily Jun-Aug, 1.30pm Sat & Sun Sep-May) of Suomenlinna depart from here.

Near the tourist office you'll find a **hostel** (09-684-7471; www.hostelhelsinki.fi; Suomenlinna C9; dm/s/d/tr from €25/55/70/90; reception 8am-3.30pm Mon-Sat, to 2pm Sun; @) , a supermarket and Suomenlinna's distinctive **church** (www.helsinginkirkot.fi; 10am-4pm daily Jun-Aug, 11.30am-1.30pm Wed, noon-4pm Thu-Sun Sep-May). Built by the Russians in 1854, it served as a Russian Orthodox place of worship until the 1920s, when it became Lutheran. It doubles as a lighthouse – the beacon was originally gaslight, but is now electric and still in use.

From the main quay, a blue-signposted walking path connects the key attractions. By the bridge that links Iso Mustasaari and the main island, Susisaari, is **Suomenlinna-Museo** (adult/child €8/5; 10am-6pm May-Sep, 10.30am-4.30pm Oct-Apr), a two-level museum covering the history of the fortress.

The most atmospheric part of Suomenlinna, **Kustaanmiekka**, is at the end of the blue trail. Exploring the old bunkers, crumbling fortress walls and cannons will give you an insight into this fortress, and there are plenty of grassy picnic spots. Monumental King's Gate was built in 1753–54 as a two-storey fortress wall, which had a double drawbridge and a stairway added. In summer you can get a water bus back to Helsinki from here, saving you the walk back to the main quay.

Several other museums dot the islands, including the absorbing **Ehrensvärd-Museo** (adult/child €5/2; 10am-5pm Jun-Aug, 11am-4pm May & Sep), once the home of Augustin Ehrensvärd, who designed the fortress. Outside, Ehrensvärd's elaborately martial tomb sits opposite **Viaporin Telakka**, a picturesque shipyard where sailmakers and other workers have been building ships since the 1750s. The dry dock holds up to two dozen boats; these days it's used for the maintenance of wooden vessels.

Along the shore from here is another fish out of water. The **Vesikko** (adult/child €7/4; 11am-6pm May-Sep) is the only WWII-era submarine remaining in Finland. It saw action against the Russians, and it's fascinating to climb inside and see how it all worked. Needless to say, there's not much room to move.

Back on Iso Mustasaari is **Sotamuseo Maneesi** (www.sotamuseo.fi; adult/child €7/4; 11am-6pm May-Sep), which has a comprehensive overview of Finnish military hardware, from bronze cannons to WWII artillery. Quite a contrast is the nearby **Suomenlinna Toy Museum** (040-500-6607;

> **HELSINKI AT A GLANCE**
>
> **Area** 745 sq km (greater urban area)
>
> **Departure tax** none
>
> **Money** euro (€)
>
> **Official languages** Finnish, Swedish
>
> **Visa** Generally not required for stays of up to 90 days; some nationalities will need a Schengen visa.

https://lelumuseo.fi/toymuseum; Suomenlinna C66; adult/child €7/3; 11am-6pm late-Jun–mid-Aug, shorter hours rest of year, closed early Jan-Feb; Suomenlinna), a delightful private collection of hundreds of dolls and almost as many teddy bears, which has an on-site cafe.

There are several places to eat and drink. **Suomenlinnan Panimo** (020-742-5307; www.panimoravintola.fi; Suomenlinna C1; mains €24-29, set menu €49; noon-10pm Mon-Sat, to 6pm Sun Jun-Aug, shorter hours Sep-May; ), by the main quay, brews a clutch of excellent beers, including a hefty porter, and offers good food to accompany it.

Cosy and snug in winter and spilling onto a sunny terrace in summer, **Bastion Bistro** (040-179-9890; www.bastion.fi/bistro; Suomenlinna C8; mains €18-25; 11am-5.30pm Mon-Thu, to 10pm Fri & Sat, noon-6pm Sun; Suomenlinna) is housed in a historic Russian military building a five-minute walk from the city ferry terminal. Finnish craft beers and a good selection of organic wines complement a varied à la carte menu that includes pizzas. For something lighter, the warm and welcoming aromas of hot soup, house-made bread and fresh cinnamon buns greet visitors to **Cafe Silo** (040-535-6610; www.silo.fi; Suomenlinna C10; snacks & light meals from €9; 10am-4pm Tue-Sun; Suomenlinna). Open daily in a wooden house in the old Russian merchants' quarter, the cafe faces visitors as they walk from the city ferry quay through the jetty barracks tunnel.

Taking a picnic is a great way to make the most of Suomenlinna's grass, views and (hopefully) sunshine. At around 5.15pm it's worth finding a spot to watch the enormous Baltic ferries pass through the narrow gap between islands.

**Tuomiokirkko** CHURCH

(Lutheran Cathedral; www.helsinginseurakunnat.fi; Unioninkatu 29; 9am-midnight Jun-Aug, to 6pm Sep-May) FREE One of Carl Ludvig Engel's finest creations, the chalk-white neoclassical Lutheran cathedral presides over Senaatintori (Senate Sq). Created to serve as a reminder of God's supremacy, its high flight of stairs is now a popular meeting place. Zinc statues of the 12 Apostles guard the city from the roof of the church. The spartan, almost mausoleum-like interior has little ornamentation under the lofty dome, apart from an altar painting and three stern statues of Reformation heroes Martin Luther, Philipp Melanchthon and Mikael Agricola.

**Uspenskin Katedraali** CHURCH

(Uspenski Cathedral; www.hos.fi/uspenskin-katedraali; Kanavakatu 1; 9.30am-4pm Tue-Fri, 10am-3pm Sat, noon-3pm Sun) FREE The eye-catching red-brick Uspenski Cathedral towers above Katajanokka island. Built as a Russian Orthodox church in 1868, it features classic golden onion domes and now serves the Finnish Orthodox congregation. The high, square interior has a lavish iconostasis with the Evangelists flanking panels depicting the Last Supper and the Ascension.

**★Kiasma** GALLERY

(029-450-0501; www.kiasma.fi; Mannerheiminaukio 2; adult/child €15/free, 1st Fri of month free; 10am-6pm Tue & Sat, to 8.30pm Wed-Fri, to 5pm Sun) One in a series of elegant, contemporary buildings in this part of town, curvaceous, metallic Kiasma, designed by Steven Holl and finished in 1998, is a symbol of the city's modernisation. It exhibits an eclectic collection of Finnish and international contemporary art, including digital art, and has excellent facilities for kids. It includes a theatre and a hugely popular glass-sided cafe and terrace, yet the most successful thing about it is that it's been embraced by the people of Helsinki.

**★Ateneum** GALLERY

(029-450-0401; www.ateneum.fi; Kaivokatu 2; adult/child €17/free; 10am-6pm Tue & Fri, to 8pm Wed & Thu, to 5pm Sat & Sun) Occupying a palatial 1887 neo-Renaissance building, Finland's premier art gallery offers a crash course in the nation's art. It houses Finnish paintings and sculptures from the 'golden age' of the late 19th century through to the 1950s, including works by Albert Edelfelt, Hugo Simberg, Helene Schjerfbeck, Pekka Halonen and the von Wright brothers. Pride of place goes to the prolific Akseli Gallen-Kallela's

### HELSINKI CARD

If you plan to see a lot of sights, the Helsinki Card (www.helsinkicard.com) gives you free travel, entry to more than 30 attractions in and around Helsinki, plus discounts on day tours. Available for one, two or three days at €49, €61 or €71, it's cheaper to buy online. Otherwise get it at the tourist office, hotels, the ubiquitous R-kioski shops and transport terminals.

## HELSINKI IN...

### One Day

Finns are the world's biggest coffee drinkers so, first up, it's a caffeine shot with a *pulla* (cinnamon bun) at a classic cafe in the city centre. Then head to the **Kauppatori** (p183) market square and the adjacent **Kauppahalli** (p191) market building. Put a picnic together and boat out to the island fortress of **Suomenlinna** (p183). Back in town, check out the **Lutheran Cathedral** on Senaatintori (Senate Sq) and nearby **Uspenski Cathedral**. Take the metro to legendary **Kotiharjun Sauna** (p187) for a pre-dinner sweat. Eat traditional Finnish cuisine at **Kuu** (p189) or **Olo** (p189).

### Two Days

With a second day to spare, investigate the art and design scene. Head to the **Ateneum** for the 'golden age' of Finnish painting, then see contemporary works at still-iconic **Kiasma**. Feet tired? Catch **tram 3** (p187) for a circular sightseeing trip around town, before browsing **design shops** (p190) around Punavuori. In the evening, head up to **Maxine** (p190) for a chic evening out or to rock hotspot **Bar Loose** (p190) for some wilder, heavy-decibel fun.

triptych from the Finnish national epic, the *Kalevala,* depicting Väinämöinen's pursuit of the maiden Aino.

**★Kansallismuseo** MUSEUM

(National Museum of Finland; ☎029-533-6000; www.kansallismuseo.fi; Mannerheimintie 34; adult/child €12/free, 4-6pm Fri free; ⏲11am-6pm Tue & Thu-Mon, to 8pm Wed May-Aug, shorter hours rest of year) Built in National Romantic art nouveau style and opened in 1916, Finland's premier historical museum looks a bit like a Gothic church with its heavy stonework and tall, square tower. It was given a major renovation in 2019, and its highlights include the exceptional prehistory exhibition and the Realm, covering the 13th to the 19th century. You'll also find a fantastic hands-on area for kids, Workshop Vintti.

**Helsingin Kaupunginmuseo** MUSEUM

(Helsinki City Museum; www.helsinginkaupunginmuseo.fi; Aleksanterinkatu 16; ⏲11am-7pm Mon-Fri, to 5pm Sat & Sun) FREE This museum complex spreads over five buildings from different eras, including Sederholmin talo, Helsinki's oldest central building (dating from 1757 and built by a wealthy merchant). They're linked by a contemporary structure, along with four other museums at separate locations. The must-see of the bunch is the main museum. Its collection of 450,000 historical artefacts and more than one million photographs is backed up by entertaining information piecing together Helsinki's transition from Swedish to Russian hands and on into independence.

**Temppeliaukion Kirkko** CHURCH

(☎09-2340-6320; www.temppeliaukionkirkko.fi; Lutherinkatu 3; adult/child €3/free; ⏲9.30am-5.30pm Mon-Thu & Sat, to 8pm Fri, noon-5pm Sun Jun-Aug, shorter hours Sep-May) Hewn into solid stone, the Temppeliaukion church, designed by Timo and Tuomo Suomalainen in 1969, feels close to a Finnish ideal of spirituality in nature – you could be in a rocky glade were it not for the stunning 24m-diameter roof covered in 22km of copper stripping. The acoustics are exceptional; regular concerts take place here. Opening times vary, depending on events and seasons, so check online before visiting. There are fewer tour groups to navigate around midweek.

**Seurasaaren Ulkomuseo** MUSEUM

(Seurasaari Open-Air Museum; ☎029-533-6911; www.kansallismuseo.fi/en/seurasaari-openair museum; Seurasaari; adult/child €10/3, May & Sep adult €7; ⏲11am-5pm Jun-Aug, 9am-3pm Mon-Fri, 11am-5pm Sat & Sun mid-late May & early–mid-Sep, closed mid-Sep–mid-May) Situated 5.5km northwest of the city centre, this excellent island-set museum has a collection of 87 historic wooden buildings transferred here from around Finland. There's everything from haylofts to a mansion, parsonage and church, as well as the beautiful giant rowboats used to transport churchgoing communities. Prices and hours refer to entering the museum's buildings, where guides in traditional costume demonstrate folk dancing and crafts. Otherwise you're free to roam the picturesque wooded island, where there are several cafes.

# Helsinki



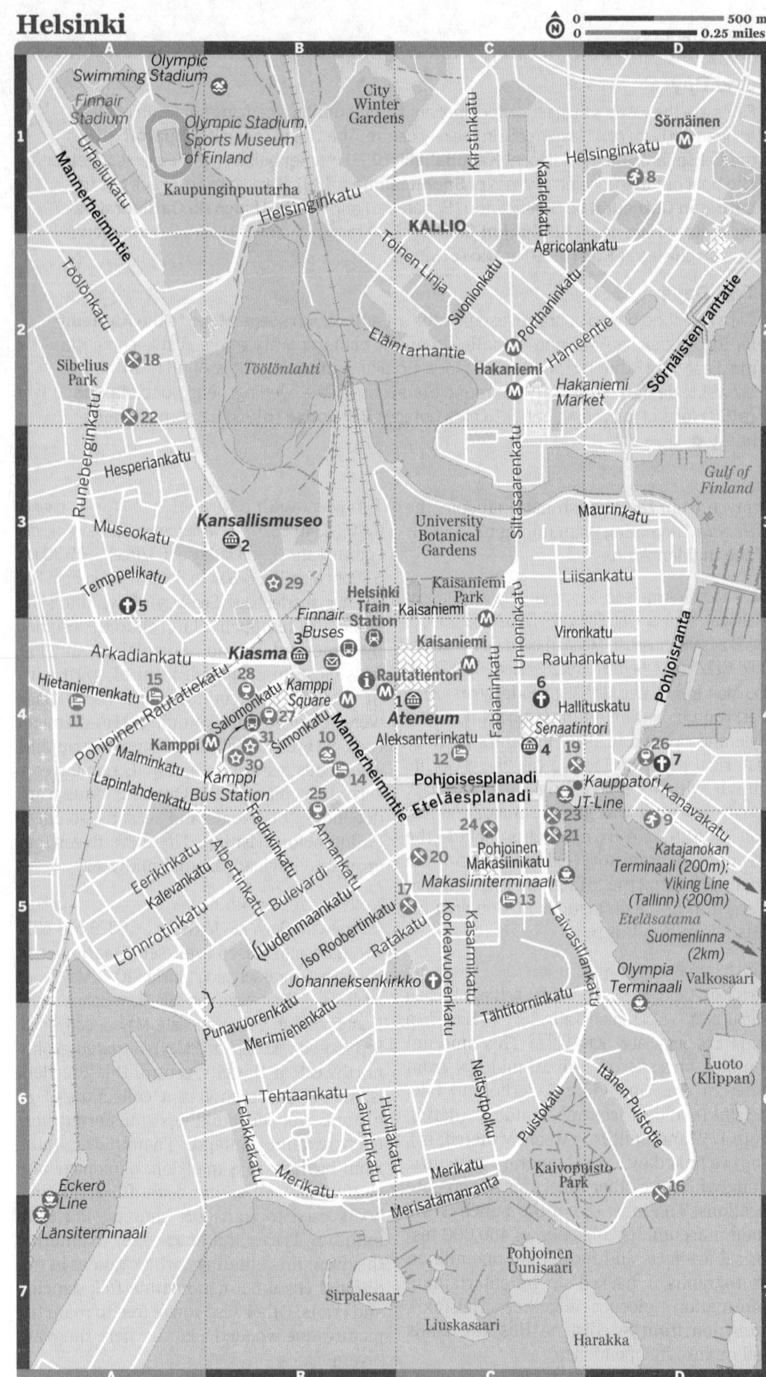

0 500 m
0 0.25 miles
Olympic Swimming Stadium
Finnair Stadium
Olympic Stadium, Sports Museum of Finland
City Winter Gardens
Kaupunginpuutarha
Helsinginkatu
KALLIO
Sörnäinen
Mannerheimintie
Urheilukatu
Kirstinkatu
Kaarlenkatu
Agricolankatu
Toinen Linja
Suonionkatu
Porthaninkatu
Hämeentie
Sörnäisten rantatie
Töölönkatu
Eläintarhantie
Hakaniemi
Hakaniemi Market
Sibelius Park
Töölönlahti
Runeberginkatu
Hesperiankatu
Siltasaarenkatu
Gulf of Finland
Kansallismuseo
University Botanical Gardens
Maurinkatu
Museokatu
Temppelikatu
Kaisaniemi Park
Liisankatu
Helsinki Train Station
Finnair Buses
Kaisaniemi
Unioninkatu
Vironkatu
Arkadiankatu
Kiasma
Rautatientori
Rauhankatu
Pohjoisranta
Hietaniemenkatu
Pohjoinen Rautatiekatu
Kamppi Square
Salomonkatu
Fabianinkatu
Hallituskatu
Ateneum
Senaatintori
Kamppi
Simonkatu
Aleksanterinkatu
Malminkatu
Kamppi Bus Station
Pohjoisesplanadi
Eteläesplanadi
Kauppatori
JT-Line
Kanavakatu
Lapinlahdenkatu
Fredrikinkatu
Annankatu
Pohjoinen Makasiinikatu
Katajanokan Terminaali (200m); Viking Line (Tallinn) (200m)
Eerikinkatu
Albertinkatu
Kalevankatu
Bulevardi
Makasiiniterminaali
Uudenmaankatu
Eteläsatama
Lönnrotinkatu
Iso Roobertinkatu
Ratakatu
Korkeavuorenkatu
Kasarmikatu
Laivasillankatu
Suomenlinna (2km)
Olympia Terminaali
Valkosaari
Johanneksenkirkko
Punavuorenkatu
Merimiehenkatu
Tähtitorninkatu
Luoto (Klippan)
Tehtaankatu
Telakkakatu
Laivurinkatu
Huvilakatu
Neitsytpolku
Puistokatu
Itäinen Puistotie
Kaivopuisto Park
Merikatu
Eckerö Line
Merisatamanranta
Länsiterminaali
Pohjoinen Uunisaari
Sirpalesaari
Liuskasaari
Harakka

## Activities

One of the joys of Helsinki is grabbing a bike and taking advantage of its long waterfronts, numerous parks and comprehensive network of cycle lanes.

Numerous summer cruises leave from the Kauppatori (p183). A 1½-hour jaunt costs around €20; dinner cruises, bus–boat combinations and sunset cruises are all available. Most go past Suomenlinna and weave between other islands. Cruises run from May to September; there's no need to book, just turn up and pick the next departure.

**★Sky Wheel** AMUSEMENT PARK
(www.skywheel.fi; Katajanokanlaituri 2; adult/child €13/9.50; ⏲10am-9pm Mon-Fri, to 10pm Sat, 11am-7pm Sun May-Oct, shorter hours Nov-Apr) Rising above the harbour, this Ferris wheel offers a fantastic panorama over central Helsinki from a height of up to 40m during the 10-minute 'flight'. A truly unique experience is the **SkySauna gondola**, allowing you to enjoy a sauna and sightsee simultaneously: one hour (up to four people, from €240) includes towels, drinks and use of a ground-level Jacuzzi and lounge.

**★Kotiharjun Sauna** SPA
(☎09-753-1535; www.kotiharjunsauna.fi; Harjutorinkatu 1; adult/child €14/8; ⏲2-8pm Tue-Sun) Helsinki's only original public wood-fired sauna dates back to 1928. It's a classic experience, where you can also get a scrub down and massage (from €30). There are separate saunas for men and women; bring your own towel or rent one (€3). It's a 150m stroll southwest of the Sörnäinen metro station.

**Yrjönkadun Uimahalli** SWIMMING
(www.hel.fi; Yrjönkatu 21B; adult/child swimming €5.50/2.50, swimming plus sauna €14/7; ⏲men 6.30am-8pm Tue & Thu, 7am-8pm Sat, women noon-8pm Sun & Mon, 6.30am-8pm Wed & Fri, closed Jun-Aug) For a sauna and swim, these art deco baths are a Helsinki institution – a fusion of Nordic elegance and Roman tradition. There are separate hours for men and women. Nudity is compulsory in the saunas; bathing suits are optional in the pool. Bring your own towel, or rent one for €4.

## Tours

An excellent budget option is to do a circuit of the city on **tram 2** or **tram 3**. You can download a network map from the HSL website (www.hsl.fi).

**Natura Viva** KAYAKING
(☎010-292-4030; www.naturaviva.fi; Harbonkatu 13, Vuosaari; 4½hr tour €78, kayak hire per 2hr €25; ⏲May-Sep) Located in Vuosaari, east of the city centre, Natura Viva runs various paddling excursions around the Helsinki archipelago. It's beginner-friendly and pick-ups can be arranged from the centre of town. You can also rent kayaks here to choose your own adventure.

## Helsinki

**Top Sights**
1 Ateneum ... C4
2 Kansallismuseo ... B3
3 Kiasma ... B4

**Sights**
4 Helsingin Kaupunginmuseo ... C4
5 Temppeliaukion Kirkko ... A3
6 Tuomiokirkko ... C4
7 Uspenskin Katedraali ... D4

**Activities, Courses & Tours**
8 Kotiharjun Sauna ... D1
9 Sky Wheel ... D5
10 Yrjönkadun Uimahalli ... B4

**Sleeping**
11 Both ... A4
12 GLO Hotel Kluuvi ... C4
13 Hotel Fabian ... C5
14 Hotel Finn ... B4
15 Hotelli Helka ... A4

**Eating**
16 Café Ursula ... D6
17 Fafa's ... C5
18 Kuu ... A2
19 Restaurant Olo ... C4
20 Skiffer Erottaja ... C5
21 Soppakeittiö ... C5
22 Tin Tin Tango ... A2
23 Vanha Kauppahalli ... C5
24 Zucchini ... C5

**Drinking & Nightlife**
25 Bar Loose ... B5
26 Holiday ... D4
27 Maxine ... B4
28 Teerenpeli ... B4

**Entertainment**
29 Musiikkitalo ... B3
30 Semifinal ... B4
31 Tavastia ... B4

**Happy Guide Helsinki** WALKING, CYCLING
(044-502-0066; www.happyguidehelsinki.com; tours, per person from €25) Happy Guide Helsinki runs a range of original, light-hearted but informative cycling and walking tours around the city. Just some of its bike-tour options include berry picking or a sunset sauna tour; walking tours range from an old-town tour to food and craft-beer tours. Meeting points are confirmed when you book.

## Festivals & Events

**Helsinki Päivä** CULTURAL
(Helsinki Day; www.helsinkipaiva.fi) Celebrating the city's anniversary on 12 June, Helsinki Päivä brings many free events to the city, with food stalls, concerts, theatre and dance performances, art exhibitions, workshops, cinema screenings, sports events and wellness activities.

**Helsingin Juhlaviikot** PERFORMING ARTS
(Helsinki Festival; www.helsinginjuhlaviikot.fi; mid-Aug–early Sep) This three-week arts festival features chamber music, jazz, theatre, opera and more at venues throughout the city.

**Flow Festival** MUSIC
(www.flowfestival.com; Suvilahti; 3-day pass from €175) Over three days on a weekend in mid-August, Flow Festival sees indie, hip-hop, electronic and experimental music rock the suburb of Suvilahti, adjacent to Kallio.

**Baltic Herring Fair** FOOD & DRINK
(Kauppatori; early Oct) Delicious salted and marinated herring is traded at this fair on Helsinki's main market square, the Kauppatori (p183), in the first week of October. It's been going since 1743.

## Sleeping

Accommodation is expensive in Helsinki. From mid-May to mid-August, bookings are strongly advised.

**Both** HOSTEL €
(09-1311-4334; https://chooseboth.fi; Hietaniemenkatu 14; dm/s/d/tr from €31/58/85/109; May-Sep; ) Finnish students live well, so take advantage of this summer residence: a clean, busy, environmentally sound spot with neat rooms, a sauna and draft sketches by Tove Jansson on the walls. Its 326 modern en-suite rooms come with kitchenettes and Finnish textiles. Dorms sleep up to three, continental breakfast costs just €6.50 and HI members get a 10% discount.

★ **Hotelli Helka** HOTEL €€
(09-613-580; www.hotelhelka.com; Pohjoinen Rautatiekatu 23; s/d/ste from €138/158/228; ) One of Helsinki's best midrange hotels, the Helka has friendly staff and excellent facilities, including parking if you can bag one of the 28 spots. Best are the rooms, with Alvar Aalto–designed furniture, quality Hilding Anders beds and plenty of light from the floor-to-ceiling windows. Saunas are situated on the top floor, adjoining the rooftop terrace.

**Hotel Finn** HOTEL €€
(09-684-4360; www.hotellifinn.fi; Kalevankatu 3B; s/d without breakfast €109/119; ) High up in a central building, this friendly two-floor hotel is upbeat, with helpful service and art from young Finnish photographers on the walls. The 37 rooms all differ, but all are bright, with modish wallpaper and tiny bathrooms, and some are furnished with recycled materials. Rates vary widely.

**Hotel Fabian** HOTEL €€€
(09-6128-2000; www.hotelfabian.com; Fabianinkatu 7; d €184-350; ) In a central but quiet location, Fabian has elegant 'Comfort' (ie standard) rooms with a restrained modern design, higher-grade 'Style' rooms (some with French balconies) and top-range 'Lux' rooms equipped with kitchenettes. Staff are super-helpful. There's no restaurant, but a chef cooks breakfasts to order. Kids under six stay for free, under 12s cost an extra €20 and under 18s an extra €50.

**GLO Hotel Kluuvi** HOTEL €€€
(010-344-4400; www.glohotels.fi; Kluuvikatu 4; s/d from €195/215; ) On a pedestrian street in the heart of town, GLO Hotel Kluuvi has 184 rooms with clean, contemporary lines, including gleaming timber floors. The 'smart doubles' are compact, at 13 sq metres, but beds are comfortable – if there's not much price difference between those and the 'comfort double', go for the latter, as you get quite a bit more space.

## Eating

Helsinki has an extensive range of restaurants, whether for Finnish classics, modern Suomi cuisine or international dishes. Cafes offer some of the cheapest lunchtime options and there are plenty of self-catering opportunities, including large, seven-day supermarkets and, better yet, Helsinki's produce-laden outdoor markets in summer and wonderful market halls year-round.

A good resource is the website www.eat.fi, which plots restaurants on a map of town: even if you can't read all the reviews without online translation, you'll soon spot which ones are the latest favourites.

**Zucchini** VEGETARIAN €
(Fabianinkatu 4; mains €9-13; 11am-4pm Mon-Fri; ) One of the city's original and most popular vegetarian cafes, Zucchini is a top-notch lunch spot; queues out the door aren't unusual. Steaming soups banish winter chills, while freshly baked quiche on the sunny terrace is a summer treat. Year-round you can choose soup or a salad/hot dish, or both. At least one vegan dish features on the daily changing menu.

**Skiffer Erottaja** PIZZA €
(45-344-5351; www.skiffer.fi; Erottajankatu 11; pizzas €14-17; 11am-9pm Mon & Tue, to 10pm Wed-Fri, 1-10pm Sat, 1-8pm Sun; ) Nautical-themed artworks brighten the low-lit interior of this out-of-the-ordinary pizza joint. Choices include the Vincent Vegan (spicy beans with avocado and fresh salsa) and Surf & Turf (crayfish and chorizo), and smaller kids' pizzas are available for €10. It's a popular meeting spot, so be prepared to wait for a table.

**Fafa's** FAST FOOD €
(www.fafas.fi; Iso Roobertinkatu 2; mains €10-12; 11am-10pm Mon-Thu, to 5am Fri & Sat, noon-2am Sun; ) Fafa's is a cut above the usual kebab places – everything is organic, with meat, vegetarian and vegan pitas, as well as salads (gluten-free breads are also available). There are 15 branches in all throughout Helsinki, including this one on Iso Roobertinkatu, which stays open until the wee hours on weekends.

**Tin Tin Tango** CAFE €
(www.tintintango.fi; Töölöntorinkatu 7; dishes €9-12; 7am-midnight Mon-Fri, 9am-midnight Sat, 10am-9pm Sun; ) This buzzy neighbourhood cafe, decorated with prints from the quiffed Belgian boy reporter's adventures, has a bit of everything. There's a laundry and a sauna, as well as lunches, brunches and cosy tables where you can sip a drink or get to grips with delicious, generously stuffed rolls. The welcoming, low-key, bohemian vibe is the real draw, though.

## PRICE RANGES

### Sleeping

The following price ranges refer to the cost of a double room.

**€** less than €80

**€€** €80–180

**€€€** more than €180

### Eating

The following price ranges refer to the cost of a main meal.

**€** less than €17

**€€** €17–27

**€€€** more than €27

**Café Ursula** CAFE €€
(www.ursula.fi; Ehrenströmintie 3; lunch buffet €12, mains €13-16; 9am-7pm Mon-Thu, to 8pm Fri & Sat, to 6pm Sun; ) Offering majestic views over the Helsinki archipelago, this upmarket cafe has marvellous outside summer seating. In winter you can sit in the modern interior and watch the ice on the sea. Along with daily specials, dishes range from elaborate open sandwiches to portobello burgers with goat's cheese and sweet-potato fries to Russian-style bavette steaks and grilled Baltic herring.

★**Kuu** FINNISH €€
(09-2709-0973; www.ravintolakuu.fi; Töölönkatu 27; mains €22-28, 3-course lunch menu €29; 11.30am-midnight Mon-Fri, 2pm-midnight Sat, 4-11pm Sun) Traditional Finnish fare is given a sharp, contemporary twist at Kuu, which creates seasonal dishes from local ingredients that could include reindeer fillet with celeriac puree and blackcurrant sauce, or liver with lingonberries and bacon sauce. Wines aren't cheap, but there are some interesting choices. Its casual bistro sibling, KuuKuu, is located 800m south.

★**Restaurant Olo** FINNISH €€€
(010-320-6250; www.olo-ravintola.fi; Pohjoisesplanadi 5; tasting menus short/long from €93/133, with paired wines €187/279; 6pm-midnight Tue-Fri, from 4pm Sat) At the forefront of New Suomi cuisine, Michelin-starred Olo occupies a handsome, 19th-century harbourside mansion. Its memorable seasonal degustation menus incorporate both the forage ethos and molecular gastronomy, and may feature culinary jewels such as

Icelandic salmon with wasabi and apple, or Finnish quail with forest mushrooms. Book a few weeks ahead.

## Drinking & Nightlife

Finns don't mind a drink and Helsinki has some of Scandinavia's most diverse nightlife. In winter locals gather in cosy bars, while in summer early-opening beer terraces sprout up all over town.

The centre's full of bars and clubs, with the Punavuori area around Iso Roobertinkatu one of the most worthwhile for trendy alternative choices.

Helsinki has a dynamic club scene that's always changing. Some club nights have age limits (often over 20), so check event details on websites before you arrive.

**Teerenpeli** PUB

(www.teerenpeli.com; Olavinkatu 2; ⌚noon-2am Sun-Thu, to 4.30am Fri & Sat; 📶) In a long, split-level space with low lighting and a mix of social and intimate seating, this excellent pub serves superb ales, stouts and berry ciders from its microbrewery in Lahti. The highish prices keep it fairly genteel, and there's a minimum age limit of 20. It's right by Kamppi bus station.

**Bar Loose** BAR

(☎044-739-8117; www.barloose.com; Annankatu 21; ⌚6pm-midnight Tue, to 4am Wed, Thu & Sun, to 5am Fri & Sat; 📶) The scarlet-coloured interior seems too fancy for a rock bar, but that's what Bar Loose is, with portraits of guitar heroes lining one wall and an eclectic crowd upstairs, served by two bars. Downstairs is a club area, with live music most nights followed by DJs spinning everything from metal to mod/retro classics. Drinks are decently priced.

**Maxine** BAR, CLUB

(www.maxine.fi; 6th fl, Kamppi Shopping Centre, Urho Kekkosenkatu 1A; ⌚10pm-4am Fri & Sat; 📶) On the top of Kamppi shopping centre, this classy venue makes the most of the inspiring city views. It's divided into three sections, with a bar area – a great spot for a sundowner – and two dance floors, one of which (the name, Kirjasto, or Library, gives it away) is quieter. Over 22s only.

★**Holiday** BAR

(www.holiday-bar.fi; Kanavaranta 7; ⌚4-11pm Wed & Thu, to 2am Fri & Sat; 📶) Even on the greyest Helsinki day, this colourful waterfront bar transports you to more tropical climes with vibrant rainforest wallpaper and plants, tropical-themed cocktails such as frozen margaritas and mojitos (plus two dozen different gins) and a seafood menu that includes softshell crab. A small market is often set up out the front in summer, along with ping-pong tables.

## ☆ Entertainment

As the nation's big smoke, Helsinki has the hottest culture and nightlife. Music is particularly big here, from metal clubs to opera. The latest events are publicised in *Helsinki This Week*, which is available at tourist offices, shopping centres, the airport, the railway station and the ferry terminal.

For concerts and performances, you can also check ticketing site **Lippupiste** (www.lippu.fi).

★**Musiikkitalo** CONCERT VENUE

(Helsinki Music Centre; ☎020-707-0400; www.musiikkitalo.fi; Mannerheimintie 13; priced by event; ⌚box office 9am-6pm Mon-Fri, 9.30am-5pm Sat & 1hr before performances) Home to the Helsinki Philharmonic Orchestra, Finnish Radio Symphony Orchestra and Sibelius Academy, the glass- and copper-fronted Helsinki Music Centre, opened in 2011, hosts a diverse program of classical, jazz, folk, pop and rock. The 1704-capacity main auditorium, visible from the foyer, has stunning acoustics. Five smaller halls seat 140 to 400. Buy tickets at the door or from www.ticketmaster.fi.

**Tavastia** LIVE MUSIC

(☎09-7746-74200; www.tavastiaklubi.fi; Urho Kekkosenkatu 4; ⌚8pm-1am Sun-Thu, 9pm-4am Fri, to 4.30am Sat) One of Helsinki's legendary rock venues, going strong since 1970, Tavastia attracts both up-and-coming local acts and bigger international groups, with a band virtually every night of the week. Most gigs start at 9pm; doors open two hours beforehand. Also check out what's on at its adjoining venue, **Semifinal** (☎09-7746-7420; www.tavastiaklubi.fi; Urho Kekkosenkatu 6; ⌚8pm-1am Sun-Thu, 9pm-2am Fri, 8pm-4am Sat), where new talent and young local bands take the stage.

## Shopping

Helsinki is a design epicentre, from fashion to furniture and homewares. Its hub is the Design District Helsinki (https://designdistrict.fi), spread out between chic Esplanadi to the east, retro-hipster Punavuori to the south and Kamppi to the west. Hundreds of shops, studios and galleries are mapped on its website; you can also pick up a map at the tourist office.

In summer there are food stalls, fresh produce and expensive berries at the Kauppatori, but the real picnic treats are in the **Vanha Kauppahalli** (www.vanhakauppahalli.fi; Eteläranta 1; ⌚8am-6pm Mon-Sat, 10am-5pm Sun; ✎) nearby. Built in 1889, some of it is touristy these days (reindeer kebabs?), but it's still a traditional Finnish market, where you can get filled rolls, cheese, bread, fish and an array of typical snacks and delicacies. Here you'll also find **Soppakeittiö** (soups €9-11; ⌚11am-5pm Mon-Sat; ✎), a great soup bar with famously good bouillabaisse.

# UNDERSTAND HELSINKI

## Helsinki Today

Regularly featuring at the top of world's most liveable cities ratings, Helsinki has long graduated from a shy provincial wannabe to a global lifestyle icon lauded by trendsetting publications such as *Monocle*. The economy might be going up and down with the rest of the eurozone, but overall the place feels as stable and confident as Switzerland, with Zurich-level prices to back up that impression. As in the rest of Europe, the political debate revolves around immigration, refugees and how much power should be delegated to Brussels. Coalition governments are the norm in Finland, and the current alliance, formed in 2019, comprises the Social Democratic Party, Centre Party, Green League, Left Alliance and Swedish People's Party of Finland.

Russia is another hot issue. For two decades the city has benefited from its proximity to St Petersburg, serving as a weekend shopping destination for rich and middle-class Russians (Finns head in the other direction in search of cheap booze). But deteriorating relations between the Kremlin and the West have renewed debate about Finnish neutrality, a sacrosanct principle since the end of WWII. More people now argue in favour of Finland joining NATO, but that's still a long way from becoming a reality.

## History

Founded in 1550 by the Swedish king Gustav Vasa, Helsinki was to be a rival to the Hansa trading town of Tallinn. For more than 200 years it remained a backwater suffering from various Russian incursions, until the Swedes built the sea-fortress Sveaborg in 1748 to protect this eastern part of their empire. When the Russians took control of Finland in 1809, a capital closer to St Petersburg was required to keep a closer eye on Finland's domestic politics. Helsinki was chosen – in large part because of the sea fortress (now called Suomenlinna) just outside the harbour – and so in 1812 Turku lost its long-standing status as Finland's capital and premier city.

In the 19th and early 20th centuries Helsinki grew rapidly in all directions. German architect Carl Ludvig Engel was called on to dignify the city centre, which resulted in the neoclassical Senaatintori (Senate Sq). The city suffered heavy Russian bombing during WWII, but in the postwar period Helsinki recovered and went on to host the Summer Olympic Games in 1952.

These days, the capital is so much the centre of everything that goes on in Finland that its past as an obscure market town is totally forgotten.

# SURVIVAL GUIDE

## ℹ Directory A–Z

Tourist info is downloadable at www.myhelsinki.fi.

Between June and August, multilingual 'Helsinki Helpers' – easily spotted by their lime-green jackets – are a mine of tourist information.

Internet access at various public libraries is free. Large parts of the city centre have free wi-fi, as do many bars and cafes – some also have terminals for customers' use. Public telephones are nonexistent.

**Helsinki Airport Tourist Office** (www.myhelsinki.fi; Terminal 2, Helsinki-Vantaa Airport; ⌚10am-8pm Mon-Sat, from noon Sun) Tourist information in the arrivals halls, Terminal 2.

**Helsinki City Tourist Office** (☎09-3101-3300; www.myhelsinki.fi; Kaivokatu 1, Central Railway Station; ⌚9am-7pm Mon-Fri, 10am-5pm Sat & Sun) Busy multilingual office in the Central Railway Station, with reams of information on the city. Also has an office at the airport.

## Getting There & Away

### AIR

**Helsinki-Vantaa Airport** (www.helsinki-vantaa.fi), 19km north of the city, is Finland's main air terminus. Direct flights serve many major European cities and several intercontinental destinations.

**Finnair** (☎ 09-818-0800; www.finnair.fi) covers 15 Finnish cities, usually at least once per day.

### BOAT

International ferries link Helsinki with Stockholm (Sweden), Tallinn (Estonia), St Petersburg (Russia) and destinations in Germany and Poland. Ferry tickets may be purchased at the terminal, from a ferry company's office or website or, in some cases, from the city tourist office. Book well in advance during the high season (late June to mid-August) and at weekends. There are five main terminals, three close to the centre:

**Katajanokan terminal** (Katajanokan) Served by trams 5 and 4.

**Olympia terminal** (Olympiaranta 1) Served by trams 2 and 3.

**Länsiterminaali** (West Terminal; Tyynenmerenkatu 8) Served by trams 7 and 6T.

**Makasiiniterminaali** (Eteläranta 7) Served by trams 1A and 2.

**Hansaterminaali (Vuosaari)** Served by buses 90 and 90A.

The following companies operate ferries to Tallinn:

**Eckerö Line** (☎ 06000-4300; www.eckeroline.fi; Länsiterminaali) Two to three daily car ferries (adult from €12, car from €24, 2½ hours) from Länsiterminaali.

**Tallink** (☎ 0600-15700; www.tallinksilja.com) Runs eight services daily (one way adult €27 to €41, vehicle €37 to €46, two hours), from Länsiterminaali.

**Viking Line** (☎ 0600-41577; www.vikingline.com; Katajanokan Terminaali) Operates car ferries (adult €26 to €39, vehicle plus two passengers €99, 2½ hours) from Katajanokan terminal.

### BUS

Purchase long-distance and express bus tickets at **Kamppi Bus Station** (☎ 0200-4000; www.matkahuolto.fi; Salomonkatu) or on the bus itself. Long-distance buses also depart from here to all of Finland.

### TRAIN

Helsinki's **train station** (Rautatieasema; www.vr.fi; Kaivokatu 1) is central and easy to find your way around. It's linked by subway to the metro (Rautatientori stop), and is a short walk from the bus station.

The train is the fastest and cheapest way to get from Helsinki to major Finnish centres. There are also daily trains (buy tickets from the international counter) to the Russian cities of Vyborg, St Petersburg and Moscow.

## Getting Around

### TO/FROM THE AIRPORT

The Ring Rail runs from Helsinki Airport to the city centre in about 30 minutes and costs €4.60. Buy tickets from machines located on the platform.

There are also door-to-door **airport taxis** (☎ 0600-555-555; www.airporttaxi.fi), which need to be booked the previous day, before 6pm, if you're leaving Helsinki (one to two people €22 to €42, depending on destination). A normal cab should cost €45 to €65.

### BICYCLE

With a flat inner city and well-marked cycling paths, Helsinki is ideal for cycling. Pick up the free *Ulkoilukartta* Helsinki cycling map at the tourist office, or view it online at www.ulkoilukartta.fi.

Launched in 2016, Helsinki's shared-bike scheme, City Bikes (www.hsl.fi/citybikes), has some 1500 bikes at 150 stations citywide. Bikes are €5/10 for a day/week pass; the first 30 minutes are free, then it's €1 for each additional 30 minutes per ride. Register online.

### PUBLIC TRANSPORT

The city's public transport system, **HSL** (www.hsl.fi), operates buses, metro and local trains, trams and a ferry to Suomenlinna. A one-journey fare within central Helsinki costs €4 when purchased on board, €2.80 when purchased in advance. The easiest ways to pay are with a chargeable HSL smartcard, or the HSL app. HSL cards are available from service points listed on the website at a cost of €5; make sure you bring ID to make the purchase. Charge the card, and simply scan it on board a vehicle to pay. The HSL app is free to download, and also works by preloading and scanning.

Day or multiday tickets for up to seven days (24/48/72 hours €8/12/16) are the best option if you're in town for a short time.

### TAXI

Hail cabs on the street or at taxi stands, or phone **Taksi Helsinki** (☎ 010-00700; www.taksihelsinki.fi).

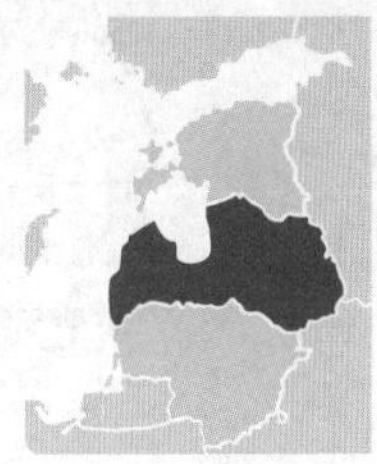

# Latvia

☎ 371 / POP 1.95 MILLION

**Includes ➡**



## Best Places to Stay

- Hotel Bergs (p217)
- Jakob Lenz (p216)
- Neiburgs (p216)
- Dome Hotel (p216)
- Light House (p230)

## Best Places to Eat

- Istaba (p220)
- 36.Line (p231)
- 3 Pavaru (p218)
- Valtera (p218)
- Aparjods (p264)

## Why Go?

A tapestry of sea, lakes and woods, Latvia is best described as a vast, unspoiled parkland with just one real city – its cosmopolitan capital, Rīga. The country might be small, but the amount of personal space it provides is enormous. You can always secure a chunk of pristine nature all for yourself, be it for trekking, cycling, berry-picking or dreaming away on a white-sand beach amid pine-covered dunes. But should you desire something urban, then Rīga, with its legendary art nouveau architecture and round-the-clock diversions, will delight in every way.

Having been invaded by every regional power, Latvia has more cultural layers and a less homogenous population than its neighbours. People here fancy themselves to be the least pragmatic and the most artistic of the Baltic lot. They prove the point with myriad festivals and a merry, devil-may-care attitude – well, a subdued Nordic version of it.

## When to Go

- In June, the all-night solstice sends locals flocking to coastal cottages for midnight sun. Latvians shake off their winter doldrums with a vengeance as they take full advantage of the long days to live life outdoors.
- Refusing to let summer go, Rīgans sip lattes under outdoor heat lamps at the season's last alfresco cafes in September and October. At the beaches, parkas are the outerwear of choice.
- Spend the winter holidays in the birthplace of the Christmas tree in Rīga's Old Town. Expect plenty of warming hot drinks at the various outdoor seasonal markets.

# Latvia Highlights

1 **Rīga** (p196) Gawking at the menagerie of devilish gargoyles that inhabit the city's art nouveau treasures.

2 **Old Rīga** (p196) Losing yourself in the Unesco-protected maze of cobblestones, church spires and gingerbread trim.

3 **Cape Kolka** (p235) Listening to the waves pound this awesomely remote cape, which crowns the lonely Kurzeme coast.

4 **Cēsis** (p266) Peering from the walls of the medieval castle, then plunging into nearby Gauja National Park.

5 **Kuldīga** (p246) Weaving among historic buildings before feeling the spray from Europe's widest – and maybe shortest – waterfall.

6 **Rundāle Palace** (p252) Sneaking away from the capital and reliving aristocratic decadence.

7 **Liepāja** (p242) Walking the fascinating Port Promenade before getting lost in the vastness of a great Baltic beach.

8 **Jūrmala** (p227) Lazing away long summer nights on a legendary white-sand beach.

# RĪGA

POP 641,400

The Gothic spires that dominate Rīga's Old Town might suggest austerity, but it is the flamboyant art nouveau that forms the flesh and the spirit of this vibrant cosmopolitan city, the largest of all three Baltic capitals. While medieval Old Rīga echoes to the rumble of year-round tourist feet, the neighbourhoods just outside the canal ring echo to the sounds of hustle and bustle. Here the convivial laughs of good times can be heard in cool cafes, cutting-edge restaurants and a whole collection of welcoming bars and pubs.

While Rīga at first seems to share the northern attributes for quiet and reserve, you'll soon find that there's some powerful energy here as Rīgans enjoy their city.

Standing next to its namesake gulf, Rīga is a short ride from toney seaside resort, Jūrmala, which comes with a stunning white-sand beach. And it's only a little further to uncrowded Saulkrasti. If you are craving solitude and a pristine environment, gorgeous sea dunes and blueberry-filled forests begin right outside the city boundaries.

## History

If Rīga were a human, it would be keeping a stack of expired passports issued in its name by a dozen states and empires.

It was born German in 1201. Bishop Albert von Buxhoevden (say that fast three times) founded Rīga as a bridgehead for the crusade against the northern 'heathens' – the Balts, the Slavs and Finno-Ugric people. Thus Rīga became a stronghold for the Knights of the Sword and the newest trading junction between proto-Russia and the West. When Sweden snagged the city in 1621, it grew into the largest holding of the Swedish Empire (even bigger than Stockholm!). Then the Russians snatched Latvia from Sweden's grip and added an industrial element to the bustling burg. By the mid-1860s Rīga was the world's biggest timber port and Russia's third city after Moscow and St Petersburg.

The 20th century saw the birth of cafes, salons, dance clubs and a thriving intellectual culture, which acquired a distinct Latvian flavour after the country became independent in 1918. All of that ended with the Soviet occupation in 1940. WWII left the city bombed and without its two largest communities – the Germans, who resettled into Germany, and the Jews, who were slaughtered in the Holocaust. But somehow, Rīga's indelible international flavour managed to rise up from the rubble, and even as a part of the USSR, Rīga was known for its forward thinking and thriving cultural life.

Today, Rīga's cosmopolitan past makes it one of the cornerstones of the Baltic and the heart of Latvia.

### LATVIA AT A GLANCE

**Currency** euro (€)

**Language** Latvian, also Russian and English (unofficial)

**Capital** Rīga

**Area** 64,589 sq km

## Sights

Rīga sits along the Daugava River, which flows another 15km north before dumping into the Gulf of Rīga. Old Rīga (Vecrīga), the historic heart of the city, stretches 1km along the river's eastern side and 600m back from its banks. This medieval section of town is mostly pedestrian, with curving cobbled streets and alleys.

Kaļķu iela heads away from the river and turns into Brīvības bulvāris (Freedom Blvd) when it hits the picturesque ring of parkland that insulates the medieval centre from the gridiron of grand boulevards just beyond. The copper-topped Freedom Monument, in the middle of Brīvības bulvāris, is the unofficial gateway into Central Rīga. This part of the city, constructed in the 19th and 20th centuries, sports wide avenues, imposing apartment blocks and plenty of art nouveau architecture. At the outer edges of the city centre, European grandeur begins to fade into Soviet block housing and *microrajons* (suburbs).

### Old Rīga (Vecrīga)

The curving cobbled streets of Rīga's medieval core are best explored at random. Once you're sufficiently lost amid the tangle of gabled roofs, church spires and crooked alleyways, you will begin to uncover a stunning, World Heritage–listed realm of soaring cathedrals, gaping city squares, crumbling castle walls and, yes, many, many fellow tourists.

### Rātslaukums

Rātslaukums is a fine place to start one's exploration of the old city. Stop by the tourist information centre, located in Blackheads House, for useful brochures and maps.

**Blackheads House** HISTORIC BUILDING

(Melngalvju nams; Map p198; ☎6704 3678; www.melngalvjunams.lv; Rātslaukums 7; adult/child €6/3; ⏰10am-6pm) Built in 1344, the original house was bombed in 1941 and flattened by the Soviets seven years later. Somehow the original blueprints survived and an exact replica of this fantastically ornate structure was completed in 2001 for Rīga's 800th birthday.

**Town Hall** HISTORIC BUILDING

(Map p198; Rātslaukums) Rīga's historic town hall was destroyed in WWII and rebuilt from scratch in 2003. A **statue of St Roland**, the city's patron, takes pride of place on the square in front of it. It, too, is a replica of the original, erected in 1897, which now stands in St Peter's Church.

**Latvian Riflemen Monument** MONUMENT

(Map p198; Latviešu Strēlnieku laukums) Latvian Riflemen Sq, on the west side of the future home of the Occupation Museum, is dominated by the imposing and controversial statue honouring Latvia's Riflemen, who formed the core of Russia's Red Army in 1918. Some of them served as Lenin's personal bodyguards, and yet most returned to the newly independent Latvia.

**Mentzendorff's House** HISTORIC BUILDING

(Mencendorfa nams; Map p198; ☎6721 2951; www.mencendorfanams.com; Grēcinieku iela 18; adult/child €6/2; ⏰10am-5pm May-Sep, 11am-5pm Wed-Sun Oct-Apr) Built in 1695 as the home of a wealthy German glazier, this sparsely furnished house offers insight into everyday life for Rīga's successful merchants. There's a permanent exhibition of contemporary glass art downstairs and temporary exhibitions are held in the attic. Note the intricate leaded glass windows.

### Pēterbaznīca Laukums

**★St Peter's Church** CHURCH

(Sv Pētera baznīca; Map p198; ☎67181 941; www.peterbaznica.riga.lv; Skārņu iela 19; adult/child €9/3; ⏰10am-7pm Tue-Sun May-Sep, to 6pm Oct-Apr) Forming the centrepiece of Rīga's skyline, this Gothic church is thought to be around 800 years old, making it one of the oldest medieval buildings in the Baltic. Its soaring red-brick interior is relatively unadorned, except for heraldic shields mounted on the columns. A colourful contrast is provided by the art exhibitions staged in the side aisles. At the rear of the church, a lift whisks visitors to a viewing platform 72m up the copper-clad steeple.

The church's austere Gothic outlook is softened by baroque sculptures, added in the 17th century, along with the spire that instantly became a signature element of Rīga's skyline. In 1721 the spire was destroyed in a blaze, despite Russian emperor Peter I personally rushing to the scene to extinguish the fire. A legend says that when it was re-erected in 1746, builders threw glass from the top to see how long the spire would last; a greater number of shards meant a very long life. The glass ended up landing on a pile of straw and broke into just two pieces. The spire ended up being destroyed again in WWII. When it was resurrected again, the ceremonial glass chucking was repeated, and this time it was a smash hit. Today St Peter's is garlanded by stylish restaurants and cafes.

**Museum of Decorative Arts & Design** MUSEUM

(Dekoratīvi lietisķās mākslas muzejs; Map p198; ☎6732 4461; www.lnmm.lv; Skārņu iela 10/20; adult/child €5/2.50; ⏰11am-5pm Tue & Thu-Sun, to 7pm Wed) The former St George's Church houses a museum devoted to applied art from the art nouveau period to the present, including an impressive collection of

### OH CHRISTMAS TREE

Rīga's Blackheads House was once known for its wild parties; it was, after all, a clubhouse for the Blackheads guild of unmarried German merchants. On a cold Christmas Eve in 1510, the squad of bachelors, full of holiday spirit (of all kinds), hauled a huge pine tree up to their clubhouse and smothered it with flowers. At the end of the evening they burned the tree in an impressive blaze. From then on, decorating the 'Christmas tree' became an annual tradition, which eventually spread across the globe (it's probably for the best that the burning part never really caught on).

An octagonal commemorative plaque, inlaid in cobbled Rātslaukums, marks the spot where the original tree stood.

## Old Rīga (Vecrīga)

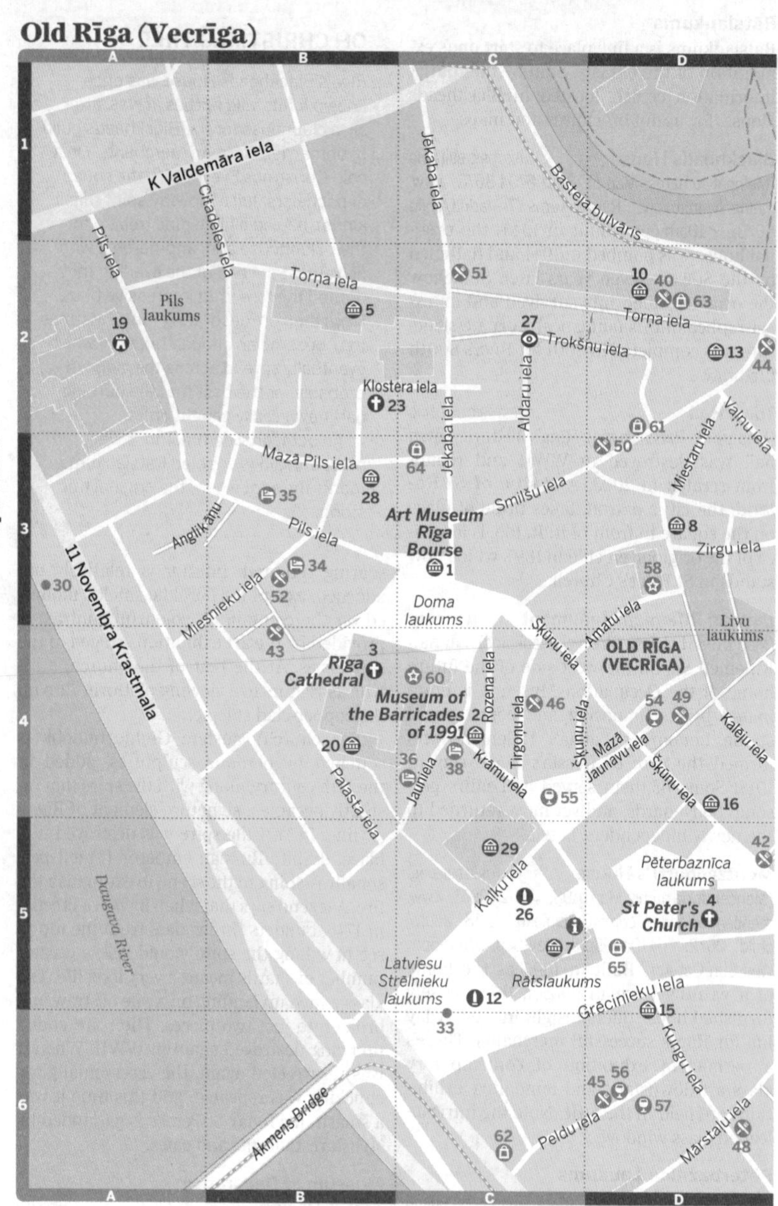


furniture, woodcuts, tapestries and ceramics. The building's foundations date back to 1207, when the Livonian Brothers of the Sword erected their castle here. Since the rest of the original knights' castle was levelled by rioting citizens at the end of the same century, it is the only building that remains intact from the birth of Rīga.

**St John's Church** CHURCH

(Jāņa baznīca; Map p198; ☎2563 5565; www.janabaznica.lv; Skārņu iela 24; ⏰10am-6pm Fri-Sun) A 13th- to 19th-century amalgam of

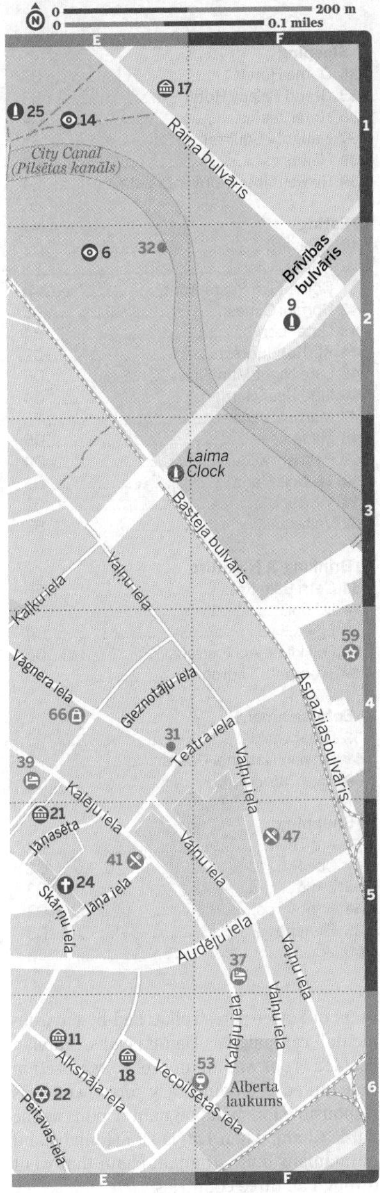


Gothic and baroque styles, the church was first mentioned when the citizens installed catapults on its roof and successfully dispersed attacking Livonian knights. Initially run by Dominican monks, it was pillaged during the reformation. After a stint as stables and granary, it was handed over to the Lutherans, who remain in control. Next to the church, an archway leads into **Jāņa sēta** (St John's courtyard), which contains the preserved remains of a 13th-century monastery wall.

It was here that Bishop Albert von Buxhoevden, who founded Rīga in 1201, set up his residence. So if you are looking for the city's exact birthplace, it is about the first spot that comes to mind. Note the curving lines above the red-brick gates – they are said to depict the back of the donkey that drove Jesus into Jerusalem. The gist of it is – follow the Christ.

**Rīga Porcelain Museum** MUSEUM

(Map p198; ☎6701 2944; http://porcelanamuzejs.riga.lv; Kalēju iela 9/11; adult/student €2.50/1; ⏱11am-6pm Tue-Sun) This quirky museum houses a collection of porcelain assembled in now-defunct local porcelain factories from Soviet times. One was run by Russians hailing from the famous Gzhel factory near Moscow, the other by local Germans. As a result, the Rīga style of porcelain-making grew as a fusion of these two schools.

### Kalēju Iela & Mārstaļu Iela

Zigzagging Kalēju iela and Mārstaļu iela are dotted with ornate reminders of the city's legacy as a wealthy northern European trading centre. Several of the old merchants' manors have been transformed into museums.

**Latvian Photography Museum** MUSEUM

(Latvijas fotogrāfijas muzejs; Map p198; ☎6722 2713; www.fotomuzejs.lv; Mārstaļu iela 8; adult/child €4/2; ⏱10am-5pm Wed & Fri-Sun, noon-7pm Thu) Occupying a historic merchant's house from 1500, this little museum displays early images from Rīga along with changing exhibitions of contemporary photography. There's also a camera obscura and an interesting display on local lad Valters Caps (1905–2003), the inventor of the miniature Minox camera so beloved by Cold War spies.

**Rīga Synagogue** SYNAGOGUE

(Map p198; ☎6721 4507; www.jews.lv; Peitavas iela 6/8; ⏱10am-5pm Sun-Fri) Built in 1905, this art nouveau–style synagogue was the only one to survive the Nazi occupation – to torch it in the tightly packed Old Town would have put neighbouring buildings at risk. It reopened for worship during the Soviet period but was damaged by bomb

## Old Rīga (Vecrīga)

**Top Sights**
1 Art Museum Rīga Bourse ... C3
2 Museum of the Barricades of 1991 ... C4
3 Rīga Cathedral ... B4
4 St Peter's Church ... D5

**Sights**
5 Arsenāls Exhibition Hall ... B2
6 Bastion Hill ... E2
7 Blackheads House ... C5
8 Cat House ... D3
9 Freedom Monument ... F2
10 Jacob's Barracks ... D2
11 Latvian Photography Museum ... E6
12 Latvian Riflemen Monument ... C5
13 Latvian War Museum ... D2
14 Memorials to Victims of 20 January 1991 ... E1
15 Mentzendorff's House ... D5
16 Museum of Decorative Arts & Design ... D4
17 Museum of the Occupation of Latvia ... E1
18 Popular Front Museum ... E6
19 Rīga Castle ... A2
20 Rīga History & Navigation Museum ... B4
21 Rīga Porcelain Museum ... E5
22 Rīga Synagogue ... E6
23 St James' Cathedral ... B2
24 St John's Church ... E5
25 Statue of Rūdolfs Blaumanis ... E1
26 Statue of St Roland ... C5
27 Swedish Gate ... C2
28 Three Brothers ... B3
29 Town Hall ... C5

**Activities, Courses & Tours**
Eat Rīga ... (see 31)
30 Kugitis Jelgava ... A3
31 Rīga Bike Tours & Rent ... E4
32 Rīga By Canal ... E2
33 Rīga City Tour ... C6

**Sleeping**
34 Dome Hotel ... B3
35 Grand Palace Hotel ... B3
36 Hotel Justus ... C4
37 Naughty Squirrel ... F5
38 Neiburgs ... C4
39 Rixwell Hotel Konventa Seta ... E4

**Eating**
40 3 Pavaru ... D2
41 Chez Olivier ... E5
Dome Fish Restaurant ... (see 34)
42 Domini Canes ... D5
43 Gutenbergs ... B4
44 KD Konditoreja ... D2
45 Late Night Munchies ... D6
46 Lido Beer Garden ... C4
47 Martina's Bakery ... F5
48 Milda ... D6
49 Pelmeņi XL ... D4
50 Tēvocis Vaņa ... D3
51 V Ķuze ... C2
52 Valtera ... B3

**Drinking & Nightlife**
53 Cetri Balti Krekli ... F6
54 DJ Bar ... D4
55 Egle ... C4
56 Folkklubs Ala Pagrabs ... D6
57 Trompete Taproom ... D6

**Entertainment**
58 Great Guild ... D3
59 Latvian National Opera ... F4
60 Rīga Cathedral ... C4

**Shopping**
61 Ars Tela ... D2
62 Cita Rota ... C6
63 Etmo ... D2
64 Hobbywool ... C3
65 Pienene ... D5
66 Upe ... E4

attacks by neo-Nazis in the 1990s, following independence. It was fully restored in 2009 and is now protected by police 24/7. Inside, there is beautiful ornamentation modelled on ancient Egyptian and Assyrian-Babylonian styles.

**Popular Front Museum** MUSEUM
(Tautas frontes muzejs; Map p198; ☎6722 4502; http://lnvm.lv; Vecpilsētas iela 13-15; ⊙10am-5pm Tue-Sat) FREE A branch of the National History Museum, this exhibition involving interactive multimedia technology covers the period of the third Atmoda (national awakening): the struggle for independence in the years of Soviet perestroika. Led by environmental campaigner Dainis Ivans, Latvian People's Front was an umbrella organisation that united pro-democracy forces and was responsible for such poignant actions as the Baltic Chain, when Latvians, Estonians and Lithuanians built a human chain that went through all three countries.

### Livu Laukums

Lively Livu laukums is near the busiest entrance to Old Rīga along Kaļķu iela. A colourful row of 18th-century buildings lines the square – most of which house cafes and restaurants.

**Cat House** HISTORIC BUILDING

(Kaķu māja; Map p198; Miestaru iela 10/12) The spooked black cats mounted on the turrets of this 1909 art nouveau–influenced building have become symbols of Rīga and Instagram stars. On any tour, you'll likely hear a tale about how the building's owner had the cats' butts aimed at the neighbouring Great Guild across the street after he was rejected for membership. The tale is completely false but thanks to guides in need of a good story it now has nine lives.

### Doma Laukums

**★Rīga Cathedral** CHURCH

(Rīgas Doms, The Dome Church; Map p198; ☎6722 7573; www.doms.lv; Doma laukums 1; €3; ⏲10am-5pm daily May-Sep, 11am-5pm Wed-Sat Oct-Apr) Founded in 1211 as the seat of the Rīga diocese, this enormous (once Catholic, now Evangelical Lutheran) cathedral is the largest medieval church in the Baltic. The architecture is an amalgam of styles from the 13th to the 18th centuries: the eastern end, the oldest portion, has Romanesque features; the tower is 18th-century baroque; and much of the rest dates from a 15th-century Gothic rebuild. The glazed black bricks are a symbol of the Hanseatic architecture.

During Soviet times services were forbidden, but the building, along with its huge 6768-pipe organ, built in 1884, underwent a careful reconstruction in 1983. It was used as a classical-music venue, which it very much remains now, although services are held again and it's the home of the Lutheran archbishop of Latvia.

The floor and walls of the huge interior are dotted with old stone tombs – note the carved symbols denoting the rank or post of the occupant. Eminent citizens would pay to be buried as close to the altar as possible. In 1709 the cholera and typhoid outbreak that killed a third of Rīga's population was blamed on a flood that inundated the tombs, whereupon new burials were banned. The serene cloisters provide a breather from the tourist-mobbed streets of Rīga.

**Rīga History & Navigation Museum** MUSEUM

(Rīgas vēstures un kuģniecības muzejs; Map p198; ☎6735 6676; www.rigamuz.lv; Palasta iela 4; adult/child €5/1; ⏲10am-5pm Wed-Sun May-Sep, 11am-5pm Tue-Sat Oct-Apr) Founded in 1773 and situated in the old Rīga Cathedral monastery, this engaging museum presents the sweep of local history, from the Bronze Age all the way to WWII. Artefacts, including lovely pre-Christian jewellery and beautiful furnishings and clothing from the art nouveau period, help tell the story. A highlight is the beautiful neoclassical Column Hall, built when Latvia was part of the Russian Empire. Kids of all ages love the rooms full of ship models.

**★Art Museum Rīga Bourse** MUSEUM

(Mākslas muzejs Rīgas Birža; Map p198; ☎6732 4461; www.lnmm.lv; Doma laukums 6; adult/child €3/0.50; ⏲10am-6pm Tue-Thu, Sat & Sun, to 8pm Fri) Rīga's lavishly restored 1852 stock exchange building is a worthy showcase for the city's art treasures. The elaborate facade features a coterie of deities that dance between the windows, while inside, gilt chandeliers sparkle from ornately moulded ceilings. The Asian section features beautiful Chinese and Japanese ceramics and an Egyptian mummy, while the main halls are devoted to Western art, including a Monet painting and a scaled-down cast of Rodin's *The Kiss*.

**★Museum of the Barricades of 1991** MUSEUM

(1991 gada barikāžu muzejs; Map p198; ☎6721 3525; http://barikades.lv; Krāmu iela 3; admission by donation; ⏲10am-5pm Mon-Fri, 11am-5pm Sat) Latvia's independence came after enormous struggles. One of the most remarkable stories involves the barricades built by thousands of citizens around important public buildings in Rīga. In January 1991, Latvians from every walk of life came together to prevent the Soviets from taking over the capital, a stunning display of heartfelt commitment to a greater cause. This excellent museum is run by the organisation of barricade veterans. It's a moving – and professionally curated – account of this pivotal time.

**Three Brothers** HISTORIC BUILDING

(Trīs brāļi; Map p198; ☎museum 6722 0779; www.archmuseum.lv; Mazā Pils iela 17, 19 & 21; ⏲museum 9am-5pm Mon-Fri) FREE Tallinn has its Three Sisters, so Rīga has dubbed three of its old stone houses the Three Brothers. These architectural gems conveniently line up in a photogenic row and exemplify Old Rīga's diverse collection of architectural styles. No 17 is over 600 years old, making it the oldest dwelling in town. Note the tiny windows on the upper levels – Rīga's

LANGUAGE

| | | |
|---|---|---|
| **Hello (good day)** | *Labdien* | *lab-dee-in* |
| **Hi (informal)** | *Sveiki* | *svay-kee* |
| **How are you?** | *Kā jums klājas* | *kah yooms klah-yus* |
| **Thank you** | *Paldies* | *paul-dee-iss* |
| **Please/you're welcome** | *Lūdzu* | *lood-zoo* |

property taxes during the Middle Ages were based on window size.

The 17th-century No 19 houses the **Latvian Museum of Architecture**, which offers temporary exhibitions about the capital's extraordinary buildings and shows decorations from lost Old Town buildings in the hidden courtyard.



**St James' Cathedral** CATHEDRAL
(Sv Jēkaba katedrāle; Map p198; 2999 1637; www.jekabakatedrale.lv; Klostera iela; 7am-1pm & 2.30-6pm Mon-Sat, to 7.30pm Sun) Built in 1225, this church has ping-ponged many times between Catholic and Protestant, and has been home to many languages and communities, including Germans, Swedes, Poles and Estonians. Most notably, it was here that Latvians first heard a mass in their own tongue during its Lutheran stint in 1523. Exactly 400 years later it was handed back to the Catholics to be used as their cathedral.

### Pils Laukums

**Rīga Castle** CASTLE
(Rīgas pils; Map p198; Pils laukums 3) Built in 1330 as the headquarters of the grand master of the Livonian Order, this building has been much mutated over the years and now only looks properly castley from certain angles. It was badly damaged in a 2013 fire, but after a massive renovation it is once again the official residence of the Latvian president. Peer past the ceremonial guards out front for a peek at the inner sanctum.

**Arsenāls Exhibition Hall** GALLERY
(Map p198; 6735 7527; www.lnmm.lv; Torņa iela 1; adult/child €4/2; 11am-5pm Tue, Wed & Fri, to 8pm Thu, noon-5pm Sat & Sun) Behind a row of granite heads depicting Latvia's most prominent artists, the imperial arsenal, constructed in 1832 to store weapons for the Russian tsar's army, is now a prime spot for international and Latvian art exhibitions.

### Torņa Iela

From Pils laukums, photogenic Torņa iela makes a beeline for City Canal (Pilsētas kanāls) at the other end of Old Rīga. Almost the entire north side of the street is flanked by the custard-coloured **Jacob's Barracks** (Jēkaba Kazarmas; Map p198; Torņa iela 4), built as an enormous warehouse in the 16th century. A few cafes and boutiques now inhabit the refurbished building.

**Swedish Gate** GATE
(Zviedru vārti; Map p198; Torņa iela 11) Built into the city's medieval walls in 1698 while the Swedes were in power, this arched gate is the only one left in Old Rīga. Set in the largest surviving section of the town walls, it leads into Trokšnu iela, Old Rīga's narrowest and most atmospheric street.

**Latvian War Museum** MUSEUM
(Latvijas kara muzejs; Map p198; 6722 3743; www.karamuzejs.lv; Smilšu iela 20; 10am-6pm Apr-Oct, to 5pm Nov-Mar) FREE The round Powder Tower dates back to the 14th century and is the only survivor of the 18 original towers that punctuated the old city walls. Nine Russian cannonballs from 17th- and 18th-century assaults are embedded in its walls. In the past the museum has served as a gunpowder store, a prison, a torture chamber and a frat house. The museum details the political and military history of Latvia from medieval times to NATO and the present day.

## Central Rīga (Centrs)

As Kaļķu iela breaks free from the centuries-old jumble of turrets and towers, it turns into Brīvības bulvāris (Freedom Blvd), and continues to neatly cut the city centre into two equal parts. An emerald necklace of lush parks acts as a buffer between the medieval walls and the large-scale gridiron of stately boulevards. Central Rīga's memorable sights include the flamboyant art nouveau district, the sprawling Central Market housed in mammoth zeppelin hangars and the iconic Freedom Monument.

### Along City Canal

**Pilsētas Kanāls (City Canal)** PARK
(Map p204) Pilsētas kanāls, the city's old moat, once protected the medieval walls

from invaders. Today the snaking ravine has been incorporated into a thin belt of stunning parkland splitting Old and Central Rīga. Stately Raiņa bulvāris follows the rivulet on the north side, and used to be known as 'Embassy Row' during Latvia's independence between the world wars.

Raiņa has once again assumed its dignified status, with the *bleu blanc rouge* fluttering at No 9. Additional diplomatic estates face the central park and moat on Kronvalda bulvāris and Kalpaka bulvāris.

**Bastion Hill** (Bastejkalns; Map p198) lies along the banks of Pilsētas kanāls near Brīvības, and is the last remnant of medieval Rīga's sand bulwark fortifications. People love to climb the circling path.

North of Bastejkalns across the canal are poignant reminders of Latvia's tragic last century. Five red stone slabs lie as **memorials to the victims of 20 January 1991** (Map p198); they were killed here when Soviet troops stormed the nearby Interior Ministry. Nearby is the 1929 **Statue of Rūdolfs Blaumanis** (1863–1908). One of Latvia's greatest writers, the short story *In the Shadow of Death* is one of his most famous works. In 1941 after Nazis occupied the city, Jews were chased and beaten on this now-serene spot.

On 18 November 1918 Latvia declared its independence at the baroque **National Theatre** (Nacionālais teātris; Map p204), at the junction of the canal and K Valdemāra iela. The beloved Latvian National Opera (p224), which resembles Moscow's Bolshoi Theatre, sits at the other end of the park near K Barona iela.

**Freedom Monument** MONUMENT

(Brīvības piemineklis; Map p198; Brīvības bulvāris) Affectionately known as 'Milda', Rīga's Freedom Monument towers above the city between Old and Central Rīga. Paid for by public donations, the monument was designed by Kārlis Zāle and erected in 1935 where a statue of Russian ruler Peter the Great once stood.

At the base of the monument there is an inscription that reads *'Tēvzemei un Brīvībai'* (For Fatherland and Freedom), accompanied by granite friezes of Latvians singing and fighting for their freedom.



## RĪGA IN...

### Two Days

Start your adventure in the heart of the city at **Blackheads House** (p197) in Rātslaukums. Spend the rest of the morning wandering among the twisting cobbled lanes that snake through medieval **Old Rīga** (p196). Stop into **Rīga Cathedral** (p201) and learn the city's history at the enjoyable **Rīga History & Navigation Museum** (p201). After a leisurely lunch, wander beyond the ancient walls, passing the **Freedom Monument** as you make your way to the grand boulevards that radiate away from the city's core. Head to the **Quiet Centre** (p207), where you'll find some of Rīga's finest examples of art nouveau architecture on Alberta iela. Don't miss the **Rīga Art Nouveau Museum** (p208).

On your second day, browse the bounty of the Latvian countryside at **Rīga Central Market** (p210), and buy some smoked fish, berries or cheese as a snack. Next ride the elevator to the **Latvian Academy of Science Observation Deck** (p210). Then take a relaxing **boat ride** (p215) along the Daugava and the city's inner canals. Head up to Central Rīga for drinks and a meal. In the evening, if the opera is in season, treat yourself to some of the finest classical music in Europe.

### Four Days

After completing the two-day itinerary above, spend day three in your swimsuit along the silky sands in **Jūrmala** (p227), Latvia's uber-resort town. Rent a bike in the afternoon and explore **Ķemeri** (p232), where spa relics coexist with natural beauty in the national park. Back in Rīga, head up to Miera iela to enjoy the city's best pubs.

Your fourth day can be spent exploring some of Rīga's lesser-known nooks, or you can make tracks to **Gauja National Park** (p258) for an action-packed day of castle-ogling mixed with natural beauty. Start in **Sigulda** (p258) to get the blood rushing on the Olympic bobsled track, swing through **Turaida** (p261), then make your way to the fortress ruins and walkable streets of **Cēsis** (p266) before returning to the capital.

## Central Rīga (Centrs)

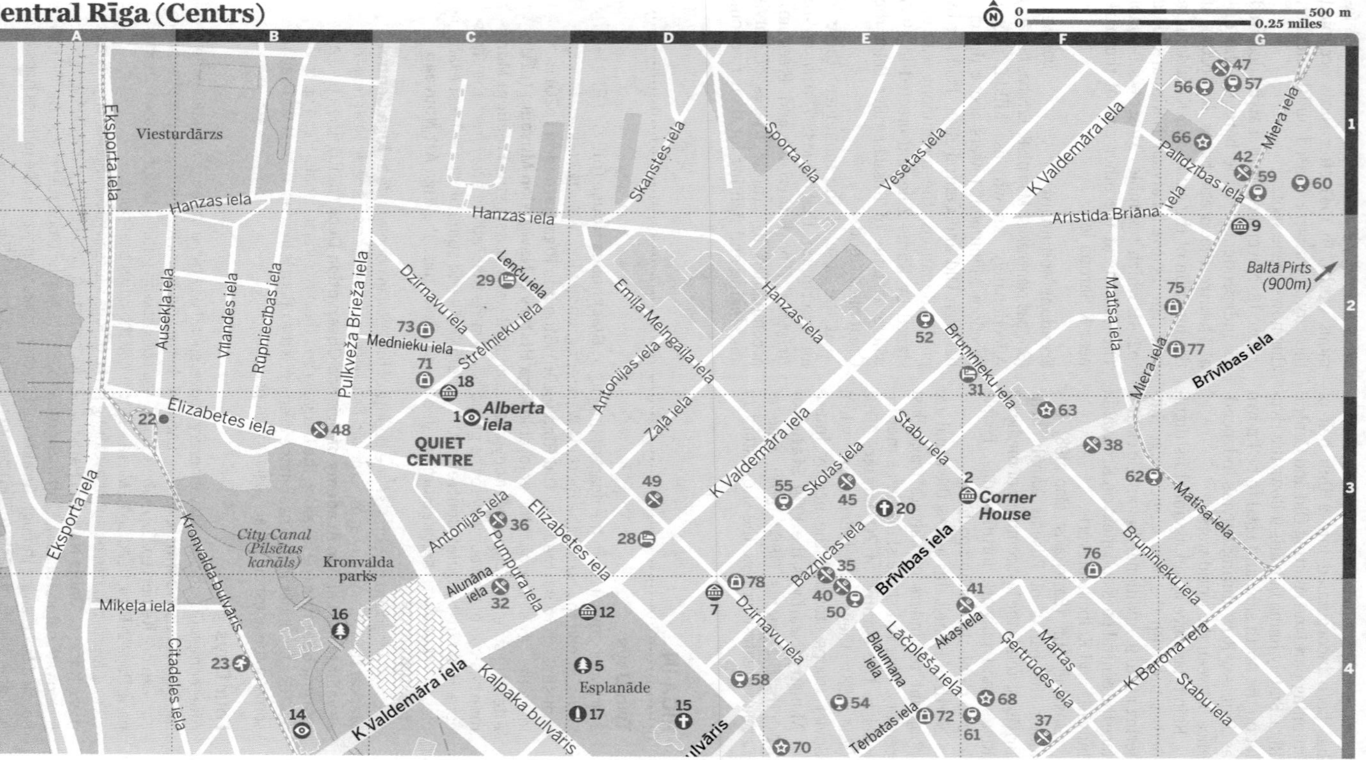

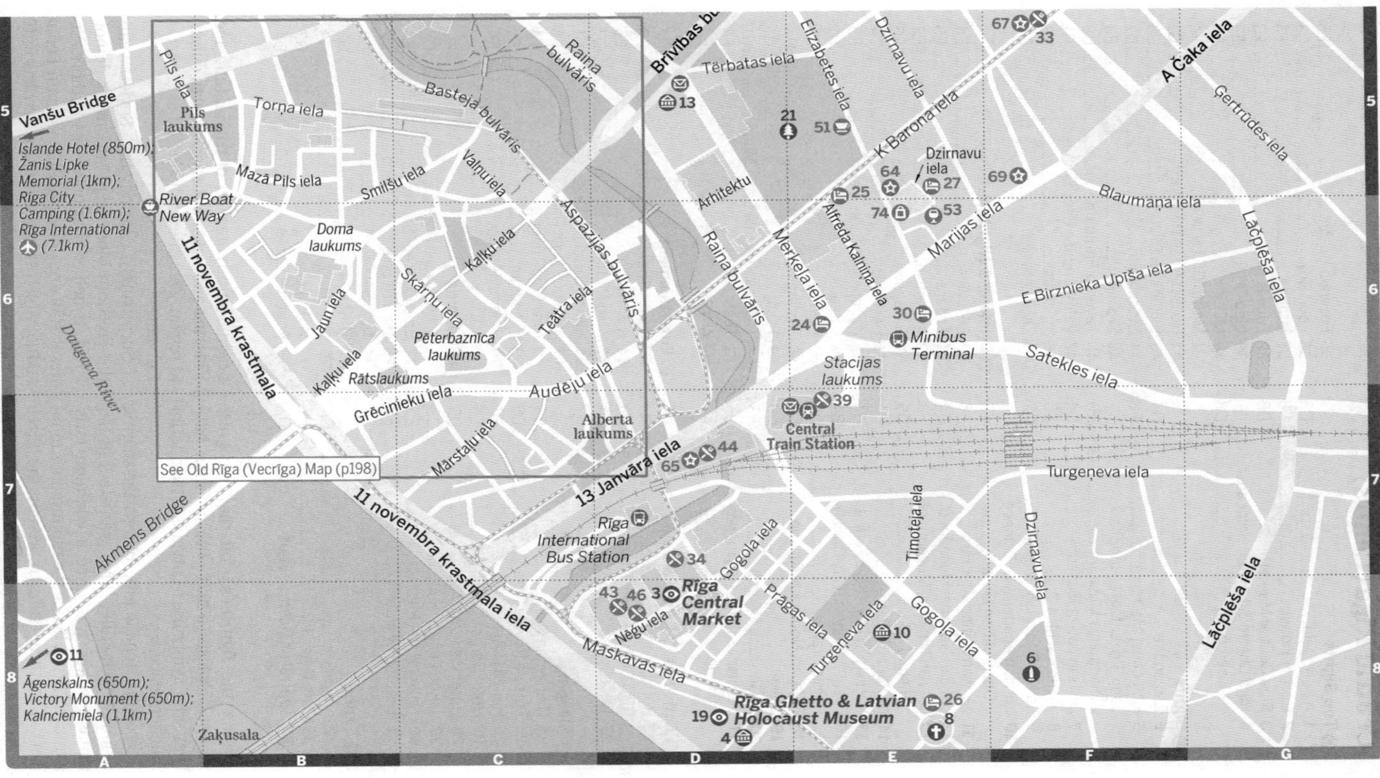

A
B
C
D
E
F
G
5
6
7
8
Vanšu Bridge
Islande Hotel (850m); Žanis Lipke Memorial (1km); Rīga City Camping (1.6km); Rīga International (7.1km)
Daugava River
Akmens Bridge
Āgenskalns (650m); Victory Monument (650m); Kalnciemiela (1.1km)
11
Zaķusala
Pils iela
Pils laukums
River Boat New Way
11 novembra krastmala
Torņa iela
Mazā Pils iela
Smilšu iela
Doma laukums
Jaun iela
Kaļķu iela
Rātslaukums
Grēcinieku iela
Pēterbaznīca laukums
Skārņu iela
Valņu iela
Kaļķu iela
Basteja bulvāris
Raiņa bulvāris
Aspazijas bulvāris
Teātra iela
Audēju iela
Alberta laukums
Mārstaļu iela
See Old Rīga (Vecrīga) Map (p198)
13 Janvāra iela
Rīga International Bus Station
11 novembra krastmala iela
Maskavas iela
Nēģu iela
43
46
3 Rīga Central Market
34
Gogoļa iela
Prāgas iela
19
4
Rīga Ghetto & Latvian Holocaust Museum
Turgeņeva iela
10
Gogoļa iela
Timoteja iela
26
8
6
Dzirnavu iela
Turgeņeva iela
Lāčplēša iela
Central Train Station
39
Stacijas laukums
44
65
Raiņa bulvāris
Merķeļa iela
24
Minibus Terminal
30
Satekles iela
E Birznieka Upīša iela
Marijas iela
Alfrēda Kalniņa iela
74
53
Dzirnavu iela
27
64
25
K Barona iela
Elizabetes iela
51
21
Tērbatas iela
Arhitektu
13
Brīvības bu
Dzirnavu iela
69
67
33
A Čaka iela
Ģertrūdes iela
Blaumaņa iela
Lāčplēša iela

## Central Rīga (Centrs)

**Top Sights**

1 Alberta Iela ... C3
2 Corner House ... F3
3 Rīga Central Market ... D8
4 Rīga Ghetto & Latvian Holocaust Museum ... D8

**Sights**

5 Esplanāde ... D4
6 Holocaust Memorial ... F8
Janis Rozentāls & Rūdolfs Blaumanis Museum ... (see 18)
7 Jews in Latvia Museum ... D4
8 Jēzus Baznīca ... E8
9 Laima Chocolate Museum ... G2
10 Latvian Academy of Science Observation Deck ... E8
11 Latvian National Library ... A8
12 Latvian National Museum of Art ... D4
13 Latvian National Museum of History ... D5
14 National Theatre ... B4
15 Nativity of Christ Cathedral ... D4
16 Pilsētas Kanāls (City Canal) ... B4
17 Rainis Statue ... D4
18 Rīga Art Nouveau Museum ... C2
19 Spīķeri ... D8
20 St Gertrude Church ... E3
21 Vērmanes dārzs (Vērmanes Garden) ... E5

**Activities, Courses & Tours**

22 Retro Tram ... A3
Riga Culture Free Tour ... (see 17)
23 Taka Spa ... B4

**Sleeping**

24 Cinnamon Sally ... E6
25 Europa Royale Rīga ... E5
26 Hanza Hotel ... E8
27 Hotel Bergs ... E5
28 Hotel Valdemārs ... D3
29 Jakob Lenz ... C2
30 Tallink Hotel Riga ... E6
31 Teater City Hotel ... F2

**Eating**

32 Aragats ... C4
33 Cafe Osīriss ... F5
34 Centrālais Gastro Tirgus ... D7
35 Fazenda Bazārs ... E3
36 Food Box ... C3
37 Istaba ... F4
38 Lauvas Nams ... F3
39 Lido Origo ... E7
40 Miit ... E4
41 Moltto Grill & Wine ... F4
42 Rocket Bean Roastery ... G1
43 Siļķītes un Dillītes ... D8
44 Stockmann ... D7
45 Stockpot ... E3
46 Taverna Pumpkin ... D8
47 Valmiermuiža Beer Embassy ... G1
48 Vincents ... B3
49 Zivju Lete ... D3

**Drinking & Nightlife**

50 Alķīmiķis ... E4
51 Apsara ... E5
52 Autentika ... E2
53 Garage ... E6
54 Herbārijs ... E4
55 Kaņepes Kultūras Centrs ... E3
56 Labietis ... G1
57 Piens ... G1
58 Skyline Bar ... D4
59 Taka ... G1
60 Tallinas Kvartāla Ezītis Miglā ... G1
61 Teātra Bārs ... F4
62 Ziemeļu Enkurs ... F3

**Entertainment**

63 Dailes Theatre ... F3
64 K Suns ... E5
65 Kino Citadele ... D7
66 KK fon Stricka Villa ... G1
67 Mūzikas nams Daile ... F5
68 New Rīga Theatre ... F4
69 Palladium ... F5
70 Splendid Palace ... E4

**Shopping**

71 Art Nouveau Rīga ... C2
72 Bold Concept Store ... E4
73 Elina Dobele ... C2
74 Jāņa Sēta ... E6
75 M50 ... G2
76 Manilla ... F3
77 Mr Page ... G2
78 Robert's Books ... D4

Among the figurines, you may recognise that of Lāčplēsis (p222) – the half-man, half-bear who symbolises Latvians' struggle for independence.

A copper female Liberty tops the soaring monument, holding three gold stars in her hands ('Milda' was once a common girls' name in Latvia, hence the monument's moniker). The three stars represent the three original cultural regions of Latvia: Kurzeme, Vidzeme and Latgale (Latvia's fourth cultural region, Zemgale, is dismissed as a part of Kurzeme).

Surprisingly, during the Soviet years the Freedom Monument was never demolished. It helped that one of its authors, Ernests Štālbergs, designed Rīga's main Lenin statue, which stood further up Brivibas until it was removed in 1991. However, all through the Soviet period, Milda was strictly off limits to Latvians, and people trying to place flowers at the base were persecuted.

Two soldiers stand guard at the monument throughout the day and perform a modest changing of the guards every hour on the hour from 9am to 6pm.

### Park Belt

**Esplanāde** PARK

(Map p204) The expansive Esplanāde is a large park dotted with tall trees, wooden benches and open-air cafes. The Latvian National Museum of Art graces it on one side, while the cupolas of the Russian Orthodox cathedral majestically rise on the other. The park used to be teeming with Soviet-era sculpture; the **Rainis Statue** (Map p204; Esplanāde) is the only vestige of that era.

**Latvian National Museum of Art** GALLERY

(Latvijas Nacionālā mākslas muzeja; Map p204; ☎6732 4461; www.lnmm.lv; K Valdemāra iela 10a; adult/child €6/3; ⏰10am-6pm Tue-Thu, to 8pm Fri, to 5pm Sat & Sun) Latvia's main gallery, sitting on the edge of the Esplanāde's leafy grounds, is an impressive building that was purpose-built in a baroque-classical style in 1905. The paintings form a who's-who of Latvian art from the 18th to late 20th centuries. Watch for temporary exhibitions.

**Nativity of Christ Cathedral** CHURCH

(Kristus Piedzimšanas katedrāle; Map p204; ☎6721 1207; www.pravoslavie.lv; Brīvības bulvāris 23; ⏰7am-7pm) Its polished gilded cupolas gleaming through the trees, this Byzantine-styled Orthodox cathedral (1883) adds a dazzling dash of Russian bling to the skyline. During the Soviet period the church was converted into a planetarium, but it's since been restored to its former use. Mind the dress code – definitely no shorts; women are asked to cover their heads.

**Vērmanes dārzs (Vērmanes Garden)** PARK

(Map p204) From Brīvības, pass the swirls of colour at the 24-hour **flower market** along Tērbatas iela to find the inviting Vērmanes dārzs. During the summer months, local bands perform in the small **outdoor amphitheatre**, and artisans set up shop along the brick walkways, amidst the chess matches, cafes and inviting benches.

**Museum of the Occupation of Latvia** MUSEUM

(Latvijas Okupācijas muzejs; Map p198; ☎6721 1030; www.omf.lv; Raiņa bulvāris 7; admission by donation; ⏰11am-6pm) This museum colourfully details Latvia's Soviet and Nazi occupations between 1940 and 1991. Some of the exhibits are disturbing, including first-hand accounts of the murder of Rīga's once-substantial Jewish population, a re-creation of a gulag cell and many photographs that detail the atrocities. Latvia's active resistance of the 1950s, the passive resistance of the 1970s and the pivotal popular resistance of the early 1990s are fully detailed. There are daily tours in English at 2pm and 4pm (€3).

The museum is currently in the former US embassy. It was previously in the stark Soviet-era building on Rātslaukums in Old Rīga and is meant to return there when renovations are complete after 2021.

### Quiet Centre

Just when you thought that Old Rīga was the most beautiful neighbourhood in town, the city's magnificent art nouveau district (focused around Alberta iela, Strēlnieku iela and Elizabetes iela) swoops in to vie for the prize. Rīga boasts over 750 art nouveau buildings, making it the city with the most art nouveau architecture in the world.

**★Alberta Iela** ARCHITECTURE

(Map p204) Like a huge painting that you can spend hours staring at, as your eye detects more and more intriguing details, this must-see Rīga sight is in fact a rather functional street with residential houses, restaurants and shops. Art nouveau (p209), otherwise known as Jugendstil, is the style, and the architect responsible for many of the buildings is Mikhail Eisenstein (father of filmmaker Sergei Eisenstein).

Named after the founder of Rīga, Bishop Albert von Buxhoevden, the street was Eisenstein's gift to Rīga on its 700th anniversary. A jolly man, his bon vivant personality comes through in his exuberant work. See the full range of his talents on display in five adjoining buildings he designed from No 2a to No 8.

In particular, note **Alberta iela 2a**, constructed in 1906: serene faces with chevalier helmets stand guard atop the facade, which noticeably extends far beyond the actual roof of the structure. Screaming masks and horrible goblins adorn the lower sections amid clean lines and surprising robot-like shapes. Most noticeable are the two stone satyr phoenix-women that stand guard at the front.

The three heads on **Alberta iela 4** are, well, head-turners. If you look carefully, you'll see a nest of snakes slithering around their heads, evoking Medusa. All six eyes seem transfixed on some unseen horror, but only two of the faces are screaming in shock and fear. Two elaborate reliefs near the entrance feature majestic griffins, while ferocious lions with erect, fist-like tails keep watch on the roof. The enigmatic woman's face over the entrance may be the most-photographed image in Rīga.

Further down the street, the Rīga Graduate School of Law at **Alberta iela 13** attracts photographers like a starlet at Cannes. Another Eisenstein, it mixes Jugendstil with the Italian Renaissance – the facade has far too much texture: true art nouveau gives facades the flatness of a theatre backdrop. Peacocks, tangled shrubs and bare-breasted heroines abound, while cheery pastoral scenes are depicted in relief on Erykah Badu–like turbans atop the giant yawning masks. The triangular summit is a mish-mash of nightmarish imagery: lion heads taper off into snake tails (like Chimera), sobbing faces weep in agony and a strange futuristic mask stoically stares out over the city from the apex.

### Rīga Art Nouveau Museum MUSEUM

(Rīgas jūgendstila muzejs; Map p204; ☎6718 1465; www.jugendstils.riga.lv; Alberta iela 12; adult/child €9/5; ⏲10am-6pm Tue-Sun) If you're curious about what lurks behind Rīga's imaginative art nouveau facades, stop by here to see the restored apartment of Konstantīns Pēkšēns (a local architect responsible for over 250 of the city's art nouveau buildings). The interiors depict a middle-class apartment from the 1920s, right down to the dark and tiny maid's room. In the basement there are multimedia exhibits about art nouveau. Enter from Strēlnieku iela; push No 12 on the doorbell.

Note the spectacular staircase, geometric stencils, rounded furniture, original stained glass in the dining room and the still-functioning stove in the kitchen. There's also a free 10-minute video detailing the city's distinct decor.

Check out the centre's website for details about art nouveau walking routes around town.

### Janis Rozentāls & Rūdolfs Blaumanis Museum MUSEUM

(Map p204; ☎6733 1641; http://memorialiemuzeji.lv; Alberta iela 12; €1.50; ⏲11am-6pm Wed-Sun) Surmount the wonderfully lavish stairwell up to the 5th floor to find the former apartment of Janis Rozentāls, one of Latvia's most celebrated painters, who lived here with his wife, Elli Forssell (a famous Finnish singer), and his friend Rūdolfs Blaumanis (the famous Latvian writer). Enter from Strēlnieku iela; push No 9 on the doorbell.

### Jews in Latvia Museum MUSEUM

(Map p204; ☎6728 3484; www.jewishmuseum.lv; Skolas iela 6, 3rd flr; ⏲11am-5pm Sun-Thu year-round, plus Fri May-Sep) FREE This small and rather informal space briefly recounts the city's history of Jewish life until 1945 through artefacts and photography. Rīga's Jewish population (unlike that of Vilnius) was very much integrated into the rest of society. You'll find a teeny kosher cafe in the basement (entrance on Dzirnavu iela) selling traditional treats like *challa* bread and gefilte fish.

### ★Corner House MUSEUM

(Former KGB compound; Stūra Māja; Map p204; ☎6615 4276; http://okupacijasmuzejs.lv/en/kgb-building; Brīvības iela 61; adult/student €10/4; ⏲10am-5.30pm Mon, Tue, Thu & Fri, noon-7pm Wed, 10am-4pm Sat & Sun) A real-life house of horrors, this imposing fin de siècle building is remembered by generations of Latvians as the local headquarters of the notorious Soviet secret police – NKVD/KGB. Arbitrary arrests, torture, executions – it all happened here. It's now an exhibition dedicated to victims and perpetrators of political repression. A sign outside reads 'KGB imprisoned, tortured, executed and humiliated its victims'. English-language tours are usually in the mornings, but confirm in advance.

Older Rīgans remember the lines of people who would form along the grey street outside the building hoping to get word about their missing loved ones. On the building at Brīvības iela 70, you can still see the metal brackets used for KGB cameras that recorded the faces of anyone who ventured near the Corner House.

### Latvian National Museum of History MUSEUM

(Latvijas Nacionālais vēstures muzejs; Map p204; ☎6722 1357; www.lnvm.lv; Brīvības bulvāris 32; adult/student €3/1.50; ⏲10am-5pm Tue-Sun)

## ART NOUVEAU 101

Ask a Rīgan where to find the city's world-famous art nouveau architecture and you'll likely get this answer: 'Look up!' More than 750 buildings in Rīga (more than any other city in Europe) boast this flamboyant and haunting style of decor. Art nouveau, also known as Jugendstil, meaning 'Youth Style', is named after a Munich-based magazine called *Die Jugend*, which popularised the design in its pages.

Art nouveau's early influence was Japanese print art disseminated throughout Western Europe, but as the movement gained momentum, the style became more ostentatious and free-form – design schemes started to feature mythical beasts, screaming masks, twisting flora, goddesses and goblins. The turn of the 20th century marked the height of the art nouveau movement as it swept through every major European city.

The art nouveau movement in Rīga can be divided into three pronounced phases:

**Eclectic Decorative Art Nouveau** The first phase occurred from 1900 to 1905. The primary focus was the facade rather than the interior, as highly ornate patterns were imported from Germany by the local architects who studied there. The intricate sculpture work was also locally designed, mostly by August Volz, who did his apprenticeship in Germany.

**National Romanticism** After the failed Russian revolution of 1905, local architects developed designs with nationalistic flair. Styles reflected Latvian ethnographic motifs. An affinity for natural materials flourished as urban facades were left unpainted to show the greys and browns of the building materials. Although this rather un-art-nouveau style was only popular for four years, it coincided with a boom in the city's wealth, and thus a lot of structures exhibit this style.

**Perpendicular Art Nouveau** The final phase flourished from around 1908 to 1912. The style was a hybrid design between the existing art nouveau traits and a return to classical motifs (presented in a heavily stylised fashion). An accentuation on verticality was pronounced, with soaring lines past a profusion of balconies and bay windows that draw your eyes right up to the sky.

In Rīga, the most noted Jugendstil architect was Mikhail Eisenstein, who flexed his artistic muscles on Alberta iela (p207). Another prolific contributor was Eižens Laube, whose wooden house (p211) on Ķīpsala still amazes.

This museum traces Latvian history from the Stone Age to the hipster age. If the exhibits have a temporary feel it's because the museum is meant to return to the Rīga Castle, where it was previously located.

**St Gertrude Church** CHRISTIAN SITE

(Svētās Ģertrūdes baznīca; Map p204; ☎6727 5707; www.gertrude.lv; Ģertrūdes iela 8; ⏰9am-6pm) FREE This gracious red-brick neo-Gothic church is dedicated to St Gertrude, the patron saint of travellers. Surrounded by flamboyant art nouveau architecture, its austere 19th-century interior is a stark counterpoint. St Gertrude's is also a musical venue. Its organ, built in 1906, is one of the city's best and classical-music concerts take place regularly.

Note the art nouveau gem at Ģertrūdes iela 10. Try to count the panoply of faces on the 1903 facade.

### Miera Iela

Miera iela is the hip and happening main street of Rīga's creative tribes. A former industrial district, it has a charming assortment of cafes, craft shops and bookstores. Head down side streets and alleys for industrial chic drinking spaces and nightspots. It's easily reached by tram 11.

**Laima Chocolate Museum** MUSEUM

(Map p204; www.laimasokoladesmuzejs.lv; Miera iela 22; adult/child €7/5; ⏰10am-6pm Tue-Sun) Your sweet tooth might come to life blocks away from the historic Laima chocolate factory as the sweet cocoa smell permeates the entire area. Founded in 1921 by Vilhelms Kuze, it turned the entire nation into chocolate addicts. The modest on-site museum is mostly geared to children, who learn the process of chocolate-making and then blackmail their parents in the adjacent chocolate shop, where you can scoop up all the popularly priced chocolates you can carry.

You can also book a class where you'll learn to make your own box of chocolates (adult/child €16/14).

**Maskavas Forštate**

Separated from Old Town by the Central Railway Station, Rīga's 'Moscow Suburb' is one of its oldest central districts, though, unlike the rest of the centre, it looks like it never quite got over the economic hardships of the Soviet era. The place also feels haunted because of its dark history – it was the site of the Jewish ghetto during the Nazi occupation of Latvia. One bright spot is Rīga's lovely Central Market.



**★Rīga Central Market** MARKET

(Rīgas Centrāltirgus; Map p204; ☎6722 9985; www.rct.lv; Nēģu iela 7; ⏲7.30am-6pm Mon-Sat, to 5pm Sun) Haggle for your huckleberries at this vast market, housed in a series of WWI Zeppelin hangars and spilling outdoors as well. It's an essential Rīga experience, providing bountiful opportunities both for people-watching and to stock up for a picnic lunch. Although the number of traders is shrinking, the colourful abundance here activates visitor's foraging instincts. The best way to enjoy the market is to simply do your best to get lost amidst the bounty and browse away the day.

In operation since 1570, the riverside market flourished during the mid-1600s when the city outgrew Stockholm to become the largest stronghold of the Swedish Empire. Laden with goods, boats travelling down the Daugava would meet those traversing the Baltic Sea for a mutually beneficial exchange.

In 1930 the market moved to its current location on the border of Central Rīga and the Russified Maskavas neighbourhood to make use of the railway, which replaced the river as the principal trade route. Confronted with the market's ever-growing size, the city of Rīga decided to bring in five enormous 35m-high German-built Zeppelin hangars from the town of Vainode in western Latvia.

Today you'll find a hip food court and lots of Latvian foods. Look for all manner of pickled treats, unusual cheeses, luxurious smoked fish, wild berries, unusual mushrooms and much more.

**★Rīga Ghetto & Latvian Holocaust Museum** MUSEUM

(Map p204; ☎6799 1784; www.rgm.lv; Maskavas iela 14a; suggested donation adult/child €5/2; ⏲10am-6pm Sun-Thu, to 2pm Fri) The centrepiece of this arresting and challenging museum is a wooden house with a reconstructed flat, like those that Jews had to move into when the Nazis established a ghetto in this area of Rīga in 1941. The central courtyard has a railway wagon similar to the kind that brought Jews from Germany to Rīga to be killed. Nearby, there is a photographic exhibition detailing the Holocaust in Latvia (p232) with the faces of those killed.

Elsewhere, well-curated exhibitions explore the Holocaust across Europe. A tiny on-site cafe offers kosher refreshments.

**Latvian Academy of Science Observation Deck** HISTORIC BUILDING

(Map p204; ☎2008 8097; www.panoramariga.lv; Akadēmijas laukums 1; adult/child €6/free; ⏲10am-10pm Apr-Nov) This Stalinesque tower is a not-so-welcome Soviet-era present from Moscow, which has seven towers just like it, only bigger. Construction of what is often dubbed 'Stalin's birthday cake' commenced in 1951 but wasn't completed until 1961, by which time Stalin had run out of birthdays. Overall it has 21 storeys and is 107m tall. But the best feature is on floor 15, where you can enjoy sweeping views of all of Rīga from a vantage point 65m up on the viewing terrace.

Once back on the ground, those with an eagle eye will spot hammers and sickles hidden in the convoluted facade. There is an excellent little bookshop on the ground floor with many interesting academic titles.

**Spīķeri** AREA

(Map p204; Maskavas iela 6) The shipping yard behind the Central Market is the latest district to benefit from a generous dose of gentrification. These crumbling brick warehouses were once filled with swinging slabs of hanger meat; these days you'll find start-up companies.

**Jēzus Baznīca** CHURCH

(Map p204; ☎6722 4123; www.jezusdraudze.lv; Elijas iela 18; ⏲9am-noon Sun, 2-8pm Tue, 9.30am-3pm Wed, noon-6pm Thu) FREE It would be a classical-style Lutheran church like many others if it wasn't made entirely of wood, which makes it a unique architectural gem that dominates the quiet and pretty square.

**Holocaust Memorial** MONUMENT

(Map p204; Dzirnavu iela 124) This moving Holocaust Memorial is on the site of a large 1871 synagogue that was burned to the ground on 4 July, 1941 during WWII, with the entire congregation locked inside. No one survived and all that remains today is the foundation. A concrete monument is dedicated to the Latvians who risked their lives to help hide Jews during the war.

## Outlying Neighbourhoods

Those who venture beyond Rīga's inner sphere of cobbled alleyways and over-the-top art nouveau will uncover burgeoning neighbourhoods, some excellent sights and a handful of other areas that help paint a fuller picture of this varied capital.

### Ķīpsala

Just a quick 10-minute walk west over Vanšu Bridge from Old Rīga, quiet Ķīpsala is Rīga's own little island. Gentrification has restored the beautiful old wooden houses that were once homes to fishing families. Abandoned factories have been turned into trendy loft apartments. The tree-lined riverside along Balasta dambis (note the restored wooden houses at Nos 60 to 66) is a great spot for a languid stroll and to take photos of the city centre across the Daugava River. On a balmy day, pause at the large **beach** (Balasta dambis 24) and hope for a passing freighter to provide some surf.

★**Žanis Lipke Memorial** MUSEUM

(☎6720 2539; www.lipke.lv; Mazais Balasta dambis 8; ⊙noon-6pm Tue-Fri & Sun, noon-6pm Sat) FREE There is hardly a place in Latvia that can tell such a poignant and optimistic story as this quietly stunning memorial. Žanis Lipke saved over 50 Jews from certain death during the Nazi occupation: he found a job with the German air force, which allowed him to smuggle people out of the Rīga ghetto under the pretext of using them as labourers. He hid them in a bunker under the woodpile next to his house – now the site of this memorial.

Lipke was helped by his wife and a whole network of volunteers, some of whom played with death by walking into the ghetto to pose as the runaways during the headcount. The memorial building is a masterpiece of understated design that amplifies the details of the story as it unfolds. Lipke's descendants still live next door.

**Laube's House** HISTORIC BUILDING

(Zvejnieku iela 14a) A rare example of an all-wood art nouveau building, this 1909 four-storey apartment house was built as worker housing. Now renovated for the better-heeled, originally it had scores of tiny three-room flats for families. It was the work of the prolific art nouveau architect Eižens Laube.

### Pārdaugava

Beyond the river, Rīga becomes markedly lower and quieter. Old wooden houses mix with newer ones, made of stone.

### TOP DAY TRIPS FROM RĪGA

Leave Rīga's jumble of art nouveau goblins and swirling church spires behind and explore Latvia's other gems: flaxen shorelines, rambling palaces, quaint provincial villages and forests full of shady trees.

**Jūrmala** (p227) A top summer beach destination for decades, with genteel restaurants and historic charm. Take a suburban train on the Tukums line, get off at Majori station, and you'll be smack in the middle of the white sand in 30 minutes flat.

**Saulkrasti** (p255) Untouched beaches, dunes and forests, with just enough life to find a cafe. This spectacular coast is only an hour by train on the Skulte line to the Pabaži stop on the Vidzeme Coast.

**Sigulda** (p258) It's hard not to be enchanted by the castles here, hidden within the pine forests of Gauja National Park. Adrenaline junkies will get their fix with an endless array of activities, such as bobsledding and zip-lining. Sigulda is only 1¼ hours away by bus or train (the Valmiera line).

**Cēsis** (p266) Latvia's most appealing medieval town has a fabulous castle and great places to eat. It's only two hours by train on the Valmiera line.

**Rundāle Palace** (p252) Latvia's miniature version of Versailles (but without the crowds) is a stunning homage to aristocratic ostentatiousness. Drive yourself or book a bus tour for the 75km jaunt. (Public buses are too complex for a quick trip.)

★**Kalnciema Kvartāls** AREA

(☎6761 4322; www.kalnciemaiela.lv; Kalnciema iela 35; ⏲10am-4pm Sat year-round, plus Sun Dec) A lovingly restored courtyard with several vintage wooden buildings is home to creative cafes, shops and restaurants. It's also home to a fantastic Saturday market that attracts some of the top food and produce vendors from across the region. Browse smoked meats, cheeses, vegetables, pastries and even spirits. The baked goods are extraordinary. At other times there are concerts, performances, art exhibitions and street food festivals. The airport bus (22) passes right outside.

**Latvian National Library** LIBRARY

(Castle of Light; Map p204; ☎2202 2920; www.lnb.lv; Mūkusalas iela 3; ⏲9am-8pm Mon-Fri, 10am-5pm Sat & Sun) FREE Looking like a ski-jump ramp designed by Swarovski, this recent Rīga landmark is a prophesy fulfilled. A feature of many Latvian fairy tales, the Castle of Light was drowned when the age of darkness came, but it would rise again from the waters of the Daugava in the new golden age of enlightenment and freedom. Architect Gunnars Bikkerts made it happen in 2014. The library has regular worthwhile special exhibitions.

**Victory Monument** MEMORIAL

(Okupācijas piemineklis; ☎6718 1696; Uzvaras bulvāris 15; ⏲24hr) FREE This sprawling green space (now mostly used as a soccer field) is home to the Victory Monument, which was built by the Soviets to commemorate the heroism of their soldiers in WWII. This is a divisive symbol, with members of the Russian community gathering here in the tens of thousands every 9 May to celebrate what they see as the victory over fascism. But for most ethnic Latvians, it is the symbol of Soviet occupation. Tram 10 stops here.

## Mežaparks

Woodsy Mežaparks (literally 'Forest Park' in Latvian), along Lake Ķīšezers, 7km north of the centre, is Europe's oldest planned suburb. Built by the Germans in the 20th century, this 'garden city', originally called Kaiserwald, was the go-to neighbourhood for wealthy merchants looking to escape the city's grimy industrial core. The atmosphere hasn't changed all that much over the last 100 years – tourists will find prim country homes, gorgeous art nouveau facades and lazy sailboats gliding along the lake.



## City Walk
## Rīga's Art Nouveau

**START** LATVIAN NATIONAL OPERA
**END** ALBERTA IELA
**DISTANCE** 2.6KM; TWO HOURS

This walk covers the best art nouveau architecture in Rīga. Start at the ❶ **Latvian National Opera** (p224) and enter the city's medieval core on Teātra iela; pause at ❷ **Teātra iela 9**, the Italian Embassy, to admire the facade's pantheon of Greek figures – two ragged older men (Prometheus perhaps) frantically clutch their necks while supporting the convoluted wrought-iron balcony above. Look up high to spot Atlas with the world on his shoulders.

Further south, get a coffee to fuel your walk at ❸ **Chez Olivier** (p217), the entrance of which is under a Jugendstil tree. Walk up Kalēju iela to ❹ **Kaļķu iela 14**: from the fox at the top, see how many critters you can count on this 1907 building. Turn northwest to find seemingly restrained ❺ **Šķūņu iela 6**, but look closely at the entrance and you'll find some strong infants and plenty of stained glass. Next, at 1902 ❻ **Šķūņu iela 12/14** you'll spot a variety of Ds hidden on the plant-covered front – the initial of the original owner. You can barely see the dog standing guard at the top.

Now head to one of Old Rīga's most popular sites, the ❼ **Cat House** (p201). Leave the selfie-snapping crowds for ❽ **Smilšu iela 3**. A number of topless figures decorate the exterior here; some are obviously women, but others are less definitive.

At 1902's ❾ **Smilšu iela 8**, two women stand atop a protruding bay carrying an elaborate crown of leaves. A large mask of a melancholy woman with her eyes shut hovers over the entrance – a common theme in the Eclectic Decorative art nouveau.

Considered to be one of the finest examples of Jugendstil in Old Rīga is ❿ **Smilšu iela 2**. The 1902 exterior features hybrid creatures including intertwining vines that morph, like a mermaid's tail, into the torso of two caryatids. The architect of this masterpiece was the undisputed Jugendstil king, Konstantīns

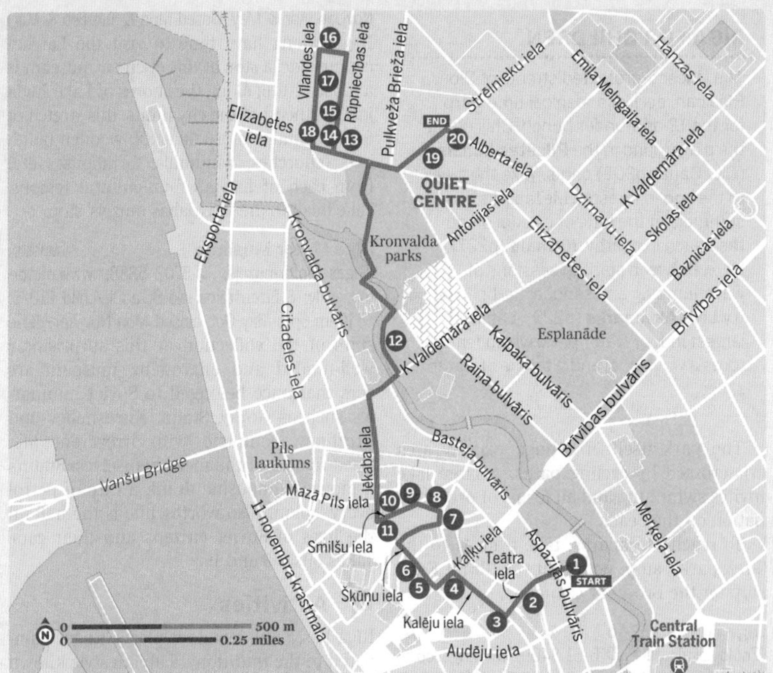



Pēkšēns, who designed over 250 art nouveau buildings in Rīga.

Across the street, ⓫ **Smilšu iela 1/3** is a pastiche of contrasting styles reflective of the building's use as shops (floors one and two), offices (three and four) and apartments (the rest).

Walk north on Jēkaba iela and exit Old Rīga. Cross K Valdemāra iela and head towards the pleasant ⓬ **Kronvalda parks**, wasting no time on the yawning Soviet piazza in between. Follow the canal, then walk through the park to the Quiet Centre art nouveau district.

Turn west to ⓭ **Elizabetes iela 13**, a 1904 Eclectic Decorative apartment building (note the typically asynchronous window styles). Across the street, ⓮ **Rūpniecības iela 1** (1903) mixes Florentine (the ground floor), Greek and other styles; note the woman with the lyre. The 1908 ⓯ **Rūpniecības iela 3** is the work of Pēkšēns and is an early example of the Perpendicular art nouveau style. Symmetry was the thing, as you can see from the bay windows set on a grid.

⓰ **Vīlandes iela 16** is another Pēkšēns' Perpendicular-style with a corner turret that rockets up to the sky and plenty of Latvian symbols in the detailing between floors two and three. Heading south, it's Pēkšēns again at ⓱ **Vīlandes iela 10**. A good example of National Romanticism art nouveau, it has numerous female figures depicted in ways that recall a Greek frieze (flowing robes, garlands of flowers). See if you can find the satyr. The street's last stop is ⓲ **Vīlandes iela 2**. If you think you've seen it before, you have: this is the mirror-image backside of Rūpniecības iela 1.

From here, head east along Elizabetes iela and turn northeast, walking to ⓳ **Strēlnieku iela 4a**. Here, art nouveau's crown prince, Mikhail Eisenstein, has run amok: just too many styles to count compete for attention on this 1905 building. Still, you're just steps away from the best work of Eisenstein, who only designed 20 buildings in Rīga, a fraction of the prolific Pēkšēns.

At ⓴ **Alberta iela** (p207), turn the corner. You're now in the middle of the much-acclaimed Rīga art nouveau line-up. Take your time savouring the masterpieces on this street, then retire to one of several appealing cafes and decompress from all the flamboyance over a refreshing beverage.

## RĪGA FOR CHILDREN

The Unesco-protected streets of Old Rīga can feel like a magical time warp for the 12-and-under bunch. Chill out at the playground in the **Pilsētas kanāls** (City Canal; p202) parks. Take the tykes to the **zoo** in forested Mežaparks or, in summer, let the little ones cool off on the beach in nearby **Jūrmala** (p227). Here, between spirited sessions of wave-jumping and sandcastle-building, try **Līvu Akvaparks** (p229), Latvia's largest indoor water park, which features a wave pool and a tangle of water slides.

The park itself is a huge woodsy area crisscrossed by cycling paths. A large lake invites swimming and all forms of procrastination on the beach.

To reach Mežaparks, take tram 11 to the 'Mežaparks' stop; get off at the 'Brāļu Kapi' stop for the Brothers' Cemetery.

**Rīga National Zoo** ZOO
(Zoologiskais dārz; ☎6751 8409; www.rigazoo.lv; Meža prospekts 1; adult/child €7/5; ⊙10am-7pm Jun-Aug, to 5pm Sep-May) Set in a hilly pine forest in Mežaparks, Rīga National Zoo has a modest collection of animals, including an assortment of tropical fauna, as well as the usual cast of Noah's ark. Tram 11 stops at the zoo.

**Rīga Brethren Cemetery** CEMETERY
(Rīgas Brāļu kapi; ☎6718 1692; http://en.rigasbralukapi.lv; Aizsaules iela 1b; ⊙8am-8pm) FREE The Brothers' Cemetery features a monument by Kārlis Zāle (the designer of the Freedom Monument) dedicated to the Latvian soldiers who died during WWI and the battles for independence between 1915 and 1920. It's a vast, mournful spot that, when combined with the larger parks area around it, makes for a thoughtful stroll on an autumn day. Tram 11 stops nearby.

### Northern Neighbourhoods

The Rīga Motor Museum and the Latvian Ethnographic Open-Air Museum orbit Rīga's central core several kilometres out.

**Latvian Ethnographic Open-Air Museum** MUSEUM
(Latvijas etnogrāfiskais brīvdabas muzejs; ☎6799 4106; www.brivdabasmuzejs.lv; Brīvības iela 21; adult/child €4/1.40; ⊙10am-8pm May-Oct, 10am-5pm Nov-Jan, Apr & May, closed Mon & Tue Feb & Mar) If you don't have time to visit the Latvian countryside, a stop at this open-air museum is a must. Sitting along the shores of Lake Jugla just northeast of the city limits, this stretch of forest contains more than 100 wooden buildings (churches, windmills, farmhouses etc) from each of Latvia's four cultural regions. Take bus 1 to the 'Brīvdabas muzejs' stop.

**Rīga Motor Museum** MUSEUM
(Rīgas Motormuzejs; ☎6702 5888; www.motormuzejs.lv; S Eizenšteina iela 8; adult/child €10/5; ⊙10am-6pm May-Oct, closed Mon Nov-Apr) The stars of the collection at this surprisingly well-funded and engrossing museum are cars that once belonged to Soviet luminaries such as Gorky, Stalin, Khrushchev and Brezhnev, complete with irreverent life-sized figures of the men themselves. Stalin's armoured limousine drank a litre of petrol every 2.5km. Also worthwhile is the hall on the lives of Soviet citizens and their cars. Takes buses 5 and 15.

## Activities

Rīga has a few standout places to get pampered in the traditional Latvian style known as *pirts* (p264). A highlight of the experience is being whipped by dried birch branches while sweating it out in temperatures beyond 40°C (over 100°F).

★**Baltā Pirts** SPA
(☎6727 1733; www.baltapirts.lv; Tallinas iela 71; sauna from €10; ⊙8am-8pm Wed-Sun) Popular with locals, Baltā Pirts combines traditional Latvian relaxation techniques (the name means 'white birch') with a subtle design scheme. They've been in the *pirts* game since 1908 and now also offer yoga and other therapies.

**Taka Spa** SPA
(Map p204; ☎6732 3150; www.takaspa.lv; Kronvalda bulvāris 3a; 45min massage €60; ⊙10am-9pm Mon-Fri, to 7pm Sat & Sun) Taka Spa offers luxurious massages, wraps, scrubs and sauna treatments. Try the signature 'opening ritual' in which clients move between saunas and plunge pools while drinking herbal teas.

## Tours

Many operators offer tours around Rīga as well as day trips to popular sights nearby.

★**Rīga Bike Tours & Rent** CYCLING
(Map p198; ☎2246 9888; www.rigabiketours.com; Riharda Vagnera iela 14; tours €20, bike rental per

3hr €7; ⌚10am-6pm May-Sep) Daily three-hour bicycle tours of Rīga on two different routes. Longer cycling tours of Latvia are also on offer. Its helpful office has signage for the Rīga Explorers Club on the window. Bikes include helmets.

**Riga Culture Free Tour** CULTURAL TOUR
(Map p204; ☎2883 4052; www.rigaculturefreetour.lv; Rainis Statue, Esplanāde; ⌚noon; ) FREE A daily two-hour English-language walk conducted by local cultural experts. It departs from the Rainis statue (p207) on Esplanāde.

**Eat Rīga** FOOD & DRINK
(Map p198; ☎2246 9888; www.eatriga.lv; Riharda Vāgnera iela 14; tours from €20) Offers tasting tours and themed itineraries covering topics like Black Balzām. Also offers cooking classes.

**Retro Tram** RAIL
(Map p204; ☎6710 4817; www.rigassatiksme.lv/en/services/retro-tram; Ausekļa iela; €2; ⌚Sat & Sun May-Sep) Ride aboard a restored tram that begins at the tram stop on Ausekļa iela, then meanders through the art nouveau district and on to Mežaparks.

**Rīga By Canal** BOATING
(Map p198; ☎2591 1523; www.rigabycanal.lv; near Bastion Hill; adult/child €18/9; ⌚10am-7pm May–mid-Oct) Enjoy a different perspective of the city aboard the 1907 vintage *Darling,* a charming wooden canal cruiser. There are three other boats in the fleet that paddle along the city canal circling Old Town and the Daugava River. The dock is just east of Bastion Hill.

**Kugitis Jelgava** CRUISE
(Map p198; ☎2553 8809; www.kugitisjelgava.lv; 11 Novembra Krastmala; adult/child €10/5; ⌚11am-11pm) Choose from a fleet of three boats for a panoramic cruise on the Daugava River. Thrill to the towering cranes in the port and ponder the retro style of the fishing houses on Ķīpsala.

**Rīga City Tour** BUS
(Map p198; ☎2665 5405; www.citytour.lv; Rātslaukums; tour €20; ⌚9.30am-4pm) A hop-on, hop-off double-decker bus that wends its way through Rīga, stopping at 15 spots on both sides of the Daugava River. Circuits last 60 to 90 minutes and the route begins at Rātslaukums, but you can hop on anywhere.

## Festivals & Events

Rīgans will find any excuse to celebrate, especially during the summer months when the city's parks host festivals almost every weekend. Check out www.liveriga.com for a complete list of local events.

**Rīga Opera Festival** MUSIC
(Rīgas Operas festivāls; www.opera.lv; Aspazijas bulvāris 3, Latvian National Opera; ⌚mid-Jun) The Latvian National Opera's showcase event takes place over two weeks and includes performances by world-renowned talents.

★**Midsummer Celebration** CULTURAL
(11 Novembra Krastmala; ⌚23 Jun) FREE Latvians return to their pagan roots while celebrating the solstice on 23 June. Crowds gather until the wee hours along the embankment of the Daugava River for bands, folk singers, DJs and much more.

**Rīga Jūrmala Music Festival** MUSIC
(https://riga-jurmala.com; ⌚mid-Jul–Aug) Over four summer weekends, major names in classical music perform at a variety of venues across Rīga and Jūrmala. The festival's first year was 2019, but it got off to a huge start and is likely to be an important stop on the European culture circuit.

★**Rīga City Festival** CULTURAL
(www.rigassvetki.lv; ⌚mid-Aug) FREE Rīga all but shuts down for this huge free festival held on the third weekend in August. The parks and waterfront are taken over by scores of activities: from big-name bands to fireworks to traditional bread baking to carnival acts for kids, there is nonstop action. You can't help but be moved watching older Rīgans weep while they sing along with folk songs from their youth.

**Festival of Light** LIGHT SHOW
(www.staroriga.lv; ⌚mid-Nov) Held around National Day celebrations in November, this festival of lights lifts spirits as Rīga begins to face the long winter ahead. Myriad civic buildings and public objects are lit up during the long nights.

★**Christmas Tree Path** CHRISTMAS
(www.eglufestivals.lv; ⌚Dec) FREE Rīga claims to be the city that originated the Christmas tree, thus at Christmas each year, locals decorate an ornate tree in Rātslaukums amid much ado. Festive, artful and magical trees in myriad styles are set up across Rīga: pick up a map from the tourist information centre.

## Sleeping

Both Old Rīga and Central Rīga lend themselves well to pedestrians. For short visits, Old Rīga is the most popular choice, but consider Central Rīga as you can dip in and out of Old Town and are still close to some of the most interesting places to eat and drink.

The choice of rental apartments is almost unlimited, which is good because visitors to Rīga greatly favour rental accommodation. It's easy to find fine places in Old Town and Central Rīga for under €50 a night. There's no reason to stay further out.

### Old Rīga (Vecrīga)

**Naughty Squirrel** HOSTEL €
(Map p198; 6722 0073; www.facebook.com/NSBhostel; Kalēju iela 50; dm/r from €12/35; ) A shot of booze at check-in sets the tone at Rīga's capital of backpackerdom, which buzzes with travellers. Plush pillows and blankets in private rooms and homey wooden bunks in dorms make the place feel anything but institutional.

**Hotel Justus** HOTEL €€
(Map p198; 6721 2404; www.hoteljustus.lv; Jauniela 24; r from €70; ) A tidy, small hotel in the very heart of Old Town. An elevator whisks you up to the 4th-floor rooms with angled ceilings that follow the roofline. Furniture is ornate without being frou-frou.

**Rixwell Hotel Konventa Seta** HOTEL €€
(Map p198; 6000 8700; www.konventa.lv; Kalēju iela 9/11; r from €65; ) The location, inside a 15th-century convent in the heart of medieval Rīga, is unbeatable. Rooms are as small and prim as a nun's cell (in fact the last nuns only left in 1938) and the hotel sprawls over several alleys.

★**Neiburgs** HOTEL €€€
(Map p198; 6711 5522; www.neiburgs.com; Jauniela 25/27; r €105-200; ) Occupying one of Old Rīga's finest art nouveau buildings, Neiburgs blends preserved details with contemporary touches to achieve its signature boutique-chic style. Try for a room on one of the higher floors – you'll be treated to a view of a colourful clutter of gabled roofs and twisting medieval spires.

**Dome Hotel** HOTEL €€€
(Map p198; 6750 9010; www.domehotel.lv; Miesnieku iela 4; r from €175; ) It's hard to imagine that this 17th-century structure was once part of a row of butcheries. Today a gorgeous wooden staircase leads guests up to a charming assortment of uniquely decorated rooms.

**Grand Palace Hotel** HISTORIC HOTEL €€€
(Map p198; 6704 4000; www.grandpalaceriga.com; Pils iela 12; r from €125; ) You'll find no better place to be pampered than the lavish Grand Palace. Rooms have a luxurious, contemporary verve. Look for limos out front as it's *the* address for visiting dignitaries. There's a health club and sauna.

### Central Rīga (Centrs)

**Cinnamon Sally** HOSTEL €
(Map p204; 2204 2280; www.cinnamonsally.com; Merķeļa iela 1; dm/r from €12/30; ) Convenient for the train and bus stations, Cinnamon Sally comes with helpful staff and a common area cluttered with sociable characters. The relentless effort to create a homey atmosphere includes a no-shoes-inside policy. Rooms are simply decorated with blond-wood furniture and have two to six beds.

**Riga City Camping** CAMPGROUND €
(6706 7519; www.rigacamping.lv; Ķīpsalas iela 8; sites per adult/child/tent €5/2/6; mid-May–mid-Oct; ) Located on Ķīpsala across the river from Old Rīga, this large campground is close to the city centre and offers plenty of open, mostly shade-free space behind Rīga's exhibition halls. Facilities are basic and include a laundry. Discounts are available for those staying more than four nights.

★**Jakob Lenz** INN €€
(Map p204; 6733 3343; www.guesthouselenz.lv; Lenču iela 2; s/d from €35/40, without bathroom from s/d €25/30; ) Tucked away along a random side street on the fringes of the art nouveau district, this great find offers 25 adorable rooms and a generous breakfast in the morning.

#### LONG-TERM RENTALS

Planning on sticking around town for a while? Check out Rent in Riga (www.rentinriga.lv) for a detailed listing of available (and red tape–free) apartments in town; select Centrs or Vecrīga to find a flat in the core of the city. You can get a very nice flat for €500 per month.

**Europa Royale Rīga** HOTEL €€
(Map p204; ☎6707 9444; www.europaroyale.com; K Barona iela 12; r from €60; P ❄ 📶) This ornate 1876 manse retains much of its 19th-century opulence with sweeping staircases, high ceilings, and a grand bar and breakfast room. Of the 60 rooms, the bay-window rooms are best.

**Hanza Hotel** HOTEL €€
(Map p204; ☎6779 6040; www.hanzahotel.lv; Elijas iela 7; r from €45; P 📶) East of Rīga Central Market in a quiet neighbourhood, this tidy hotel has 80 comfortably large rooms with plenty of light, from both the large windows and the adjustable reading lights. It overlooks the cobblestone square with Jēzus Baznīca.

**Hotel Valdemārs** HOTEL €€
(Map p204; ☎6733 4462; www.valdemars.lv; K Valdemāra iela 23; r from €85; ❄ 📶) Part of an art nouveau block, this 83-room hotel is an excellent choice for those who want to be in the heart of all the Central Rīga action. Rooms are corporate-comfortable.

**Teater City Hotel** HOTEL €€
(Map p204; ☎6731 5140; www.cityhotel.lv; Bruņinieku iela 6; r from €50; 📶 🏊) An imposing art nouveau gem, the Teater has seven storeys of comfortable rooms. Those on the top floor have fine city views. There's a small sauna and pool.

**Tallink Hotel Riga** HOTEL €€
(Map p204; ☎6709 9760; www.tallinkhotels.com; Elizabetes iela 24; r from €75; ❄ 📶) This 256-room hotel could not be more centrally located. The rooms are modern and the included breakfast buffet is immense. The hotel is owned by the Stockholm ferry company; there are good packages available.

★ **Hotel Bergs** HOTEL €€€
(Map p204; ☎6777 0900; www.hotelbergs.lv; Elizabetes iela 83/85, Bergs Bazārs; ste from €203; P ❄ 📶) A refurbished 19th-century building embellished with a Scandi-sleek extension, the 37 spacious rooms at the Hotel Bergs embody the term 'luxury'. It's at the heart of Bergs Bazārs, which features a few hip venues.

## Eating

Rīga's dining scene is a good reason to visit. You'll find a range of interesting and creative eateries, generally serving excellent meals at much lower prices than other European capitals to the west. Some of the best restaurants, cafes and bakeries take the bounty from Latvia's countryside and transform it in ways that bring a contemporary flair to Latvian traditions.

### Old Rīga (Vecrīga)

Restaurants in Old Town are aimed at tourists, so expect Latvian standards that are heavy on the traditional, as well as crowd-pleasing continental favourites. Given the lively crowds, don't be surprised if the drinks lists are longer than the food menus. Prices are closer to Western European norms than elsewhere in Rīga.

**V Ķuze** CAFE €
(Map p198; ☎6732 2943; www.kuze.lv; Jēkaba iela 20/22; snacks €4; ⊙10am-9pm; 📶) Step back to 1910 in this *dahling* little cafe, where the art nouveau–styled cabinet positively groans under the weight of cakes and chocolate truffles. It's named after chocolatier Vilhelms Ķuze, who died after being deported to Siberia after WWII. Tables out front overlook a park.

**Chez Olivier** CAFE €
(Map p198; ☎2696 9566; www.facebook.com/chezoliviercafe/; Kalēju iela 23; snacks from €3; ⊙8am-8pm) On the ground floor of a boldly coloured 1903 art nouveau building, this corner cafe serves fine coffee and pastries with French flair through the day. There are also smoothies and tea. Just look for the tree-shaped portico over the door with the sun on the facade above.

**Lido Beer Garden** LATVIAN €
(Lido Alus Seta; Map p198; ☎6722 2431; www.lido.lv; Tirgoņu iela 6; mains €4-6; ⊙11am-10pm; 📶) The pick of the Lido litter (Rīga's ubiquitous smorgasbord chain), this woodsy charmer feels like an old Latvian brewhouse. In summer, the front opens up and tables spill onto the cobbled street forming the namesake 'beer garden'. Enjoy tasty traditional fare and house-brewed beer.

**KD Konditoreja** CAFE €
(Map p198; ☎2695 9096; Smilšu iela 20; mains €4-7; ⊙8am-9pm) The bentwood chairs are just one traditional detail at this old-time cafe. The coffee is excellent and the baked goods fresh; get anything with rhubarb when in season. Lunch offers old favourites such as *kartupeļu pankūkas ar kūpinātu lasi* (potato pancakes with smoked salmon).

**Martina's Bakery** BAKERY €
(Map p198; ☎6721 3314; www.bekereja.lv; Vaļņu iela 28; snacks €1-5; ⊙8am-8pm) It could still be 1930 in the Old Rīga branch of this popular local bakers. Ponder the huge loaves of traditional bread, then wander over to the display cases with popularly priced treats. Nab a seat inside or out, and enjoy a warm beverage and something sweet.

**Late Night Munchies** BURGERS €
(Map p198; ☎2233 3839; https://munchies.lv; Peldu iela 21; mains €4-6; ⊙11am-11pm Sun-Wed, to 3am Thu-Sat) Not only does this tidy little hole in the wall have one of the best URLs ever, it lives up to its name. Staff – far more sober than most of the customers – take pride in making huge, juicy, condiment-dripping burgers.

**Pelmeņi XL** RUSSIAN €
(Map p198; ☎6722 2728; www.xlpelmeni.lv; Kaļķu iela 7; mains €2-4; ⊙9am-11pm Mon-Thu, 10am-4am Fri-Sun) A Rīga institution for budget travellers and after-hours partiers, this extra-large self-serve eatery stays open extra-late, offering tasty *pelmeņi* (Russian-style dumplings stuffed with meat) amid Flintstones-meets-Gaudí decor. Portions are priced by weight.

**Milda** LATVIAN €€
(Map p198; ☎2571 3287; www.restoransmilda.lv; Kungu iela 8; mains €8-25; ⊙noon-11pm Tue-Sun) Centred on Latvia, but with guest stars from Lithuania and Belarus, this traditional restaurant serves slightly glammed-up versions of the sort of local fare you'd enjoy on Sundays at granny's. Potato dumplings filled with meat, eel with mashed potatoes, pork stew cooked for 24 hours – these are just some of the warming dishes on offer. Nice sidewalk terrace, good dark beer.

**★Valtera** LATVIAN €€€
(Map p198; ☎2952 9200; www.valterarestorans.lv; Miesnieku iela 8; mains €15-22; ⊙noon-10pm Mon-Thu, to 11pm Fri & Sat) The country comes to the city: that's the motto at this modern restaurant that works with a bevy of small-scale producers in Latvia's lush hinterlands. Meats, cheeses, vegetables, fruits, breads – they all have peerless provenance. The menu changes constantly, reflecting what's fresh. Service is smooth, the wine list good. Flowers line the outside deck.

**3 Pavaru** MODERN EUROPEAN €€€
(Map p198; ☎2037 0537; www.3pavari.lv; Torņa iela 4, Jacob's Barracks; mains €18-27; ⊙noon-11pm) The stellar trio of chefs who run this show have a jazzy approach to cooking, with improvisation at the heart of the compact, ever-changing menu. The emphasis is on experimentation, seasonal freshness and artful visual presentation that would have made Mark Rothko or Joan Miró proud. There are appealing terrace tables.

**Dome Fish Restaurant** SEAFOOD €€€
(Map p198; ☎6750 9010; www.zivjurestorans.lv; Miesnieku iela 4; mains €18-27; ⊙7am-11pm Mon-Fri, 8am-11pm Sat & Sun; 📶) The Dome Hotel's restaurant quickly reminds diners that Rīga sits near bodies of water that are full of delicious fish. Service is impeccable and dishes (including some meat and vegetarian options) are expertly prepared. An ever-changing five-course menu (€55) demonstrates the kitchen's talents. Book ahead to dine under the stars on the rooftop deck.

**Gutenbergs** LATVIAN €€€
(Map p198; ☎6721 1776; http://restaurant-gutenbergs.lv; Doma laukums 1; mains €13-25; ⊙1-11pm) Go one better than dining with a view – dine *in* the view! The Hotel Gutenbergs' rooftop terrace in the heart of Old Rīga perches between soaring spires and gingerbread trim. The menu focuses on local favourites, fresh seafood and steaks. When the temps tumble, the retractable roof closes. There's a long wine list and the bar shares the great views.

**Domini Canes** EUROPEAN €€€
(Map p198; ☎2231 4122; www.dominicanes.lv; Skārņu iela 18/20; mains €9-20; ⊙10am-11pm) Tables sprawl across the square at this upmarket but relaxed restaurant facing the rear of St Peter's Church. The bistro-style menu includes fresh seafood, grilled meats and plenty of fresh Latvian produce.

**Tēvocis Vaņa** RUSSIAN €€€
(Uncle Vanya; Map p198; ☎2788 6963; www.unclevanya.lv; Smilšu iela 16; mains €15-27; ⊙11am-11pm) Russia puts on its friendly Chekhovian hat in this quaint restaurant that dishes up a fairy-tale-ish assortment of *bliny* pancakes, *pelmeņi* dumplings and *kholodets* (jellied meat) that, together with a plate of pickles, is an inseparable aspect of any competent *samogon* (village vodka) drinking experience. The streetside terrace is Siberia-sized.

## EAT & DRINK LIKE A LATVIAN

Some highlights of Latvian cuisine:

**Berries** If you were to count the total area of blackberry bushes and cranberry marshes, it would likely cover a large chunk of Latvia. Berries are sold at markets all over the country, or look for little set-ups by intrepid pickers featuring the fruits of their labour.

**Mushrooms** A national obsession; mushroom-picking takes the country by storm during the first showers of autumn.

**Smoked fish** Dozens of fish shacks dot the Kurzeme coast – look for the veritable smoke signals rising above the tree line. Grab 'em to go; they make the perfect picnic. Or hit the Rīga Central Market.

**Rye bread** Apart from being tasty and heartier than their wheat peers, these large brown (even black) loafs have aesthetic value too, matching the dark wood of Latvia's Nordic interiors nicely. There are myriad variations, some utterly covered in whole grains.

**Alus** For such a tiny nation there's definitely no shortage of *alus* (beer) – each major town has its own brew. Among the top choices: Rīga's Labietis and Valmiera's Valmiermuiža.

**Kvass** A beloved beverage made from fermented rye bread. It's surprisingly popular with kids.

**Black Balzām** This jet-black, 45%-proof concoction is a secret recipe of more than a dozen unusual herbs and spices. A shot a day keeps the doctor away, so say most of Latvia's pensioners. Try mixing it with a glass of cola to take the edge off.

## Central Rīga (Centrs)

Rīga's most creative chefs can be found in Central Rīga. Enjoy a mouthwatering mix of cutting-edge kitchens, traditional favourites and welcoming cafes. Even if you're staying in Old Rīga, you'll want to venture beyond the canals to try some of the best meals that Latvia has to offer. Note that prices here are on average much less than Old Rīga.

### ★Miit — CAFE €

(Map p204; ☎2889 1351; www.miit.lv; Lāčplēša iela 10; mains €4-7; ⏰7am-9pm Mon, to 11pm Tue-Thu, to 1am Fri, 9am-11pm Sat, 10am-6pm Sun; ✎) Rīga's hipster students head here to sip espresso and blog about Nietzsche amid comfy couches and blond-wood minimalism. Weekday breakfast (8am to 11.30am) and weekend pancake brunch (11am to 4pm) are pure morning joy. The lunch menu changes daily and everything is vegetarian.

### Food Box — KEBAB €

(Map p204; ☎2820 5998; www.foodbox.lv; Antonijas iela 6; mains €4-6; ⏰11am-7pm Mon-Fri, noon-6pm Sat; 📶) Mismatched tables perch unsteadily on a sidewalk cracked by a lovely old shade tree at this very popular kebab shop. From the pitas to the piquant grilled meat, everything is made in-house. Staff are cheery and the tea is free. Note, it's really on Pumpura iela, despite the official address.

### Stockpot — LATVIAN €

(Map p204; ☎2783 2165; www.stockpot.lv; Ģertrūdes iela 6; mains €4-8; ⏰11am-8.30pm Mon-Fri; ✎) Step down a few steps – just metres from St Gertrude Church – to some of the freshest fare in Rīga. Local and seasonal produce dictates what's on offer, so check the website for the menu as it changes daily. Expect soups, salads, sandwiches and hot mains with international flair, all served in the sparkling white dining room.

### Lido Origo — LATVIAN €

(Map p204; ☎2782 3316; www.lido.lv; Origo shopping centre 2; mains €4-7; ⏰10am-9pm; 📶) Rīgans of all stripes stop by this bustling cafeteria, just a few metres from the ticket windows in the mall at the Central Train Station. Lido's unbeatable combination of high-quality Latvian favourites and low prices is on full display. Grab a tray and head down the cafeteria line.

Tables outside overlook the big station square, where at times there's live entertainment, meaning Lido diners can enjoy bargain-priced dinner-theatre.

**Taverna Pumpkin** LATVIAN €
(Ķirbis Taverna; Map p204; ☎2733 8814; Centrāltirgus iela 3, Hall 2, Rīga Central Market; mains €3-9; ⏰10am-5pm) This is the place to finally have grey peas: the national dish of savoury stewed beans is scrumptious at this simple and tidy bar/cafe catering to shoppers and market workers. The menu highlights other Latvian standards. Get a friend and enjoy the cheese and smoked meat board.

**Centrālais Gastro Tirgus** FOOD HALL €
(Central Gastro Market; Map p204; ☎2807 8666; https://centralais.lv; Centrāltirgus iela 3, Rīga Central Market; mains €3-10; ⏰11am-9pm Sun-Thu, to 11pm Fri & Sat) Rīga Central Market now has a food court, and it's somewhat upscale. Over 20 stalls cook up fare from around the world, including sushi, pho, pasta, burgers, baked goods and a lot more. Two bars serve inventive cocktails, all in an effort to prove this market is not your parents' market.

**Stockmann** SUPERMARKET €
(Map p204; ☎6707 1222; www.stockmann.lv; 13 Janvāra iela 8; ⏰9am-10pm) This slightly upscale supermarket has an excellent deli section: the perfect complement for your foraging foray at the Rīga Central Market, whether it's for a picnic or a feast in your holiday apartment.

**Siļķītes un Dillītes** SEAFOOD €€
(Map p204; ☎2639 1122; www.facebook.com/SilkitesUnDillites; Centrāltirgus iela 3, Rīga Central Market; mains €6-15; ⏰10am-5pm) If exploring the fish stalls at the Rīga Central Market puts you in the mood for some excellent fresh seafood, you're in luck. Right next to the fish hall, this scallop-sized little cafe serves up superb seafood dishes. Start with a plate of smoked fish, have some hearty fish soup and then tuck into perfectly grilled salmon.

It's located in the passage between the fish and vegetable departments of the market.

**Cafe Osīriss** CAFE €€
(Map p204; www.cafeosiris.lv; K Barona iela 31; mains €8-23; ⏰8am-11pm Mon-Sat, 10am-11pm Sun; 📶) Despite Rīga's mercurial cafe culture, Osīriss is a legendary stalwart. The green faux-marble tabletops haven't changed since the mid-1990s and neither has the clientele: angsty artsy types scribbling in their Moleskines and past prime ministers plotting their return to power. The traditional fare, such as *kartupeļu pankūkas* (potato pancakes), is some of Rīga's best. Enjoy the champagne bar.

**Aragats** GEORGIAN €€
(Map p204; ☎2910 9732; http://aragats.lv; Alunāna iela 2a; mains €5-20; ⏰noon-10pm Tue-Thu, to 11pm Fri & Sat year-round, plus noon-7pm Sun Sep-May) Sample some great cuisine from the Caucasus, which proves that life gets spicier when you go south. Start with an appetiser of pickled vegetables – the perfect chaser for your home-brewed *chacha* (Georgian vodka). Then, make nice with the family as they dish up fresh herbs at your table to mix with the savoury stew and grilled meats.

**Moltto Grill & Wine** BISTRO €€
(Map p204; ☎6730 5900; http://moltto.lv; Ģertrūdes iela 20; mains €8-18; ⏰11am-11pm Mon-Sat) Savour the cultured Ģertrūdes iela street life on the large shaded terrace at this hip, Italian-style cafe. Have some bruschetta with a glass of wine from the long list, or delve into some spicy bouillabaisse or other Med-influenced main.

**Zivju Lete** SEAFOOD €€
(Map p204; ☎2029 1653; https://zivjulete.lv; Dzirnavu iela 41; mains €8-16; ⏰noon-11pm) From fish and chips to towering seafood platters, every day the line-up changes depending on what sails in on the fishing fleet. This contemporary cafe has clean-lined bare brick walls, gleaming wooden floors and date-friendly tables for two.

**Fazenda Bazārs** MODERN EUROPEAN €€
(Map p204; ☎6724 0809; www.fazenda.lv; Baznīcas iela 14; mains €11-18; ⏰9am-10pm Mon-Fri, from 10am Sat, from 11am Sun) Although right in the centre, this place feels like you've discovered a warm tavern in the middle of nowhere. Complete with a tiled stove, this wooden house oozes charm and the food on offer feels as homey as it gets, even with the global influences. All that's lacking on the big outdoor terrace is the sound of crickets.

★**Istaba** CAFE €€€
(The Room; Map p204; ☎6728 1141; www.facebook.com/galerijaISTABA; K Barona iela 31b; mains €17; ⏰restaurant noon-11pm) Like every other country north of Antarctica, Latvia has TV chefs. Here, the beloved Mārtiņš Sirmais

runs an idiosyncratic restaurant that's part housewares salon, part performance space and part fine-dining retreat. There's no set menu – you're subject to the cook's fancy – but expect lots of little plates that add up to a feast.

**Vincents** EUROPEAN €€€

(Map p204; ☎6733 2830; www.restorans.lv; Elizabetes iela 19; mains €30-40; ⊙6-10pm Tue-Sat) This toney restaurant has served royalty and rock stars (Japanese emperor Akihito, Prince Charles, Elton John) amid its eye-catching van Gogh–inspired decor. The head chef, Oskars Sprukts, is a stalwart of the Slow Food movement and crafts his ever-changing menu mainly from produce sourced directly from small-scale Latvian farmers. Great wine list; book ahead.

**Koya** BISTRO €€€

(☎2775 7255; http://koyarestaurant.com; Andrejostas iela 5k-15; mains €12-28; ⊙noon-10pm Mon-Sat, 11am-6pm Sun) Part of a sleek row of waterside bistros overlooking the Passenger Ferry Terminal and the Daugava River in the Andrejosta neighbourhood, Koya has a large and protected terrace with fine views. Dishes mix Asian and European flavours and are beautifully presented.

**Hercogs Ģimenes Restorāns** SEAFOOD €€€

(☎6787 3804; www.hercogi.lv; Balasta dambis 70, Ķīpsala; mains €13-25; ⊙noon-10pm; 👪) This renovated brick former chalk factory has a stellar position right on the Daugava River on Ķīpsala. Whether you're in the dining room with the front that opens up in summer or down on the floating dining area, the views of Old Rīga are stunning. The seafood is fresh and artfully presented. Book ahead for weekend brunch.

### Miera Iela

The renovated – and not-so-renovated – industrial spaces in the Miera iela neighbourhood on the east side of Central Rīga are home to some of the city's most enjoyable places to eat and drink.

★**Rocket Bean Roastery** CAFE €

(Map p204; ☎2021 5120; www.rocketbeanroastery.com; Miera iela 29/31; mains €4-7; ⊙8am-9pm Mon, to 10pm Tue-Thu, to 11pm Fri & Sat, to 6pm Sun; 📶) 'What kind of Colombian beans would you like?' Yes, these people are serious about coffee – they roast their own. The bare-brick vibe is attractive, as are the streetside tables. Besides baked goods through the day, there's a lunch buffet (€8) featuring fresh and healthy fare.

**Lauvas Nams** CAFETERIA €

(Map p204; ☎6731 2661; Brīvības iela 82; meals €3-5; ⊙24hr) Generations of Rīgans have stopped for a bite at this round-the-clock retro cafeteria where a sign proclaiming 'Brezhnev ate here' would not be out of place. Simple Latvian fare – think pork stew and potatoes – is displayed at the small counter and comes in large portions.

★**Valmiermuiža Beer Embassy** BRASSERIE €€

(Valmiermuižas alus vēstniecība; Map p204; ☎2865 6111; www.valmiermuiza.lv; Aristida Briāna iela 9a; mains €9-13; ⊙3-11pm Sun-Tue, to 1am Wed & Thu, to 2am Fri & Sat) One of Lavia's favourite craft brewers, Valmiermuiža, has a craft kitchen in this renovated industrial space. Creative dishes include excellent popular fare like fresh fish and chips. Sample the range of in-house beers and brews from other top breweries and enjoy the Rīga Central Market pickles. This is ground zero for a superb pub crawl.

## Drinking & Nightlife

To party like a Latvian, assemble your friends and pub crawl your way through the city, stopping at haunts for rounds of beer, belly laughter and, of course, Black Balzām. After dark, many bars and cafes transform into grittier venues with pumping beats. Note that Rīga's craft beer scene is booming, with fine local brews like Labietis on tap all over.

### Old Rīga (Vecrīga)

On summer evenings, the beer gardens of Old Rīga echo with shouts in all the languages of Europe and beyond.

★**Folkklubs Ala Pagrabs** BAR

(Map p198; ☎2779 6914; www.folkklubs.lv; Peldu iela 19; ⊙noon-4am Mon-Wed, to 7am Thu-Sat, 2pm-4am Sun) A huge cavern filled with the bubbling magma of relentless beer-infused joy, folk-punk music, dancing and Latvian nationalism, this is an essential Rīga drinking venue. The bar strives to reflect the full geography and diversity of Latvian beer production, but there is also

## LĀČPLĒSIS: THE NATIONAL HERO

It usually doesn't take more than a few days in Latvia before you pass a Lāčplēša street (there is one in every town) or drink a glass of Lāčplēša beer. So what's in the name?

Lāčplēsis dates back to ancient sagas and the imagination of 19th-century Latvian writer Andrejs Pumpurs. Today, he's Latvia's main national hero, thought to be chosen by ancient gods to save the land from invaders. (Latvia's greatest military award is called the Order of Lāčplēsis.)

The son of a man and a she-bear, Lāčplēsis inherited his mother's ears, which serve as a secret source of supernatural faculties. As a young man, he slaughters an aggressive bear by ripping its mouth apart with his bare (human) hands. This is when people start calling him Lāčplēsis. The word means 'bear slayer' and contains enough letters with diacritic signs to look quintessentially Latvian. You can find a sculpture of him (and the slaughtered bear) at the bottom of Rīga's Freedom Monument (p203).

From here the story gets very cinematic. Lāčplēsis takes on the evil Germans, who are trying to impose their will on the Latvians. Next he sails to Germany and rescues his lover. But just as he's about to marry her, the Germans send their Dark Knight to bust up the ceremony. He and Lāčplēsis fight and both tumble to their doom in the Daugava. Fade to black.

plenty of local cider, fruit wine and *šmakouka* moonshine. The 'No Instagram!' rule is reason enough to pop in. Among the snacks and cheap meals, the *kartupeļu pankūkas* are superb.

**Egle** BEER GARDEN

(Map p198; ☎2200 6800; www.spogulegle.lv; Kaļķu iela 1a; ⊙11am-1am Mon-Sat, to midnight Sun) Split between a noisier half with live music most nights (everything from folk to rockabilly), and a quieter half (which generally closes earlier), this is the best of Old Rīga's open-air beer gardens. It's an open-air mall of imbibing pleasures complete with artworks and flowers.

**Trompete Taproom** BAR

(Map p198; ☎2574 5299; www.trompete.lv; Peldu iela 24; mains €10-16; ⊙noon-midnight Sun-Thu, to 1am Fri & Sat) The name means trumpet and you'll hear Louis Armstrong blowing his as you pass by the speakers outside. The bar has a big courtyard and cosy rooms inside for listening to live jazz most nights. The beer list is good, as are the burgers and many plates of appetisers made for sharing.

**Cetri Balti Krekli** BAR

(Map p198; ☎2868 8488; www.krekli.lv; Vecpilsētas iela 12; cover €2; ⊙10pm-6am Fri & Sat) Dance to pop and disco in a big courtyard or inside under the lasers at this big bar that books top-notch DJs. Be ready for sets of the same Latvian music you hear being hummed on buses.

**DJ Bar** BAR

(Map p198; www.djbar.lv; Mazā Jaunavu iela 5; ⊙4pm-1am Mon-Thu, to 4am Fri & Sat, 4-10pm Sun) Specialising in electronic underground, this tiny bar hiding in a tiny lane lets young DJs master their talent under the condition that the music is quiet enough to encourage, rather than prevent, a conversation over cocktails and wine.

### Central Rīga (Centrs)

Distances in Rīga are short, so you can easily wander about between venues.

**★Kaņepes Kultūras Centrs** BAR

(Map p204; ☎2940 4405; www.kanepes.lv; Skolas iela 15; ⊙3pm-2am or later) This crumbling former musical school is now a culture centre with a fabulous bar. Choose from an alluring line-up of craft beers, then grab a mismatched old wooden chair inside or a comfy perch on the big wrap-around terrace. The energy here is palpable and wild dancing regularly erupts. Some nights there's art-house films, other nights improv theatre.

**Alķīmiķis** PUB

(Map p204; ☎2668 6828; www.facebook.com/AlkimikisAlus; Lāčplēša iela 12; ⊙noon-11pm Sun-Wed, to 1am Thu-Sat) This unassuming barn-red wooden building is the modest cover for some of Rīga's most audacious brews. The wizards at Alķīmiķis (which fittingly means Alchemist) are always pushing the envelope with beer styles. Grab one of the tiny tables outside or settle back in the friendly confines inside.

**Teātra Bārs** BAR
(Map p204; ☎2591 6519; Lāčplēša iela 26; ⏲6pm-midnight Sun-Thu, to 4am Fri & Sat) Opposite a popular theatre, this grungy cavern is a beloved ancient local institution with gobs of atmosphere, right down to the tiny, mismatched wooden tables. It attracts some of the best crowds in Rīga: actors, artists, students, bus drivers, basically anyone. Weekend live music packs the smallish dance area, which gets wild in the wee hours.

**Autentika** CLUB
(Map p204; ☎2834 8453; www.facebook.com/autentika.b2; Bruņinieku iela 2; ⏲noon-10pm Sun-Tue, to 1am Wed & Thu, to 5am Fri & Sat) Set in a veteran old wooden building, this cultural space is a local hub for all things indie. Free-spirited locals mingle on mismatched furniture inside and out, while enjoying cocktails, weekend brunch, art exhibitions, emerging live bands and more. Check the Facebook page for events.

**Garage** WINE BAR
(Map p204; ☎2662 8833; www.vinabars.lv; Elizabetes iela 83/85, Berga Bazārs; ⏲10am-midnight) Apart from a semi-industrial fit-out (polished concrete floors, metal chairs), there's nothing even vaguely garagey about this chic little place with candles on the tables and a fountain outside. It's equal parts wine bar and cafe (the coffee's excellent), serving tapas and a limited selection of mains.

**Herbārijs** BEER GARDEN
(Map p204; ☎2734 3393; Dzirnavu iela 67, Gallerija Riga; ⏲11am-11.30pm Sun-Thu, to 1am Fri & Sat) Soaring high over the grand boulevards of Central Rīga, on the 8th-floor roof of the Gallerija Riga shopping mall, Herbārijs is a big open-air space with a Med-beach vibe. Enjoy the dome of sky overhead day and night.

**Skyline Bar** COCKTAIL BAR
(Map p204; ☎6777 2288; www.skylinebar.lv; Elizabetes iela 55; ⏲noon-2am Mon-Wed, to 3am Thu-Sat, 11.30am-2am Sun; 📶) Skyline Bar sits on the 26th floor of the Radisson Blu Hotel Latvija and offers sweeping views of Rīga. The glammed-up interior verges on self-parody: you expect Austin Powers to wander through. The crowd is a mix of expense-account types, tourists and people who can't pass a mirror without looking. DJs spin tunes from 9pm to 3am Thursday to Saturday.

**Apsara** TEAHOUSE
(Map p204; ☎6721 2436; www.apsara.lv; Elizabetes iela 74, Vērmanes dārzs; ⏲noon-10pm) A charming wooden cottage set within the park, Apsara is a veritable library of rare teas imported from beyond the Himalaya. Daintily sip your imported brews while relaxing on the floor amid a sea of pastel pillows or outside on the big porch.

## Miera Iela

**★ Labietis** BEER HALL
(Map p204; ☎2565 5958; www.labietis.lv; Aristida Briāna iela 9a-2; ⏲4-11pm Mon-Wed, to 1am Thu, to 3am Fri, 1pm-3am Sat, 1pm-midnight Sun) With a minimalist design that makes it feel a bit like a Gothic church, this place is on a mission to promote more obscure Latvian breweries and local craft beer. There are eight taps and several lines are usually devoted to the house brews, which many consider Latvia's best. Find Labietis down a grungy alley; several other good nightspots are nearby.

**Tallinas Kvartāla Ezītis Miglā** BEER GARDEN
(Map p204; ☎2307 0474; www.facebook.com/tallinasezitis; Miera ielas 34; ⏲11am-1am Sun-Thu, to 4am Fri & Sat) The moribund former headquarters of the city's ambulance service has been transformed into an events space with a huge and hidden inner courtyard. Right in the centre is this outpost of the popular chain of cheery pubs Ezītis Miglā (Hedgehog in the Mist). Rickety wooden tables spread out over the cracked concrete; the bar serves comfort food and craft cocktails.

There are other pop-up pubs here in the Tallinn Quarter and the entire space echoes with parties late into the night. There's a second entrance at Tallinas St 10.

**Piens** CLUB
(Milk; Map p204; ☎6601 6300; http://piens.nu; Aristida Briāna iela 9; ⏲11am-midnight Mon, Tue & Sat, to 5am Wed, to 2am Thu & Fri) This barclub in an old factory is surrounded by a few other excellent bars. There's an appealing mix of eclectic decor, sunny terraces and live music. Acts range from rock to industrial acid.

**Ziemeļu Enkurs** MICROBREWERY
(Northern Anchor; Map p204; ☎2072 2200; www.ziemeluenkurs.lv; Matīsa iela 8; ⊙4-11pm Mon-Thu, 2pm-1am Fri & Sat, noon-11pm Sun) Above a bike shop in a courtyard off a busy street, this innovative brewery has eight core beers available year-round and an ever-rotating cast of new beers dreamt up by the brewmaster. Who can resist the Touched by a Seal (*Roņa Pieskāriens*) brown ale? A big balcony surveys neighbourhood action.

**Taka** BAR
(Map p204; ☎2667 1629; www.facebook.com/takabars; Miera iela 10; ⊙3pm-midnight Mon-Wed, 3pm-2am Thu, 3pm-3am Fri, noon-2am Sat, 6-11pm Sun; 📶) An old-timer in the hipsterish Miera iela area, Taka sports bright murals on the walls and extra-comfy couches. It's an excellent place to try craft beers from Latvia's best small brewers. Or try the homemade apple wine, while listening to the underground music.

## ☆ Entertainment

Check www.liveriga.com for opera, ballet, guest DJs, live music and other events around town. Also look for free listings guides. The tourist information centre in the Blackheads House can help visitors book tickets at any Rīga venue.

### Opera, Ballet & Theatre

Rīga's ballet, opera and theatre season breaks for summer holidays (between June and September), although there's always the star-studded Rīga Jūrmala Music Festival (p215).

**★New Rīga Theatre** THEATRE
(Jaunais Rīgas Teātris; Map p204; ☎6728 3323; www.jrt.lv; Lačplēša iela 25; ⊙box office 11am-7pm) Important and contemporary repertory theatre. Attracts big names like Mikhail Baryshnikov, who premiered his play *White Helicopter* here in 2019. Many performances are in English or available in simultaneous translation through headphones.

**Dailes Theatre** THEATRE
(Map p204; ☎6727 9566; www.dailesteatris.lv; Brīvības iela 75; ⊙box office 11am-7pm) Rīga's largest modern theatre; it retains many of its original architectural elements from the Soviet era. Presents a varied calendar of contemporary plays and groups.

**Latvian National Opera** OPERA, BALLET
(Latvijas Nacionālajā operā; Map p198; ☎6707 3777; www.opera.lv; Aspazijas bulvāris 3) With a hefty international reputation as one of the finest opera companies in all of Europe, the national opera is the pride of Latvia. It's also home to the Rīga Ballet; locally born lad Mikhail Baryshnikov got his start here. Performances happen most nights of the week.

### Concert Venues

**★Rīga Cathedral** CLASSICAL MUSIC
(Map p198; ☎6721 3213; www.doms.lv; Doma laukums 1; tickets free-€20; ⊙hours vary) Short organ concerts are held in the evening throughout the week, with lengthier performances on Friday nights. Buy tickets in advance in summer.

**Great Guild** CLASSICAL MUSIC
(Map p198; ☎6722 4850; www.lnso.lv; Amatu iela 6; ⊙box office noon-7pm Mon-Fri) Home to the acclaimed Latvian National Symphony Orchestra, Great Guild dates to 1854.

**Palladium** LIVE MUSIC
(Map p204; ☎6728 4516; www.palladium.lv; Marijas iela 21) The architecturally significant Palladium is a modernised venue that holds 2000 and attracts top acts.

**KK fon Stricka Villa** ARTS CENTRE
(Map p204; ☎6601 6300; www.fonstrickavilla.lv; Aristida Briāna iela 9) This old and dishevelled mansion with a weedy yard hosts events through the year. During summer there are evening concerts (often on Wednesday) spanning genres (pop, acid, hip-hop, jazz etc) that spill outside onto the grass under the trees. Many are free. It's one of Rīga's great scenes.

**Arena Rīga** LIVE MUSIC
(☎6738 8200; www.arenariga.com; Skantes iela 21) This is the main venue for the most popular spectator sports: ice hockey and basketball. The 10,000-seat venue also hosts dance revues and concerts.

**Mūzikas nams Daile** CONCERT VENUE
(Map p204; ☎2495 9495; http://dailesnams.lv; K Barona iela 31) This former cinema is a concert venue, specialising in acoustic and classical music.

### Cinemas

As ever more films are dubbed into Latvian, theatres indicate if films are in their original language with subtitles or dubbed. Most cinemas have assigned seating.

**K Suns** CINEMA
(Map p204; ☎2923 1633; www.kinogalerija.lv; Elizabetes iela 83/85, Bergs Bazārs) An artsy cinema that shows mostly indie films.

**Kino Citadele** CINEMA
(Map p204; ☎1189; www.forumcinemas.lv; 13 Janvāra iela 8) Rīga's multiplex has stadium seating, 14 screens and a cafe on the top floor, high above the Stockmann supermarket. Expect Hollywood fare, with many films dubbed in Latvian. Buy tickets online.

**Splendid Palace** CINEMA
(Map p204; ☎6718 1143; www.splendidpalace.lv; Elizabetes iela 61) Obscured from view by Soviet Lego architecture, this art deco gem specialises in art house, festival retrospectives and Latvian films.

## Shopping

Latvians love their shopping malls (a palpable marker of globalisation), but travellers will be pleased to find a wide assortment of small, locally owned shops that specialise in all sorts of Latvian items – knits, crafts, spirits and fashion.

Old Rīga has few shops left catering to residents, everything is aimed at visitors. For the most interesting shops, head to the tonier streets of Central Rīga, such as Brīvības iela and Miera iela, and the genteel byways of the Quiet Centre.

And don't forget Rīga Central Market (p210), with its plethora of vendors selling food and non-food items, plus the more upscale Kalnciema Kvartāls (p212) across the river.

★**Elīna Dobele** FASHION & ACCESSORIES
(Map p204; ☎2230 1197; www.elinadobele.com; Mednieku iela 7; ⊙11am-7pm Mon-Sat) Renowned local designer Elīna Dobele specialises in exquisite handmade shoes for men and women. They're true artisanal products, as artful as the nearby art nouveau gems. She also designs and sells accessories and frocks.

★**Robert's Books** BOOKS
(Map p204; www.robertsbooks.lv; Dzirnavu iela 51; ⊙11am-10pm Mon-Fri, noon-8pm Sat & Sun) As much a cafe and cultural centre as it is a bookshop, the namesake owner used to write for the *Economist*. Browse used and new titles, especially esoteric titles in English. The coffee and tea are excellent; enjoy a cup over conversation in the courtyard.

**Mr Page** BOOKS
(Map p204; ☎2641 1292; www.mrpage.lv; Miera iela 4; ⊙11am-8pm Mon-Sat, noon-5pm Sun) Slip on white cotton gloves and caress the books in this elegant shop that treats tomes like works of art – and in fact many are. Browse beautiful titles on art and design (most in English). The kids' section will spoil them.

**Jāņa Sēta** BOOKS
(Map p204; ☎2700 0062; www.mapshop.lv; Elizabetes iela 85a, Bergs Bazārs; ⊙10am-7pm Mon-Fri, to 5pm Sat) The largest travel bookstore in the Baltics overflows with a bounty of excellent maps (many published in-house), souvenir photo books and guidebooks.

**M50** FASHION & ACCESSORIES
(Map p204; ☎2411 5990; www.m50.lv; Miera iela 17; ⊙11am-7pm Mon-Fri, to 5pm Sat) Take your pick of pleasures at this bifurcated shop: browse designer housewares on one side and delve into exquisite belts, bags and jewellery on the other. If your energy lags, get a coffee from the cute cafe.

**Manilla** STATIONERY
(Map p204; ☎2200 9101; https://manilla-dizaina-papirlietas.business.site; Tērbatas iela 55; ⊙11am-7pm Mon-Fri, to 4pm Sat) You might just forsake email: lovely handmade stationery and paper goods of all kinds are on offer here. Go on, write a letter.

**Art Nouveau Rīga** GIFTS & SOUVENIRS
(Map p204; ☎6733 3030; www.artnouveauriga.lv; Strēlnieku iela 9; ⊙10am-7pm) Right by Alberta iela, this place sells a variety of art nouveau designer decor items, souvenirs, guides and postcards.

**Pienene** HANDICRAFTS
(Map p198; ☎2929 8748; www.studijapienene.lv; Kungu iela 7/9; ⊙10am-8pm) 'The Dandelion' is an airy boutique in the heart of Old Rīga where visitors can sample locally produced beauty products, try on floaty scarves and sniff scented candles.

**Upe** MUSIC
(Map p198; ☎6720 5509; www.upeveikals.lv; Vāgnera iela 5; ⊙11am-7pm Mon-Fri, to 4pm Sat) Classical Latvian tunes play as customers peruse traditional instruments and CDs of local folk, rock and experimental music.

**Hobbywool** ARTS & CRAFTS
(Map p198; ☎2707 2707; www.hobbywool.com; Mazā Pils iela 6; ⊙10am-6pm Mon-Sat, 11am-3pm Sun) The slogan at this colourful little shop is 'Knit like a Latvian'. Given that locals have a long history of creating beautiful, brightly coloured knitted shawls, mittens and socks to ward off the bitter winters, that's a good goal.

### RĪGA PASS

If you have a long list of sights and activities on your checklist, pick up a Rīga Pass. Perks include free public transport, free or discounted admission to some museums and a free walking tour of Old Rīga. Cards are available for purchase at the tourist office, the airport and several major hotels. Prices for one-/two-/three-day cards are €25/30/35. Check www.liveriga.com for more information.

**Etmo** DESIGN
(Map p198; ☎2913 4999; www.etmo.lv; Torņa iela 4-3a; ⏰11am-6pm) Modern homewares, clothing and accessories by Latvian artisans and designers are hand-picked and curated by the shop's owner. If your aesthetic is clean and contemporary and you're after a unique souvenir to take (or wear) home, look here.

**Ars Tela** DESIGN
(Map p198; ☎6733 4545; www.arstela.lv; Smilšu iela 18; ⏰10am-6pm Mon-Sat, 11am-5pm Sun) Latvian textiles are woven using old-world handlooms at this design shop. Inspired by the scenes of the countryside, the earth-toned fabrics have traditional patterns and are fused with other fine fibres such as silk and cashmere, making for exquisite scarves, sweaters, blankets and more.

**Bold Concept Store** CLOTHING
(Map p204; ☎2925 6045; www.boldconceptstore.lv; Blaumaņa iela 7; ⏰11am-7pm Mon-Fri, noon-6pm Sat) The design lives up to the name at this stark grey and white store that stocks goods from top Baltic designers. Browse the spectacular clothing and accessories.

**Cita Rota** FASHION & ACCESSORIES
(Map p198; ☎2033 3773; www.citarota.lv; 11 Novembra Krastmala 29; ⏰10am-7pm Mon-Fri, to 4pm Sat) Old Believers symbols and other designs from Latvia's past are the basis for the look at this unique Old Town shop. Clothes, jewellery and interior design items from a variety of local designers are on offer.

## Information

### INTERNET ACCESS

Fast internet access and full office services, including copying and printing, are available at **Copy Pro** (☎2924 0166; www.copypro.lv; Raiņa bulvāris 17; ⏰24/7).

Most cafes offer free wi-fi to patrons or have password-free access.

### MEDICAL SERVICES

**ARS** (☎6720 1006; www.ars-med.lv; Skolas iela 5; consultation from €32) English-speaking doctors; 24-hour consultation available.

### MONEY

ATMs are easily found across Rīga.

### POST

Look for blue storefronts with 'Pasta' written on them. See www.pasts.lv for more info.

**Central Post Office** (Map p204; Brīvības bulvāris 32; ⏰7.30am-7pm Mon-Fri, 9am-3pm Sat)

**Post Office** (Map p204; Central Train Station; ⏰9am-7pm)

### TOURIST INFORMATION

**Tourist Information Centre** (Map p198; ☎6703 7900; www.liveriga.com; Rātslaukums 6; ⏰10am-6pm) In a corner of the Blackheads House, dispenses popular tourist maps and oodles of other information. Books entertainment, tours and day trips. Sells the Riga Pass discount card.

**1188** (www.1188.lv) Lists virtually every establishment in Rīga and the rest of Latvia. The site also provides up-to-date information on Rīga nightlife and traffic plus bus and transit info.

## Getting There & Away

### AIR

**Rīga International Airport** (Starptautiskā Lidosta Rīga; ☎1817; www.riga-airport.com; Mārupe District; 🚌22) is in the suburb of Skulte, 13km southwest of the city centre. It's the primary hub for air travel to the country. Latvia's national carrier, airBaltic (www.airbaltic.com), offers direct flights to 70 destinations within Europe.

### BOAT

Rīga's **passenger ferry terminal** (Eksporta iela 3a) is located about 1km north of Akmens Bridge. About 100m east is a tram stop from where you can catch trams to Old Town and beyond. **Tallink** (www.tallinksilja.com) has car ferry service to Stockholm (passenger from €69, 18 hours, daily) on large comfortable ships.

You can reach Jūrmala on a scenic ride aboard the **River Boat New Way** (Map p204; ☎2644 5180; http://rigaship.lv; 11 Novembra Krastmala; one-way adult/child €20/10, return €30/15; ⏰daily May-Sep). The journey takes two hours and departs from the river in front of Old Town.

### BUS

Buses for destinations across Latvia and beyond depart from Rīga's modern **international bus station** (Rīgas starptautiskā autoosta; Map p204; ☎9000 0009; www.autoosta.lv; Prāgas iela 1), located behind the railway embankment near the Central Market. There is extensive international service (p286). Major companies like Ecolines (www.ecolines.net) and Lux Express (www.luxexpress.eu) have offices here. Ticket machines make buying domestic tickets a breeze.

Small buses to the region around Rīga depart from the bare-bones **Minibus Terminal** (Map p204; Satekles iela) across from the central train station.

All bus schedules and fares can be found at www.1188.lv.

### TRAIN

Rīga's **central train station** (Centrālā stacija; ☎6723 2135; www.pv.lv; Stacijas laukums 2) is convenient to Old and Central Rīga plus public transport. It's housed within a modern shopping mall with a good supermarket, just outside Old Town.

The information office (open 7am to 7pm), to the far right facing the ticket windows, is very helpful. Use www.1188.lv and the national railways' site (www.ldz.lv) for schedule and fare info.

International trains head from Rīga to Moscow (16 hours), St Petersburg (15 hours) and Minsk (nine hours) daily.

Rīga has six suburban lines. Of most use to travellers is the Dubulti–Sloka–Ķemeri–Tukums Line, which runs through the entire length of Jūrmala, and the Sigulda–Cēsis–Valmiera Line, which can take you into the heart of Gauja National Park. The Skulte line is convenient for Saulkrasti.

## Getting Around

### TO/FROM THE AIRPORT

The cheapest way to get from Rīga airport to the centre is bus 22 (€2, 25 minutes), which runs at least every 30 minutes and stops at several points around town including the Stockmanns complex and on the river side of Old Town.

A taxi ride between the airport and the centre typically costs about €15. Use the queue with cabs from the reliable Baltic Taxi, Bolt and Red Cab.

### BICYCLE

Pedal around town with **Sixt Bicycle Rental** (Sixt velo noma; ☎6767 6780; www.sixtbicycle.lv; per 30min/day €1.30/13). It has self-service stands across Rīga and the first 30 minutes are free. You can rent the bikes for one-way trips between Rīga and Jūrmala. The 'Next Bike' app makes using the bikes a breeze.

Rīga Bike Tours & Rent (p214) also rents bikes.

### CAR & MOTORCYCLE

Municipal and private parking in the centre of Rīga costs between €2 and €3 per hour. If you need to drop a car in Rīga for longer, consult www.europark.lv – it runs parking lots all around the city.

### PUBLIC TRANSPORT

The centre of Rīga is too compact for most visitors to bother with public transport, but trams, buses or trolleybuses are essential if you're venturing a little further out. For routes and schedules, consult www.rigassatiksme.lv. Note that buses and trolleybuses (which run on overhead wires) may have the same route number but run on entirely different routes. Don't confuse them.

Fares are paid by e-tickets called e-talons. You can buy and refill them at Narvessen convenience stores, vending machines on board newer trams, at the Opera House stop and in the underground pass by the train station. A single journey costs €2; unlimited tickets are available for 24 hours (€5), three days (€10) and five days (€15). A 10-trip ticket is €10.90.

### TAXI

Insist on having the meter on before you set off in a taxi; note that rates vary between operators. From Old Town to Miera iela the fare could be about €7. Some freelance taxis are dubious, so stick to ones summoned by app or phone. Each of these outfits has English-speaking operators and a handy app:

**Baltic Taxi** (☎2000 8500)
**Bolt/Taxify** (☎8999)
**Red Cab** (☎8383)

# AROUND RĪGA

It's hard to believe that long stretches of flaxen beaches and shady pine forests lie just 20km from Rīga's metropolitan core. Both Jūrmala and Ķemeri National Park make excellent day trips from Rīga.

## Jūrmala

POP 48,600

Jūrmala (pronounced *yoor*-muh-lah) is a 32km-long series of townships strung along a beautiful white-sand beach. The heart of the action is at the townships of Majori and Dzintari. A 1km-long pedestrian street, Jomas iela, connects these two districts and is considered to be Jūrmala's main drag, with loads of visitor-centric venues.

# Around Rīga

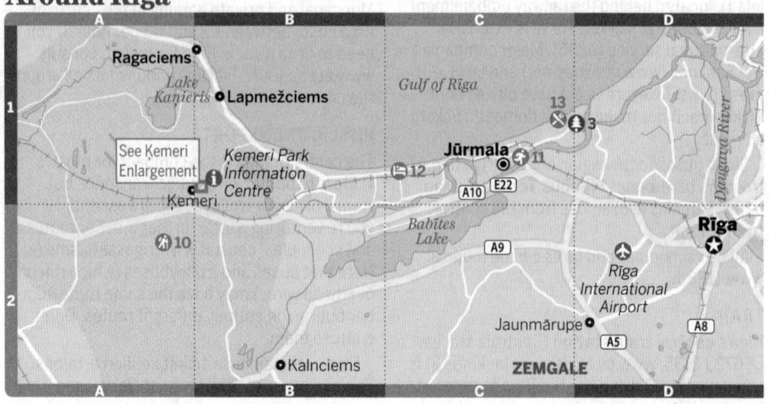


## Around Rīga

**Top Sights**

1 Biķernieki Memorial ........ E1

**Sights**

2 Hotel Ķemeri ........ F1
3 Jūrmala Open Air Museum ........ D1
4 Ķemeri Park ........ F1
5 Latvian Ethnographic Open-Air Museum ........ E1
6 Lizard Spring ........ F1
7 Rīga Motor Museum ........ E1
8 Salaspils Concentration Camp Memorial ........ E2
9 St Peter-Paul Orthodox Church ........ F1

**Activities, Courses & Tours**

10 Great Ķemeri Bog Boardwalk ........ A2
11 Līvu Akvaparks ........ C1

**Sleeping**

12 Alba Hotel ........ C1

**Eating**

13 36.Line ........ C1

Across the resort towns the narrow streets are lined with Prussian-style wood villas dating to the 19th century, lending Jūrmala an attractive, genteel air. Even during the height of communism, Jūrmala was a popular retreat, always a place to 'sea' and be seen. These days, on summer weekends, vehicles clog the roads as jet-setters and day-tripping Rīgans flock to the resort town for some serious fun in the sun.

Amidst all the clamour, the beach remains the focus. Few developments have encroached on the bluffs behind the sand, giving it an unspoiled atmosphere interrupted only by the odd beach cafe and the ever-present squeals of delight from beachgoers of all ages.

## Sights

Besides its Blue Flag beach, Jūrmala's main attractions are its colourful art nouveau **wooden houses**, distinguishable by frilly awnings, detailed facades and elaborate towers. There are over 4000 wooden structures found throughout Jūrmala (most are summer cottages), but you can get your fill of wood by taking a leisurely stroll along **Jūras iela**, which parallels Jomas iela between Majori and Dzintari.

**Jūrmala Beach** BEACH

Jūrmala's ribbon of white sand stretches for 24km. The sand is hard-packed and ideal for walking – or packing into sand sculptures or castles – and the water is calm and shallow. Note, however, that even in August the winds can be brisk and you may be disheartened to see people wearing parkas. Unlike some beach resorts, most of the sand is open for you and your towel. The smattering of cafes have a few loungers you can use.

**Jūrmala Open Air Museum** NATURE RESERVE

(Jūrmalas brīvdabas muzejs; ☎6775 4909; www.jbmuzejs.lv; Tīklu iela 1a; ⊙10am-6pm May-Sep, to 5pm Oct-Apr) FREE Before the clothing of choice in Jūrmala was the bikini (with or

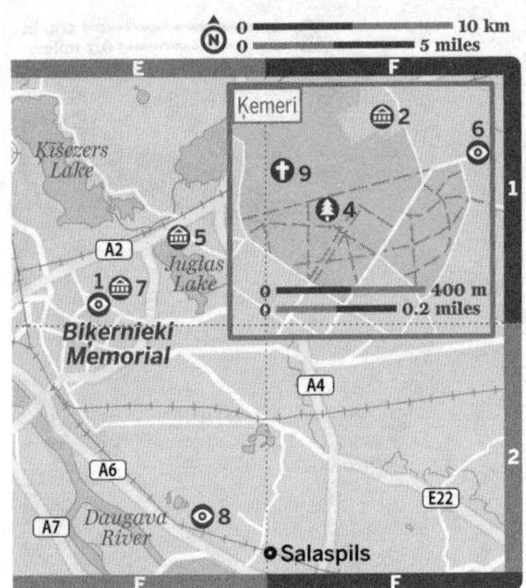


without a parka), the peninsula was home to fishing people who eked out a living through endless days of work. Get insight into the lives of these hardy folk at this open-air museum at Jūrmala's far east end, which recreates a fishing village. On summer Thursdays, demonstrations show how fish were smoked – sampling is encouraged! The adjoining **Ragakāpa Nature Park** has trails through the forests and dunes.

**Jūrmala City Museum** MUSEUM
(☎6776 1915; www.muzeji.lv/lv/museums/jurmala-city-museum/; Tirgoņu iela 29; ⊙10am-5pm Wed-Sun) FREE This well-funded museum features a cool permanent exhibit detailing Jūrmala's colourful history as *the* go-to resort town in the former USSR. One popular section details children enjoying Jūrmala through the decades.

**Art Rezidence 'Inner Light'** GALLERY
(☎2711 7240; http://yermolayev.eu; Omnibusa iela 19; adult/child €5/3; ⊙11am-5pm) Local Russian artist Vitaliy Yermolayev runs this studio out of his home and dabbles with a secret recipe for glow-in-the-dark paint by creating portraits that morph when different amounts of light strike the painting. You can linger over a glass of French wine in the tiny bar.

## Activities

Jūrmala's first spa opened in 1838, and since then the resort has been known as the spa capital of the Baltic. Treatments are available at a variety of hotels and hulking Soviet-era sanatoriums going west along the beach towards Ķemeri National Park. Many places to stay offer combined spa and sleeping deals. Don't expect a plethora of water sports. The lack of surf, the shallow water and the bracing temps keep people on the sand.

**Baltic Beach Hotel & Spa** SPA
(☎6777 1441; www.balticbeach.lv; Jūras iela 23/25; treatments from €20; ⊙7am-10pm) The huge spa at the beachfront resort has three rambling storeys full of massage rooms, saunas, yoga studios, swimming pools and spa pools. On a 'spa journey' you'll be dunked in waters from frigid to steaming.

**Līvu Akvaparks** WATER PARK
(☎6775 5636; www.akvaparks.lv; Viestura iela 24; 1-day adult/child €29/20; ⊙11am-10pm Mon-Fri, 10am-10pm Sat & Sun Jun-Aug, shorter hours Sep-May) At this massive, family-friendly water park in Lielupe, located near the bridge to the Rīga highway (A10), large areas are enclosed and open all year.

## Festivals & Events

Jūrmala has a packed summer events calendar. Check out www.visitjurmala.lv for details.

**Jomas Street Festival** STREET CARNIVAL
(www.visitjurmala.lv; ⊙mid-Jul) FREE Jūrmala's annual city festival celebrates the main drag in Majori. The fun includes music, theatre, dance and general frolic. Don't miss the sand-sculpture contest on the beach.

## Sleeping

Accommodation choices range from simple hostels away from the beach to hotels in historic wooden guesthouses near the sand. There are fewer large modern resorts than you'd expect. Holiday apartments and rooms are listed by the score on booking sites and are the most common way people stay in Jūrmala. Pay attention to the location, as many are far from the beach.

**Parus** HERITAGE HOTEL €€
(☎6776 2391; www.parus.lv; Smilšu iela 2; s/d from €55/60; 📶) One of those Prussian villas that form the face of Jūrmala, this pretty green-coloured wooden house has 12 traditionally decorated rooms that come in various shapes and sizes. The beach is just a dune away.

**Alba Hotel** HOTEL €€
(☎6751 2632; www.albahoteljurmala.lv; Dārzu iela 9; r from €40; P📶) This small, modern hotel has very large rooms (some with small

## Jūrmala

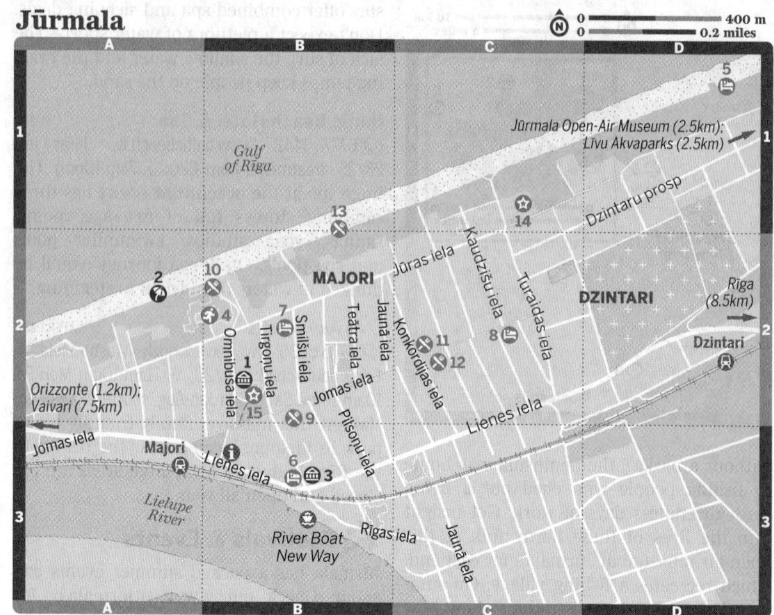


## Jūrmala

**Sights**
1 Art Rezidence 'Inner Light'.................... B2
2 Jūrmala Beach.............................................. A2
3 Jūrmala City Museum ................................ B3

**Activities, Courses & Tours**
4 Baltic Beach Hotel Spa.......................... B2

**Sleeping**
5 Light House.................................................. D1
6 MaMa Boutique Hotel............................... B3
7 Parus................................................................ B2
8 Villa Joma.................................................... C2

**Eating**
9 De Gusto ........................................................ B2
10 Il Sole............................................................. B2
11 Lighthouse.................................................. C2
12 Sue's Asia .................................................... C2
13 Summertime .............................................. B1

**Entertainment**
14 Dzintari Concert Hall............................... C1
15 Jūrmala Culture Centre .......................... B2

balconies), a relaxing garden and a popularly priced cafe. It's in the quiet western end of Jūrmala and is a five-minute walk from the beach.

★**Light House** BOUTIQUE HOTEL €€€
(☎6751 1445; www.lighthousejurmala.lv; Gulbenes iela 1a; r high/low season from €660/180; P ❄ 📶) This striking seaside hotel offers luxurious respite with a global flair. Its 11 rooms – each with terrace access and Baltic Sea views – are themed after a different destination, such as Indonesia, Africa, Spain, and other regions in Latvia. Elegant furnishings and authentic, tasteful decor capture the spirit of each geographical muse. Amenities include a private beach.

**MaMa Boutique Hotel** BOUTIQUE HOTEL €€€
(☎6776 1271; www.hotelmama.lv; Tirgonu iela 22; r €65-200; 📶) Traditional wood outside, mod – and even odd – inside. The bedroom doors have thick, mattress-like padding on the interior and the suites themselves are a veritable blizzard of white drapery with a mix of silver paint and pixie dust accents in the ultramodern furnishings and amenities. This full-service hotel lays on the luxury and has an acclaimed restaurant.

**Villa Joma** BOUTIQUE HOTEL €€€
(☎6777 1999; www.villajoma.lv; Jomas iela 90; s/d from €100/110; 📶) This inviting hotel sports 15 compact rooms that come in quirky

configurations; try for one with a skylight. Villa Joma is right on the main drag and has a lovely garden terrace in the back to catch some rays. The attractive and airy ground-floor restaurant is popular.

## Eating & Drinking

Stroll down Jomas iela and take your pick from warm-weather beer tents, cafe terraces and trendy restaurants. There are a number of summertime beach cafes perched on the sand at regular intervals, ranging from very basic to hip and stylish. On long summer nights, most restaurants and cafes keep serving drinks to cheery patrons long into the evening.

**De Gusto** CAFE €
(2024 2328; www.de-gusto.lv; Jomas iela 46; snacks from €2; 9am-8pm; ) An excellent small bakery and cafe right in the heart of Majori on the main street. The tables out front are prime people-watching territory.

**Summertime** CAFE €
(2022 0061; off Teātra iela, Jūrmala Beach; mains €4-7; 11am-10pm May-Sep; ) Typical of the summer beach cafes, this big place is about 50m back from the high tide line. There are fab sandy views from the huge wooden terrace or you can get a sun lounger and enjoy your beer (as well as various grilled meats and sandwiches) in blissful repose.

**Lighthouse** EUROPEAN €€
(2636 0603; www.hol.lv; Jomas iela 63; mains €7-16; 11am-10pm; ) Nab a tree-shaded table outside this sleek bar and restaurant with a front that opens up to the pedestrian quarter. The contemporary menu matches the contemporary decor: sandwiches, salads and grilled mains are all good. Breakfast is served until 1pm; there's a good wine list and a kids' menu.

**Sue's Asia** ASIAN €€
(6775 5900; www.suesasia.lv; Jomas iela 74; mains €9-19; noon-10pm) Sue's is beloved by locals for its fairly authentic, albeit toned down, South Asian cuisine. Enjoy curries or tender butter chicken amid statues of praying deities.

**★36.Line** LATVIAN €€€
(2201 0696; www.36line.com; Līnija 36; mains €12-50; 1-11pm; ) Popular local chef Lauris Alekseyevs delivers modern twists on traditional Latvian dishes and fresh seafood at this innovative restaurant occupying a perch above the sand at the eastern end of Jūrmala. Enjoy the beach, then switch to casual attire for lunch or glam up for dinner. In the evening, DJs spin beats. There's also a beach cafe down by the water.

**Il Sole** ITALIAN €€€
(Jūras iela 23/25; mains €14-30; 11am-11pm) A very popular restaurant at the Baltic Beach Hotel & Spa, Il Sole has much-sought-after ocean-side seating and a long list of Italian dishes matched with Italian wines. The Florentine decor is rather cheesy, but you'll hardly notice while staring out at the sunset glow.

## Entertainment

**★Dzintari Concert Hall** LIVE MUSIC
(Dzintari Koncertzāle; 6776 2005; www.dzintarukoncertzale.lv; Turaidas iela 1) This legendary open-air concert hall (there is a roof, but no walls) dates back to 1897. Now modernised, there are two stages – one large and one small – and shows through the year, with summer seeing shows almost every night. Look for big-name performers, bands and orchestras, as well as films and musical theatre.

**Jūrmala Culture Centre** PERFORMING ARTS
(Majori Kultūras nams; 6776 2403; www.facebook.com/jurmalaskultcentrs; Jomas iela 35; ) Hosts films, small music concerts and various arts and craft exhibitions.

## Information

**Tourist Office** (6714 7900; www.visitjurmala.lv; Lienes iela 5; 9am-5pm Mon-Fri, 10am-5pm Sat & Sun) Located across from Majori train station, this helpful office has information outlining walks, bike routes and attractions.

## Getting There & Around

### BICYCLE

**Sixt** (www.sixtbicycle.lv; per day €13) has several locations across Jūrmala, including one near Majori station. Bikes can be hired for one-way trips between Jūrmala and Rīga.

### BOAT

The most scenic way to travel between Rīga and Jūrmala is by the **River Boat New Way** (29237123; http://rigaship.lv; one-way adult/child €20/10, return €30/15; daily May-Sep). Along the two-hour journey you'll be transfixed by the Daugava River, the busy harbour and the vast reed-lined sparkling waters of the Lielupe,

## REMEMBERING THE HOLOCAUST

After their invasion in June 1941, the Nazis began rounding up Jews in Rīga. Later that year, trains began arriving with German, Czech and Austrian Jews who had been ordered east (the Polish death camps didn't open until 1942). In December, the Nazis began slaughtering Jews in the forests around Rīga. Thousands at a time were taken into the woods and shot, often with the help of Latvians loyal to the Germans.

Of the nearly 100,000 Jews living in Latvia before the war, fewer than 5000 survived. Another 20,000 Jews were brought from the west and killed.

In Rīga, the Rīga Ghetto & Latvian Holocaust Museum (p210) is an essential stop for understanding the Holocaust. The nearby Holocaust Memorial (p211) details one atrocity, while the Žanis Lipke Memorial (p211) on Ķīpsala recounts the efforts of one Latvian to save the lives of Jews. Other important holocaust memorials can be found in Daugavpils (p271) and near Liepāja (p243). For more information, see http://memorialplaces.lu.lv.

Between 1941 and 1944, the Nazis – aided by Latvians – shot more than 35,000 Jews at 55 different sites in this forest. It is one of several killing sites that ring Rīga. In 2001 the large and impressive **Biķernieki Memorial** (Biķernieku memoriāls; Bikernieku iela 70) was opened here deep in the woods, about 200m south of the busy road. Stones list the names of places in Europe from where Jews were brought to be killed here. Paths through the now silent trees lead to other killing sites. Some 6km east of central Rīga, the memorial is a thoughtful and contemplative place. Bus 15 stops nearby.

In October 1941 the Nazis sent 1800 German Jews to Latvia to build a concentration camp at Salaspils, 18km southeast of Rīga. Over 1000 died during the construction. Ultimately, the Germans used the camp for Latvian prisoners and Russian POWs. Upwards of 2000 people died here. In 1967 the huge Soviet-style **Salaspils Concentration Camp Memorial** (Salaspils novads) was opened. A monument to commemorate the Jews who died here was added in 2004. To get here by public transport, take a suburban train on the Ogre–Aizkraukle line to Dārziņi (not Salaspils) station. It's a 15-minute walk from the station to the *piemineklis* (memorial).

the circuitous channel behind the Jūrmala peninsula. In Jūrmala, the boat departs from a dock just east of the Majori train station.

### CAR

The east end of Jūrmala is only 20km west of Rīga via the modern A10 highway. However, on sunny summer weekends, the road can become hopelessly clogged with sun-seekers, so take the train instead. Parking is usually not a problem – except on sunny summer weekends.

Motorists driving into Jūrmala must pay a €2 toll per day from April to September when they reach the resort's outskirts. Confounding but multilingual automated machines dispense receipts.

### TRAIN

Jūrmala is on the Tukums suburban line from Rīga. Among several options, the Majori station (€1.40, 30 minutes) is in the heart of the action. Trains run two to three times per hour (roughly 6am to 10.30pm).

# Ķemeri

The old spa town of Ķemeri (pronounced kyeh-meh-ree or tyeh-meh-ree, depending on who you ask) could not have a more polarised split personality. On the one hand, it's the centre of Latvia's most popular natural area, **Ķemeri National Park** (Ķemeru nacionālais parks; ☎6673 0078; www.kemerunacionalaisparks.lv), which offers great walks and vast expanses of untouched lakes, forests and bogs; on the other, it's the local equivalent of Pompeii (albeit much younger) – a former resort area that's now in ruins.

Though the pungent smell of rotten eggs still wafts through the air, Ķemeri was once known for its curative mud and spring water, and by the end of the 19th century was attracting visitors from across Europe. By the 1930s, the town was in full bloom, with lavish and artful facilities. Today, plans inch along to erase the destruction wrought by its near-abandonment during the post-WWII Soviet era, when such bourgeois places were shunned.

Rent a bicycle to explore Ķemeri's natural and historic wonders.

## Sights & Activities

**Ķemeri Park** PARK

(off Emīla Dārziņa iela) The former resort's central park offers melancholy hints of what once was and what might be again. Amidst the manicured lawns are dishevelled features in need of some love, like the once-stunning **Love Island Rotunda** and the faded **wrought-iron bridges** with romantic names such as Bridge of Sighs or Bridge of Caprices. Shed a tear for the ruins that were once the **Bathing Facility**.

**Lizard Spring** SPRING

(Turistu iela 2b) The area's spring water is perfectly potable and supposedly quite healthy. Try filling your water bottle at the Lizard, a stone sculpture at the mouth of a spring that trickles into the river. Sip your pungent brew and hope for the best.

**St Peter-Paul Orthodox Church** CHURCH

(Katedrāles iela 1) Built in 1893 and now beautifully restored, St Peter-Paul Orthodox Church is the oldest place of worship in Ķemeri and, if you look closely, you'll notice that this large wooden structure was constructed entirely without nails.

**Hotel Ķemeri** HISTORIC BUILDING

(Tukuma iela) You can't miss the Hotel Ķemeri. Known as the 'White Ship', it was built during Latvia's brief period of independence in the 1930s, and has one of the most impressive facades outside Rīga. At the moment, only the sparkling white exterior can be appreciated, while plans for a full renovation drag on.

★ **Great Ķemeri Bog Boardwalk** WALKING

(Lielais Ķemeru purva dēļu celiņš; off A10) This fascinating 3.5km boardwalk circuit takes you through the otherworldish Ķemeri marsh, a landscape of multicoloured moss, dark deep puddles and a huge variety of plants, including insect-catching sundews. There's also a watchtower, where serious birders try to spot a golden plover or a curlew. The walk is 3.4km southwest of the Ķemeri train station. The parking area has a summertime info booth.

## Information

**Ķemeri Park Information Centre** (☎2642 4972; www.kemerunacionalaisparks.lv; Meža iela; ⏰10am-5pm Wed-Sun May-Oct) In the historic Forest House, built in 1933 during the resort's glory years, the info centre is housed in the former Mosquito restaurant, named in honour of Ķemeri's most prolific resident. It has a playground and a picnic area, and there's an engrossing 600m **Melnalkšņu Bog Boardwalk** through the surrounding dense, swampy forest of black alders. Signs provide engrossing natural details (one explains the tough life of moss). The centre is 2.5km northeast of the train station.

## Getting There & Around

Ķemeri is easily accessible from Rīga (and abuts the west end of Jūrmala). Trains run almost hourly (€2, one hour) to the 1922 **Ķemeri Station** (off Tukuma iela) on the Rīga–Tukums line via Jūrmala. Bikes are an ideal way to see Ķemeri and the national park. Rent one from **Ķemeri Takas** (☎2923 9273; http://velonoma.lv; off Tukuma iela, Ķemeri Station; bike rental per hour/day €3/12; ⏰10am-7pm May-Oct) at the station.

# WESTERN LATVIA (KURZEME)

Kurzeme is miles and miles of jaw-dropping natural beauty. The region's sandy strands of desolate coastline are tailor-made for an off-the-beaten-track adventure. A constellation of coastal towns – Kolka, Ventspils, Pāvilosta and Liepāja – provide pleasant breaks between the large stretches of awesome nothingness. Get back to nature and enjoy some smoked fish from the Gulf of Rīga.

Inland, you'll revel in the Latvian devotion to the countryside in historic Kuldīga and the surrounding lands, dotted with ancient churches and manor houses.

Kurzeme was once run by the namesake Cours, a rebellious tribe known for teaming up with the Vikings for raids and battles. During the 13th century, German crusaders ploughed through, subjugating the Cours. When the Livonian Order collapsed under assault from Russia's Ivan the Terrible in 1561, the Order's last master, Gotthard Kettler, salvaged Courland and neighbouring Zemgale as his own personal fiefdom. Many other personalities and powers have controlled this fertile but thinly populated land through the centuries, but its inherent stoic independent spirit is undiminished.

# Western Latvia (Kurzeme)

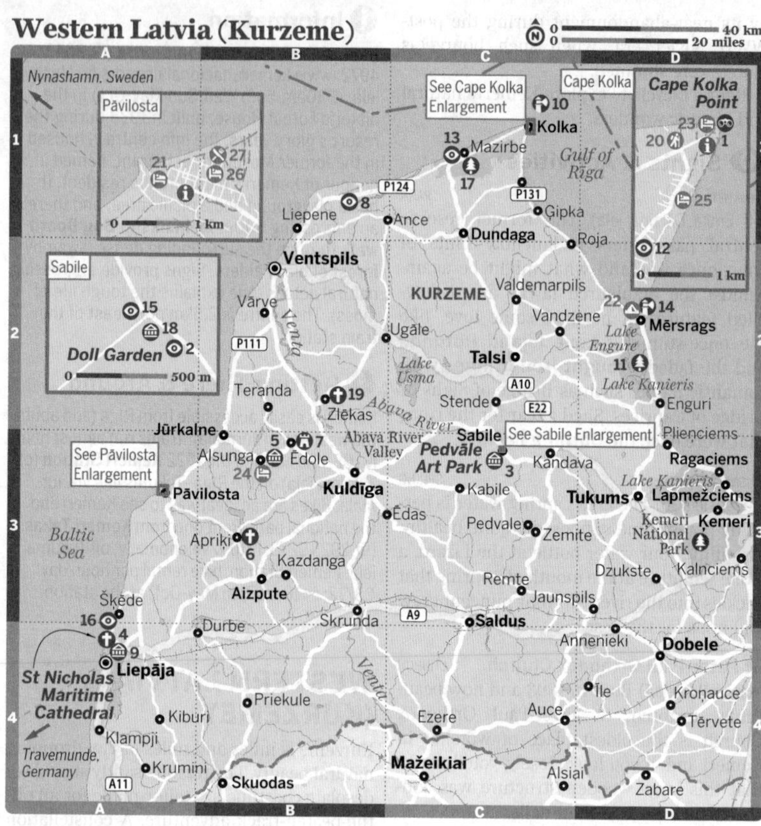


# Western Latvia (Kurzeme)

**Top Sights**

1 Cape Kolka Point .......... D1
2 Doll Garden .......... A2
3 Pedvāle Art Park .......... C3
4 St Nicholas Maritime Cathedral .......... A4

**Sights**

5 Alsunga District Museum .......... B3
6 Apriķi Lutheran Basilica .......... B3
7 Ēdoles Pils .......... B3
8 Irbene Radio Telescope .......... B1
9 Karosta Prison .......... A4
10 Kolka Lighthouse .......... C1
11 Lake Engure Nature Park .......... D2
12 Livonian Community House .......... D2
13 Livonian People's House .......... C1
14 Mērsrags Lighthouse .......... D2
15 Sabile Synagogue .......... A2
16 Šķēde Dunes Holocaust Memorial .......... A3
17 Slītere National Park .......... C1
18 Wooden Toy Museum .......... A2
19 Zlēku Baznīca .......... B2

**Activities, Courses & Tours**

20 Kolka Pine Trail .......... D1
Pāvilosta Serf Club .......... (see 21)
Rietumkrasts .......... (see 4)

**Sleeping**

21 Āķagals .......... A1
22 Noras .......... D2
23 Saules Mājas .......... D1
24 Spēlmaņu Krogs .......... B3
25 Ūši .......... D1
26 Vēju Paradize .......... B1

**Eating**

Sabiles Sidra Nams .......... (see 18)
Tējnīca Sapņotava .......... (see 24)
27 Wunderland .......... B1

## Kurzeme Gulf Coast

The coast along the Gulf of Rīga running to Kolka is a mix of windy, remote stretches and tiny fishing villages. Close to Jūrmala, a growing prosperity is evident in new holiday homes. It's a good place to get out in nature without straying far from the capital.

### Sights & Activities

The coast road sticks close to the water for almost all of the 123km between Jūrmala and Cape Kolka. The best way to see the sights is to pick a random road and head out to the water, which is invariably a calm, cerulean blue. The largest town, Roja (pop 3600), is little more than a small commercial fishing area.

**Lake Engure Nature Park** NATURE RESERVE
(☎6316 1701; http://eedp.lv; off P131, Bērzciems; 24hr) FREE The third-largest lake in Latvia, Engure is a bird haven with almost 200 species calling the lake home. The vistas stretch far to the horizon across the shallow waters, and the only sound you'll hear other than bird calls is the breeze in your ears. The 5km-long **Orchid Trail** runs along the lake shore and through the dense conifer forest. A boardwalk extends into the lake to a viewing tower. There are over 20 species of the namesake plants.

**Mērsrags Lighthouse** LIGHTHOUSE
(Mērsraga bāka; Bākas iela 60) Built in 1875 out of cast iron, this 21m-tall lighthouse stands over a popular **beach** that mixes gravel patches with white sand and dunes. The views of the gulf from this small point are sweeping.

### Sleeping & Eating

Going northwest along the gulf coast from Jūrmala, your sleeping options are limited. A few campgrounds, modest guesthouses and holiday rentals are all you'll find.

Between Jūrmala and Kolka on the gulf coast, eating opportunities dwindle right along with the population density, although you're never far from a basic supermarket. Be sure to save time for a stop in **Ragaciems**, where there's a pod of vendors right by the P128. Several sell myriad varieties of smoked fish while others specialise in tasty Latvian fare such as pickles, grilled meats and rye bread. It's truly picnic heaven.

★**Noras** CAMPGROUND €€
(☎2003 7000; https://noras.lv; Bākas iela 58, Mērsrags; cottages €70-90; May-Sep; P) What a beachside campground should be, the widely spaced sites in the shadow of the lighthouse are good for pitching tents. However, it's the cabins that really appeal: each sleeps four and has sleeper-sofas, a loft with a bed, kitchen facilities, a private bathroom and a nice terrace. You can rent stand-up paddleboards (SUPs), boats and bikes.

### Getting There & Away

Buses run in each direction along the gulf coast road (for most of its length, designated the P131) about every two hours. Riding nonstop from the Jūrmala area to Kolka will cost €5 and take about 2½ hours.

## Cape Kolka (Kolkasrags)

Enchantingly desolate and hauntingly beautiful, a journey to Cape Kolka (Kolkasrags) feels like a trip to the end of the earth. It's here that the Dižjūra (the Great Sea, or Baltic Sea) meets Mazjūra (the Little Sea – the Gulf of Rīga) in very dramatic fashion.

The village of Kolka, 1km south of the Cape, is spread out and bland, but it does have a good cultural centre and places to get food.

### Sights & Activities

The entire Cape Kolka region, including Slītere National Park (p239), is laced with hiking and cycling trails, especially along the beaches.

★**Cape Kolka Point** VIEWPOINT
(Cape Kolka; parking €1.50; 24hr; P) Watching the Baltic swells crash into the blue swells of the Gulf of Rīga is mesmerising. Find a spot away from the summertime crowds on the narrow beach; a 1km trail follows the beach southwest to the more serene environs of the Pine Trail, where there is uncrowded free parking. Local vendors sell crafts from small stalls.

**Kolka Lighthouse** LIGHTHOUSE
Centuries ago, bonfires were lit at the cape's tip to guide sailors around the protruding sandbar. Today, the solar-powered lighthouse guides vessels to safety. The scarlet tower, built in 1884, sits on an artificial island 6km offshore.

VALERIJS KOSTRECKIS/GETTY IMAGES ©

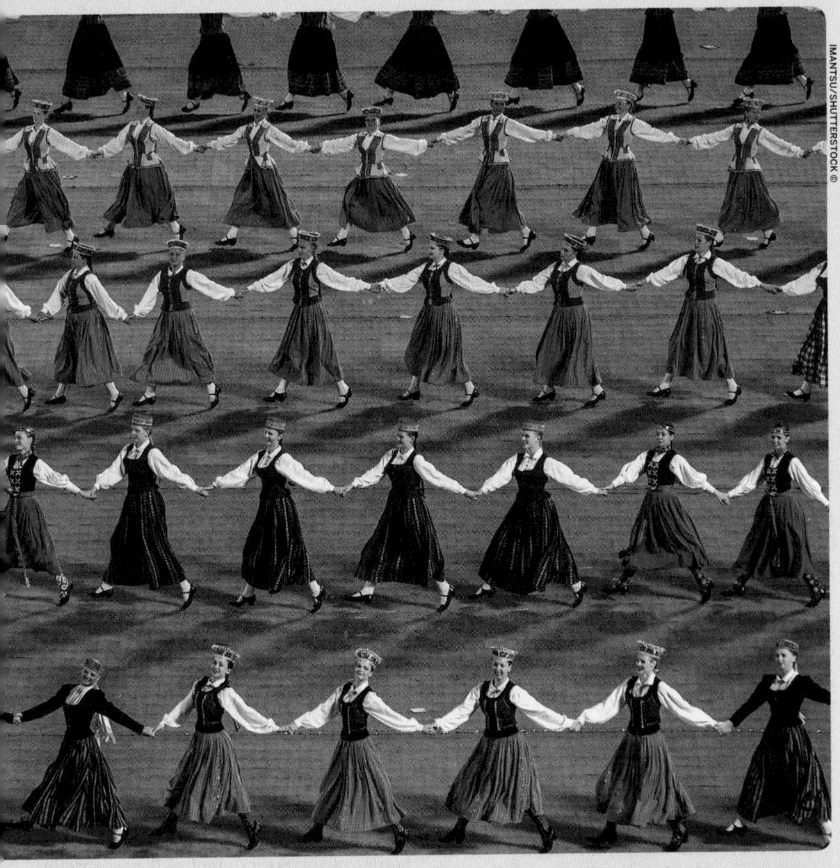

**1. Cēsis Castle (p266), Gauja National Park**
Explore the pretty grounds and dramatic towers of this medieval castle.

**2. Latvian Song and Dance Festival (p282), Rīga**
Celebrate traditional dance at this Unesco-recognised week-long festival, held every five years.

**3. Classic Latvian dishes (p283)**
Tuck into a nourishing bowl of grey peas – a national favourite.

**4. Pedvāle Art Park (p250), Sabile**
Walk among spectacular, large-scale artworks, such as *Chair,* a giant seat made from oil drums.

### THE LAST OF THE LIVS

Kurzeme is home to some of the last remaining Livs, Finno-Ugric peoples who first migrated to northern Latvia 5000 years ago. Although many Latvians are descended from this fishing tribe, fewer than 200 Livs remain in Latvia today, clustered in the fishing villages along the Baltic coast south of Cape Kolka. Hungary, Finland and Estonia also have small Liv populations, but they consider this area to be their homeland and return every August for the **Liv Festival** at the Livonian People's House in Mazirbe. Kolka also has a good Liv cultural centre.

**Livonian Community House** CULTURAL CENTRE
(☎2940 2093; http://livones.kolka.lv; P131, Kolka; ⏲9.30am-6pm daily Jun-Aug, 10am-5pm Tue-Sat Sep-May) FREE This modern centre provides a good introduction to local Livonian culture, including their love of berries, songs and their unique red-checked wool socks. There is also regional tourism info.

**Kolka Pine Trail** HIKING
(Cape Kolka, off P124) Over this 1.8km trail you'll experience Cape Kolka's virgin beaches, dunes and pine forest. The looping trail begins and ends at the free parking lot just northwest of the traffic circle where the P124 meets the P131. A highlight is the 15m-tall **watchtower** with grand views of the Cape.

## Sleeping & Eating

The Kolka area has some fun idiosyncratic places to sleep as well as holiday rentals.

Don't leave without stopping by one of the roadside stalls selling smoked fish. There is a small summer cafe at the Cape Kolka Point parking area and a supermarket in town for picnic and camping supplies.

**Ūši** GUESTHOUSE €
(☎2947 5692; www.kolka.info; off P131, Kolka; s/d €28/38, sites per person/car €4/2; P 📶) Across from the Russian Orthodox church and near the water, Ūši has two simple but prim rooms and a spot to pitch tents in the flower-filled garden. With advance notice, the very welcoming owner will prepare a meal with local specialities (€7). You can rent bikes (€8.50 per day) and camping gear.

**Saules Mājas** GUESTHOUSE €€
(☎2836 8830; http://saulesmajas.com; Cape Kolka; r €50; P) Accommodation here is in sea-facing barrel-shaped huts on a small dune under trees on the beach. The houses are quite charming and have one-way glass so you can enjoy the exceptional view but beachgoers can't enjoy you. There are shared toilets and showers in a separate building.

## Information

**Cape Kolka Visitors Centre** (☎2914 9105; http://kolkasrags.lv; Cape Kolka Point; ⏲10am-6pm daily May–mid-Oct, Fri-Sun mid-Oct–Apr; 📶) Small but good tourist office in the parking lot of Cape Kolka Point. Sells refreshments and simple snacks, and has good maps for hiking and cycling.

Livonian Community House in Kolka is another good source of info.

## Getting There & Away

The best way to explore Cape Kolka is with your own wheels.

To reach the town of Kolka from Rīga, buses (€6.25, 3½ to 4½ hours, five daily) either follow the gulf coast road via Roja, or run through Talsi and Dundaga (inland). To/from Kuldīga, Ventspils or Liepāja you must switch buses in Talsi.

# Northern Baltic Coast

During Soviet times the entire coast north of Ventspils was zoned off as a heavily guarded border of the Soviet empire. It was strictly out of bounds to civilians, lest they get in boats and sail to Sweden. The region's development was thus stunted and today the string of desolate coastal villages has a distinctly anachronistic feel – as though they've been locked away in a time capsule.

Today, this stagnation is a boon for visitors as the coast here has almost no development. The coast road (P124) links a quiet series of one-street villages like a string of pearls. Rusty Soviet remnants occasionally dot the landscape, but they feel more like abstract art installations than reminders of harder times. The west-facing beaches offer unforgettable sunsets over the churning sea and stark, sandy terrain.

## Sights & Activities

Superb 18th-century wooden buildings line the sand-paved streets in pleasant **Košrags**. The equally small **Mazirbe** has a gorgeous strip of dune-backed beach, typical of this coast. Hiking and biking trails wend along the sand, under the pines and back into the rolling terrain of the green hinterlands.

**Slītere National Park** NATIONAL PARK
(☎6328 6000; www.slitere.lv; off P125; parking free, lighthouse adult/child €1.50/0.70; ⊙lighthouse 10am-6pm Tue-Sun Jun-Aug) Slītere National Park protects 265 sq km of land back from the coast on the Kolka peninsula. The park's focal point is the **Slītere Lighthouse**, a towering red spire that acts as the gatekeeper to the park's rugged, often tundra-like expanse, home to wild deer, elk, buzzards and beavers. Displays at the lighthouse detail the rich natural beauty and history of the region. There are many hiking trails.

The **Slītere Nature Trail** starts at the lighthouse and runs for 2.2km. Part is on a boardwalk through lush wetlands, while another section wends through 100-year-old pines shading vast expanses of ferns.

**Irbene Radio Telescope** HISTORIC SITE
(VIRAC, Irbenes radioteleskops; ☎2923 0818; http://virac.venta.lv/en; off P124, Irbene; adult/child €7/4; ⊙hours vary Jun-Oct) This Cold War–era site contains a large radio telescope now run by an academic institute and used for astronomical studies. Hidden in the forest 24km north of Ventspils, the Irbene facility was used by the Soviets to spy on American satellites. Today, the huge 600-tonne, 32m-dish mounted on a 25m-tall concrete base is open at certain times for tours. To visit, call or email at least three days in advance to book a spot on a tour.

You can also stop by the building the tours depart from to see if they have any spots available on the day. Just driving into Irbene is an adventure as you pass by blocks of abandoned Soviet housing that look like Chernobyl.

**Livonian People's House** CULTURAL CENTRE
(Livlist rovkuoda; ☎2860 3233; Mazirbe; ⊙11am-4pm Jun-Aug) FREE Opened with great pride in 1939, this art deco-ish cultural centre hosts gatherings of Liv descendants (the Liv Festival on the first Saturday in August draws crowds from the Livonian diaspora worldwide) and has exhibitions on their culture. In summer there's usually a small cafe that opens.

### Getting There & Around

There's no public transport along the 80km-long coast road (P124) between Kolka and Ventspils so you'll need your own wheels.

## Ventspils

POP 38,100

Outside of Rīga, Ventspils is one of Latvia's most dynamic cities. It has a gentrifying waterfront that's replacing a grim industrial past and a long beach backed by lovely parklands. Take a dip in the Baltic, relax on the sands, ride a bike through the dunes, visit a museum, imbibe at a cafe and soon you'll discover a couple of days have passed.

This big and busy port has a maritime legacy that dates back to the 13th century. It was a key member of the Hanseatic League through the 16th century and a vital ice-free port in Soviet times.

### Sights & Activities

With a detour or two around industrial sites, the walk west from the centre along the south bank of the Venta River passes by historic fishing boats and offers a fascinating dip into the city's maritime past. Eventually you'll reach the Southern Promenade after passing through the old **Ostgals** neighbourhood, which recalls when Ventspils was merely a humble fishing village dotted with wooden abodes.

Sights are just spread out enough that exploring Ventspils by bike is both practical and rewarding.

★**Ventspils Beach** BEACH
For Ventspils, the wide stretch of dazzling white sand south of the Venta River is its main treasure. During the warmer months, beach bums of every ilk – from nudists to kiteboarders – line the pristine Blue Flag sands to absorb the sun's rays. It's backed by a belt of dunes and a lush manicured park.

**Southern Promenade** PIER
Extending out into the Baltic Sea, the Southern Promenade follows a breakwater with thrilling views of huge freighters passing close by. The walk is capped by a lighthouse and anchored by Ventspils beach.

**Seaside Open-Air Museum** MUSEUM
(Piejūras brīvdabas muzejs; ☎6362 4467; http://muzejs.ventspils.lv; Riņka iela 2; adult/child museum €2.50/1.50, train €3/2; ⊙10am-6pm

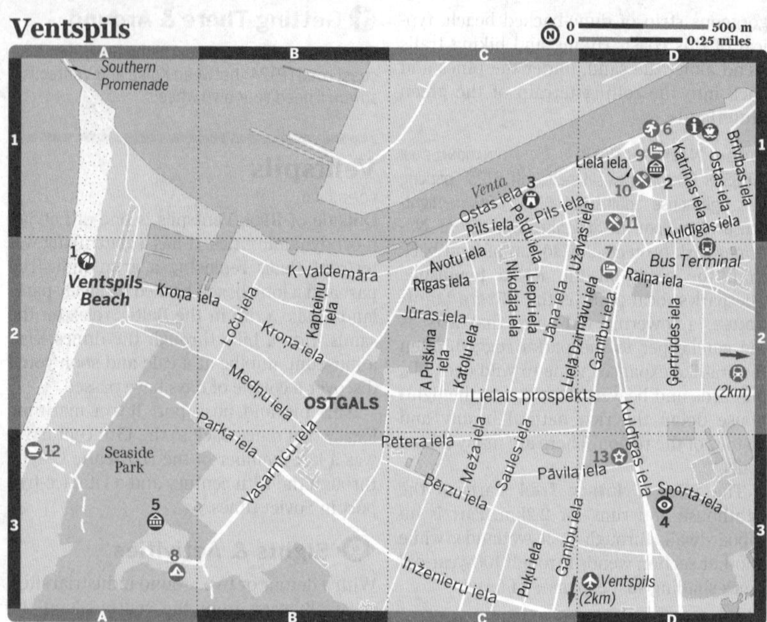


## Ventspils

**Top Sights**
1 Ventspils Beach ........ A2

**Sights**
2 House of Crafts ........ D1
3 Livonian Order Castle ........ C1
4 Reņka Garden ........ D3
5 Seaside Open-Air Museum ........ A3

**Activities, Courses & Tours**
6 Hecogs Jēkabs Boat ........ D1
Vent Velo ........ (see 8)

**Sleeping**
7 Kupfernams ........ D2
8 Piejūras Kempings ........ A3
9 Viesu Nams Zītari ........ D1

**Eating**
10 Kārumnieks ........ D1
Krogs Zītari ........ (see 9)
11 Skroderkrogs ........ D1

**Drinking & Nightlife**
12 Surf Saulīte ........ A3

**Entertainment**
13 Concert Hall Latvia ........ D3

Tue-Sun May-Oct, by appointment winter) For centuries, life in Kurzeme revolved around seafaring and fishing. Occupying vast parkland territory, this museum features a collection of fishing crafts, anchors and traditional log houses, brought from nearby coastal villages. A bonus attraction is a narrow-gauge railway, which recreates a line built by the occupying Germans in 1916. The route runs for over 2km through the city's parks.

**Livonian Order Castle** CASTLE
(Livonijas ordeņa pils; 6362 2031; www.ventspilsmuzejs.lv; Jāņa iela 17; adult/child €3/1.50; 10am-6pm Tue-Sun) This blocky building doesn't look obviously castle-like from the outside, but the 13th-century interior is home to an entertaining interactive local history and art museum. During Soviet rule the castle was used as a prison, and an exhibit in the stables recounts its horrors.

**House of Crafts** MUSEUM
(Amatu māja; 6362 0174; Skolas iela 3; adult/child €1/0.50; 10am-6pm Tue-Sat) Visitors can learn about the handicrafts of Kurzeme

in this 18th-century school building. Watch local artisans spin yarns (literally) and clay bowls, before purchasing something to take home.

**Hecogs Jēkabs Boat** BOATING
(☎2635 3344; cnr Ostas iela & Tirgus iela; adult/child from €1.60/0.70; ⊙May-Oct) This two-level boat sails around the mouth of the Venta River on 45-minute excursions that get close to the port action. Longer trips sail up the river.

**Vent Velo** CYCLING
(☎2758 3888; http://ventvelo.lv; Vasarnīcu iela 56; bicycle rental per hour €2.50; ⊙8am-8pm) Located at Piejūras Kempings, this place has a range of bikes and related gear available. Ask for a map showing all the routes along the beaches and waterfront.

## Sleeping

**Piejūras Kempings** CAMPGROUND €
(☎6362 7925; www.camping.ventspils.lv; Vasarnīcu iela 56; sites per person €5, 4-person cottage from €58; @) This charming campus of grassy campsites and pine cottages is in a park not far from the beach. There's an on-site laundry and bicycle rental, plus tennis, volleyball and basketball courts.

**Kupfernams** B&B €
(☎2767 7107; www.hotelkupfernams.lv; Kārļa iela 5; s/d from €25/35; ) This charming vintage wooden house in the centre of Ventspils has a set of cheery upstairs rooms with slanted ceilings opening onto a communal lounge. Below, there's a cafe and a hair salon (which doubles as the reception).

**Viesu Nams Zītari** GUESTHOUSE €€
(☎2570 8337; www.facebook.com/KrogsZitari; Tirgus iela 11; r from €50) There are several well-appointed rooms in this 300-year-old timber-framed house adjoining the popular Krogs Zītari beer garden. The location on the market square can't be more central. Rooms have a woodsy theme, from the floors to the modern furniture.

## Eating & Drinking

Be sure to enjoy a locally brewed Užavas beer.

★**Kārumnieks** BAKERY €
(☎2942 4860; www.facebook.com/pg/ventspilskarumnieks; Lielā iela 20; mains from €3; ⊙9am-6pm Mon-Sat) Buy a treat for your stroll along the waterfront or just escape the drizzle in the warm confines of this old family-run bakery known for its tasty cakes, pastries, chocolates and more.

**Krogs Zītari** LATVIAN €€
(☎2570 8337; www.facebook.com/KrogsZitari; Tirgus iela 11; mains €7-15; ⊙noon-10pm) Tucked in the courtyard of a pretty timber-framed German house, this beer garden serves large portions of meat- and seafood-heavy fare.

**Skroderkrogs** LATVIAN €€
(☎6362 7634; Skroderu iela 6; mains €6-13; ⊙11am-10pm) Enjoy Latvian comfort food in a leafy park setting. The terrace is a summer delight, while inside there's a vintage vibe with lashings of rural charm. The fresh seafood is always good.

**Surf Saulīte** CAFE
(Ventspils Beach; ⊙10am-10pm Jun-Aug) Right on the sand, this summer cafe serves up smoothies, good coffee, draft beer and ice cream. Hang out under the awning or take in the rays on the rooftop deck.

## Entertainment

**Concert Hall Latvia** CONCERT VENUE
(Koncertzāle Latvija; ☎2654 6213; www.koncertzalelatvija.lv; Lielais prospekts 1) A stunning architectural statement, this new concert and music hall hosts everything from pop to classical performances.

## Information

**Tourist Information Centre** (☎6362 2263; www.visitventspils.com; Dārzu iela 6; ⊙8am-7pm Mon-Fri, 10am-7pm Sat, 10am-4pm Sun Jun-Aug, 8am-6pm Mon-Fri, 10am-4pm Sat & Sun Sep-May; ) An excellent and friendly resource in the ferry terminal.

## Getting There & Away

Ventspils' **bus terminal** (☎6362 9904; Kuldīgas iela 5) has services to/from Rīga (€7.55, three to four hours, hourly), Kuldīga (€3, 1¼ hours, six daily) and Liepāja (€5.20, 2¼ to three hours, six daily) via Jūrkalne.

Stena Line (www.stenaline.lv) operates a ferry service to Nynäshamn, Sweden (passenger from €19, car and driver from €49, 8½ hours), one to two times daily from the modern ferry terminal.

# Pāvilosta

POP 3100

This sleepy beach town, located halfway between Ventspils and Liepāja, exudes a chilled-out California surfer vibe despite its location on the chilly Baltic Sea. Summer

## AN ISLAND OF SUITI CULTURE

In the middle of a rough triangle formed by Ventspils, Kuldīga and Liepāja is an island of Catholicism in the middle of Lutheran Kurzeme. The Suiti people here speak a distinct dialect and stick to their traditions: at least some of the locals show up for Sunday mass in their centuries-old traditional attire, which includes a kind of tartan poncho worn by women over scarlet dresses.

At the very heart of Suiti identity lies singing. What experts call 'many-voiced drone' is interrupted with a kind of rap, in which the soloist satirises those present in the audience for looking untidy, absent-minded or lazy. The text is entirely improvisational.

The capital of the Suiti is Alsunga, which is 12km east of another Suiti village, Jūrkalne, which lies on the main coastal road (P111).

days are filled with windsurfing, kiteboarding, surfing and sailing interspersed with beach naps and beers. Evenings are long and languid. Rent a holiday apartment and sit back amidst the hum of crickets.

The tourist office can line up a local source for water-sports activities. Few have any fixed addresses, as more often than not, they're out enjoying the surf. From a weathered garage at the end of the town's main drag, **Pāvilosta Serf Club** (2644 4934; dagnisb@windsurf.lv; Dzintaru iela 1; hours vary) rents gear for riding the Baltic.

## Sleeping & Eating

**Vēju Paradize** INN €€

(2644 6644; www.veju-paradize.lv; Smilšu iela 14; s/d from €45/50; restaurant 2-9pm daily Jun-Aug, Sat & Sun May & Sep; P) 'Wind Paradise' has 17 tidy rooms that are simple, yet feel distinctly beachy. Aloe plants are a clever touch, especially if you've spent one too many hours splashing around in the sea. Vēju's on-site restaurant, open during summer, features fresh seafood and European cuisine. Guests enjoy a fabulous breakfast buffet.

The place runs a fleet of traditional wooden boats, available for hire.

**Āķagals** GUESTHOUSE €€

(2202 3242; www.facebook.com/aakagals; Dzintaru iela 3; r from €45, mains €5-8; restaurant noon-7pm; P) By night, listen to the surf crashing just over the dune from your room, which is finished in all-natural wood. By day, enjoy stacks of delicious Latvian cuisine on varnished picnic tables made from thick logs. There's a large swing set, windswept dunes and a lookout tower out the back to keep you busy while you await your meal.

★ **Wunderland** CAFE €

(2258 9000; Kalna iela 43; mains €4-9, campsite €2; 11am-11pm Jun-Aug; P) This bamboo hut is one of the best places on the coast to revel in the summer beach vibe. Right on the beach, it's a surfer hang-out where you can hear groovy tunes late into the night courtesy of the loaner guitar. They make their own cranberry juice, cider, kombucha and even gin. Lunch specials change daily and range from burgers to vegan.

Campsites are on a sandy expanse and are bargain priced.

## Information

**Tourist Office** (www.pavilosta.lv; Dzintaru iela 2; 7.30am-9pm Jun-Aug, to 7pm Sep-May) Located along the main road to the docks, near the bus stop.

## Getting There & Away

Intercity buses link Pāvilosta to Liepāja (€2.65, one hour, four daily) and Ventspils (€3.25, one hour, four daily). Buses stop in front of the tourist office.

# Liepāja

POP 69,400

Liepāja doesn't fit any cliche – it's a port city of gritty red-brick warehouses with a gentrifying waterfront, and home to both a notorious old Soviet prison and one of the country's most beautiful beaches. Its rough-around-the-edges vibe translates into grungy musical sounds that reflect the city's own slow self-discovery.

Founded by the Livonian Order in the 13th century, Latvia's third-largest city only flourished after Tsar Alexander III deepened the harbour and built a gargantuan naval port at the end of the 1800s. After WWII, the Soviets occupied what was left of the bombed-out city and turned it into a vast strategic military base, the legacy of which is still crumbling today.

## Sights & Activities

Walk along Liepāja's waterfront to see where the city has been and where it's going. Head north for its post-apocalyptic Soviet legacy and to the beach for fun and frolic.

### City Centre & Waterfront

Liepāja's city centre is an uneven mix of old and new, but the parks are lovely. The **Port Promenade** along the south bank of the Tirdzniecības Canal is well worth a stroll. Walk west from Rīgas iela bridge and check out the growing collection of historic naval boats, old trawlers and modern tugs moored amidst eddies of gentrification.

**Peter's Market** MARKET
(☎6342 3517; http://petertirgus.lv; Kuršu iela 5; ⏲8am-6pm Mon-Sat, to 4pm Sun) Vendors have touted their wares here since the mid-17th century. The market expanded in 1910, when an art nouveau–style pavilion was constructed adjacent to the square. Today you'll find stalls inside and out at this bustling complex, selling everything from second-hand clothes and beautiful handicrafts to fresh, locally grown produce and baked goods.

**House of Craftsmen** MUSEUM
(☎2654 1424; www.saivaart.com; Dārza iela 4/8; ⏲10am-5pm Mon-Fri) FREE Check out the largest piece of amber art in the world, plus legions of old women knitting scarves, mittens and blankets available for purchase. The jeweller, based on the 2nd floor, makes unusual (and beautiful) earrings and necklaces.

**Liepāja Museum** MUSEUM
(Liepājas muzejs; ☎2960 5223; www.liepajasmuzejs.lv; Kūrmājas prospekts 16; ⏲10am-6pm) FREE Features a variety of impressive displays, such as an interactive exhibit that brings to life the tough lives of people living in the South Kurzeme in the 19th century. Another recalls the six months in 1918 and 1919 when Liepāja was the capital of Latvia as the nation fought for its independence.

**Liepāja Under Occupation Museum** MUSEUM
(☎6342 0274; K Ukstiņa iela 7; ⏲10am-6pm Wed-Sun) FREE Traces the bloody history of the Soviet and Nazi occupations in Latvia, with an emphasis on Liepāja. Captions are in Latvian, but no words are needed to explain the powerful images of the 1939–40 deportations to Siberia (an estimated 2000 people from Liepāja were deported), the genocide committed against Latvian Jews (over 5000 massacred in and around the city) and the 1991 fight for independence.

### Beach

A green belt acts as a buffer between the soft white dunes and tatty urban core.

★**Liepāja Beach** BEACH
This Blue Flag beach is a fabulous place for a dip. The fine white sand is over 50m in width and the shore stretches for 8km. In summer you'll find a few beach cafes and water-sports operators.

**Seaside Park** PARK
(Jūrmalas Park) Ancient trees, manicured flower beds, water features, elegant walkways and cycling trails make this 3km-long park the very definition of an urban oasis. To the east are the once-elegant 19th-century wooden holiday homes, to the west are the shimmering sands of the beach. Festivals large and small are held here all summer long.

### Karosta

Off limits to everyone during the Soviet occupation, Karosta, 4km north of central Liepāja, is a former Russian naval base encompassing about one-third of Liepāja's

OFF THE BEATEN TRACK

#### ŠĶĒDE DUNES HOLOCAUST MEMORIAL

The beauty obscures the horror. Some 10km north of Liepāja, off a long dirt coastal road, is a **memorial** (off Lībiešu iela, Šķēde) at a place of death. Amidst a flawless white-sand beach and dunes protected by pine forests, there is a large memorial to the more than 3000 local Jews shot here by the Nazis from September 1941 to February 1942. Signs show blurry photos of terrified men, women and children moments before they were killed. The open area is dominated by a 2005 sculpture that stretches across gravel and forms a Star of David. It's a contemplative spot, the silence only broken by the sound of the sea.

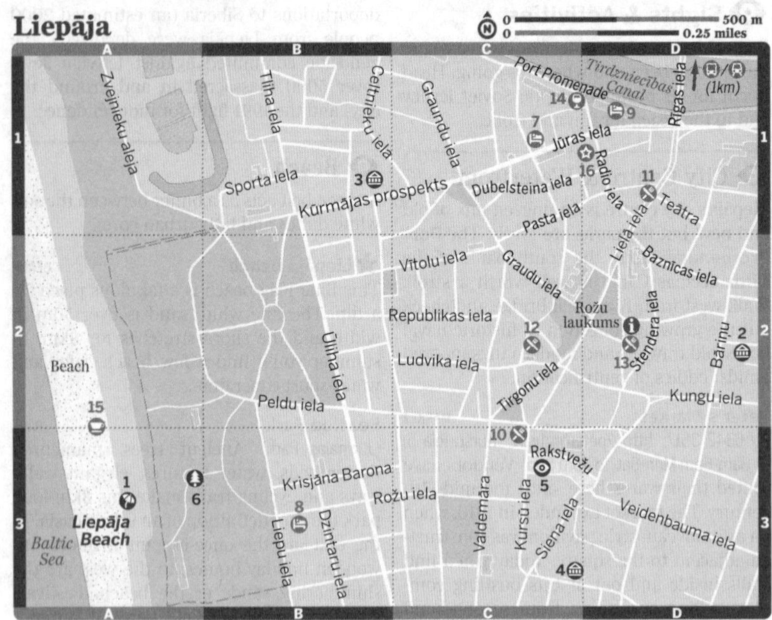


## Liepāja

**Top Sights**
1 Liepāja Beach .......... A3

**Sights**
2 House of Craftsmen .......... D2
3 Liepāja Museum .......... B1
4 Liepāja Under Occupation Museum .......... C3
5 Peter's Market .......... C3
6 Seaside Park .......... A3

**Sleeping**
7 Fontaine Hotel .......... C1
8 Hotel Roze .......... B3
9 Promenade Hotel .......... D1

**Eating**
10 Boulangerie Liepāja .......... C3
11 Kafejnīca Darbnīca .......... D1
12 Pastnieka Māja .......... C2
13 Roma Beķereja .......... D2

**Drinking & Nightlife**
14 Fontaine Palace .......... C1
15 Red Sun Buffet Beach Bar .......... A2

**Entertainment**
16 Great Amber Concert Hall .......... D1

city limits. From ageing army barracks to ugly Soviet-style concrete apartment blocks (many abandoned), evidence of the occupation still remains. As sights are fairly far apart, Karosta is best explored by bicycle or car. There is a nice beach, so take your swimsuit along.

**★ St Nicholas Maritime Cathedral** CHURCH
(www.morskoj-sobor.lv; Katedrāles iela 7; ⏲8am-5pm & during evening services) **FREE** The stunning cathedral, with its bulbous cupolas, shines like a precious stone through the grey concrete of the decrepit Soviet apartment blocks that surround it on all sides. Built in 1901 in the Russian revival style, the cathedral was restored in the 1990s. Proper attire is required (no shorts etc).

**Karosta Prison** HISTORIC BUILDING
(Karostas cietums; ☎2636 9470; www.karostascietums.lv; Invalīdu iela 4; adult/child €6/4.50; ⏲9am-7pm daily Jun-Aug, 10am-6pm daily May & Sep, noon-4pm Sat & Sun Oct-Apr) Gluttons for punishment will get a bellyful in this creepy old Soviet-era prison, which operated right up until 1997. Built in 1900 as an infirmary, it was quickly turned into a military prison, even before the building

was completed. Tours depart on the hour, detailing the history of the prison, which was used to punish disobedient soldiers. A range of more extreme 'experiences' is also on offer for groups of 10 or more (booking essential).

**Rietumkrasts** WATER SPORTS
(☎2918 7779; http://rietumkrasts.lv; Ziemeļu mols, Karosta; kiteboard rental per hour €10; ⊙noon-7pm) Just north of one of Karosta's main breakwaters, this water-sports outfit has a fine position at the south end of a long beach. Rentals include kiteboards, surfboards, SUPs, kayaks and e-bikes. The on-site cafe has a beach view and serves fresh takes on Latvian standards.

## Festivals & Events

**Summer Sound** MUSIC
(https://summersound.lv; Seaside Park; ⊙early Aug) Rock, hip-hop and electronic music reverberate off the dunes at this big two-day festival near the beach.

## Sleeping

**Fontaine Hotel** GUESTHOUSE €
(☎6342 0956; www.fontaine.lv; Jūras iela 24; r with/without bathroom from €40/25; P 📶) This funky place set in a charming 18th-century wooden house feels like a second-hand store, from the kitschy knick-knack shop used as the reception to the 20-plus rooms stuffed to the brim with rock memorabilia, dusty oriental rugs, bright tile mosaics, Soviet propaganda and anything else deemed appropriately offbeat. There's a communal kitchen and chill-out space in the basement.

★**Hotel Roze** GUESTHOUSE €€
(☎6342 1155; https://en.parkhotelliepaja.lv; Rožu iela 37; r €48-70; P 📶) Stylish and comfortable, this pale-blue wooden guesthouse near the sea was once a 19th-century summer home for the elite, and still has a certain art nouveau styling. Rooms are spacious, and each is uniquely decorated with antique wallpaper and sheer drapery. There's a fine garden, good views of Seaside Park and a small restaurant.

**Promenade Hotel** LUXURY HOTEL €€€
(☎6348 8288; www.promenadehotel.lv; Vecā Ostmala 40; r €80-150; P ❄ 📶) The poshest hotel in Kurzeme is in an enormous harbour warehouse that was once used to store grain. Many rooms have grand views of the port, and all have sedate decor with comfortable, traditionally styled furniture. As you'd guess, the hotel is on the promenade.

## Eating

The best place to browse for food and drink is along the Port Promenade.

**Roma Beķereja** BAKERY €
(☎2636 2233; https://arthotelroma.lv; Zivju iela 3; snacks from €3; ⊙8am-6pm) Attached to the stylish Art Hotel Roma, this Italian-style cafe has a fabulous terrace on Liepāja's main drag. The coffee is suitably excellent and there are many delectable pastry and sandwich choices.

**Kafejnīca Darbnīca** CAFE €
(☎2681 1313; www.facebook.com/darbnicacafe/; Lielā iela 8; mains €4-6; ⊙9am-9pm Mon & Tue, to 11pm Wed & Thu, to 2am Fri, 10am-2am Sat, 11am-5pm Sun) A local hipster hang-out, this cafeteria-cum-bar serves burgers, Asian noodle dishes and Latvian faves. At night it turns into a bar with a great selection of Latvian beers on tap and a good soundtrack. The decor is retro and funky.

**Boulangerie Liepāja** BAKERY €
(www.boulangerie.lv; Kuršu ielā 2; mains €5; ⊙10am-7pm Mon-Sat, to 6pm Sun) In the morning you'll see croissant and coffee addicts hanging around outside the door waiting for this tiny place to open. A queue inevitably forms as staff lay out freshly baked pastry, eclairs and macaroons. On a warm day, try to get a seat on the roof terrace. There is also a menu of more filling dishes such as omelettes.

**Pastnieka Māja** LATVIAN €€
(Postman's House; ☎6340 7521; www.pastniekamaja.lv; Brīvzemnieka iela 53; mains €7-15; ⊙11am-11pm) This polished two-level restaurant with a big and inviting terrace is housed in the city's old post office. The menu features traditional Latvian favourites, as well as crowd-pleasers like Caesar salad and various pastas. Order a pint of Līvu Alus, the local beer.

## Drinking & Entertainment

Liepāja is the centre of Latvia's rock-music scene. Its gritty surrounds have fuelled decades of bands famous and obscure. Taking in a concert with a sweaty, heaving crowd is a must.

★**Fontaine Palace** BAR
(☎6348 8510; www.fontainepalace.lv; Dzirnavu iela 4; ⊙24hr) A legendary music venue across

the Baltics, there is live music almost every night in this former port warehouse. The never-closing bar extends over two levels and out onto a big terrace. Management also runs a couple of adjoining food venues, including the cheap and somewhat cheerful munchies-satisfying **Delisnack**.

**Red Sun Buffet Beach Bar** CAFE
(www.facebook.com/redsunbuffet; Liepāja Beach) The beach outpost of the popular city-centre cafe brings a bit of style to the strand. Grab a seat on the large covered patio that opens on to the Baltic or snap up a lounger on the sand. It's open all year, so you can watch storms brew over the Baltic. It's west of the tennis courts.

**Great Amber Concert Hall** CONCERT VENUE
(Koncertzāle Lielais Dzintars; ☎6342 4555; http://lielaisdzintars.lv; Radio iela 8) This bold seven-storey concert hall is a vision in amber glass that's meant to mark the start of a shinier future for Liepāja. It books all manner of acts, from music to theatre.

## Information

**Tourist Information Centre** (☎2940 2111; www.liepaja.travel; Rožu laukums 5/6; ⊙9am-7pm Mon-Fri, 10am-6pm Sat, 10am-4pm Sun) A comprehensive centre for local and regional information. Has tour information and routes.

## Getting There & Around

**Liepāja Bus Station** (☎6342 2754; Rīgas iela 71) is linked by tram 1 with Lielā iela in the centre. Bus services include Rīga (€9, 3½ to 4½ hours, two to three hourly), Kuldīga (€4, 1¾ to 2½ hours, seven daily) and Ventspils (€5.20, 2¼ to three hours, six daily).

Stena Line operates ferries to Travemünde, Germany (passenger from €26, car and driver from €79, 28 hours, four weekly).

The optimistically named Liepāja International Airport has one flight five days a week to/from Rīga on Air Baltic.

The Tourist Information Centre rents bicycles for €2 per hour and €10 per day.

# Kuldīga

POP 12,900

Lovely Kuldīga would be a hit even if it didn't have its own Niagara of sorts, what Latvians rather archly call 'the widest waterfall in Europe'. Kuldīga is remarkably well preserved and it's easy to feel the centuries slip away as you wander its historic streets, chill in its inviting parks and scamper along its riverside paths.

In its heyday, Kuldīga (or Goldingen, as its German founders called it) served as the capital of the Duchy of Courland (1596–1616), but it was badly damaged during the Great Northern War and never quite able to regain its former lustre. Today, this blast from the past may easily be one of your favourite Latvian discoveries.

## Sights

Pedestrianised Liepajas iela is Old Town's main commercial drag. It's an uneven but visually interesting mix of buildings from the 17th through the 20th centuries. The south end of Baznīcas iela presents a tableau of restored buildings that looks like a 19th-century impressionist painting.

**★Old Brick Bridge** BRIDGE
(Kuldīgas ķieģeļu tilts; Stendes iela) The vaulted arches of the 1874 red-brick bridge are one of Kuldīga's favourite sites. At 154m, it's the third-longest brick bridge in Europe.

**★Kuldīga Waterfall** WATERFALL
(Ventas Rumba) Spanning 249m, Ventas Rumba is branded Europe's widest waterfall, though it's far from the tallest. Its subtle beauty becomes compelling the longer you look at it and enjoy the sparkling river, the calming sound of tonnes of water cascading over the precipice and the refreshing feel of the mist on a summer day.

In spring, crowds come from near and far to watch vimba (a type of migratory bream) jump the falls on their migration from the Baltic.

**Town Garden** PARK
(Pils iela) Finely manicured and with great views of the waterfall, Kuldīga's park has multifaceted appeal. Moody **castle ruins** from the 13th century are watched over by the 1735 **Castle Watchman's House** (Pils iela 4). Legend has it that the house was the site of executions and beheadings during various violent interludes. Pause to appreciate the 22 large stone sculptures in the park carved by the late Līvija Rezevska. These evocative pieces have names like Granny, Love and the Piper.

In summer, the Kuldīga District Museum sponsors the **Goldingen Knight open-air cinema**, which screens films on Friday and Saturday nights one hour after sunset. For schedules, see www.kuldigasmuzejs.lv/s41.

## Kuldīga

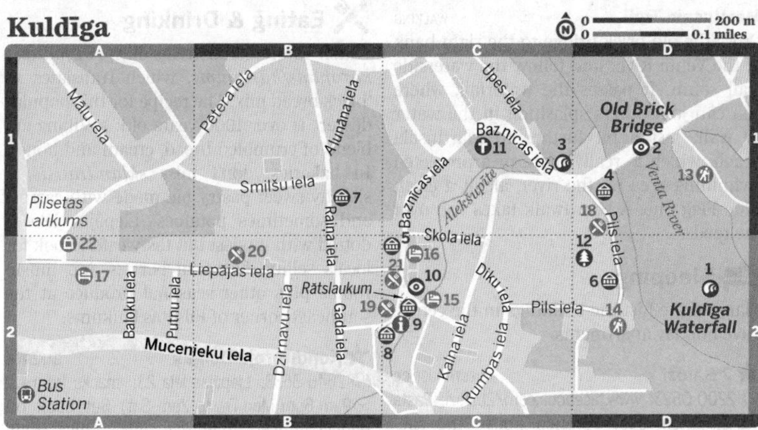


### Kuldīga

**Top Sights**
1 Kuldīga Waterfall D2
2 Old Brick Bridge D1

**Sights**
3 Alekšupīte Waterfall C1
4 Castle Watchman's House D1
5 Duke Jakob's Pharmacy C2
6 Kuldīga Historic Museum D2
7 Kuldīga Synagogue B1
8 New Town Hall C2
9 Old Town Hall C2
10 Old Wooden House C2
11 St Katrīna's Church C1
12 Town Garden D2

**Activities, Courses & Tours**
13 Mārtiņsala Trail D1
14 River Venta Trail D2

**Sleeping**
15 2 Baloži C2
16 Hotel Metropole C2
17 Jēkaba Sēta A2

**Eating**
18 Bangert's D1
19 Goldingen Room C2
20 Konditoreja Daigas B2
21 Kursas Zeme C2
Pagrabiņš (see 9)

**Shopping**
22 Kuldīgas Labumi A2

**Kuldīga Historic Museum** MUSEUM
(Kuldīgas novada muzejs; ☎6335 0179; www.kuldigasmuzejs.lv; Pils iela; ⏰10am-6pm Tue-Sun) FREE This engaging museum is housed in what a local legend 'claims' was a Russian pavilion from the 1900 World Exhibition in Paris. The 2nd floor recreates the apartment of a rich early-20th-century local family and features an international playing-cards collection in the 'master's room'.

**St Katrīna's Church** CHURCH
(☎6332 4394; http://kuldigas.lelb.lv; Baznīcas iela 31/33; €0.50; ⏰11am-5pm May-Sep) The most important church in town: Katrina (St Catherine) is Kuldīga's patron saint and protector, and is featured on the town's coat of arms. The church dates to 1252 and was rebuilt in the mid-1600s. Inside it's atmospherically musty; you can climb the tower for good views. The stroll from here to the Town Garden is a delight.

**Alekšupīte Waterfall** WATERFALL
(off Baznīcas iela) Disappointed in the modest height of Kuldīga's waterfall? Head over to what is – yes! – Latvia's tallest waterfall (4.2m). Sure it's lined with concrete and was once used for a mill, but the cascade is one more tick in the town's checklist of charm.

## Activities

**River Venta Trail** WALKING
(Pils iela) This beautiful signposted path starts south of the Town Garden and follows the course of the Venta River past the falls for 2.4km. It ends at the Ganību iela bridge over the river.

**Mārtiņsala Trail** WALKING

Cross the old brick bridge to the right bank of the Venta River and follow the waterside trail south. It passes the waterfall, where you can join others splashing in the water or walk just a bit further to Mārtiņsala beach, which is really more of a protected swimming area on the river, albeit a clean Blue Flag one. A boardwalk takes you over the reeds.

## Sleeping

Many of the historic buildings in the centre have holiday apartments.

**★ 2 Baloži** GUESTHOUSE €€

(2200 0523; www.facebook.com/2balozi; Pasta iela 5; r from €45) Perched above the Alekšupite stream, this old wooden house has rooms designed in the laconic Scandinavian style with lots of weathered wood, creating a contemporary yet nostalgic ambience.

**Jēkaba Sēta** GUESTHOUSE €€

(2863 1122; www.jekabaseta.lv; Liepājas iela 36; s/d from €37/44; P) This typical Latvian inn, complete with a pub, has standard-looking rooms with wooden furniture. The location is on the main pedestrian strip near the edge of Old Town.

**Hotel Metropole** HOTEL €€

(6335 0588; www.hotel-metropole.lv; Baznīcas iela 11; r from €65; P) Featuring a modern pale palette, the rooms here are spacious, especially the double-decker ones overlooking pedestrian Rātslaukums. This is Kuldīga's main full-service hotel.

## Eating & Drinking

Watch for regional treats like *rupjmaizes kārojums/kārtojums,* which translates as 'black bread mix'. The recipe for this popular dessert is over 1000 years old: a Viking-era blend of crumbled bread, cream and honey. In bakeries, don't miss *sklandrausis,* a slightly sweet pastry pie made with carrots and sometimes potatoes. Liepājas iela is dotted with modest but tasty cafes. Look for locals selling beautiful berries and mushrooms plus other seasonal produce at the southeast corner of Pilsētas laukums.

**★ Konditoreja Daigas** BAKERY €

(2646 3533; Liepājas iela 23; snacks from €1; 9am-6pm Mon-Fri, to 2pm Sat) Set back off pedestrianised Liepājas iela, this small one-woman bakery has fabulous baked goods at amazing prices. In between customers, the baker can be seen working her magic in the tiny kitchen. Tarts, pastries, rolls and more are fresh from the oven. The choices vary through the day. Coffee is good and there are a couple of tables.

**Kursas Zeme** CAFE €€

(2960 1000; Baznīcas iela 6; mains €8-20; 10am-10pm Sun-Thu, to 11pm Fri & Sat) This sprightly modern cafe serves good burgers, pasta, salads and other crowd-pleasers. The *kiploku grauzdiņi* (Latvian garlic bread) is superb. There's a full bar with a creative drinks menu and good coffee.

**Pagrabiņš** PUB FOOD €€

(6632 0034; www.pagrabins.lv; Baznīcas iela 5; mains €5-15; 11am-11pm Mon-Thu, to 3am

### KULDĪGA'S HISTORIC BUILDINGS

Kuldīga has many notable structures dotting the centre. Go on a stroll to discover these and others.

**Old Town Hall** (Rātslaukums) This renovated 16th-century wood building is now home to the Tourist Information Centre. Outside, a statue popular for selfies portrays Evalds Valters, a beloved film star.

**New Town Hall** (Rātslaukums 5) Built in 1860 in Italian Renaissance style, the New Town Hall is at the southern end of the Rātslaukums, the town square.

**Old Wooden House** (Baznīcas iela 7) Dating from 1670, this veteran (the oldest in town) has a weathervane featuring a unicorn.

**Duke Jakob's Pharmacy** (Baznīcas iela 10) A half-timbered icon, this 1622 structure is now a residence.

**Kuldīga Synagogue** (1905 Gada iela 6) Stately and stolid, this 1875 structure was home to Kuldīga's Jewish community until the Holocaust. It now houses the town's library and arts centre.

OFF THE BEATEN TRACK

## AROUND KULDĪGA

The hinterlands around Kuldīga boast many remote treasures: little villages and splendid churches that are worth seeking out. Many are reached by dirt roads. Note that the churches rarely have visiting hours. Call the number listed and a caretaker or even a designated schoolchild will meet you and open it up. An offering of €5 to €10 in the donation box is appropriate.

**Apriki** The stolid **Apriki Lutheran Basilica** (2802 3132, 6344 8004; Apriki) in this tiny village predates its first recorded mention in 1640. The interior is a stunner: it's a perfectly proportioned flamboyant fantasy in blue, gold and white. Note the 2nd-floor pews so the barons would not have to associate with the peasants.

**Ēdole** The namesake **Ēdoles Pils** (6332 1251; http://edolespils.lv; Ēdole; museum adult/child €5/2, r from €55, mains €7-15; museum 10am-7pm) is the centre of everything in this hamlet. It's part manor house, part castle dating to 1264. It has a park-like setting, a proper restaurant and hotel rooms. Explore the complex and stop by the museum for insight into baronial life.

**Zlēkas** On a little hill, the proud white 1645 **Zlēku Baznīca** (2625 7521; off P123, Zlēkas) looks mundane outside but inside is a national treasure: the towering 17th-century altarpiece is a masterpiece of wood carving. Ornate decor throughout is befitting of what was once the private church of the baronial von Behr family.

Fri & Sat, noon-11pm Sun; ) Pagrabiņš inhabits a cellar that was once used as the town's prison. Today a variety of dishes are served under low-slung alcoves lined with honey-coloured bricks. In warmer weather, enjoy a beer on the large verandah, which sits atop the trickling Alekšupīte stream.

**Goldingen Room** ITALIAN €€
(6332 0721; www.facebook.com/goldingenroom; Baznīcas iela 2; mains €6-12; 11am-8pm Sun-Thu, to 10pm Fri & Sat) This stylishly designed restaurant – Nordic woodwork with a pinch of Ikea – serves good pizza and fresh Italian classics. The large outside deck in front is the place to be in summer.

**Bangert's** EUROPEAN €€
(2912 5228; www.bangerts.lv; Pils iela 1; mains €10-21; noon-9pm Sun-Thu, to 10pm Fri & Sat; ) In a vintage house on the Town Garden, this proper restaurant serves a formal menu of fresh fish and meaty mains. Book ahead in the summer for a table in the open-air gazebo with grand views of the waterfall.

### Shopping

**Kuldīgas Labumi** GIFTS & SOUVENIRS
(2547 3680; Pilsētas laukums 7a; 9.30am-6pm Mon-Fri, to 4pm Sat) *Labumi* roughly translates as 'goodies' and that's what you'll find in this little shop selling locally produced crafts and foodstuffs. Pick out some pickles, then browse the polychromatic wool mittens.

### Information

**Tourist Information Centre** (6332 2259; www.visit.kuldiga.lv; Rātslaukums, Old Town Hall; 9am-5pm Mon-Fri, to 3pm Sat & Sun) Good regional info. On many days women work traditional looms in an adjoining room.

### Getting There & Away

From the **bus station** (6332 2061; Adatu iela 9), buses run to/from Rīga (€7, 2½ to 3½ hours, 10 daily), Liepāja (€4, 1¾ hours, seven daily) and Ventspils (€3, 1¼ hours, six daily).

Rent bicycles at **Velo Noma** (2950 5958; Baznīcas iela 5; bike rental per hour/day €2.50/10; 10am-6pm May-Sep).

## Alsunga

POP 1300

The heart of Suiti culture (p242) is an appealing little town. Stop by the **Alsunga District Museum** (2642 5015; http://alsunga.lv/lv/muzeji; Skolas iela 11a; adult/child €1.50/0.50; 11am-4pm Mon-Fri, 11am-3pm Sat & Sun Jun-Sep, closed Mon Oct-May) to learn all about the local customs and people. Then imbibe and join the fun at two unmissable eateries/venues/funfests.

**Spēlmaņu Krogs** GUESTHOUSE €€
(2617 9298; www.spelmankrogs.lv; Pils iela 7; s/d from €30/45, mains €5-15; 10am-9pm; ) This traditional inn, standing next to Livonian castle ruins, offers simple rooms and

copious meals. Mini-festivals celebrating Suiti music and food take place most weekends. It gets raucous and is always a hoot.

**Tējnīca Sapņotava** CAFE €
(Tea House Dreamgirl; ☎2550 5075; http://sapnotava.lv; Skolas iela 11a; mains from €4; ⏲11am-10pm) On the lawn in front of the town museum is this dream of a cafe, a vision in white wood and glass. Run by the intrepid Dace Oberšate-Veisa, it's more cultural happening than mere teahouse (although they have dozens of house-made herbal concoctions). Concerts happen outside. Enjoy snacks, burgers and baked goods. There's a full bar.

### Getting There & Away

There are five buses daily between Kuldīga and Alsunga (€2, 45 minutes).



## Sabile

POP 1400

Sabile would be just another sleepy cobbled-street Latvian village if its eccentric residents weren't on a mission to find any available method of making it unique. Outdoor artworks big and small plus some juice of the grape are but some of the highlights. The tiny centre is looking spiffier by the year and is good for a wander, especially as a pause on the way to Kuldīga.

The town anchors the Abava Valley, which was created when crescent-shaped glaciers receded at the end of the last ice age. Gnarled oaks and cute villages dot the gushing streams, rewarding people who explore the little lanes at random.

### Sights

★ **Pedvāle Art Park** GALLERY
(Pedvāles mākslas parks; ☎2913 3374; www.pedvale.lv; off Brīvības iela; adult/child €3/2.50; ⏲10am-6pm May-Oct, to 4pm Nov-Apr) Located 1.5km south of the centre, this open-air art extravaganza was founded by Ojars Feldbergs, a Latvian sculptor. Pedvāle showcases over 100 thought-provoking installations on 100 hectares of rolling hills. Every year the pieces rotate, reflecting the theme of the year. Standout works include *Chair*, an enormous seat made from bright blue oil drums; and the iconic *Petriflora Pedvalensis*, a bouquet of flowers whose petals have been replaced with spiral stones. The site is anchored by an old manor house.

★ **Doll Garden** LANDMARK
(Rīgas iela 17) FREE Latvia's answer to the Chinese terracotta army is entirely comprised of straw-filled unarmed civilians. Local folk artist Daina Kučera has filled a roadside garden with over 200 winsome straw dolls dressed as people of all ages and walks of life – from schoolchildren to policemen to village people (there are even some cute bunnies). Kučera is around most of the time, chatting about her work and collecting donations. The garden is just east of the centre.

**Wooden Toy Museum** MUSEUM
(☎2654 2227; Kuldīgas iela 1; ⏲by appointment) Well, this one is way cooler than just another small collection of toys from around the world. The owner, drawing teacher Andris Millers, makes mind-boggling kinetic wooden sculptures. With his absurdist sense of humour, Millers and his creations are a bit of a DIY Monty Python show, but you'll need a translator if you don't speak Latvian or Russian.

**Sabile Synagogue** ARTS CENTRE
(Strauta iela 4) The imposing 1890 synagogue that hasn't seen any services since the Jewish population was killed in the Holocaust is being restored so it can be transformed into an art centre.

### Eating & Drinking

**Sabiles Sidra Nams** LATVIAN €
(☎2836 7928; www.sabilessidrs.lv; Rīgas iela 11; mains €4-8; ⏲11am-6pm Wed-Thu & Sun, to 8pm Fri & Sat) The best lunch option in the area, this welcoming wood house offers tastings of the local cider and wine (you'll have seen the vineyards in the surrounding hills). The menu features local cheese and other specialities plus burgers, soups and salads. Everything is fresh and homemade. Grab a sunny table out on the porch.

### Getting There & Away

Sabile is a stop on the bus route connecting Kuldīga (€2.20, 45 minutes, hourly) with Rīga (€5, two hours, hourly).

# SOUTHERN LATVIA (ZEMGALE)

A long strip of land between Rīga and the Lithuanian border, southern Latvia has been dubbed the 'bread basket' of Latvia for its plethora of arable lands and mythical forests. The region is known as Zemgale,

## Southern Latvia (Zemgale)

### Southern Latvia (Zemgale)

**Top Sights**
1 Institute of Horticulture....A1

**Sights**
2 Bauska Castle....C2
3 Castle Ruins....A1
4 Jaunpils Castle....A1
5 Pokaiņi Forest....A1
6 Rundāle Palace....C2
7 Tērvete Nature Park....A2

**Sleeping**
8 Baltā Māja....C2
9 Hotel Mežotne Palace....C2
Jaunpils Castle Hotel....(see 4)

**Eating**
Rundāle Palace Restaurant....(see 6)

named after the defiant Baltic Semigallian (or Zemgallian) tribe who inhabited the region before the German conquest at the end of the 1200s. The Semigallians were a valiant bunch, warding off the impending crusaders longer than any other tribe. Before retreating to Lithuania, they even burned down all of their strongholds rather than surrender them to the invaders.

From the 16th to the 18th centuries, the region (along with Kurzeme) formed part of the semi-independent Duchy of Courland, whose rulers built a mind-boggling palace in Rundāle. Today, the summer palace is Zemgale's star attraction, and a top day trip from Rīga. Further east, the Daugava River Valley is a verdant expanse with a wide ribbon of water and a few worthy sights.

## Bauska

POP 8700

Once an important seat in the Duchy of Courland, these days Bauska is best known as the jumping-off point for the splendid Rundāle Palace. But before you make the hop, consider checking out the local castle.

**Bauska Castle** CASTLE

(Bauskas pils; ☎2001 1880; www.bauskaspils.lv; Pilskalna iela; castle free, museum adult/child €4/2; 9am-7pm daily May-Sep, 9am-6pm Oct, 11am-5pm Tue-Sun Nov-Apr) Bauska Castle sits on a picturesque hillock squeezed between two rivers – the Mūsa and Mēmele – that flow parallel to each other. It is actually two castles melded together. The oldest part is in ruins and dates to the Livonian Order in the 15th century. The newer portion is a fortified manor house built by the Duke of Courland in the 16th century and is mostly intact. A museum covers the entire tangled history of the castle and the region.

Take a good look at the grey blocks along the facade of the newer castle section, which is in the midst of a renovation. The blocks appear to be bulging out of the wall, but that's an optical illusion – the bottom left corner of each brick has been scraped with a chisel to trick the viewer into thinking that they are seeing a shadow.

During the 18th century an Italian by the name of Magno Cavala moved to Bauska in search of a new business venture. He was something of a Casanova (and a conman), and started collecting the water at the junction of the two rivers near the castle. He claimed that the water was a pungent love potion and made a fortune scamming the poor townspeople.

To find the castle ruins from the bus station, walk west to the central roundabout along Zaļā iela then continue west along Uzvaras iela for a total distance of 1.5km.

## Getting There & Away

Bauska's **bus station** (Slimnīcas iela 11) offers two to three buses per hour between 6.10am and 10.40pm to/from Rīga (€3, 70 minutes to two hours).



# Rundāle Palace

Built as a grand residence for the Duke of Courland, this magnificent **palace** (Rundāles pils; ☎6396 2274; www.rundale.net; Rundāle Parish; adult/child from €11/3.50; ⏲palace 10am-6pm, park 10am-7pm) is a monument to 18th-century aristocratic ostentatiousness, and is rural Latvia's architectural highlight. It was designed by Italian baroque genius Bartolomeo Rastrelli, who is best known for the Winter Palace in St Petersburg. About 40 of the palace's 138 rooms are open to visitors, as are the wonderful formal gardens. Detailed displays inside the palace offer fascinating insight into its design and restoration.

Ernst Johann Biron started his career as a groom and lover of Anna Ioanovna, the Russian-born Duchess of Courland. She gave him the duchy when she became Russian empress, but he stayed with her in St Petersburg, becoming the most powerful political figure of the empire. In 1736 he commissioned the Italian architect Bartholomeo Rastrelli to construct his summer residence near Bauska.

Russian authors later blamed Biron for ushering in an era of terror, but many historians believe his role in the persecution of the nobility was exaggerated. On her deathbed, the empress proclaimed Biron the Regent of Russia, but two months later his rivals arrested him and sentenced him to death by quartering. The sentence was commuted to exile. The unfinished palace stood as an empty shell for another 22 years when, pardoned by Catherine II, Ernst Johann returned home. Rastrelli resumed the construction and in 1768 the palace was finally finished. Ernst Johann died four years later at the age of 82. A succession of Russian nobles inhabited (and altered) the palace after the the Duchy of Courland was incorporated into the Russian Empire in 1795.

The palace was badly damaged in the Franco-Russian War in 1812 and again during the Latvian War of Independence in 1919 – what you see now is the result of a painstaking restoration that began in 1972 and ended in 2015.

The castle is divided into two halves; the **East Wing** was devoted to formal occasions, while the **West Wing** was the private royal residence. The **Royal Gardens**, inspired by the gardens at Versailles, were also used for public affairs. The rooms were heated by a network of 80 porcelain stoves, although the castle was mostly used during the warmer months.

Definitely spend an extra €3 and opt for the 'long route' option when buying the ticket. Unlike the short route, it includes the duke's and duchess' private chambers, which is your chance to peek into the everyday life of 18th-century aristocrats as well as to admire the opulent interior design. Even the duke's chamber pot, adorned with a delightful painting of swimming salmon, is on display. Outside, the palace and park are surrounded by lush apple orchards.

## Sleeping & Eating

There are basic guesthouses and one actual palace near Rundāle. However, most people visit on day trips from Rīga.

Rundāle Palace has several restaurants and cafes inside the grounds. There are basic cafes and a convenience store around the parking area.

**Baltā Māja** GUESTHOUSE €

(☎6396 2140; www.hotelbaltamaja.lv; Rundāle; r from €25; P 📶) The 'White House' is a quaint guesthouse and cafe sitting in the Rundāle Palace's Tudor-style servants' quarters near the entrance to the grounds. The rooms are small and have basic country decor. The cafe serves basic Latvian fare.

★ **Hotel Mežotne Palace** HISTORIC HOTEL €€€

(☎6396 0711; www.mezotnepalace.com; Mežotne; r €65-150; P ❄ 📶) Live like Duke Ernst Johann and stay at Mežotne Palace, about 2km north of Rundāle, on the far bank of the Lielupe River. The palace was built in a classical style from 1797 to 1802 for Charlotte von Lieven, the governess of Russian empress Catherine II's grandchildren. After many years in disrepair, it was transformed into a hotel and a popular restaurant in 2001. Rooms are stocked with aristocratic collectables – think cast-iron bed frames, swinging chandeliers and carefully curated antiques.

**Rundāle Palace Restaurant** CAFETERIA €€
(☎2922 7369; http://rundale.net; mains €12-17; ⏰10am-6pm May-Oct, shorter hours rest of year) Located in the palace basement, this vaguely formal restaurant serves old-school Latvian fare suitable for a special occasion. Other palace eating options include a simpler restaurant and a lovely summertime cafe in the gardens.

### Getting There & Away

Various tour operators run day trips to Rundāle Palace from Rīga. By bus, you'll need to transfer at Bauska (12km east). To reach the palace, take a bus to the Rundāles pils stop (€1, 25 minutes, every one to three hours).

## Dobele

POP 9300

Provincial Dobele, in the far western corner of Zemgale, is the gateway to a vast acreage of mythical forests and meandering rivers. The town is centred around its ruined castle. Just outside, you can sample some of the produce you see growing in profusion throughout the region.

**★Institute of Horticulture** GARDENS
(☎2865 0011; www.darzkopibasinstituts.lv; Graudu iela 1; museum adult/student €4/3; ⏰9am-7pm Mon-Fri, 11am-3pm Sat & Sun) These massive gardens draw throngs of visitors each spring when the scores of fruit trees are in bloom. There are apricot, cherry and plum orchards, as well as one of Europe's largest collections of lilacs. A museum tells the history of the gardens and a shop offers plants, seeds and shoots for sale. But the real reason to visit is the selection of house-made ice cream made with the farm's fruit. It's smooth, creamy and not to be missed.

**Castle Ruins** CASTLE
(Brīvības iela; ⏰24hr) FREE These impressive Livonian Order castle ruins, which date back to the 1300s, are well worth a stop. This brick bastion was built over the original site of an earlier Semigallian stronghold. In 1289 the Semigallians incinerated their own castle and fled to Lithuania rather than surrender the structure to the invading crusaders. A monument commemorates their departure. The site today is surrounded by a nice park.

### Getting There & Away

Dobele is easily accessible by bus from Rīga (€3.25, 1½ hours, two to three per hour). It's the main transfer point for service around the region.

## Around Dobele

Mysterious sites deep in the forest and large nature parks highlight the lush lands around Dobele. Although it is possible to get around by bus, you'll find it much easier to explore with your own wheels.

### Tērvete

The village of Tērvete barely qualifies as such. The real draw here is the multifaceted **Tērvete Nature Park** (☎6372 6212; www.mammadaba.lv; off P103; adult/child €5.50/4; ⏰9am-7pm; 👪), which protects three ancient mounds, including the impressive 13th-century **Tērvete Castle Mound** that was abandoned by the Semigallians after several battles with the Livonian Order. Nearby **Klosterhill** was first inhabited over 3000 years ago by Semigallian ancestors, and **Swedish Hill** was constructed by the Livonian Order in the 13th century.

The main pull is the **Fairy Tale Forest**, a magical grove of fir trees inhabited by wood-carved figures. There are two main clusters: one is dedicated to the characters of Latvian fairy tales, another – the Dwarfs' Town – is a toy village complete with log houses and a mill, where children can play dwarfs (while you can play a busy Snow White).

A costumed witch entertains children in the summer with games and potions. If weather permits, you can also go for a swim in a lake at the far end of the forest. The area can be explored on foot, aboard a park train (€1.50) or by bicycle, available for hire (€10) at the information centre at the entrance where there is also a simple cafe.

There are about seven buses a day from Dobele bus station to Tērvete (€1.15, 30 minutes).

## Pokaiņi Forest

It's one of Latvia's biggest unsolved mysteries: in the mid-'90s a local historian discovered stone cairns throughout the **Pokaiņi Forest** (www.mammadaba.lv; V1128; adult/child €2.50/2, per car €2; ⊙toll booth 10am-7pm) and realised that the rocks had been transported to the forest from faraway destinations. Historians have theorised that Pokaiņi was an ancient sacred ground used in proto-pagan rituals more than 2000 years ago. There are 15km of walking trails through the forest, with themes including mystical healing, the seasons and the zodiac.

Pokaiņi Forest is best reached by car or bicycle. The reserve is 16km southwest of Dobele.

There are two buses daily from Dobele to Īle, which stop at the entrance to the visitor's centre (€0.85, 20 minutes).

## Jaunpils

The small but perfectly medieval **Jaunpils Castle** (☎6310 7082; www.jaunpilspils.lv; ⊙10am-8pm May-Sep, shorter hours other times) FREE is unique in the fact that it has largely retained its original look since 1301, when it was founded by the master of the Livonian Order, Gotfried von Roga. For four centuries until the break-up of the Russian Empire in 1917, it was the home of the German baronial family von der Recke. Ponder the small museum, wander the sprawling manicured grounds or just revel in the atmosphere inside.

You can even spend the night! The **Jaunpils Castle Hotel** (☎2610 1458; www.jaunpilspils.lv; r €60-120, dm €15; ⊙tavern 10am-8pm; P 📶) has four private rooms with brick floors, baldachin-covered beds and real fireplaces. Some rooms share bathrooms and there are also dorm beds. The 'medieval tavern' in the castle premises serves quality Latvian fare.

Jaunpils is 21km northwest of Dobele. There are four buses daily from Dobele (€2, 45 minutes).

# Daugava River Valley

Latvia's serpentine Daugava River, known as the 'river of fate', winds its way through Latgale, Zemgale and Vidzeme before passing Rīga and emptying out in the Gulf of Rīga. For centuries the river was Latvia's most important transport and trade corridor for clans and kingdoms further east. Its namesake valley is a sylvan ribbon through the heart of Latvia.

Driving out of Rīga, east towards Daugavpils, you can choose the modern E22 highway or the much more scenic old A6, which wanders through riverside towns and villages, with the Daugava in full view much of the time. Obviously the A6, with its succession of sights and river vistas all the way to Daugavpils, is the more rewarding choice.

## Sights

**Kokenhausen** RUINS

(Kokneses pilsdrupas; off A6, Koknese; adult/child €1.60/0.80) Stop at Koknese to admire the ruins of Kokenhausen, a medieval castle. It has a stunning location overlooking the confluence of the Daugava and Perse Rivers, and is a good stop to appreciate the valley's beauty. Built by German crusaders beginning in 1209, what remains today is extensive enough to suggest the huge fortress that once stood here. The surrounding park is pleasant for a riverside stroll. A model in a small information office shows the castle in its prime.

**Garden of Destiny** MEMORIAL

(Likteņdārzs; ☎6728 9535; http://liktendarzs.lv; off A6, Koknese; parking €2, site entry by donation; ⊙8am-5pm Mon-Fri, 9.30am-6pm Sat & Sun May-Oct, 9.30am-4pm Sat & Sun Apr & Nov) Grandly named the Garden of Destiny, this sprawling project on an island in the river celebrates Latvia as a nation and opened for the centennial in 2018. Designed by acclaimed Japanese gardener-cum-philosopher Shunmyu Masuno, a 2.5km trail links areas with portentous names such as Alley of Destiny, House of Silence and Stream of Tears. Still a work in progress, there are vast new gardens and features that honour the country while recalling recent history.

**Teiči Nature Reserve Watchtower** NATURE RESERVE

(Teiču Dabas Rezervāts Skatu Tornis; A12, Atašienes pagasts; ⊙24hr) FREE Stop at this roadside watchtower for sweeping views of the 20,000-hectare Teiči Nature Reserve, which boasts the largest moss marsh in the Baltics. The hard-to-miss 27m-tall tower is 9km east of the turn to Atašiene via the P62.

### Eating

**Liepkalni Maiznīca** LATVIAN €
(☎2613 4952; www.liepkalni.lv; A6, Liepsalās; mains €4-8; ⏲8am-10pm) Follow the other cars and turn off the A6 for this wildly popular roadside bakery and cafe. Liepkalni has busy bakers (you can watch them in action) and a shop where you can buy all manner of Latvian breads, pastries and snacks at bargain prices. There's a fine cafe and picnic tables with a scenic location on the river. It's 115km southeast of Rīga via the A6.

# NORTHEASTERN LATVIA (VIDZEME)

When Rīga's urban hustle fades into a pulsing hum of chirping crickets, you've entered northeastern Latvia. Known as Vidzeme, or 'the Middle Land', to locals, the country's largest region is an excellent sampler of what Latvia has to offer. Forest folks can hike, bike or paddle through the thicketed terrain of Gauja National Park, beach bums will revel on white-sand beaches on the coast and history buffs will be sated with a generous sprinkling of castles throughout.

## Vidzeme Coast

Vidzeme's stone-strewn coast is often seen from the car – or bus – window by travellers on the Via Baltica (the A1 highway) en route between Rīga and Tallinn – a real shame! Those who take time to explore will be rewarded with beguiling beach towns, a desolate strand of craggy cliffs and pebble beaches carved from aeons of pounding waves. It's a nature-lovers dream.

### Saulkrasti

A quick 44km jaunt from Rīga, Saulkrasti is an ideal day trip for those who want to enjoy glistening white sand, clear blue water and pristine dunes covered with pine forests. Among the rewards is a sea that gets deep enough to swim in before you walk all the way to Sweden. Much of the beach here has won Blue Flag designation. The lack of mass development provides a sylvan respite from the hubbub of the capital, and the streets are a quiet panoply of gentrified holiday homes.

Saulkrasti, which means 'sunny coast', is actually several beachside villages strung along the railway line and parallel beach road, which running north is named Rīgas iela, Ainažu iela and Tallinas iela in succession.

### Sights & Activities

There are over 10km of flat cycling and walking trails along the Saulkrasti beaches. Nature paths wander through the pine forests in the dune behind the shore.

★**Baltā Kāpa** VIEWPOINT
(White Dune; off Rīgas iela) These striking pine-covered cliffs loom above a pristine white-sand beach dissected by a glistening stream. This is one of the most enchanting places along the entire Latvian coast, and the wooden walkway along the 18m-high cliffs affords sweeping views of the Gulf of Rīga. The **Sunset Trail** runs for 4km north through the pine forest along the ridge of the dune. Baltā Kāpa is 1.2km northwest of the Inčupe train station and 1.4km southwest of the Pabaži station.

**Pabaži Beach** BEACH
(Pabaži) Among many fine beaches, the one directly west of the Pabaži train station and the A1 highway has bright white sand, shallow, pine-covered dunes and very little commercial development anywhere nearby. Of course, you can wander north or south along the long Saulkrasti strand.

**Bicycle Museum** MUSEUM
(☎2888 3160; www.velomuseum.lv; Rīgas iela 44a; adult/child €2.50/1.50, bicycle rental per 1/24hr €2.50/15; ⏲10am-6pm Apr-Aug, other times by appointment) Explore this lovely collection of retro bicycles, including a 130-year-old specimen assembled in Latvia. Better yet, choose from a range of modern rental bicycles to explore the region, which is ideal for cycling. The owner is an excellent resource of local info. The museum is close to the Pabaži train station.

### Sleeping & Eating

Rental apartments and rooms can be found all along the string of Saulkrasti villages.

There are supermarkets for picnic supplies near the Pabaži and Saulkrasti train stations. The latter also has a couple of modest cafes in the minute village centre. There are only a few beach cafes or snack bars on the wonderfully unspoiled sand. Day-trippers can bring something enticing for lunch from Rīga.

## Northeastern Latvia (Vidzeme)

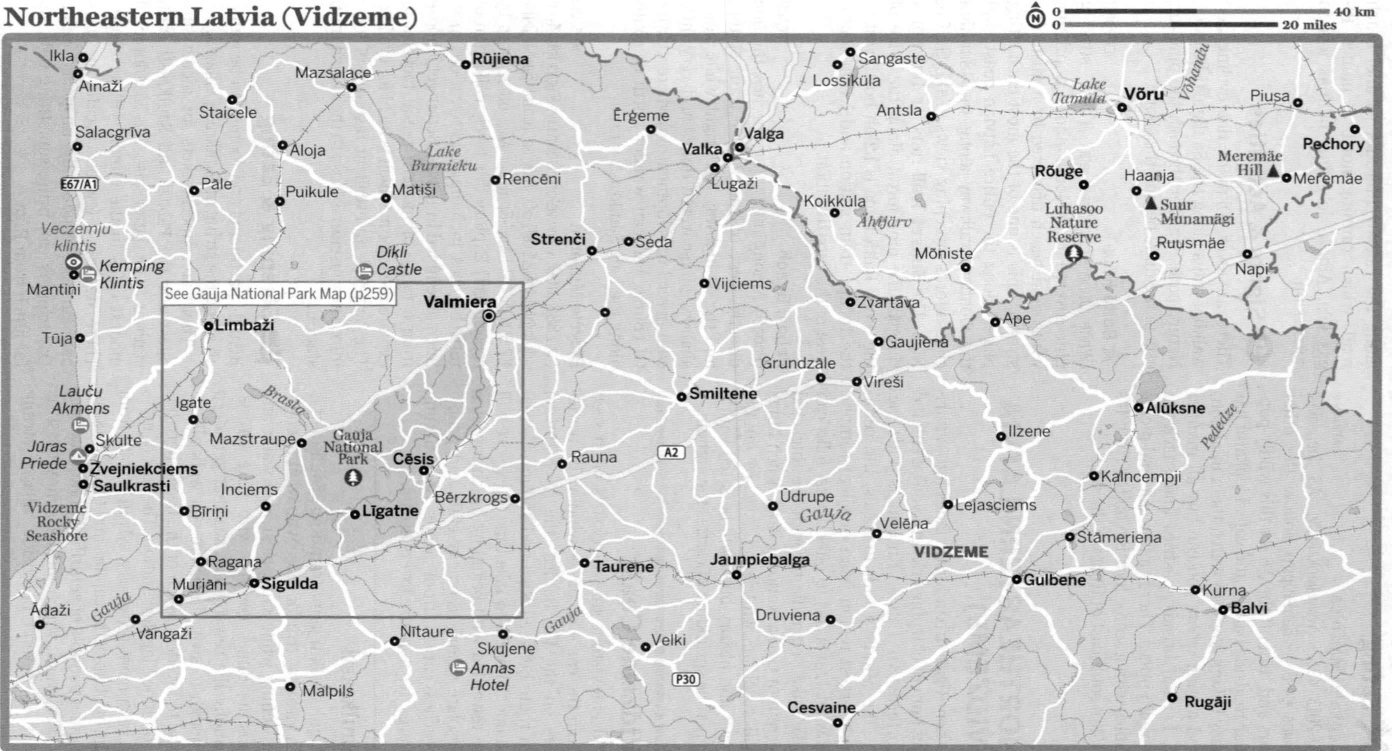

**Jūras Priede** CAMPGROUND €
(☎2700 8353; www.juraspriede.lv; Ūpes iela 56a, Zvejniekciems; sites per person €7.50, cabin from €40; P 📶) Pitch your tent or rent a log cabin just off the beach in Zvejniekciems, at the northern end of the Saulkrasti region. It's on the north side of Zvejniekciems harbour, and there is a cafe on the premises. The railway station is a good 4km away and the stop for Rīga buses is 1.4km east on Tallinas iela.

**Pine Resort** HOTEL €€
(☎6690 0623; www.pineresort.lv; Rīgas iela 28; r from €60; ⊙May-Sep; P 📶) Located on a quiet plot well off Rīgas iela, this small hotel is close to the best beach. Rooms in the three-storey building have balconies and come in various sizes. There's a small bar and cafe with a terrace, as well as a playground. Warm up from the brisk Baltic beach breezes in the sauna. Pabaži station is 800m northeast.

**Cafe Lagūna** CAFE €
(☎2617 8744; off Vidrižu iela; mains €4-12; ⊙9am-7pm May-Sep) Nestled under the pines, this glass-fronted cafe with a large wooden terrace is an unobtrusive gem right on the sand. There is excellent coffee and other beverages, plus a menu of snacks and meals that breaks away from the rubbery hot dog and crisps cliche. Head here at sunset and have a fresh salmon sandwich with some refreshing fruit. It's about 800m west of Saulkrasti train station.

**Restaurant Baltā Kāpa** CAFE €€
(☎2666 8061; www.baltakapa.lv; Kāpu iela 1; mains €6-15; ⊙11am-10pm) The multilevel decks at this contemporary cafe are much sought after on balmy summer days. The food is fresh and modern with salads, sandwiches and mains such as pasta, seafood and grilled meats. The coffee drinks and cocktails are refreshing. The cafe is next to the Rīgas iela and is right at the parking area for Baltā Kāpa.

### Getting There & Around

Saulkrasti stretches along the Skulte railway line. Coming from Rīga, the first station is Inčupe, followed by Pabaži, Saulkrasti and Zvejniekciems at the northern end. Trains to/from Rīga run at least hourly (€2, one hour). Travelling by car, take the Tallinn highway (E67/A1) for about 35km and exit onto the coast road, Rīgas iela, at Lilaste, which is at the south end of Saulkrasti. Rent a bike from the Bicycle Museum.

## Northern Vidzeme Coast

North of the Saulkrasti strip – which ends around Zvejniekciems – the coast is mostly wild, with quiet beaches, long stretches of dunes and pine forest, and the odd campground and guesthouse. The only two towns of any size, Salacgrīva and Ainaži, are useful places to get gas or a quick snack as you near the Estonian border on the A1 highway.

### Sights

**Veczemju klintis** NATURAL FEATURE
(Red Cliffs; Mantiņi) Veczemju klintis, halfway between Saulkrasti and Salacgrīva, is a dramatic spot for a picnic and a walk. The jagged cliffs have a deep reddish hue and are the highlight of this 14km stretch of protected coast known as the Vidzeme Rocky Seashore. Rippled sands undulate between tiny capes and caverns. Look for a tiny, dirt road just south of the point where the A1 runs right along the water, then head south along the bluffs for 4km.

You can also follow signs for the campground 'Klintis'.

### Festivals & Events

**Positivus** MUSIC
(www.positivusfestival.com; Sporta iela, off A1; ⊙late Jul) A major event on Latvia's summer calendar, Positivus draws big names and bigger crowds for three days of live music that ranges from folk to funk. Stages are set up in a beachside pine forest 2km north of Salacgrīva, close to the Estonian border. Al fresco camping is the favoured means of accommodation.

### Sleeping & Eating

**Laučų Akmens** RESORT €€
(☎26350536; www.laucakmens.lv; Lauči; campsite per person €9, apt €45-120, mains €7-16; ⊙restaurant 9am-9pm; P 📶) This beachfront complex has sweeping views of the Gulf of Rīga. The range of apartments, from simple units in an older building to ones called 'Sunset Apartments' in a modern building, have gorgeous views and decor courtesy of Ikea. The restaurant is excellent and serves local favourites made with locally sourced ingredients (call to confirm opening hours if you're visiting between October and April).

It's 7km north of Zvejniekciems, deep in a quiet oceanfront forest west of the A1. Watch for signs.

**Kemping Klintis** HOLIDAY PARK €€

(☎2785 2476; www.klintis.lv; Mantiņi; sites €5, cabins from €50, mains €7-15; ⏲sites Apr-Oct, restaurant 9am-9pm May-Sep) Close to the Veczemju klintis amidst the Vidzeme Rocky Seashore, this campground has cute little cabins set amidst the pine trees. There are picnic sites and an excellent restaurant, Rankuļrags, which features local ingredients like mushrooms and seafood in hearty country fare. Follow the signs posted along the A1 then follow the dirt roads west.

### Getting There & Away

Regular buses plying the A1 from Rīga stop at Salacgrīva and Ainaži. However, to explore the coast, you'll need your own wheels to traverse the mostly smooth, dirt roads.



## Gauja National Park

A stunning region encompassing virgin pines and the rushing Gauja River, Latvia's first national park (www.gnp.gov.lv) mixes urban areas with pristine countryside, extending from castle-strewn Sigulda to quiet Valmiera, passing woodsy Līgatne and picture-perfect Cēsis along the way.

Founded in 1973, Gauja National Park is Latvia's third most popular destination, after Rīga and Jūrmala. Sigulda and Cēsis are popular day trips from the capital, and whether you have hours or days, you'll find opportunities for hiking, biking, canoeing, river rafting and a slew of other sports. Happily, there is no entrance fee to enter the park.

Watch for wild mushrooms on menus across the region.

## Sigulda

POP 11,400

The gateway to the Gauja Valley boasts two castles and numerous great hikes and activities. It's very spread out, so bring your walking shoes.

### Sights

Sigulda sprawls between its three castles, with most of the action occurring on the east side of the Gauja River near the Sigulda Castle complex. Take your own walking tour for an abridged version of Sigulda's greatest hits, and be sure to include the cable car for awesome views of the valley.

★**Sigulda Castle Complex** CASTLE

(Siguldas pils komplekss; ☎6797 1335; www.tourism.sigulda.lv; Pils iela 16; ⏲9am-8pm daily May-Sep, 9am-5pm Mon-Fri, to 7pm Sat & Sun Oct, 9am-5pm Nov-Apr) The city of Sigulda has done a fine job developing the historic buildings at its core into one unmissable complex. The highlight is the **Livonian Order Castle** (Pils iela 16; adult/child €2/1; ⏲9am-8pm daily May-Sep, 9am-5pm Mon-Fri, to 7pm Sat & Sun Oct, 9am-5pm Nov-Apr), which was constructed between 1207 and 1209 by the Livonian Brothers of the Sword. Its evocative ruins are being restored and are worth an exploration.

Some sections are complete and you can walk along the ramparts and ascend a tower with wonderful views over the forested Gauja Valley.

See if you can spy Krimulda Manor and Turaida Castle poking through the trees.

#### THE ROSE OF TURAIDA

Sigulda is home to many legends. One especially melancholy one involves Maija Roze (May Rose), a little girl who was taken into Turaida Castle after she was found among the wounded following a battle in the early 1600s. She grew into a beautiful young woman and was courted by men from far and wide, but her heart belonged to Viktors, a humble gardener at nearby Sigulda Castle. They would meet in secret at Gūtmaņa Cave, halfway between the two castles.

One day, a particularly desperate soldier among Maija Roze's suitors lured her to the cave with a letter forged in Viktors' handwriting. When Maija Roze arrived, he kidnapped her. Maija Roze pleaded with the soldier and offered to give him the scarf from around her neck in return for her freedom. She claimed it had magical protective powers, and to prove it, she told him to swing at her with his sword. It isn't clear whether or not she was bluffing or if she really believed in the scarf's powers – either way, the soldier took his swing and killed her.

The soldier was captured, convicted and hanged for his crime. In the centuries since, documents have been found that seem to give credence to this story that lacks a fairy-tale ending. Today, a small stone memorial (p261) commemorates Maija Roze.

## Gauja National Park

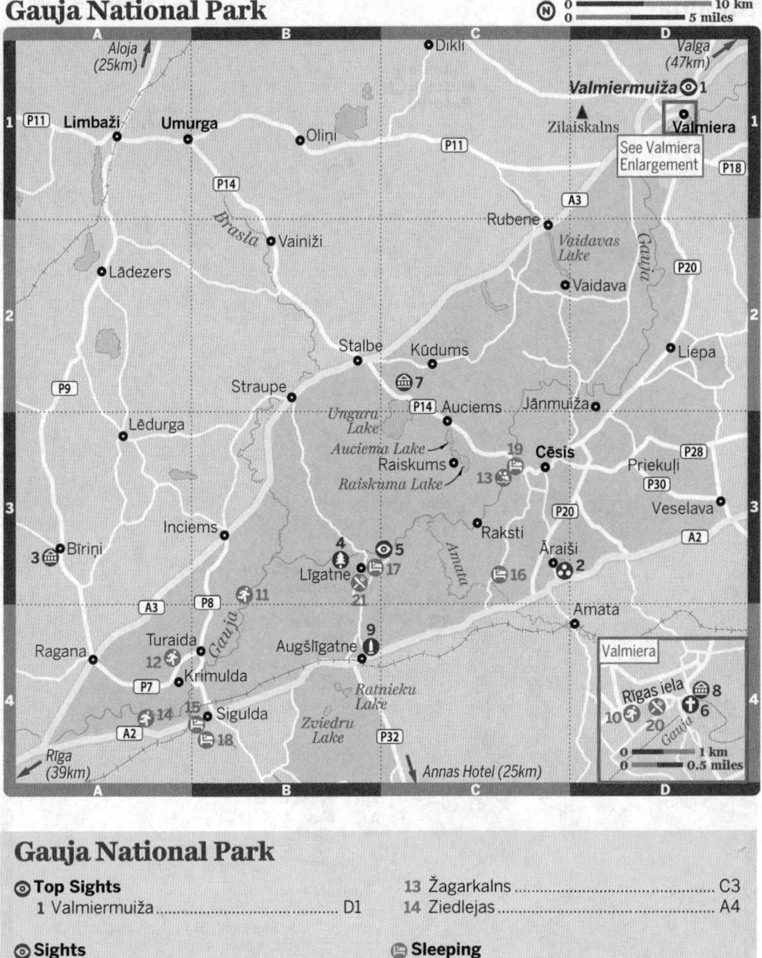


## Gauja National Park

**Top Sights**
1 Valmiermuiža .......... D1

**Sights**
2 Āraiši Archaeological Park .......... C3
3 Bīriņi Castle .......... A3
4 Līgatne Nature Trails .......... B3
5 Soviet Secret Bunker .......... C3
6 St Simon's Church .......... D4
7 Ungurmuiža .......... C2
8 Valmieras Muzejs .......... D4
9 Vienkoču Parks .......... B4

**Activities, Courses & Tours**
10 Eži Veikals .......... D4
11 Jaunzāģeri .......... B3
12 Reiņa Trase .......... A4
13 Žagarkalns .......... C3
14 Ziedlejas .......... A4

**Sleeping**
15 Hotel Aparjods .......... B4
16 Kārlamūiža .......... C3
17 Lāču Miga .......... B3
18 Spa Hotel Ezeri .......... B4
19 Villa Santa Hotel .......... C3

**Eating**
Aparjods .......... (see 15)
20 Vecpuisis .......... D4
21 Vilhelmīnes dzirnavas .......... B3

**Information**
Tourist Information Centre .......... (see 21)

At the front of the complex, the 1878 neo-Gothic **manor house** was the home of Russian prince Dimitri Kropotkin, the man responsible for turning Sigulda into a tourist haven. It now houses Sigulda district council and is not open to the public. The complex's grounds have some lovely gardens; historic auxiliary buildings are

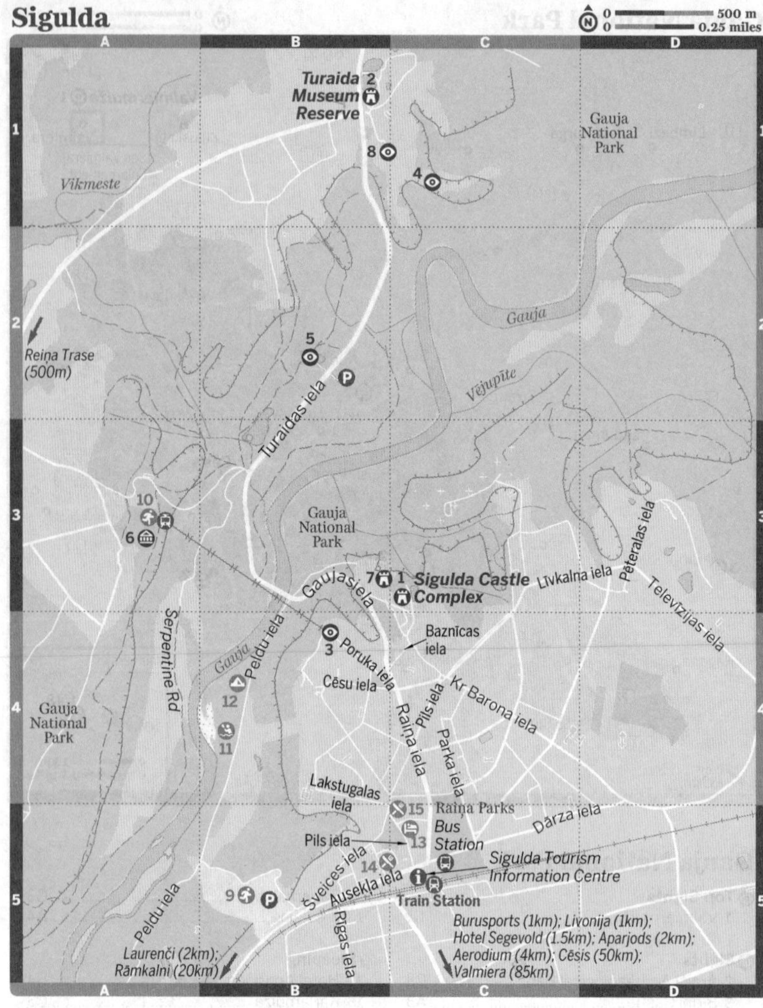


## Sigulda

**Top Sights**
1 Sigulda Castle Complex ... C3
2 Turaida Museum Reserve ... B1

**Sights**
3 Cable Car ... B4
4 Folk Song Garden ... C1
5 Gūtmaņa Cave ... B2
6 Krimulda Manor ... A3
7 Livonian Order Castle ... B3
8 Turaida Rose Headstone ... B1

**Activities, Courses & Tours**
9 Bobsled Track ... B5
10 Cable Car Zipline ... A3
11 Makars Tourism Bureau ... B4

**Sleeping**
12 Camping Siguldas Beach ... B4
13 Hotel Sigulda ... C5

**Eating**
14 Jāņa Tirgus ... B5
15 Kaķu Māja ... C5

**Drinking & Nightlife**
Valmiermuiža Beer Garden ... (see 1)

now home to excellent restaurants, cafes and shops with working artists.

**★Turaida Museum Reserve** CASTLE
(Turaidas muzejrezervāts; ☎6797 1402; www.turaida-muzejs.lv; Turaidas iela 10; adult/child summer €6/1.15, winter €3.50/0.70; ⏲9am-8pm May-Sep, 10am-7pm Apr & Oct, 10am-5pm Nov-Mar) Turaida means 'God's Garden' in ancient Livonian, and this green knoll capped with a fairy-tale castle is certainly a heavenly place. The red-brick castle with its tall cylindrical tower was built in 1214 on the site of a Liv stronghold. A museum inside the castle's 15th-century granary offers an interesting account of the Livonian state from 1319 to 1561; additional exhibitions can be viewed in the 42m-high Donjon Tower and the castle's western and southern towers.

The rest of the reserve features a variety of buildings that have been transformed into small galleries and exhibits. It's worth stopping by the smith house, where you can try forging metal. There is a real blacksmith on hand who sells his crafts, and guests can try pounding Liv pagan symbols into small chunks of iron.

In the graveyard of the pretty wooden church (1750) is the grave of Maija Roze (p258), an ill-fated beauty known as the 'Rose of Turaida' and the subject of a tragic legend. Look for the onyx **headstone** bearing the inscription 'Turaidas Roze 1601–1620'.

The nearby **Folk Song Garden** is dotted with 26 sculptures dedicated to epic Latvian heroes immortalised in the *dainas,* poetic folk songs that are a major Latvian tradition.

**Gūtmaņa Cave** CAVE
(☎6130 3030; off Turaidas iela; ⏲24hr) FREE More grotto than cave, this 19m-deep fissure in the earth is most famous for its role in the tragic legend of the Rose of Turaida. Most tourists visit to peruse the inordinate amount of graffiti spread along the walls – some of it dates back to the 16th century. Many legends are attached to the spring-fed water flowing out of the cave. There's a paid parking area and small information office (9am to 5pm) on the east side of Turaidas iela.

**Cable Car** CABLE CAR
(☎2802 0088; www.cablecar.lv; Poruka iela 14; one-way adult/child €8/5; ⏲10am-6.20pm May-Oct, to 5pm Nov-Apr) Enjoy terrific views by catching a ride on the cable car over the Gauja River. From the Sigulda side, it departs from a rocky precipice south of the bridge and heads towards Krimulda Manor. The ride is 1km in length and 43m above the river.

**Krimulda Manor** HISTORIC BUILDING
(☎2911 1619; http://krimuldasmuiza.lv; Mednieku iela 3) The sprawling, crumbling Krimulda estate includes a neoclassical manor house from 1822, whose proud columns look out onto modest gardens. Inside you can get a very simple room for the night (from €40) or a hostel bed (€13). About 300m north are the tree-shaded ruins of a 14th-century **medieval castle** that was destroyed in 1601. The manor is 200m south of the cable car station.

## Activities

Canoeing or otherwise floating down the lazy Gauja River is a top activity in the region. Many trips end in Sigulda (which is downstream from the rest of the park) and you can join a tour that begins with transport from Sigulda upstream.

Other activities include exciting options like zip lines and a bobsled track. Hiking and cycling are very popular and there are myriad routes to choose from. You'll also find plenty of touristy activities like thrill rides and adventure parks.

### Canoeing & Boating

Floating down the peaceful Gauja River is a great way to observe this pristine area away from modern life. There are campgrounds all along the stretch of river from Cēsis to Sigulda. Team up with one of the outfitters within the national park that organises boat trips along the Gauja, or you can just head upstream, hop into an inner tube, and float back to town.

Trips cover most sections of the river, although few start in Sigulda and continue southwest. Most begin in Līgatne or Cēsis.

**Jaunzāģeri** WATER SPORTS
(☎2200 2033; www.jaunzageri.lv/; V89, Gauja River; canoe rental per day from €30; ⏲May-Sep) A virtual oasis along the river, Jaunzāģeri has a remote location midway between Līgatne and Sigulda. You can rent canoes, kayaks and rafts, which include transport from Sigulda or back to Līgatne and Cēsis. The site is deeply shaded by trees and there are campsites (per person €5) and cabins (from €35). Best of all, there is an authentic *pirts,* the traditional black sauna (€50). It's a magical spot.

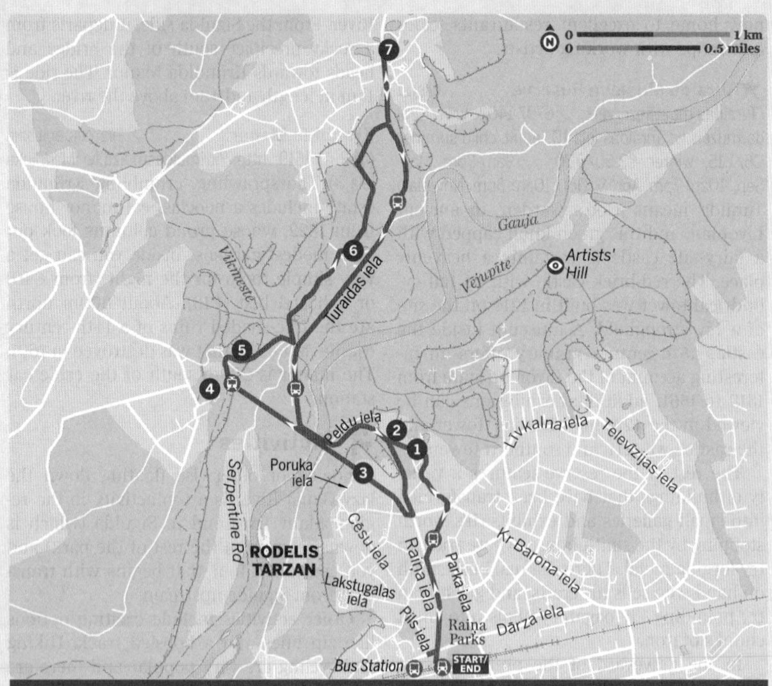




# Town Walk
# Three Castles Tour

**START** SIGULDA TRAIN STATION
**END** SIGULDA BUS STATION
**LENGTH** 6.6KM; 5½ HOURS

The town's three main castle reserves and one legendary cave can easily be tackled in an afternoon.

From the train station, walk down Raiņa iela and linden-lined Pils iela until you reach the **1 Sigulda Castle Complex** (p258), built on the orders of Russian prince Dmitry Kropotkin, who developed Sigulda as a resort town. He was killed by a revolutionary terrorist in 1879, when the construction commenced. Check out the ruins and reconstructed sections of the **2 Livonian Order Castle** (p258) towards the rear, which was constructed in 1207 by the Order of the Brethren of the Sword, but was severely damaged in the 18th century during the Great Northern War. Stop at the beer garden or grab an ice cream from one of the excellent cafes.

Now follow Poruka iela to the rocky precipice and take the **3 cable car** (p261) over the scenic river valley to **4 Krimulda Manor** (p261), a once-elegant 19th-century estate that's making an effort to attract tourists. Check out the views from the rear terrace.

Walk north to the nearby crumbling ruins of **5 Krimulda Medieval Castle**, then follow Serpentine Rd to **6 Gūtmaņa Cave** (p261). Immortalised by the legend of the Rose of Turaida, it's the largest cave/grotto in the Baltic. Take some time to read the myriad inscriptions carved into the walls and dip your hand in the cool spring water.

Now head up to the **7 Turaida Museum Reserve** (p261). The towering medieval castle was erected in the 13th century for the Archbishop of Rīga over the site of an ancient Liv stronghold. Climb the ancient tower for sweeping views of Gauja National Park, then explore the grounds, filled with whimsical sculptures depicting Latvian fairy-tale characters. Pause at the cafe and then catch any bus with 'Siguldas AO' on the front back to back to Sigulda bus station (€0.60, about every 75 minutes).

**Laivojam** KAYAKING
(☎2652 9812; www.laivojam.lv; kayak rental from €40) Good outfit that rents kayaks and canoes for trips of many lengths. Rates include transport to the starting point from Sigulda, plus life jackets and other gear. There is no office: all details are arranged when you book.

**Makars Tourism Bureau** CANOEING
(☎2924 4948; www.makars.lv; Peldu iela 2; river tour from €30; ⊙hours vary) Runs canoe and kayak tours, ranging from four hours to seven days, on the Gauja River that end in Sigulda. Rafting starts at €10 for a 45-minute trip. It also runs a campground (per person €6) and you can rent camping gear.

### Hiking & Cycling

Sigulda is prime hiking territory. A popular (and easy) route is the 40-minute walk from Krimulda Castle to Turaida Museum Reserve via Gūtmaņa Cave. Or you can head south from Krimulda and descend to **Little Devil's Cave** and **Big Devil's Cave**, cross the river via a footbridge, and return to Sigulda (about two hours). Note the black walls in Big Devil's Cave, which are believed to be from the fiery breath of a travelling demon that took shelter here to avoid the sunlight.

East of Sigulda castle, try the well-marked loop that joins **Peter's Cave**, **Satezele Castle Mound** and **Artists' Hill**; it takes about 1½ hours. The panoramic view of Turaida Castle and the Gauja River valley from Artists' Hill is spectacular.

Tourist offices have numerous brochures and booklets outlining walks, hikes and cycling routes in the region lasting from under an hour to many days.

One excellent bike route follows forest trails along the Gauja River to Līgatne. It covers 23km and takes about two hours. Several outfitters around Sigulda offer bicycle and mountain-bike rentals.

**Reiņa Trase** CYCLING
(☎2927 2255; www.reinatrase.lv; Krimuldas novads; bicycle rental per 3hr €7; ⊙8am-5pm) Just north of Sigulda, the local golf club doubles as a bicycle rental shop.

### Thrill Sports

**Bobsled Track** ADVENTURE SPORTS
(Bob trase; ☎6797 3813; www.bobtrase.lv; Šveices iela 13; adult/child €10/7; ⊙noon-5pm Sat & Sun May-Sep & Nov–mid-Mar) Sigulda's 1200m bobsled track has a fine legacy as the Latvians score above their weight in bobsleigh (they've won three Olympic medals since 2014). In winter, you can fly down the 16-bend track at 80km/h in a five-person Vučko **soft bob**. Summer thrill-seekers can ride a wheeled **summer bob**.

**Cable Car Zipline** ADVENTURE SPORTS
(☎2838 3333; http://zipline.lv; Poruka iela 14; bungee jump adult/child €55/15; ⊙10am-6pm May-Oct) Make like the cable car and zoom over the Gauja River on a mile-long zip line. Wave to the birds.

## Festivals & Events

**Sigulda Opera Festival** MUSIC
(☎6797 1335; www.opersvetki.lv; ⊙late Jul) The evocative Livonian Order Castle ruins serve as a backdrop for the country's top opera festival.

## Sleeping

What Sigulda lacks in quantity of hotel rooms, it makes up for in vacation rooms and apartment rentals. Try to stay near the river or train station so you can walk to everywhere of interest.

**Camping Siguldas Beach** CAMPGROUND €
(Kempings Siguldas Pludmale; ☎2924 4948; www.makars.lv; Peldu iela 2; per person/tent/car/caravan €6/3/3/6; ⊙mid-May–mid-Sep) Pitch your tent in the grassy camping area beside a sandy beach along the Gauja. Two-person tents can be hired for €5 per day. There's a second camping area up the river in Līgatne that's owned and operated by Makars as well.

**Hotel Aparjods** HOTEL €€
(☎6797 2230; www.aparjods.lv; Ventas iela 1; s/d from €45/55; P📶) Tucked behind the busy main road 1.5km away from the centre, Aparjods is a modern complex of barn-like structures with reed-and-shingle roofing. The rooms, however, aren't as characterful and are ready for a new generation of furniture. Breakfast is included and served in the excellent on-site restaurant.

**Spa Hotel Ezeri** RESORT €€
(☎6797 3009; www.hotelezeri.lv; Siguldas pagasts Ezeri; r €75-100; P📶🏊) The luxurious Ezeri, 2km south of the centre, offers all manner of ways to treat your body, including a small swimming pool, a rooftop sun deck and an elaborate spa that offers a traditional *pirts* sauna. Rooms are fairly simple, with a contemporary decor that's easy on the eyes.

DON'T MISS

## PIRTS, THE WONDERFULLY TRADITIONAL SAUNA

Cast modesty aside and indulge in Latvia's most Latvian tradition, the *pirts*. A *pirts* is Latvia's version of the sauna, and while somewhat similar to the Finnish sauna, there are many elements that set this sweaty experience apart. A traditional *pirts* is run by a sauna master, who cares for her attendees while performing choreographed branch beatings that feel almost shamanistic in nature. While you lie naked and prone, the sauna master swishes branches in the air to raise the humidity then lightly beats a variety of wildflowers and branches over your back and chest. *Pirts* are much hotter and more humid than their Finnish counterparts – a branch-beating session usually lasts around 15 minutes before one exits the sauna to jump in a nearby body of water (lake, pond or sea). The aroma of the sauna is also very important – sauna masters take great care to create a melange of herbs and spices to accent the air. In general, an afternoon at a *pirts* involves multiple sweat sessions interspersed with leaps in cool water – beer, herbal tea and snacks are essential accompaniments.

Most traditional saunas are in the countryside at private cottages. However, you can find authentic *pirts* in Sigulda at the Spa Hotel Ezeri (p263) and Hotel Aparjods (p263). In the countryside, try **Ziedlejas** (2610 5993; https://ziedlejas.lv; off A2, Krimuldas; spa treatment from €150; by appointment), which is 7km west of Sigulda, and most delightfully, the riverside Jaunzāģeri (p261). Around three hours of sauna with plenty of tea and snacks costs €50 to €150 per person.

**Hotel Sigulda** HOTEL €€
(6797 2263; www.hotelsigulda.lv; Pils iela 6; r €60-125; P ) Right in the centre of town, this is the oldest hotel in Sigulda – it was built by the Russian baron who had dreams of turning the little hamlet into an exciting tourist destination. While the old stone-and-brick facade is quite charming, the rooms are mostly basic Scandi stark.

## Eating & Drinking

Sigulda's dining options are expanding, led by the many choices at the renovated Sigulda Castle Complex.

**Jāņa Tirgus** FOOD HALL €
(2233 6033; www.facebook.com/pg/JanaTirgus; Krišjāņa Valdemāra iela 2; mains €3-10; 8am-8pm) This modern market hall near the train station has a good range of vendors selling prepared foods, from burgers to seafood. Other stalls sell local produce (the blueberries are heavenly), baked goods, smoked fish and honey from the region. Dine under the skylit roof or prepare a picnic.

**Kaķu Māja** LATVIAN €
(Cat's House; 2661 6997; www.cathouse.lv; Pils iela 8; mains €4-8; restaurant 8am-9pm daily, disco 10pm-2am Fri & Sat; ) The 'Cat's House' has a long CV: cafeteria, bakery, cafe and nightclub. Get a tray and load up on cheap Latvian fare or get one of the good coffee drinks and enjoy it with a freshly baked tart. Very centrally located, it has a fine outdoor terrace, and a nearby pizzeria and rooms for rent (from €35).

★ **Aparjods** INTERNATIONAL €€
(Ventas iela 1; mains €11-35; noon-10pm) The namesake hotel's popular restaurant serves an excellent range of Latvian and European specials made with locally sourced ingredients. Service is excellent and there's a good beer and drinks list. In summer the front opens up to the outside, while at other times a roaring fire warms the dark-wood dining room. At busy times be sure to book.

**Valmiermuiža Beer Garden** BEER GARDEN
(2734 4025; Pils iela 16, Sigulda Castle Complex; 11am-8pm Sun-Thu, to 10pm Fri & Sat Jun-Aug, noon-8pm Fri-Sun May & Sep) The castle's 19th-century brewery lives again, thanks to one of Latvia's best craft breweries, Valmiera-based Valmiermuiža. Sample their range of beers and enjoy creative snacks and smoked meat dishes.

## Information

**Sigulda Tourism Information Centre** (6797 1335; www.tourism.sigulda.lv; Ausekļa iela 6; 9am-7pm May-Sep, to 6pm Oct-Apr; ) Located within the train station, this very helpful centre has stacks of information about activities and accommodation. It stocks a huge range of official information on the national park.

## Getting There & Away

The best way to reach Sigulda is via the centrally located **train station** (Ausekļa iela). Roughly one train per hour (between 6am and 9pm) travels the Rīga–Sigulda–Cēsis–Valmiera line. Destinations from Sigulda include Rīga (€1.90, 1¼ hours).

Buses make the 50km run between Sigulda's **bus station** (off Ausekļa iela), next to the train station, and Rīga (€2.75, 1¼ hour, every 30 minutes between 7am and 10.30pm).

## Getting Around

Sigulda's attractions are quite spread out and after a long day of walking you'll enjoy the handy bus service that links the train station, Sigulda Castle Complex and Turaida Museum Reserve (€0.60).

# Līgatne

POP 1000

Deep in the heart of the Gauja National Park, little Līgatne is a twilight zone of opposite extremes. The town's collection of defunct and ugly industrial relics sprouts up from a patchwork of picturesque pine forests and cool blue rivulets. The old village is a tidy little gem and is right on the swift-flowing Līgatne River, a tributary of the Gauja. (The grim paper mill and worker housing is just north.)

## Sights

**Līgatne Nature Trails** NATURE RESERVE

(☎2832 8800; www.ligatnesdabastakas.lv; adult/child €3.60/2.10; ⊙9am-6pm Apr-Oct, to 4pm Nov-Mar) An odd cross between a nature park and a zoo, here elk, deer, bison and wild boar roam in open-air enclosures in the forest. From the parking area, a 4km trail links the main sights, which include several small cages holding some sad-eyed badgers and other critters. Along the way are observation stops and a 22m-high tower with good views of the birch and conifer forests and the Gauja River. It's 4km by bike from the town centre.

**Soviet Secret Bunker** HISTORIC SITE

(Padomju Slepenais Bunkurs; ☎6416 1915; www.bunkurs.lv; Skaļupes; guided tours adult/child €13.20/11.20; ⊙tours at noon, 2pm, 4pm Sat & Sun, 3pm Mon-Fri) What poses as a dreary rehabilitation centre is in fact a top-secret Soviet bunker, known by its code name, the Pension. When Latvia was part of the USSR, it was one of the most important strategic hideouts during a time of nuclear threat. Remarkably, almost all of the bunker's 2000 sq m still look as they did when it was in operation, making it a scarily authentic USSR time capsule.

Tours in English are offered on weekends and include a (surprisingly tasty) Soviet-style lunch served within the bunker's cafeteria. Note the plastic flowers on the table – they've been adorning the dining hall since 1982.

**Vienkoču Parks** SCULPTURE

(☎2932 9065; www.vienkoci.lv; adult/child €4/3; ⊙10am-6pm) Rihards, a local wood carver, has filled a 10-hectare park with his unique creations. Short trails snake past modern art installations, a classical garden, model houses and displays about wooden shipbuilding. Buy yourself a hand-crafted wooden bowl. The park is right off the A2, at the Līgatne turn.

## Sleeping & Eating

**Lāču Miga** GUESTHOUSE €€

(☎6415 3481; www.lacumiga.lv; Gaujas iela 22; r €36-56; P 🛜) Built in a large log chalet, the 'Bears' Den' stays true to its moniker with a gargantuan plush teddy bear positioned at the front entrance. Slews of stuffed bears welcome guests in the 12 rooms. The house is 1.5km from the historic centre.

**Vilhelmīnes dzirnavas** LATVIAN €

(☎2755 1311; Spriņģu iela 1; mains €5-10; ⊙10am-9pm) Located in the historic centre, Līgatne's most atmospheric restaurant serves up traditional food and drink such as beet soup, homemade meatballs and *kvass* (an alcoholic drink made from rye bread). On balmy days, sit outside on the covered terrace and watch bicycling tourists whizz past.

## Information

**Tourist Information Centre** (☎6415 3169; www.visitligatne.lv; Spriņģu iela 2; ⊙10am-6pm May-Sep) Very helpful and offers great advice for exploring the area, including pointing you in the direction of several small local museums.

## Getting There & Away

There are hourly buses to Sigulda (€1, 15 minutes) and Cēsis (€1.40, 30 minutes). Four trains daily stop at Līgatne station on their way to/from Rīga (€2.65, 1½ hours), Sigulda (€0.70, 10 minutes) and Cēsis (€1.55, 30 minutes). The train station is 6.5km south of the historic centre.

## Cēsis

POP 18,100

With its stunning medieval castle, cobbled streets, green hills and landscaped gardens, Cēsis is simply the cutest little town in Latvia. There's a lot of history here, too: it started eight centuries ago as a Livonian Order stronghold in a land of unruly pagans, and saw horrific battles right under (or inside) the castle walls. Although it makes a perfect day trip from Rīga, Cēsis is worth a longer stay, especially since there is the whole of Gauja National Park around it to explore.

### Sights

**★Cēsis Castle** CASTLE
(Cēsu pils; ☎2831 8318; www.cesupils.lv; Pils laukums 9; adult/child €8/4.50; ⏲10am-6pm daily May-Sep, to 5pm Tue-Sun Oct-Apr) Cēsis Castle is actually two castles in one. The moody dark-stone towers belong to the increasingly restored old castle. Founded by Livonian knights in 1214, it was sacked by Russian tsar Ivan the Terrible in 1577. The newer castle, the stolid 18th-century manor house, was once inhabited by the dynasty of German counts von Sievers and now houses a museum that features original fin-de-siècle interiors. In summer there is a demonstration garden showing how people ate 500 years ago.

After visiting the castle, take a walk through the landscaped **castle park** (Lenču iela 9a). Nearby is the hilltop **Russian Orthodox Church of Transfiguration** (Palasta 22), which the von Sievers built at their family cemetery (like many Germans on Russian service they converted to Orthodoxy).

**St John's Church** CHURCH
(Svētā Jāņa baznīca; www.cesujana.lelb.lv; ⏲10am-5pm) Switch on your imagination in this 13th-century church where armour-clad Livonian knights prayed and buried their dead in what was then a lonely island of Christianity surrounded by the lands of pagans. Currently under restoration, it's the home of the town's Lutheran community and the church contains tombs of the order's grand masters and top bishops.

### Activities

Many people rate the section of the Gauja River between Cēsis and Līgatne – lined with dramatic sandstone outcrops and especially verdant forest – as the most scenic. There is also some winter skiing in the area – think bunny slopes and top-notch cross-country.

**Žagarkalns** CANOEING
(☎2626 6266; www.zagarkalns.lv; Mūrlejas iela 12; canoe rental per trip from €45; ⏲hours vary by season; 👪) From its attractive riverside campground (€6 per person), 3km west of the centre, this adventure company rents canoes, kayaks and bikes for trips in the area, including the not-to-be-missed Cēsis–Līgatne river run. Rates include gear and transport. In winter, they have several gentle pistes, including one that goes through a forest, and a separate safe area for children to learn skiing.

**Cēsis Inside** WALKING
(☎2910 9965; www.cesisinside.lv; tours from €20) Experienced local guide Sigita Kletniece leads walking tours through historical Cēsis and out in the countryside around the river and national park. Experiences can include traditional pie-making, beer-tasting, castle-climbing and much more.

#### ĀRAIŠI

Photogenically set on an islet in the middle of Āraiši Lake, **Āraiši Archaeological Park** (☎2566 9935; http://amata.lv/araisu-arheologiskais-parks/; Āraišu ezerpils; adult/child €2/1; ⏲9am-7pm daily Apr-Oct, 10am-4pm Thu-Sun Nov-Mar) is a reconstruction of a fortified settlement inhabited by Latgallians, an ancient tribe that called the region home in the 9th and 10th centuries. A wooden walkway leads across the water to the unusual village, which was discovered by archaeologists in 1965.

Peering across the lake are the ruins of **Āraiši Stone Castle** (Āraišu mūra pils), built by Livonians in the 14th century and destroyed by Ivan IV's troops in 1577. From here, a path leads to a reconstructed Stone Age settlement – there are a couple of reed dwellings and earth ovens for roasting meat and fish. The fortress and castle, together with the iconic 18th-century **Āraiši windmill** (Āraišu vējdzirnavas), are signposted 1km along a dirt track from the main road and form the **Āraiši Museum Park** (Āraišu muzejparks). The complex is 7km south of Cēsis.

# Cēsis

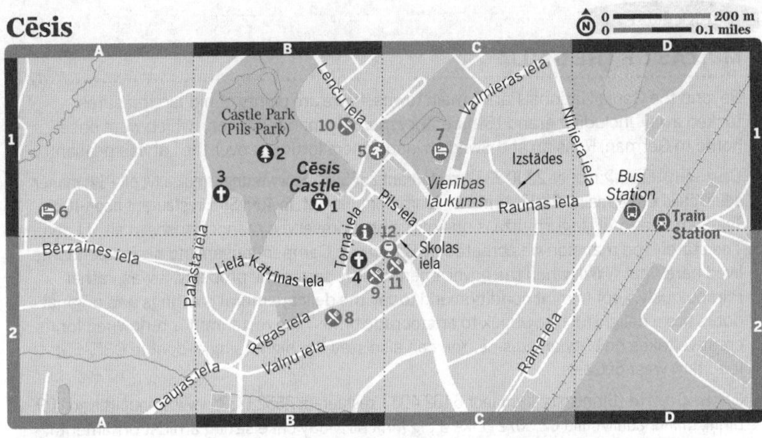


## Cēsis

**Top Sights**
1 Cēsis Castle ........ B1

**Sights**
2 Castle Park (Pils Park) ........ B1
3 Russian Orthodox Church of Transfiguration ........ B1
4 St John's Church ........ B2

**Activities, Courses & Tours**
5 Ezi Veikals ........ B1

**Sleeping**
6 Glūdas Grava ........ A1
7 Hotel Cēsis ........ C1

**Eating**
8 Cafe Priede ........ B2
9 Cēsu Maize ........ B2
10 Mākslas Telpa Mala ........ B1
11 Vinetas un Allas Kārumlādes ........ C2

**Drinking & Nightlife**
12 Trimpus Craft Brewery ........ C2

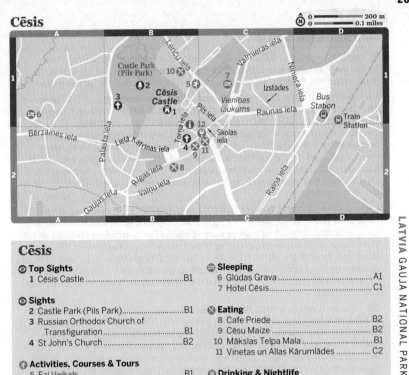

**Ezi Veikals** CYCLING
(☎2657 3132; www.veikals.ezi.lv; Pils laukums 1; bike/e-bike per day €10/25; ⏲9.30am-6pm Mon-Fri, 10am-4pm Sat) Good central source for rental bikes of many types, including e-bikes.

## Festivals & Events

There are concerts and festivals almost every weekend during the summer; visit http://cesufestivals.lv for details.

## Sleeping

Cēsis' popularity means that the selection of accommodation is ever-expanding, both in the historic town centre and in the lovely countryside.

**Hotel Cēsis** HOTEL €€
(☎6412 0122; www.hotelcesis.com; Vienības laukums 1; r from €55; P 📶) Though the exterior is vaguely neoclassical, the inside features rows of corporate-standard hotel rooms. The in-house restaurant serves good Latvian and European cuisine in a formal setting or on the lovely terrace overlooking manicured gardens.

**Kārlamūiža** HERITAGE HOTEL €€
(☎2616 5298; www.karlamuiza.lv; Kārļi; r from €55; P 📶) In the village of Kārļi, the barons von Sievers bought this country house in 1777 to go with their castle in Cēsis, 12km to the northeast. Reborn as a gentrified country hotel, the two-storey stone-sided building surrounded by an apple orchard has rustic-style rooms of varying size. Sit on the terrace and revel in the silence.

The restaurant is much heralded for its locally sourced cuisine.

**Glūdas Grava** APARTMENT €€
(☎2703 6862; www.gludasgrava.lv; Glūdas iela 6a; r from €55; P 📶) Each of the five studios with glassy front walls and individual entrances in a renovated brick garage is equipped with a kitchen and sleeps up to four people. It's close to the centre and you can relax on the outdoor terrace. Bike rentals available.

DON'T MISS

## MUIŽAS OF THE GAUJA

Beyond the Gauja National Park's main towns, there are plenty of hidden treasures tucked away, including grand 18th-century *muižas* (manor houses), which were once home to German, Russian and Swedish landowners lording it over the Latvian peasantry.

**Ungurmuiža** (☎manor 2200 7332, restaurant 2565 2388; www.ungurmuiza.lv; off P14; manor adult/child €3/2, mains €8-17; ⏱manor 10am-6pm Tue-Sat, to 4pm Sun, restaurant noon-10pm Tue-Sun) Beautiful Ungurmuiža is one of the best preserved manor houses in all of Latvia. The stately red mansion was created by Baron von Campenhousen and his descendants lived here until WWII, when the government swiftly seized the property. It was, rather miraculously, kept in mint condition and today the delicate mural paintings and original doors are a delightful throwback to aristocratic times. The restaurant is renowned for its creative takes on Latvian cuisine. You can also stay the night (single/double €35/55). It's 14km west of Cēsis.

**Bīriņi Castle** (Bīriņu pils; ☎manor 6402 4033, restaurant 2652 1733; www.birinupils.lv; off P9, Bīriņi; manor adult/child €2.50/2) Like a big pink birthday cake sitting amidst ornamental gardens, historic Bīriņi Castle governs a scenic tract of land overlooking a tranquil lake. The baronial estate has been transformed into an opulent hotel swathed in a Renaissance style focused around the grand foyer staircase. Daytime visitors can savour the opulence on a tour or boat ride. The restaurant serves traditional baronial fare (mains €11 to €25) and rooms (€65 to €95) come in several luxurious flavours. It's 20km northwest of Sigulda.

**Dikli Castle** (Diķu pils; ☎6402 7480; www.diklupils.lv; Dikli; r €70-125; ⏱restaurant 2-10pm Fri & Sat, other times by reservation; P 📶) It was here, in 1864, that a priest organised Latvia's first Song Festival, which gives Dikli Castle an important place in the nation's history. The current neobaroque aristocratic manor has been transformed into a luxurious retreat with hotel rooms and a lavish spa known for its herbal treatments. Visitors can enjoy strolls in the 20-hectare park, boat rides, and tours detailing the history and restoration of the manor. The restaurant (mains €17 to €23) is one of Latvia's best. It's 20km northwest of Valmiera.

**Annas Hotel** (☎6418 0700; www.annashotel.com; Annas; apt from €135; ⏱restaurant 9am-10pm; P 📶) Dating from the 18th century, Annas Hotel is a boutique property that fuses historical charm with thoroughly modern motifs. It's all about relaxation, and the hotel provides just that through spa sessions and lovely grounds peppered with trees and ponds. The restaurant (mains €17 to €26) is known for its complex, seasonal menu. It's 40km southeast of Sigulda.

**Villa Santa Hotel** HOTEL €€€
(☎6417 7177; www.villasanta.lv; Gaujas iela 88; r from €90; P 📶) Once used by the Russian nobility as holiday homes, three 19th-century wooden buildings have been transformed into a lovely hotel deep in the woods, near a river ravine, just west of the centre. Banishing decades of grim municipal furnishings, the rooms feature a mix of appealing modern and traditional-style furniture. The restaurant is also good.

## Eating & Drinking

Cēsis is becoming a great destination for food lovers. Day-trippers will be spoiled for lunch choices.

★ **Cēsu Maize** BAKERY €
(☎2641 2803; www.facebook.com/cesu.maize/; Rīgas iela 18; bread from €6; ⏱10am-6pm Mon-Fri, to 2pm Sat) This tiny craft bakery is always warm, humid and redolent with the scents of freshly baking bread. Hearty loaves made with whole grains and rye are close to the Latvian soul and here the big loaves are almost spiritual. Everything is locally grown and organic. Work your way through the generous samples.

**Mākslas Telpa Mala** CAFE €
(☎2610 1945; www.facebook.com/telpamala; Lenču iela 11; mains €3-5; ⏱noon-10pm Wed & Thu, to 2am Fri & Sat, to 6pm Sun; 📶) A haven for artists and art lovers, order a drink, open

a book and sit for a spell. There are regular gallery exhibitions and readings. Meals are simple, cheap and mostly vegan. Expect a hip soundtrack.

**Vinetas un Allas Kārumlādes** CAFE €

(☎2837 5579; Rīgas iela 12; snacks €2-5; ⏰8.30am-9pm Mon-Sat, 10am-6pm Sun) Nail your sweet tooth at this fancy bake shop and cafe. Look for pies, muffins and tarts made with local berries and rhubarb. There are over a dozen flavours of cake, as well as little sweets that are works of art. Sit back with a coffee or a glass of wine.

**Cafe Priede** CAFE €€

(☎2721 2727; www.facebook.com/kafepriede/; Rīgas iela 27; mains €5-12; ⏰11am-10pm) Overlooking the main square and fountain, this modern cafe has a seasonal menu with dishes crafted from local produce: it's all very fresh and inventive. Stop in for a coffee, a drink or a meal. Local artists are featured in the decor.

★**Trimpus Craft Brewery** MICROBREWERY

(☎2300 2000; https://trimpus.lv; Lielā Skolas iela 6; ⏰4-11pm Mon-Sat, 2-9pm Sun Jun-Aug, closed Sun-Tue Sep-May) This subterranean brewery has a great street terrace in the summer and a rotating line-up of house-made beers, sodas and ciders. Sour beers are a speciality.

## Information

**Tourism Information Centre** (☎2831 8318; www.tourism.cesis.lv; Baznīcas laukums 1; ⏰10am-6pm May-Sep, to 5pm Oct-Apr; 📶) Well versed in the many ways to first enjoy Cēsis, then explore the national park.

## Getting There & Away

Cēsis' **bus station** (Raiņa iela) and **train station** (Raiņa iela) share the same location, just east of the centre. There are five trains per day each way on the line from Rīga (€3.50, two hours). Towns served from Cēsis include Sigulda (€2, 40 minutes) and Valmiera (€1.55, 30 minutes).

Two or three buses per hour ply the route from Cēsis to Rīga (€4.15, two hours), stopping in Līgatne and Sigulda (€1.85, 45 minutes).

# Valmiera

POP 22,800

This pleasant university town often features as the starting point for boat trips on the Gauja River. The town is famous for its beer, which you must try here if you haven't elsewhere in Latvia.

## Sights & Activities

★**Valmiermuiža** BREWERY

(☎tour booking 2026 4296; www.valmiermuiza.lv; Dzirnavu iela 2; tours adult/child €9/3; ⏰tours daily with advance booking) See how one of Latvia's best-known craft beers is made on an entertaining tour: expect friendly guides and plenty of samples. Enjoy hearty pints and Latvian favourites with a seasonal twist in the **Beer Kitchen**, a lively cafe (open Friday evenings and from 10am Saturday and Sunday). Valmiermuiža is just north of the city centre, past Viestura laukums.

**Valmieras Muzejs** MUSEUM

(☎6422 3620; https://valmierasmuzejs.lv; Bruņinieku iela 3; adult/child €1.40/free; ⏰10am-5pm Mon-Sat) Exhibits at this enjoyable museum complex along the Gauja River are housed in eight historical buildings. Also on the grounds are medieval castle ruins and a herbal garden demonstrating how people made medicine and flavoured food hundreds of years ago.

**St Simon's Church** CHURCH

(Svētā Sīmaņa Baznīca; ☎6420 0333; www.simanadraudze.lv; Bruņinieku iela 2; tower adult/child €2/0.50; ⏰11am-6pm) Dating to 1283, St Simon's shelters medieval burial tombs, an altarpiece, *The Temptation* (1842), a pulpit from 1739 and an 1886 pipe organ.

**Eži Veikals** ADVENTURE SPORTS

(☎6420 7263; www.ezi.lv; Rīgas iela 43; bike/e-bike per day €10/25, canoe rental from €40; ⏰9am-7pm Mon-Fri, to 4pm Sat) If you need to rent a canoe, raft or bicycle for your Gauja National Park adventure (such as the 45km float to Cēsis), check out the selection here. It's located next to a popular skate park.

## Eating

**Vecpuisis** CAFE €€

(☎2611 0026; https://vecpuisis.lv; Leona Paegles iela 10; mains €7-12; ⏰11am-10pm Wed-Sun) Boasting a fabulous terrace overlooking a park, this genteel cafe in an elegant old building serves locally sourced seasonal fare. The menu melds Latvian and European favourites.

## Getting There & Away

Valmiera is on the train line with Cēsis, Sigulda and Rīga (€4.20, 2½ to three hours, five daily). There are hourly buses to/from Cēsis (€1.80, 45 minutes).

# SOUTHEASTERN LATVIA (LATGALE)

Welcome to the breadbasket. Latgale, Latvia's southeast region, is dissected by the mighty Daugava and dotted with scenic lakes hidden in the depths of a thick forest. German knights failed to capture Latgale at the dawn of Latvia's history, which sent the region along a rather different historical path than the rest of the country. Russian, Polish and Jewish influences are felt more strongly here, while locals tend to think of themselves as Latgalean first and Latvian second. It's a fertile land of farmers, who speak a distinct dialect, which many believe should be branded a separate language.

Latgale's two main cities, Daugavpils and Rēzekne, are slowly shedding their grey Soviet clothes and putting on a modern cosmopolitan outfit. Latgale is a good addition to an itinerary that includes Lithuania to the south and the Daugava River Valley (p254) to the west.

## Daugavpils

POP 85,000

Latvia's second-largest city has a walkable old centre and a don't-miss old fortress on the Daugava River. Predominantly Russian-speaking, Daugavpils was once a provincial Russian imperial town with a thriving Jewish community. Today it struggles with population loss as ethnic Russians have moved across the nearby border.

The city's greatest celebrity, Mark Rothko, travelled across the ocean to become one of America's most notable 20th-century artists. A contemporary art centre honours his work and legacy.

### Sights

Daugavpils has an interesting historical centre that's a disharmonious mix of old brick buildings, the odd art nouveau gem, grumpy Soviet-era piles and a few 1990s mirrored-glass oddities. It's well worth a stroll, and in the evening you'll have plenty of company as locals promenade along the mostly pedestrian Rīgas iela.

The city's incongruous centrepiece, the Soviet-era modernist Park Hotel Latgola, provides a sweeping 360-degree panorama from its top-floor restaurant and bar – a good place for a local overview.

**★Daugavpils Fortress** FORTRESS

(off Daugavpils iela; 24hr) FREE This impressive riverside citadel is enjoying an ongoing renovation that's recreating its historic atmosphere. Look for the restored **Nicholas Gate** near the excellent Mark Rothko Art Centre. Built on the orders of tsar Alexander I on the eve of the Napoleonic wars, the fortress served as an imperial stronghold during two Polish insurrections in the 19th century and as a home away from home for tsars exploring their realm. It's a 3km walk northwest of the centre along the river.

Although the architecture is rather utilitarian, you can make out Gothic and Egyptian motives in the decor of its four gates – all named after Russian royals. The fortress itself survived two centuries of wars and revolutions largely intact, but the beautiful 18th-century Jesuit cathedral that stood in the middle was destroyed by WWII bombardment, its ruins later cleared by the Soviets, who instead built a cluster of ugly generic apartment blocks for the military. A plaque outside the main gate states that Tatar poet Musa Jalil languished here from September to October 1942, in what was then the Nazi concentration camp Stalag-340. Inside, a memorial marks the site where local aristocrat Leon Plater was executed by the tsar's soldiers for leading the Polish revolt in the area in 1863.

**Daugavpils Mark Rothko Art Centre** ARTS CENTRE

(6543 0250; www.rothkocenter.com; Mihaila iela 3; adult/child €8/4; 11am-7pm Wed-Sat, to 5pm Tue & Sun) The old imperial Russian arsenal inside Daugavpils Fortress is now an excellent contemporary art gallery honouring Daugavpils native Mark Rothko. The permanent collection includes hundreds of works by visiting artists, as well as some Rothko originals and displays about the artist's work. It also hosts myriad temporary exhibitions.

The 1st floor is dedicated to Rothko, whose surrealist and abstract works led him to stardom in America, where he emigrated at age 10 in 1913 (he died in New York City in 1970). An interactive multimedia exhibition recapping Rothko's biography and explaining the historical context of his childhood years is followed by a small display of Rothko's original works representing 'multiform', the series that he

## DAUGAVPILS' LOST JEWISH HERITAGE

A census conducted in 1897 showed that 46% of Daugavpils (then known as Dvinsk) residents were Jews, which made them the largest, if not the most powerful, community. The city was teeming with Jewish-run businesses, as well as cultural, religious and political institutions. In the streets, Yiddish could be heard more often than Russian, Latvian or Polish.

There are only a few hundred Jews left now, and few are descended from the original Jewish inhabitants. When the Nazis seized Daugavpils in 1941, they drove 14,000 local Jews into a ghetto that was located in an outpost of the Rīga Citadel on the far side of the river. Gradually, nearly all these people were executed, or starved and worked to death.

One killing ground, the **Railwaymen's Garden** (Preču iela 30a), is just 1.5km southeast of the Daugavpils synagogue, near railway tracks and close to Church Hill. A plaque at the forlorn site notes 'In July 1941, the Nazis executed here more than 1000 of Daugavpils Jews'. Barely 100 people survived till the Soviet army recaptured the city. The synagogue has a small museum about local Jewish history.

created in the later period of his life. The 2nd floor is dedicated to contemporary Latvian artists. There is a good cafe situated on-site.

**Daugavpils Synagogue** SYNAGOGUE
(☎2954 8760; www.jewishlatgale.lv; Cietokšņa iela 38; €5; ⊙by appointment, Thu-Sun) FREE The city's main synagogue was built in 1850 and beautifully restored in 2005, thanks to the contributions of Mark Rothko's children. Arrange a visit (by phone or email) with local historian Josifs Ročko, who maintains a small on-site museum about local Jewish history.

**Church Hill** CHRISTIAN SITE
Churches of four main local Christian denominations congregate near each other on a small hill dissected by busy 18 Novembra iela. Lutherans flock into the red-brick neo-Gothic **Martin Luther Cathedral** (18 Novembra iela 66), while Catholics congregate at pure-white **Holy Virgin Cathedral** (Andreja Pumpura iela 11a). Both are east of the Russian Orthodox **Cathedral of Princes Boris & Gleb** (Tautas iela 2) and the gold-domed Old Believer's **Novostroyensky Church of Resurrection, Holy Virgin & St Nikola** (Puškina iela 16a).

The first three are open to visitors during business hours. Church Hill is about 2km east of the centre.

**Daugavpils Lead Shot Factory** HISTORIC BUILDING
(DSR; ☎2776 6655; www.dsr.lv; Varšavas ielā 28; tour adult/child €5.50/3.50, admission only €1.50; ⊙10am-5pm daily Jun-Aug, Wed-Sun Sep-May) As you'll learn at this tall brick tower built in 1886, ammunition used to require gravity. Molten lead was poured from the top of the tower, and by the time the drops reached the bottom, they solidified into perfectly round balls, ready to be used in guns. You won't see the actual process, but they'll turn on century-old machines for you and let you climb the tower. Check English-language tour times. It's about 2km east of the centre on a hill.

## Sleeping

Staying in the centre allows you to enjoy the local street life.

**★Mark Rothko Art Centre Residences** GUESTHOUSE €€
(☎6543 0250; www.rothkocenter.com; Mihaila iela 3; s/d from €30/40; P 📶) Here is your chance to spend a real night at the museum. Although intended for resident and visiting artists, rooms at the art centre incorporate architectural details of the historic building. Decor fittingly features primary colours in a stark design. You also get the run of the Daugavpils Fortress. Reserve rooms through www.booking.com.

**Homelike Hotel** HOTEL €€
(☎6582 4000; www.homelikehotel.lv; Mihoelsa iela 66; r from €40; P ❄ 📶) Perfectly located, this small three-storey hotel is in a renovated building just off the main pedestrian street. Rooms are modern, although cynics should note that the walls bear treacly bromides such as 'Fill a house with love and it becomes a home'. Don't bother springing for a balcony room: the view is of an alley. Good breakfast included.

## Southeastern Latvia (Latgale)

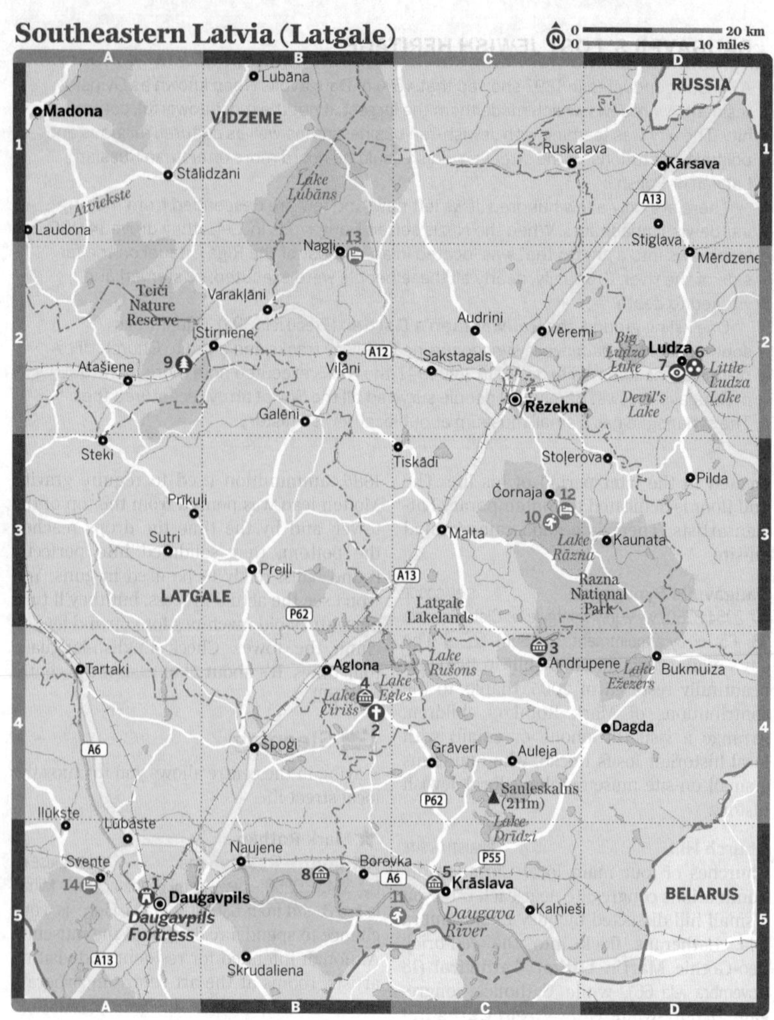




**Villa Ksenija** GUESTHOUSE €€
(☎6543 4317; www.villaks.lv; Varšavas iela 17; s/d from €50/58; P ) Occupying a stately mansion that was built in 1876, this hotel provides a relatively plush, if not very central, option 2km east of the Daugavpils centre. The rooms are comfortable and have period-style furniture, but the garden is the best feature – take breakfast here on a warm day.

**Sventes Muiža** HOTEL €€
(Jaunsvente Manor; ☎6542 7822; www.svente-hotel.lv; Alejas iela 7, Svente; r from €45; @ ) Count Michael Plater-Ziberg, a scion of Latgale's most prominent aristocratic family, had just two years before WWI broke out to enjoy the grand estate house he built for himself 13km west of Daugavpils. It's now a welcoming countryside hotel with a good restaurant and, slightly off-topic, a museum of WWII vehicles and tanks. The grounds are park-like.

**Park Hotel Latgola** HOTEL €€
(☎6540 4900; www.hotellatgola.lv; Ģimnāzijas iela 46; r €45-85; P ) The city's centrepiece and also its largest building, this 10-storey Soviet monument sports modern corporate hotel-style rooms behind

## Southeastern Latvia (Latgale)

**Top Sights**
1 Daugavpils Fortress....A5

**Sights**
2 Aglona Basilica....B4
3 Andrupene Farmstead Museum....C4
4 Bread Museum....B4
Daugavpils Mark Rothko Art Centre....(see 1)
5 Kraslava Castle....C5
6 Ludza Castle....D2
7 Ludza Craftsmen Centre....D2
8 Slutišķi Old-believers' Farmstead....B5
9 Teiči Nature Reserve Watchtower....A2

**Activities, Courses & Tours**
10 Buru Guru....C3
11 Klajumi Stables....C5

**Sleeping**
Aglonas Cakuli....(see 4)
12 Ezerkrasti....C3
13 House Stikāni....B2
Mark Rothko Art Centre Residences....(see 1)
14 Sventes Muiža....A5

**Eating**
Café Kristīne....(see 7)

its glitzed-up facade. It's situated right on the pedestrian street.

### Eating & Drinking

Try a shot of Latgale's own liquor, the potent (about 100 proof) *šmakovka:* it's clear, but your head won't be. It's made locally by enthusiasts who often add their own flavourings to the mix.

**★Cafe Imbir** CAFE €
(☎2450 9965; www.facebook.com/pg/kafeimbir; Saules iela 39; mains €3-7; ⊙10am-7pm Tue-Sun) Resplendent in white, this city-centre cafe has a couple of tables out front on the street. Inside you'll find excellent coffee, daily specials, light meals and luscious baked goods, plus surprises like board games.

**Vēsma** PUB FOOD €€
(☎2200 9991; Rīgas iela 49; mains €5-12; ⊙11am-10pm Sun-Thu, to midnight Fri & Sat) This big cafe offers genuine cafe culture with tables on a wide terrace overlooking the main pedestrian zone. (Or rise above it all on the roof deck.) Dishes span the world, from sushi to pizza, but stick close to home and opt for the Latgale dishes, which are flagged on the menu. There's a long drinks menu.

**Gubernators** RUSSIAN €€
(☎6542 2455; www.gubernators.lv; Lāčplēša iela 10; mains €5-9; ⊙11am-midnight) Sporting rustic decor with a hint of Soviet nostalgia, this cellar restaurant serves Russian *pelmeņi* dumplings and excellent Russian-style sour vegetable soup (*solyanka*), plus many more Eastern European favourites, along with its own brand of beer.

**Artilērijas Pagrabi** BAR
(www.facebook.com/ArtilerijasPagrabi; Rīgas iela 22; ⊙from 7pm Wed-Sun) This easy-going subterranean place sees itself as something of a Latvian cultural bastion in the east, its fire power generated by great local beer and regular live gigs featuring bands (mostly rock) from Latvia and lands beyond the frontier. The burgers are popular.

### Information

**Tourist Office** (www.visitdaugavpils.lv; Rīgas iela 22a; ⊙10am-6pm daily Apr-Sep, closed Sun Oct-Mar) Well stocked with information detailing sights and activities across Latgale.

### Getting There & Away

Train services from the **train station** (Stacijas iela 44), at the east end of Rīgas iela, include Rīga (€7, 3½ hours, three daily) and Minsk in Belarus (€31, nine hours, three weekly). There is a handy weekends-only service twice a day to Vilnius (€9, 2¾ hours).

From the centrally located **bus station** (☎6542 3000; www.buspark.lv; Viestura iela 10), buses run to/from Rīga (€9, 3½ hours, hourly) and Rēzekne (€4, 1½ to two hours, six daily), as well as Vilnius in Lithuania (€13, 3½ hours, two daily).

## Around Daugavpils

The gently rolling hills around Daugavpils are threaded with rivers connecting some pastoral lakes. Atmospheric tiny hamlets seem unchanged in decades. Population loss means you'll see plenty of old abandoned farms and often have the roads to yourself.

OFF THE BEATEN TRACK

### ON HOME SOIL

Latvians remain attached to their land to a great extent. And not just any land, but particular farmsteads owned by their parental families. Many urbanites still have relatives running a farm, which often comes with fruit gardens, a large chunk of forest and a lake. Summer months are spent in the countryside with their grandparents, aunts and uncles. This ongoing attachment can be explained by the fact that cities and towns were for centuries run by conquerors – Germans, Russians or Swedes.

The en-masse migration of ethnic Latvians into urbanised areas only began in the 19th century. However, the situation in the countryside became chaotic beginning with WWII and continued with the later collectivisation of farms and the forced migration of thousands of farming families to Siberia. Since 1991 there have been extraordinary efforts made to sort out land claims and return farms to their original families. The process has been fraught for myriad reasons, one of which is that farms are uneconomic: you'll see many abandoned farmhouses as you drive around rural Latvia.

American writer Inara Verzemnieks writes movingly about her family's struggles to come to terms with their recent past and ties to a eastern Latvian farm in *Among the Living and the Dead: A Tale of Exile and Homecoming on the War Roads of Europe*.

If you want to learn more about traditional rural life, head to **Andrupene Farmstead Museum** (☎2645 8876; laukuseta@inbox.lv; Skolas iela 5, Andrupene; adult/child €3/1; ⊙9am-5pm Tue-Fri, 10am-2pm Sat), which occupies a farm that remains unaltered since the 1920s, when many Latvians received generous chunks of land in the agrarian reform. Contact them in advance to arrange a traditional Latgale dinner served with traditional bread they bake on the spot.

The village of Andrupene is located 30km east of Aglona, near Dadga. You'll need your own wheels to get there.

## Slutišķi

POP 100

Sitting on the bank of the Daugava, this bucolic hamlet of log cabins has a lovely riverfront setting and is populated by Russian Old Believers. It served as an unlikely catalyst of Latvia's Third Atmoda (National Awakening), which led to the restoration of independence in 1991. A newspaper article criticising the Soviet government's plan to build a hydropower station and flood Slutišķi generated public outcry that turned its author, Dainis Īvans, into an instant hero. Soon he was the leader of Latvian Popular Front, a movement that made the liberation happen.

Slutišķi is surrounded by **Daugavas Loki nature park**, which protects a particularly beautiful stretch of the gracefully bending Daugava. One of the scattered farms has been transformed into the **Slutišķi Oldbelievers' Farmstead** (☎2653 2508; http://naujenesmuzejs.lv; Slutišķi; adult/child €1.50/1; ⊙10am-7pm Wed-Sun May-Sep, 8am-5pm Tue-Fri Oct-Apr), which details local life dating back to the 1700s. Outside the fir-log building are exhibits about local farming and good signboards detailing local life. Nearby is a picnic area as well as riverside trails.

### Getting There & Away

Slutišķi is located near the village of Markova, 28km east of Daugavpils on the A6 to Krāslava. The turn is well signposted. It's about 800m to the parking area in the park. The village is then about a 500m walk. The route is good for bikes.

## Krāslava

POP 7900

Just 6km north of the Belarus border, sleepy Krāslava is a picturesque town of wooden houses set amid the green hills embracing the Daugava. A former domain of the Polish Plater family, Krāslava has always been an intriguing multicultural melting pot. Its coat of arms displays five oars symbolising five local communities: Poles, Latvians, Belarusians, Russians and Jews. The latter used to be the largest group, but virtually all of them perished in the Holocaust.

The small town centre, down the hill from the castle, has a couple of modest cafes.

**Krāslava Castle** MUSEUM

(☎6562 3586; Pils iela; adult/child €2/1; ⊙grounds 24hr, museum 10am-5pm Mon-Sat, to 2pm Sun) Occupying a key vantage point, Krāslava's 'castle' is really a modest manor house. Its historic interior is closed to visitors, but the floral-scented grounds are pretty and good for strolling. Part of the complex, the small **History and Art Museum** has displays outside showing pictures of local life since the 1850s. A nearby tourist information office (www.visitkraslava.com) sells local crafts.

**Klajumi Stables** HORSEBACK RIDING
(☎2947 2638; www.klajumi.lv; 2-/4-/7-day tours €125/310/585, 1hr ride €20) Ilze, the owner of Klajumi Stables, comes from an equestrian family and offers a variety of activities from multiday riding tours to short countryside jaunts. The adorable, large guest cottages (from €50) look like gingerbread houses and have beautiful, rural settings. One comes with a sauna (that doubles as a shower), a kitchenette and a loft bedroom with satellite TV. Toilets are located in outdoor huts. The stables are 8km southwest of Krāslava, near Kaplava.

### Getting There & Away

Krāslava is on the road leading from Daugavpils to Vitsebsk in Belarus. Buses for Daugavpils are hourly (€2.35, one hour). There are two morning buses a day to Aglona (€2, one hour).

## Aglona

POP 870

Teeny Aglona, sitting on an isthmus between two large placid lakes, is one of the most visited towns in all of Latvia. But that only becomes apparent for a few days around 15 August, when thousands of Catholic pilgrims from across Eastern Europe arrive to celebrate Assumption Day in the town's basilica. At other times, Aglona is a quiet village with a good bakery/museum and houses noted for their lush vegetable and flower gardens.

### Sights

**Aglona Basilica** CHURCH
(☎6538 1109; www.aglonasbazilika.lv; Ciriša iela 8; ⊙7am-8pm) More than 300 years ago, a group of wandering Dominican monks discovered a healing source hidden among a thicket of spruce trees ('Aglona' means 'spruce tree' in an old dialect). It became a place of pilgrimage and, although the sulphur fount lost its apparent power a century later, the water from the source is still regarded as a product of divine intervention and is used in rituals. On Assumption Day, enormous numbers of Catholic pilgrims celebrate mass here.

Today's basilica is a twin-towered whitewashed cathedral standing in a vast grass courtyard, created for Pope John Paul II's visit in 1993 to bestow the title of Basilica Minoris (Small Basilica) upon the holy grounds. One of the basilica's 10 altars guards a sacred icon of the Virgin Mary, said to have saved Aglona from the plague in 1708. Mass is held at 7am, noon and 7pm Monday to Saturday and at 10am, noon and 7pm on Sunday. Rosary is held at 11am Monday to Saturday and at 9am on Sunday.

**Bread Museum** MUSEUM
(Aglonas maizes muzejs; ☎2928 7044; Daugavpils iela 7; adult/child €4/2; ⊙8.30am-4pm Mon-Fri, 9am-2pm Sat & Sun) Learn about the history and traditions surrounding traditional Latgalian dark rye bread, a local staple, and try your hand at milling grain and baking. Little English is spoken, so call ahead to arrange a complimentary translator. Even if you don't have time for the one-hour presentation, be sure to buy a fresher-than-fresh loaf of gorgeous bread still warm from the large oven. Peek through the window into the kitchen to watch the bakers hard at work.

### Sleeping

**Aglonas Cakuli** GUESTHOUSE €
(☎2933 3422; http://aglonascakuli.lv; Ezera iela 4; r with/without bathroom from €40/35; 📶) Near the bread museum in town, this comfy family-run guesthouse is right on Lake Cirišs. It has eight rooms, a playground for kids and a sauna. You can arrange for a boat on the lake as well as meals. They also rent lakeside cottages near the basilica.

### Getting There & Around

Aglona is 9km off the main road between Daugavpils and Rēzekne (Rte A13). There are two buses a day to/from Daugavpils (€3, one hour) and two to Krāslava (€2, one hour). For Rēzekne and Rīga, change at Preiļi (€1.50, 35 minutes, seven daily).

## Rēzekne

POP 28,100

Rēzekne furtively pokes its head up from a giant muddle of derelict factories and generic block housing. The town took a heavy beating during WWII, when most of its historic buildings were pulverised by artillery fire. It's worth a stop, however, for some historic sights and good places to eat and drink. Frequent trains and buses also make it a convenient jumping-off point to explore the quiet lakeland further south.

## Sights

**Gors** CULTURAL CENTRE
(☎6463 3303; http://latgalesgors.lv; Pils iela 4; ⊙hours vary) An elegant and modern addition to the middle of town, Gors is a large cultural centre. Art exhibitions, cultural displays, concerts, films, poetic readings – you name it – take place regularly.

**Green Synagogue** SYNAGOGUE
(☎2659 5017; http://sinagoga.lv; Krāslavas iela 5; donations accepted; ⊙10am-3pm Wed & Sat) Close to Latgales iela and the old Jewish quarter, this 1845 synagogue is indeed green. Restored inside and out to past wooden glory, there are displays about local Jewish culture through the centuries and the stolid wooden architecture popular throughout Latgale. There's a good cafe across the street.

**Māra** MONUMENT
(Atbrīvošanas aleja 93) In the middle of the town's square stands Māra, a statue twice destroyed by the Soviet authorities in the 1940s and only re-erected in 1992. Its inscription 'Vienoti Latvijai' means 'United Latvia'.

**Latgales iela** STREET
(Latgales iela) The town's oldest street is lined with dozens of charming brick facades constructed by wealthy Yiddish merchants several hundred years ago.

## Sleeping

**Kolonna** HOTEL €€
(☎6460 7820; www.hotelkolonna.com; Brīvības iela 2; r from €54; P 📶) This corporate-style hotel has 41 comfortable rooms in a stately art deco building in the centre, near Latgales iela. The attached Rozalija restaurant serves European standards as well as Latgale specialities. It has a fine patio.

## Eating & Drinking

**Ausmeņa Kebabs** MIDDLE EASTERN €
(☎2011 2200; Rancāna iela 41; mains €3-5; ⊙11am-10pm Sun-Thu, to 2am Fri & Sat) It's hard to explain how a kebab shop could have grown into a local institution known for its bohemian drinks and fervent pro-Latvian spirit, but there you are. Turkish-style kebabs come in their pita-wrapped takeaway forms, as well as served on a plate with chips. It's one street northeast of the central square and has a large, covered terrace.

**Marijas Cafe** LATVIAN €€
(☎2651 4420; Atbrīvošanas aleja 88; mains €5-17; ⊙11am-11pm) The best restaurant in town is just south of the central square and back off the main drag. There's a casual cafe menu as well as more substantial meals such as steaks, pasta and a long list of Latvian and local faves. The bar area and dining room have arched brick and stone walls. Outside there's a sunny terrace. Service is smooth.

**Fresh Terase** BEER GARDEN
(☎2065 5740; www.facebook.com/freshterase; Atbrīvošanas aleja 142; mains €4-8; ⊙5-11pm Mon-Fri, 1-11pm Sat & Sun) A real beer garden! Enjoy excellent local brews under fruit trees laden with apples at this popular spot at the north end of town. The menu includes grilled meats, snacks and sandwiches.

## Information

**Tourist Information Centre** (☎6460 7609; www.rezekne.lv; Krasta iela 31, Zeimuļs Creative Centre; ⊙10am-6pm Mon-Fri, to 4pm Sat) An excellent tourist office located in the new Zeimuļs Creative Centre, a striking modern structure just across from the remains (think piles of stones) of Rēzekne Castle. There is a good cafe in the complex as well as an observation deck with sweeping views of Latgale.

## Getting There & Away

The **bus station** (Latgales iela 17) has services to/from Daugavpils (€4, 1½ to two hours, six daily) and Rīga (€10, four to 4½ hours, six daily), among other destinations.

**Rēzekne II train station** (Stacijas iela) has services to Rīga (€7, 3½ hours, two daily).

Exploring the region around Rēzekne will mostly require your own wheels.

# Around Rēzekne

The thinly populated lands around Rēzekne include dozens of lakes, including two large ones: Lakes Rāzna and Lubāns. Both offer water sports and idyllic rural retreats amidst the green countryside. The former is also the centrepiece of one of Latvia's four national parks. You'll want your own wheels to explore the lakes.

## Lake Rāzna

**Rāzna National Park** was established in 2007 to protect the blue waters of Lake Rāzna, Latvia's second-largest lake. Still mostly undeveloped, the park is a quiet preserve protecting roughly 530 sq km of verdant lakelands. Infrastructure like visitor centres and hiking trails remain in the future, although there is a designated cycling route fully encircling the lake. Discovering a few quiet beaches on a bike ride is an ideal way to spend a day, although you'll need to bring your own bike.

The small old fishermen's villages around Lake Rāzna were founded by Russian Old Believers, who gave them Slavic-sounding names.

**Buru Guru** BOATING

(2983 3890; http://buruguru.lv; Dukstigala Bay, Čornaja, off P55; sailing tour for up to 20 people €180, sleeping per night €100) Join Captain Andris Strutskis for a lake voyage on his ocean-going sailing boat *Sea Esta*. Unless you travel in a large group, it makes sense to enquire in advance about the possibility of sharing the sailing tour price with other travellers. The boat is also available as a romantic floating hotel.

**Ezerkrasti** GUESTHOUSE €

(2641 1207; www.raznasezerkrasti.lv; Dukstigals, Tilīši, Čornajas pagasts, off P55; per person from €30; ) At the mouth of Dukstigals Bay, you'll find Ezerkrasti Resort: this lush green property dotted with charming wooden cottages in a variety of shapes and sizes offers volleyball, paddleboats, a lake for swimming, and an indoor pool and sauna. It's 20km southeast of Rēzekne.

## Lake Lubāns

Latvia's largest lake is very shallow, its shores covered in reeds and encircled by a fir tree forest so dark and wild you can shoot films about Siberia here. Around 180 species of birds, including swans and eagles, nest here and there are several watchtowers in the area for spotting.

Three kilometres south of the tiny village of Īdeņa, look for the **Teirumnīku Swamp Trail**. It runs for 800m into pristine wetlands near the lake.

**Baka Water Tourism Centre** WATER SPORTS

(2666 3358; https://baka.rezeknesnovads.lv; Kvāpāni; kayak or bicycle rental per hour €6; 9am-7pm Tue-Sun May-Sep) This striking water-sports centre with a lighthouse motif is on a very quiet bit of Lake Lubāns. The three-storey building anchors a range of activities that include SUP, kayaks, waterskiing and more, or you can rent a bike and try the new waterside cycling route. Ask about renting a room looking over a sea of reeds (from €60). It's 43km northwest of Rēzekne.

**Zvejnieki** GUESTHOUSE €

(2830 1143; www.zvejnieki.lv; Īdeņa, Nagļi pagasts; dm from €8, 8-person cottage €64) Offers beds in atmospheric wooden houses scattered around its property. Excellent Latgale meals made with produce from the garden and lake fish (smoked or fresh) can be arranged in advance. Also, ask about a whole range of available activities, including fishing, birdwatching and guided nature hikes, when you book. It's 40km northwest of Rēzekne on an isthmus in the lake.

**House Stikāni** GUESTHOUSE €€

(2867 1971; ilze@dabastures.lv; Bernāni, Rēzeknes novads; r from €50) Century-old apple trees shade this vintage wooden house in the village of Bernāni in a remote corner of Lake Lubāns. Bird-spotters and nature hikers will revel in the quiet beauty. There are four basic rooms and meals are available. It's 38km northwest of Rēzeknes.

## Ludza

POP 8000

Little Ludza, just a hop from the Russian border, was founded in 1177, making it the oldest town in Latvia. Located at the junction of two lakes (known as Big Ludza Lake and Little Ludza Lake), the small village and trading post grew around a 14th-century castle. Today Ludza feels like a frontier post, with quiet streets at the tail end of the country. You can't get closer to rural life than here.

**Ludza Craftsmen Centre** CULTURAL CENTRE

(2946 7925; www.ludzasamatnieki.lv; Tālavijas iela 27a; 9am-5pm Mon-Fri, to 2.30pm Sat) This centre in an old brick and wood building set back from the street features a great array of locally made handicrafts, including beautiful wool garments and gloves. The centre has three attached workshops in which local artisans perfect their trade. If you ring ahead, you too can try your hand at time-honoured methods of wool spinning, pottery making and sewing. There's a collection of old tools to peruse and a traditional Latgalian costume to try on for picture taking.

**Ludza Castle** RUINS

(Lielā Ezerkrasta iela 19) Built by German crusaders in 1399 to protect the eastern front of the Livonian Order, the castle has been in ruins since 1775. Today the melange of crumbling crimson brick and smoky grey boulders is both haunting and beautiful, and makes a great place for a picnic overlooking the church spires and rivulets down the hill. Nearby are the twin towers of the reconstructed Church of the Assumption.

**Café Kristīne** CAFE €

(☎6578 1326; Baznīcas iela 25; mains €4-7; ⏰10am-7pm Mon-Fri, 11am-8pm Sat, noon-5pm Sun) This old-fashioned cafe serves Latvian favourites (get your grey peas here!) made from local produce. Try a local speciality such as *gulbešnīki* (stuffed potato dumplings). The coffee is good and there are sunny tables outside on the small square.

### ℹ Getting There & Away

Ludza is located 26km east of Rēzekne along Rte A12 as it makes its way into Russia. Buses to Rēzekne (€1.70, 40 minutes) run through the day; some continue to Daugavpils.

# UNDERSTAND LATVIA

## Latvia Today

The legacy of Latvia's history is inescapable today. The small nation remains haunted by the series of invasions and occupations around WWII, when the population was decimated by war, the Holocaust, people fleeing as refugees and forced deportations. Five decades of stagnation during the Soviet occupation have not been fully reversed in the almost 30 years later. Travel down any street in the country outside the very core of Rīga and you'll still see one decayed building after another.

Adding to the uncertainty is the ever-present fear of Russia's intentions. Despite membership in the EU and NATO, people remember the two occupations in the last 80 years. The narrow gap between Belarus and Kaliningrad along the Polish–Lithuanian border looks very small and very far away at times.

Even as Rīga exudes energy from new business ventures and a thriving creative community, the nation's overall population continues to decline. The population loss of 1% a year is the second highest in the EU after Bulgaria. Young people, well versed in English in Latvia's public schools, leave for seemingly brighter futures elsewhere in the EU.

Many are looking forward to the Rail Baltica (p427) project, which will link the Baltic nations by high-speed rail to Poland and Western Europe, lessening their isolation, both perceived and real. If nothing else, closer integration with Europe could allow more people to discover Rīga's beauty, the lush countryside and the fantastical coastline and beaches.

## History

### The Beginning

The first signs of modern humans in the region date back to the Stone Age, although Latvians descended from tribes that migrated north from around Belarus and settled on the territory of modern Latvia around 2000 BC. These tribes settled in coastal areas to fish and take advantage of rich deposits of amber, which was more precious than gold in many places until the Middle Ages.

Eventually, four main Baltic tribes evolved: the Selonians, the Letts (or Latgals), the Semigallians and the Cours. From the latter three the names of three of Latvia's four principal regions are derived: Latgale, Zemgale and Kurzeme. The fourth region, Vidzeme (Livland), derived its name from the Livs, a Finno-Ugric people unrelated to the Balts.

During succeeding centuries of foreign rule these tribes merged into one Latvian identity. They were pagan until the 13th century, when German knights forced them into the Christian fold with sword and fire. But pagan traditions have lingered up until the present day, with Midsummer celebrated as the most important national holiday.

### GREY SKIES ARE GONNA CLEAR UP...

Since 1991, Latvia's environmental climate has improved by leaps and bounds, largely due to tax reforms, an infusion of EU and private money, and the collapse of Soviet-era heavy industry. More than 1300 wastewater treatment plants have been built, which has increased the purity of river waters – the Daugava and Lielupe Rivers are now deemed 'good-quality'.

Latvia's water and sewage reforms are restoring the Baltic Sea and Gulf of Rīga to their former swimmable state. The European Blue Flag water safety and purity ranking (with its rigorous criteria) has been awarded to over 20 beaches, including ones at Jūrmala, Ventspils, Liepāja, Saulkrasti and Rīga.

Stringent rules, both EU and Latvian, regulate auto and truck emissions, pesticide and fertiliser use on farms and myriad other polluting practices.

## Christianity

Arriving in Latvia in 1190, the first Christian missionaries tried to persuade the pagan population to convert. It was an uphill battle: as soon as the missionaries left, the new converts jumped into the river to wash off their baptism. In subsequent years more missionaries would arrive, and more Latvians would submit and then renounce Christianity.

In 1201, at the behest of the pope, German crusaders, led by Bishop von Buxhoevden of Bremen, conquered Latvia and founded Rīga. Von Buxhoevden also founded the Knights of the Sword, who made Rīga their base for subjugating Livonia. Colonists from northern Germany followed, and during the first period of German rule, Rīga became the major city in the German Baltic, thriving from trade between Russia and the West and joining the Hanseatic League (a medieval merchant guild) in 1282. Furs, hides, honey and wax were among the products sold westward from Russia through Rīga. Indigenous Baltic inhabitants were sidelined from the regional politics and urbanisation.

Power struggles between the Church, knights and city authorities dominated the country's history between 1253 and 1420. Rīga's bishop, elevated to archbishop in 1252, became the leader of the Church in the German-conquered lands, ruling a good slice of Livonia directly and further areas of Livonia and Estonia indirectly through his bishops. The Church clashed constantly with knights, who controlled most of the remainder of Livonia and Estonia, and with German merchant-dominated city authorities who managed to maintain a degree of independence during this period.

## Sweden, Poland & Russia

The 15th, 16th and 17th centuries were marked with battles and disputes about how to divvy up what would one day become Latvia. The land was at the crossroads of several encroaching empires and everyone wanted to secure the area as a means of gaining a strategic upper hand. It was at this time that Martin Luther posted his theses and Lutheran ideals flooded east. Rīga quickly became a centre for the Reformation and merchant elites adopted the doctrine. Fervent religious movements spawned the emergence of written Latvian.

Western Latvia grew in influence and power under the Duchy of Courland, a semiautonomous kingdom governed by the capable Duke Kettler, who established far-flung colonies in the Gambia and on Tobago. At this time, southeastern Latvia was grabbed by Poland, and Sweden took Rīga and the northeast. The Russians barged in at the end of the 1620s and gobbled everything up during the Great Northern War (1700–21).

## National Awakening

The idea of a cohesive national identity began around the 17th century, when the peasant descendants of the original tribes started to unite under the name 'Latvia'. By the mid-19th century, the sentiment grew stronger as the first newspapers printed their issues in Latvian and the first Song and Dance Festival started up. Farmers flocked to the big city and demanded equal rights. Political parties emerged to organise worker strikes to oust the remaining German aristocracy. Democratic leaders would later call this push for freedom the 'Latvian Revolution'.

## A Taste of Freedom

Out of the post-WWI confusion and turmoil arose an independent Latvian state, declared on 18 November 1918. By the 1930s Latvia had achieved one of the highest standards of living in all of Europe. In 1934 a bloodless coup, led by Kārlis Ulmanis, Latvia's first president, ended the power of parliament. Installing himself as dictator, Ulmanis ruled with a certain benevolence that didn't tolerate extremists from the left or right.

The Soviets were the first to recognise Latvia's independence, but the honeymoon didn't last long. Soviet occupation began in 1939 with the Molotov-Ribbentrop Pact. Nationalisation, killings and mass deportations to Siberia followed. In July 1941, Latvia was occupied by Nazi Germany, which proceeded to kill or deport an estimated 175,000 Latvians, mostly Jews, by 1945.

## Soviet Rule

When WWII ended the Soviets marched back in, claiming to 'save' Latvia from the Nazis. A series of deportations (over 40,000 people) began anew as the nation was forced to adapt to communist ideologies. Smoke-spewing factories were swiftly erected and farms were collectivised. Thousands fled to the West. Notions of individuality were stripped away as country cottages and cosmopolitan urban buildings were 'nationalised', forcing everyone into drab apartment blocks.

The first public protest against Soviet occupation was on 14 June 1987, when 5000 people rallied at Rīga's Freedom Monument to commemorate the 1941 Siberia deportations. New political organisations emerged in the summer of 1988. The Popular Front of Latvia (PLF) quickly rose to the forefront of the Latvian political scene. Less than two months later, on 23 August 1989, two million Latvians, Lithuanians and Estonians formed a 650km human chain from Vilnius, through Rīga, to Tallinn, to mark the 50th anniversary of the Molotov-Ribbentrop Pact. This iconic moment continues to be celebrated worldwide.

In early 1991, a series of stand-offs between tens of thousands of Latvians in Rīga and Soviet forces culminated in several killings. Locals had banded together to build barricades around key civic institutions to prevent the Soviets from seizing control. The resulting violence left scars that are still part of the Latvian psyche today.

## Independence

When Russian democratic forces led by Boris Yeltsin came out as winners in a stand-off, known as the August Coup, Latvia was finally free to go its own way. The country declared independence on 21 August 1991, and on 17 September 1991 Latvia, along with Estonia and Lithuania, joined the UN and began taking steps to consolidate its newfound nationhood. Democratic elections were held in 1993 and the new government, headed by Guntis Ulmanis (a farmer and descendant of Kārlis Ulmanis), lurched from crisis to crisis, while a game of prime minister roulette followed the devastating crash of the country's largest commercial bank.

In 1999 Vaira Vīķe-Freiberga, a Latvian by birth but who spent most of her life in Canada, won the presidential election with her promise of propelling the country towards EU membership. It was a tough uphill battle as the nation shook off its antiquated Soviet fetters, and on 1 May 2004 the EU opened its doors to the fledgling nation. Latvia also joined NATO that year, which has irritated Russia ever since.

Long the Baltic laggard (and the poorest country in the EU), Latvia registered the highest economic growth in the EU in 2004, 2005, 2006 and 2007, even though thousands of Latvians left for jobs in Ireland and elsewhere. However, the global economic crisis that swept across the world at the end of 2008 caused a brutal recession in Latvia, as much of the nation's spectacular economic growth turned out to be illusionary. The subsequent years were spent clearing the rubble caused by the economic collapse.

Now on a course of moderate economic growth, Latvia steers a centrist course with turns to the left and right via coalition governments cobbled together from myriad political parties. Though the Greens were ascendant in the mid-2010s, following the 2018 elections, power shifted to the centre-right.

## The People

Don't expect cheery hellos from strangers, but under the reticence, Latvians are a friendly and welcoming bunch. The guardedness in the culture is a response to centuries of foreign rule and has helped preserve the unique Latvian language and culture through changing times. Any lingering provincialism is fading, especially in Rīga. English is taught at every level and during every year of school. More and more people under the age of 50 have worked for at least a spell abroad.

About two-thirds of the population is ethnically Latvian, the highest since the 1930s. Ethnic Russians comprise about 25% and mostly live in and around Rīga.

Latvian women were traditionally responsible for preserving the hearth and home by passing on traditional songs, recipes, legends and tales. The men, enriched by these closely kept customs, would guard the land. Today, women remain a strong presence in the household but also have a prominent role in politics and business. Almost one-third of parliament is female (higher than the EU average) and Latvia's most noted president was Vaira Vīķe-Freiberga. In business, more than half of Latvian companies with 10 or more employees are run by women.

Latvians generally adore nature and continue to incorporate their ancient pagan traditions and customs into everyday life, despite being members of the Lutheran Church (ethnic Russians are mainly Orthodox or Old Believers). Superstitious beliefs are quite common and often linked to the wildlife that shares the land. In rural Latvia, families place tall wooden poles in their yard to attract nest-building storks, which are believed to bring children. Latvians also love flowers; if you go to a birthday party or are invited into someone's home, always bring a bouquet (but make sure it's an odd number of flowers – even numbers are reserved for funerals).

### ONLINE RESOURCES

**1188** (www.1188.lv) An excellent resource with comprehensive info on transport, business listings, accommodation, dining, traffic reports, taxis and much more.

**Magnetic Latvia** (www.latvia.travel) National tourism website.

**Latvia Institute** (www.li.lv) Provides details on events plus high-level information targeted at foreign visitors.

**Lonely Planet** (www.lonelyplanet.com/latvia) Destination information, hotel bookings, traveller forum and more.

**lsm.lv** (https://eng.lsm.lv) Latvia's public broadcasters offer news and weather in English.

## The Arts

### Cinema

*The Fisherman's Son* (Zvejnieka dēls), made in 1940, marked both the beginning and the end of an era in Latvian filmmaking. It was the nation's first full-length sound film, but it was one of the last major works before WWII and the subsequent years of oppression. At the beginning of the USSR period, the state-owned Rīga Documentary Film Studio created heaps of movies, mostly laden with propaganda. After Stalin's death in 1953, directors earned more freedom, but it wasn't until the 1980s that pastiche and parody became commonplace. Most of the films up until then were adaptations of famous Latvian legends and modern novels.

Latvian director Jānis Streičs has produced a number of films pertinent to Latvia's turbulent past. *Limousine in the Colour of Summer Solstice Night* (1981) and *The Child of Man* (1991) remain popular for their blend of irony and comedy. The latter, about a boy growing up and falling in love in Soviet-occupied Latvia, won the Grand Prix at San Remo in 1992 and was nominated for an Academy Award for best foreign film in 1994. Streičs' more recent film, *The Mystery of the Old Parish Church* (2000), addresses the prickly issue of locals

### TOP MUSIC FESTIVALS

Latvians love their summer music festivals. Many take place under the long twilight and starry nights in beautiful natural settings. Among the more notable are the following:

**Ezera Skaņas** (Lake Sounds; www.ezeraskanas.lv; off P81, Kāla Ezers) It's the Baltic Burning Man! Latvia's most unusual – and ethereal – music festival takes place at dawn on one summer morning each August. Ticket-holders gather on boats and along the shores of Kāla Ezers, a remote lake in the countryside 130km east of Rīga. As light breaks at about 4am, performers begin singing and playing from rafts on the water. It's as magical as it is unusual. Buy tickets well in advance.

**Positivus** (p257) One of Latvia's largest music festivals, Positivus draws big names performing a range of styles, from folk to funk. It's held over three days in a pine forest near the beach north of Salacgrīva, close to the Estonian border.

**Summer Sound** (p245) Rock, hip-hop and electronic music reverberate off the dunes at this big two-day festival at Liepāja's beach in western Latvia.

Not to be outdone by the hinterlands, Rīga has appealing music festivals (p215) over the course of the year.

collaborating with Nazi and Soviet occupiers during WWII.

At the end of the Soviet era, the long-form documentary film *Is it Easy to be Young?* by Juris Podnieks became one of the cultural icons of the Soviet *perestroika* period. In 2010 Antra Cilińska shot a film featuring *Is it Easy to be Young?* characters, now in their 40s, recapping two decades of their lives after the collapse of the USSR.

Also worth noting is Laila Pakalnina, whose 1998 feature film *The Shoe,* about occupied Latvia, was an official selection at the Cannes 1998 film festival. Pakalnina's 1996 film *The Mail* shows the isolation of Latvia, as symbolised by the lonely delivery of the morning mail.

Latvia's tortured past continues to inspire filmmakers today. The harrowing life of Melānija Vanaga, who was deported by the Soviets along with thousands of others to slave camps in Siberia in 1941, is the basis for Viestur Kairish's *The Chronicles of Melanie* (2016). It's available on streaming services. Dāvis Sīmanis dramatised the incredible efforts by Rīga's Zanis Lipke and his family to save Jews from the Nazis in 2018's *The Mover.*

## Latvian Song & Dance

Traditional folk songs have always played an integral role in Latvian culture, although the recognition of music as an established art form did not come about until the mid-19th century. In 1869 Jānis Cimze started cataloguing folk tunes, some dating back 1000 years, and his collection of 20,000 melodies became the basis for Latvia's first song festival, where thousands of singers joined together in huge choirs to celebrate traditional folk music. During the Soviet occupation the song festivals were pivotal in forging a strong sense of national identity and pride, and became part of the battle cry that rallied Latvians to fight for independence.

The Unesco-recognised Latvian Song and Dance Festival is held in Rīga every five years (the next one is in 2023) and is a week-long celebration of the nation's cultural soul. However, you need not wait till then, as there are an ever-growing number of music festivals all year long. At even the smallest of festivals, expect to see young and old Latvians grow misty eyed as they sing along with folk favourites.

The National Opera (p224) is the home of the Rīga Ballet, which produced Mikhail Baryshnikov and Alexander Godunov during the Soviet years. The opera itself is considered to be one of the finest in Europe and cheap seats have made it accessible to the public, who regard the theatre with the utmost respect.

Latvia struck it big at the Eurovision contest in 2002 when Marie N (Marija Naumova) took home the grand prize. The tiny nation has finished in the top 10 an impressive 10 times since 2000. Instrumenti are a popular and witty electronic music duo that have performed worldwide.

## Art & Architecture

Of Latvia's spectrum of visual arts, visitors will be most awestruck by the collection of art nouveau architecture (p209) in Rīga. The capital has more Jugendstil (the German word favoured locally) buildings than any other European city – 750 buildings and counting (as renovations continue).

Jānis Rozentāls, Latvia's first major painter, lived in Rīga's art nouveau district and his former home has since been transformed into a museum (p208). The abstract expressionist, Daugavpils-born Mark Rothko, was arguably the most famous Latvian artist around the world. Although he grew up in the USA, interest in the artist and his oeuvre are celebrated in his hometown, including at an eponymous cultural centre (p270).

For other Latvian painters, check out the collection of the Latvian National Museum of Art (p207), which includes the strange mesmerising snow and ice landscapes by its first director Vilhelms Purvitis and lush expressionist works by Ludolfs Liberts. Also look out for the works of Miervaldis Polis, who was a leading nonconformist underground artist in the Soviet era, but more recently earned a reputation as a 'court artist' by painting postindependence Latvian leaders.

# Food & Drink

Traditional food in Latvia is very hearty. For centuries, eating was a utilitarian task rather than an art and a pleasure. But times have changed, especially in Rīga. Latvia is a major food producer, from berries to bread, pickles to mushrooms, and pork to silky smoked fish. From bounteous markets to a new crop of creative eateries helmed by creative cooks, look for fresh and interesting fare.

## Favourite Foods

A walk through a Latvian market, such as Rīga's Central Market, will quickly reveal Latvia's bounty of local foods. In season discover mountains of berries, apples, rhubarb and other produce. Throughout the year smoked fish (herring, pike, trout or salmon) are a treasure and the great variety available fills display cases. Top dairy products include *biezpiens* (cottage cheese), *siers* (a cheddery cheese) and *rūgušpiens* (curdled milk).

Mushroom-picking is a national obsession. There are over 300 edible varieties found in Latvia's sprawling forests, and in the countryside you'll see people out and about with plastic buckets foraging. Pickled foods are a staple and who makes the best fresh cucumbers pickled with garlic and dill is much debated. Latvians are intrepid beekeepers and many farms have beehives and honey-production facilities.

No visit to Latvia is complete without eating plenty of the national staple, rye bread (*rupjmaize*). The huge, dark-brown crusted loaves come in myriad variations, many with whole grains such as barley and wheat. On cold days, a slice of bread and bowl of hearty grey peas stewed with pork and onions (which is *so* much better than

### DO IT YOURSELF: BLACK BALZĀM COCKTAILS

The trademarked clay bottle of Black Balzām makes a fine gift and conversation starter – especially once tasting begins. Some people love the black secret concoction with its throat-warming high alcohol content and bittersweet flavour. Others loathe it, comparing its medicinal taste (it was the creation of a pharmacist in 1752) to the unloved cough syrups of their youth. Recent brand extensions such as the treacly blackcurrant version are definitely acquired tastes.

Besides straight shots (hardcore elements mix it with vodka...), Black Balzām makes an interesting addition to cocktails:

**Black Mojito** Mix one part Black Balzām with four parts lemon-lime soda, add half a smashed lime and a drizzle of fruit syrup. Serve over crushed ice.

**Lazybones** Add a shot of Black Balzām to a cold glass of cola.

**Black Shake** Toss a shot of Black Balzām into a vanilla milkshake.

## EAT YOUR WORDS

These days, most restaurants have English menus, but why not impress your server and order your savoury sausage in Latvian? Start with these basic phrases and names.

### Useful Phrases

| | | |
|---|---|---|
| **A table for ... people, please.** | *Lūdzu galdu ... personām.* | *loo*-dzu *gahl*-du ...*per*-so-nahm |
| **Do you have a menu?** | *Vai jums ir ēdienkarte?* | vai yums ir *eh*-dean-kar-te |
| **I'm a vegetarian.** | *Es esmu veģetārietis/te.* (m/f) | es es-mu ve-gye-tah-reah-tis/te |
| **What do you recommend?** | *Ko jūs iesakat?* | kwo yoos *eah*-sah-kut |
| **I'd like ...** | *Es vēlos ...* | es *vaa*-lwos ... |
| **The bill, please.** | *Lūdzu rēķinu.* | *loo*-dzu *reh*-kyi-nu |

### Food Glossary

| | | |
|---|---|---|
| **beefsteak with fried onions** | *sīpolu sitenis* | see-po-luh see-ten-ees |
| **beetroot soup (similar to borscht)** | *biešu zupa* | bee-eh-shu zoo-pa |
| **diced vegetable salad in sour cream and mayonnaise** | *dārzeņu salāti* | *dar*-zen sa-*la*-tee |
| **dumplings** | *pelmeņi* | pell-me-nee |
| **fish soup** | *zivju zupa* | zeev-yoo zoo-pah |
| **fresh grated cabbage** | *kāpostu salāti* | *kah*-post sa-*la*-tee |
| **fried pork chop with potatoes and pickled and fresh vegetables** | *karbonāde ar piedevām* | kar-bo-*nah*-deh ar pee-eh-dev-*am* |
| **fried salmon with potatoes and pickled and fresh vegetables** | *cepts lasis ar piedevām* | tsepts lah-sees ar pee-eh-dev-*am* |
| **grey peas with pork and onions** | *pelēkie zirņi ar speķi* | peh-*leh*-kee-eh zeer-nee ar speh-kyi |
| **hunter's sausages (pork)** | *mednieku desiņas* | med-nye-kuh deh-see-nyas |
| **meatballs** | *kotletes* | kot-leh-tess |
| **pickled herring with sour cream, egg and beetroot** | *siļķe kažokā* | seel-kye kah-djo-*kah* |
| **salmon in cream sauce** | *lasis krējuma mērcē* | lah-sis *kreh*-ma mehr-tse |
| **salmon in mushroom and dill sauce** | *lasis sēņu un diļļu mērcē* | lah-sis *seh*-nyu oon di-lyu mehr-tse |
| **sausage (usually smoked)** | *desa* | deh-sa |

it sounds) is a ticket to inner warmth and contentment.

For sweets: berries and rhubarb are turned into scrumptious fruit pies and *kūka* (tarts). Ancient Cour Viking dessert recipes made from sweet creams and dark breads can still be found in western Latvia. Be sure to try *rupjmaizes kārojums/kārtojums,* which tastes like Black Forest cake. Locally beloved Laima-brand chocolates are cheap and tasty.

### Top Tipples

Latvia's famous Black Balzām – an insidious jet-black, 90-proof liquor flavoured with some 24 fairy-tale ingredients (such as linden flower and Peruvian balsamic oil) – should be tried at least once.

Latvia has a long brewing tradition, in no small part due to its centuries of German influence. Two popular local brewers of lager are Aldaris and Bauskas Alus. Craft brewers are proliferating. Top choices to look for include Ārpus, Barda, Labietis, Malduguns and Valmeira's own Valmiermuiža.

Rīga has several excellent bars and brewpubs specialising in local craft beers. Elsewhere most bars will have at least a couple of interesting local brews in addition to bland international brands.

## Where to Eat & Drink

Rīga's range of dining and eating options rivals any other European city of its size, but elsewhere – with the exception of Jūrmala and a few other larger towns – the choices are limited as locals on limited budgets take their meals at home.

*Restorāns* (restaurants) in Latvia are generally sit-down affairs, while *kafejnīca* (pronounced ka-fay-*neet*-za; cafes) are multipurpose facilities where patrons enjoy a coffee, a faster meal or drinks in the evening. Bars, especially in Rīga and other major cities, often offer a full menu of dishes. For quick, self-service choices, keep an eye out for *pelmeņi* (dumpling) and pancake shops, cafeteria-style venues such as some of the links in the Lido restaurant chain, and supermarkets, namely Rimi, which sells to-go snacks and meals. Small towns have local restaurants that mix hearty fare with international staples like burgers and pizza.

A Latvian *brokastis* (breakfast), available from sunrise to around 11am, usually consists of bread and cheese, cold meat and smoked fish. *Pusidienās* (lunch) and *vakariņas* (dinner) are more substantial affairs, with heartier Baltic staples. Restaurants serve lunch at midday. Dinner tends to be around 7pm, although it can be later during long summer nights.

# SURVIVAL GUIDE

## Directory A–Z

### ACCOMMODATION

- Book ahead during the high season (summer). Rates drop significantly in the colder months.
- Rīga has a huge selection of hotels and apartments.
- Outside of Jūrmala, beachfront accommodation is not as common as you'd expect.
- Check out www.camping.lv for details on places to pitch a tent.

### ACTIVITIES

Latvia's vast forests are great for hiking, cycling, camping, birdwatching, berry-picking, mushrooming and canoeing during the warmer months. The Latvian coast is an almost uninterrupted stretch of untrammelled white-sand beaches backed by pine-covered dunes.

Water sports are enjoyed along the Gulf of Rīga and the Kurzeme Coast. In winter, skiing – primarily cross-country – is popular.

Latvians enjoy nature walks and a growing number of trails are being developed in places such as Ķemeri National Park.

### CUSTOMS REGULATIONS

Latvian customs rules are in line with EU rules for the Schengen Area. Check the regulations at www.vid.gov.lv/en/customs.

### EMBASSIES & CONSULATES

The following useful diplomatic offices are in Rīga:

**Belarusian Embassy** (☎6732 5321; www.latvia.mfa.gov.by; Jēzusbaznīcas 12; ⏲9am-1pm & 2-6pm Mon-Fri)

**Russian Consulate** (☎6721 2579; www.latvia.mid.ru; Skolas iela 20-16; ⏲visas by appointment)

### INTERNET ACCESS

Almost all accommodation in Latvia has free wi-fi. Many restaurants, cafes and bars offer wi-fi – just ask for the password. Some, like the Lido chain, have open networks. There are also free wi-fi networks in many public spaces and city centres.

### MAPS

- Excellent printed country and city maps of Latvia are published by Rīga-based Jāņa sēta (www.kartes.lv) and are sold widely. There is also a useful app.
- Free national, regional and local maps are available at tourist offices and can be downloaded (www.latvia.travel).
- Note that Google Maps can be weak on road hierarchies and may provide directions that include rough, dirt roads when better, paved options are close by. Double-check routes with a printed map.

### EATING PRICE RANGES

The following price ranges refer to a main course.

**€** less than €7

**€€** €7–15

**€€€** more than €15

## SLEEPING PRICE RANGES

The following price ranges refer to a double room with bathroom.

**€** less than €40

**€€** €40–90

**€€€** more than €90

### MONEY

- Latvia uses the euro.
- ATMs are easy to find and credit cards are widely accepted.

### POST

Latvia's **postal service** (www.post.lv) has offices in most towns. Service is reliable; mail to North America takes about 10 days, and within Europe about a week.

### PUBLIC HOLIDAYS

**New Year's Day** 1 January
**Easter Friday & Monday** March/April
**Labour Day** 1 May
**Restoration of Independence Day** 4 May
**Mothers' Day** Second Sunday in May
**Whitsunday** A Sunday in May or June
**Līgo Day** (Midsummer festival) 23 June
**Jāņi** (Summer Solstice) 24 June
**National Day** 18 November; anniversary of the 1918 Proclamation of the Republic of Latvia
**Christmas** (Ziemsvētki) 24–26 December
**New Year's Eve** 31 December

### TELEPHONE

- Latvian telephone numbers have eight digits; landlines start with 6 and mobile numbers start with 2.
- There are no area codes.
- Latvia's country code is 371.

### TOURIST INFORMATION

- Latvia's national tourist organisation, Magnetic Latvia (www.latvia.travel), has good information online.
- Most towns and cities in Latvia have a tourist office, open during normal business hours (at the very least), with extended hours during the summer. Most have English-speaking staff and oodles of useful brochures and maps for the entire country, as well as regional info for the Baltics.
- Check out the website of the Latvia Institute (www.li.lv) for in-depth cultural and economic information.

## Getting There & Away

### AIR

International air service to Latvia is through Rīga International Airport (p226), about 13km southwest of the city centre. Liepāja International Airport (www.liepaja-airport.lv) has one connecting flight with Rīga five times weekly.

Several major European airlines serve Rīga. Latvia's national carrier, airBaltic (www.airbaltic.com), offers direct flights to over 60 destinations within Europe, including Tallinn and Vilnius.

### LAND

Latvia is in the EU's Schengen Area, which means there are no border controls between it and both Estonia and Lithuania. However, carry your travel documents with you at all times, as random border checks do occur.

#### Bus

Major international bus companies serving Rīga include Ecolines (www.ecolines.net) and Lux Express (www.luxexpress.eu). Fares vary widely: compare prices on www.1188.lv.

Destinations from Rīga with daily service include the following:

- Berlin (18½ hours)
- Kaliningrad (eight hours)
- Minsk (nine to 10 hours)
- Moscow (14 hours)
- Tallinn (4¼ to 4¾ hours)
- Tartu (four hours)
- Vilnius (four to 4½ hours)
- St Petersburg (11 hours)
- Warsaw (11 hours)

#### Car

Rental cars are usually allowed to travel around the Baltics, but confirm details with your rental provider.

#### Train

International trains head from Rīga to Moscow (16 hours), St Petersburg (15 hours) and Minsk (nine hours) daily.

For Tallinn to/from Rīga, there is a daily quick connection at Valga (6½ hours overall). For Vilnius to/from Rīga, there is a weekend-only connection with a stopover in Daugavpils (overall times vary).

### SEA

Regular car and passenger ferry services include Rīga–Stockholm, Liepāja–Travemünde, Germany, and Ventspils–Nynäshamin, Sweden.

## Getting Around

### BUS

Buses are the main mode of public transport for much of Latvia. Check schedules and fares at www.autoosta.lv and www.1188.lv.

### CAR & MOTORCYCLE

Driving is on the right-hand side. Headlights must be on at all times. Be sure to ask for '*benzene*' when looking for a petrol station – *gāze* means 'air'. Some roads linking important towns outside Rīga are unpaved.

Major car-rental firms operate in Rīga and at the airport. Most can arrange for the car to be delivered to your hotel or apartment address. Contracts usually allow the car to be driven in the three Baltic countries, although there are variations; confirm when reserving. Rīga-based firms may offer cheaper rates.

**Car Rent Riga** (☎2958 0448; www.carsrent.lv) Cash-only, with a €200 deposit. Cars delivered in the Rīga area.

**EgiCarRent** (☎2570 5475; www.egi.lv) Minimum rental period is three days. Cars delivered anywhere in Rīga.

### TRAIN

Train travel is convenient for destinations near Rīga, including Jūrmala, Saulkrasti, Sigulda and Cēsis. Service is limited for destinations further afield, with the exception of Daugavpils.

Check schedules and fares at www.pv.lv and www.1188.lv.

# Lithuania

370 / POP 2.85 MILLION

**Includes ➡**



## Best Places to Stay

➡ Hotel Pacai (p309)

➡ Artagonist (p309)

➡ Miškiniškės (p329)

➡ Miško Namas (p379)

➡ Michaelson Boutique Hotel (p368)

## Best Places to Eat

➡ Nineteen18 (p311)

➡ Senoji Kibininė (p323)

➡ Uoksas (p348)

➡ Sweet Root (p312)

➡ Tik Pas Joną (p381)

## Why Go?

Blame it on the Baltic sea breeze or the almost endless midsummer days: Lithuania has an otherworldly quality. In the southernmost of the Baltic States, beaches are spangled with amber and woodlands are alive with demonic statues. Medieval-style mead and traditional woodcarving never went out of style.

Offsetting Lithuania's reverence of tradition is a spirited counterculture, particularly in compact capital Vilnius. A city of churches and baroque finery, Vilnius' cobblestoned charms haven't gone unnoticed by tourists. Second city Kaunas also draws visitors with its rough-and-ready charm, as does spa resort Druskininkai, where 19th-century architecture nudges against brooding Soviet buildings.

As Europe's last country to be Christianised, pagan history still soaks the land. Sand-dune-studded Curonian Spit, splintering from the Baltic coast, is awash in folklore and draws cyclists, hikers and beach-goers. Cloaking much of Lithuania are lakes, forests of birch and pine, and pancake-flat farmland, where there's ample space to breathe.

## When to Go

➡ Lithuania is at its best in high summer when days are long, nights are short and the Baltic Sea is splash-worthy. Don't miss Klaipėda's four-day Sea Festival.

➡ Sometimes spring arrives late but is good for canoeing and hiking sans mosquitoes.

➡ September through November sees many sunny days, with turning leaves adding a splash of colour, though nights are chilly. Culture reaches a crescendo with classical music festivals and Vilnius' annual Mama Jazz festival.

# VILNIUS

☎5 / POP 576,400

There is a dreamy quality to Vilnius (vil-nyus), especially in the golden glow of a midsummer evening. Lithuania's capital has an Old Town of rare authenticity: marvellously intact, its cobbled streets are lined with weather-worn period buildings that hide cafes, boutiques and dainty guesthouses.

Vilnius doesn't hide its scars. The city was once nicknamed the 'Jerusalem of the north' but its Jewish community was largely destroyed in WWII. Reminders of loss are everywhere: museums and memorials dedicated to the Holocaust, former ghettos, preserved KGB torture chambers and cemeteries filled with the war dead.

Yet optimism shines through despite past horrors. It's a compact, walkable city that feels like a big village, with plenty of green spaces, and a lively night scene, yet nighttime shrouds its baroque spires in near-silence. And this is no Eastern European antique: artists, punks and a self-declared micro-nation keep Vilnius cutting-edge.

## History

Legend says Vilnius was founded in the 1320s, when Lithuanian grand duke Gediminas dreamt of an iron wolf that howled with the voices of 100 wolves – a sure sign to build a city as mighty as their cry. In fact, the site had already been settled for 1000 years.

A moat, a wall and a tower on Gediminas Hill protected 14th- and 15th-century Vilnius from Teutonic attacks. Tatar attacks prompted inhabitants to build a 2.4km defensive wall (1503–22), and by the end of the 16th century Vilnius was among Eastern Europe's biggest cities. Three centuries on, industrialisation arrived: railways were laid and Vilnius became a key Jewish city. Occupied by Germany during WWI, it became an isolated pocket of Poland afterwards. WWII ushered in another German occupation and the death knoll for its Jewish population. After the war, Vilnius' skyline was filled with new residential suburbs populated by Lithuanians from other parts of the country, alongside immigrant Russians and Belarusians. In the late 1980s the capital was the focus of Lithuania's push for independence from the USSR, achieved in 1990.

Vilnius has fast become a European city. In 1994 its Old Town became a Unesco World Heritage Site and 15 years later shared the prestigious title of European Capital of Culture with the Austrian city Linz. In between, much of Old Town has been sensitively restored.

### LITHUANIA AT A GLANCE

**Currency** euro (€)

**Language** Lithuanian

**Capital** Vilnius

**Area** 65,300 sq km

## Sights

Vilnius is a compact city and most sights are easily reached on foot. Those visiting for a couple of days will scarcely move out of Old Town, where folk-artist workshops and designer boutiques jostle for attention with a treasure trove of architecture. Stay a couple more days and the New Town beckons, with its museums, shops and riverside action.

Begin your exploration of the city at epicentral Cathedral Sq, with Gediminas Hill rising behind it. Southward lies the cobbled Old Town, bisected by Pilies gatvė. Heading west, Gedimino prospektas drives through the heart of the New Town to parliament, and has several museums and notable buildings.

## Gediminas Hill

**Gediminas Castle & Museum** MUSEUM

(Gedimino Pilis ir Muziejus; Map p296; ☎5-261 7453; www.lnm.lt; Gediminas Hill, Arsenalo gatvė 5; adult/child €5/2; ⏲museum 10am-9pm, castle hill 7am-9pm) With its hilltop location above the junction of the Neris and Vilnia Rivers, Gediminas Castle is the last of a series of settlements and fortified buildings occupying this site since Neolithic times. This brick version, built by Grand Duke Vytautas in the early 15th century, harbours an engaging museum about the city with successive floors elaborating on past centuries of warfare, medieval weaponry and contemporary history. For most visitors, the highlight is the 360-degree panorama of Vilnius from the roof.

**Gediminas Hill** HILL

(Map p296) Vilnius was founded on 48m-high Gediminas Hill, topped since the 13th century by a red-brick tower. To reach the top of the hill, clamber up the rocky steps behind the cathedral's southeastern side or take the historic **funicular** (Map

# Lithuania Highlights

❶ **Vilnius** (p289) Wandering the backstreets of the beautiful baroque capital, looking for that perfect bar.

❷ **Curonian Spit National Park** (p372) Cycling, swimming in the Baltic Sea or exploring settlements on this spit.

❸ **Aukštaitija National Park** (p328) Fishing, boating, bathing and berrying in Lithuania's beloved lakeland.

❹ **Kaunas** (p338) Exploring Lithuania's vibrant, arty town with a gorgeous historic heart.

**5 Hill of Crosses** (p355) Paying your respects to this eerie spiritual place of remembrance.

**6 Druskininkai** (p332) Taking the healing waters at Lithuania's leading spa resort.

**7 Nemunas Delta** (p382) Losing yourself in the whispering rushes, teeming birdlife and perfect serenity.

**8 Žemaitija National Park** (p389) Visiting a former Soviet nuclear missile base before cycling through woods.

# Vilnius

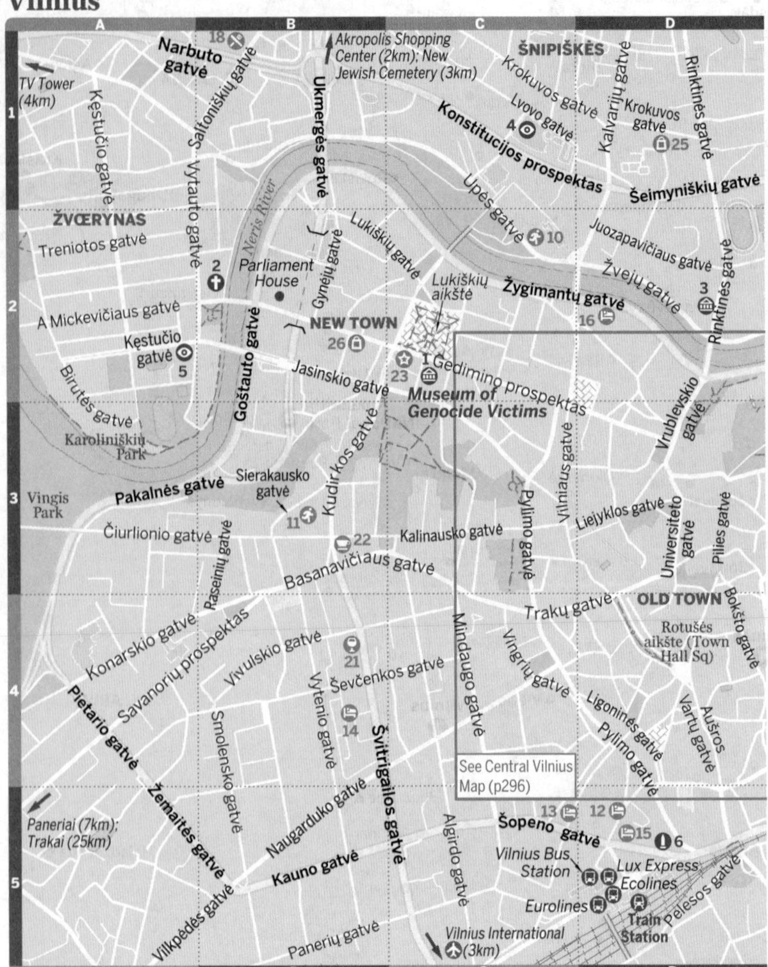


p296; ☎5-261 7453; www.lnm.lt; Arsenalo gatvė 5; adult/student €2/1; ⏲10am-7pm May-Sep, to 5pm Oct-Apr), saving you a steep walk.

**Museum of Applied Art** MUSEUM

(Taikomosios Dailės Muziejus; Map p296; ☎5-262 8080; www.ldm.lt; Arsenalo gatvė 3a; adult/student €2/1; ⏲11am-6pm Tue-Sat, to 4pm Sun) The Old Arsenal, built in the 16th century and restored in the 1980s, houses temporary exhibitions and a permanent collection showcasing 15th- to 19th-century Lithuanian sacred art. Many pieces were discovered in Vilnius Cathedral in 1985 after being hidden in the walls by Russian soldiers in 1655. Because of fear that they'd be seized by the Soviets, the works, valued at €11 million, remained a secret until 1998, when they were finally displayed to the world.

## ⦿ Cathedral Square

**★Cathedral Square** SQUARE

(Katedros aikštė; Map p296) Katedros aikštė buzzes with local life. In the 19th century markets and fairs were held here and a moat ran around what is now the square's perimeter so that ships could sail to the cathedral door. Within the moat were walls and towers, the only remaining part of

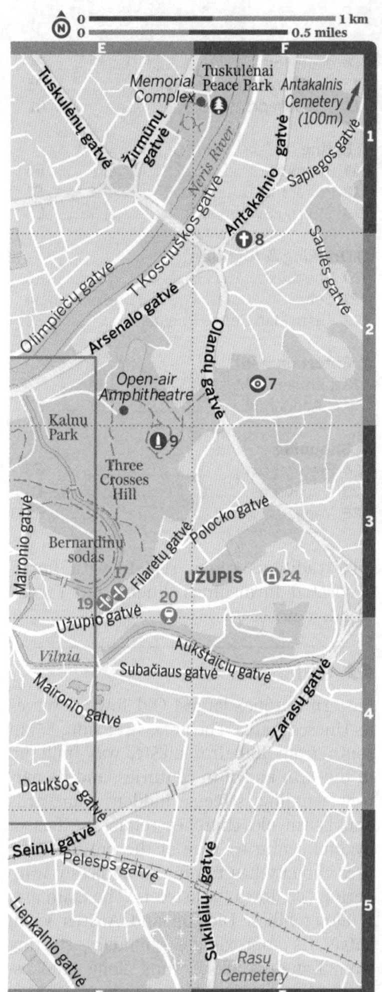


which is the 57m-tall belfry (p294) near the cathedral's western end. In front of the entrance to the Royal Palace, at the square's eastern end, is an equestrian **statue of Gediminas** (Katedros aikštė), built on an ancient pagan site.

Behind the grand old duke, Bernardinų sodas leads to **Three Crosses Hill** and **Kalnų Park**.

### ★Palace of the Grand Dukes of Lithuania — MUSEUM

(Valdovų Rumai; Map p296; ☎5-262 0007; www.valdovurumai.lt; Katedros aikštė 4; full admission €5.50, per exhibition €2-3, guided tour €20-30; ⏲10am-6pm Mon-Wed & Sun, to 8pm Thu-Sat) If you only see one museum in Vilnius, make it this one. On a site that has been settled since the 4th century AD stands the latest in a procession of fortified palaces, repeatedly remodelled, destroyed and rebuilt. The baroque palace, built for the 17th-century grand dukes, has been faithfully revamped to house an atmospheric museum of art and history. Visitors with several hours can opt for full admission, accessing four 'routes' through Lithuanian history; otherwise choose one or two.

Route I walks you through two millennia of Lithuanian history. Guided through the strata of the palace's foundations, visitors can see the bones of successive episodes in the history of the building and the nation. A second route explores the splendidly reconstructed ceremonial halls of the grand duchy, complete with the crimson velvet of the throne room and remarkable wooden ceilings, while routes three and four take you through a thicket of halberds and swords dating back to the time of the grand dukes. This gleaming white complex is a potent symbol of revitalised, independent Lithuania.

### ★Vilnius Cathedral — CATHEDRAL

(Vilniaus Arkikatedra; Map p296; ☎5-269 7800; www.katedra.lt; Katedros aikštė 1; cathedral admission free, crypt tours adult/child €6/4; ⏲7am-7pm, crypt tours 10am-5pm) Stately Vilnius Cathedral, divorced from its freestanding belfry (p294), is a national symbol and the city's most instantly recognisable building. Known in full as the Cathedral of St Stanislav and St Vladislav, this columned neoclassical cathedral occupies a spot originally used for the worship of Perkūnas, the Lithuanian thunder god.

Register in advance to tour the crypts, the final resting place of many prominent Lithuanians including Vytautas the Great (1350–1430).

The first wooden cathedral was built here between 1387 and 1388; after several episodes of destruction and reconstruction, the present edifice was erected in the late 18th century. Note the greyish stone on the exterior, showing the older parts of the building.

The reconstruction followed the original Gothic floor plan and incorporated St Casimir's and the Valavičius family chapels in the late 18th century. **St Casimir's Chapel**, with its baroque cupola, coloured marble and frescoes of the saint's life, is the cathedral's showpiece.

## Vilnius



From 1950 the Soviets used the cathedral as a warehouse, gallery and concert venue, before its reconsecration in 1989.

**★ Cathedral Bell Tower** HISTORIC BUILDING
(Map p296; ☎8-600 12080; www.bpmuziejus.lt; Katedros aikštė; adult/student €5/3; ⏲10am-7pm Mon-Sat May-Sep) Climb the creaky stairs into the free-standing belfry of Vilnius Cathedral, once part of the city's 13th-century defences. Towering 57m high, it's one of the city's oldest brick buildings as well as Vilnius' most recognisable landmark. Bells dating back to the 15th century dangle in the small exhibition space, but the primary reasons to navigate the narrow ladders and stairwells are the priceless views across the city. At 5pm, listen to the bells ring for several minutes.

**National Museum of Lithuania** MUSEUM
(Lietuvos Nacionalinis Muziejus; Map p296; ☎5-262 7774; www.lnm.lt; Arsenalo gatvė 1; adult/child €3/1.50; ⏲10am-6pm Tue-Sun) This wide-ranging museum (inside the New Arsenal) exhibits art and artefacts from Lithuanian life from Neolithic times to the present day. Early history is revealed in 2nd millennium BC arrowheads and 7th-century grave hauls (signage isn't always good), while the lives of well-to-do Lithuanians of recent centuries are unveiled with velvet-lined sleds and elaborately painted furniture. The highlight is the colourful folk traditions room, replete with floral-decorated furnishings, linens and carved wooden crosses.

## Old Town

Eastern Europe's largest Old Town deserves its Unesco status. The area, stretching 1.5km south from Katedros aikštė, was built up in the 15th and 16th centuries, and its narrow winding streets, hidden courtyards and lavish old churches retain the feel of bygone centuries. One of the purest pleasures the city has to offer is aimlessly wandering Old Town backstreets. The main axis is along Pilies, Didžioji and Aušros Vartų gatvė. Its approximate boundary, starting from Katedros aikštė, runs along Stuokos-Gucevičiaus, Liejyklos, Vilniaus, Trakų, Pylimo, Bazilijonų, Šv Dvasios, Bokšto, Maironio, Radvilaitės and Šventaragio streets – an area of roughly 1 sq km.

### Pilies Gatvė

Cobbled Pilies gatvė (Castle St) – the hub of tourist action and the main entrance to Old Town from Katedros aikštė – buzzes with buskers, souvenir stalls and the odd beggar. Until the 19th century the street was separated from the square by the lower castle wall, which ran across its northern end. Only a gate in the wall connected the two. Notice the 15th- to 17th-century brickwork of Nos 4, 12 and 16 towards the northern end of the street.

### House of Signatories
MUSEUM

(Signatarų Namai; Map p296; ☎5-231 4437; www.lnm.lt; Pilies gatvė 26; adult/concession €2/1; ⏲10am-6pm Tue-Sat) Lithuania's Declaration of Independence was signed here on 16 February 1918. Today, across 14 rooms of this 18th-century house, you'll find a reverent exhibition of materials relating to the National Movement and the signatories themselves. Independence didn't last long; by 1920 the Poles had retaken Vilnius and the city was only returned to the Lithuanian heartland in 1939 as a 'gift' by Stalin.

## Vilnius University

### ★Vilnius University
HISTORIC BUILDING

(Vilniaus Universitetas; Map p296; ☎5-219 3029; www.muziejus.vu.lt; Universiteto gatvė 3; campus adult/child €1.50/0.50, bell tower €3/1.50; ⏲campus 9am-6pm Mon-Sat, bell tower 10am-7pm May-Sep) Founded in 1579 during the Catholic Counter Reformation, Vilnius University was run by Jesuits for two centuries. During the 19th century it became one of Europe's greatest centres of learning, and the university survived shutdown by Tsar Nicholas I, rebranding under Soviet rule and closure by the Nazis. Its spectacular architectural ensemble includes a 64m bell tower, baroque church, courtyard and fresco-laden hall, all of which are open to visitors.

### ★Sts Johns' Church
CHURCH

(Šv Jonų Bažnyčia; Map p296; www.jonai.lt; Šv Jono gatvė 12; campanile €3; ⏲10am-5pm) The full name is 'Church of St Johns, St John the Baptist and St John the Apostle and Evangelist', but 'Sts Johns' (plural) will do nicely. Founded in 1387, it predates the 16th-century university within which it is situated, although the present late-baroque structure was built following an 18th-century fire. Its freestanding campanile is the tallest structure in Old Town, and contains a Foucault's Pendulum demonstrating the rotation of the earth. Views from the top are splendid.

## Central Old Town

Old Town is bisected by Pilies gatvė, which becomes Didžioji gatvė as you head south. This street widens into Rotušės aikštė, the site of the former town hall and effective heart of Old Town. Along this axis, worthwhile sights, museums and churches are spread out on both the eastern and western sides.

### St Anne's Church
CHURCH

(Šv Onos Bažnyčia; Map p296; www.onosbaznycia.lt; Maironio gatvė 8-1; ⏲10.30am-6.30pm Tue-Sat, 8am-7pm Sun) Flamboyant and Gothic St Anne's Church, a vision of undulating lines and red-brick arches, was built in 1500 on the site of a wooden church that burned to the ground. Today it's among Vilnius' most famous buildings; the turreted facade (marrying 33 different kinds of brick) inspires countless photo ops from the grassy plaza opposite. Inside, rib vaults trace graceful lines of brick through a rosy interior. Napoleon was reportedly so charmed that he wanted to relocate the church to Paris.

Dwarfing St Anne's is the Bernadine Church, one of Vilnius' oldest Gothic buildings.

### Bernadine Church & Monastery
CHURCH

(Šv Pranciškaus Asyžiečio Parapija; Map p296; ☎5-262 6004; www.bernardinuansamblis.lt; Maironio gatvė 10; ⏲7am-7pm Mon-Fri, from 8am Sat & Sun) The massive buttresses and towering walls of this, one of the most impressive churches in Vilnius, are capable of providing defence as well as worship. After successive periods of extension and improvement in the 17th and 19th centuries, it came to a prosaic end when the Soviets converted it into a warehouse. The Bernadine community regained their building after independence, restoring it to its former Flamboyant Gothic and Brick Gothic glory, and adding trails for sightseers wishing to explore the complex.

### Toy Museum
MUSEUM

(Map p296; ☎8-604 00449; www.zaislumuziejus.lt; Šiltadaržio gatvė 2; adult/child €5/3; ⏲noon-10pm Tue, to 6pm Wed-Fri, 11am-4pm Sat; 👪) This excellent museum is a fun romp through the ages for kids and adults alike. Acquaint yourself with 12th-century games and peruse the extensive collection of Soviet toys.

### Presidential Palace
PALACE

(Map p296; ☎5-266 4011; www.president.lt; S Daukanto gatvė 3; ⏲tours 9am-2.30pm Sat, to 12.45pm Sun) FREE The Bishops of Vilnius' Palace in the 16th century, this classical edifice now houses the president and chancellery. It gained its current Russian empire style early in the 19th century, and was used

> **ℹ COMBO TICKET**
>
> Combined tickets for the St Michael the Archangel Church museum and the belfry and crypts at Vilnius Cathedral are €14/8. If you want to visit two out of the three attractions, the price is €10/6.

# Central Vilnius

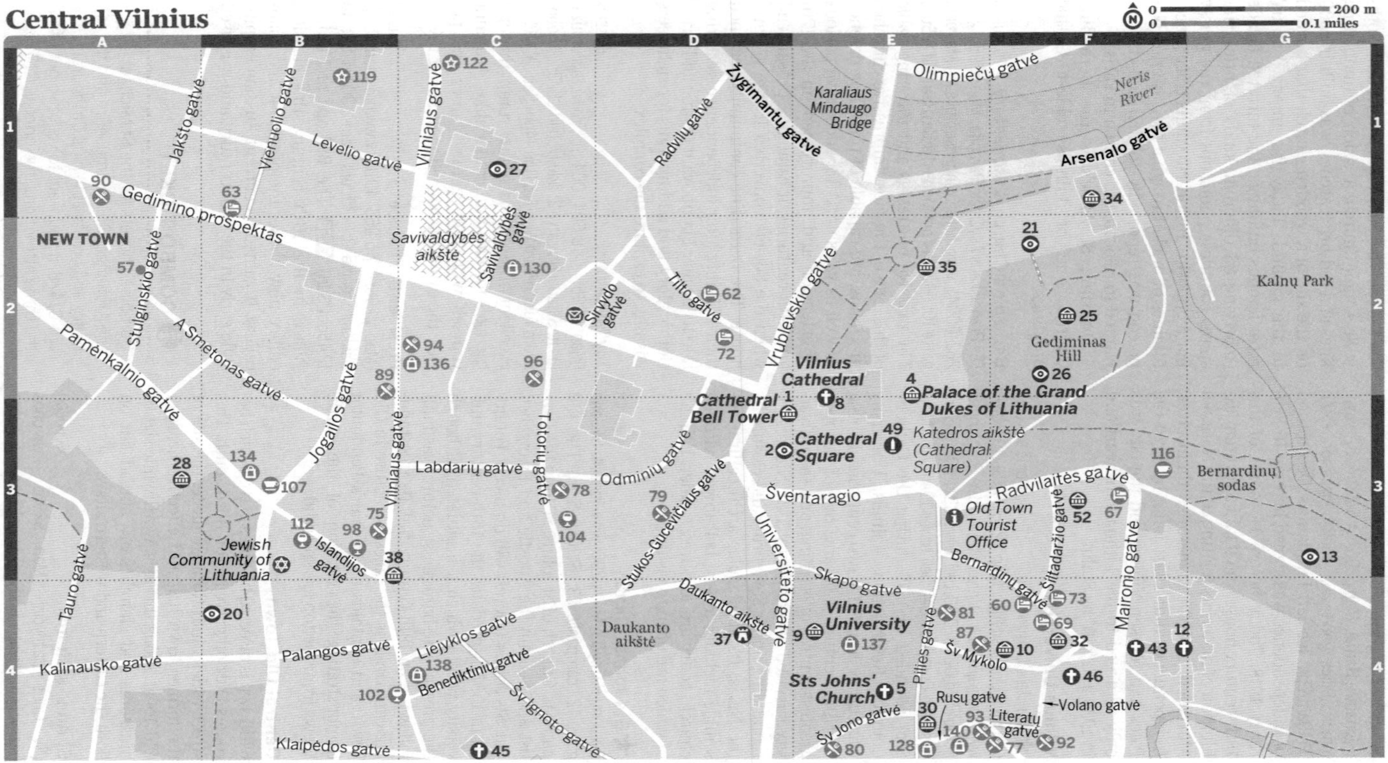

0 200 m
0 0.1 miles

A B C D E F G
1 2 3 4

Olimpiečų gatvė
Neris River
Karaliaus Mindaugo Bridge
Žygimantų gatvė
Arsenalo gatvė
Kalnų Park
Radvilų gatvė
Vilniaus gatvė
Vienuolio gatvė
Jakšto gatvė
Levelio gatvė
Gedimino prospektas
NEW TOWN
Savivaldybės aikštė
Savivaldybės gatvė
Stulginskio gatvė
A Smetonas gatvė
Pamėnkalnio gatvė
Jogailos gatvė
Širvydo gatvė
Tilto gatvė
Vrublevskio gatvė
Gediminas Hill
Vilnius Cathedral
Cathedral Bell Tower
Palace of the Grand Dukes of Lithuania
Cathedral Square
Katedros aikštė (Cathedral Square)
Labdarių gatvė
Totorių gatvė
Odminių gatvė
Šventaragio
Stukos-Gucevičiaus gatvė
Universiteto gatvė
Radvilaitės gatvė
Bernardinų sodas
Old Town Tourist Office
Šiltadaržio gatvė
Maironio gatvė
Bernardinų gatvė
Jewish Community of Lithuania
Islandijos gatvė
Tauro gatvė
Skapo gatvė
Daukanto aikštė
Daukanto aikštė
Vilnius University
Liejyklos gatvė
Palangos gatvė
Kalinausko gatvė
Benediktinių gatvė
Šv Ignoto gatvė
Klaipėdos gatvė
Sts Johns' Church
Pilies gatvė
Šv Mykolo
Rusų gatvė
Literatų gatvė
Volano gatvė
Šv Jono gatvė

1 2 4 5 8 9 10 12 13 20 21 25 26 27 28 30 32 34 35 37 38 43 45 46 49 52 57 60 62 63 67 69 72 73 75 77 78 79 80 81 87 89 90 92 93 94 96 98 102 104 107 112 116 119 122 128 130 134 136 137 138 140

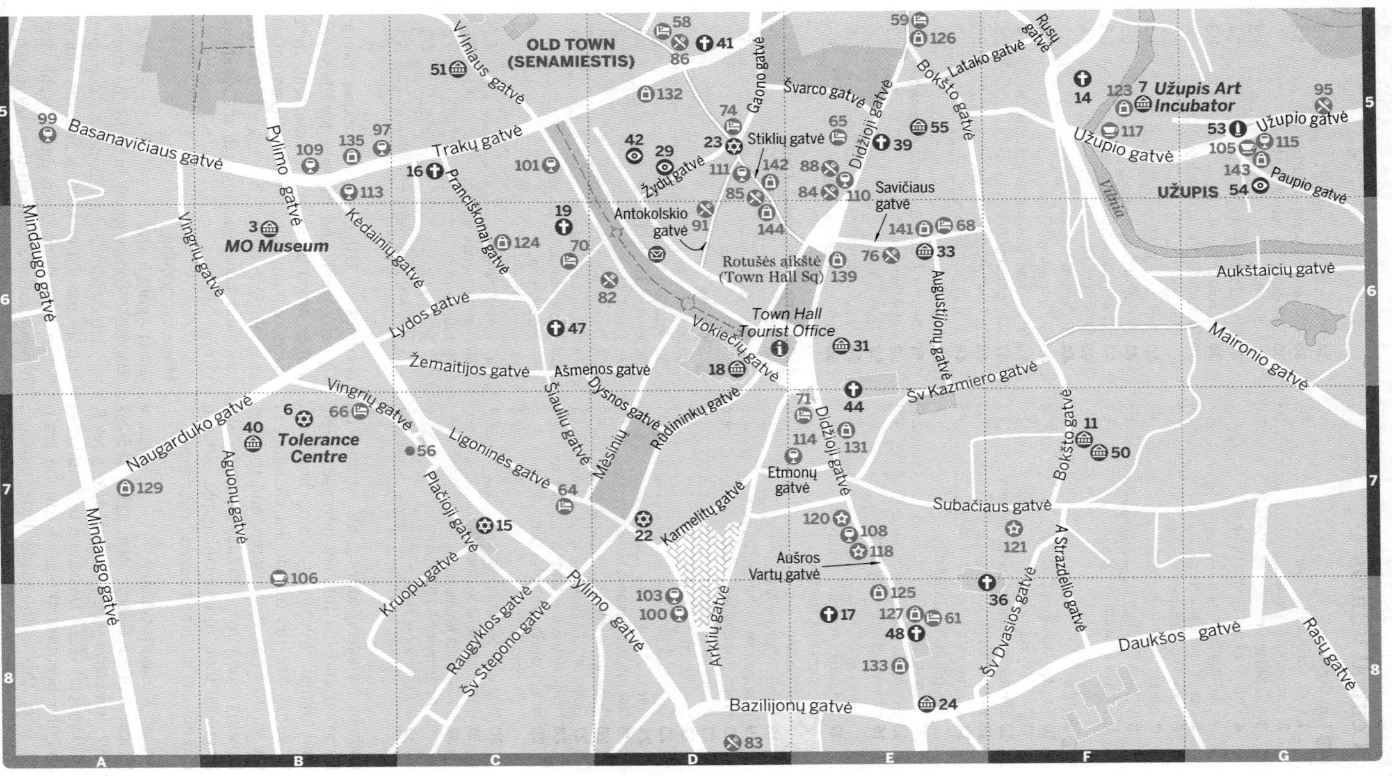
OLD TOWN (SENAMIESTIS)
UŽUPIS
Užupis Art Incubator
Vilnia
MO Museum
Tolerance Centre
Town Hall
Tourist Office
Rotušės aikštė (Town Hall Sq)
Mindaugo gatvė
Basanavičiaus gatvė
Vingrių gatvė
Pylimo gatvė
Aguonų gatvė
Naugarduko gatvė
Kėdainių gatvė
Lydos gatvė
Žemaitijos gatvė
Plačioji gatvė
Kruopų gatvė
Raugyklos gatvė
Šv Stepono gatvė
Ligoninės gatvė
Šiaulių gatvė
Ašmenos gatvė
Dysnos gatvė
Mėsinių
Rūdninkų gatvė
Karmelitų gatvė
Arklių gatvė
Bazilijonų gatvė
Aušros Vartų gatvė
Etmonų gatvė
Didžioji gatvė
Vokiečių gatvė
Antokolskio gatvė
Žydų gatvė
Trakų gatvė
Pranciškonai gatvė
Vilniaus gatvė
Gaono gatvė
Stiklių gatvė
Švarco gatvė
Savičiaus gatvė
Bokšto gatvė
Latako gatvė
Rusų gatvė
Augustijonų gatvė
Šv Kazmiero gatvė
Subačiaus gatvė
Šv Dvasios gatvė
A Strazdelio gatvė
Daukšos gatvė
Rasų gatvė
Maironio gatvė
Aukštaičių gatvė
Užupio gatvė
Paupio gatvė
A
B
C
D
E
F
G
5
6
7
8

## Central Vilnius

**Top Sights**
1 Cathedral Bell Tower ... D3
2 Cathedral Square ... D3
3 MO Museum ... B6
4 Palace of the Grand Dukes of Lithuania ... E2
5 Sts Johns' Church ... E4
6 Tolerance Centre ... B7
7 Užupis Art Incubator ... F5
8 Vilnius Cathedral ... E3
9 Vilnius University ... E4

**Sights**
10 Amber Museum-Gallery ... F4
11 Artillery Bastion ... F7
12 Bernadine Church & Monastery ... F4
13 Bernardinų sodas ... G3
14 Cathedral of the Theotokos ... F5
Chapel of the Gates of Dawn ... (see 24)
15 Choral Synagogue ... C7
16 Church of Our Lady of the Assumption ... C5
17 Church of the Holy Trinity (Uniates) & Basilian Monastery ... E8
18 Contemporary Art Centre ... D6
19 Evangelical Lutheran Church ... C6
20 Frank Zappa Memorial ... B4
21 Funicular to Gediminas Hill ... F2
22 Gate to Large Ghetto ... D7
23 Gate to Small Ghetto ... D5
24 Gates of Dawn ... E8
25 Gediminas Castle & Museum ... F2
26 Gediminas Hill ... F2
27 Government Building ... C1
28 Holocaust Exhibition ... A3
29 House of Gaon Elijahu Ben Shlomo Zalman ... D5
30 House of Signatories ... E4
31 Kazys Varnelis Museum ... E6
32 Mickiewicz Memorial Apartment & Museum ... F4
33 MK Čiurlionis House ... E6
34 Museum of Applied Art ... F1
35 National Museum of Lithuania ... E2
36 Orthodox Church of the Holy Spirit ... F8
37 Presidential Palace ... D4
38 Radvilos Palace ... B3
39 Russian Orthodox Church of St Nicholas ... E5
40 Samuel Bak Museum ... B7
41 Shrine of Divine Mercy ... D5
42 Site of Great Synagogue ... D5
43 St Anne's Church ... F4
44 St Casimir's Church ... E7
45 St Catherine's Church ... C4
46 St Michael the Archangel Church ... F4
47 St Nicholas Church ... C6
48 St Teresa's Church ... E8
49 Statue of Gediminas ... E3
50 Subačiaus Gate ... F7
51 Theatre, Music & Cinema Museum ... C5
52 Toy Museum ... F3
53 Užupis Angel ... G5
54 Užupis Republic Constitution ... G5
55 Vilnius Picture Gallery ... E5

**Activities, Courses & Tours**
56 All Sides of Vilnius Bike Tour ... C7
57 Feel Z City ... A2

**Sleeping**
58 Apia Hotel ... D5
59 Artagonist ... E5
60 Bernardinu B&B ... F4
61 Domus Maria ... E8
62 Dvaras Manor House ... D2
63 Fabrika Hostel ... B1
64 Grotthaus ... C7
65 Hotel Pacai ... E5
66 Hotel Rinno ... B7
67 Hotel Vilnia ... F3
68 Jimmy Jumps House ... E6
69 Litinterp ... F4
70 Mikalo House ... C6
71 Radisson Blu Royal Astorija ... E7

both by Napoleon (during his advance on Moscow) and his Russian adversary, General Mikhail Kutuzov (chasing him back to Paris). See the ceremonial changing of the guard every day at 6pm, and the flag-hoisting ceremony on Sunday at noon. Visits by guided tour (in Lithuanian, plus English in summer) must be booked in advance.

**Amber Museum-Gallery** MUSEUM
(Gintaro Muziejus-Galerija; Map p296; ☎5-262 3092; www.ambergallery.lt; Šv Mykolo gatvė 8; ⌚10am-7pm) FREE Dedicated to Baltic gold and the beautiful things it can be crafted into, this enthusiastic little museum occupies a 17th-century baroque house. Upstairs you'll find trinkets, jewellery and amber brigantines; in the basement, huge pieces of many-hued amber, kilns and other archeological finds. The descent into the basement takes you through the strata of Vilnius' history.

**Make Everything Great Again Mural** PUBLIC ART
(Map p292; Šopeno gatvė) In 2016 the mural by artist Mindaugas Bonanu, depicting Trump and Putin kissing and the slogan 'Make Everything Great Again', went viral. It was a satirical take on the 1979 image of

72 Senatoriai Hotel ... D2
73 Shakespeare ... F4
74 Stikliai ... D5

**Eating**
75 Ali Šokoladinė ... B3
Amandus ... (see 59)
76 Balzac ... E6
77 Beigelistai ... F4
78 Blue Lotus ... C3
79 CAPO ... D3
80 Ertlio Namas ... E4
81 Etno Dvaras ... E4
82 Gyoza ... D6
83 Halės Market ... D8
84 Kitchen ... E5
85 Lokys ... D5
86 Meat Lovers' Pub ... D5
87 Mykolo 4 ... E4
88 Nineteen18 ... E5
89 Pinavija ... B2
90 Radharanė ... A1
91 René ... D6
92 Saint Germain ... F4
Selfish Bistro ... (see 75)
93 Senamiesčio Krautuvė ... E4
94 Senoji Kibininė ... C2
95 Sweet Root ... G5
96 Vegafe ... C2

**Drinking & Nightlife**
97 Alaus Biblioteka ... B5
98 Alchemikas ... B3
99 Amy Winehouse ... A5
100 Apoteka Bar ... D8
101 BeerHouse & Craft Kitchen ... C5
102 Bubbles Champagneria ... B4
103 Bukowski ... D8
104 Būsi Trečias ... C3
105 Coffee1 ... G5
106 Crooked Nose & Coffee Stories ... B7
107 Elska Coffee ... B3
108 In Vino/Portobello ... E7
109 King & Mouse ... B5
110 Nomads ... E5
111 Notre Vie ... D5
112 Opium ... B3
113 Pabo Latino ... B5
114 Prohibicija ... E7
115 Špunka ... G5
116 StrangeLove ... F3
117 Užupio kavinė ... F5

**Entertainment**
118 Jazz Cellar 11 ... E7
119 Lithuanian National Opera & Ballet Theatre ... B1
120 Lithuanian National Philharmonic ... E7
121 Tamsta ... F7
122 Vilnius Congress Concert Hall ... C1

**Shopping**
123 4 Boobs Studio ... F5
124 Amatų Gildija ... C6
125 Amber Museum ... E8
126 Aukso Avis ... E5
127 Aušros Vartų Meno Galerija ... E8
128 Balta Balta ... E4
129 Black Ceramics Centre ... A7
130 Gedimino 9 ... C2
131 House of Naïve ... E7
132 Humanitas ... D5
133 Jonas Bugailiškis ... E8
134 Juozas Statkevičius ... B3
135 Lietuviški Drabužiai ... B5
136 Lino Namai ... C2
137 Littera ... E4
138 Moustache Boutique ... C4
139 Ramunė Piekautaitė ... E6
140 Sauluva ... E4
141 Senųjų Amatų Dirbtuvės ... E6
142 Terra Recognita ... D5
143 Vilniaus Puodžių Cechas ... G5
144 Vitražo manufaktūra ... D6

Brezhnev kissing East German President Erich Honecker that was eventually painted on the Berlin Wall. After the Trump/Putin mural was vandalised, it was repainted to show the two exchanging a 'shotgun' of marijuana smoke. The wall is now repainted pink and bears the message 'Make Empathy Great Again'.

**Vilnius Picture Gallery** MUSEUM

(Vilniaus Galerija Paveikslų; Map p296; ☎5-212 0841; www.ldm.lt/en/vpg; Didžioji gatvė 4; adult/child €3/1.50; ⏲11am-6pm Tue-Sat, noon-5pm Sun) Built in the early 17th century, with substantial additions in the 19th, the Chodkeviciai Palace now houses a permanent exhibition of Lithuanian art from the 16th to the 19th centuries. Temporary exhibitions showcase specific Lithuanian movements, artists and mediums.

**Kazys Varnelis Museum** MUSEUM

(Map p296; ☎5-279 1644; www.lnm.lt; Didžioji gatvė 26; adult/concession €3/1.50; ⏲10am-6pm Tue-Sat) During his 50 years in the US, Kazys Varnelis earned fame and fortune with his optical and three-dimensional paintings. This museum shows his personal collection of paintings, furniture, sculptures, maps and books, including works by Dürer, Goya and Matteo Di Giovanni. Visits are by appointment only, so call beforehand.

## JEWISH VILNIUS

Before WWII, Vilnius was a top Jewish centre for learning in Europe, known as the 'Jerusalem of the East'. But by the end of the war, little remained of a once-vibrant community. Vilnius' main Jewish and Holocaust-related sights are administered by the Vilna Gaon State Jewish Museum (www.jmuseum.lt). The buildings include the Holocaust Museum, the Tolerance Centre, the Paneriai Memorial Museum (p322) in the Paneriai Forest and the Samuel Bak Museum. Two more branches of the museum are due to open in the future.

The Soviets destroyed several Jewish cemeteries in the 1950s. The **old Jewish cemetery** (Krivių gatvė) where Rabbi Gaon Elijahu was originally buried was ripped up in 1957 and turned into Žalgiris Stadium. The tombstones were recycled as paving stones; the steps leading up Tauro Hill to the Trade Union Palace on Mykolaičio-Putino gatvė were originally built from Jewish gravestones. In 1991 the Jewish community retrieved many of these desecrated markers; a handful are now on display at the site of the old cemetery. **Discover Jewish Vilnius** is a useful Android app.

**Holocaust Museum** (Holokausto Ekspozicija; Map p296; ☎5-262 0730; www.jmuseum.lt; Pamėnkalnio gatvė 12; adult/child €3/1.50; ⏲9am-5pm Mon-Thu, to 4pm Fri, 10am-4pm Sun) The Holocaust Museum tells the unvarnished account of the destruction of Lithuania's once-vibrant Jewish community, the Litvaks, through a collection of photos, documentation and first-hand accounts. Situated in the so-called 'Green House', the displays lack modern interactive touches but are perhaps all the more moving for it. Many of the items here were donated by survivors and victims' families.

**Tolerance Centre** (Tolerancijos Centras; Map p296; ☎5-212 0112; www.jmuseum.lt; Naugarduko gatvė 10/2; adult/concession €4/2; ⏲10am-6pm Mon-Thu, to 4pm Fri & Sun) The Tolerance Centre is one of the main branches of the Vilna Gaon Jewish State Museum. The building, which has been at various stages a refuge, a concert hall and a theatre, exhibits Litvak (Lithuanian Jewish) art and cultural and historical collections. It serves as a helpful adjunct to the Holocaust Museum: its exhibitions focus less on the Holocaust and more on Jewish

**St Michael the Archangel Church** CHURCH
(Church Heritage Museum; Map p296; ☎5-269 7803; www.bpmuziejus.lt; Šv Mykolo gatvė 9; adult/child €6/4; ⏲11am-6pm Tue-Sat) This grand early-17th-century chuch, built by the Sapiega family, now houses a wonderful museum of sacral art. The building itself, with its single Gothic nave, coloured-marble high altar and alabaster statuary, is a rare example of late-Renaissance architecture in Vilnius. The exhibition includes religious art, liturgical vessels and rare manuscripts, plus a precious monstrance and reliquaries from Vilnius Cathedral.

**Mickiewicz Memorial Apartment & Museum** MUSEUM
(Mickevičiaus Memorialinis Butas-muziejus; Map p296; ☎5-279 1879; www.mb.vu.lt; Bernardinų gatvė 11; adult/child €2/1; ⏲10am-5pm Tue-Fri, to 2pm Sat & Sun) 'Lithuania, my fatherland...' is from Poland's romantic masterpiece *Pan Tadeusz*. Its Polish author Adam Mickiewicz (1798–1855) – muse to Polish nationalists in the 19th century – grew up near Vilnius and studied at the university (1815–19) before being exiled for anti-Russian activities in 1824. The rooms where he wrote the well-known poem *Grażyna* (Lithuanian: *Gražia;* a Polish name for a woman with Lithuanian roots meaning 'beauty') are now filled with some of the poet's letters.

**MK Čiurlionis House** HISTORIC BUILDING
(Map p296; ☎5-262 2451; www.mkcnamai.lt; Savičiaus gatvė 11; adult/concession €2/1; ⏲10am-4pm Mon-Fri) FREE Inside the former home of the great artist and composer are a handful of Čiurlionis reproductions, worth taking a peek at if you can't make it to the National Čiurlionis Art Museum in Kaunas.

### Aušros Vartų Gatvė

Vilnius' oldest street – which leads south out of Didžioji gatvė to the Gates of Dawn – is laden with churches and gift shops.

**Gates of Dawn** HISTORIC BUILDING
(Aušros Vartai; Map p296; ☎5-212 3513; www.ausrosvartai.lt; Aušros Vartų gatvė 12; ⏲6am-7pm) FREE The southern border of Old Town is marked by the last standing of five 16th-century portals that were once built into the city walls. A suitably grand way to enter Old Town, the focal point of the Gates of Dawn

history and culture over the centuries leading up to WWII. A small permanent exhibit on the Jewish avant-garde in Vilnius between the wars is enlightening.

**Samuel Bak Museum** (Map p296; ☎5-212 0112; www.jmuseum.lt; Naugarduko gatvė 10; adult/child €4/2; ⏰10am-6pm Mon-Thu, to 4pm Fri & Sun) Art gallery showcases the bold, vivid, somewhat surrealist paintings of renowned artist Samuel Bak, whose works were first exhibited in 1942 in the Vilnius ghetto.

**Choral Synagogue** (Choralinė Sinagoga; Map p296; ☎5-261 2523; www.lzb.lt; Pylimo gatvė 39; €1; ⏰10am-4pm Mon-Fri, to 2pm Sun) This synagogue, built in 1903, is the city's only Jewish house of worship to survive WWII intact (the Nazis used it as a medical store). Prayers in the Misnagdim (counter-Hasidic) tradition are heard daily.

**Gate to Large Ghetto** (Map p296; Rūdninkų gatvė 18) A plaque and map at No 18 mark the site of the entrance to the Large Ghetto, in which 29,000 Litvaks (Lithuanian Jews) were imprisoned by the Nazis between 1941 and 1943.

**Gate to Small Ghetto** (Map p296; www.jewishcenter.lt; Stiklių gatvė 12) This was once the entrance to the main Jewish quarter, which lay in the streets west of Didžioji gatvė. Today only street names like Žydų (Jews) and Gaono (Gaon) serve as reminders of those days, while a small plaque marks the site of the gate to the ghetto, liquidated in 1941.

**Site of Great Synagogue** (Map p296; Žydų gatvė 1-2) The Great Synagogue of Vilna, built in the 1630s on the site of an earlier synagogue, was destroyed by the Soviets in the 1950s, after the Nazis had a go in WWII. Today there's a map of the Vilnius ghetto at the site.

**House of Gaon Elijahu Ben Shlomo Zalman** (Map p296; Žydų gatvė 5) A plaque marks the former house of the famous 18th-century Talmudic scholar.

**Site of New Jewish Cemetery** (Map p292) A memorial marks the spot of Vilnius' 19th-century Jewish cemetery, destroyed by the Soviets in the 1950s.



is the Chapel of Mary the Mother of Mercy, housing the 'Vilnius Madonna'. Framed in silver, this 17th-century painting of the Virgin Mary attracts pilgrims from across Europe.

**Chapel of the Gates of Dawn** CHAPEL

(Map p296; www.ausrosvartai.lt; Aušros Vartų gatvė 12; ⏰6am-7pm, Mass 9am in Lithuanian, 10am in Polish Mon-Sat, 9.30am Sun in Lithuanian) Above the Gates of Dawn you'll find this 18th-century chapel, aka the Gates of Dawn Chapel of Mary the Mother of Mercy. Inside is a venerated painting of the Virgin Mary, known as the *Madonna of the Gates of Dawn*, believed to date from the early 17th century. It is revered equally by the Catholic, Orthodox and Uniate (Greek Catholic) faiths and has evolved into one of Eastern Europe's leading pilgrimage destinations.

**Orthodox Church of the Holy Spirit** CHURCH

(Stačiatikių Šv Dvasios Cerkvė; Map p296; ☎5-212 7765; Aušros Vartų gatvė 10; ⏰10am-5pm) The peachy facade gives an understated first impression but there's an electric atmosphere inside Lithuania's chief Russian Orthodox church. The 16th-century sanctuary was given a dazzling baroque makeover in the 18th century; note the iconostasis with jewel tones and gold filigree. In front of the altar lie the preserved bodies of three 14th-century martyrs, Sts Anthony, Ivan and Eustachius, their feet peeping out beneath ornate shrouds. Adjoining are male and female Orthodox monasteries, the only ones in the country.

**Artillery Bastion** MUSEUM

(Artilerijos Bastėja; Map p296; ☎5-261 2149; www.lnm.lt; Bokšto gatvė 20/18; adult/concession €4/2; ⏰10am-6pm Tue-Sun) This revamped 17th-century fortification houses a rich collection of weaponry and armour through the ages and the atmospheric tunnels are a joy to wander.

**Church of the Holy Trinity (Uniates) & Basilian Monastery** CHURCH

(Map p296; ☎5-212 2578; Aušros Vartų gatvė 7; ⏰hours vary) Through the elaborate Basilian Gates lie this 16th-century church and monastery, mixing baroque, Gothic and Russian Byzantine styles. The Uniates are an order that sought to unite the Eastern and Western churches. Mass is held only in Ukrainian.

**St Teresa's Church** CHURCH

(Šv Teresės Bažnyčia; Map p296; ☎5-212 3513; www.ausrosvartai.lt; Aušros Vartų gatvė 14; ⏲7am-7pm) This Carmelite church is early baroque outside and ornate late baroque inside. Underneath its entrance is a chamber for the dead, which contains some fine examples of baroque tombs, but it's usually locked.

### Vokiečių Gatvė & Around

Vokiečių gatvė, the wide boulevard running northwest from Rotušės aikštė, is lined with restaurants that sprawl out onto the square, and also features a couple of impressive churches.

**St Casimir's Church** CHURCH

(Šv Kazimiero Bažnyčia; Map p296; ☎5-212 1715; www.kazimiero.lt; Didžioji gatvė 34; ⏲10am-6.30pm Mon-Sat, 8am-6.30pm Sun Apr-Sep, 4-6.30pm Mon-Sat, 8am-2pm Sun Oct-Mar) This striking church is the city's oldest baroque place of worship. St Casimir's dome and cross-shaped ground plan defined a new style for 17th-century churches when the Jesuits built it between 1604 and 1615. It was destroyed and rebuilt several times over the centuries.

**Contemporary Art Centre** MUSEUM

(SMC, Šiuolaikinio Meno Centras; Map p296; ☎5-212 1945; www.cac.lt; Vokiečių gatvė 2; adult/child €4/2; ⏲noon-8pm Tue-Sun) With 2400 sq metres of space for photography, video, installations and other exhibits, plus a program of lectures, live music and film screenings, this is the largest centre for contemporary art in the Baltics. There's free entry on Wednesday, and different pricing for special events.

**WISH UPON A...**

...star? No. Not in Vilnius. Rather, a stone tile bearing the word *stebuklas* (miracle). It marks the spot on Cathedral Sq where the human chain – formed between Tallinn (Estonia) and Vilnius by two million Lithuanians, Latvians and Estonians to protest Soviet occupation in 1989 – ended. To make a wish, do a clockwise 360-degree turn on the tile. Unfortunately, superstition forbids us from revealing the location of this elusive-but-lucky spot, meaning you have to search for it yourself. Hint: we *did* tell you it was on Cathedral Sq...

**St Nicholas Church** CHURCH

(Šv Mikalojaus Bažnyčia; Map p296; ☎5-262 3069; www.mikalojus.lt; Šv Mikalojaus gatvė 4; ⏲1-6.30pm Mon-Fri, 7.30am-3pm Sun) Lithuania's oldest church, this red-brick Gothic pile was built by German Christians around 1320, when the country was still pagan. From 1901 to 1939 it was the only church in Vilnius where Mass was held in Lithuanian. It's remarkably well preserved (bar the addition of baroque features in recent centuries) and definitely worth a visit.

### Vilniaus Gatvė & Around

At the confluence of Vokiečių gatvė, Vilniaus gatvė and Dominikonų gatvė stand some sizeable church and monastery complexes dating from the 17th and 18th centuries.

**★MO Museum** GALLERY

(Map p296; ☎8-609 83764; www.mo.lt; Pylimo gatvė 17; adult/student/child under 7 €7/3.50/free; ⏲10am-8pm Sat-Mon, Wed & Thu, to 10pm Fri) Opened in October 2018, this assemblage of contemporary Lithuanian art and photography is the country's first private museum. An orderly union of sharp angles, polished glass and white plaster, the ultramodern gallery was designed by visionary Daniel Libeskind, the architect behind Berlin's Jewish Museum. Around 5000 20th-century artworks are assembled within, freshened by rotating exhibitions and occasional cultural events.

**Radvilos Palace** MUSEUM

(Radvilų Rūmai; Map p296; ☎5-212 1477; www.ldm.lt; Vilniaus gatvė 24; adult/student €3/1.50; ⏲11am-6pm Tue-Sat, noon-5pm Sun) This 17th-century palazzo houses the foreign fine-arts section of the Lithuanian Art Museum.

**Theatre, Music & Cinema Museum** MUSEUM

(Teatro, Muzikos ir Kino Muziejus; Map p296; www.ltmkm.lt; Vilniaus gatvė 41; adult/student €2/1.45; ⏲11am-6pm Tue-Fri, to 7pm Wed, to 4pm Sat) Artefacts of Lithuanian song, stage and screen are the stars of this museum. Three centuries of notable instruments – including the *pūslinė* (a primitive Baltic string instrument made from animal bladders) and several *kanklės* (plucked, fretted string instruments) – are exhibited, alongside curios of Lithuanian and Soviet film, and a large collection documenting the national theatre.

**Frank Zappa Memorial** MEMORIAL

(Map p296; Kalinausko gatvė 1) West of Vilniaus gatvė, rock 'n' roll legend Frank

## LANGUAGE

| | | |
|---|---|---|
| **Hello** | *Sveiki* | *svay*-ki |
| **Hi (informal)** | *Labas* | *lah*-bahs |
| **How are you?** | *Kaip gyvuojate?* | *kaip*-gee-vu-aw-*yah*-ta |
| **Goodbye** | *Sudie* | *su*-deah |
| **Thank you** | *Dėkoju* | deh-*kaw*-yu |
| **I'm lost** | *Aš paklyd(usi/ęs)* | ahsh-*pah*-klee-d(usi/as) |

Zappa is immortalised in a bronze bust atop a 4.2m-high stainless-steel pole. It was the world's first memorial to the offbeat American who died in 1993. Look carefully for it in the parking lot, as it doesn't jump out at you. Take a look at the graffiti on the walls surrounding the lot while you're here.

### East of Gediminas Hill

**Antakalnis Cemetery** CEMETERY

(Antakalnio Kapinės; off Karių kapų gatvė; ⏲9am-dusk) In this leafy suburb, little-visited by tourists, Antakalnis Cemetery is the final resting place of Lithuanian luminaries and locals lost to war. Brutalist, art-nouveau and modernist headstones give the cemetery, a half-hour walk east of the centre, the feel of an open-air sculpture gallery. Those killed by Soviet special forces on 13 January 1991 are memorialised by a sculpture of the Madonna. A taxi or Bolt service from the train station costs around €6.

Another memorial honours Napoleonic soldiers who died of starvation and injuries in Vilnius while retreating from the Russian army. The remains of 2000 of them were only found in 2002.

Hundreds of Polish soldiers' graves, including many unknown soldiers, are also located here. Former president Algirdas Brazauskas's grave is a bit abandoned atop a hill slope, in a newer area of the cemetery.

**Three Crosses** MONUMENT

(Trys Kryžiai; Map p292; T Kosciuskos gatvė) Crosses were first erected in the 17th century, in memory of a group of monks martyred by pagans three centuries earlier. The current crosses replace three bulldozed by the Soviets; their twisted remains can be seen below the current set. Walk up the hill from T Kosciuskos gatvė, and enjoy fabulous views of the city, particularly good here at sunset.

**St Peter & Paul Church** CHURCH

(Šv Apaštalų Petro ir Povilo Bažnycla; Map p292; ☎5-234 0229; Antakalnio gatvė 1; ⏲6am-6.30pm) Don't be fooled by the uninspiring exterior of this church. Its baroque interior – a riot of over 2000 stuccoes created by Italian sculptors between 1675 and 1704 – is the finest in the country. The church was founded by Lithuanian noble Mykolas Kazimieras Paca, whose tomb is on the right of the porch.

### Užupis

The cheeky independent republic remains the arty epicentre of Vilnius, with numerous small galleries and quirky street art to discover.

★**Užupis Art Incubator** GALLERY

(Map p296; ☎8-622 75805; www.umi.lt; Uzupio gatvė 2a; ⏲11am-5pm Mon-Fri, outdoor gallery 24hr) One of two branches of the creative powerhouse of the Užupis Republic, the Galera shows exciting temporary exhibitions by local talent and invites artists from around the world to engage in a dialogue about art. Outside the gallery, the riverbank and the adjacent garden are open-air galleries created by talent from Užupis and further afield. There's a grand piano and stone cairns on the river, a giant rocking horse and stone sculpture along the path, and other installations.

**Užupis Republic Constitution** LANDMARK

(Užupio Respublikos Konstitucija; Map p296; www.uzhupisembassy.eu; Paupio gatvė) The 'Republic' of Užupis's Constitution is engraved in English, French, Lithuanian and several other languages on plaques running along Paupio gatvė. It guarantees citizens, among other things, the right to hot water, to be free, to be happy (or unhappy) and to love. Cats, on the other hand, have the right *not* to love their owners. Death, however, is not an obligation.

The self-declared, unofficial Republic of Užupis (Užupio Republika) came into existence in the late 1990s, when the neighbourhood was growing into a hive of artistic and counter-culture activity. The tongue-in-cheek micronation continues to celebrate its 'Independence Day' annually on 1 April.

**Užupis Angel** MONUMENT

(Map p296; Užupio gatvė) Since its erection in 2002, this statue of a trumpeting angel has come to symbolise Vilnius' quirkiest district.

## New Town

The 19th-century New Town (Naujamiestis) stretches 2km west of the cathedral and Old Town. Here the medieval charm of Old Town is replaced by wide boulevards and pockets of lush parkland.

### Gedimino Prospektas

Sandwiched between the Roman Catholic Cathedral's dramatic skyline and the silver domes of the Russian Orthodox **Church of the Saint Virgin's Apparition** (Znamenskaya Tserkov; Map p292; A Mickevičiaus gatvė 1), fashionable Gedimino is the main street of modern Vilnius. Its 1.75km length is dotted with shops, a theatre, banks, hotels, restaurants, offices, a few park squares and the seats of various official bods, including the Lithuanian **Government Building** (Map p296; www.lrv.lt; Gedimino prospektas 11) and Parliament House. Laid out in 1852, it's had 11 name changes since: the Tsarists named it after St George, the Poles after Mickiewicz, and the Soviet rulers first after Stalin, then Lenin.

★**Museum of Genocide Victims** MUSEUM

(Genocido Aukų Muziejus; Map p292; ☎5-249 8156; www.genocid.lt/muziejus; Aukų gatvė 2a; adult/concession €4/1, photography €2; ⏲10am-6pm Wed-Sat, to 5pm Sun) This former headquarters of the KGB (and before them the Gestapo, Polish occupiers and Tsarist judiciary) houses a museum dedicated to thousands of members of the Lithuanian resistance who were murdered, imprisoned or deported by the Soviet Union from WWII until the 1960s. Backlit photographs, wooden annexes and a disorienting layout sharpen the impact of past horrors outlined in graphic detail. Most unsettling is the descent to the prison cells, and one especially padded to muffle sounds coming from within.

### South of Gedimino Prospektas

**Kenessa** HOUSE

(Map p292; Liubarto gatvė 6; ⏲hours vary) West of Jasinskio gatvė across the Neris River is this *kenessa,* a traditional Karaite (sect of Turkic Jews) prayer house, built in 1911. It's one of three *kenessas* surviving in Lithuania.

### Šnipiškės

On the north bank of the Neris, the quarter of Šnipiškės has been transformed: the tatty Soviet concrete blocks have gone and in their place is a new skyline of skyscrapers, including the **Europa Tower** (Map p292; Konstitucijos Prospektas 7) on the Europa Business & Shopping Centre, which – at 129m – is the Baltic's tallest skyscraper.

This new business district, dubbed 'Sunrise Valley', continues to grow apace, with high-rises and construction sites popping up among the relics of Soviet architecture.

**Energy & Technology Museum** MUSEUM

(Map p292; ☎5-278 2085; www.muziejai.lt; Rinktinės gatvė 2; adult/child €4/2; ⏲10am-6.30pm Tue-Sat) Vilnius' first power station, in operation from 1903 to 2003, now houses exhibitions on energy, technology and their historical development. The original machinery used for power generation has been preserved and is particularly impressive.

## Outside the Centre

**TV Tower** TOWER

(Televizijos Bokštas; ☎5-252 5333; www.tvbokstas.lt; Sausio 13-osios gatvė 10; adult/child €8/5; ⏲observation deck 11am-11pm Tue-Sat, to 9pm Sun & Mon; 🚌1, 3, 7 ,16) It's hard to miss the 326m TV tower on the city's western horizon. This tall needle symbolises Lithuania's strength of spirit: on 13 January 1991 the Soviet army killed 12 pro-Independence resisters here, with Lithuanian TV continuing to broadcast until troops burst through the tower door. There are memorials to those killed near the tower, and a revolving restaurant and observation deck, the Milky Way, at 165m. Admission for adults rises to €11 on weekends. Take a trolleybus here.

## Activities

Aside from walking and cycling, Vilnius offers something you don't find everywhere – hot-air ballooning. Specialised tour companies can also take you on day trips to Ignalina nuclear power plant and have you drive a tank and shoot various weapons at a gun range.

★**Oreivystės Centras** BALLOONING

(Map p292; ☎5-273 2703; www.ballooning.lt; Upės gatvė 5; per person €99) Dedicated to the promotion and development of hot-air ballooning in Lithuania, the Ballooning Centre also sells flights over Vilnius, Trakai,

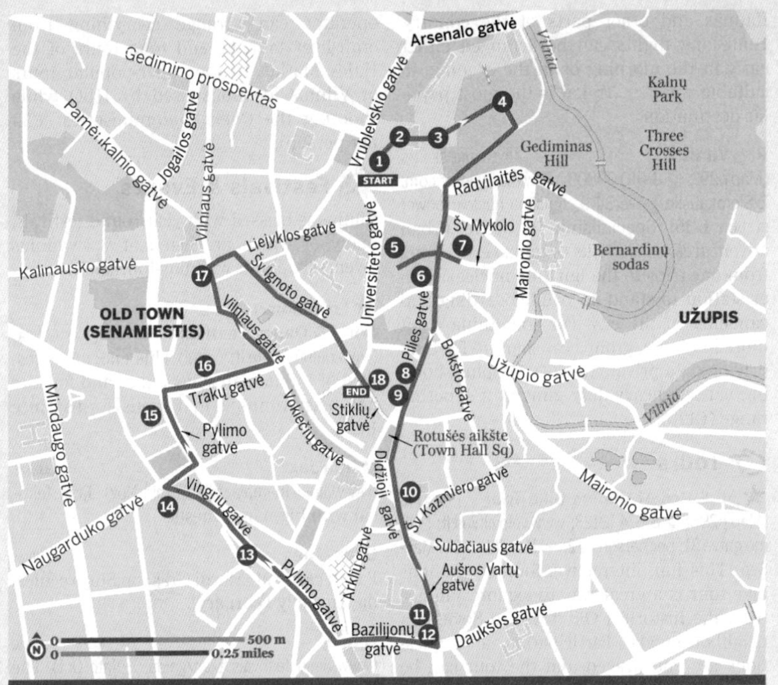


# City Walk
# The Best of Vilnius

**START** CATHEDRAL SQ
**END** ROTUŠES AIKŠTĖ
**DISTANCE** 4.9KM; 8 HOURS

Eastern Europe's largest Old Town is made for meandering.

Begin on **1 Cathedral Square**, taking in its magical tile, **2 Cathedral** (p293) and **3 Grand Dukes' Palace** (p293) before taking the funicular up to the **4 castle** (p289) on Gediminas Hill. From the tower survey the city then hike down into Old Town along Pilies gatvė. To get a feel for historic Vilnius, cut right onto Skapo gatvė and stop by the centuries-old **5 Vilnius University** (p295) and scale the bell tower at **6 Sts Johns' Church** (p295). Try some 19th-century Lithuanian recipes at **7 Mykolo 4** (p312), then proceed south along Didžioji gatvė, stopping to peruse Lithuanian fashion at the **8 Moustache Boutique** (p316). Admire the iconic **9 St Casimir's Church** (p302) off Rotušes aikštė and then continue south along Aušros Vartų, before stopping by the **10 Jonas Bugailiškis** (p317) workshop to check out his wooden carvings, and finishing up at the sacred **11 Gates of Dawn** (p300).

Duck through the Gates of Dawn and turn west on Bazilijonų gatvė before heading north along Pylimo gatvė and admiring the beautiful **12 Choral Synagogue** (p301) on the way. Proceed further north and detour slightly to the **13 Tolerance Centre** (p300) for an immersion in Jewish culture, then head further up Pylimo gatvė to discover the best of Vilnius' contemporary art at **14 MO Museum** (p302). Afterwards, stop for an afternoon beer at **15 Alaus Biblioteka** (p313), across the street. Continue east along Trakų gatvė, then cut through onto Stiklių gatvė for a glimpse of Jewish Vilnius. Browse boutiques such as one-of-a-kind **16 Terra Recognita** (p316) before rejoining Didžioji gatvė and opting for pre-dinner cocktails at **17 Nomads** (p313). Finish off with a contemporary Lithuanian meal at **18 Nineteen18** (p311), then find an outdoor terrace off Rotušes aikštė for evening people-watching.

Kaunas and other parts of the country. Hour-long flights can be arranged either early in the morning or in the evening, in suitable weather. Trakai is the most popular destination.

**PlayVilnius** ADVENTURE SPORTS
(Map p292; ☎8-610 00809; www.play-vilnius.com; Z Sierakausko gatvė 34-9; Ignalina nuclear power station €115) Specialising in active urban adventures, these folks organise everything from day trips to the Ignalina nuclear power station to stand-up paddleboarding and canoeing in the city. For something a bit more hardcore, groups can sign up for tank driving on a private track (€75), plus shooting various heavy-duty guns at a shooting range (€120).

## Tours

★**All Sides of Vilnius Bike Tour** CYCLING
(Map p296; ☎8-674 12123; www.velovilnius.lt; Pylimo gatvė 31; per person €22; ⊙11am Mon-Sat May-Sep) This fun, interactive, four- to six-hour bike tour is a great way to explore Vilnius, from the historical Old Town to Soviet-era neighbourhoods. Participation and questions are encouraged and the tour can be tailored towards specific interests.

**Vilnius With Locals** CULTURAL
(www.likealocalguide.com) Explore various aspects of Vilnius' history and culture with these enthusiastic, knowledgeable guides. The Jewish Vilnius tour (€12 per person) is sensitively done; another offering includes the Lithuanian Food Tour, a comprehensive look at traditional and nontraditional dining in Vilnius. Book online.

**Feel Z City** CULTURAL
(Map p296; ☎8-618 27926; www.feelzcity.com; Stulginskio gatvė 5) This enthusiastic local operator can arrange everything from craft-beer tastings and food tours of the Halės Market to the super-popular tours of Vilnius locations used by HBO while shooting the *Chernobyl* miniseries (€39 per person).

## Festivals & Events

Vilnius is blessed with year-round festivals, many of which are listed at www.vilnius-events.lt and www.vilnius-tourism.lt.

★**Lithuanian Song & Dance Festival** CULTURAL
(www.dainusvente.lt; ⊙Jul) This enormous festival of Lithuanian song, dance and folklore has been running in various forms since 1923.

**Mama Jazz** MUSIC
(www.vilniusmamajazz.lt; ⊙mid-Nov) Jazz festival with big-name guests.

**Užgavėnės** CARNIVAL
Pagan carnival (Mardi Gras) on Shrove Tuesday (usually February).

**Gaida** MUSIC
(www.vilniusfestivals.lt/en/gaida; ⊙late Oct) The biggest and most important contemporary and experimental music festival in the Baltics.

**Vilnius Festival** MUSIC
(www.vilniusfestivals.lt; ⊙Jun) Classical music, jazz and folk concerts in Old Town courtyards.

**Vilnius International Film Festival** FILM
(www.kinopavasaris.lt; Savanorių prospektas 7, Forum Cinemas Vingis; ⊙Mar) This celebration of celluloid is also known as Kino Pavasaris ('Cinema Spring'). The bulk of the screenings take place at Forum Cinemas Vingis, plus three other cinemas.

### THE UŽUPIS REPUBLIC

The cheeky streak of rebellion pervading Lithuania flourishes in Vilnius' bohemian heart, where artists, dreamers, drunks and squatters in Užupis have declared a breakaway state. The Užupis Republic (Užupio Republika) was officially, in an unofficial sense, born in 1998. The state has its own tongue-in-cheek president, anthem, flags and a 41-point constitution.

On April Fool's Day, citizens of the Užupis Republic celebrate their wholly unofficial state. Border guards wearing comical outfits stamp passports at the main bridge and the Užupis president makes speeches in the quarter's small square – the intersection of Užupio, Maluno and Paupio gatvės where the republic's symbol, the **Angel of Užupis**, stands. Increasingly hip, the neighbourhood continues to fill with galleries, restaurants and folk-artist workshops.

### VILNIUS IN...

#### Two Days

Spend the first day exploring Old Town, not missing the **Vilnius Cathedral** (p293), **Pilies gatvė**, the **Gates of Dawn** (p300) and the **university's 13 courtyards**, followed by lunch on an Old Town terrace. At dusk, hike (or ride the funicular) up **Gediminas Hill** (p289) for a city-spire sunset. On the second day, stroll around the **Užupis Republic**, visit the **Museum of Genocide Victims** (p304) and take in some of the sights of Jewish Vilnius.

#### Four Days

Depending on your interests, spend more time discovering **Jewish Vilnius**, take in the contemporary art at **MO Museum** (p302) and explore Vilnius' terrific dining and craft-beer scenes. Finish up with a spot of **shopping**: scour the city for linen, amber and Lithuanian fashion. You can also squeeze in a half-day trip by train to **Trakai** (p320) to check out the picture-perfect castle and paddle on the lake.

**Kaziukas Crafts Fair** CULTURAL
(www.kaziukomuge.lt; 4 Mar) Dating back to the 17th century, this festival of craft and culture comes to Old Town on St Casimir's Day, with stalls dotted about the medieval streets and squares.

**New Baltic Dance** DANCE
(www.dance.lt; early May) Contemporary dance festival.

**Christopher Summer Festival** MUSIC
(www.kristupofestivaliai.lt; Jul & Aug) Classical music festival with numerous events across the city.

**Capital Days** PERFORMING ARTS
(Gedimino prospektas; Sep) Three-day music and performing-arts festival, with stages set up along Gedimino prospektas.

**Sirenos** THEATRE
(www.okt.lt; mid-Sep–mid-Oct) This international theatre festival takes place at several venues across the city.

## Sleeping

For a small capital, Vilnius has plenty of accommodation options. Old Town has characterful places to stay for all budgets – guesthouses, homey hostels and centuries-old boutique hotels – just don't expect a parking space. Beyond Old Town, business hotels and upmarket chains are also well represented.

★ **Jimmy Jumps House** HOSTEL €
(Map p296; 5-231 3847; www.jimmyjumpshouse.com; Savičiaus gatvė 12-1; dm €13-18, d/tr without bathroom incl breakfast from €31/39; ) Movie nights, pub crawls, beer pong, tank-driving tours, free waffles...this clean, well-run, centrally located hostel is justifiably popular among backpackers who enjoy a crush-a-beer-can-against-the-forehead party vibe. The pine-wood bunks are in modest four- to 12-bed rooms, but hands-on service, lockers, a sociable lounge, games and a well-priced bar add up to money well spent.

**Mikalo House** HOSTEL €
(Map p296; 8-651 65037; www.mikalohouse.com; Šv Mikalojaus gatvė 3; dm/d/q €11/28/48; ) Apart from the superb location on a quiet little street in the heart of Old Town, this homey place is run by the ever-helpful Valdas who really makes travellers feel welcome. Choose between a six-bed dorm, a snug twin or a quad. The morning coffee and fresh croissants are a nice touch, too.

**25 Hours Hostel** HOSTEL €
(Map p292; 8-609 58560; www.hostel25hours.lt; Sodų gatvė 9; dm/s/d from €14/20/30; ) Handy for the bus and train stations, this friendly hostel distinguishes itself from the rest of Vilnius' budget scene with its vast, colourful dorms with quality beds and bunks, oversized sofas for lounging about and spotless private rooms. It's a sociable place without being a party hostel.

**Litinterp** B&B €
(Map p296; 5-212 3850; www.litinterp.lt; Bernardinų gatvė 7-2; s/d/tr without bathroom €23/40/54, d/tr with bathroom €46/60; office 8.30am-9pm Mon-Fri, 9am-3pm Sat; ) This bright, clean and friendly establishment has a wide range of options in the heart of Old Town. Rooms with shared bathroom can be a little cramped, but those with en suite are generously large. Guests can check in after office hours providing they give advance notice, and mini-kitchens and a left-luggage service are available. Breakfast is €3.50.

**Fabrika Hostel** HOSTEL €

(Map p296; ☎5-203 1005; www.facebook.com/fabrikahostelvilnius; Gedimino prospektas 21; dm/d €15/45; 📶) There's much to love about this this stylish, colourful hostel on the 6th floor of a historic building (no lift). There's a buzzy feel to the spacious common areas and kitchen, and nice little touches in the good-sized dorms and rooms, including individual power sockets and reading lights.

**Come to Vilnius** HOSTEL €

(Map p292; ☎8-620 29390; Šv Stepono gatvė 15; dm/d/tr €17/37/45; @📶) Bright colours, timber furnishings, proximity to transport and perks such as free pancakes, hot drinks and towels are the draws at this six-room, family-run hostel.

★ **The Joseph** BOUTIQUE HOTEL €€

(Map p292; ☎8-610 77500; www.facebook.com/theJosephLT; Žygimantų gatvė 11; s/d €88/97; 📶) Consisting of just seven individually styled rooms in a 19th-century building, the Joseph has won many fans with its exceptional service and decor. Expect original brick walls and heavy wooden beams with mirrored headboards and contemporary art by Lithuanian and French artists. Breakfast (€9) is cooked to order and delivered to your room.

The hotel is due to open more rooms in the same building by 2020.

**Apia Hotel** HISTORIC HOTEL €€

(Map p296; ☎5-212 3426; www.apia.lt; Šv Ignoto gatvė 12; r €75-135; P@📶) This smart, fresh and friendly hotel occupies some prime real estate in the heart of Old Town. Choose from courtyard or cobbled-street views among the hotel's 12 rooms, but if you're after a balcony, reserve room 3 or 4.

**Bernardinu B&B** GUESTHOUSE €€

(Map p296; ☎5-261 5134; www.bernardinuhouse.com; Bernardinų gatvė 5; d €50-60, d/tr with shared bathroom from €49/75; P📶) Baroque flourishes and original frescoes make every room unique at this friendly, family-owned B&B, stylishly restored within an 18th-century townhouse. Old timber flooring and ceilings have been carefully preserved, and stripped patches of brick allow you to see through the patina of the years. Breakfast (€7) is brought to your door.

**Domus Maria** GUESTHOUSE €€

(Map p296; ☎5-264 4880; www.domusmaria.lt; Aušros Vartų gatvė 12; s/d/tr/q incl breakfast from €60/77/108/121; P📶) Austere and occasionally spooky, the guesthouse of the Vilnius archdiocese is housed in a former 17th-century monastery. Rooms are plain but ample, history almost echoes along the long corridors, and the location at the foot of Old Town artery Aušros Vartų gatvė couldn't be better. Two rooms, 207 and 307, have views of the Gates of Dawn – book far in advance.

**Hotel Vilnia** HISTORIC HOTEL €€

(Map p296; ☎5-203 4455; www.hotelvilnia.lt; Maironio gatvė 1; d/ste €94/175; 📶) An enviable location near the Cathedral Sq, a beautiful 19th-century facade and spacious rooms flooded with plenty of natural light are among the perks here. The thoroughly contemporary restaurant, serving refined European cuisine, is an extra bonus.

**eLoftHotel** HOTEL €€

(Map p292; ☎5-266 0730; www.elofthotel.lt; Ševčenkos gatvė 16; s/d/tr €55/60/84; P@📶) This pleasant little hotel, which boasts 'ecological materials throughout', is a good choice for those who appreciate the greater quiet (15 minutes' walk) outside Old Town. Room price includes continental breakfast, the triples come with kitchenette and there's even a common kitchen and sauna.

**Senatoriai Hotel** HOTEL €€

(Map p296; ☎5-212 6491; www.senatoriai.lt; Tilto gatvė 2a; s/d €80/90; P@📶) This small, homey hotel's location so close to the cathedral is either a boon or a bane, depending on how much you enjoy the sound of the 5pm bells. Rooms are generally spacious and feature heavy leather furniture and decent beds. It also offers good Lithuanian cooking in its restaurant, a laundry service and online discounts in slow periods.

**Grotthaus** HOTEL €€

(Map p296; ☎5-266 0322; www.grotthusshotel.com; Ligoninės gatvė 7; s/d/ste €68/80/132; P📶) Step through the red-canopied entrance of this buttercup-yellow boutique townhouse to find Villeroy & Boch bathtubs, 19th-century *Titanic*-style fittings, Italian-made furniture, and curtains allegedly made with the same fabric as that used by the Queen of England! The Old Town location is top notch, and even the standard singles and doubles are a decent size.

**Hotel Rinno** HOTEL €€

(Map p296; ☎5-262 2828; www.rinno.lt; Vingrių gatvė 25; s/d from €64/75; P❄@📶) This

## VILNIUS FOR CHILDREN

Vilnius is great for kids: it's welcoming, relatively small-scale and has enough boat tours, hot-air balloons, castles and pizza to keep them satisfied.

- Vilnius Tourism has downloadable maps of kid-friendly spots, from playgrounds and ice rinks to museums of interest to little ones; see www.vilnius-tourism.lt/en/what-to-see/vilnius-for-you.
- With a hill to clamber on and medieval treasures inside the museum, Gediminas Castle & Museum (p289) is a hit with most age groups.
- The Toy Museum (p295) is a lot of fun for kids of all ages, with everything from 12th-century games to Soviet toys.
- In cold weather the **Akropolis shopping centre** (5-238 7711; www.akropolis.lt; Ozo gatvė 25; 10am-10pm; ) – with a cinema, ice-skating rink and soft-play area for under-12s – has you covered.
- Museum and public-transport tickets are usually half-price for kids.

charismatic little independent combines spacious, carpeted rooms with desks and armchairs, and a handy location (between Old Town and the train and bus stations) at a fair price. Breakfast is served in the pleasant and private backyard.

**Panorama Hotel** HOTEL €€
(Map p292; 5-233 8822; www.hotelpanorama.lt; Sodų gatvė 14; s/d from €51/54; P@) Beneath the kitsch veneer of this Soviet-era hotel you'll find well-maintained, good-value accommodation and some fabulous views of Old Town and surrounding hills from the pricier rooms. Decor won't make your social media posts, but the location is super handy for trains and long-distance buses.

★ **Hotel Pacai** DESIGN HOTEL €€€
(Map p296; 5-277 0000; www.hotelpacai.com; Didžioji gatvė 7; d from €180; P@) Staying at luxurious Pacai, in a restored 17th-century palace, you slumber beneath the same timber beams as past nobles - except nowadays there's modern art decking the walls, and individually styled chambers have discreet sundecks and lustrous marbled bathrooms. Murals, centuries-old statuary and vaulted corridors preserve the history, and with two of Vilnius' top restaurants on-site, Pacai is a gourmet epicentre, too.

★ **Artagonist** DESIGN HOTEL €€€
(Map p296; 5-243 0000; www.artagonist.lt; Pilies gatvė 34; s/d/ste from €93/118/203; ) With its giant mural and glass dome, the atrium at the Artagonist takes your breath away as you step inside. Each of the individually styled rooms features original art by Lithuanian talent as well as high ceilings typical of a 19th-century merchant house. Of the rooms, our favourite is the junior suite, with its spacious terrace overlooking Pilies gatvė.

**Stikliai** BOUTIQUE HOTEL €€€
(Map p296; 5-264 9595; www.stikliaihotel.lt; Gaono gatvė 7; s/d/ste €148/158/304; P@) The cream of the crop among Vilnius hotels, this boutique choice is managed by the Relais & Chateaux chain. Tucked down a picture-postcard cobbled street in the old Jewish quarter, it offers luxurious rooms in a 17th-century building with an abundance of charm and bold splashes of bright colour.

**Shakespeare** BOUTIQUE HOTEL €€€
(Map p296; 5-266 5885; www.shakespeare.lt; Bernardinų gatvė 8/8; s/d/apt from €88/127/190; P) This former printing house turned boutique hotel comprises 30 individually styled rooms. Perks include its tasteful eclecticism of decor, thoughtful touches like naming the rooms for literary and cultural figures (Winston Churchill, Dostoevsky, Aristotle), and the switched-on staff who give it a true distinction. Most importantly, antiques, books and quality furniture make the rooms delightful to spend time in.

**Dvaras Manor House** BOUTIQUE HOTEL €€€
(Map p296; 5-210 7370; www.dvaras.lt; Tilto gatvė 3-1; s/d from €84/106; P) Hospitality began here in the late 18th century, when heritage-listed Dvaras Manor offered five guest rooms and an ale shop. Things have developed since then: it now boasts eight plush rooms, with satellite TV, antique-style chairs and supremely comfortable beds. Best of all, you're in easy striking distance of the cathedral, castle and all the Old Town sights.

**Radisson Blu Royal Astorija** HOTEL €€€

(Map p296; ☎5-212 0110; www.radissonblu.com; Didžioji gatvė 35/2; r/ste from €137/272; P 📶 🏊) The Radisson is an excellent splurge, exuding character and housed within a building dating from the early 20th century. The central location, overlooking St Casimir's Church, is a plus, as are the popular wintertime Sunday brunches. Opt for the new-style premium rooms to get statement wallpaper, patios and bright pops of crimson. Of the classic rooms, pay a little extra for Old Town views.

## Eating

Whether you're craving rustic Lithuanian classics like *cepelinai* (parcels of thick potato dough stuffed with cheese and meat) and *kepta duona* (deep-fried rye bread with garlic), or inventive pan-European menus with pairing cocktails, Vilnius has it covered. Most restaurants are in Old Town: expect vaulted cellars, artful cafes serving homespun recipes and bright, contemporary restaurants serving global cuisine.

★ **Ali Šokoladinė** CAFE €

(Map p296; ☎8-683 35877; www.alisokoladine.lt; Vilniaus gatvė 31; cakes €4-6; ⏰10am-9pm) There's a designer boutique feel to this place, where customers are as likely to sip a coffee or glass of wine beneath the crimson splashes of contemporary art as they are to order the edible works of art – the pistachio eclairs, the perfect cubes of handmade chocolate, the elaborate cakes.

**Beigelistai** BAGELS €

(Map p296; ☎8-682 10971; www.facebook.com/beigelistai; Rusų gatvė 7; bagels €1-4.30; ⏰9am-7pm) Moderately distressed furniture and movie posters greet you at this snug NY-style bagel shop. Freshly baked daily, their fillings cater to all tastes – from zaatar and olive oil and braised beef to peanut butter and banana, hummus and veggies. Good coffee, too.

**Radharanė** VEGETARIAN €

(Map p296; ☎5-212 3186; www.radharane.lt; Gediminio prospektas 32; soups/mains €3/5; ⏰11am-9pm Mon, Tue & Thu-Sat, from 11.30am Wed & Sun; 🌿) Nourishing vegetarian food and swift service create a reviving experience at this contemporary restaurant. There's ample choice, from samosas and chickpea masala to cream-drenched paneer (cheese) dishes. The menu is largely Indian-inspired but there are always a few Lithuanian staples, such as chilled beetroot soup and potato pancakes. Vegans, rarely well catered for in Lithuania, have plenty of options.

**Pinavija** CAFE €

(Map p296; ☎8-676 44422; www.pinavija.lt; Vilniaus gatvė 21; coffee/pastries €1.60/2; ⏰9am-8pm; 📶 👪) With caramel-striped awnings, flowers throughout, a stunning array of cakes and pastries and good coffee, this smart bakery-cafe is a lovely place to refuel. There's even a snug kids' area, complete with Wendy house and toys, and soothing jazz for the more mature clientele. Try the Lithuanian cookies with cottage cheese and walnuts, or chocolate and nutmeg.

**Senoji Kibininė** LITHUANIAN €

(Map p296; www.kibinas.lt; Vilniaus gatvė; mains €3-5; ⏰9am-9pm Mon-Fri, 10am-9pm Sat, 10am-8pm Sun; 🌿) You can fill up on *cepelinai* or potato pancakes here, but its real thing is *kibinai:* pasties traditional to the country's Turkic Karaite minority that deserve to share the fame of their Cornish rivals. Whether it's mutton, chicken and mushroom, or spinach and curd you fancy, these toothsome shortcrust pockets are ideal after a few drinks in Old Town.

★ **Balzac** FRENCH €€

(Map p296; ☎8-614 89223; www.facebook.com/balzacvilnius; Savičiaus gatvė 7; mains €12-19; ⏰11.30am-11pm Sun-Wed, to midnight Thu-Sat) This faithfully *français* bistro serves classic French dishes in an elegantly distressed setting: melt-in-mouth duck confit with lentils, *tournedos de boeuf* (beef tenderloin wrapped in bacon) and its signature *tarte tatin* (caramelised apple cake). The dining area is small, so book to avoid disappointment.

★ **Panorama Gourmet** FOOD HALL €€

(Map p292; www.panorama.lt/en/gourmet; Saltoniškių gatvė 9; mains from €8; ⏰10am-10pm) Vilnius' best food court, inside the eponymous shopping mall, is a favourite haunt of local foodies. Standout offerings include steaks by Bučeris, Gan Bei City dumplings, wood-fired pizza pie and Pizza 360 and elaborate cakes at Pinavija. Oh, and the pistachio eclairs at Ali Šokoladinė are pastry perfection. It's well worth the walk (or short Bolt ride) northwest of the centre.

★ **Etno Dvaras** LITHUANIAN €€

(Map p296; ☎8-656 13688; www.etnodvaras.lt; Pilies gatvė 16; mains €6-12; ⏰11am-midnight; 🌿)

Yes, this is a chain. Yes, the cutesy 'Lithuanian countryside' theme is over the top. But we love this temple to Lithuanian stodge with all our hearts. There is something immensely satisfying about its monumental stacks of potato pancakes, slabs of pork roast, generous spreads of dumplings and superlative *cepelinai*. Your waistline won't thank you but your taste buds will.

**Gyoza** JAPANESE €€

(Map p296; ☎8-688 89997; www.facebook.com/gyozavilnius; Vokiečių gatvė 14; mains €6-10; ⏲11am-10pm Mon-Thu, to 11pm Fri, noon-11pm Sat, to 10pm Sun) All clean lines and edgy contemporary art, this thimble-sized, charcoal-and-crimson dumpling bar serves five types of moreish gyoza (Japanese dumplings) with individual dipping sauces, a supporting cast of poke bowls, *tonkatsu* and a handful of Japanese snacks, plus hot and cold sake and a small, carefully chosen selection of Japanese craft beer. It's hard to improve on perfection.

**Blue Lotus** THAI, INDIAN €€

(Map p296; ☎8-626 27196; www.bluelotus.lt; Totorių gatvė 16; mains €7-15; ⏲11.30am-11pm Mon-Thu, to midnight Fri, noon-midnight Sat, to 10pm Sun; ✍) Awaft with the scents of galangal and garam masala, Blue Lotus is one of those rare places that executes two distinct cuisines with aplomb within a subtly exotic interior. The tom yum soup and curries pack authentic heat and there are plenty of tofu, aubergine, chickpea and vegetable dishes to tempt the meat-averse.

**CAPO** SICILIAN €€

(Map p296; ☎8-612 99932; www.elcapo.lt; L Stuokos-Gucevičiaus gatvė 7; pizza €7-10; ⏲11am-11pm Mon-Wed, to 1am Thu & Fri, noon-1am Sat, to 11pm Sun; ✍) Authentic Sicilian cuisine is on offer at this trendy bar with angular black metal sconces, ceiling-high wine racks, dimmed lighting and an insistent, pulsating beat. The wood-fired pizzas topped with high-quality ingredients are particularly good.

**René** BELGIAN €€

(Map p296; ☎5-212 6858; www.restoranasrene.lt; Antokolskio gatvė 13; mains €9-13; ⏲11am-11pm; 📶) René Magritte is the patron saint of this place, which showcases *'La Cuisine de la Biere'*, and wonky, surrealist brickwork. Staff wear bowler hats and patrons are encouraged to draw on paper tablecloths, in between tucking into *moules marinière* and sausages roasted in beer.

**Meat Lovers' Pub** PUB FOOD €€

(Map p296; ☎8-652 51233; www.meatloverspub.lt; Šv Ignoto gatvė14; mains €7-22; ⏲11.30am-midnight Mon-Fri, noon-midnight Sat, noon-8pm Sun; 📶) Order lager, wheat beer or dark ale. Nibble fried cheese and moreish smoked ribs. Find that you're thirsty again, and start the cycle anew. Meat Lovers' Pub delivers exactly what it promises: unapologetically carnivorous pub food, such as German sausages, T-bone steaks and juicy burgers, in a convivial setting that somehow suits everyone from merry-making groups to solo travellers with books.

**Vegafe** VEGAN €€

(Map p296; ☎8-659 77411; www.jogosmityba.lt; Totorių gatvę 3; mains €8; ⏲11am-10pm Mon-Fri, from noon Sat & Sun; ✍) Adhering to vegan and ayurvedic principles (no garlic, no onion), Vegafe is on the swankier end of the conscious-eating spectrum. The setting is all clean design, and the food – perhaps a riotous plate of spring greens or *momos* (Tibetan dumplings) – is as delicious as it is virtuous. Wash it down with a nonalcoholic ginger wine.

**Kitchen** INTERNATIONAL €€

(Map p296; ☎8-688 80558; www.facebook.com/kitchenvilnius; Didžioji gatvė 11; mains €8-14; ⏲11.30am-midnight) This stylish, stripped-back place, accessed through a carriageway from bustling Didžioji gatvė, does inventive contemporary food with an emphasis on what's in season locally. That might be cold yoghurt soup with cucumber, or something tasty with the spring's first asparagus. The kitchen operates on reduced hours in summer.

**Lokys** LITHUANIAN €€

(Map p296; ☎5-262 9046; www.lokys.lt; Stiklių gatvė 8; mains €12-20; ⏲noon-midnight) Track down the big wooden bear to make merry in the vaulted 16th-century cellars of a former merchant's house. As a 'hunter's restaurant', it does a strong line in game, including roast venison and boar, game sausages with cabbage, quail with pear and cowberry, and even beaver stewed with mushrooms. Buckwheat with chanterelles is a veggie-pleasing stunner.

★**Nineteen18** BALTIC €€€

(Map p296; ☎8-608 08950; www.nineteen18.lt; Didžioji gatvė 7; tasting menu €115; ⏲6pm-midnight Wed-Sat) Helmed by renowned chef Matas Paulinas, this is one of Lithuania's most memorable dining experiences. The pared-down decor contrasts vividly with the imaginative, beautiful dishes kept secret until they're placed in front of you. The concept is reimagined Baltic cuisine and clean flavours. Pair the dishes with carefully chosen wines or wonderfully original nonalcoholic beverages, made in-house. Book well ahead.

**★Šturmų Švyturys** SEAFOOD €€€
(Map p292; ☎8-656 98000; www.sturmusvyturys.lt; Užupio gatvė 30; per person €35; ⏰noon-10pm) Serving only wild-caught fish (eel, bream etc) from the Curonian Lagoon, this nautically themed restaurant feeds you whatever happens to be fresh on the day. The super-short menu includes their legendary fish soup, three types of fish (typically grilled and served with a vegetable medley) and dessert. Bring a friend, as dishes are meant for two.

**★Sweet Root** LITHUANIAN €€€
(Map p296; ☎8-685 60767; www.sweetroot.lt; Užupio gatvė 22; 7-course degustation €75; ⏰6-11pm Wed-Sat) 🌿 Led by the seasons, Sweet Root pairs locally sourced ingredients – pike and nettles, beetroot leaves and chanterelles – and presents them in a smart modern dining room. It's an evening-long degustation experience, elevated to greater heights if you opt for wine pairing (€55). A menu of ingredients for you to cross out as you go along adds a touch of whimsy.

**Saint Germain** MEDITERRANEAN €€€
(Map p296; ☎5-262 1210; www.saintgermain.lt; Literatų gatvė 9; mains €17-40; ⏰11am-11pm) Focusing largely on Italian and French fare, and serving wine-friendly snacks such as oysters and scallop bruschettas, this stylish wine bar-bistro is tucked away on one of Old Town's nicest cobbled streets. If you want to enjoy your Ligurian-style *zander* (pike-perch; baked in foil with tomatoes, olives, potatoes and pine nuts) on the summer terrace, book ahead.

**Ertlio Namas** LITHUANIAN €€€
(Map p296; ☎8-690 33300; www.ertlionamas.lt; Šv Jono gatvė 7; 4-/6-course tasting menu €35/45; ⏰5-10pm Mon-Thu, to 11pm Fri, 1-11pm Sat, 1-10pm Sun) Dining here is stepping back in time. Each of the imaginatively re-created, centuries-old recipes (trout with saffron bagel, roe-deer sausage with pumpkin pudding) comes with an elaborate backstory, so you're coming here to learn the ways of 17th-century nobles as much as for exciting flavours.

**Selfish Bistro** SEAFOOD €€€
(Map p296; ☎8-656 11330; https://selfish.business.site; Vilniaus gatvė 29; mains €15-28; ⏰5-11pm Mon-Thu, 2pm-1am Sat, 2-11pm Sun) As much a nightspot as a bistro, Selfish is all mood lighting, oysters on ice and glasses of bubbly – from champagne to cava to crémant. You can get something more substantial – seafood risotto, perhaps, or snacks to share – or you can be shellfish and have a dozen or two bivalve molluscs all to yourself.

**Mykolo 4** LITHUANIAN €€€
(Map p296; ☎8-688 22210; www.mykolo4.lt; Šv Mykolo gatvė 4; mains €15-25; ⏰noon-10.30pm Mon-Fri, to 10pm Sat) This heavy wooden-beamed, brick-walled bistro specialises in dishes inspired by 19th-century 'bourgeois' recipes and framed by the availability of seasonal ingredients. During cooler days, Jerusalem artichoke and buckwheat soup and slow-cooked lamb are delightful belly-warmers, while blueberry-marinated herring and goat's cheese and beetroot dumplings are among the lighter fare.

**Amandus** LITHUANIAN €€€
(Map p296; ☎8-675 41191; www.amandus.lt; Pilies gatvė 34; tasting menu €60; ⏰7-10pm) Chef Deivydas Praspaliauskas is one of the high priests of modern Lithuanian cuisine. His chefs work their magic in an open kitchen in a whimsical cave-like basement, decorated with pop art. The monthly changing tasting menu revolves around seasonal ingredients; expect the likes of beetroot with goat's cheese, duck with lingonberries and desserts trailing theatrical dry-ice smoke. Reserve ahead.

### Self-Catering

Self-catering is easy, with a supermarket on every second street corner, a superb market and numerous speciality shops.

**★Halės Market** MARKET €
(Halės Turgavietė; Map p296; ☎5-262 5536; www.halesturgaviete.lt; Pylimo gatvė 58; ⏰7am-6pm Tue-Sat, to 3pm Sun) Traditional market stalls mingle effortlessly with on-trend cafes at Halės Turgavietė, one of the city's oldest food markets, staffed by Russian traders. The glossy metal and glass construction, completed in 1906, is a delightful place to mingle and meander. Browse glistening fruit and veg, honeys and jams, or head into the pungent interior for cheeses, meats and *churchkhela* (Georgian/Turkish sweet). Inside the main hall there are several casual places to eat and even craft beer on tap.

**Senamiesčio Krautuvė** DELI €

(Map p296; ☎5-231 2836; www.senamiesciokrautuve.lt; Literatų gatvė 5; ⏲10am-8pm Mon-Sat, 11am-5pm Sun) Look no further than this quiet hobbit-hole deli for the very best Lithuanian comestibles, many unique to the country. Wicker baskets brim with fruit and vegetables, cheeses and yoghurts fill the chiller cabinets, and jars of honey and jam line the shelves. Grab breads and cookies to eat on the hoof while admiring the arty tributes along Literatų gatvė.

**Kmyninė** BAKERY €

(Map p292; ☎8-640 49042; www.facebook.com/kmynine; Užupio gatvė 38; bread/cookies per kilo €3.50-7; ⏲7.30am-9pm Mon-Fri, from 8am Sat & Sun; 📶) This sweet little bakery, named for the caraway seeds so beloved in Central and Eastern Europe, is a great place to pick up moist, sweet rye breads, Lithuanian cookies and *sakotis,* the traditional cake that looks a little like a Christmas tree.

## Drinking & Nightlife

Lined with terraces in summer, Vokiečių gatvė is a sociable starting point; as the night wears on, bar crawl along Totorių or Vilniaus gatvė. Vilnius has a small but lively clubbing scene, with DJ-led electronica and alternative rock and metal well represented in warehouse-like venues.

★**Apoteka Bar** COCKTAIL BAR

(Map p296; ☎8-675 53565; www.apotekabar.lt; Visų Šventųjų gatvė 5; ⏲6pm-midnight Sun-Thu, to 2am Fri & Sat) Find the cosy nook in a stone alcove or perch around the bar beneath the heavy wooden beams before tasting some of Vilnius' most imaginative mixology. Some of the cocktails take you on a trip around the world, some are classic reimagined, while others – like Forager – are autumn in a glass.

★**Alaus Biblioteka** CRAFT BEER

(Map p296; ☎5-212 6874; www.beerlibrary.lt; Trakų gatvė 4; ⏲5pm-midnight Tue-Sat) With 17 rotating Lithuanian and international craft brews on tap and the bar staffed by knowledgeable staff, this might be your idea of heaven, especially if you're keen on the idea of drinking a lambic sour or a Trappist ale while surrounded by books. You'll have to tackle steep stairs afterwards, though.

★**Nomads** COCKTAIL BAR

(Map p296; ☎8-676 08911; www.facebook.com/nomadsbar; Didžioji gatvė 5; ⏲5pm-2am Sun-Thu, to 3am Fri & Sat) This intimate little cocktail bar with velvet bar stools runs with a globe-roaming theme, with each of their nine cocktails (changing every month) driven by ingredients from a particular country and culture. A Lithuanian concoction might



### VILNIUS' COFFEE SCENE

There are no shortages of places to get your caffeine fix in the Lithuanian capital, from branches of Caffeine Roasters and Huracan Coffee chains to quirky speciality coffee shops. Here are five of the best:

**Crooked Nose & Coffee Stories** (Map p296; ☎8-670 81803; www.crooked-nose.com; Šaltinių gatvė 20; ⏲10am-4pm Thu-Sat) Come here to try three different small batch roasts every week and browse copies of *Drift* magazine for coffee devotees.

**StrangeLove** (Map p296; ☎8-626 69218; www.facebook.com/strangelovevilnius; B Radvilaitės gatvė 6B; ⏲8am-9pm Mon-Thu, to 10pm Fri, 10am-10pm Sat, 10am-8pm Sun; 📶) 🍃 An all-white interior, mellow jazz in the background and delectable cakes all make for excellent accompaniments to the sustainably sourced coffee.

**Coffee1** (Map p296; ☎8-610 60160; www.facebook.com/coffee1.lt; Užupio gatvė 9; ⏲7.30am-8pm Mon-Fri, 8am-8pm Sat, 9am-8pm Sun) Quasi-industrial-themed coffee shop, with great cakes (including vegan ones) and split-level seating (laptop-toters on the bottom tier).

**Elska Coffee** (Map p296; ☎8-608 21028; www.facebook.com/elska.coffee; Pamėnkalnio gatvė 1; ⏲7am-9pm Mon-Fri, 8am-8pm Sat & Sun; 📶) Distressed, artfully mismatched furniture, excellent coffee, hipster chow such as avocado toast and chia-seed pudding, as well as a pocket-sized library and adjoining gallery of modern art.

**Taste Map Coffee Roasters** (Map p292; ☎8-626 80483; www.tastemap.lt; M K Čiurlionio gatvė 8; ⏲7am-8pm Mon-Fri, 9am-8pm Sat, 10am-7pm Sun; 📶) This smart coffee shop in western Vilnius is the favourite haven of the laptop-toting set. They also roast their own beans.

### TOP VILNIUS PANORAMAS

For a breathtaking cityscape try the following:

**Gediminas Castle** (p289) While sightseeing.

**Sts Johns' Church** (p295) For 360-degree views of Old Town from its free-standing campanile.

**Oreivystės Centras** (p304) Go high above the city in a hot-air balloon.

**Three Crosses** (p303) Best for hilltop sunset views of Old Town.

**TV Tower** (p304) For sunset vistas.

feature blackcurrant wine and beetroot, while a Brazilian offering revolves around *cachaça* (sugar-cane firewater).

**BeerHouse & Craft Kitchen** CRAFT BEER
(Map p296; 8-614 44436; www.beer-house.lt; Vokiečių gatvė 24; 5pm-midnight Mon-Wed, to 2am Thu & Fri, 2pm-midnight Sat & Sun) This labyrinth of medieval cellars stocks a staggering 300 bottled beers from around the world, as well as 20 keg brews from local microbreweries. The pub grub is also excellent.

**Alchemikas** COCKTAIL BAR
(Map p296; 8-612 99800; Islandijos gatvė 1; 7pm-2am Mon-Thu, to 4am Fri & Sun) Dedicated to serious mixology, 'the Alchemist' turns base materials into golden evenings for many a Vilnius hipster. It's very popular and the limited space runs out quickly; Wednesday and Thursday are less insanely busy than weekends.

**Šnekutis** PUB
(Map p292; 8-687 76247; www.facebook.com/baraisnekutis; Polocko gatvė 7a; 10am-11pm) The Užupis branch of this local institution is an atmospheric wooden shack decorated with antlers, carvings and assorted bric-a-brac. There are around a dozen rotating craft beers on tap, all from local producers, served alongside belly-filling, traditional Lithuanian snacks: fried bread, smoked pigs' ears and other munchies.

**Prohibicija** CRAFT BEER
(Map p296; 8-655 12666; www.facebook.com/prohibicijapub; Arklių gatvė 6; 5pm-midnight Tue-Thu, to 2am Fri & Sat) Part of the Etmonų Posesija Creative Cluster – a multipurpose space reminiscent of a Budapest ruin pub, featuring a ceramics studio, tattoo artist and pizza – this tiny craft-beer bar specialises in Danish and limited-edition Lithuanian brews. Join the locals at the outdoor tables (if you don't mind the smoke).

**Amy Winehouse** WINE BAR
(Map p296; 8-640 33111; www.facebook.com/amywinehousevilnius; Basanavičiaus gatvė 14a; 6pm-2am Sun-Thu, to 4am Fri & Sat) It's hard to resist this bohemian wine bar, named after the bouffant-haired chanteuse herself, with inexpensive Prosecco on tap and a good array of wines from the Old and New worlds. The light-strung terrace is perfect for summer nights.

**Bubbles Champagneria** WINE BAR
(Map p296; 8-647 72557; www.facebook.com/bubbles.champagneria; Vilniaus gatvė 35; 5pm-1am Mon, to 2am Tue-Thu, to 4am Fri & Sat) The cool black interior lets you focus on the bubbly in your glass as you sample one (or two, or seven…) or the dozens of champagne, crémant, cava and other sparkling wines on offer. There are champagne cocktails, too, and oysters to slurp down alongside them. Dress up; the locals do.

**Bukowski** BAR
(Map p296; 8-640 58855; www.facebook.com/bukowskipub; Visų Šventų gatvė 7; 4pm-2am Mon-Thu, to 4am Fri & Sat, to midnight Sun) The eponymous Barfly is the spiritual patron of this charismatic boho bar in a less-trodden pocket of Old Town. It has a back terrace for finer weather, great beers on tap, a full program of poetry, music and other events, and a welcoming, unpretentious atmosphere. One of Vilnius' best.

**Špunka** BAR
(Map p296; 8-652 32361; www.spunka.lt; Užupio gatvė 9; 3-10pm Tue-Sun, from 5pm Mon) This tiny, charismatic bar does a great line in craft ales from Lithuania and further afield. If you need sustenance to keep the drink and chat flowing, crunchy beer snacks, charcuterie platters and garlic bread are close at hand.

**King & Mouse** BAR
(Map p296; 5-203 2552; www.kingandmouse.lt; Trakų gatvė 2; 5pm-1am) While a collection of more than 300 whiskies (and whiskeys) from around the world is its forte, this bar also does great cocktails and food. Knowledgeable staff, outdoor area atwinkle with fairy lights and a welcoming atmosphere make this one of Old Town's sweetest spots to refuel.

**Soho** GAY & LESBIAN
(Map p292; ☎8-699 39567; www.sohoclub.lt; Švitrigailos gatvė 7/16; cover charge varies; ⏲10pm-6am Fri & Sat) Proud, friendly and party-obsessed, Soho proudly bills itself as Lithuania's 'most popular' (and pretty much only) LGBTQ club. On a regular night, DJs play house and pop; on special nights, live performers take over.

**Pabo Latino** CLUB
(Map p296; ☎5-262 1045; www.pabolatino.lt; Trakų gatvė 3/2; cover charge varies; ⏲9pm-3am Thu, to 5am Fri & Sat) Forgive the cheesy themes ('Girls Night Out!', 'Be My Latin Lover!'): if you want to salsa till the wee hours, and don't mind a cocktail or two, this technicolour cavern promises all sorts of fun. Super-popular with locals.

**Būsi Trečias** MICROBREWERY
(Map p296; ☎8-618 11266; www.busitrecias.lt; Totorių gatvė 18; ⏲11am-11pm Sun-Wed, to midnight Thu, to 2am Fri & Sat) Locals know this split-level microbrewery-pub is a great place to get a cheap, sustaining Lithuanian lunch. It also offers charismatic wooden decor, 12 varieties of beer (including lime, raspberry and caramel, though the dark ale is our favourite) and courtyard tables for the warmer months.

**Opium** CLUB
(Map p296; ☎8-691 41205; www.facebook.com/opiumclub; Islandijos gatvė 4; admission €3-5; ⏲11pm-6am Fri & Sat) This compact venue – which serves food in the daylight hours – is for serious clubbers. Some of Vilnius' best DJs as well as international acts play electro, techno and house.

**Užupio kavinė** CAFE
(Map p296; ☎5-212 2138; www.uzupiokavine.lt; Užupio gatvė 2; ⏲10am-11pm; 📶) The plum spot on the Vilnia, next to the main bridge into Užupis, is the best thing about this cafe-bar. In summer, grab a table on the deck overlooking the art installations on the river (they tend to book up fast) and watch the bohos and tourists stream by. The cosy interior is equally fun in winter, sometimes with impromptu live entertainment.

**In Vino/Portobello** WINE BAR
(Map p296; ☎5-212 1210; www.facebook.com/invinobaras; Aušros Vartų gatvė 7; ⏲4pm-2am Sun-Thu, to 4am Fri & Sat) This hugely popular Old Town venue has split: the glamorous wine bar In Vino remains, but has yielded half its space to the English-style 'pub' Portobello. On one side of the courtyard you'll find candlelit tables and a fantastic range of wines by the glass; on the other, it's pints of craft beer and red phone boxes.

**Notre Vie** WINE BAR
(Map p296; ☎8-6142 4521; www.notrevie.lt; Stiklių gatvė 10; ⏲1pm-midnight Mon-Wed, to 3am Thu-Sat, to 1am Sun; 📶) Wedged into one of the prime crossroads in the twisting streets of Old Town is this charismatic little wine bar, offering Old and New World wines by the glass, plus cheese, charcuterie, quesadillas and other wine-friendly snacks.

## ☆ Entertainment

As a cultured, bookish city, Vilnius' theatre scene is high quality, though most performances are in Lithuanian. The live music scene's all the better for being small scale, with good jazz clubs and gigs across genres. See www.vilnius-tourism.lt for a calendar of events.

### Theatre & Classical Music

Mainstream theatre – from both Lithuania and abroad – is performed at several locations in town. Most companies shut down for the summer season. Buy tickets at venue box offices.

**Lithuanian National Opera & Ballet Theatre** OPERA
(Lietuvos Nacionalinis Operos ir Baleto Teatras; Map p296; ☎5-262 0727; www.opera.lt; Vienuolio gatvė 1; ⏲box office 10am-7pm Mon-Fri, to 6.30pm Sat, to 3pm Sun) This stunning (or gaudy,

### GAY & LESBIAN VILNIUS

Vilnius is a hub for LGBT+ rights activism in Lithuania, having hosted the country's first pride parade in 2010. People in Vilnius are generally more accepting of diversity than elsewhere in the country, where conservative and prejudicial attitudes are common. Nonetheless, many travellers may prefer to keep a low profile – as do many local LGBT+ people.

The scene is generally low-key, with only a few clubs in Vilnius catering exclusively or mostly to a gay clientele; the most popular is Soho. The Vilnius-based Lithuanian Gay League (www.lgl.lt) maintains a list of restaurants, bars, hotels and entertainment venues and Friendly City (www.friendlycity.info) has compiled listings of LGBT+-friendly businesses.

depending on your taste) Soviet-era building, with huge, cascading chandeliers and grandiose dimensions, is home to Lithuania's national ballet and opera companies. You can see world-class performers for as little as €10.

**Vilnius Congress Concert Hall** CONCERT VENUE
(Map p296; ☎5-262 8127; www.lvso.lt; Vilniaus gatvė 6/16; ⏰box office noon-7pm Mon-Fri, 11am-4pm Sat) The home of the Lithuanian State Symphony Orchestra, this chunky geometric pile near the Neris hosts symphonies, chamber music, opera and more. Leading Lithuanian and international performers can be seen for a song.

**Lithuanian National Philharmonic** CLASSICAL MUSIC
(Lietuvos Nacionalinė Filharmonija; Map p296; ☎5-266 5233; www.filharmonija.lt; Aušros Vartų gatvė 5; ⏰box office 10am-7pm Tue-Sat, to noon Sun) Lithuania's premier venue for orchestral, chamber and sacral music. But it's not all classical: prominent international jazz acts often ply their trade here.

**Lithuanian Music & Theatre Academy** CLASSICAL MUSIC
(Lietuvos muzikos akademija; Map p292; ☎5-261 2691; www.lmta.lt; Gedimino prospektas 42) Nurturing Lithuania's young musical, terpsichorean and theatrical talent, the Academy also stages hundreds of free performances each year. It's spread over four buildings, but the classical pile at number Gedimino prospektas 42 is the main one.

### Live Music

**Jazz Cellar 11** LIVE MUSIC
(Map p296; ☎8-684 11382; www.vilniusjazzclub.lt; Aušros Vartų gatvė 11; ⏰8pm-1am Thu-Sat) Closed over the summer season, in the darker months this atmospheric cellar hosts live jazz acts – both homegrown talent and acts from abroad. Cover charge varies, depending on who's playing.

**Tamsta** LIVE MUSIC
(Map p296; ☎5-212 4498; www.tamstaclub.lt; Subačiaus gatvė 11a; cover charge varies; ⏰7pm-midnight Wed & Thu, to 2am Fri & Sat Sep-Apr) Live music by local musicians ranging from rock to rock 'n' roll to jazz with inspired jamming some nights. The long bar gets pretty packed most evenings. Note the club shuts down during summer (June to August).

## Shopping

Crafts and clothes boutiques dotted around Old Town offer linens, deli produce, amber creations and wood-carved souvenirs. There are also quirky shops selling age-old Lithuanian crafts, plus gifts and accessories by up-and-coming Lithuanian designers.

### Old Town

★ **Amatų Gildija** CERAMICS
(Craft Guild; Map p296; ☎5-212 0520; www.amatugildija.lt; Pranciškonų gatvė 4; ⏰11am-7pm Tue-Sat) Dedicated to preserving and teaching traditional techniques of ceramics, Amatų Gildija is a hive of industry and beautiful handicrafts. It's an open workshop, (commercial) gallery and teaching space set below street level, and always abuzz with quiet, concentrated activity. While it's mainly about pots, it also teaches and displays woodworking, weaving and other crafts.

**Amber Museum** JEWELLERY
(Map p296; ☎5-212 1988; www.ambergift.lt; Aušros Vartų gatvė 9; ⏰10am-6pm Mon-Fri, to 3pm Sat) Displays the wares of top jewellers working with Baltic Gold in a room itself decorated with more than 500kg of amber.

★ **Terra Recognita** JEWELLERY
(Map p296; ☎5-231 3907; www.terrarecognita.lt; Stiklių gatvė 7; ⏰10am-10pm) Artist and designer Saulius Vaitiekūnas has been making striking, unusual jewellery from Baltic stone for many years and there's a great deal of symbolism to his works. The jewellery shop doubles as a gallery for his other art.

**Balta Balta** GIFTS & SOUVENIRS
(Map p296; ☎8-618 78022; www.baltabalta.com; Pilies gatvė 32; ⏰11am-7pm) Hand-crafted scarves, hats, soft toys, cushions and clothes, made from natural fibres by local artists.

**Moustache Boutique** FASHION & ACCESSORIES
(Map p296; ☎8-613-89738; www.facebook.com/moustacheboutique; Vilniuaus gatvė 28; ⏰11am-7pm Mon-Fri, to 5pm Sat) Design workshop, specialising in unique streetwear for men and women by Lithuanian designers. Some unusual accessories and gifts, too.

**4 Boobs Studio** CERAMICS
(Map p296; ☎8-621 54640; www.facebook.com/4boobsceramics; Užupio gatvė 2a; ⏰noon-8pm Mon-Fri) Wonderful contemporary ceramic creations are available at this Užupis studio. You can also sign up for a pottery course.

## THE BEST OF FOLK ART IN VILNIUS

Lithuanian folk art is alive and well, as the clutch of enchanting folk-artist workshops in and around Old Town proves.

**Senųjų Amatų Dirbtuvės** (Old Crafts Workshop; Map p296; ☎8-613 81889; www.seniejiamatai.lt; Savičiaus gatvė 10; ⊙11am-7pm Tue-Sun) The tools, materials, processes and final results of a whole range of traditional crafts – weaving, papermaking, bookbinding, leather-working and metalworking – are lovingly displayed in this fantastic, welcoming little shop. Affiliated with the Fine Crafts Association of Vilnius, it's a wonderful place to learn these time-worn skills, or pick up a beautiful Lithuanian keepsake.

**Black Ceramics Centre** (BCC; Map p296; ☎8-699 42456; www.ceramics.w3.lt; Naugarduko gatvė 20) This building contains both the workshop and retail outlet for the Black Ceramics Centre, dedicated to preserving and teaching the ancient Lithuanian art of black ceramics.

**Jonas Bugailiškis** (Map p296; ☎8-652 36613; www.bugailiskis.com; Aušros Vartų gatvė 17-10; ⊙by arrangement) Lithuanian artist Bugailiškis turns out all manner of weird and beautiful things from his workshop: sculptures, ornate crosses and even musical instruments.

**Sauluva** (Map p296; ☎8-686 43906; www.sauluva.lt; Literatų gatvė 3; ⊙10am-7pm) A 'Joint Stock Company' selling handicrafts in amber, metal, ceramics, textiles and other materials. Great for unusual and educational toys, with multiple branches around town.

**Vilniaus Puodžių Cechas** (Vilnius Potters' Guild; Map p296; ☎8-659 99040; Paupio gatvė 2-20; ⊙11am-7pm Tue-Fri, noon-6pm Sat) Traditional ceramic manufacturing and handicrafts are on display here.

**Vitražo manufaktūra** (Map p296; ☎5-212 1202; www.stainedglass.lt; Stiklių gatvė 6-8; ⊙1-7pm Mon-Fri, from 11am Sat-Sun) Exquisite stained-glass sculptures, wall murals and mobiles fill this creative stained-glass workshop. Daily demonstrations noon to 4pm.

**Lino Namai** HOMEWARES

(Linen House; Map p296; ☎5-212 2322; www.siulas.lt; Vilniaus gatvė 12; ⊙10am-7pm Mon-Fri, to 6pm Sat, 11am-5pm Sun) Lino Namai sells linen from Siūlas, the oldest flax mill in the country, renowned for high-quality table and bed linen. You'll also find accessories and a few pieces to wear. There's another branch on Pilies gatvė 38.

**Aukso Avis** FASHION & ACCESSORIES

(Map p296; ☎5-261 0421; www.facebook.com/auksoavis; Pilies gatvė 38; ⊙11am-8pm Mon-Fri, to 7pm Sat, to 5pm Sun) This gallery, established by Vilnius fashion designer Julija Žilėniene, sells bags, T-shirts, wall murals and jewellery (think necklaces in felt or wool) made from a rich range of materials.

**Ramunė Piekautaitė** FASHION & ACCESSORIES

(Map p296; ☎5-231 2270; www.ramunepiekautaite.com; Didžioji gatvė 20; ⊙11am-7.30pm Mon-Fri, to 6pm Sat, to 4pm Sun) A swanky boutique showcasing locally designed business, leisure and bridal wear.

**House of Naïve** GIFTS & SOUVENIRS

(Map p296; ☎8-616 99665; www.houseofnaive.com; Didžioji gatvė 38; ⊙11am-7pm Mon-Fri, to 4pm Sat & Sun) This polished store specialises largely in women's fashion by Lithuanian designers – linen suits, shirts, dresses – but also handmade footwear, stylish handbags and locally made chocolate that comes in unusual flavours.

**Humanitas** BOOKS

(Map p296; ☎5-262 1153; www.humanitas.lt; Dominikonų gatvė 5; ⊙10am-6pm Mon-Fri, to 4pm Sat) Wonderfully stocked with art, design, architecture and titles on all things Lithuanian.

**Aušros Vartų Meno Galerija** ARTS & CRAFTS

(Map p296; ☎5-240 5007; www.avmenogalerija.lt; Aušros Vartų gatvė 12; ⊙9am-9pm) Good spot to look for locally made souvenirs, including paintings, lace and arts and crafts.

**Littera** BOOKS

(Map p296; ☎5-212 1988; Universiteto gatvė 3; ⊙9am-6pm Mon-Fri, 10am-3pm Sat) You'll find the university bookshop, which sells souvenirs too, in MK Sarbievijus courtyard.

**Lietuviški Drabužiai** FASHION & ACCESSORIES
(Map p296; Trakų gatvė 6; ⏲10am-6pm) Come here for streetwear with bold designs by Lithuania's up-and-coming young designers, statement backpacks and purses, and colourful socks – we particularly like the Trump/Putin Make Everything Great Again socks, based on the infamous Vilnius mural.

**Freaky Foxx** JEWELLERY
(Map p292; ☎8-682 28229; www.freakyfoxx.com; Polocko gatvė 38; ⏲by appointment) At this Užupis design studio you can find some wonderfully unique porcelain jewellery made by local artisans. Call ahead.

**Vaga** BOOKS
(Map p292; ☎5-249 8392; www.vaga.lt; Gedimino prospektas 9; ⏲10am-7pm Mon-Fri, to 4pm Sat & Sun) Great map selection and good coffee.

## New Town

**Lino Kopos** FASHION & ACCESSORIES
(Map p292; www.giedrius.com; Krokuvos gatvė 6; ⏲10am-7pm Mon-Fri, to 4pm Sat) The local master of linen is Giedrius Šarkauskas. Inspired by life's natural cycle, the designer produces collections sewn solely from linen. Accessories are made from amber, wood, leather and linen.

**Juozas Statkevičius** FASHION & ACCESSORIES
(Map p296; www.statkevicius.com; Paménkalnio gatvė 2-1; ⏲10am-6pm Mon, from 9am Tue-Fri) 'Josef Statkus' is a big local name in cutting-edge fashion and costume design, with representatives in Paris, New York and Moscow.

## Information

### MEDIA

**Vilnius in Your Pocket** (www.inyourpocket.com) is a quality city guide published every two months, available as PDF download, as an app or in bookshops, tourist offices and newspaper kiosks (€1).

### MEDICAL SERVICES

Pharmacies are easy to find all over town and medicine is inexpensive.

**Baltic-American Medical & Surgical Clinic** (☎5-234 2020; www.bak.lt; Nemenčinės gatvė 54a; ⏲24hr) English-speaking healthcare inside Vilnius University Antakalnis hospital.

**University Emergency Hospital** (Santaros Klinikos; ☎5-236 5000; www.santa.lt; Santariškių gatvė 2; ⏲24hr) This teaching hospital takes serious and emergency cases.

### MONEY

The following all have ATMs accepting Visa and MasterCard. ATMs can also be found throughout the city.

**Citadele Bankas** (☎5-213 5454; www.keitykla.lt; Gedimino prospektas 26; ⏲8am-5pm Mon-Fri) Lithuania's Amex representative exchanges currency.

**SEB Vilniaus Bankas** (www.seb.lt; Vokiečių gatvė 9; ⏲9am-5.30pm Mon-Fri) Also has a branch on **Gedimino** (www.seb.lt; Gedimino prospektas 12; ⏲8am-5pm Mon-Fri).

**Swedbank** (www.swedbank.lt; Gedimino prospektas 56; ⏲9am-5.30pm Mon-Thu, to 4.30pm Fri) Exchanges currency.

### ONLINE RESOURCES

**Vilnius** (www.vilnius.lt) Informative city municipality website.

**Vilnius Old Town Renewal Agency** (www.vsaa.lt) The latest on the Old Town renovation.

**Vilnius Tourism** (www.vilnius-tourism.lt) Tourist office website; brilliant up-to-the-minute capital guide.

### POST

**Branch Post Office** (Map p296; www.post.lt; Vokiečių gatvė 7-13; ⏲10am-6pm Mon-Fri) Handy for Old Town.

**Central Post Office** (Centrinis Paštas; Map p296; www.post.lt; Gedimino prospektas 7; ⏲8.30am-7pm Mon-Fri, 9am-2pm Sat) Has the longest hours.

### TOURIST INFORMATION

**Airport Tourist Office** (☎5-230 6841; www.vilnius-tourism.lt; Rodūnios kelias 2-1; ⏲10am-1.30pm & 2.30-8pm) Not as extensive as the offices in town, but a handy first port of call when arriving in Vilnius.

**Old Town Tourist Office** (Map p296; ☎5-262 9660; www.vilnius-tourism.lt; cnr Pilies & Radvilaitės gatvė; ⏲9am-noon & 1-6pm) The head office of Vilnius' tourist information service has free maps, transport advice and can help book accommodation. The Vilnius City Card (per 24/72 hours €15/30) is on sale here, as well as online.

**Town Hall Tourist Office** (Map p296; ☎5-262 6470; www.vilnius-tourism.lt; Didžioji gatvė 31; ⏲9am-1pm & 2-6pm) Good for maps, brochures, bike rentals, accommodation booking, advice and more.

## Getting There & Away

### AIR

**Vilnius International Airport** (Tarptautinis Vilniaus Oro Uostas; ☎6-124 4442; www.vno.lt; Rodūnios kelias 10a; 📶; 🚌1, 2) lies 5km south of the centre. There are no domestic flights within Lithuania. Noteworthy airlines operating out of Vilnius include AirBaltic, including five daily flights to Rīga and one or two daily to Tallinn; Lufthansa, with direct flights to international hub airport Frankfurt; and budget airline Ryanair, linking Vilnius with destinations including Barcelona, Berlin, Dublin, London and Oslo.

### BUS

**Vilnius Bus Station** (Vilniaus Autobusų Stotis; Map p292; ☎1661; www.autobusustotis.lt; Sodų gatvė 22; ⊙5am-10.45pm) is just south of Old Town, across from the train station. Inside its ticket hall, domestic tickets are sold from 6am to 7pm, and information is available. Timetables are displayed on a board here and on the handy website. The station also has a *bagažinė* (left-luggage service) charging €2 per item per day (5.25am to 9pm Monday to Friday, 7am to 8.45pm Saturday and Sunday).

Several bus lines run from here to international destinations. Buses to destinations within Lithuania, and to Rīga (Latvia) and Tallinn (Estonia), include the following:

| DESTINATION | COST (€) | DURATION (HR) | FREQUENCY (PER DAY) |
|---|---|---|---|
| Druskininkai | 12-13.50 | 2-2½ | 14 |
| Ignalina | 6.50 | 2 | 14 |
| Kaliningrad | 21 | 8 | daily |
| Kaunas | 6.60-10 | 1½-1¾ | every 15min 5.45am-11pm |
| Kernavė | 2.50 | 1-1¼ | 6 |
| Klaipėda | 18-22 | 4-5¼ | 15 |
| Minsk | 13-14 | 3¾-4½ | 14 |
| Molėtai | 5 | 1-1½ | 16 |
| Palanga | 20-23 | 4¼-6 | 8; more via Klaipėda |
| Rīga (Latvia) | 17-23.60 | 4¼-5¼ | 7 |
| Šiauliai | 13-14 | 3-4¾ | 10; more via Kaunas |
| Tallinn (Estonia) | 27-35 | 9¼ | 2 |
| Visaginas | 8.50 | 2¾ | 14 |

International bus companies include:

**Ecolines** (Map p292; ☎5-213 3300; www.ecolines.net; Geležinkelio gatvė 15; ⊙8.30am-9.30pm) Serves large cities across Europe.

**Eurolines** (Map p292; ☎5-233 5277; www.eurolines.lt; Sodų gatvė 22; ⊙6.30am-9.30pm) A reliable long-distance carrier with services to Rīga, Tallinn, Warsaw (Poland) and Lviv (Ukraine).

**Lux Express** (Map p292; ☎5-233 6666; www.luxexpress.eu; Sodų 20b-1; ⊙8am-7pm Mon-Fri, from 9am Sat & Sun) Luxurious coaches connecting Vilnius with Rīga, Tallinn, St Petersburg, Warsaw and Helsinki.

### CAR & MOTORCYCLE

Twenty-four-hour petrol stations are plentiful in Vilnius. If you hire a car and intend to cross a border, check whether you're insured to do so. Most car rentals have branches in town as well as at the airport.

**Autobanga** (☎5-212 7777; www.autobanga.lt; Arklių gatvė 24; per day from €25)

**Avis** (☎5-232 9316; www.avis.com; Rodūnios kelias 2, Vilnius International Airport; ⊙6am-1.15am)

**Europcar** (☎5-250 3425; www.europcar.com; Rodūnios kelias 2, Vilnius International Airport; ⊙9am-midnight)

**Sixt** (☎5-239 5636; www.sixt.lt; Rodūnios kelias 2, Vilnius International Airport; ⊙8am-midnight Mon-Fri, 10am-5pm Sat & Sun)

### TRAIN

Elegantly styled after Vilnius Cathedral, the **train station** (Geležinkelio Stotis; ☎5-269 3722; www.litrail.lt; Geležinkelio gatvė 16) is equipped with ATMs, supermarket, information desks and storage lockers (from €2 to €4, depending on size).

There is no direct or convenient rail link between Vilnius and Rīga or Tallinn. Direct daily services within Lithuania to/from Vilnius include:

| DESTINATION | COST (€) | DURATION (HR) | FREQUENCY (DAILY) |
|---|---|---|---|
| Ignalina | 4.40 | 1½-1¾ | 7-8 |
| Kaunas | 3.60-5 | 1-1½ | 9 |
| Klaipėda | 14.50-17.40 | 3¾-4¼ | 5 |
| Minsk (Belarus) | 18 | 3 | 2 |
| Šiauliai | 9.70-11.60 | 2¼-2½ | 5-6 |
| Trakai | 1.60 | 30min | 15 |

## ℹ Getting Around

### TO/FROM THE AIRPORT

The airport is reachable by bus, train and taxi/Bolt.

**Bus** Buses 1 and 2 run between the airport and train station, as does bus 3G which continues through central Vilnius, crosses the Žaliasis bridge and terminates in the northern district of Fabijoniškės. Buy a ticket (€1 from the driver); have small change handy.

**Train** Trains run to/from the central station roughly once an hour between 6am and 10pm. Tickets cost €0.70 and the trip takes less than 10 minutes; buy on board or at the train station.

**Taxi & Bolt** Taxi rates vary depending on whether you hail one from out the front of the arrivals hall (about €15), or call a reputable firm in advance (around €10). Download the Bolt (www.bolt.eu) app for cheaper rides.

### BICYCLE

Vilnius is becoming increasingly bike-friendly, although bike lanes are rarer outside Old Town and along the banks of the Neris. Orange Cyclocity stations dot the city and the tourist office has free cycling maps.

**Cyclocity** (☎8-800 22008; www.cyclocity.lt; ⏰Apr-Oct) Bikes can be easily hired and returned at the many Cyclocity stations across Vilnius. Either credit cards or Cyclocity Cards (available by advance subscription) can be used to hire a bike. A three-day ticket costs €2.90 and the first half-hour is free, then charges are between €0.39 to €3.39 per 30 minutes.

**Velo-City** (☎8-674 12123; www.velovilnius.lt; Palangos gatvė 1; ⏰10am-8pm Apr-Sep, by appointment Oct-Mar) This well-established bike-hire operation on the edge of Old Town has decent, well-maintained bikes; rental costs €5 for the first hour, then €1 per hour afterwards.

You'll find electric scooters all over town. Download the Bolt (www.bolt.eu) and CityBee (www.citybee.lt) apps and you'll be zipping around in no time.

### CAR & MOTORCYCLE

There is little need to drive around Vilnius, given the proliferation of other modes of transport, the tangle of one-way streets in Old Town and the heavy congestion.

Street parking around the centre can be hard to find and is expensive: some car park rates are €1.20 per hour, others run to €2 per hour. Tickets need to be bought from a machine and displayed on the dashboard.

### PUBLIC TRANSPORT

The city is efficiently served by buses and trolleybuses from 5am to midnight; Sunday services are less frequent. Single-trip tickets cost €1 when bought from the driver. If you get a *Vilniečio kortelė* (electronic ticket) for €1.50, single journeys cost €0.65 for up to 30 minutes or €0.90 for up to 90 minutes; or you can buy 24-/72-/120-hour passes for €5/8/12 (www.vilniusticket.lt). Public transport is free if you have a Vilnius City Card (sold in tourist offices). Fare evaders risk a fine.

Faster minibuses shadow most routes. They pick up/drop off passengers anywhere en route (not just at official bus stops) and can be flagged down on the street. Tickets cost €1 from the driver.

Much of Old Town is closed to traffic, which is delightfully walkable.

Read more at www.vilniustransport.lt and find routes at www.stops.lt. There are transport maps available at tourist offices.

### TAXI

Bolt (www.bolt.eu) is the Baltics' version of Uber. Download the app for inexpensive rides.

Taxi rates in Vilnius vary; they are generally cheaper if ordered in advance by phone than if hailed directly off the street or picked up at a taxi stand. Ask the hotel reception desk or restaurant to call one for you. Reliable companies include:

**Ekipažas** (☎1446; www.ekipazastaksi.lt)
**Martono Taksi** (☎240 0004)
**Mersera** (☎278 8888)

# AROUND VILNIUS

The centre of Europe, a fairy-tale castle and ancient castle mounds lie within easy reach of the capital. There is also the trip to Paneriai, the site of the biggest Holocaust massacres on Lithuanian territory.

## Trakai

☎528 / POP 4480

A red-brick Gothic castle, rising like an apparition from the waters of Lake Galvė, is the crowning attraction of Trakai. Spread along a 2km-long peninsula only 28km from Vilnius, this attractive little town is an enormously popular day trip.

With practically the entire town gazetted as a **national park** (www.seniejitrakai.lt), it's fitting that Trakai's very name derives from the Lithuanian word for a forest glade. Its castle roosts on one of 21 islands in Lake Galvė, which opens out from the northern end of the peninsula. The 82-sq-km protected area also encompasses the ruins of an earlier fortification among its reed-fringed lakes.

Grand Duke Gediminas is thought to have made Trakai his capital in the 1320s and Kęstutis based his 14th-century court here. Beyond the castle, there's outstanding natural beauty and Karaite culture, architecture and cuisine, belonging to a Judaic minority group who have lived in Trakai since medieval times.

### Sights

**★Trakai Castle** CASTLE
(Trakų Pilis; ☎528-53 946; www.trakaimuziejus.lt; adult/concession €8/4; ⏰10am-7pm; 👪) Stepping across the wooden walkway to Trakai's

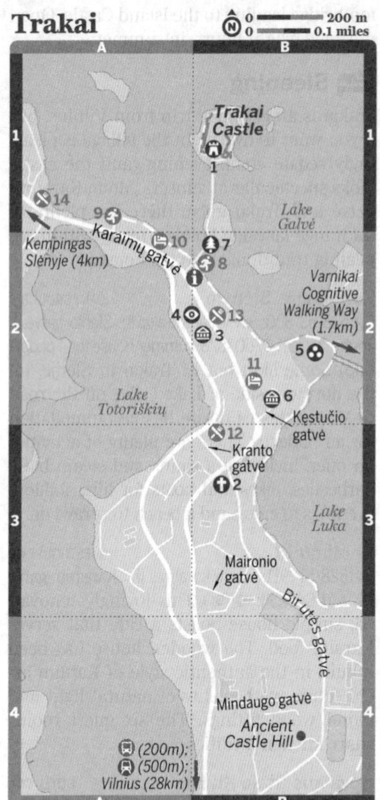


Gothic castle is like tripping into a fairy tale. The castle is estimated to date from around 1400, when Grand Duke Vytautas needed stronger defences than the peninsula castle afforded. Arranged between its coral-coloured brick towers, the excellent **Trakai History Museum** conveys the flavour of past eras: chainmail, medieval weapons, 19th-century embroidery and glassware, plus talking knights, projected onto the stone walls.

In summer the courtyard is a magical stage for concerts and plays. Archery and shooting ranges offer the chance to learn how you'd have fared as a castle defender.

The castle's prominence as a holy site is reflected in its collection of religious art.

**Karaite Ethnographic Museum** MUSEUM
(Karaimų Etnografinė Paroda; ☎528-55 286; www.trakaimuziejus.lt; Karaimų gatvė 22; adult/child €2/1; ⏲10am-6pm Wed-Sun) Displaying traditional dress, arresting photographs and items from daily life, this small ethnographic museum traces the ancestry of the Karaites, a Judaic

## Trakai

**Top Sights**
1 Trakai Castle ........ B1

**Sights**
2 Church of the Visitation of the Blessed Virgin Mary ........ B3
3 Karaite Ethnographic Museum ........ B2
4 Kenessa ........ A2
5 Peninsula Castle ........ B2
6 Sacred Art Exhibition ........ B2
7 Trakai Historical National Park ........ B2

**Activities, Courses & Tours**
8 Boating ........ B2
9 Irkluojam SUP Rental ........ A1

**Sleeping**
10 Apvalaus Stalo Klubas ........ A2
11 Karaimų 13 ........ B2

**Eating**
Bona Lounge ........ (see 10)
12 Kiubėtė ........ B3
13 Kybynlar ........ B2
14 Senoji Kibininė ........ A1

sect and Turkic minority originating in Baghdad, which adheres to the Law of Moses. Around the year 1400, Lithuanian Grand Duke Vytautas brought 383 Karaite families from the Crimea to Trakai, installing them as castle guards. They later took on occupations including horse breeding, handicrafts and agriculture. Only about 60 Karaite people still live in Trakai and their numbers – fewer than 280 throughout Lithuania – are dwindling rapidly.

**Church of the Visitation of the Blessed Virgin Mary** BASILICA
(www.trakubaznycia.lt; Birutės gatvė 5; 9am-6.30pm) Founded around the same time as Trakai Castle, and also by Grand Duke Vytautas, this 15th-century parish church has a richly decorated baroque altar and a large collection of ecclesiastical art. Its centrepiece is the Trakai Mother of God, a revered image thought to have been donated by Vytautas himself.

**Kenessa** RELIGIOUS SITE
(Karaimų gatvė 30; admission by donation) This well-maintained wooden prayer house, with its interior dome, is a rare surviving example of Karaite architecture. Arrange a visit at the Karaite Ethnographic Museum.

**Peninsula Castle** RUINS
(www.piliakalniai.lt) The peaceful ruins of the Peninsula Castle, built from 1362 to 1382 by the medieval Duke Kęstutis and destroyed

in the 17th century, are around 700m south of the Island Castle. The peninsula itself is dotted with old wooden cottages, many built by the Karaites, and offers great views of the main castle, town and lakes.

**Sacred Art Exhibition** MUSEUM
(Sacralineo Meno Muziejus; ☎528-53 945; www.trakaimuziejus.lt; Kęstučio gatvė 4; adult/student €3/1.50; ⊙10am-5pm Wed-Sun) This small exhibition space, housed in a former Dominican chapel, displays a range of religious and sacral objects, including altarpieces, crosses, monstrances and chalices.

## Activities

The tourist office has information about a plethora of activities, including boating, horse riding, hot-air ballooning (arranged in Vilnius) and sailing. It also hires out bikes (per hour/day €3/14) and has maps for a 14km cycling route around the main sights. Winter offers horse-drawn sled rides, skiing and ice-fishing.

**Irkluojam SUP Rental** WATER SPORTS
(☎8-656 22822; www.irkluojam.lt; 2hr €12) On the lakeshore, some 300m north of the bridge to the castle, these guys rent stand-up paddleboards and offer instruction.

**Varnikai Cognitive Walking Way** WALKING
For a lovely stroll out of Trakai, head for this botanical-zoological preserve with its interpretive trail, 4km east of town. To get here, follow the signs marked 'Varnikų Gamtos Takas' across two lake bridges.

**Boating** BOATING
(☎8-6095 1305) Pick up a pedalo (per hour €6) or rowing boat (per hour €5) near the footbridge leading to the Island Castle. Open during daylight hours, in summer.

## Sleeping

Trakai is an easy day trip from Vilnius, but if you want to overnight the village is pleasingly sedate come evening (and the castle looks spectacular at sunset). Along Karaimų gatvė and Trakų gatvė there are plenty of midrange lakeside hotels – many within appealing traditional wooden houses.

**Kempingas Slėnyje** CAMPGROUND €
(☎528-53 380; www.camptrakai.lt; Slėnio gatvė 1; adult/car/tent €7.50/5/3, summer house for 4 people €40) Some 5km out of Trakai in Slėnje, on the northern side of Lake Galvė off the road to Vievis, this campsite has accommodation for all budgets. There are plenty of activities on offer, including a sauna and steam bath, barbecues, bikes and boats for hire, folklore evenings to enjoy and a beach to sprawl on.

**Karaimų 13** GUESTHOUSE €€
(☎528-51 911; www.karaimai.lt; Karaimų gatvė 13; s/d €43/58; @ 🛜) This lovingly renovated, simple house boasts a cafe that serves Karaite food. The wooden house has been rebuilt in the authentic style of Karaim architecture, with plenty of natural light and blond wood fittings. The six guest rooms share kitchen facilities.

**Apvalaus Stalo Klubas** HOTEL €€€
(☎528-55 595; www.asklubas.lt; Karaimų gatvė 53a; r €78-198; @ 🛜 🏊) Perfectly situated lakeside, this hotel has unrivalled views of the castle, and it's the ideal place to romance your sweetie. Choose a room in either the more elegant French-provincial Ežeras villa, with comfy furnishings and bold colours on the walls, or the

OFF THE BEATEN TRACK

### PANERIAI HOLOCAUST MEMORIAL

Some 11km southwest of Vilnius, the pine forest site of Paneriai is notorious as the site of approximately 100,000 murders – by subunits of the Nazi secret police and their Lithuanian assistants. It's a sombre, thought-provoking place.

Around 70% of those killed in Paneriai were Jewish. Other victims were Lithuanian and Polish soldiers and partisan fighters, Roma, prisoners of war and priests.

A small **museum** (☎tours 8-699 90384; www.jmuseum.lt; Agrastų gatvė 15; ⊙9am-5pm Tue-Sun May-Sep, by appointment Oct-Apr) FREE details the practicalities of the massacres, with eyewitness reports detailing how they unfolded. The killings began with the execution of 348 people on 11 July 1941; that month alone, around 5000 people were killed. A walking path connects Jewish, Soviet and Polish monuments and locations associated with the killings, such as prison bunkers and pits where victims were shot.

Daily trains travel between Vilnius and Paneriai station (€0.70, 10 minutes, one to three hourly). To reach the museum, make a right down Agrastų gatvė and walk for 1km.

DON'T MISS

### LITHUANIA'S TATAR HERITAGE

Towards the end of the 14th century, Grand Duke Vytautas invited Crimean Tatar Muslims (Lipka Tatars) to settle in pagan Lithuania, providing additional defence against the threat of the Christian Teutonic Knights.

The Lipka Tatars settled around Vilnius, Trakai and Kaunas, and while today they number just over 3000, their heritage is still visible in the form of surviving mosques and monuments and their contribution to the country's cuisine (*chebureki*).

You can visit one of the sites of original Tatar settlements on the southeastern outskirts of Vilnius. The historic village of Nemėžis is home to an attractive wooden **mosque** (Nemėžis Masjid; Totorių gatvė 4, Nemėžis; ⌚hours vary) dating back to the early 20th century that survived Soviet occupation as a munitions store. Look for one of the most beautiful copies of the Quran near the *mihrab* (prayer niche), and for the ancient Tatar cemetery out back.

more workaday, modern (and slightly cheaper) digs at the Karaimai villa. There's also an excellent restaurant, Bona Lounge.

## Eating

Trakai is renowned for its Karaite cuisine, imported by the Turkic Judaic sect in the 15th century. *Kibinai* (pasties filled with meat or mushrooms) are the speciality here.

**Senoji Kibininė** KARAITE €
(☎528-55 865; www.kibinas.lt; Karaimų gatvė 65; pasties from €1.60, mains €5-9; ⌚10am-10pm) Draped with antiques, wall paintings and wood-carved finery, the interior of this traditional house is an understandably popular place for the full Karaite culinary experience. It's worth braving the crowds for the superlative *kibinai* (Karaite pasties) with multiple fillings, plus a supporting cast of soups, salads and dumplings.

★**Bona Lounge** INTERNATIONAL €€
(☎8-699 13769; www.bona.lt; Karaimų gatvė 53a; mains €10-22; ⌚noon-11pm Jun-Sep, to 10pm Thu-Sun Oct-May; ☎) With mostly unobstructed views of the castle, Bona has the best sunset seats in town. The ubiquitous *kibinai* (Karaite pasties) aside, the short and sweet menu specialises in more adventurous fare than its Trakai brethren – from grilled catfish with asparagus and portobello mushrooms with blue cheese to cold cucumber soup with wasabi crisp. Decent original cocktails, too.

**Kybynlar** KARAITE €€
(☎8-698 06320; www.kybynlar.lt; Karaimų gatvė 29; pasties from €2.20, mains €7-14; ⌚noon-9pm Mon, 11am-9pm Tue-Thu & Sun, 11am-10pm Fri & Sat) Best known for the eponymous *kibinai* (pasties stuffed with lamb, beef and other goodies), this is Trakai's best spot for traditional Karaite cuisine. There's also lamb and date stew, stuffed grape leaves and baked chicken-and-cheese stacks, fragrant with cinnamon. It gets busy but a shot of *krupnik* (clove-scented, honeyed vodka) alleviates the wait. Alternatively, grab *kibinai* from the takeaway counter.

**Kiubėtė** LITHUANIAN €€
(☎528-59 160; www.kiubete.lt; Trakų gatvė 2; mains €7-9; ⌚10.30am-11pm) Offering a mix of Lithuanian and Karaite fare, Kiubėtė has a lovely location opposite Lake Totoriškių, on the quieter side of the Trakai peninsula.

## Information

**Police** (☎528-32 230; Vytauto gatvė 57) Located in the centre of Trakai.

**Tourist Office** (☎528-51 934; www.trakai-visit.lt; Karaimų gatvė 41; ⌚9am-6pm May-Sep, 8am-5pm Mon-Fri, 10am-5pm Sat & Sun Oct-Apr) Stocked with brochures, staffed by English speakers who can organise everything from boat trips to accommodation, and with an adjoining handicrafts shop.

## Getting There & Away

Trains travel between Trakai's **train station** (Trakų geležinkelio stotis; ☎7005 5111; www.litrail.lt; Vilniaus gatvė 5) and Vilnius (€1.80, 35 minutes, nine to 10 daily). Regular buses also link Vilnius to the Trakai bus station (€2, 30 minutes, at least two hourly).

# Kernavė

☎382

The quiet town of Kernavė (ker-nar-veh) is home to one of Lithuania's most important historical sites, the Kernavė Cultural Reserve.

A. ALEKSANDRAVICIUS/SHUTTERSTOCK ©

ANGEL VILLALBA/GETTY IMAGES ©

CRAIG HASTINGS/SHUTTERSTOCK ©

3

YEVGEN BELICH/SHUTTERSTOCK ©

**1. Cepelinai (p400)**
Sample a Lithuanian speciality: *cepelinai* are parcels of thick potato dough stuffed with cheese and meat.

**2. Vilnius (p294)**
Stroll the picture-perfect Old Town streets of Lithuania's capital.

**3. Witches' Hill (p375), Juodkrantė**
Examine the bewitching wooden sculptures on this forest-clad hill.

**4. Trakai Castle (p320)**
Step back in time at this spectacular island castle.

## Sights

**Kernavė Cultural Reserve** ARCHAEOLOGICAL SITE
(Kernavės Kultūrinio Rezervato; ☎382-47 385; www.kernave.org; Kerniaus gatvė; ⏲info office 10am-6pm Wed-Sun) FREE Deemed an 'exceptional testimony to 10 millennia of human settlements in this region' by Unesco, which made it a World Heritage site in 2004, Kernavė is a must-see. Thought to have been the spot where Mindaugas (responsible for uniting Lithuania for the first time) celebrated his coronation in 1253, this cultural reserve comprises four old castle mounds and the remains of a medieval town.

The sprawling reserve sits on the southern edge of town, facing the Neris River, and gives a good sense of why the site was chosen. While the museum and guided tours are highly worthwhile, there's nothing to stop you simply wandering up and down the hill-forts at your leisure.

The official opening hours are for the info office; you can wander into the reserve anytime.

**Archaeological & Historical Museum** MUSEUM
(Archeologijos ir Istorijos Muziejus; ☎382-47 385; www.kernave.org; Kerniaus gatvė 4a; adult/child €2/1, tours €20; ⏲10am-6pm Tue-Sun Apr, May, Sep & Oct, Wed-Sun Jun-Aug, to 4pm Nov-Mar) This absorbing museum traces the history of the area from 9000 BC to the 13th and 14th centuries AD. There is a wealth of artefacts on display – pottery, Iron Age tools, intricate horn seals – but the highlights are the gilded head decorations, silver jewellery from Russia and cowrie shells from the Indian Ocean that indicate just how far trade had spread during Kernavė's heyday.

## Festivals & Events

**Rasos Feast** CULTURAL
(⏲23 Jun) This midsummer festival brings medieval fun and frolics to Kernavė – axe throwing, catapulting, mead making and floating flower wreaths down the river. Pyres burn all night.

**International Festival of Experimental Archaeology** CULTURAL
(www.kernave.org; ⏲Jul) This three-day festival, held annually in early July, involves the presentation of ye olde crafts: Stone Age fire-starting techniques, bronze casting, yarn dyeing, Viking age smithing and much more.

## Sleeping

Kėrnave is an easy day trip from Vilnius, but it's worth lingering overnight, particularly if attending a summer festival. There's a hotel and a couple of guesthouses.

★**Gallery Guest Rooms** GUESTHOUSE €
(☎8-616 36291; Vilniaus gatvė 8; s/d/tr €30/33/37; 📶) Bright quilts on beds, plenty of art scattered about the house, and a flower-filled garden that doubles as a steampunk sculpture gallery greet guests at this centrally located guesthouse. The owner will feed you a home-cooked breakfast and maybe even dumplings.

## Eating

**Kernavės Slėnis** INTERNATIONAL €
(☎8-674 38052; www.facebook.com/kernaves.slenis; Vilniaus gatvė 14b; mains €7-12; ⏲noon-9pm Sat & Sun) Overlooking a pond, this weekend-only restaurant offers crowdpleasers such as big plates of ribs and lasagne.

## Getting There & Away

To get to Kernavė, follow the road through Dūkštos from Maisiagala on the main road north to Ukmergė, or take a minibus from Vilnius (€2.50, one hour, six daily).

# Europos Parkas Sculpture Park

Some 21km north of Vilnius, off the Utena road, is **Europos Parkas** (☎5-237 7077; www.europosparkas.lt; Europos Parkas gatvė; adult/child €11/6; ⏲10am-sunset). Leading contemporary sculptors, including Sol LeWitt and Dennis Oppenheim, show over 100 works in wooded parkland (bring mosquito repellent). These include the largest sculpture in the world made entirely from TV sets (3000 of them); it's also a maze, leading to a fallen statue of Lenin.

The sculpture park was the brainchild of Lithuanian sculptor Gintaras Karosas, inspired by the 'Centre of Europe' tag. Every year international workshops are held here, attracting artists from all over the world.

To get here, take bus 66 (marked Skirgiskes/Europos Parkas) from the Zalgirio stop on Kalvarijų gatvė (€1, 35 minutes, nine to 12 daily).

# EASTERN & SOUTHERN LITHUANIA

Some of Lithuania's most spectacular scenery is found in the deep forests of the country's eastern and southern corners, with a lake district that extends into Belarus and Latvia.

Aukštaitija National Park is Lithuania's oldest, framed by the 900-sq-km Labanoras-Pabradė Forest. Dzūkija, in the far south, is the biggest national park, surrounded by the 1500-sq-km Druskininkai-Varėna Forest. Both parks are blessed with an abundant berry crop in early summer, while mushrooms sprout by the bucketful from early

## Eastern Lithuania

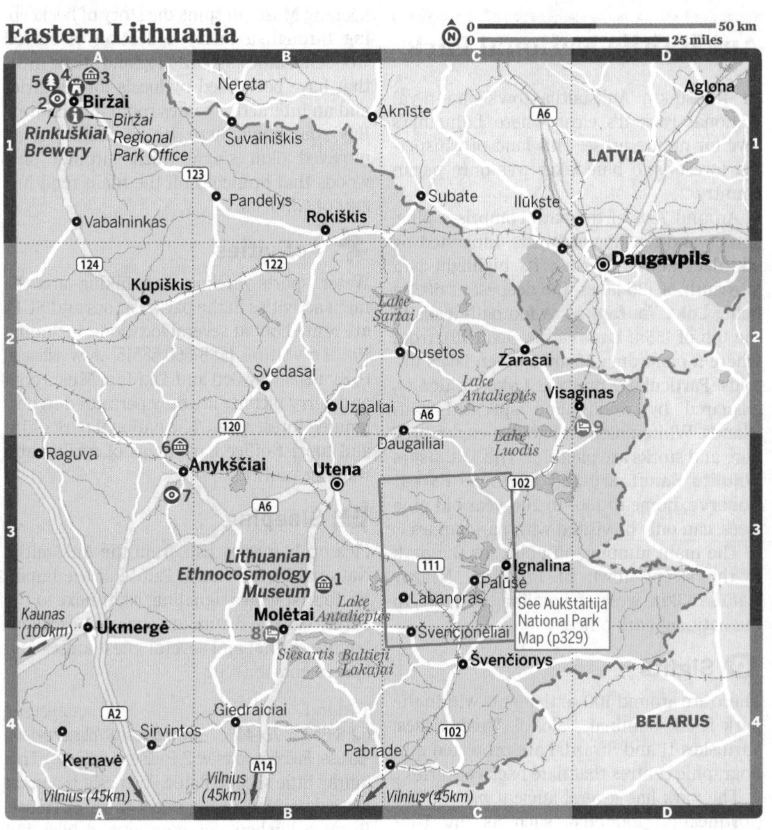


## Eastern Lithuania

**Top Sights**

1 Lithuanian Ethnocosmology Museum ........ B3
2 Rinkuškiai Brewery ........ A1

**Sights**

3 Astravas Manor ........ A1
4 Biržai Castle ........ A1
5 Biržai Regional Park ........ A1
6 Horse Museum ........ A3
Molėtai Astronomical Observatory ........ (see 1)
7 Puntukas Stone ........ A3

**Sleeping**

8 Gerugnė ........ B4
9 Idile B&B ........ D2
Spa-Hotel Gabriella ........ (see 9)

**Eating**

Ikura ........ (see 9)
Senoji Užeiga ........ (see 8)

spring until late autumn, and both parks are heaven for canoeists, cyclists and hikers.

Close to the Dzūkija National Park is the spa resort of Druskininkai, where Lithuanians indulge in the likes of warm honey massages. The Grūtas sculpture park next door, with its busts of Lenin, Stalin and the gang, is a breath of Soviet nostalgia.

# Aukštaitija National Park

☎386

In 406-sq-km Aukštaitija (owk-shtai-ti-ya) National Park it's clear where Lithuania's love for nature arose. This land of whispering forests and blue lakes was once pagan country.

Around 70% of the park comprises pine, spruce and deciduous forests, inhabited by elk, deer and wild boar. Its highlight is a labyrinth of 126 lakes, the deepest at 60.5m being **Lake Tauragnas**. A footpath leads to the top of 155m **Ladakalnis** (Ice Hill), from where a panorama of some seven lakes unfolds. Particularly pretty is **Lake Baluošas**, ensnared by woods and speckled with islands. White-tailed and golden eagles prey here and storks are plentiful. The **Trainiškis Wildlife Sanctuary** and **Ažvinčiai Forest Reserve**, home to 150- to 200-year-old pine trees, can only be visited with park guides.

The main jumping-off point for the park is the sleepy town of **Ignalina**. Nearby **Palūšė**, 3km west of Ignalina, is home to the national park office.

## Sights

There are around 100 settlements within the park itself: Šuminai, Salos ll, Vaišnoriškės, Varniškės II and Strazdai are protected ethnographic centres that date back centuries.

The park has several ancient *piliakalnis* (fortification mounds), such as the **Taurapilio mound** on the southern shore of Lake Tauragnas, and some quaint wooden architecture, including a fine church and bell tower at Palūsė. Around Lake Lūšiai a wooden sculpture trail depicts Lithuanian folklore.

**Ginučiai Watermill** HISTORIC BUILDING
(☎386-47 478; Ginučiai; adult/student €2/1; ⏲10am-6pm Tue-Sat May-Sep) This 19th-century mill in Ginučiai retains its original mechanism, and you can poke around its interior and check out the ye olde farming equipment in the attic. If there are enough visitors, the curator may do a demo of how grain used to be ground. It's possible to overnight here as well.

**Museum of Ancient Beekeeping** MUSEUM
(Senorinės Bitininkystės Muziejus; ☎8-686 12105; www.biciumuziejus.lt; Stripeikių kaimas, Stripeikiai; adult/concession €2/1; ⏲10am-6pm Wed-Sun May–mid-Oct; 👪) Stripeikiai's Ancient Beekeeping Museum spins the story of beekeeping through a merry collection of carved wooden statues, historic log and straw hives that have been used by locals for centuries and an interactive games room for children. Buy your honey here. It's reachable via an unpaved 5km single track through pine woods that branches off the main road just east of Ginučiai.

## Activities

Water sports, cycling and hiking are the main activities in the park. Canoes and SUPs are rented out at several locations, including **Palūšė valtinė** (☎8-650 58515; www.valtine.lt; ⏲8am-8pm May-Oct) and Tiki Inn. Mushroom and berry picking are only permitted in designated forest areas. The national park office and tourist office have maps of cycling and walking trails.

## Sleeping

Pick up homestay lists from the Aukštaitija National Park Office in Palūšė or the Ignalina Tourist Office. Ignalina, right next to the park's eastern boundary, has an excellent boutique hotel and several guesthouses and apartments for rent.

**Tiki Inn** GUESTHOUSE €
(☎8-652 72444; www.paluse.lt/place/tiki-inn-paluse; Pašakarvio gatvė 2, Palūšė; d €45; 📶) This quirky little slice of Baltic Polynesia is a great lakeside option in the sweet town of Palūšė. It has a kitchen, common area, a beautiful terrace for watching the sunset, and is as welcoming as you could possibly hope for. Also rents kayaks and paddle-boards. Prices can rise, depending on the season and demand.

**Žuvėdra** HOTEL €
(☎8-686 09069; www.zuvedra.com; Mokyklos gatvė 11, Ignalina; s/d/q €29/50/72; 🅿📶) This small hotel on the shores of Lake Paplovinis is an excellent in-town choice, within easy walking distance of the tourist office in Ignalina. The helpful staff can arrange activities including bike and boat rental, and the restaurant serves decent Lithuanian food (mains €6 to €8).

## Aukštaitija National Park

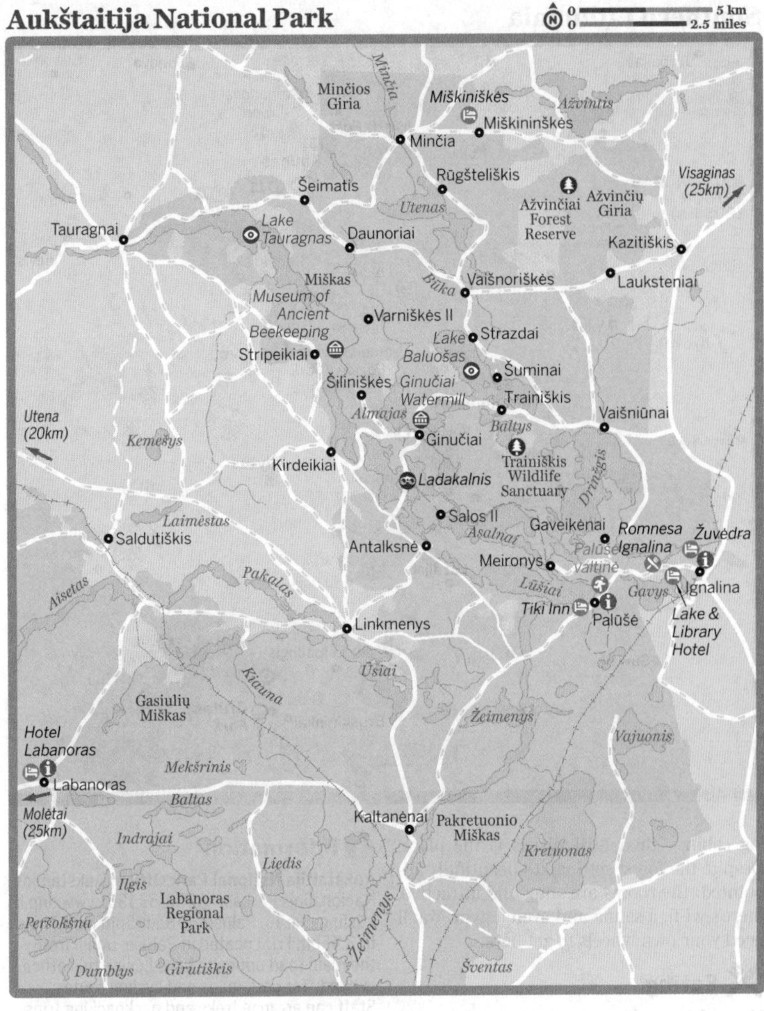


**Ginučiai Watermill** GUESTHOUSE €
(☎8-616 29366; www.anp.lt; Ginučių 22; d €35) This 19th-century watermill offers stripped-back rooms with clean wood interiors and almost perfect serenity. Bring your own food to cook in the kitchen, and end the evening relaxing by the fire or in the sauna. It's open from April to October, weather-dependent, and you can book through the national park office (p330).

★ **Lake & Library Hotel** BOUTIQUE HOTEL €€
(☎8-686 97248; www.facebook.com/lakeandlibraryhotel; Turistų gatvė 30b, Ignalina; d from €53; P 📶) Overlooking the white-sand beach of Gavys Lake, this delightful boutique hotel is the area's loveliest. The hosts go out of their way to make guests feel welcome, the breakfast spread is terrific and all the rooms are individually styled, with a quirky mix of chandeliers, contemporary art and book-filled shelves. Owners can help arrange visits to the Ignalina nuclear power station.

**Miškiniškės** CABIN €€
(☎8-616 00692; www.miskiniskes.lt; d/apt €55/130; 📶) If you've ever harboured wilderness survival fantasies – canoeing and hiking all day among the spruce and pine, eating heartily then sleeping deeply in a

## Southern Lithuania

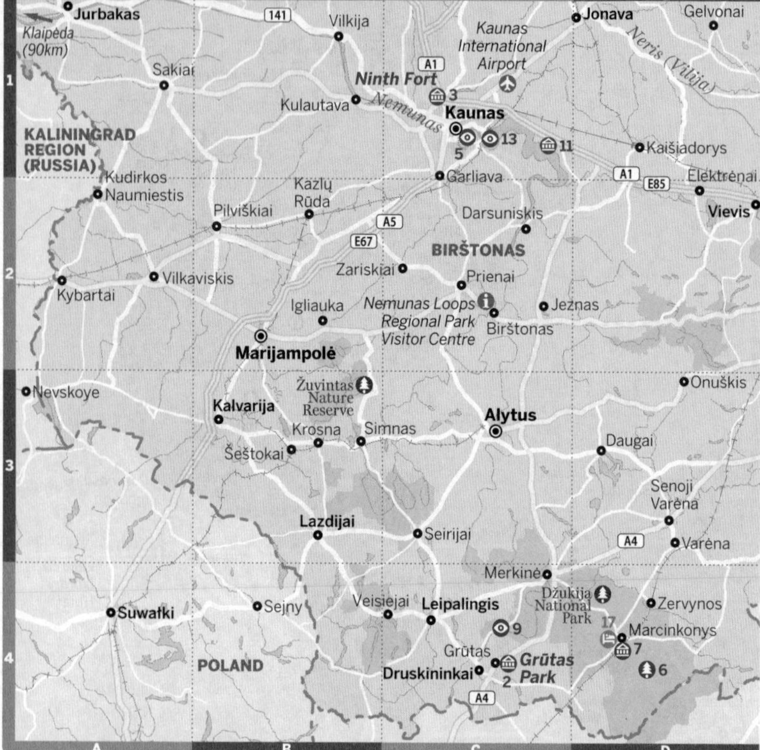


log cabin – then Miškiniškės is the place. Despite the forest setting, it's beautifully appointed: the rooms are snug and attractive, there's wi-fi, a sauna and even a gym. You'll need your own wheels to get here.

## Eating

Most of the park's accommodation is geared towards self-caterers, though home-cooked meals can be arranged at homestays. There is one excellent restaurant in Ignalina.

★ **Romnesa Ignalina** LITHUANIAN €
(☎8-600 26354; www.romnesa.lt; Strigailiškis; mains €4-8; ⏰11am-8pm Sun-Thu, to 10pm Fri & Sat; 📶🌶) On the western outskirts of Ignalina, Romnesa really delivers when it comes to creative Lithuanian cuisine. The Old Testament-thick menu features such culinary delights as baked pike-perch with spinach, boletus stew, and pork chops with chanterelle sauce. Spuds in various forms are well represented and the homemade *gira* (kvass) is terrific.

## Information

**Aukštaitija National Park Office** (Aukštaitijos Nacionalinis Parkas; ☎386-53 135; www.anp.lt; Lūšių gatvė 16, Palūšė; ⏰8am-5pm Mon-Thu, to 3.45pm Fri) Located in Palūšė, uphill from the main road opposite Lake Lūsiai, this office is handy for park maps and cycling routes. Staff can arrange treks and backpacking trips by boat, English-speaking guides (€15 per hour for groups of up to 20) and even skiing, fishing, horse riding and sledging.

**Ignalina Tourist Office** (☎386-52 597; www.ignalina.info; Ateites gatvė 23; ⏰9am-6pm Mon-Fri year-round, plus 9am-1pm & 2-6pm Sat, 10am-3pm Sun Jun-Aug) Located in Ignalina's main square, this centre sells maps and provides information on the park's activities and accommodation.

## Getting There & Away

Hop on a bus (€6.50, two hours, 14 daily) or train (€4.40, 1½ to 1¾ hours, seven to eight daily) from Vilnius to Ignalina. Several buses travel daily between Ignalina and Palūšė (€1, 10 minutes).

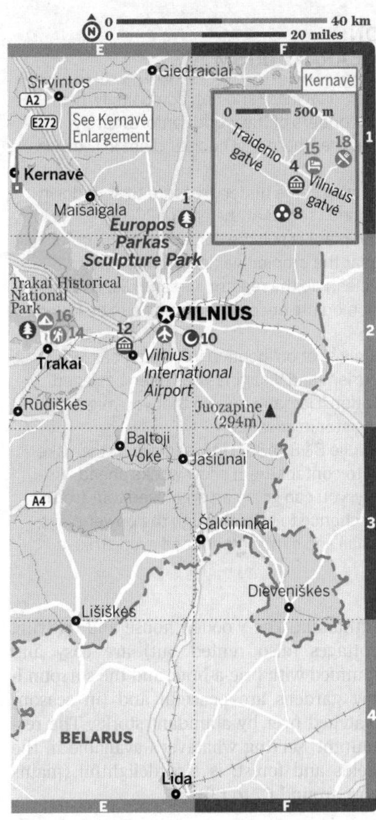


## Southern Lithuania



# Visaginas & Ignalina Nuclear Power Station

386 / POP 19,600

The purpose-built worker-housing town of Visaginas is as Soviet as you'll get outside the borders of Russia. Built in 1975 for employees at the former Ignalina Nuclear Power Station nearby, it's packed with identical-looking blocks of flats amid forest.

In its heyday around 5000 shift workers were shuttled between Visaginas and the former plant, about 3km east of the town centre. A Geiger counter recorded the day's radiation level and Russian was the lingua franca on the streets.

The shutting down of the Ignalina nuclear power station in 2009 plunged the town into uncertainty, though a boost in nuclear tourism may change the Visaginas' fortunes.

## Sleeping & Eating

**Idile B&B** B&B €

(8-652 04493; www.idile-visaginas.com; Energetikų gatvė 5; s €27, d €32-60; P) The only low-rise building in Visaginas, this friendly B&B comprises a melange of simple rooms, a short walk from the beach of Visaginas Lake. Bicycles are available for rent and helpful owners can assist with arranging a visit to the Ignalina nuclear power station if you contact them in advance. There's a buffet breakfast.

**Spa-Hotel Gabriella** HOTEL €

(386-70 171; www.gabriella.lt; Jaunystės gatvė 21; s/d €38/44; P) The Gabriella, as the name suggests, offers massage and spa options, but isn't as fancy as the name implies, with a distinctly Soviet vibe and unsmiling service. There's also a decent restaurant – one of a handful of options in town.

**Ikura** SUSHI €

(8-602 41241; www.ikura.lt; Taikos prospektas 72; sushi sets €5-7; noon-9pm) Come to the Visaginas branch of the reliable Lithuania-wide sushi chain for well-executed dragon (eel

### IGNALINA NUCLEAR POWER STATION: FROM DECOMMISSIONING TO NUCLEAR TOURISM

In its day the Ignalina Nuclear Power Station near Visaginas (and not, confusingly, near Ignalina the town) was one of the technological wonders of the world. Unfortunately, though, the design was similar to the one used at the Chernobyl nuclear plant in Ukraine, which suffered a catastrophic meltdown in 1986.

After Lithuania joined the EU in 2004, the country came under pressure to shut down the two reactors. The plug was pulled on the second reactor at the end of 2009.

Though power is no longer produced here, the plant is still the subject of some controversy. Foremost is the question of who will bear the prohibitive decommissioning costs, including the billions of euros needed to clean up the reactor site and dispose of redundant radioactive material. More information on the decommissioning can be found at www.iae.lt.

The 2019 *Chernobyl* miniseries on HBO (largely shot on location in Vilnius) has led to a massive rise in public interest in nuclear tourism and Visaginas has been besieged by visitors wishing to visit the nuclear power station. Demand is such that you might be waiting for months for a slot, and you have to register in advance.

It's possible to arrange visits with the help of Idile B&B (p331) in Visaginas or the Lake & Library Hotel (p329) in Ignalina, but you have to contact them a few weeks ahead. Visits from Visaginas cost around €60; alternatively, you can go on an organised tour from Vilnius with PlayVilnius (p306). Tours give you a chance to walk through the power plant, clad in protective gear, look around the turbine hall and control room and even strike a pose on top of the actual nuclear reactor.

and shrimp), sakura (salmon, shrimp, mango sauce), spicy tuna and other rolls.

### ℹ Getting There & Away

From **Visaginas Train Station** (Visagino geležinkelio stotis; Taikos prospektas), just north of town, there are services to Vilnius (€6, 2¼ hours, six daily). There are also buses to Vilnius (€8.50, 2½ hours, 13 daily) via Ignalina.

## Labanoras Regional Park

Southwest of Aukštaitija is 528 sq km of pretty parkland dotted with 285 lakes. At its heart sits the lovely Labanoras, the largest of the many traditional villages within the park. Canoeing is a grand pastime in the park, particularly on the Lakaja River in the southern section, while cycling is a wonderful way to get around the many trails that cut through pine forest. Bikes need to be brought in from outside; the national park office (p330) in Palūšė can help with bike hire, in season.

Accommodation in the park is limited to a handful of homestays and one delightful hotel-restaurant in Labanoras village.

★**Hotel Labanoras** BOUTIQUE HOTEL €
(☎8-655 70918; www.hotellabanoras.lt; camping €5, d/tr €50/70; 📶) This charming hotel-restaurant takes you to the heart of rural Lithuania. The wooden house and outlying cottages (also rented out) are cosy and jammed with bric-a-brac, and the surrounding gardens are peaceful and (in season) watched over by abundant storks. The restaurant, serving whatever's available in the fields and forest, is also delightful (mains cost around €7 to €9).

### ℹ Information

**Labanoras Regional Park Information Centre** (☎387-47 142; www.labanoroparkas.lt; Seniūnijos gatvė 19; ⏲8am-5pm Mon-Fri year-round, plus 9am-5pm Sat summer) A trove of information on the flora, fauna and geography of Labanoras, the centre has advice for walkers, bikers, kayakers and foragers. It can also help you find canoes and kayaks for hire (usually around €15 per day).

## Druskininkai

☎313 / POP 16,100

The reputation of Druskininkai's healing mineral waters dates back centuries and reached its zenith in the 1800s. During the days of the USSR, the old and ailing sought miracle cures at the famous health resort. Today it attracts well-heeled visitors seeking a quick detox from city life, particularly Lithuanians and tourists from Poland, Belarus and Russia.

Stark Soviet-era buildings remain, but Druskininkai's 19th-century elegance is being restored: timber houses have carved gables and fronts awash in yellow and pastel green. Parks, fountains and promenades form the town's leafy centre. Most refreshing of all, the town is hugged by forests of tall fir and birch and lies only a few kilometres from Dzūkija National Park.

## Sights

**★Grūtas Park** MUSEUM

(Grūto Parkas; ☎8-682 42320; www.grutoparkas.lt; Grūtas; adult/child €7.50/4; ⏰9am-10pm Jun-Aug; 👪) With Soviet-era statues of Lenin, Stalin and prominent Lithuanian members of the Communist Party that once dominated Lithuanian towns lining the forest trails, Grūtas Park pays black-humoured homage to a dark period of history. Watchtowers pipe marching songs and a train with cattle car is a sobering reminder of mass deportations. There are three exhibition buildings in the park, displaying socialist-realist art, newspapers and USSR maps.

It's 8km east of Druskininkai; take bus 2 via Viečiūnai (two to five daily).

Grūtas Park's surreal mix of setting and subject matter satirises the era neatly. The park was the idea of Viliumas Malinauskas, a former collective farm head who made a fortune canning mushrooms then won the loan of hated objects like statues from the Ministry of Culture.

This open-air **sculpture gallery**, featuring heroic statues of Soviet partisans and Communist League of Youth Members, makes for great photo ops, and there's a big playground for kids.

**Museum of Armed Resistance & Exile** MUSEUM

(www.druskininkukulturoscentras.lt; Vilniaus alėja 24; ⏰1-5pm Tue-Sun) FREE A simple, two-room museum on the upper floor of the Cultural Centre tells an incredible history: the forced deportation of Lithuanians to Siberia and the bravery of partisan fighters against Soviet rule. Items like fur-lined skis and ornaments carved during exile bring to life their stories of struggle.

**Girios Aidas** MUSEUM

(Echo of the Forest; ☎313-53 901; MK Čiurlionio gatvė 116; adult/child €2/1; ⏰10am-6pm Wed-Sun) Two kilometres east of town, Girios Aidas has been home to a museum and collection of pagan- and nature-themed wood carvings since 1972.

**MK Čiurlionis Memorial Museum** MUSEUM

(☎313-52 755; www.ciurlionis.lt; MK Čiurlionio gatvė 41; adult/child €2.50/1.25; ⏰11am-6pm Tue-Sat, to 4pm Sun) The life and works of Lithuania's renowned painter-musician MK Čiurlionis are paid homage at this attractive museum in a residential neighbourhood. His treasured possessions (including a piano) are exhibited across four small buildings. The artworks in the little gallery are copies, not originals.

**Joy of All Who Sorrow Church** CHURCH

(Laisvės Aikštė; ⏰hours vary) The tear-shaped domes of this 19th-century timber Russian Orthodox church, picked out in blue, white and gold, dominate Laisvės aikštė.

**Mineralinio Vandens Biuvetė** FOUNTAIN

(per cup €0.10; ⏰11am-2pm & 3-7pm) The magical powers of local mineral water can be tested at the Dzūkija Fountain, inside the Mineralinio Vandems Biuvetė, a round green building with mosaic floor and stained-glass windows on the footpath running along the Nemunas River. Of particular note is a 1960s image of Eglė, Queen of Serpents.

### STORKS

Eastern Lithuania, indeed the entire country, is prime stork-sighting territory. Lithuania has approximately 13,000 pairs, giving it the highest-density stork population in Europe.

Measuring 90cm in height, this beautiful long-legged, wide-winged creature is breathtaking in flight. Equally marvellous is the catwalk stance it adopts when strutting through meadows in search of frogs to feast on. It sleeps standing on one leg.

The arrival of the stork from Africa each year marks the start of spring. Lithuanians celebrate this traditional protector of the home with Stork Day (25 March), the day farmers traditionally stir their seeds, yet to be planted, to ensure a bigger and better crop.

Storks on their return home usually settle back into the same nest they have used for years. Some are splayed out across wooden cartwheels, fixed on tall poles by kindly farmers keen to have their farmstead blessed by the good fortune the stork brings.

# Druskininkai

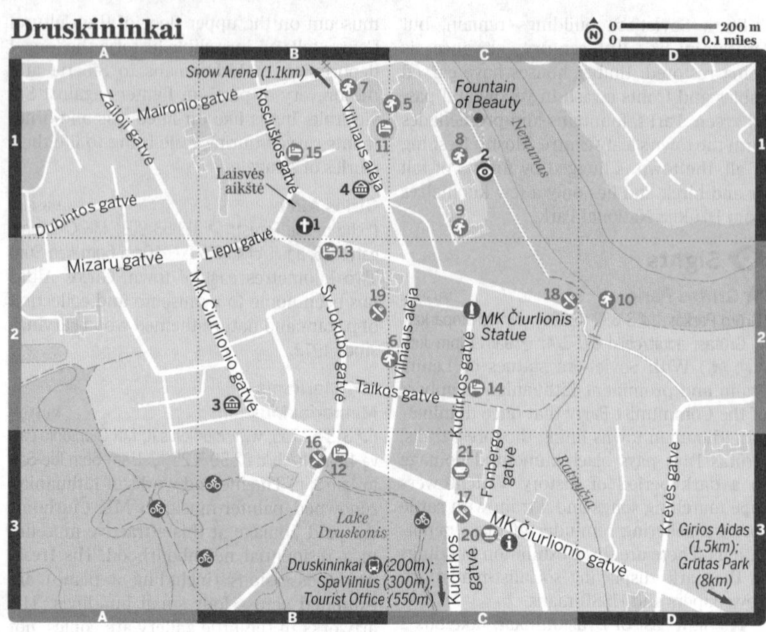




## Druskininkai

**Sights**
1 Joy of All Who Sorrow Church ........ B1
2 Mineralinio Vandens Biuvetė ........ C1
3 MK Čiurlionis Memorial Museum ........ B2
4 Museum of Armed Resistance & Exile ........ B1

**Activities, Courses & Tours**
5 Aqua Park ........ C1
6 Bike Rental ........ C2
7 Cable Car ........ B1
8 Druskininkai Health Resort ........ C1
9 Europa Royale Spa ........ C1
10 Steamboat Druskininkai ........ D2

**Sleeping**
11 Aqua Hotel ........ B1
12 Art Hotel ........ B3
13 Dalija ........ B2
14 Hotel Druskininkai ........ C2
15 Regina ........ B1

**Eating**
16 Etno Dvaras ........ B3
17 House ........ C3
18 Kolonada ........ C2
19 Toli Toli Druskininkai ........ B2

**Drinking & Nightlife**
20 Boulangerie ........ C3
21 City Coffee ........ C3

## Activities

The two main activities in Druskininkai are freewheeling around and relaxing in spas (p336). In summer, several spots in town and by the lake rent electric scooters, hoverboards and boats.

**Bike Rental** CYCLING
(☎8-686 87022; Laisvės alėja 10; bikes per hour/day €3/10, buggies per 30/60min €7/12; ⏰8am-9pm) Between May and October bikes and buggies can be hired at the corner of Vilniaus and Laisvės alėjas, or opposite the tourist office at MK Čiurlionio gatvė 52.

**Steamboat Druskininkai** CRUISE
(☎8-612 26982; www.gelme-druskininkai.lt; Taikos gatvė 51; adult/child €12/6; ⏰2.30pm Tue-Sun May-Oct) Tranquil three-hour cruises for the Liškiava Monastery leave from the Druskininkai dock.

**Cable Car** CABLE CAR
(Lynu Kelias; www.lynukelias.lt; Vilniaus alėja 13-2; one-way/round-trip €3/5; ⏰10am-7pm Sun-Thu, to

10pm Fri & Sat) Operating both during summer and the ski season, this cable car soars above the houses and pine forests surrounding Druskininkai as it links the Aqua Park and the Snow Arena winter-sports complex.

## Sleeping

Druskininkai is rich in midrange hotels, with a few budget guesthouses and numerous apartments for rent. Regardless of budget, even where hotels don't boast their own facilities, they often offer discount vouchers to spas or the Aqua Park.

**Dalija** GUESTHOUSE €
(313-51 814; www.dalijahotel.lt; Laisvės aikštė 21; d/tr/q €40/50/58; ) This charming, spick-and-span timber guesthouse is superb value. It's right in the heart of Druskininkai, overlooking a beautiful wooden church. Rooms come with satellite TV and mini-kitchen.

★ **Art Hotel** BOUTIQUE HOTEL €€
(8-677 99229; www.arthotel.lt; Šv Jokūbo gatvė 9; d/f/apt €65/79/97; ) The pick of Druskininkai's non-spa accommodation, this wooden mansion comprises spacious studios in soothing blues and whites and high-beamed apartments, ideal for families, livened up by bold contemporary art.

**Hotel Druskininkai** SPA HOTEL €€
(313-51 200; www.grandspa.lt; V Kudirkos gatvė 43; r/ste from €94/142; ) The Druskininkai is certainly one of the most stylish hotels in town. Behind its striking glass-and-wood facade are modern rooms bathed in natural light, a Turkish bath, a Jacuzzi bubbling with Druskininkai mineral water and a hotel gym. The location is excellent, close to the centre, the river and the spas.

**Aqua Hotel** HOTEL €€
(313-59 195; www.aquapark.lt; Vilniaus alėja 13-1; s/d/apt from €80/89/189; ) If you're mainly in Druskininkai for a family romp at Aqua Park, this may be the place to stay. The rooms are nicely furnished, breakfast and buffet supper are included, you're surrounded by diversions (bowling, spas, the waterpark itself), and excellent packages are available online. Prices rise on Friday, Saturday and holidays.

**Regina** SPA HOTEL €€
(313-51 243; www.regina.lt; Kosciuškos gatvė 3; s/d/tr/q incl breakfast from €56/60/100/118; ) A grande dame of Druskininkai's hotel scene, Regina has rooms in a pleasing classical style with just a whiff of antique glamour. It also has one of the best breakfast buffets in town and a luxuriant little spa (massage from €30).

## Eating

**Boulangerie** CAFE €
(8-633 35555; www.kepyklele.lt; MK Čiurlionio gatvė 63; cakes €2-3; 9am-7pm) You'll find decent coffee as well as ice cream, Lithuanian cookies and cakes at this French-style bakery and cafe, just next to the tourist office.

**House** INTERNATIONAL €€
(8-679 14738; www.thehouse.lt; MK Čiurlionio gatvė 61; mains €5-15; 9am-11pm Sun-Thu, to midnight Fri & Sat; ) A pleasant summer terrace, good service and a crowd-pleasing menu that covers most bases (superlative takes on burgers, pasta, risottos, salads, grilled meats) make this Druskininkai's top restaurant.

**Kolonada** EUROPEAN €€
(8-662 06062; www.sventejums.lt/kolonada; Kudirkos gatvė 22; mains €7-13; 11am-11pm Sun-Thu, to 1am Fri & Sat) One of Druskininkai's best locations is graced by one of its best kitchens at this terraced parkside restaurant. In good weather, grab a table overlooking the gardens and tuck into a salmon salad or pork neck with boletus foraged from Dzūkija National Park. The serenity is best accompanied by oolong tea or a colourful fruit-topped cocktail.

**Toli Toli Druskininkai** INTERNATIONAL €€
(8-684 96378; www.facebook.com/tolitolidruskininkai; Vilniaus alėja 8; mains €6-14; noon-10pm Wed & Thu, to midnight Fri & Sat, 10am-9pm Sun; ) Offering an ambitious menu tinged with Middle Eastern (falafel, shakshuka), global flavours (chicken tikka masala, pancakes with bacon and maple syrup) and good cocktails, this friendly spot with eclectic decor gets very busy in the evenings. There's a kids' menu too.

**Etno Dvaras** LITHUANIAN €€
(8-656 19953; www.etnodvaras.lt; MK Čiurlionio gatvė 55; mains €5-9; 11am-10pm Mon-Thu, to midnight Fri, 10am-midnight Sat, 10am-11pm Sun) Part of a Lithuanian chain of countrified restaurants, this branch delivers some of the tastiest traditional cooking in town. The speciality here are hearty *cepelinai* – parcels of potato dough lathered with bacon-studded sour cream. Bonus: it's by the lake and has outdoor seating.

## TOP DRUSKININKAI SPAS

Druskininkai is dotted with spas. But beware, though, not all are swish. Here's a quick guide to help you:

**Aqua Park** (☎313-52 338; www.akvapark.lt; Vilniaus alėja 13-2; 2hr water entertainment adult/child from €11/9; ⊙noon-10pm Mon-Thu, noon-11pm Fri, 10am-11pm Sat, 10am-9pm Sun) Families need look no further than this humid wonderland, which brings together six waterslides (the longest over 200m), spas, saunas, a wave pool, kids' play area and more. Prices rise during summer and on weekends and public holidays.

**SpaVilnius** (☎313-53 811; www.spa-vilnius.lt; K Dineikos gatvė 1; massage per hour from €60; ⊙8am-10pm) Located inside an eight-storey hotel, the Druskininkai branch of SpaVilnius is a little tucked away from the centre of things, and all the more relaxing for it. Treatments include amber baths, hydrotherapy, massages and even cosmetic surgery. Double rooms start from €95.

**Europa Royale Spa** (☎313 42221; www.europaroyaledruskininkai.lt; Vilniaus alėja 7; treatments €7-50; ⊙9am-9pm) The contemporary spa at the eponymous hotel offers a range of treatments, from salt-room sessions for asthmatics to kinesiotherapy, and a plethora of massages and wraps.

**Druskininkai Health Resort** (Druskininkų gydykla; ☎313-60 508; www.akvapark.lt; Vilniaus alėja 11; treatments €13-84; ⊙8am-8pm, to 7pm Sun) Lymph-drainage, hot-stone massage and baths (whirling, herbal, mineral, mud and even vertical) are all on the menu at this well-maintained, vividly green, Soviet-era spa. Some even come seeking treatment for more serious ailments – cardiovascular, cutaneous, vestibular, endocrinal and more.

## Drinking & Nightlife

**City Coffee** COFFEE

(☎8-647 29545; www.facebook.com/rghtcoffee; V Kudirkos gatvė 37; ⊙9am-9pm Mon-Sat, to 8pm Sun; 📶) The mellow tinkling of the piano in the background and walls covered in sketches of European cities in days of yore create a welcoming atmosphere at Druskininkai's best coffee shop. There are speciality teas for purchase and a pleasant outdoor terrace.

## ℹ Information

**SEB Bankas** (MK Čiurlionio gatvė 40; ⊙8am-5pm Mon-Fri) Currency exchange inside, ATM outside.

**Tourist Office** (☎313-51 777; www.info.druskininkai.lt; MK Čiurlionio gatvė 65; ⊙10am-1pm & 1.45-6.45pm Tue-Sat, 10am-1pm Sun) Brochures, bike rental (from €6) in summer, accommodation booking and advice. There's another **tourist office** (☎313-60 800; www.info.druskininkai.lt; Gardino gatvė 3; ⊙8.30am-12.15pm & 1-5.15pm Mon-Fri) near the bus station.

## ℹ Getting There & Away

From the **bus station** (☎313 51 333; Gardino gatvė 1; ⊙5.15am-6.50pm) there are daily direct buses to/from Vilnius (€12 to €13.50, two to 2½ hours, 14 daily), Kaunas (€10 to €13, 2½ to 3½ hours, 15 daily), Klaipėda (€24 to €27, five to 6¾ hours, two daily) and Palanga (€25 to €28, 5½ to 7¼ hours, two daily). More Klaipėda and Palanga departures via Vilnius and Kaunas.

Reaching Šiauliai (€23 to €28, six hours) requires changing buses in Kaunas.

Three-hour Steamboat Druskininkai (p334) cruises for the Liškiava Monastery leave from the Druskininkai dock during the summer months.

# Dzūkija National Park

☎310

The 555-sq-km Dzūkija (dzoo-ki-ya) National Park (Lithuania's largest) is a nature-lover's paradise. Four-fifths of it is swathed in pine forest, cover for 48 lakes. The Ūla and Grūda Rivers, perfect for a day of canoeing, flow through it, and an abundance of mushrooms and berries grow here in season.

In addition to natural reserves, the park houses ethnographic and cultural reserves, plus protected villages such as **Zervynos** and **Liškiava**. **Merkinė**, 10km further down the Nemunas River, is the starting point for the 12km **Black Potters' Trail** (Merkinė) around workshops where pots as black as soot are made from red clay. The extraordinary colour comes from pine-wood resin fired with the pot in an outdoor kiln.

Marcinkonys, some 34km northeast of Druskininkai, is home to the second of the park's two visitor centres.

Tradition is still very strong in this part of the country. Woodcarving and basket weaving are flourishing trades in the villages, linen and wool is handmade, and crops are still harvested with scythes.

## Sights

**Čepkeliai Strict Nature Reserve** NATIONAL PARK
(Čepkelių Valstybinis Gamtinis Rezervatas; www.cepkeliai-dzukija.lt; adult/child €1.50/0.75) The 112-sq-km Čepkeliai reserve, the largest area of untouched nature in Lithuania, is a glorious wet wilderness of bogs, black alder swamps, Cladinoso-callunosa forest and lakes, home to more than 4000 species of animals and plants (including lynx and wolves).

Visits are limited: apply and pay the necessary fees at the Marcinkonys Visitor Centre (p338). Between April and June, visits to the nature reserve are only possible with accredited guides.

**Dzūkija National Park Ethnographic Homestead** MUSEUM
(Dzūkijos Nacionalinio Parko Etnografinė Sodyba; ☎310-39 169; Miškininkų gatvė 6, Marcinkonys; adult/child €1.50/0.75; ⏰8am-5pm Mon-Thu, to 3.45pm Sat) Housed in an early-20th-century homestead, this exposition explores the everyday life, traditions and material culture of Dzūkian people. There are great examples of woodcarving, weaving, basket-making and beekeeping.

**Liškiava Monastery** MONASTERY
(Liškiavos Švč Trejybės Bažnyčia; Liškiava; adult/child €2/1; ⏰1-7pm Mon-Fri, noon-7pm Sat, 1-5pm Sun) Commanding a verdant loop of the Nemunas River, 9km north of Druskininkai, this former Dominican monastery is famous for its seven rococo-style altars and its crypt with glass coffins.

## Sleeping

There are 15 traditional homesteads scattered about the villages, ideal for travellers wishing to experience rural Lithuanian life. Check www.gamta.cepkeliai-dzukija.lt for the complete list.

**Rūta Sakalienė Homestead** HOMESTAY €
(Rūtos Sakalienės kaimo turizmo sodyba; ☎8-615 34306; www.sakalai.lt; Marcinkonys; per person €35) Life at this homestead is as traditional as it gets. The lodgings are basic, there's an outdoor privy instead of a flushing toilet, you wash in the creek and warm yourself by the wood fire. Homemade meals available, courtesy of the welcoming owners. There's a bit of a language barrier, so brush up on your Lithuanian!

DON'T MISS

### STARGAZING NEAR MOLĖTAI

One of Lithuania's oldest towns, Molėtai (mo-ley-tai) is the jumping-off point for one of Lithuania's most unusual museums and an observatory, located near town.

The **Lithuanian Ethnocosmology Museum** (Lietuvos etnokosmologijos muziejus; ☎383-45 424; www.etnokosmomuziejus.lt; Žvaigždžių gatvė, Kulionys; adult/child €2.40/1.60, night tours €6-8; ⏰8am-4.30pm Mon-Fri) explores the cosmos's connection to cultural ideas of hell, heaven and earth in its bubble-shaped exhibition centre. If you attend the night tours with English-speaking guides, two hours after sunset, you can peek through the two giant telescopes. Nearby, the **Molėtai Astronomical Observatory** (Molėtų astronomijos observatorija; ☎383-45 444; http://mao.tfai.vu.lt/sci; Kulionys) FREE boasts northern Europe's largest telescope; book your free visit in advance online or by phone.

To reach both, catch a bus from Molėtai to Utena, ask to be let off at the 'etnokosmologijos muziejus' turn-off (signposted 10km north of town) and follow the road to the right for another 4km.

In town, you can bed down at the hospitable **Gerugnė** (☎698 13423; www.gerugne.lt; Vilniaus gatvė 66; d/tr €36/45; 📶) guesthouse; a short walk away, **Senoji Užeiga** (☎676 04463; www.senojiuzeiga.lt; Vilniaus gatvė 29; mains €4.50-6.50; ⏰8am-8pm) serves generous portions of Lithuanian classics.

Buses from Vilnius (€5, one to 1½ hours, 16 daily) stop at the **Moletai Bus Station** (www.moletuautobusai.lt; Vilniaus gatvė 2).

## Information

**Merkinė Visitor Centre** (☎310-57 245; www.dzukijosparkas.lt; Vilniaus gatvė 3; ⊙8am-noon & 12.45-5pm Mon-Fri, to 3.45pm Sat) Tons of information on the surrounding environment and traditional village culture, plus walks, accommodation, cycling and canoeing. English-speaking guides for mushrooming or berrying can also be arranged at around €15 per hour, or €60 per day.

**Marcinkonys Visitor Centre** (☎310-44 466; www.dzukijosparkas.lt; Miškininkų gatvė 61; ⊙8am-noon & 12.45-5pm Mon-Fri, 8am-noon & 12.45-3.45pm Sat) The visitor centre in Marcinkonys can advise on walking, cycling and canoeing and is the starting point for the 14km Zackagiris Sightseeing Route (Zackagirio Takas) plus shorter (7km and 10.5km) walks. Access to the Čepkeliai Strict Nature Reserve can also be arranged here. A voluntary €1 contribution is levied.

## Getting There & Around

The Steamboat Druskininkai (p334) makes trips between Druskininkai and Liškiava during the summer months.

Buses to/from Druskininkai and Vilnius stop at the Merkinė intersection (Merkinės kryžkelė; €3, 30 minutes, four daily), 2km east of Merkinė town centre. Three daily trains to/from Vilnius stop at Zervynos (€4.20, 1¾ hours) and Marcinkonys (€4.50, two hours).

Cycling is a wonderful way to explore the park, and bikes can easily be hired in Druskininkai, in season. The Druskininkai tourist office (p336) also has excellent free maps for cyclists.

# CENTRAL LITHUANIA

Within easy reach of the capital, central Lithuania is home to the country's thriving second city, as well as one of the country's oddest sights.

Proud Kaunas, the alternative Lithuanian capital between WWI and WWII and the country's perpetual 'number two' city, holds court in the heart of the country. Its Old Town is as intriguing as its mass of museums and art galleries, and there is no better place to base yourself for central-country forays. Within easy reach of Kaunas is Birštonas, a tiny spa town where both jazz and mud treatments are serious business, plus Kėdainiai, Lithuania's 'Cucumber Capital' with an adorable Old Town.

Still in the process of reinvention is Šiauliai, once a closed city in Soviet times that sheltered the USSR's largest military base outside Russia. Most tourists make the pilgrimage here for the papal-blessed Hill of Crosses, 10km to the north, and leave awed by the strength and devotion of the Lithuanian people.

## Kaunas

☎37 / POP 374,600

Although during its centuries of existence, Kaunas (kow-nas) mostly played second fiddle to Vilnius, this up-and-coming city is no slouch. Strategically wedged at the confluence of the Nemunas and Neris Rivers, Kaunas gained a taste for the limelight during a brief spell as Lithuania's capital in the interwar period; the town owes some of its most attractive art deco architecture to this era.

A beautiful, cobbled Old Town aside, Kaunas is densely packed with museums and some of the country's best galleries, with bold street art jumping out at you from multiple locations. It's here that you'll find some terrific bars, a superb dining scene and that staple of hipsters: third-wave coffee shops. As Kaunas builds towards its stint as European Capital of Culture for 2022, this plucky city is getting bolder by the day.

### History

Legend has it that Kaunas was founded by the son of tragic young lovers. Beautiful maiden Milda let the Holy Eternal Flame go out while caring for her lover Daugerutis; sentenced to death by vengeful gods they fled to a cave, where Milda gave birth to Kaunas.

Archaeologists believe the city dates from the 13th century and until the 15th century was in the front line against the Teutonic Order in Lithuania's west. Kaunas became a successful river port in the 15th and 16th centuries. German merchants were influential here, and there was a Hanseatic League office. During the interwar period it became the capital of Lithuania, as Vilnius lay in Polish hands. Its strategic position is the main reason it was destroyed 13 times before WWII – when it once again received a battering.

### Sights

Rotušės aikštė, the square wedged between the Nemunas and Neris Rivers, is the historic heart. From here pedestrianised Vilniaus gatvė runs east to meet the city's main axis, Laisvės alėja – also pedestrianised. Pick up a copy of *Wallographer's Notes* from the tourist office to go hunting for the best street art.

## Old Town

### Rotušės Aikštė & Around

This large, open square at the heart of Old Town is lined with pretty 15th- and 16th-century German merchants' houses and is centred on the 17th-century former town hall. In the square's southwestern corner stands a statue of the patriot-poet Maironis.

**Town Hall** HISTORIC BUILDING
(Kauno Rotušė; Rotušės aikštė 15) Old Town's tallest tower (53m) rises from Kaunas' Town Hall, an elegant white layer-cake of a building. Built in the mid-16th century, the hall has served as a theatre, a magazine, prison and palace over the years. Nowadays it is mainly used for official events, though it's also a favourite photo-op for visitors stopping by the tourist office inside.

The first two floors also serve as a wedding hall (Saturdays usually see a procession of brides and grooms in their finery) and there's a small town museum in the cellar.

**House of Perkūnas** HISTORIC BUILDING
(Perkūno Namas; ☎8-641 44614; www.perkunonamas.lt; Aleksoto gatvė 6; adult/student €2/1; ⏱10am-5pm Mon-Fri) With ornate arches and

## Central Lithuania

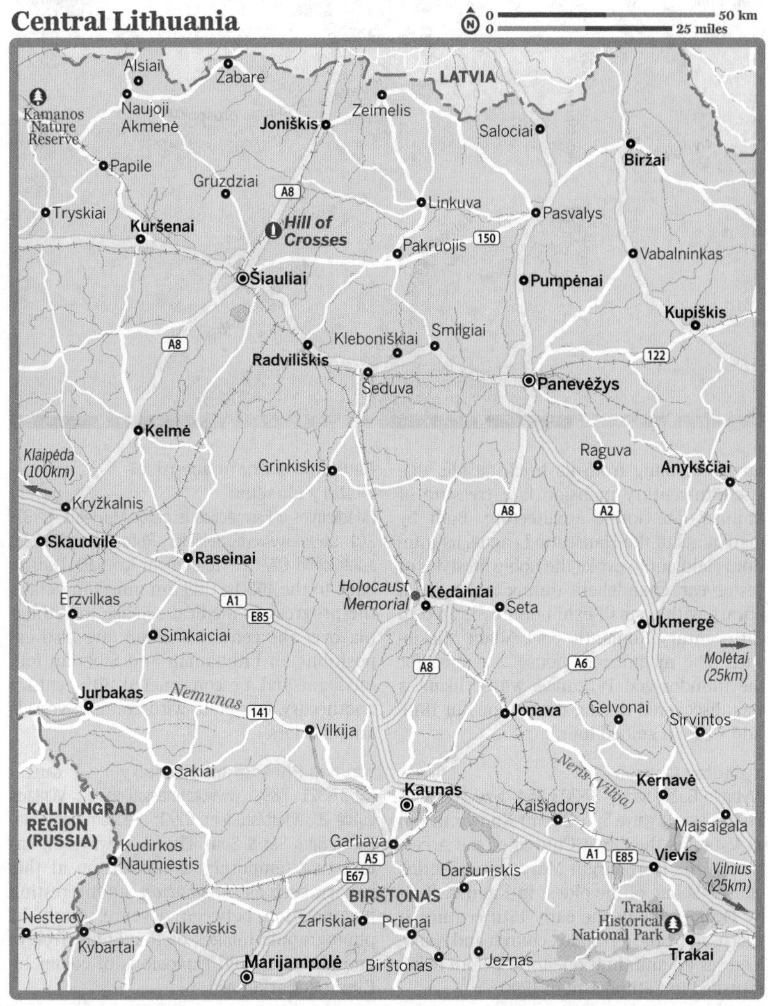

## Kaunas

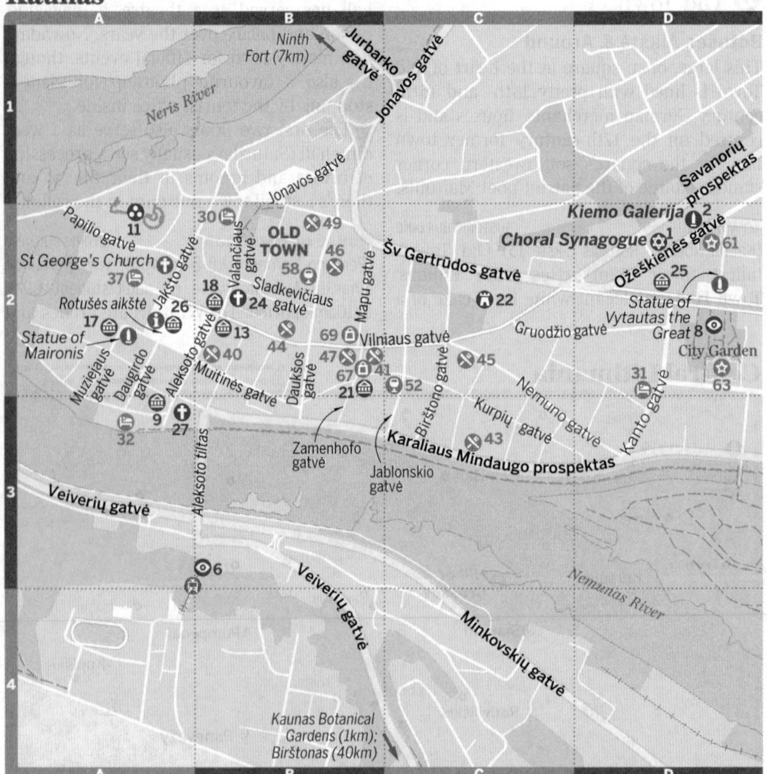


turrets rippling from its brick facade, this late-15th-century mansion is a treasure of Kaunas' late-Gothic architecture. Built by merchants of the Hanseatic League, its interior is laid out to evoke the noble lifestyles of yesteryear: chandeliers, dining tables and a library with a small exhibition dedicated to 19th-century Romantic poet Adam Mickiewicz. The magnificent house is named for the thunder god Perkūnas, whose likeness was discovered during renovations in 1818. Add €1 for a guided tour.

**Vytautas Church** CHURCH

(Vytauto Bažnyčia; ☎37-203 854; www.vytautine.lcn.lt; Aleksoto gatvė 5; ⏰2-7pm) Known in full as Vytautas the Great Church of the Accession of the Holy Virgin Mary, this red-brick church is one of the oldest in Kaunas. Built by Franciscans in the early 15th century, it was used by the Orthodox church and Napoleon (as an ammunition store) before being returned to Catholicism in 1990.

**Medicine & Pharmaceutical History Museum** MUSEUM

(Medicinios ir Farmacijos Istorijos Muziejus; ☎37-201 569; www.muziejai.lt; Rotušės aikštė 28; adult/child €2/1; ⏰10am-5pm Tue-Sat) Dating back to the 1930s, this fun museum details the progress of medical science in Lithuania over the centuries. There are also expositions on Lithuanian and Siberian folk medicine and a reconstructed 19th-century apothecary, complete with ceramic vessels and clay jars.

**Kaunas Photography Gallery** GALLERY

(☎37-321 789; www.kaunasgallery.lt; Vilniaus gatvė 2; adult/student €2/1; ⏰11am-6pm Tue-Fri, to 5pm Sat & Sun) There's always an interesting temporary exhibition on at this gallery, such as *Integration*, an interesting juxtaposition between obscure, dimly lit photographic images of Remigijus Treigys and abstract, bold explosions of colour by Eimutis Markūnas.

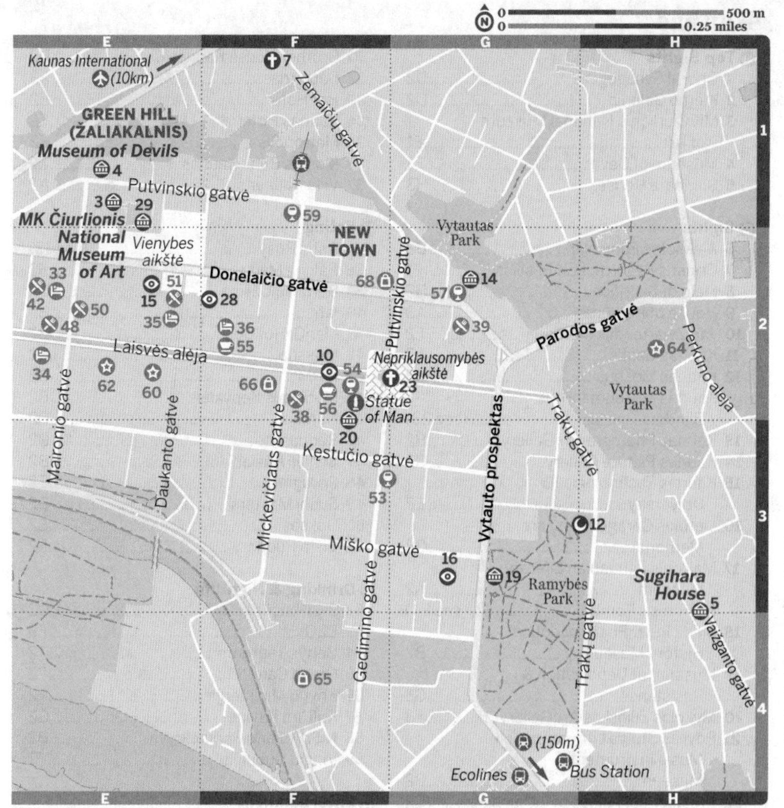




**Maironis Lithuanian Literary Museum** MUSEUM
(Maironio Lietuvių Literatūros Muziejus; ☎37-206 842; www.maironiomuziejus.lt; Rotušės aikštė 13; adult/child €3/1; ⏱9am-5pm Tue-Sat) Even travellers unenthused by turn-of-the-20th-century literature will be enchanted by this museum dedicated to Lithuanian luminary Maironis (aka Jonas Mačiulis). The museum is inside a beautifully attired 18th-century mansion, bought and furnished by Maironis in 1909. Highlights include the rococo Red Room (actually baby blue) and the Great Dining Room, gloriously decorated with traditional heraldry rendered in bold graphic art.

**Aleksotas Funicular** FUNICULAR
(Aleksoto Funikulierius; ☎37-391 086; Amerikos Lietuvių 6; €0.70; ⏱7am-noon & 1-4pm Mon-Fri, from 10am Sat) This historic funicular at the southern end of Aleksoto Tiltas (Aleksoto Bridge) dates from 1935 and the viewing platform at the top affords great rooftop views of Old Town (best in the morning).

**Kaunas Castle** RUINS
(☎37-300 672; www.kaunomuziejus.lt; Papilio gatvė; adult/child €2.50/1.20; ⏱10am-6pm Tue-Sat, to 4pm Sun) A reconstructed tower, sections of wall and part of a moat are all that remain of 14th-century Kaunas Castle, an important bastion against Teutonic attacks around which the town originally grew. There's an exibition on the history of the castle, a reconstructed dungeon, plus the opportunity to try your hand at old Lithuanian games and archery.

## Vilniaus Gatvė & Around

Vilniaus gatvė is Old Town's charming main artery.

**Presidential Palace of Lithuania** PALACE
(Istorinė Lietuvos Prezidentūra; ☎37-201 778; www.istorineprezidentura.lt; Vilniaus gatvė 33; adult/student €5/2.50; ⏱10am-5pm Tue-Fri, to 7pm Thu, 11am-4pm Sat & Sun, gardens 8am-9pm

## Kaunas

**Top Sights**
1 Choral Synagogue........D2
2 Kiemo Galerija........D2
3 MK Čiurlionis National Museum of Art........E1
4 Museum of Devils........E1
5 Sugihara House........H3

**Sights**
6 Aleksotas Funicular........B3
7 Christ's Resurrection Basilica........F1
8 Field of Sacrifice........D2
9 House of Perkūnas........A3
10 Jan Zwartendijk Memorial........F2
11 Kaunas Castle........A2
12 Kaunas Mosque........H3
Kaunas Museum for the Blind........(see 23)
13 Kaunas Photography Gallery........B2
14 Kaunas Picture Gallery........G2
15 Kaunas Technological University........E2
16 Lietūkis Garage Massacre Memorial........G3
17 Maironis Lithuanian Literary Museum........A2
Maironis's Tomb........(see 24)
18 Medicine & Pharmaceutical History Museum........B2
19 Museum of Deportation & Resistance........G3
20 Mykolas Žilinskas Art Gallery........F3
21 Povilas Stulga Lithuanian Folk Music Instruments Museum........B2
22 Presidential Palace of Lithuania........C2
23 St Michael the Archangel Church........G2
24 Sts Peter & Paul Cathedral........B2
25 Tadas Ivanauskas Zoological Museum........D2
26 Town Hall........A2
27 Vytautas Church........A3
28 Vytautas Magnus University........F2
29 Vytautas the Great War Museum........E1

**Sleeping**
30 Apple Economy Hotel........B2
31 Brother House Kaunas........D2
32 Daugirdas........A3
33 Hof Hotel........E2
34 Kaunas Hotel........E2
35 Metropolis........E2
36 Monk's Bunk Kaunas........F2
37 Villa Kaunensis........A2

**Eating**
Antis Rūsy........(see 13)
38 Baking Mad........F2
39 Bernelių Užeiga........G2
40 Ieti........B2
41 ManGi Hot Dogs........B2
42 Moksha........E2
43 MOMO Grill........C3
44 Motiejaus Kepyklėlė........B2
45 Nüman........C2
46 Radharanė........B2
47 Senieji Rūsiai........B2
48 Spruginė........E2
49 Sushi Masters........B2
50 Uoksas........E2
51 Višta Puode........E2

**Drinking & Nightlife**
52 2½ Ubuolio........C2
53 B2O........F3
54 Genys Taproom........F2
55 Green Cafe........F2
56 Knygų Ministerija........F2
57 Kultūra Kavinė........G2
58 NiShA Bar'o Perspektyva........B2
59 Vingiu Dubingiu........F1

**Entertainment**
60 Džem Pub........E2
61 Kaunas Philharmonic........D2
62 Kaunas State Drama Theatre........E2
63 Kaunas State Musical Theatre........D2
64 O Kodėl Ne?........H2

**Shopping**
65 Akropolis........F4
66 Ali Šokoladinė........F2
67 Egidijaus Rudinsko Grafikos Galerija........B2
68 kARTu........F2
69 Livi Design........B2

daily) This handsome 19th-century building was the seat of government for the Republic of Lithuania between the wars. Restored to its original grandeur, it now houses an exhibition on independent Lithuania including historic photos, gifts given to past presidents, collections of family silver and presidential awards. Statues of former presidents also stud the palace garden.

**Povilas Stulga Lithuanian Folk Music Instruments Museum** MUSEUM
(Lietuvos Tautinės Muzikos Muziejus; ☎37-422 295; www.kaunomuziejus.lt; Zamenhofo gatvė 12; adult/child €2.50/1.20; ⏲10am-6pm Tue-Fri, to 4pm Sat) This museum shows that almost any raw material can be turned into a musical instrument. Housed in a 16th-century Gothic house, the wonderful 7000-piece collection includes wood and bone flutes, unusual reed

pipes, three-string cellos, and both basic and elaborately carved *kanklės* (zithers).

**Sts Peter & Paul Cathedral** CHURCH
(Šventų Apaštalų Petro ir Povilo Arkekatedra Bazilika; ☎37-324 093; www.kaunoarkikatedra.lt; Vilniaus gatvė 1; ⏲7am-7pm Mon-Fri, 8am-6pm Sat & Sun) With its single tower, this church owes much to baroque reconstruction, especially inside, but the original 15th-century Gothic shape of its windows remains. The largest Gothic building in Lithuania, it was probably founded by Vytautas around 1410 and now has nine altars. The **tomb of Maironis** stands outside the south wall.

## New Town

Kaunas expanded east from Old Town in the 19th century, giving birth to the modern centre and its striking 1.7km pedestrian street, **Laisvės alėja** (Freedom Ave).

Independent Lithuania's first parliament convened in 1920 at the Kaunas State Musical Theatre, the former State Theatre Palace overlooking **City Garden** (Miestos Sodas) at the western end of Laisvės alėja, which was created in 1892.

★**Kiemo Galerija** PUBLIC ART
(Ožeškienės gatvė 25) FREE Artist Vytenis Jakas moved into this courtyard over a decade ago and turned it into an ever-evolving art project, creating murals and transferring onto walls the photos of Jewish families that lived here before WWII. The 'Stick Your Memory' wall encourages you to join in and contribute a sentimental knick-knack to the chaotic yet joyful collage.

**St Michael the Archangel Church** CHURCH
(Šv Archangelo Mykolo Rektoratas; ☎37-226 676; Nepriklausomybės aikštė 14; ⏲9am-5pm) The Soviets turned this blue-domed neo-Byzantine church, which fills the sky so dramatically at the eastern end of Laisvės alėja, into a stained-glass museum. Built for the Russian Orthodox faith in 1893, St Michael's was reopened to Catholic worshippers in 1991.

The church catacombs have been converted into the **Kaunas Museum for the Blind** (adult/student €3/1.50; ⏲10am-2pm Mon-Fri) – allowing visitors to experience a sightless world.

**Mykolas Žilinskas Art Gallery** MUSEUM
(Mykolo Žilinsko Dailės Galerija; ☎37-322 788; www.ciurlionis.lt/m-zilinskas-art-gallery; Nepriklausomybės aikštė 12; adult/child €5/2.50; ⏲11am-5pm Tue, Sat & Sun, to 7pm Wed-Fri) This art museum on three floors is based on the private collection of Mykolas Žilinskas, but is now operated by the National Čiurlionis Art Museum. The collection is strongest on European art from the 17th to the 20th centuries and boasts Lithuania's only Rubens.

**Tadas Ivanauskas Zoological Museum** MUSEUM
(Tado Ivanausko Zoologijos Muziejus; ☎37-200 292; www.zoomuziejus.lt; Laisvės alėja 106; adult/child €3/2; ⏲11am-7pm Tue-Sun) With over 250,000 specimens spread over three floors, this museum covers the animal kingdom from the imposing taxidermy mammals (bison, muskox, big cats, hippos, primates) to varied birdlife, and even a paleontological section full of mammoth remains. It was founded in 1919 by Tadas, a famous Lithuanian naturalist, and the displays are thorough and well organised, but you leave with a wistful feeling that you'd rather have seen these creatures alive and in the wild.

**Kaunas Mosque** MOSQUE
(Kauno Mečetė; www.islamasvisiems.lt; Totorių gatvė 6; ⏲1.30-11pm Sat-Thu, from noon Fri) This small mosque is one of four in Lithuania and the only one made of brick in the Baltics, constructed here to replace the original wooden mosque from 1860.

## Vienybės Aikštė & Around

Vienybės Aikštė (Unity Sq) houses **Kaunas Technological University** (Kauno technologijos universitetas; ☎37-300 000; www.ktu.edu; K Donelaičio gatvė 73) and the smaller **Vytautas Magnus University** (Vytauto didžiojo universitetas; ☎37-222 739; www.vdu.lt/en; K Donelaičio gatvė 58), first founded in 1922 and refounded in 1989 by a émigré Lithuanian.

★**MK Čiurlionis National Museum of Art** GALLERY
(MK Čiurlionio Valstybinis Dailės Muziejus; ☎37-229 475; www.ciurlionis.lt; Putvinskio gatvė 55; adult/student €5/2.50, audio guide €4; ⏲11am-5pm Tue, Sat & Sun, to 7pm Wed-Fri) One of Lithuania's oldest and grandest galleries, Kaunas' leading art museum (founded 1921) is the place to acquaint yourself with the dreamlike paintings of Mikalojus Konstantinas Čiurlionis (1875–1911), one of the country's greatest artists and composers. Elsewhere in the sizeable gallery are contemporary sculpture exhibitions, Lithuanian folk and

### THE HEROES OF KAUNAS

Beloved Lithuanian pilots Steponas Darius and Stanislovas Girėnas died on 15 July 1933, just 650km short of completing the longest nonstop transatlantic flight at the time. Two days after the duo set off from New York, 25,000 people gathered at Kaunas airport for their triumphant return. They never arrived. Their orange plane *Lituanica* crashed in Germany; see the wreckage in the Vytautas the Great War Museum. After being embalmed, then hidden during Soviet occupation, the bodies came to rest at **Aukštieji Šančiai Cemetery** (Ašmenos 1-oji gatvė 1) in 1964.

The small **Museum of Deportation & Resistance** (Rezistencijos ir tremties muziejus; ☎37-323 179; Vytauto prospektas 46; adult/child €1.75/1.20; ⏰9am-5pm Tue-Fri, to 4pm Sat) documents the resistance spirit embodied by the Forest Brothers, who fought the Soviet occupation from 1944 to 1953. Led by Jonas Žemaitis-Vytautas (1909–54), somewhere between 50,000 and 100,000 men and women went into Lithuania's forests to battle the regime. The museum staff estimates that one-third were killed, and the rest captured and deported (in total 150,000 Lithuanians were sent to Soviet territory during this time).

One of the most desperate anti-Soviet actions was the suicide of Kaunas student Romas Kalanta, commemorated by the **Field of Sacrifice** (Miesto Sodas). On 14 May 1972 he doused himself in petrol and immolated himself in protest at communist rule.

religious art, 16th- to 20th-century European works and Lithuanian landscapes and portraits from the 1900s to 1940s.

**★Museum of Devils** MUSEUM
(Velnių Muziejus; ☎37-221 587; www.ciurlionis.lt; Putvinskio gatvė 64; adult/child €5/2.50; ⏰11am-5pm Tue, Sat & Sun, to 7pm Wed-Fri) This museum is devoted to the Devil, Lucifer, Satan, the fallen angel, the seducer, the cajoler, with over 3000 statuettes, carvings, masks and other images, collected over the years by landscape artist Antanas Žmuidzinavičius (1876–1966). There's a light-hearted exploration of the Horned One in various mythologies, plus a look at celebrations held to drive away darkness and evil, from Walpurgis Night and Shrovetide to Halloween.

**Kaunas Picture Gallery** GALLERY
(Kauno Paveikslų Galerija; ☎37-221 789; www.ciurlionis.lt; Donelaičio gatvė 16; adult/student €5/2.50; ⏰11am-5pm Tue, Sat & Sun, to 7pm Wed-Fri) This branch of the many-tentacled Čiurlionis museum (p343) exhibits works by 20th-century Lithuanian artists, including a particularly poignant Lithuania In Exile exhibition by émigré artists. Most explanations are in Lithuanian but the art does the talking: 1920s and '30s watercolours depict bucolic countryside and fishing villages along with treasured artworks like a vivid triptych by 20th-century painter Adomas Galdikas, plus engaging temporary exhibitions.

**Vytautas the Great War Museum** MUSEUM
(Vytauto Didžiojo Karo Muziejus; ☎37-320 765; www.kariuomene.kam.lt/lt/karo_muziejus.html; Donelaičio gatvė 64; adult/child €2/1; ⏰10am-5pm Tue-Sun) Maintained by the Lithuanian Army, this museum keeps exhibitions on the history of weapons, Lithuanian military history, the period of the Grand Duchy and more. Of particular interest is the wreckage of the *Lituanica,* in which Steponas Darius and Stanislovas Girėnas died while attempting to fly nonstop from New York to Kaunas, in 1933.

**Christ's Resurrection Basilica** CHURCH
(Kauno Paminklinė Kristhaus Prisikėlimo Bašničia; ☎37-322 583; www.prisikelimas.lt; Zemaicių gatvė 316; ⏰11.30am-6.30pm Mon-Fri, from 11am Sat & Sun) There's an austerity, symmetry and simplicity to this white-washed concrete cathedral, built over a period of 70 years from 1934 onwards, though its Functionalist style divides opinion. A Nazi paper warehouse, then a radio factory under the Soviets, it was finally consecrated in 2004. Take the stairs (€1.20) or the lift (€2.40) to the upstairs terrace for great views of the city.

## Outside the Centre

The outskirts of Kaunas are home to a diverse range of attractions, from a poignant WWII memorial and museum to a gorgeous monastery and a taste of ye olde Lithuania at an open-air museum.

**★Ninth Fort** MUSEUM
(IX Forto Muziejus; ☎37-377 750; www.9fortomuziejus.lt; Žemaičių plentas 73; adult/child €3/1.50; ⏰10am-6pm Tue-Sun) Lithuania's dark

20th-century history is poignantly told here, 7km north of Kaunas. Begin in the sombre, church-like gallery with striking stained glass and exhibits detailing Lithuania's suffering under the Soviets and the Nazis. Then continue uphill to the Holocaust memorial and the WWI-era fort – a hard-labour prison in the early 20th century and a centre of torture and mass killings during WWII.

Take bus 23 from Jonavos gatvė to the 9-ojo Forto Muziejus stop, then cross under the motorway.

The spot next to the vast stone Holocaust memorial is where 50,000 people – 30,000 of them Lithuanian Jews – were murdered by the Nazis, alongside Jews from other parts of Europe, plus dissident Lithuanians and Russian prisoners of war.

The fort was built in the late 19th century and was occupied by German troops during WWI. When WWI ended, it became a prison; exhibitions detail the brutality with which inmates were treated. During WWII, the fort was used as a holding pen for political prisoners before they were deported to distant parts of the Soviet Union, plus a brief stopover for Jews before they were killed en masse. Heart-wrenching displays pay tribute to individual victims of the Holocaust, detail the privations and horrors of the Kaunas ghetto and honour the Righteous Among the Nations – the Lithuanians who risked their lives to save Jews.

Enquire ahead for guided tours of different aspects of the site, including the early history of the fort and the Holocaust in Lithuania (extra charges apply, usually €5).

**Pažaislis Monastery** MONASTERY
(☎37-458 868; www.pazaislis.org; Masiulio gatvė 31; adult/child €6/3; ⏰10am-5pm Tue-Fri, to 4pm Sat Jun-Sep) Built by Camaldolese monks in the 17th century, this striking baroque monastery lies 9km east of central Kaunas, on a promontory jutting into the Kauno marios (Kaunas Sea). Given to the Russian Orthodox order by Tsar Alexander in 1831, it's a sumptuous if slightly run-down affair with a 50m-high cupola and luxurious Venetian interior made from pink and black Polish marble.

On the premises is **Monte Pacis** (☎8-655 95185; www.montepacis.lt; mains €15-19, 3-/6-course tasting menu €33/66; ⏰noon-10pm Sun-Thu, to 11pm Fri & Sat) 🍃, one of Lithuania's best fine dining restaurants.

Take trolleybus 9, or cycle the riverside path.

The monastery has had a chequered history, becoming a psychiatric hospital in the Soviet era, before reverting to its Catholic roots in 1990. It's best to visit during the Pažaislis Music Festival, between June and August.

**Open-Air Museum of Lithuania** MUSEUM
(Lietuvių Liaudies Buities Muziejus; ☎34-647 392; www.llbm.lt; L Lekavičiaus gatvė 2, Rumšiškės; adult/child €5/2.50; ⏰indoor exhibits 10am-6pm May-Oct) The open-air museum consists of re-created 18th- and 19th-century villages representing Lithuania's main regions (Dzūkija, Aukštaitija, Suvalkija, Žemaitija and Lithuania Minor). Potters, weavers and joiners demonstrate their crafts in the museum workshop and, while the indoor exhibits shut for the colder months, tours of the park can be booked throughout the year. The museum is in Rumšiškės, 25km east of Kaunas, about 2km off the Kaunas–Vilnius road. It's also accessible by bus from Kaunas (30 minutes, five daily).

## Festivals & Events

Music festivals make up many of Kaunas' social highlights.

**Kaunas Jazz Festival** MUSIC
(☎37-750 146; www.kaunasjazz.lt; Rotušės aikštė 29; ⏰Apr) Inaugurated just after the departure of the Soviets, this lively festival brings world-class jazz musicians to Kaunas for two weeks every April, before heading down the road to Vilnius.

**Operetta in Kaunas Castle** MUSIC
(☎37-203 661; www.operetta.lt; L Zamenhofo gatvė 5a; ⏰Jul) This open-air festival of opera spends several nights in the ruins of Kaunas Castle in the first week of July before heading on the road, running from May to September altogether.

**Pažaislis Music Festival** MUSIC
(☎37-203 547; www.pazaislis.lt; T Masiulio gatvė 31; ⏰May-Sep) Sprawling across the summer, this eclectic festival makes use of the splendid grounds of the 17th-century Pažaislis monastery on the shore of the Kaunas Sea. Expect symphonic and chamber performances, choral work and folk ensembles.

## Sleeping

A moderate budget is no barrier to staying in Kaunas, which has rich pickings for light wallets. The majority of accommodation options feel business-focused, but there are

## JEWISH KAUNAS

Known to be living in the Kaunas region since the 15th century, Litvaks (Lithuanian Jews) originally settled in what is the present-day neighbourhood of Vilijampolė, on the western bank of the Neris, across from Old Town. This is also where the Kovno Ghetto was located during WWII, in the area bounded by Jurbarko, Panerių and Demokratų streets. It's worth noting that much of Kaunas' interwar infrastructure and architecture owed much to the funding and expertise of its Jewish residents, most of whom then perished in the Holocaust at the hands of the Nazis and their willing Lithuanian collaborators. When the Nazis invaded Lithuania on 22 June, 1941, there were around 37,000 Jews resident in Kaunas; at the end of the war, less than 3000 survived.

Kaunas' present-day Jewish community is tiny and the mix of museums and memorials pertaining to Jewish history makes for a poignant pilgrimage.

**Choral Synagogue** (Kauno Choralinė Sinagoga; ☎8-614 03100; www.kaunasjews.lt; Ožeškienės gatvė 13; ⊙service 5.45-6.30pm daily, 10am-noon Sat) FREE Call ahead if planning to visit Kaunas' last functioning synagogue, its exterior crying out for renovation. Built in 1871, it's the only synagogue to have survived since 1941, with a remarkable dark-wood and gold bema. A memorial out front commemorates 1600 children killed at the Ninth Fort.

**Lietūkis Garage Massacre Memorial** (Miško gatvė 11) Step inside the courtyard to view the small memorial marking the spot where, on 27 June, 1941, during the first days of the Nazi occupation of the city, 'patriots' from the Lithuanian Activist Front (LAF) murdered 70 or so Jewish passers-by in front of a crowd of cheering onlookers.

**Ninth Fort** (p344) This 19th-century fort some 7km north of Kaunas was the site of mass killings and torture during WWII; this is where the majority of Kaunas' Jews perished, alongside prisoners of war and dissident Lithuanians.

**Sugihara House** (Sugiharos Namas; ☎37-332 881; www.sugiharahouse.com; Vaižganto gatvė 30; adult/student €4/2; ⊙10am-5pm Mon-Fri, 11am-4pm Sat & Sun) Kaunas-based Japanese diplomat Chiune Sugihara (1900–86) – with the help of Dutch diplomat Jan Zwartendijk – saved 6000 Jewish lives between 1939 and 1940 by issuing transit visas to stranded Polish Jews who faced the advancing Nazi terror. When the Soviets annexed Lithuania and ordered that all consulates be shut he asked for a short extension. Dubbed 'Japan's Schindler', he disobeyed orders from Tokyo for some 29 days by signing 300 visas per day, and handed the stamp to a Jewish refugee when he left. This museum tells his life story, and features video installations and stories of those he managed to save.

**Jan Zwartendijk Memorial** (Laisvės alėja 29) Come here at night to see the installation lit up in tribute to the Jewish lives saved during WWII by the heroic actions of the Dutch diplomat.

numerous charmers in their midst, from boutique guesthouses to excellent hostels, plus numerous room-sharing options.

★**Villa Kaunensis** GUESTHOUSE €
(Kaunas Archdiocese Guesthouse; ☎37-322 597; www.kaunas.lcn.lt/sveciunamai; Rotušės aikštė 21; s/d/tr without bathroom €21/29/39, tr/q with bathroom from €40/49; P❄@🛜) The location of this Catholic archdiocesan guesthouse couldn't be better, snuggled between venerable churches and overlooking the Old Town square. Rooms are a rhapsody in beige, but spacious with high ceilings and big windows. There's a communal kitchen to cook breakfast (not offered) and staff couldn't be friendlier. Book your parking space (€3) in advance.

**Monk's Bunk Kaunas** HOSTEL €
(☎8-620 99695; www.facebook.com/kaunasmonksbunk; Laisvės alėja 48-2; dm €13-15; 🛜) Kaunas' original hostel is still its best. There are only 18 beds here, spread across three spacious dorms with lockers, and a chilled-out vibe encouraging you to get to know your fellow travellers. The large guest kitchen is a boon, the owner is happy to share his local knowledge and the location is second to none.

**Metropolis** HOTEL €
(☎37-205 992; www.metropolishotel.lt; S Daukanto gatvė 21; s/d/tr/q €30/42/56/70; ) This dependable stalwart ('Lietuva' in Soviet times) on a quiet tree-lined street was undergoing a much-needed facelift at research time. Rooms are plain but well fitted out, and time-worn features (such as the sculpted-stone balconies and hefty wooden turnstile leading into the moulded-ceilinged lobby) enhance its charm. Friendly service and buffet breakfast included.

**Apple Economy Hotel** HOTEL €
(☎37-321 404; www.applehotel.lt; Valančiaus gatvė 19; s/d/q €33/44/56; ) Apple consists of 14 compact but appealing rooms with bright pops of colour. There are no frills but it's a serviceable economy option in an excellent location, tucked into a quiet courtyard on the northwestern flank of Old Town.

★**Daugirdas** BOUTIQUE HOTEL €€
(☎37-301 561; www.daugirdas.lt; Daugirdo gatvė 4; s/d/ste incl breakfast €61/65/148; ) This stylish boutique hotel, wedged between central Old Town and the Nemunas River, is one of the most charismatic in Kaunas. Parts of the building date to the 16th century, and the standard rooms are cosy and modern with good-quality beds and bathrooms with heated floors. For something extra special, luxuriate in a Jacuzzi in the timber-beamed Gothic Room.

**Hof Hotel** BUSINESS HOTEL €€
(☎37-367 999; www.hofhotel.eu; Maironio gatvė 21a; r/tr/apt €63/78/100; ) Though aimed largely at the business set, the Hof adds a few soft touches to the decor – plenty of red velvet and soft furniture to flop around on, plus flower-bedecked balconies. Complimentary buffet breakfast is a boon, and so is the location – in a quiet courtyard just off Laisvės alėja.

**Brother House Kaunas** APARTMENT €€
(☎8-615 33171; Kanto gatvė 11; r/studio/apt €39/44/59; ) Decked out in austere greys and whites, offset by the dark-wood furniture and the odd splash of modern art that borders on risqué, these contemporary rooms, studios and delightful self-contained apartments are well located for exploring central Kaunas. Ask for one towards the back if you're a light sleeper.

**Kaunas Hotel** BUSINESS HOTEL €€€
(☎37-750 850; www.kaunashotel.lt; Laisvės alėja 79; s/d/ste from €113/122/143; ) Dating back to 1892, the Kaunas is a slick operation with an eye for business clientele. Glass fronts the top floor where room 512 sports a peek-if-you-dare glass-walled bathroom overlooking tree-lined Laisvės alėja. There's also a pool, sauna and gym (free with deluxe rooms and suites, otherwise there's a €10 surcharge).

## Eating

Getting more diverse by the year, Kaunas' menu roams far beyond traditional Lithuanian cuisine. Choose between Lithuanian classics and wild game in Old Town's atmospheric cellars, or sample some of the country's boldest contemporary cuisine, as well as stellar Indian, fusion, Japanese and other offerings.

★**ManGi Hot Dogs** HOT DOGS €
(☎8-603 46129; www.mangi.lt; Vilniaus gatvė 36; hot dogs €3-7; noon-10pm Sun-Thu, to midnight Fri & Sat) Minimalist decor, hot dogs made with Angus beef and topped with imaginative toppings, plus Dutch fries, oyster shooters and the finest Lithuanian craft beer. Sometimes a combination can be just right.

**Baking Mad** BURGERS €
(☎8-693 90002; www.facebook.com/bakingmadlt; A Mickevičiaus gatvė 30; burgers €6-7; 11am-10pm Mon-Thu, to 11pm Fri & Sat, noon-7pm Sun) The owners of this burger joint opted for a *Breaking Bad* theme and ran with it a few miles: the TV screens episodes of the show, test tubes bubble on the windowsills, and a mannequin in a hazard suit and gas mask perches by the bar. The burgers aren't bad, either; try the (allegedly) spiciest burger in Lithuania.

**Radharanė** VEGETARIAN €
(☎37-320 800; www.radharane.lt/kaunas; Daukšos gatvė 28; mains €3.50-6; 11am-9pm; ) Showing an admirable commitment to plant-based sustenance, the Kaunas branch of this chain vegetarian restaurant serves a broad menu from soy goulash to Thai vegetable curry and curried aubergine. There are also curd-cheese dumplings, potato pancakes and samosas for carb-loading (and keep your eye on the dessert chiller cabinet).

**Motiejaus Kepyklėlė** BAKERY €
(☎8-616 15599; Vilniaus gatvė 7; pastries from €1.20; 7.30am-8pm Mon-Sat, 9am-7pm Sun) In a beautiful historic building, Motiejaus prepares traditional Lithuanian cakes and cookies, alongside *canelés* (French vanilla

cakes), muffins and croissants, plus coffee with a Franco-Italian flavour. Omelettes with interesting ingredients are cooked to order.

**★Moksha** INDIAN €€

(☎8-676 71649; www.facebook.com/cafemoksha; Vasario 16-osios gatvė 6; mains €6-12; ⏰11am-9pm Mon-Fri, noon-9pm Sat, noon-8pm Sun; 📶✍) Moksha reels you in with ambient, plucked-string music, chilli-spiked aromas and personable service. The young hotshot chef from Kerala cooks everything from scratch – from the Thai-style soups to mango fish curry, fresh sambals and chutneys. Most dishes are vegetarian or vegan and spice levels can be adjusted to suit your palate. There are only four tables, so it's worth making reservations.

**★Ieti** FUSION €€

(☎8-626 85228; www.ieti.lt; Rotušės aikštė 6; mains €11-20; ⏰noon-10pm Tue-Thu, to 11pm Fri & Sat, to 8pm Sun; ✍) The chef here has a light and sure touch, and a flair for ingredient pairings that sees mostly locally sourced meat and fresh produce transformed into nicely presented dishes that work very well. Hazelnuts and apple add crunch and sweetness to buckwheat risotto, trout tartare sings with red currant high notes and the tomato and peach soup delights and surprises.

**Sushi Masters** SUSHI €€

(☎8-635 09000; www.facebook.com/sushimasterskaunas; Šv Gertrūdos gatvė 39a; mains €8-13; ⏰11am-10pm Mon-Thu, to midnight Fri & Sat, noon-9pm Sun) Kaunas' best sushi place wouldn't be out of place in a world capital. Uromaki, hosomaki and futomaki rolls are freshly prepped with raw scallops, soft-shell crab and other exciting seafood, there's a nice spread of sashimi, and a congregation of Kaunas' trendies on the outdoor terrace.

**Senieji Rūsiai** EUROPEAN €€

(Old Cellars; ☎37-202 806; www.seniejirusiai.lt; Vilniaus gatvė 34; mains €11-20; ⏰11am-midnight Mon-Thu, to 1am Fri, noon-1am Sat, noon-11pm Sun; 📶) Named for its 17th-century subterranean vaults lined with frescoes, 'Old Cellars' is one of the most atmospheric places in Kaunas for a candlelit dinner. Choose fried catfish or duck with wine-poached pears to match the medieval banquet ambience, or peruse pan-Asian options like tuna steak with green-tea sauce.

Come at lunchtime for main courses priced at a wallet-pleasing €4.

**Bernelių Užeiga** LITHUANIAN €€

(☎37-208 802; www.berneliuuzeiga.lt; Donelaičio gatvė 11; mains €5-10; ⏰11am-10pm Sun-Thu, to 1am Fri & Sat) Stuffed animal heads, peasant shirts and other rustic paraphernalia support the traditional Lithuania theme here, and the voluminous menu covers Lithuanian classics – herrings every which way, cold beetroot soup, *didžkukuliai* (cannonball-like dumplings) – plus stewed venison and dramatically impaled pork, fit for a medieval banquet.

There's a second branch in Old Town, at M Valančiaus gatvė.

**Antis Rūsy** INTERNATIONAL €€

(☎8-615 45666; www.facebook.com/antisrusy; Rotušės aikštė 1; mains €7-17; ⏰11am-11pm Sun-Wed, to midnight Thu, to 2am Fri & Sat; 👪) With an enviable location on the main square, the Duck in the Cellar lets you choose between dining in the subtly lit, centuries-old cellar or on the terrace. Grilled duck with sour cherries is the speciality here, along with a supporting cast of other meat dishes and hearty soups. Kids' menu also.

**Višta Puode** LITHUANIAN €€

(☎8-693 63777; www.vištapuode.lt; Daukanto gatvė 23; mains €6-17; ⏰8am-11pm Sun-Wed, to midnight Thu-Sat; ✍) If you haven't tasted nouvelle Lithuanian cuisine – a departure from gut-busting *cepelinai,* filling enough to get you through a siege – here's your chance. The greenery-bedecked interior suggests wholesomeness and local ingredients are turned into such delights as curd dumplings with nettle sauce and Granny's country chicken soup and duck breast with rhubarb.

**MOMO Grill** STEAK €€

(☎37-297 488; www.facebook.com/steakhouse.kaunas; Karaliaus Mindaugo prospektas 18a; mains €7-19; ⏰11am-10pm Tue-Thu, to 11pm Fri & Sat, to 4pm Sun) The Kaunas branch of the Klaipėda meatery is an altar to steak. It's all exposed brick and chandeliers and prime cuts thrown on the grill just long enough to sear. The desserts are great too; try the pistachio crème brûlée.

**★Uoksas** LITHUANIAN €€€

(☎8-686 38881; www.uoksas.eu; Maironio gatvė 28; mains €17-20, 4-/6-course tasting menu €30/40) 🍃 There's an organic quality to the decor – lots of plants, chairs covered in faux lichen – the menu changes according to the seasons and chef Artūras Naidenko never repeats the same dish twice. There's a commitment to sustainable, seasonal ingredients from the Baltic Sea region and it's best to put yourself in Naidenko's hands by opting for the surprise tasting menus.

**Nüman** NEW NORDIC €€€

(☎8-611 54439; www.facebook.com/numantherestaurant; Nemuno gatvė 43; mains €13-28; ⏰6-11pm Tue-Sat) The decor at Nüman is deliberately understated to direct your attention to the food, which is an essay on the finer points of Nordic cuisine. The menu is short (six starters, four mains, two desserts) and sweet, the pairing of seasonal ingredients inspired, the presentation refined and the wine list well chosen. Book ahead.

## Drinking & Nightlife

Old Town is the place to clank glasses in vaulted pubs, seek out basement cocktail joints and make merry on outdoor tables that spill onto the cobblestones. But more avant-garde nightlife and the best craft beer lies east, in the New Town.

**★Genys Taproom** CRAFT BEER

(☎8-671 88402; www.facebook.com/genyskaunas; Laisvės alėja 21; ⏰5pm-1am Mon-Thu & Sun, to 2am Fri & Sat) A heavy-rock soundtrack, black walls and Kaunas' best craft beer is what Genys Taproom is all about. There are nine or 10 house brews on tap, from the chocolate porter, APA and IPA to the Baltic Pale Ale, and interesting seasonal experiments, such as the raspberry-milkshake ale and a sour, punchy IPA infused with fresh passion fruit.

**★B2O** BAR

(☎8-684 02200; Gedimino gatvė 30; ⏰11am-2am Mon-Thu & Sun, to 4am Fri & Sat) What sets the B2O (the new incarnation of the locally legendary BO bar) apart from its peers is the convivial atmosphere that makes you want to linger for hours, a mellow soundtrack that doesn't preclude conversation and a kicking bar-food menu with global overtones. Part of the proceeds go towards supporting Syrian war victims.

**Kultūra Kavinė** BAR

(☎8-676 25546; www.facebook.com/kauno.kultura; Donelaičio gatvė 14-16; ⏰noon-2am Tue-Sat, to midnight Sun & Mon; 📶) If revolution brews in Kaunas, they'll trace it back to Kultūra Kavinė. The town's dreamers and debaters spill out from this shabby-chic pub, smoking and sipping beers on the concrete terrace. Close to the New Town's galleries and beloved by students, this artful hangout has a raw, earnest feel and open-minded clientele. The best spot in town to mingle.

**Vingiu Dubingiu** CRAFT BEER

(☎8-636 94848; Donelaičio gatvė 41; ⏰4pm-1am Mon-Sat) Inside an old blue wooden house, this friendly bar caters to genuine beer connoisseurs. There are usually 10 rotating brews of tap, from the latest in Lithuanian craft brewing to beers from the US and Germany. Its bottled beer collection is a wonderful intro to Lithuanian craft beer, cider and more.

**2½ Ubuolio** PUB

(☎8-650 66422; www.facebook.com/2supuseobuolio; Palangos gatvė 9; ⏰5pm-2am Tue-Thu & Sun, to 4am Fri & Sat) A den for locals to glug a cold one over trivia nights and sports screenings, this cider pub in a vaulted cellar gets packed out even on weeknights and features no less than 30 different types of fermented apple brew. Good bar food and occasional live music, too.

**NiShA Bar'o Perspektyva** CRAFT BEER

(☎8-611 30030; www.facebook.com/nisha.baro.perspektyva; M Daukšos gatvė 29; ⏰3pm-midnight) This relaxed pint-sized bar is well worth seeking out for its bewildering array of bottled brews from all over the world. Whether you're after a Belgian blonde or an Icelandic Arctic pale ale, odds are, they've got it.

### COFFEE IN KAUNAS

If you're looking for a caffeine buzz, Vero Cafe is the Lithuanian equivalent of Starbucks and ubiquitous all over the city. Ditto: Caffeine Roasters. If you're looking for more of a local flavour, try one of the following:

**Green Cafe** (☎8-612 44335; www.facebook.com/greencafe.europe; Laisvės al 46; ⏰7.30am-9pm Mon-Fri, 9am-8pm Sat, 10am-7pm Sun; 📶) Best speciality coffee shop in town. Two branches in Central Kaunas.

**Knygų Ministerija** (☎8-691 61285; www.facebook.com/knyguministerija; Laisvės alėja 29; ⏰10am-9pm Mon-Sat, to 7pm Sun) Beautiful bookshop, great coffee. What's not to adore?

**Sprugine** (☎37-200 355; Laisvės al 84; doughnuts from €1; ⏰8.30am-8pm Mon-Fri, 9am-8pm Sat, 10am-7pm Sun) Local institution serving no-nonsense coffee along with freshly baked doughnuts.

## Entertainment

Kaunas has a wealth of performing-arts venues and associated companies. Check the daily newspaper *Kauno diena* (www.kaunodiena.lt) for event listings.

**Kaunas State Drama Theatre** THEATRE
(Naciolinis Kauno Dramos Teatras; ☎37-224 064; www.dramosteatras.lt; Laisvės alėja 71; ⊙box office 10.30am-7pm) Kaunas' principal dramatic venue, and one of the oldest in Lithuania, the State Drama Theatre stages classic drama productions and cutting-edge new material. Some of the productions are accompanied by English surtitles. Closed between 15 June and 15 August.

**Kaunas State Musical Theatre** THEATRE
(Muzikinis teatras; ☎37-200 933; www.muzikinisteatras.lt; Laisvės alėja 91; ⊙box office 11am-2pm & 3-6pm Tue-Sat) This handsome late-19th-century building hosts operas, operettas and other musical theatre from September to June.

**Kaunas Philharmonic** CONCERT VENUE
(Kauno filharmonija; ☎37-222 558; www.kaunofilharmonija.lt; L Sapiegos gatvė 5; ⊙box office 2-6pm Tue-Sun) Housed in the former Palace of Justice, the Kaunas Philharmonic is the city's main concert hall for classical music.

**O Kodėl Ne?** LIVE MUSIC
(☎8-670 67811; www.facebook.com/okodelnekaune; Perkūno alėja 4; ⊙3pm-1am Mon-Thu, to 3am Fri, noon-3am Sat, to midnight Sun) This rather ramshackle venue in the park tries to be all things to all people – a pleasant cafe, a hip bar, and a live-music venue staging DJ sets and other live acts. Most of the time it succeeds. The name translates as 'Why Not?' Why not, indeed?

**Džem Pub** LIVE MUSIC
(☎8-657 45003; www.dzempub.lt; Laisvės alėja 59, 5th fl; admission €5; ⊙5pm-3am Tue-Thu, to 4am Fri & Sat) With excellent views from its 5th-floor balcony and a wide choice of beers, Džem caters to a young, alternative crowd with its ever-changing program of live acts and DJs.

## Shopping

**★Ali Šokoladinė** CHOCOLATE
(☎8-678 82223; www.alisokoladine.lt; Laisvės alėja 41; ⊙9am-8pm Mon-Fri, 10am-9pm Sat & Sun) Imagine a pistachio or salted-caramel eclair so picture-perfect that you're loath to take a first bite, plus macarons in every imaginable colour and perfect cubes of handmade chocolate, sitting in their prim black gift boxes. It's all here, and it's all wonderful.

**Egidijaus Rudinsko Grafikos Galerija** ART
(☎8-688 24486; www.egidijusrudinskas.com; Kurpiu gatvė 13-2; ⊙noon-6pm Mon-Fri, to 4pm Sat) A great place to pick up beautiful lithographs, etchings and prints by the eponymous Egidijaus, whose works are fit to illustrate your favourite fantasy fiction.

**Livi Design** FASHION & ACCESSORIES
(☎8-676 10240; www.livi.lt; Vilniaus gatvė 15; ⊙11am-6pm Mon-Fri, to 4pm Sat) Smart and sassy women's streetwear by Lithuanian designers, particularly Kaunas-born Lina Sliosoraitė – Janušauskė (Livi Design). Choose between her skirts, tops and dresses, Knoto and Alpacos sweaters, trousers by K Lieb or Givali and more.

**kARTu** FASHION & ACCESSORIES
(☎8-630 75019; www.kartustudio.com; Donelaičio gatvė 24-1; ⊙11am-6.30pm Mon-Fri, to 4pm Sat) High-quality Italian leather transformed into exclusive leather bags and purses for women by Kaunas-based Lithuanian designers.

## Information

### MEDICAL

**Kauno Medicinos Universiteto Klinikos** (☎emergency 37-326 089; www.kaunoklinikos.lt; Eivenių gatvė 2; 24hr emergency) University medical clinic for emergencies. Approximately 2.5km north of the New Town; catch trolleybus 1 from the Old or New Town.

### MONEY

**DNB Nord** (Laisvės alėja 86; ⊙8am-5.30pm Mon-Thu, to 5pm Fri) Foreign exchange and ATM.

**SEB Bankas** (www.seb.lt; Laisvės alėja 82; ⊙8.30am-5pm Mon-Fri) Bank and ATM.

### TOURIST INFORMATION

**Kaunas** (www.kaunas.lt) Official city website.

**Kaunas in Your Pocket** (www.inyourpocket.com/kaunas) Annual city guide sold in hotels, art galleries and news kiosks for €1 (or download from the website).

**Tourist Office** (☎8-616 50991; www.visit.kaunas.lt; Rotušės aikštė 15, Town Hall; ⊙9am-1pm & 2-6pm Mon-Fri, 10am-1pm & 2-4pm Sat, 10am-1pm & 2-3pm Sun) Inside Kaunas' Town Hall, this friendly, multilingual tourist office can book accommodation, sell maps and guides, and arrange bicycle rental and guided tours of Old Town.

## Getting There & Away

### AIR

**Kaunas International Airport** (☎8-612 44442; www.kaunas-airport.lt; Oro uosto gatvė, Karmėlava; ⊙6am-midnight; 🚌29, 29E) is situated 10km north of the city centre and served by direct flights to/from Dublin, Frankfurt, Liverpool, London, Milan, Paris, Stockholm, Turku and Tel Aviv. Ryanair handles the bulk of the airport's traffic. Bus 29G (€1) runs to the centre of town; a taxi should cost less than €20.

### BUS

The long-distance **bus station** (Autobusų Stotis; ☎37-409 060; www.autobusubilietai.lt; Vytauto prospektas 24; ⊙ticket office 6am-9.30pm) handles intercity buses within Lithuania and buses further afield. Information is available from the timetable on the wall or online. There's also luggage storage here.

For domestic tickets, try the Eurolines subsidiary Kautra (www.kautra.lt). Buy tickets inside the main bus terminal or via www.autobusubilietai.lt.

Several companies offer international services, including Eurolines (www.eurolines.lt) and its Lux Express (www.luxexpress.lt) subsidiary. Buy tickets in the main hall. **Ecolines** (☎37-202 022; www.ecolines.net; Vytauto prospektas 27; ⊙9am-6pm Mon-Fri, to 3pm Sat) also sells tickets for international destinations.

Daily services within Lithuania and the Baltic countries include the following:

| DESTINATION | PRICE (€) | DURATION (HR) | FREQUENCY |
|---|---|---|---|
| Birštonas | 3.14 | 1 | 2-3 hourly |
| Druskininkai | 9.60-12 | 2¼-2¾ | hourly |
| Klaipėda | 15.20-17.60 | 2½-4½ | 1-2 hourly |
| Palanga | 16.15-19.40 | 3-4¼ | 11 daily |
| Panevėžys | 7.70-10.40 | 1½-2½ | 1-2 hourly |
| Rīga (Latvia) | 20-29 | 4¼-7 | 3 daily |
| Šiauliai | 10.60-12.40 | 2½-3¾ | 1-2 hourly |
| Tallinn (Estonia) | 33 | 11½ | daily |
| Vilnius | 6.60-10 | 1½-1¾ | 4-5 hourly |

### CAR

**Autobanga** (☎5-212 7777; www.autobanga.lt; Oro uosto gatvė 4) and large car-rental franchises have offices at Kaunas airport. If you're only looking to rent a car for a few hours, consider downloading the CityBee (www.citybee.lt) app.

### TRAIN

From the **train station** (Geležinkelio Stotis; ☎7005 5111; www.traukiniobilietas.lt; MK Čiurlionio gatvė 16; ⊙ticket office 4.10am-9.45pm) there are regular direct trains to/from Vilnius (€3.60 to €7, 65 minutes to 1½ hours, six daily). To get to Šiauliai you have to change either in Kaišiadorys or Vilnius. To reach Klaipėda (and Curonian Spit), you'll have to backtrack and change trains in Kaišiadorys.

## Getting Around

### CAR & MOTORCYCLE

Outside Old Town, driving in Kaunas is a relatively simple affair, with plentiful parking and few one-way streets. Old Town is a warren of small cobbled alleys, however, and parking can be pricey. Some coin meters charge you between 8am and 8pm Monday to Friday, while the ones around the main square require payment daily from 8am till midnight.

### BICYCLE & ELECTRIC SCOOTER

Kaunas is a cyclist-friendly city with a good number of cycle lanes and particularly attractive long rides along the river – east to Panemunė Park and Pažaislis Forest Park and monastery, or west for some 15km to a couple of attractive villages.

There are several bicycle rental schemes that you can use with multiple pick-up points across the city. One is Kaunas Bike (www.kaunasbike.lt), rented using the Dropbyke app. CityBee (www.citybee.lt) charges €0.50 per 30 minutes for bicycle rental and also rents electric scooters (€0.10 per minute, plus €0.50 activation fee); cars are also available for short-term rental for €5 per hour. Finally, Bolt (www.bolt.eu) rents out electric scooters at comparable prices.

### BUS & TROLLEYBUS

Buses and trolleybuses run from 5am to 11pm and tickets from the driver cost €1. Alternatively, you can buy a Kauno Kortelė (Kaunas Card) from a Kauno Spauda or Naversen kiosk for €1.50, top it up, and pay only €0.70 each time you press it to the on-board card reader. There are also three-/seven-day passes available for €5.50/10.

Minibuses shadow routes and run later than regular buses; drivers sell tickets for €1.30, and will stop wherever you wish. For information on public transport, see the Kaunas Public Transport (www.kvt.lt) website.

To get to/from the airport, take minibus 120 from the local bus station on Šv Gertrūdos gatvė or bus 29G from the stop on Vytauto prospektas. Buses depart at least once an hour between 7am and 11.30pm.

Trolleybuses 1, 5 and 7 run north from the train station along Vytauto prospektas, west along Kęstučio gatvė and Nemuno gatvė, then north on Birštono gatvė. Returning, they head east along Šv Gertrūdos gatvė, Ožeškienės gatvė and Donelaičio gatvė, then south down Vytauto prospektas to the bus and train stations.

There are also skeletal night-bus routes – 13N, 14N and 37N – from Thursday to Saturday.

### TAXI & BOLT

Several taxi companies operate in Kaunas and you're always best advised to order one in advance by phone. Try **OptiTAXI** (☎8-644 64646). Cheaper and very convenient, Bolt (www.bolt.eu) is the Baltics' answer to Uber; download the app.

# Kėdainiai

☎347 / POP 24,100

Some 55km north of Kaunas, Kėdainiai is among Lithuania's oldest towns. Its origins date back to the late 14th century; for around 300 years the town was owned by the Radvila family, one of the most powerful of the Grand Duchy of Lithuania. When Kėdainiai became one of the religious and cultural centres for Protestantism in Lithuania in the mid-16th century, that movement attracted a large Scottish population, and Scots played a prominent part in Kėdainiai's judiciary and education systems well into the 19th century. A large Jewish community contributed to the town's cultural melting pot and agriculture (Kėdainiai's known as the cucumber capital of Lithuania) until their demise during WWII.

Kėdainiai's compact, cobbled Old Town is among Lithuania's most attractive. While it's entirely possible to visit Kėdainiai on a day trip from Kaunas, it's really worth lingering overnight.

## Sights

**★Kėdainiai Regional Museum** MUSEUM

(☎347-53 685; www.kedainiumuziejus.lt; Didžioji gatvė 19; adult/concession €2/1; ⏲10am-5pm Wed-Sat, to 3pm Sun) Housed inside a former 18th-century Carmelite monastery, this is a particularly thorough introduction to the history of the region and the town. Displays run the gamut from Stone Age tools and Bronze Age weaponry to centuries-old furniture, ceramics and a multilingual multimedia presentation on Jewish Kėdainiai. One of the highlights here is a room full of elaborately carved wooden crosses – masterpieces of Lithuanian folk art by Vincas Svirskis.

**Great Market Square** SQUARE

(Didžiosios Rinkos aikštė) The square is overlooked by a particularly photogenic trio of 17th-century merchants' houses as well as the impressive town hall with a rococo sun dial in the courtyard and the Evangelical Reformed Church. Sitting in the square is a monument depicting a massive chest that symbolises the treasury of Grand Duchy of Lithuania, guarded by Radvila, the town's former hetman (military commander).

**Janina Monkutė-Marks Museum-Gallery** GALLERY

(☎347-57 398; www.jmm-muziejus.lt; J Basanavičiaus gatvė 45; adult/concession €2/1; ⏲10am-6pm Tue-Fri, to 3pm Sat) Born in Radviliškis, artist Janina Monkutė-Marks grew up in Kėdainiai and this museum showcases a permanent collection of her vibrant, joyful paintings upstairs. The ground floor stages temporary exhibitions of contemporary Lithuanian and international art.

**Arnett House** MUSEUM

(www.kedainiumuziejus.lt; Radvilų gatvė; ⏲8am-5pm Mon-Fri) FREE This 17th-century building was once owned by the Scottish merchant John Arnett and now hosts craft demonstrations. Come here to learn about the traditional trades of wood carving, wicker- and cloth-weaving, and ceramics.

**Old Market Square** SQUARE

(Senosios Rinkos Aikštė) Kėdainiai's Jewish community originally settled off this 15th-century market square in the first half of the 17th century. A wooden synagogue, built in 1655, was replaced by the **Great Summer Synagogue** in the 18th century, now an art school. Next to it is the **Small Winter Synagogue**, now a multicultural centre that hosts concerts and exhibitions. In front of it is a **Holocaust memorial** comprising a triangle of stones and an all-seeing eye.

**Holocaust Memorial** MEMORIAL

(Žydų Žudynių Vieta ir Kapas; off Rte 144) When the Nazis took control of Lithuania in July 1941, they forced the Jews of Kėdainiai, Šėta and Žeimiai communities to move into a closed ghetto. On 28 August 1941, the vast majority – 2076 Jews – was brutally murdered here and dumped in the ravine. Today the spot is

## Kėdainiai

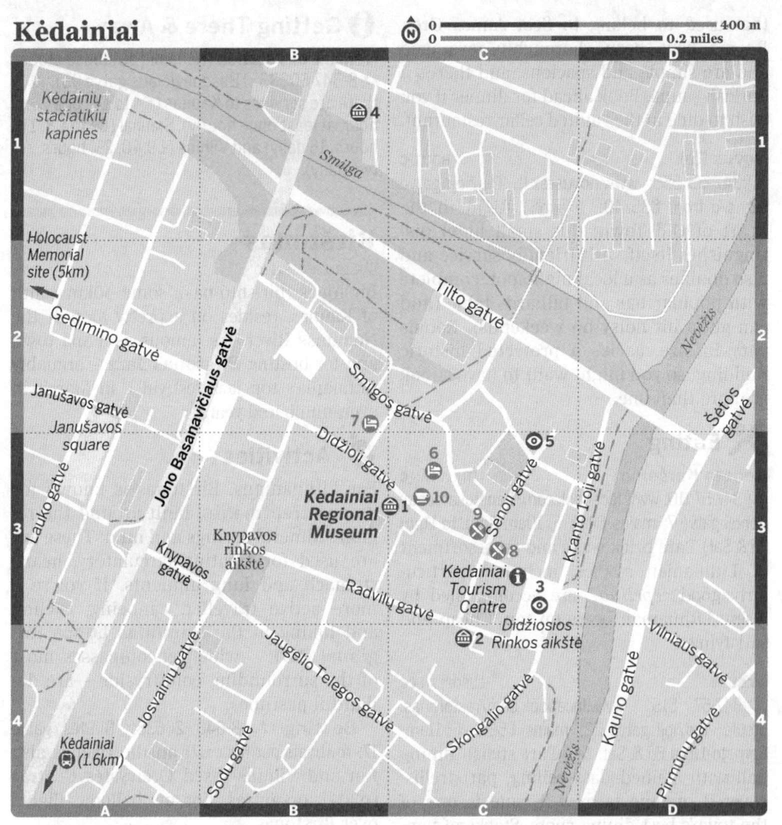


## Kėdainiai

**Top Sights**
1 Kėdainiai Regional Museum .......... C3

**Sights**
2 Arnett House .......... C4
3 Great Market Square .......... C3
4 Janina Monkutė-Marks Museum-Gallery .......... B1
5 Old Market Square .......... C3

**Sleeping**
6 Grėjaus Namas .......... C3
7 Novus Rex .......... B2

**Eating**
8 Beneto Karčema .......... C3
9 Ursule .......... C3

**Drinking & Nightlife**
10 Kavamanija .......... C3

marked by a metal board, imprinted with the names of the dead, and a small stone memorial, flanked with candles. It's signposted off Rte 144, 15km northwest of town.

## Festivals & Events

**Cucumber Festival** FOOD & DRINK
(www.kedainiutvic.lt; Jul) Taking place over several days in mid-July, this fun festival celebrates the town's favourite vegetable – the cucumber. Here's your chance to try a surprising variety of dishes made from the green wonder.

## Sleeping

**Grėjaus Namas** HISTORIC HOTEL €
(Grey's House Hotel; 347-51 500; www.grejausnamas.lt; Didžioji gatvė 36; s/d from €35/44; ) Adorned with the flag and thistle of Scotland, this historic hotel is an 18th-century mansion

that used to belong to Scot James Grey. Rooms have been thoroughly revamped and are simple and spacious, and there's a Turkish sauna. Book ahead for dinner if you wish to dine in the vaulted cellar restaurant.

**Novus Rex** HOTEL €
(☎347 55 555; www.novusrex.lt; Didžioji gatvė 52; s/d from €35/40; P❄📶) Right in the heart of Old Town, this small hotel distinguishes itself with friendly service and also doubles as a local nightspot, complete with popular bar and billiards table (and can get a bit noisy on weekends). Rooms vary in size, as it's a protected historic building, so you might want to have a look at more than one.

## Eating

**Beneto Karčema** LITHUANIAN €
(☎347-57 110; www.facebook.com/benetokarcema; Senoji gatvė 7; mains €4-7; ⏰10am-8pm, to 11pm Fri & Sat) Bare brick walls and an assortment of Lithuanian staples, including particularly good *cepelinai*, are accompanied by a few Lithuanian beers on tap. Cheap and satisfying.

**Ursule** EUROPEAN €€
(☎347-57 515; www.facebook.com/restoranas.ursule; Didžioji gatvė 22; mains €5-12; ⏰11am-8pm, to 11pm Fri & Sat; 🌿) Part stylish dining hall with stained-glass ceiling, part trellis-covered organic burrow, Ursule is one of the town's best dining spots. Stacks of pancakes and veggie burgers are joined on the menu by the likes of beetroot carpaccio with herring, Caesar salad and an array of meat- and fish-heavy mains. Service is sweet and prompt.

## Drinking & Nightlife

**Kavamanija** COFFEE
(☎8-656 86355; www.facebook.com/kavamanija; Didžioji gatvė 26; ⏰8am-8pm Mon-Fri, from 10am Sat & Sun; 📶) The one and only speciality coffee shop in town. They roast their own beans and there's a decent assortment of sweet bites to go with your brew.

## Information

**Kėdainiai Tourism Centre** (☎347-56 900; www.kedainiutvic.lt; Didžiosios Rinkos aikštė 6; ⏰8am-6pm Mon-Fri, 10am-5pm Sat, to 3pm Sun) Multilingual staff are happy to advise on Kėdainiai's attractions, accommodation and dining scene.

## Getting There & Away

From the **bus station** (Kėdainių autobusų stotis; ☎8-347 60333; J Basanavičiaus gatvė 93), there are services to Kaunas (€4 to €5, one hour, at least once hourly), Šiauliai (€7 to €8, 1¾ hours, 16 daily) and Vilnius (€9.40, 2¾ hours, two daily).

# Birštonas

☎319 / POP 4120

Birštonas (bir-shto-nas), some 40km south of Kaunas, resides on a pretty loop of the Nemunas River. It's famous as a spa town and for hosting **Birštonas Jazz** – arguably Lithuania's top jazz festival – in March in even-numbered years.

## Activities

For Lithuanians, Birštonas is known for its **spa treatments**, built around the region's mineral springs and mud. These are are used for treating circulatory, heart, stomach and lung ailments. If you're a more active traveller, canoeing, cycling and hiking in the **Nemunas Loops Regional Park** – which encompasses most of the surrounding countryside – are delightful pastimes.

**Boating** (☎8-640 26638; Birutės gatvė 17; rowboats per hour €7) on the river is also fun and Vilnius-based Oreivystės Centras (p304) organises hot-air balloon flights over Birštonas.

**Eglės Sanatorija** SPA
(☎319-42 142; www.sanatorija.lt; Algirdo gatvė 14; ⏰8am-5pm Mon-Fri) Offering spas, mud baths, week-long treatments and B&B (from €60 per night), Eglės is a well-established spa in central Birštonas, not far from the broad Nemunas River. It's excellent value: a one-hour massage can be had for as little as €30, or a mineral bath for €10, plus there's an amber spa.

**Bicycles Birštonas** CYCLING
(Dviračiai Birštone; ☎8-677 77472; Pušyno gatvė 75; per hour/day €3/10; ⏰9am-10pm May-Sep) Hire a bike in the summer months.

**Vytenis** CRUISE
(Pušyno gatvė; adult/child €12/7; ⏰3pm Sun) Leaving from the pier on Pušyno gatvė, this two-tiered pleasure craft takes up to 50 passengers for a one-hour jaunt to the Verknė River.

## Sleeping & Eating

**Hotel Audenis** HOTEL €

(☎319-61 300; www.audenis.lt; Lelijų gatvė 3; s/d €40/49; P@🛜) This very pleasant hotel has simple rooms in an array of pastel colours. Friendly staff can organise kayaking, bike rental and other pastimes, and the terraced cafe is a fine spot for a light lunch.

**Domus Hotel** HOTEL €€

(☎8-616 38104; www.hoteldomus.lt; Birutės gatvė 21; s/d/tr/f €47/60/80/100; P🛜) Overlooking the Nemunas river, this tranquil property is all simple, light-filled rooms with blond-wood furniture and friendly staff. There's no spa on-site, but guests get vouchers for a nearby spa and the breakfast buffet is excellent.

**Villa Luxuria** LUXURY HOTEL €€€

(☎8-699 64529; www.luxuria.lt; Kampiškių gatvė 8; r €75-180; P🛜🏊) Located on the banks of the Nemunas, away from the town centre and surrounded by forest, Nemuno Slėnis offers seclusion and comfort. The interior is lavish, with rooms decorated in plush, antique furniture and draped in deep, warm colours. There's a spa, restaurant and fitness centre in the complex.

**Restoranas Kurhauzas** EUROPEAN €€

(☎8-687 23801; www.facebook.com/restoranaskurhauzas; B Sruogos gatvė 2; mains €7-13; ⏲noon-10pm Tue-Fri, 10am-11pm Sat & Sun) This family-run restaurant executes dishes from its pan-European repertoire with flair and gusto. Standout mains include risotto with caramelised pear, steamed mussels, nicely grilled steak. River views from the terrace are a bonus.

## Information

**Birštonas Tourism Information Centre** (Birštono turizmo informacijos centras; ☎319-65 740; www.visitbirstonas.lt; B Sruogos gatvė 4; ⏲9am-6pm Mon-Fri, 10am-6pm Sat, to 4pm Sun) While some of the printed information isn't available in English, the helpful staff can advise on spas, river activities, hiking, accommodation and more.

**Nemunas Loops Regional Park Visitor Centre** (Nemuno kilpŭ regioninio parko; ☎319-65 610; www.nemunokilpos.lt; Tylioji gatvė 1; ⏲8am-noon & 12.45-5pm Mon-Thu, to 3.45pm Fri, 10am-4pm Sat May-Oct) Provides essential information on hiking, camping, cycling and nature-watching in the gorgeous Nemunas Loops National Park, 250 sq km of meandering waterway, forests and gentle hills. Guides can also be arranged (€22 per hour).

## Getting There & Away

From Birštonas there are buses to Kaunas (€3.15, one hour, twice-hourly) and Vilnius (€7.20, two hours, nine daily).

# Šiauliai

☎41 / POP 100,100

Visitors from far and wide descend on Lithuania's fourth-largest city, Šiauliai (show-ley) to visit the Hill of Crosses, a startling crucifix-cloaked mound north of the city. For some, it's a religious pilgrimage; others come to pay respects and erect a cross to those who've perished in recent conflicts, while curiosity draws the rest.

Aside from the legendary Hill of Crosses, Šiauliai has a few niche museums in the city centre, while Communist-era architecture lends the city a bit of a time warp feel.

## Sights

Šiauliai is home to some of Lithuania's most niche museums, all of which lie either on or near the main avenue, Vilniaus gatvė.

**★Hill of Crosses** MONUMENT

(Kryžių Kalnas; ☎41-370 860; Jurgaičiai; ⏲information centre 9am-6pm) Lithuania's fabled Hill of Crosses is a symbol of defiance as much as a pilgrimage site. More than 100,000 crosses have been planted on this low hill, many of them strung with rosary beads that rattle softly in the breeze. The tradition began during the 1831 Uprising and reached its height in the 1960s, in defiance of anti-religious Soviet rule. At night locals crept here to lay crosses, infuriating their oppressors. It's 12km north of Šiauliai (2km off Hwy A12) near Jurgaičiai.

Repeated efforts to bulldoze the hill during the 1960s and '70s didn't deter locals from placing crosses here, despite the harsh punishments for being caught. Today it is forbidden to remove a cross from the site, and any visitor may plant a cross (up to a certain size). Enterprising vendors sell simple wooden crucifixes near the visitor centre; they loan marker pens for devotees to write a family name, prayer or wish onto the cross before placing it in the soil.

Large and tiny, expensive and cheap, wood and metal, the crosses are devotional, to accompany prayers, or finely carved folk-art masterpieces. Others are memorials tagged with flowers, a photograph or other mementos of the deceased, and inscribed

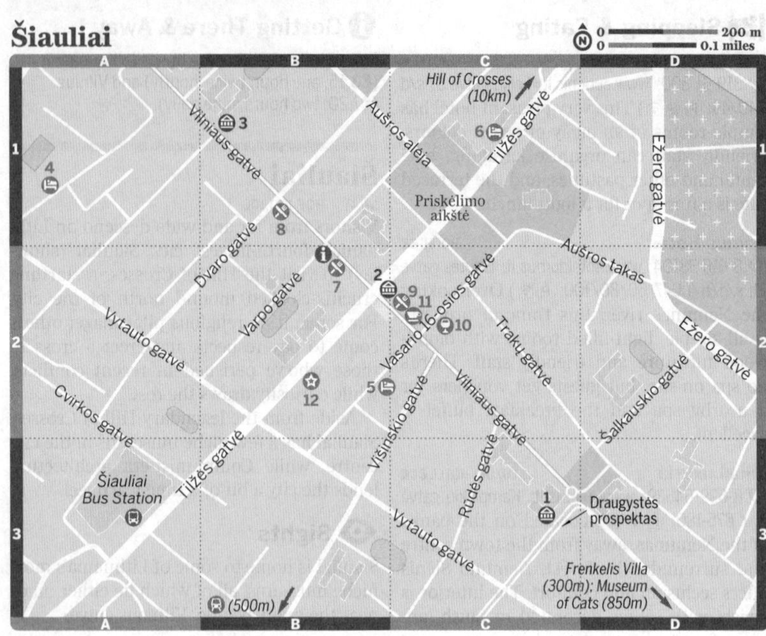




## Šiauliai

**Sights**

1 Bicycle Museum ........ C3
2 Photography Museum ........ C2
3 Radio & Television Museum ........ B1

**Sleeping**

4 Juro Guesthouse ........ A1
5 Šaulys Hotel ........ B2
6 Šiauliai College Youth Hostel ........ C1

**Eating**

7 Arkos ........ B2
8 Cask 215 ........ B1
9 Leja ........ C2

**Drinking & Nightlife**

10 Black Bar ........ C2
11 Caffeine LT ........ C2

**Entertainment**

12 Saulė ........ B2

with a sweet or sacred message. Traditional Lithuanian *koplytstulpis* (wooden sculptures of a figure topped with a little roof) intersperse the crosses, as do magnificent sculptures of the Sorrowful Christ (Rūpintojėlis). If you wish to add your own, souvenir traders in the car park sell crosses big and small. Some of the crosses are devotional, others are memorials (many for people deported to Siberia). They vary greatly in size and some are accompanied by mournful statues of the Virgin Mary. The devout come from far and wide; you may spot a memorial to 9/11 victims and another to Ukrainians killed in ongoing Russia-Ukraine conflict.

A pathway leads from the hill to a modern **chapel**; it's worth looking inside to see a view of the Hill of Crosses perfectly framed in the large window at the altar.

Legends swirl around the Hill of Crosses. Some locals claim that the mound conceals the bodies of 14th-century warriors, others swear that it's haunted by monks. It's more than likely that the hill was a pre-Christian worship site.

An alternative view of the cross-swamped hill is from inside the chapel of the modern brick **monastery**. Now home to around a dozen Franciscan monks, it was built behind the hill from 1997 to 2000. The monastery was allegedly the idea of the late Pope John Paul II, who said after visiting the hill in 1993 he would like to see a place of prayer here. Behind the altar in the church, the striking backdrop seen through the ceiling-to-floor window of the Hill of Crosses is very moving; Italian architect Angelo Polesello designed it.

From the Hwy A12, it's another 2km east from a well-marked turn-off ('Kryžių kalnas 2'). From Šiauliai, take a Joniškis-bound bus (€1.50, 10 minutes, up to seven daily) to the 'Domantai' stop and walk for 20 minutes, or grab a taxi (around €20).

By bicycle, the Hill of Crosses makes for a gentle three-hour trip out and back, mostly along paved bicycle paths that lie to the side of the main road. The tourist office hires out bikes (€1.50 per hour) and can show the route (mostly straight along the main road in the direction of Rīga, turning right at the sign for the last 2km.

**Frenkelis Villa** MUSEUM

(Ch Frenkelio Vila; ☎41-524 389; www.ausrosmuziejus.lt; Vilniaus gatvė 74; adult/child €3/1.50; ⏲10am-6pm Tue, Thu & Fri, to 7pm Wed, 11am-5pm Sat & Sun) To the east of the town centre stands Frenkelis Villa, built in art-nouveau style in 1908 for the then leather baron of Šiauliai. It survived WWII unscathed and was used as a military hospital by the Soviets from 1944 until 1993, at which time it was turned over to the city. The exterior has been spruced up, and the interior has been lovingly restored to its former glory, with dark-wood panelling and period furniture featuring heavily throughout.

**Photography Museum** GALLERY

(☎41-524 396; www.fotomuziejus.lt; Vilniaus gatvė 140; adult/child €2/1; ⏲10am-6pm Tue, Thu & Fri, to 7pm Wed, 11am-5pm Sat & Sun) Special exhibitions shine a spotlight on Lithuania's contemporary photography talent, while the gallery's permanent collection features photography from the mid-20th century plus historic photography equipment.

**Bicycle Museum** MUSEUM

(Dviračių Muziejus; ☎41-524 395; www.ausrosmuziejus.lt; Vilniaus gatvė 139; adult/child €2/1; ⏲10am-6pm Tue, Thu & Fri, to 7pm Wed,11am-5pm Sat) An endearing little museum devoted to vintage bicycles and Lithuanian cycling history is spread across three floors of a grim-looking tower block in central Šiauliai. Start by testing your own pedal power on one of the interactive exhibits, before admiring 19th-century wooden bikes, Soviet designs and more contemporary models.

**Museum of Cats** MUSEUM

(Katinų Muziejus; ☎8-683 69844; Žuvininkų gatvė 18, Jaunųjų gamtininkų centras; adult/child €1.50/0.75; ⏲10am-5pm Tue-Fri, 9am-4pm Sat) Cat-lovers will certainly want to venture out to this museum southeast of the centre to see an unusual collection of feline memorabilia, including endless displays of porcelain cats and photogenic felines on the walls. There are even a couple of live cats on the premises that shadow you as you take in the various rooms.

**Radio & Television Museum** MUSEUM

(Radijo ir Televizijos Muziejus; ☎41-524 399; www.ausrosmuziejus.lt; Vilniaus gatvė 174; adult/child €1/0.50; ⏲10am-7pm Wed, to 5pm Thu & Fri, 11am-5pm Sat) Šiauliai was home to some of Lithuania's first amateur radio operators in the 1920s, so it's a fitting locale for this eclectic collection of radios, TVs and phonographs. Particularly enjoyable are the big old radio receivers and some Soviet-era TV sets that were produced at nearby factories.

## Sleeping

**Šiauliai College Youth Hostel** HOSTEL €

(Šiaulių Kolegijos Jaunimo Navynės Namai; ☎41-523 764; www.jnn.svako.lt; Tilžės gatvė 159; s/d/tr/q €20/26/36/40; ⏲reception 7am-11pm; P 📶) This renovated former college has been turned into a somewhat sterile hostel with kitchen and TV room that's unlikely to make your social media posts, though the central location's a winner. Reception staff don't speak much English, but they do their best to help.

**Juro Guesthouse** GUESTHOUSE €€

(☎8-618 74886; www.juroguesthouse.lt; S Nėries gatvė 7; s/d/tr €30/32/36; P 📶) This spotless, well-appointed guesthouse is just a short stroll away from Vilniaus gatvė and its restaurants and the garden and communal balcony are great in summer. The owner's English is rudimentary, but she's super-helpful.

**Šaulys Hotel** HOTEL €€

(☎41-520 812; www.saulys.lt; Vasario 16-osios gatvė 40; s/d/tr/q incl breakfast €60/80/110/140; P @ 📶) This four-star establishment is Šiauliai's swankiest choice. Hidden behind its deep-red facade are suitably plush rooms in understated greys and browns, a quality 1950s-style restaurant and English-speaking staff who can organise paragliding and other outdoor activities.

## THE ART OF CRAFTING CROSSES

Crosses were once symbols of sacred fervour and national identity, both pagan and Catholic; cross crafting is the embodiment of Lithuanian contradiction.

Handed down from master to pupil, the crosses were carved from oak, the sacred pagan tree. They were made as offerings to gods, and were draped with food, coloured scarves (for a wedding) or aprons (for fertility). Once consecrated by priests, they became linked with Christian ceremonies, with unmistakable sacred significance. The crosses, which measure up to 5m in height, then became symbols of defiance against occupation.

When it comes to explaining the origin of the Hill of Crosses (p355), there are almost as many myths as crosses. Some claim it was created in three days and three nights by the bereaved families of warriors killed in a great battle. Others say it was the work of a father who, in a desperate bid to cure his sick daughter, planted a cross on the hill. Pagan traditions tell stories of sacred fires being lit here and tended by celestial virgins.

Crosses first appeared here in the 14th century. They multiplied after bloody anti-tsarist uprisings to become a potent symbol of suffering and hope.

During the Soviet era planting a cross was an arrestable offence – but pilgrims kept coming to commemorate the thousands killed and deported. The hill was bulldozed at least three times. In 1961 the Red Army destroyed the 2000-odd crosses that stood on the mound, sealed off the tracks leading to the hill and dug ditches at its base, yet overnight more crosses appeared. In 1972 they were destroyed after the immolation of a Kaunas student in protest at Soviet occupation. But by 1990 the Hill of Crosses comprised a staggering 40,000 crosses, spanning 4600 sq metres. Since Independence they have multiplied at least 10 times – and are multiplying still; some of the most recent ones include tributes to Ukrainians killed in the ongoing Russian-Ukrainian war.

In 1993 Pope John Paul II celebrated mass here (his pulpit still stands) and graced the hill a year later with a papal cross, adding his own message to the mountain of scribbled-on crosses.

## Eating

The better restaurants are clustered along central Vilniaus gatvė. Pick up groceries and fast food southwest of the centre, on the corner of Cvirkos gatvė and Tilžės gatvė.

**★Leja** EUROPEAN €€

(☎41-585 735; www.facebook.com/lejacafe; Vilniaus gatvė 138; mains €7-18; ⏲11am-11pm) There's a touch of the belle époque about Leja, from the rococo-style armchairs to the chandeliers and the mellow tinkling of the background piano. The menu is the most imaginative in town: brunch is eggs Benedict or herring tartar with wasabi ice cream. The rest of the day, choose from imaginative salads, or pasta with orange, prawns and zucchini.

**Cask 215** GASTROPUB €€

(☎8-614 90995; www.facebook.com/cask215; Vilniaus gatvė 215; mains €5-15; ⏲noon-10pm Mon & Tue, to midnight Wed & Thu, to 1am Fri & Sat, to 7pm Sun) Inside this glossy restaurant-bar, friendly servers present adept versions of American and Lithuanian fast food, from juicy burgers to pork ribs with smoky stewed beans. It's good for dinner with friends but a bit loud for an intimate tête-a-tête. The cocktail list is among the best in town.

**Arkos** LITHUANIAN €€

(☎41-520 205; www.arkos.lt; Vilniaus gatvė 213; mains €6-13; ⏲10am-midnight) Dishes appear hauled straight from a medieval banquet table in cellar restaurant Arkos. Brick vaults add to the old-timey appeal while the Lithuanian and international mains – mushroom-stuffed turkey, wine-marinated duck and gargantuan portions of grilled pork – are executed with flair. There's live music on Saturday nights.

A couple of vegetarian options are offered, too.

## Drinking & Nightlife

**★Black Bar** BAR

(☎8-642 44445; www.blackbar.lt; Vasario 16-osios gatvė 48; ⏲noon-11pm Mon-Wed, to midnight Thu, to 4am Fri & Sat, to 8pm Sun) Imagine you're on a date with a vampire. This is exactly the sort of place the stylish undead would take you to: dark wood and leather banquettes, black walls and chandeliers twinkling in the atmospheric gloom. Then there's the clever wine list, the imaginative cocktails, Lithuanian beers on tap, plus plenty of meaty gastropub dishes to sink your fangs into.

**Caffeine LT** COFFEE
(☎8-699 77541; www.caffeine.lt; Vilniaus gatvė 136; ⊙7am-10pm Mon-Thu, to 11pm Fri, 9am-11pm Sat, 9am-9pm Sun) The local branch of the popular nation-wide chain serves reliably good coffee in various forms and is decked out with fantastic photos of the region.

## ☆ Entertainment

**Saulė** CONCERT VENUE
(☎41-424 424; www.saule.lt; Tilžės gatvė 140; ⊙hours vary) Šiauliai's principal concert hall hosts chamber orchestras, ensemble choirs and more. It's worth a visit for the stained glass alone: at 200m sq, it's the largest of the kind in Lithuania and depicts the 1236 Battle of Saulė.

## ℹ Information

**Šiauliai Bankas** (☎8-700 55055; www.sb.lt; Vilniaus gatvė 167; ⊙8am-6pm Mon-Fri) A major bank outlet handy to the town centre.

**Tourist Office** (☎41-523 110; http://tic.siauliai.lt; Vilniaus gatvė 213; ⊙9am-6pm Mon-Fri, 10am-4pm Sat Sep-May, plus 10am-2pm Sun Jun-Aug) This multilingual tourist office sells maps and guides, makes accommodation bookings and provides information on the local bus network.

## ℹ Getting There & Away

### BUS

Direct services to/from the **bus station** (Šiaulių autobusų stotis; ☎8-7005 5066; Tilžes gatvė 109) include the following.

| DESTINATION | PRICE (€) | DURATION (HR) | FREQUENCY (PER DAY) |
|---|---|---|---|
| Kaunas | 10-13 | 2½-3¾ | 14 |
| Klaipėda | 12-14.50 | 3-3½ | 6; more via Kryžkalnis |
| Palanga | 11 | 3 | 3; more via Klaipėda or Kryžkalnis |
| Panevėžys | 6-7 | 1½-1¾ | 18 |
| Rīga (Latvia) | 11 | 2½ | 1; more via Panevėžys |
| Vilnius | 13-14 | 3-4¾ | 10; more via Kaunas or Panevėžys |

### TRAIN

Services to/from Šiauliai **train station** (Šiaulių geležinkelio stotis; ☎41-203 205; Dubijos gatvė 44) include Klaipėda (€6.60 to €9.70, 1¾ to three hours, six daily), Panevėžys (€4.60, 1½ hours, two daily) and Vilnius (€9.40 to €11.60, 2½ to 2¾ hours, five daily).

Travel to/from Kaunas requires changing trains in Vilnius (you're better off getting a direct bus).

# Biržai

☎450 / POP 13,800

The quiet town of Biržai (ber-zhay) – Lithuania's northernmost, and one of its oldest – sits along the shores of two beautiful lakes and the confluence of two rivers. Besides its castle, the town's claim to fame is its fantastic brewery.

## ⊙ Sights

**Biržai Castle** CASTLE
(☎450-33 390; www.birzumuziejus.lt; adult/child €3/1.50; ⊙10am-6.30pm Wed-Sat, to 5.30pm Tue & Sun) First built by Duke Kristupas Radvila in the late 16th century, Biržai Castle was largely restored in the 1980s, having been twice destroyed. Its huge, white-washed bastions striking skywards from man-made Lake Širvėnait was the seat of the Dukes of Biržai, and found itself in the front line in two wars with Sweden. The main castle and arsenal house fairly dry exhibitions of local wildlife, ethnography, military history, and the story of the castle, the Duchy and Radvilas family.

Highlights include temporary exhibitions of contemporary art, displays of traditional women's attire and musical instruments. The atmospheric cellar restaurant, **Pilies Skliautai** (☎450-33 032; www.piliesskliautai.lt; J Radvilos gatvė 3; mains €7-12; ⊙noon-9pm Tue-Sun), serves hearty renditions of traditional Lithuanian dishes.

**Biržai Regional Park** NATIONAL PARK
(www.birzuparkas.lt; entry per day/month €1/5) The region around Biržai is famous for its karst sinkholes, formed when underground water sources wash away the gypsum supporting the soil. More than 9000 of these holes, including the 12.6m-deep Cow's Cave (so-called because an unhappy bovine was swallowed up when it opened, 200 years ago) can be found in the area, many within the 146-sq-km regional park. The **park office** (☎450-32 889; Rotušės gatvė 10; ⊙8am-5pm Mon-Thu, to 3.45pm Fri, 10am-4pm Sat) sells

### SAMPLING THE NORTHERN ALES

Northern Lithuania is the land of barley-malt beer, with ale-makers keeping to ancient recipes and rituals practised by their ancestors 1000 years ago. People here drink 160L of beer a year, say proud locals. The biggest drinkers in the world, the Czechs, consume around the same amount. The Australians down around 110L per year, the Brits a meagre 100L.

Big-name brews to glug include **Horn**, brewed in Kaunas since 1853; Šiauliai-made **Gubernija** (www.gubernija.lt); and **Kalnapilis** from Panevėžys.

Lakeside Biržai, 65km north of Panevėžys and the true heart of Lithuanian beer country, hosts the annual two-day **Biržai Town Festival** in August, a madcap fiesta where the town's breweries sell their wares on the street; expect plenty of beer swilling and general drunken behaviour. Its **Rinkuškiai Brewery** (☎45-035 293; www.rinkuskiai.lt; Alyvų gatvė 8; tours €5-29; ⏰10am-8pm) can be visited, and its beer – everything from light lager to lead-heavy stout – can be bought in bulk in its factory shop and sampled at the attached restaurant. A lesser-known label to look out for in the region is the sweet **Butautų alaus bravoras**, an ale bottled in brown glass with a ceramic, metal-snap cap. It has been brewed in the village of Butautų since 1750.

entry tickets and has more information on the topography, plus walks, tours and other activities.

**Astravas Manor** HISTORIC BUILDING
(Astravo Dvaras) This once-grand Romantic estate, built by Count Mykolas Tiškevičius in 1862, is beautifully sited on the northern shore of Lake Širvėna. It's subsequently been used as a dairy, a sacking factory and a linen warehouse, but restoration of the buildings and classical park in the 1950s and '60s returned some of its original grandeur. It's not officially open to the public, but you can walk over the 525m footbridge (Lithuania's longest), admire the views and possibly have a peek inside.

## Sleeping & Eating

**Helveda** GUESTHOUSE €
(☎450-31 150; www.helveda.lt; J Janonio gatvė 7; s/d €20/40; 📶) Handy for the bus station and Biržai's main sights, this functional guesthouse is clean and quiet, even though it won't win awards for interior decoration.

**Portfolio Art Studio/Cafe** CAFE €
(☎8-627 37154; www.facebook.com/portfolio-birzai; Rotušės gatvė 12; mains €2.50-5; ⏰11am-8pm Mon-Sat, to 4pm Sun; 📶) This stylish cafe doubles as an art gallery for local talent and serves good coffee, excellent homemade gelato and a short and sweet menu of soup, salad and pizza.

★ **Alaus Kelias** INTERNATIONAL €€
(Beer Route; ☎450-35 293; www.rinkuskiai.lt; Alyvų gatvė 8; mains €7-14; ⏰noon-9pm Sun-Thu, to 11pm Fri & Sat) Next to the Rinkuškiai Brewery, the town's best and most popular restaurant is all heavy wooden beams, stone walls and beer hall ambience. You can get 15 of the brewery's offerings on tap (including a flight of nine for €10), plus expertly prepared international offerings such as chicken teriyaki and a hearty beer and bean soup.

## Information

**Tourist Office** (☎450-33 496; www.visitbirzai.lt; J Janonio gatvė 2; ⏰8am-5pm Mon-Fri, 10am-3pm Sat & Sun mid-Jun–Aug, shorter hours rest of year) Bursting with pamphlets and good advice, this friendly little centre can help arrange accommodation, local tours, cycling and walks.

## Getting There & Away

Buses run to/from Panevėžys (€5, 1¼ to 1½ hours, 14 daily), Kaunas (€14 to €17, 3½ hours, six daily), Vilnius (€14, three to 4¼ hours, hourly) and other major centres.

# Anykščiai

☎381 / POP 12,000

Lovely Anykščiai (a-neeksh-chey), 60km southeast of Panevėžys, sits on the confluence of the Šentoji and Anykšta Rivers. Fanning eastward are 76 lakes, the largest of which – **Lake Rubikiai** (9.68 sq km and 16m deep) – is freckled with 16 islands. There are some curious museums and sights near the town, and in winter the city transforms itself into that rarity of rarities, a Lithuanian ski resort.

## Sights

The chance to clamber over train cars and even to take a ride on an old narrow-gauge locomotive is arguably the town's biggest attraction, and a big draw for kids.

**★Narrow-Gauge Railway Museum** MUSEUM
(Siaurojo Geležinkelis Istorijos Ekspozicija; ☎381-54 597; www.siaurukas.eu; Viltis gatvė 2; adult/child €4/2; ⏲10am-5pm May-Oct) Housed in Anykščiai's old station, a couple of kilometres outside the town, this fun museum gives visitors the chance to ride on manual rail cars, a railway bicycle and, on weekends from May to October, take a 12km trip to Rubikiai Lake for picnics. Trains leave at 11am and return around 3pm; tickets cost €7.

A warehouse exhibit is full of beautifully restored vintage cars and motorcycles, Soviet and otherwise. The curator's passion makes up for rudimentary English.

In the original train station building, spot the train timetable from 30 years ago; back in the day, it was possible to travel from Anykščiai as far as Almaty.

**Horse Museum** MUSEUM
(Arklio Muziejus; ☎381-6237 0629; www.arkliomuziejus.lt; Muziejaus gatvė, Niūronys; adult/child €5/3; ⏲9am-5pm) Horse lovers – and kids – will want to make the journey 6km north to Lithuania's only horse museum, in the tiny village of Niūronys. Set out as a traditional farmstead, the museum displays B&W photos of horse-drawn transport in Vilnius alongside a fine collection of horse-drawn fire engines, carriages and taxis. Horse and carriage rides are available (adult/child €1.50/1) and there's a playground for bipedal fun. Buses (€0.70, 20 minutes, two daily) connect Niūronys with Anykščiai.

**Puntukas Stone** LANDMARK
(Puntuko Akmuo) A pine forest 10km south of Anykščiai contains the Puntakas Stone (Puntuko akmuo), a boulder 5.7m tall, 6.7m wide and 6.9m long, which legend says was put there by the devil. While he was trying to destroy Anykščiai's twin-steeple church, St Mathew's (1899–1909), a rooster crowed and the devil thundered to hell – prompting the boulder to hurtle down from the sky.

Nearby is the new **Treetop Walking Path**, a 300m-long steel-and-wood canopy walk for observing the pine woods (€1).

## Activities

**Kalitos Kalnas** SNOW SPORTS
(☎381-78 144; www.kalitoskalnas.lt; Kalno gatvė 25; ⏲11am-6pm Mon-Fri, 10am-7pm Sat & Sun) In winter, Anykščiai transforms itself into one of the country's few 'ski resorts'. This ski centre operates two ski lifts in season (December to March), has equipment for hire and offers skiing lessons. Throughout the rest of the year, the 'Alpine Coaster' (a sled on tracks) can still satisfy your desire to speed down a hill (adult/child €2/1.50).

## Festivals & Events

**Devilstone Music Festival** MUSIC
(www.devilstone.net; ⏲Jul) This open-air event brings all forms of hard rock to Anykščiai's Dainuva Valley for four days every July.

## Sleeping & Eating

The Anykščiai tourist office can suggest homestays and farmstays, and there are a couple of hotels, but the most common form of accommodation in town consists of private apartments for rent.

**Nykščio Namai** HOTEL €
(☎8-655 43379; www.nykscionamai.lt; Liudiškių gatvė 18; s/d €40/50; ) Keturi Kalnai is a reasonably slick modern hotel that offers excellent value in comfortable rooms that are a rhapsody in beige, livened up by some eye-jarring carpeting. Plus, there's a gym, a tennis court and a pool on-site.

**Perino Food & Wine** INTERNATIONAL €
(☎8-655 11624; Dariaus ir Girėno gatvė 8; mains €6-12; ⏲11am-10pm Thu-Sat, 10am-7pm Sun) Next to the blackcurrant wine factory, this sleek, minimalist restaurant is your own private dancer, determined to be whatever you want it to be. It mostly succeeds, particularly if you're looking for Mediterranean dishes (and some Asian-style and Mexican-style outliers). The gnocchi, creative salads, chilli con carne and lasagne are most satisfying.

**★5 Taškai** ITALIAN €€
(☎8-657 53513; www.facebook.com/5taskai; S Daukanto gatvė 5; mains €7-12; ⏲noon-8pm Tue-Fri, 11am-9pm Sat, 11am-6pm Sun) A snug wooden cottage hides a thimble-sized restaurant consisting of just three tables. As an Italian restaurant, it's a model of its kind: the short menu features several kinds of pasta and gnocchi, all beautifully presented. Finish the meal with an espresso and a light tiramisu with a potent hit of caffeine.

## Drinking & Nightlife

**Coffee Hill** COFFEE

(A Baranausko a. 2; ⌚9am-8pm Mon-Sat, to 7pm Sun) Inside the Anykščių Kultūros Centras, this sleek, minimalist cafe serves a mean espresso and a chocolate avocado cake practically guaranteed to convert you to veganism.

## Shopping

**Anykščių Vynas** WINE

(Dariaus ir Girėno gatvė 8; ⌚9am-5pm Mon-Sat) Certified by the European culinary heritage network, blackcurrant wine is the town's pride and joy, and you can buy some here, at the shop attached to the wine factory.

In the same building there's a canteen on the 2nd floor, serving cheap-as-chips *cepelinai,* borscht and other hearty staples.

## Information

**Tourist Office** (☎381-59 177; www.antour.lt; Gegužės gatvė 1; ⌚8am-5pm Mon-Sat year-round, plus 9am-4pm Sun May-Sep) At Anykščiai's extremely helpful tourist office the enthusiastic staff can help book homestays as well as advise on sights and travel info.

## Getting There & Away

With Anykščiai's rail line effectively transformed into a tourist attraction, that leaves just the bus. From the **bus station** (Anyksciu autobusu stotis; ☎381-51 333; A Vienuolio gatvė 1; ⌚6am-7pm), near the tourist office, there are buses to/from Panevėžys (€5.50, 1¼ hours, four daily), Vilnius (€9, 2½ hours, six daily), Kaunas (€8, 2¼ to 2¾ hours, 10 daily), Molėtai (€3.60, one hour, daily) and Utena (€4, one hour, four daily).

# WESTERN LITHUANIA

During the summer season (mid-May to mid-September), locals and visitors alike come to Lithuania's Baltic coastline in droves to enjoy the nearly 100km stretch of sea and white-sand beaches.

Topping the bill is Curonian Spit (Kursių Nerija), an extraordinary, slender sliver of sand on the Unesco World Heritage list that meanders into Russia. Its historical fishing villages and East Prussian past are fascinating backdrops to the real attraction: giant sand dunes and dense pine forests.

The gateway to the spit is Klaipėda, the country's third-largest city and only major port. This busy city with its tiny Old Town has its own rhythms. To the north is the party resort of Palanga, heaving with beachgoers all summer.

South of Klaipėda, the Nemunas Delta Regional Park is an oasis for birds and bird lovers. Inland, the Žemaitija National Park was once home to a secret Soviet nuclear base.

# Klaipėda

☎46 / POP 192,300

There's a distinctly German flavour to Klaipėda (klai-pey-da). Lithuania's third-largest city, formerly known as Memel, was part of the Prussian Kingdom until the region wrestled to autonomy in 1923. Buildings in the compact, cobblestoned Old Town are constructed in the German *Fachwerk* style – that is, with distinctive half-timbered facades. Beyond the orderly historic centre, the modern city sprawls into an industrial forest of cranes and shipyards, sliced in two by the Danė River as it meanders into the Baltic Sea.

Most people only catch a glimpse of Klaipėda as they rush headlong for the ferry to Curonian Spit, the birch-lined tendril of land across the lagoon. But spend a few hours – or even better, a day – and you'll be rewarded by a town as rich in historic architecture as sculptures and street art, not to mention a bevy of bars in which to sip beers by the water.

## History

Lithuania's oldest city, Klaipėda was the Prussian city of Memel until 1923. Founded in 1252 by the Teutonic Order, who built the city's first castle, it was a key trading port from the 15th century until 1629, when Swedish forces destroyed it. After the Napoleonic wars of the early 19th century, it became part of Prussia and stayed in Prussian hands until WWI. The population at this time was an even split of Germans and Lithuanians.

Under the Treaty of Versailles that ended WWI, Memel town, the northern half of Curonian Spit and a strip of land (about 150km long and 20km wide) along the eastern side of the Curonian Lagoon and the northern side of the Nemunas River were separated from Germany as an 'international territory'. It remained stateless until 1923, when Lithuanian troops marched in, annexed it, and changed the name of Memel to Klaipėda.

# Western Lithuania

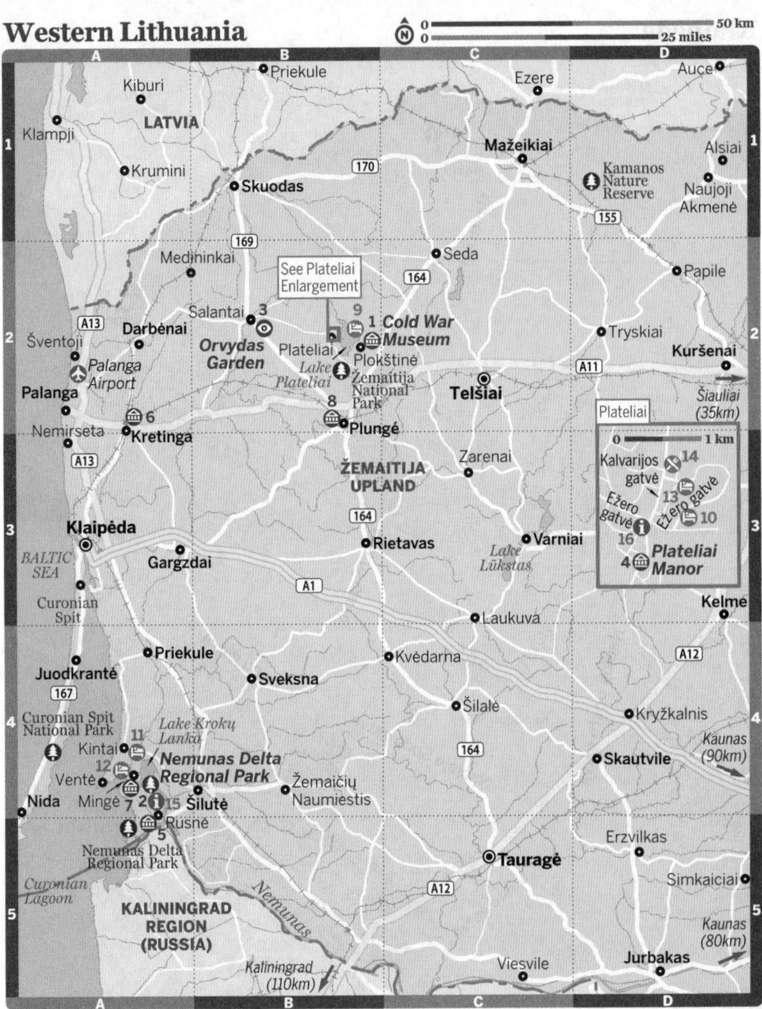


## Western Lithuania

**Top Sights**

1 Cold War Museum ........ B2
2 Nemunas Delta Regional Park ........ A4
3 Orvydas Garden ........ B2
4 Plateliai Manor ........ D3

**Sights**

5 Ethnographic Farmstead Museum ........ A5
6 Kretinga Museum ........ A2
7 Uostadvaris Polder Museum ........ A4
8 Žemaitija Art Museum ........ B2

**Sleeping**

9 Hotel Linelis ........ B2
10 Julija and Bronius Staponkai ........ D3
11 Mėlynasis Karpis ........ A4
12 Mingės Poilsis ........ A4
13 Vila Runa ........ D3

**Eating**

14 Užkandinė Plate Lyn ........ D3

**Information**

15 Regional Park Headquarters ........ A4
16 Žemaitija National Park Visitor Centre ........ D3

# Klaipėda

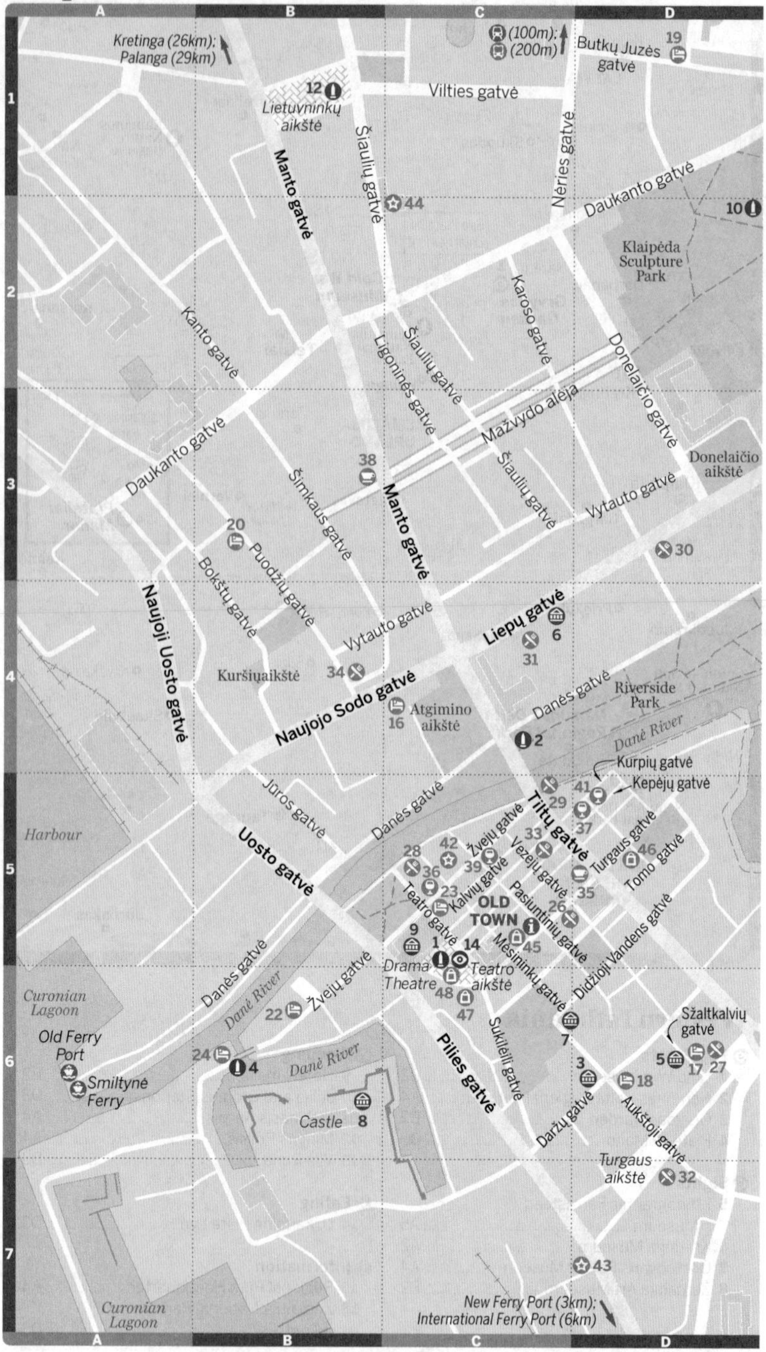

A B C D
1 2 3 4 5 6 7

Kretinga (26km); Palanga (29km)
(100m); (200m)
Butkų Juzės gatvė
19
12
Lietuvninkų aikštė
Vilties gatvė
Šiaulių gatvė
Manto gatvė
Nėries gatvė
44
Daukanto gatvė
10
Klaipėda Sculpture Park
Karoso gatvė
Kanto gatvė
Ligoninės gatvė
Šiaulių gatvė
Donelaičio gatvė
Mažvydo alėja
Daukanto gatvė
38
Manto gatvė
Šiaulių gatvė
Donelaičio aikštė
Šimkaus gatvė
Vytauto gatvė
20
Puodžių gatvė
30
Bokštų gatvė
Naujoji Uosto gatvė
Liepų gatvė
6
31
Vytauto gatvė
34
Kuršių aikštė
Naujojo Sodo gatvė
16
Atgimino aikštė
Danės gatvė
Riverside Park
2
Danė River
Kurpių gatvė
Kepėjų gatvė
41
29
Tiltų gatvė
37
Jūros gatvė
Danės gatvė
Harbour
Uosto gatvė
28
42
Žvejų gatvė
33
Vežėjų gatvė
Turgaus gatvė
46
Tomo gatvė
36
39
Kalvių gatvė
23
35
Teatro gatvė
OLD TOWN
26
Pasiuntinių gatvė
9
1
14
45
Mėsininkų gatvė
Didžioji Vandens gatvė
Drama Theatre
Teatro aikštė
48
47
Danės gatvė
Dane River
Žvejų gatvė
22
Curonian Lagoon
7
Šaltkalvių gatvė
Old Ferry Port
Smiltynė Ferry
24
4
Danė River
Piliės gatvė
Sukilėlių gatvė
3
5
17
27
18
Castle
8
Daržų gatvė
Aukštoji gatvė
Turgaus aikštė
32
43
Curonian Lagoon
New Ferry Port (3km); International Ferry Port (6km)

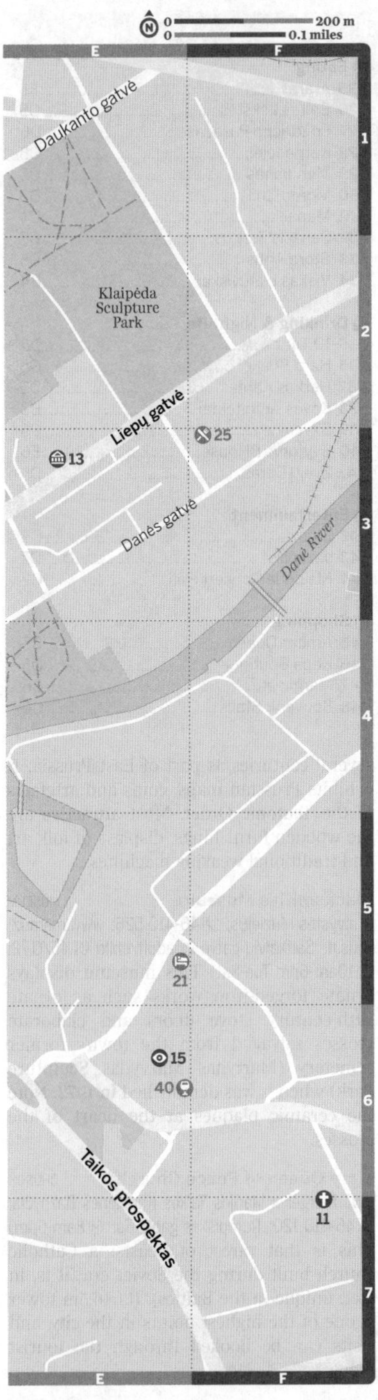


Germany eventually reclaimed Klaipėda during WWII and the city served as a Nazi submarine base. The city's strategic value ensured that it was all but destroyed during the war. After much rebuilding and repopulating, it has developed into an important city on the back of shipbuilding and fishing. In 1991 its university opened, followed in 2003 by a new cruise-ship terminal and a focus on the tourist trade.

## Sights

### Old Town

Little of German Klaipėda remains but there are some restored streets in the oldest part of town wedged between the river and Turgaus aikštė. Pretty **Teatro aikštė** (Theatre Sq) is the Old Town focus.

In front tinkles a **fountain** dedicated to Simon Dach, a Klaipėda-born German poet (1605–59) who was the focus of a circle of Königsberg writers and musicians. On a pedestal in the middle of the water stands **Ännchen von Tharau** (1912), a statue of Ann from Tharau sculpted by Berlin artist Alfred Kune (a replica; the original was destroyed in WWII) and inspired by a famous German wedding and love song originally written in the East Prussian dialect.

**Klaipėda Drama Theatre** HISTORIC BUILDING
(☎46-314 453; www.kldteatras.lt; Teatro aikštė 2; ⏲noon-6pm Tue-Sat) This fine neoclassical theatre, built in 1857, stages productions in Lithuanian. Hitler proclaimed the *Anschluss* (incorporation) of Memel into Germany from its balcony.

**Klaipėda Castle Museum** MUSEUM
(Klaipėda Pilies Muziejus; ☎46-453 098; www.mlimuziejus.lt; Priešpilio gatvė 2; adult/child €1.74/0.87; ⏲10am-6pm Tue-Sat) The castle museum is spread across four exhibition spaces around Klaipėda's castle – two of these are located in atmospherically lit tunnels and deal with the history of the castle and of Klaipėda as a port city; another features changing exhibitions of contemporary art. The highlight, however, is the **Museum 39/45** (separately priced; adult/child €1.74/0.87), a high-tech depiction of WWII and its impact on the city.

Originally built by the Teutonic Order in the 13th century, moat-protected Klaipėda Castle has a storied history befitting the

## Klaipėda

**Sights**
1 Ännchen von Tharau Statue........C5
2 Arka........C4
3 Baroti Gallery........D6
4 Black Ghost........B6
5 Blacksmith's Museum........D6
6 Clock Museum........C4
7 History Museum of Lithuania Minor........C6
8 Klaipėda Castle Museum........B6
9 Klaipėda Drama Theatre........C5
10 Klaipėda Sculpture Park........D2
11 Mary Queen of Peace Church........F7
12 Monument to Martynas Mažvydas........B1
13 Pranas Domšaitis Gallery........E3
14 Simon Dach Fountain........C5
15 Švyturys........E6

**Sleeping**
16 Amberton Klaipėda........C4
17 Friedricho Guest House........D6
18 Hotel Euterpė........D6
19 Klaipėda Hostel........D1
20 Litinterp Guesthouse........B3
21 Memel Hotel........E5
22 Michaelson Boutique Hotel........B6
23 National Hotel........C5
24 Old Mill Hotel........B6

**Eating**
25 Ararat........F3
26 Baltos Lėkštės........C5
27 Friedricho Pasazas........D6
28 Katpėdėlė........C5
29 Meridianas........C5
30 Momo Grill........D3
31 Monai........C4
32 Senasis Turgus........D7
33 Stora Antis........C5
34 Viskas Lietuviškai........B4

**Drinking & Nightlife**
35 10 Tiltų........D5
36 Hard Shake........C5
37 Herkus Kantas........D5
38 Kavos Architektai........B3
39 S7ven........C5
40 Svyturys BHouse........E6
41 Žvejų Baras........D5

**Entertainment**
42 Bluez........C5
43 Jazzpilis........D7
44 Klaipėda Concert Hall........C2

**Shopping**
45 Amber Queen........C5
46 Kopa Boutique........D5
47 Marginiai........C6
48 Souvenir Stalls........C6

region's turbulent past. Razed and rebuilt on multiple occasions, the castle was almost entirely destroyed in the late-19th century. It languished in disrepair until mid-20th-century archaeological excavations (still ongoing) renewed interest in the castle.

**Švyturys** BREWERY
(☎46-484 000; www.svyturys.lt; Kūlių Vartų gatvė 7) Klaipėda is home to the country's second-oldest brewery, where its biggest beer, Švyturys, has been brewed since 1784. Book through the tourist office or ask directly at the bar for tours of the brewery that include tastings of three or four beers (1½ to two hours, from €10 per person). Tour times are usually between 10am and 4pm from Monday to Friday, but they vary by demand.

**History Museum of Lithuania Minor** MUSEUM
(Mažosios Lietuvos Istorijos Muziejus; ☎46-410 524; www.mlimuziejus.lt; Didžioji Vandens gatvė 6; adult/child €1.45/0.72; ⏰10am-6pm Tue-Sat) This creaky-floored little museum traces the origins of 'Lithuania Minor' (Kleinlitauen), as this coastal region was known during its several centuries as part of East Prussia. It exhibits Prussian maps, coins and artefacts of the Teutonic Order. Most attractive are the wooden furnishings, displays of folk art and traditional weaving machines.

**Blacksmith's Museum** MUSEUM
(Kalvystės Muziejus; ☎46-410 526; www.mlimuziejus.lt; Šaltkalvių gatvė 2; adult/child €1.45/0.72; ⏰10am-6pm Tue-Sat) This museum displays ornate forged-iron works such as ornate 19th-century stove doors and elaborate crosses salvaged from the town's former cemetery (Martynas Mažvydas Sculpture Park) when it was demolished in 1972. Note the ceramic plaques at the heart of the crosses.

**Mary Queen of Peace Church** CHURCH
(Švč Mergelės Marijos Taikos Karalienės Bažnyčia; ☎46-410 120; Rumpiškės gatvė 6a; ⏰8am-6pm) This is that rarest of beasts: a Catholic church built during the Soviet era (it is, in fact, unique in the Baltics). Its 46.5m tower is one of the highest points in the city, and visits can be booked through the tourist office.

**Baroti Gallery** GALLERY
(Baroti Galerija; ☎46-313 580; www.barotigalerija.lt; Aukštoji gatvė 12; ⏲11am-6pm Tue-Fri, to 4pm Sat) FREE This gallery is partly housed in a converted fish warehouse dating to 1819. It has a lively program of visiting art and photography exhibitions.

## New Town

A **riverside park** skirts the northern bank of the Danė. A little further north, Liepų gatvė – called Adolf-Hitler-Strasse for a brief spell – has a few attractions of its own.

**Clock Museum** MUSEUM
(Laikrodžių Muziejus; ☎46-410 414; www.ldm.lt; Liepų gatvė 12; adult/child €2.50/1.25; ⏲noon-6pm Tue-Sat, to 5pm Sun) If you want to know what makes things tick, look no further than this niche museum that explores human measurement of time, from the earliest sundials to the latest quartz-powered Swiss watch, touching on water clocks, candle clocks and other ways of measuring time. Upstairs, the exhibition looks at the evolution of design and form in clocks over the past four centuries. The sundial garden can be worth the price of admission, on sunny days.

**Pranas Domšaitis Gallery** MUSEUM
(☎46-410 416; www.ldm.lt; Liepų gatvė 33; adult/child €2.50/1.25; ⏲noon-6pm Tue-Sat, to 5pm Sun) This gallery is renowned for the bold works by the Prussian-born expressionist painter Pranas Domšaitis (1880–1965), who spent his last years in South Africa, plus former Lithuanian artists-in-exile. Besides a wealth of Lithuanian pastoral landscapes, there are some wonderful miniatures upstairs, as well as another permanent exhibition on ornate knobs.

Domšaitis' work was famously demonised by the Nazis at the 1937 Degenerate Art Exhibition in Munich, as Hitler was not a fan.

## Beaches

Melnragė, 1km north of Klaipėda, has a pier and beach which city dwellers like to visit at sunset; **Giruliai Beach** is 1km further north. Buses 6 and 4 respectively link Manto gatvė with both. Karklė, another 1km north, is known for having amber specks wash up on its unusually stony beach after autumn storms and for the protected Dutch Cap, a 24m sea cliff.

## Activities

Klaipėda's tourist office can arrange boat trips, sailing (during July's Sea Festival), and ice fishing in winter.

## Festivals & Events

**Sea Festival** CULTURAL
(Juros Svente; ☎46-400 300; www.jurossvente.lt; ⏲Jul) Klaipėda celebrates its rich nautical heritage in late July with the flamboyant Sea Festival. The four-day event brings music, workshops, fairs and (naturally) watercraft to town.

## Sleeping

From business-hotel behemoths to atmospheric guesthouses, a hostel and numerous

### KLAIPĖDA'S SCULPTURE SCAPE

In true Lithuanian style, Klaipėda is studded with great sculptures, including 120-odd pieces from the late 1970s in the **Klaipėda Sculpture Park** (www.mlimuziejus.lt; K Donelaičio gatvė; ⏲24hr), the city's main cemetery until 1977. Not far from the park is a monumental 3.5m **sculpture** (Lietuvininkų aikštė) in granite of the eponymous Martynas Mažvydas, author of the first book published in Lithuanian in 1547.

The red granite pillar propping up a broken grey arch of almighty proportions at the southern end of Manto gatvė is Lithuania's biggest granite sculpture. Engraved with the quote, 'We are one nation, one land, one Lithuania', by local poet Ieva Simonaitytė (1897–1978), **Arka** (Arch; off Tiltų gatvė) celebrates Klaipėda joining Lithuania in 1923.

Outside the train station stands **Farewell** (Prisetočio gatvė; 2002), a moving statue of a mother with a headscarf, a suitcase in one hand and the hand of a small boy clutching a teddy bear in the other. It was given by Germany to Klaipėda to remember Germans who said goodbye to their homeland after the city became part of Lithuania in 1923.

Inside Old Town are sculptures of the **Black Ghost** (Juodasis Vaiduoklis; Žvejų gatvė) – an eerie, lantern-holding wraith clawing its way up from the water – a dog, a cat, a mouse, a spider and a disturbing red dragon, while on its outskirts reside an apple, a row of oversized yellow chairs and a boy with a dog waving off the ferries.

apartment rentals, Klaipėda's accommodation has a big range of styles and prices. Book in advance during the summer season, especially during the Sea Festival (late July).

**★Litinterp Guesthouse** GUESTHOUSE €
(☎46-410 644; www.litinterp.com; Puodžių gatvė 17; s with/without bathroom €28/23, d €46/40; P 📶) For value, this guesthouse in an 18th-century building is a standout star. High ceilings with wooden beams and sizeable beds ensure charm and comfort in equal supply, and it's efficiently run, with English-speaking staff. The 19 rooms vary from standard doubles to kitchen-equipped suites; there's a shared kitchen and enclosed parking, too. Breakfast (€3) is delivered in a little basket.

**Klaipėda Hostel** HOSTEL €
(☎8-655 94407; www.klaipedahostel.com; Butkų Juzės gatvė 7/4; dm/d/q €11/30/50; P @ 📶) This friendly hostel close to the bus station looks a bit shabby from the outside but is very homey and pleasant inside. Two small dorms with lockers sleep 12 people and there's one double and a quad. There's also a kitchen and free tea and coffee. Book in advance; no credit cards accepted.

**Memel Hotel** HISTORIC HOTEL €€
(☎46-474 900; www.memelhotel.lt; Bangų gatvė 4; s/d €40/53; 📶) Handily located right near the Švyturys Brewery, the Memel occupies a restored 19th-century heritage building. Expect high ceilings, carpeted rooms decked out in soothing pastels, helpful staff and a generous complimentary buffet breakfast.

**Old Mill Hotel** HOTEL €€
(☎46-219 215; www.oldmillhotel.lt; Žvejų gatvė 22; s/d/ste €50/78/116; 📶) Occupying two old merchants' buildings in a commanding position either side of the Klaipėda dock swing-bridge, this well-established hotel is close to the castle, Old Town and ferries to Curonian Spit. The claret-carpeted rooms are bright and generous, with quality beds and sparkling bathrooms.

**Friedricho Guest House** GUESTHOUSE €€
(☎46-391 020; www.pasazas.lt; Šaltkalvių gatvė 3; s/d/apt from €55/65/120; P 📶) This pretty guesthouse is run by the same people who operate the restaurants along Friedricho Pasažas. Accommodation ranges from snug economy rooms to luxury apartments; some of the rooms themselves are more like small apartments, with kitchenettes and sitting rooms, and are perfect for families.

**Amberton Klaipėda** HOTEL €€
(☎46-404 372; www.ambertonhotel.com; Naujoji Sodo gatvė 1; d/f from €99/120, original building s/d from €40/46, all incl breakfast; P ❄ @ 📶 🏊) Part of a four-star hotel chain, the Amberton feels institutional but compensates with amenities (spa, tennis courts, casino, pool). The experience hinges on whether you book digs in the rather worn original building or, for double the price, one of the glossier, more contemporary rooms in the 'K' centre.

**★Michaelson Boutique Hotel** BOUTIQUE HOTEL €€€
(☎46-224 413; www.hotelmichaelson.com; Žvejų gatvė 18a; r €115-165; P 📶) 🍃 With splendid views of the Danė River, this restored 18th-century warehouse has been turned into Klaipėda's most atmospheric hotel. There's an intimate feel to the 16-room place, particularly if you're staying on the top floor with its dramatically slanted roof. Decor is neutral creams and greys, original heavy wooden beams and reclaimed ancient oak floors. Great restaurant, too.

**Hotel Euterpė** HOTEL €€€
(☎46-474 703; www.euterpe.lt; Daržų gatvė 9; s/d/ste €85/110/165; P @ 📶) Our bet for the best small hotel in Klaipėda is this upscale number, tucked among former German merchant houses in Old Town. The accommodation has a neat, minimalist look; single rooms with slanted ceilings are on the snug side, but the best doubles have king-sized beds, skylights and oak floors.

**National Hotel** HISTORIC HOTEL €€€
(☎46-211 111; www.nationalhotel.lt; Žvejų gatvė 21; s/d/ste €110/125/170; ❄ 📶) As central as can be in Old Town, this revamped 19th-century hotel is all high ceilings and plenty of natural light and a mix of antique-style furnishings and modern creature comforts. Suites come with whirlpools. Although the hotel is attached to a popular bar, good soundproofing means that your repose won't be disturbed.

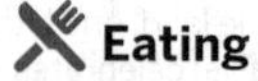

## Eating

**Katpėdėlė** LITHUANIAN €
(☎8-618 28343; www.katpedele.lt; Žvejų gatvė 12; mains €4-10; ⊙11am-10pm Sun-Wed, to 11pm Thu, to 1am Fri & Sat; 📶 👪) It may be a franchise, but Katpėdėlė does the Lithuanian standards really well, and makes the most of a brick merchant's building in a prime spot by the Danė. There are hearty potato

pancakes, the more sophisticated grilled pork neck with whiskey sauce, and soups in hollowed-out bread bowls.

**Viskas Lietuviškai** LITHUANIAN €
(☎46-216 402; Puodžių gatvė 3; mains €4-7; ⏰11am-8pm Mon-Sat, to 6pm Sun) If you're hankering after a deeply satisfying dose of potato-based stodge, look no further than this low-key neighbourhood restaurant where *cepelinai* (rugby-ball-shaped mega-dumplings of potato dough swimming in a cream and bacon sauce) are an exemplary version of Lithuania's classic dish.

**Senasis Turgus** MARKET €
(Turgaus aikšte 5; ⏰6am-6pm) A farmers market of inexpensive fresh produce is typically held daily on and just off the square. Some days you'll find old coins, stamps, Soviet badges and other assorted bric-a-brac a block up from the food market, with such novelty WWII items as bayonets and Nazi helmets.

**Ararat** ARMENIAN €€
(☎46-400 880; www.ararat.lt/restoranas; Liepų gatvė 48a; mains €7-12; ✎) This venerable Armenian restaurant is a stalwart of Klaipėda's dining scene. Grilled meats are a joy here, cooked with flair and Caucasian herbs, but vegetarians needn't feel left out: the aubergines stuffed with walnuts and pomegranate and dolma (stuffed vine leaves) lend the city a touch of the exotic. Try the brandies, too.

**Baltos Lėkštės** PIZZA €€
(☎8-624 41640; Turgaus gatvė 10; pizzas from €7; ⏰11am-10pm Tue-Sun; 📶) You can smell what may be the best pizza in Lithuania before you even step through the door. All heavy beams and a snug, cavelike, split-level interior, this place specialises in wood-fired pizza with an imaginative array of toppings.

**Friedricho Pasazas** INTERNATIONAL €€
(☎46-301 070; www.pasazas.lt; Tiltų gatvė 26a; mains €12-26; ⏰11am-1am Mon-Sat, noon-midnight Sun; 📶) Lining an arcade on the southern side of Old Town, Friedricho Pasazas invites diners to pick anything from pizza to Argentinian steak to Lithuanian dumplings. In the main restaurant, mannerly waiters lay Siberian perch, Argentinian steak and creative Mediterranean dishes onto crisp white tablecloths.

★**Momo Grill** STEAK €€€
(☎8-693 12355; www.momogrill.lt; Liepų gatvė 20; mains €13-27; ⏰11am-10pm Tue-Fri, from noon Sat; 📶) This tiny, modern, minimalist steakhouse has an equally minimalist menu. There are three appetisers (beef tartare, burrata mozzarella salad and green salad), two cuts of Uruguayan beef, seared expertly on the Josper grill, a smattering of sides, two desserts (the pistachio panna cotta is marvellous) and a well-chosen wine list. Perfect.

★**Monai** EUROPEAN €€€
(☎8-626 63362; www.restoranasmonai.lt; Liepų gatvė 4; mains €15-19; ⏰11.30am-2pm & 6-10pm Tue-Sat, 10am-4pm Sun) As Klaipėda's go-to place for on-trend Modern European cuisine, Monai's serves classic pairings of ingredients (scallops with pea puree, pike-perch with chanterelles) and beautifully presented dishes that aren't trying too hard. The menu changes with the seasons and the eggs Benedict and mimosa Sunday brunch is popular with locals.

**Stora Antis** LITHUANIAN €€€
(☎8-686 25020; www.storaantis.lt; Tiltų gatvė 6; mains €15-19; ⏰5pm-midnight Tue & Thu-Sat) Taking full advantage of an atmospheric 19th-century cellar, brick-lined Stora Antis elevates classic Lithuanian fare (baked duck, bean soup, pan-fried plaice) to haute-cuisine heights. A restaurant was first established here in 1856 and it's retained its charms, laden with antiques and bric-a-brac.

**Meridianas** EUROPEAN €€€
(☎8-601 31866; www.restoranasmeridianas.lt; Danė Embankment, near Tiltų gatvė; mains €7-24; ⏰noon-1am Mon-Sat, to 10pm Sun; 👪) The *Meridianas* – a barquentine built by Finland for the USSR as part of imposed war reparations – has been restored to the glory befitting this icon of Klaipėda, and is now moored in a prominent position on the Danė. Aboard, it's all gleaming fittings, starched tablecloths, and a pan-European menu of salads, steaks, risottos, fish and fine wine.

## Drinking & Nightlife

Port-side drinking holes and taverns are the norm in Klaipėda (read: beer, dumplings and more beer). Several bars with cocktails and live music diversify the nightlife.

★**S7ven** PUB
(☎8-653 27777; Žvejų gatvė 7; ⏰noon-11pm) The stripped-down decor and clean lines of this riverside pub mean that the focus is squarely on what it offers, which is a convivial atmosphere, fuelled by a mind-boggling collection of whiskies, craft beers from all over the country and decent burgers.

★ **Hard Shake** COCKTAIL BAR
(☎8-608 61007; www.facebook.com/hardshake; Žvejų gatvė 10; ⊙8pm-3am Thu, to 5am Fri & Sat) This cocktail bar is small in size but a giant when it comes to mixology. The list of drinks (both classic and original) is epic, and if by some freak chance you don't find what you're looking for, the bartenders can make you one according to your specifications. DJ sets keep the place lively on weekends.

**Kavos Architektai** COFFEE
(☎8-645 05022; www.kavosarchitektai.lt; Manto gatvė 9; ⊙7am-7pm Mon-Fri, 10am-4pm Sat) Klaipėda's best coffee shop is an attractive, cosy space for lingering with a coffee-table book on art and architecture. The coffee is excellent as well, and prepared umpteen ways to suit the discerning 21st-century coffee drinker. House-made ice cream too; try the sea-hawthorn flavour.

No wi-fi. Customers are actually encouraged to converse with one another. *Gasp.*

**Svyturys BHouse** BEER HALL
(☎8-648 43555; www.facebook.com/svyturysbhouse; Kūlių Vartų gatvė 7; ⊙4pm-midnight Mon-Wed, to 1am Thu, to 3am Fri, 11am-3am Sat, 11am-11pm Sun) Attached to the city's major brewery, this industrial-style beer hall serves a wide range of interesting beers (their core ones, as well as small-batch brews); check out the latest on the huge board. You can peer into the brewery itself through the glass.

**10 Tiltų** COFFEE
(☎8-698 80216; www.facebook.com/10tiltukavine; Turgaus gatvė 19; ⊙7.30am-10pm Mon-Fri, from 9am Sat & Sun; 📶) Part art gallery, part laptop-friendly hangout, this coffee shop is located inside the characterful historic pharmacy building. The delicious cakes are made in-house, the baristas are serious about their speciality coffee without worshipping the stuff, and cushions in cosy nooks encourage you to linger longer.

**Žvejų Baras** BAR
(☎8-686 60405; www.zvejubaras.lt; Kurpių gatvė 8; ⊙5pm-midnight Sun-Wed, to 2am Thu, to 4am Fri & Sat) Set aglow by lead-lined lamps, the maritime-meets-industrial vibe of this timbered portside pub lives up to the name, meaning 'Fisherman's Bar'. This is one of Klaipėda's nicest places to catch live music, sports screenings or chat over one of 16 different (mostly Lithuanian) beers.

**Herkus Kantas** PUB
(☎8-685 87338; www.facebook.com/herkuskantaspub; Kepėjų gatvė17; ⊙5pm-1am Tue-Sat) One of Klaipėda's riverside pubs, Herkus has perhaps the best location of all, opposite the iconic barquentine *Meridianis,* which is permanently moored here on the Danė. There's plenty of outdoor seating for good weather, and a cosy cellar interior with great beers (including a weekly guest ale) on tap.

## ☆ Entertainment

**Jazzpilis** LIVE MUSIC
(☎8-677 81899; www.jazzpilis.lt; Pilies gatvė 6; ⊙11am-2pm Mon-Fri, plus 6pm-1am Tue, 6-11pm Thu, 6pm-4am Fri & Sat) Exposed brick walls, scuffed wooden tables and mood lighting from a dozen lanterns set the scene at Jazzpilis, an intimate venue where international jazz acts and local experimental bands alike take to the stage. Check the website to see what's happening Tuesday, Thursday, Friday and Saturday nights.

**Bluez** LIVE MUSIC
(☎8-683 95255; www.bluez.lt; Žvejų gatvė 8; ⊙11am-10pm Mon-Thu, to 4am Fri & Sat, noon-10pm Sun) Inside a revamped warehouse on the banks of the river, this friendly bar features live music from Wednesday to Saturday nights. Bluez is a bit of misnomer, since the live acts are a mixed bag of genres. It's a good place for a cocktail, beer and charcuterie platter.

**Klaipėda Concert Hall** CONCERT VENUE
(☎46-410 561; www.koncertusale.lt; Šiaulių gatvė 36; ⊙box office 11.15am-2.30pm & 3.15-7.15pm Mon-Fri) Orchestral, choral and chamber performances are held in this handsome 19th-century building.

## Shopping

Klaipėda is known for its amber. It's also possible to pick up fine linen and artwork in town.

★ **Amber Queen** JEWELLERY
(☎46-213 390; www.amberqueen-shop.com; Turgaus gatvė 3; ⊙10am-9pm) Did you know that Colombian amber comes in emerald, ruby or even deep blue colours? This part-museum, part-jewellery shop has a remarkable range of items, from amber-accented antiques and such creations as amber sailing ships and chess sets to chunky beads and delicate contemporary jewellery in various hues of white, butter-yellow, orange, amber and even grey.

**Marginiai** GIFTS & SOUVENIRS
(☎46-410 488; Sukilėlių gatvė 4; ⏲10am-3pm Mon, to 6pm Tue-Sat) Just off Theatre Sq, this is a great place to look for delicate lacework, traditional woven sashes, linenwear, woolly mittens and contemporary art – all Lithuanian-made.

**Kopa Boutique** FASHION & ACCESSORIES
(☎8-676 56619; www.kopaboutique.lt; Turgaus gatvė 20; ⏲10am-7pm Mon-Fri, to 5pm Sat) If you're after Lithuanian couture, this boutique stocks carefully chosen items by Lithuanian designers, from womenswear to accessories.

**Souvenir Stalls** GIFTS & SOUVENIRS
(Teatro aikštė; ⏲hours vary) During warmer months, the stalls on Teatro aikštė are a good place to hunt for locally made lace items, lesser quality amber jewellery, ceramics, attractive wooden kitchen utensils and more.

## ℹ Information

**Tourist Office** (☎46-412 186; www.klaipeda info.lt; Turgaus gatvė 7; ⏲9am-6pm Mon-Fri) Exceptionally efficient tourist office selling maps and locally published guidebooks, and arranging accommodation and tours. Open weekends in summer.

## ℹ Getting There & Away

### BOAT

From Klaipėda's **International Ferry Port** (☎46-499 799; www.portofklaipeda.lt; Perkėlos gatvė 10), **DFDS Seaways** (☎46-323 232; www.dfdsseaways.lt; Baltijos prospektas 40; ⏲10am-5.30pm) runs big passenger and car ferries regularly to Kiel, Germany (from €75 per passenger) and to Karlshamn, Sweden (from €50 per passenger).

Ferries to Curonian Spit depart from different terminals, depending on whether you're a passenger on foot or bike, or if you are bringing your car onto the peninsula.

Smiltynės Perkėla (www.keltas.lt) runs a quick ferry from Klaipėda's **Old Ferry Port** (Senoji perkėla; ☎46-311 117; www.keltas.lt; Danės gatvė 1) to/from Smiltynė (per passenger/bicycle €1/free, at least hourly between 7am and 9pm) for foot passengers and cyclists. Following a hiatus in 2019, there are plans to restore the daily May–August ferry services to Nida via Juodkrantė, a trip taking about two hours (kids under seven travel free).

Drivers need to embark at the **New Ferry Port** (Naujoji perkėla; ☎46-311 117; www.keltas.lt; Nemuno gatvė 8; per foot passenger/motorbike/car €1/4.90/12.30, bicycle free) for services to Smiltynė (€12.30, one to three ferries per hour between 5am and 9pm); pay as you drive on.

### BUS

Ecolines (www.ecolines.net) sells tickets for international destinations. At the **bus station** (Autobusų Stotis; ☎46-411 547; www.klap.lt; Butkų Juzės gatvė 9; ⏲ticket office 3.30am-7.30pm) the information window has timetable information. Most buses to/from Juodkrantė and Nida depart from the ferry landing at Smiltynė on Curonian Spit.

Services to/from Klaipėda bus station include the following:

| DESTINATION | PRICE (€) | DURATION (HR) | FREQUENCY (PER DAY) |
|---|---|---|---|
| Kaliningrad (Russia) | 12 | 4½ | 2 |
| Kaunas | 15-17 | 2¾-4½ | 14 |
| Kretinga | 1.30-1.90 | 25-50min | 15 |
| Liepāja (Latvia) | 6 | 1¾ | 1 |
| Nida | 4.20-6 | 1½-2 | 3 (via Smiltynė) |
| Palanga | 1.30-2 | ½ | 20 |
| Pärnu (Estonia) | 41-51 | 9-11 | 2 (via Vilnius or Kaunas) |
| Rīga (Latvia) | 19 | 5 | 2 (more via Panevėžys or Vilnius) |
| Šiauliai | 11-13 | 3-3½ | 6 (more via Kryžkalnis) |
| Tallinn (Estonia) | 47-56 | 13½-15¾ | 3 (via Kaunas) |
| Vilnius | 18-22 | 4-5¼ | 15 |

### TRAIN

The **train station** (Klaipėdos geležinkelio stotis; ☎information 8-700 55111; www.litrail.lt; Priestočio gatvė 1; ⏲ticket office 6.10am-7pm; 🚌5, 8), 150m from the bus station, has an unusual helmeted clock tower. Daily services include trains to/from Vilnius (€17.40, four to 4¼ hours, four daily) and to/from Šiauliai (€6.60 to €9.70, 1¾ to 2¾ hours, six daily) via Kretinga (€1.50, 30 minutes).

## ℹ Getting Around

### BICYCLE

**Baltic Cycle** (☎8-615 91773; www.bbtravel.lt; Naujoji Uosto gatvė 3; per day €12; ⏲9am-6pm May-Sep, by reservation Oct-Apr) hires bikes, handy for seeing Klaipėda or Curonian Spit. Otherwise, to get around town, download the **CityBee** (www.citybee.lt) app and use it to borrow bicycles and electric scooters.

### BOAT

Everything about the **Smiltynė Ferry** (Smiltynės Perkėla; ☎46-311 117; www.keltas.lt; Nemuno gatvė 8; adult/child over 7 €12/8.40) – timetables, fares, newsflashes – is online.

The passenger ferry for Smiltynė (principal point-of-access for Curonian Spit) leaves from Old Ferry Port (p371): look for signs to 'Neringa'. It docks on the eastern side of Smiltynė, at the start of the Nida road. Ferries sail at least every half-hour between 6.30am and midnight June to August (at least hourly until 11pm the rest of the year). The crossing takes five minutes and a return passenger fare is €1 per person; bicycles and children under the age of seven sail for free.

Year-round, vehicles can use the New Ferry Port (p371), around 2km south of the mouth of the Danė River. Look for road signs to 'Neringa'. Ferries sail half-hourly between 5.40am and 1.10am and dock on Curonian Spit, 2.5km south of the Smiltynė ferry landing. Bus 1 links Klaipėda city centre with the New Ferry Port.

### BUS

Local bus tickets cost €0.80 from kiosks or €1 from the driver. Bus 8 links the train station with Manto gatvė, the city centre and the Turgaus stop, on Taikos prospektas. Bus 5 follows roughly the same route. Minibuses, which follow the same routes, can be flagged down on the street and cost €1 (or €1.30 before 6am and after 11pm).

# Curonian Spit National Park

☎469 / POP 2500

On this bewitching tendril of land, winds caress the sand dunes, pine scents the breeze and amber washes up on beaches. Designated a national park (Kuršių Nerijos Nacionalinis Parkas) in 1991, the Unesco-protected Curonian Spit trails across the Baltic Sea from Lithuania to Russian territory Kaliningrad. Pine forests populated by elk and wild boar cover about 70% of the area and only a fraction is urban; the four main villages Nida, Juodkrantė, Pervalka and Preila are known collectively as 'Neringa'. Today these fishing villages have embraced tourism, a double-edged sword that yields both their main source of income and their biggest environmental threat.

Until the first decades of the 20th century, most of the spit was German territory. The area used to have a magnetic attraction for German exiles, and continues to draw a large number of German tourists. Today locals joke that the spit's sand dunes are 'Lithuania's Sahara'.



## SHIFTING SANDS & DELICATE DUNES

Legend has it that motherly sea giantess Neringa created the spit, lovingly carrying armfuls of sand in her apron to form a protected harbour for the local fishing folk. The truth is just as enchanting. The waves and winds of the Baltic Sea let sand accumulate in its shallow waters near the coast 5000 or 6000 years ago to create an original beauty found nowhere else.

Massive deforestation in the 16th century started the sands shifting. Trees were felled for timber, leaving the sands free to roam unhindered at the whim of the strong coastal winds. At a pace of 20m a year, the sands swallowed 14 villages in the space of three centuries.

It was soon dubbed the 'Sahara of Lithuania' due to its desert state; drastic action was needed. In 1768 an international commission set about replanting. Today this remains a priority of the national park authorities. Deciduous forest (mainly birch groves) covers 20% of the national park; coniferous forest, primarily pine and mountain pine trees, constitutes a further 53%. Alder trees can be found on 2.6 sq km (3% of the park's area). Lattices of branches and wooden stakes have pinned down the sand.

But the sands are still moving – at least 1m a year. Slowly the spit is drifting into the Baltic Sea. Each tourist who scrambles and romps on Parnidis Dune (p377) – the only remaining free-drifting dune – meanwhile pushes down several tonnes of sand. With 1.5 million people visiting the dunes each year, the threat posed by them wandering off designated paths – not to mention the risk of forest fire – is high.

The dunes are also shrinking. Winds, waves and humans have reduced them by 20m in 40 years. Its precious beauty may yet be lost forever.

### SPIT RULES

- Neringa municipality entrance fee: motorbike/car July to August €5/10, September to June €5/5.
- Speed limit: 50km/h in villages, 70km/h on open roads.
- Don't romp in the dunes, pick flowers or stray off designated footpaths.
- Don't damage flora or fauna, mess with bird nests or light campfires.
- Don't pitch a tent or park a camper overnight anywhere in the park.
- Don't fish without a permit; purchase them at tourist offices.
- Beware of elk and wild boar crossing the road, and don't feed them!
- Break a rule and risk an on-the-spot fine of up to €150.
- In case of forest fire, call ☎01, 112, Smiltynė ☎8-656 35025, Juodkrantė ☎8-656 34998, Preila and Pervalka ☎8-687 27758, Nida ☎8-656 34992.

## Information

Main towns Smiltynė, Juodkrantė and Nida each have an information office, though some are seasonal. If travelling outside May to September, check with Klaipėda's helpful tourist office (p371) before boarding the ferry.

Visit Neringa (www.visitneringa.com) is a well-maintained site covering most of Neringa's attractions and facilities.

## Getting There & Around

Curonian Spit is accessible only via boat or ferry (there are no bridges linking the spit to the mainland). From Klaipėda, two ferries run regularly: a passenger ferry goes to Smiltynė from the Old Ferry Port (p371); and a vehicle ferry from the New Ferry Port (p371), 2km south of Klaipėda's Old Town, connects to a point on the spit around 2km south of Smiltynė.

You can also reach the Russian Kaliningrad Region from here. The Russian border post is 3km south of Nida on the main road and daily buses depart from Nida. Check www.visit-kaliningrad.ru for details on e-visas and tourist visas.

## Smiltynė

☎46 / POP LESS THAN 50

Though it's administratively part of Klaipėda, Smiltynė is a hop, skip and five-minute ferry ride across the thin strait that divides the rest of the city from Curonian Spit. Smiltynė is a tiny village, with an information centre and a couple of interesting museums, and it's the starting point for forays further along Curonian Spit.

### Sights

**Lithuania Sea Museum** AQUARIUM
(Lietuvos Jūrų Muziejus; ☎46-490 740; www.juru.muziejus.lt; Smiltynės gatvė 3; adult/student Jun-Aug €9/4.50, Sep-May €7/3.50; ⏲10.30am-6.30pm Tue-Sun Jun-Aug, shorter hours rest of year; 👪) This popular museum, set in a 19th-century fort, has some fascinating stuffed sea animals, as well as aquariums showcasing the marine life of the Curonian Lagoons and beyond. Animal lovers will wish to skip the live shows featuring seals, sea lions and dolphins.

**Beaches** BEACH
Grab your Speedos and take a footpath through pine forests across the spit's 1km-wide tip to a bleached-white sandy beach. From the ferry landing, walk straight ahead across the car park, then bear left towards Nida; on your right a large sign marks a smooth footpath that leads through pine forest to a women's beach (Moterų pliažas; 1km), mixed beach (Bendras pliažas; 700m) and men's beach (Vyrų pliažas; 900m). Nude or topless bathing is the norm on single-sex beaches.

**Exposition of the National Park of the Curonian Spit** MUSEUM
(Kursių Nerijos Nacionalinis Parkas Gamtos Muziejus Ekspozicija; ☎46-402 256; www.nerija.lt; Smiltynės gatvė 11; adult/child €2/1; ⏲11am-6pm Wed-Sun May-Sep) Dedicated to the flora and fauna of the park, this museum is spread across three wooden houses. Alongside stuffed examples of wild pigs, badgers, beavers and elk, there's a large collection of insects, and information on measures being taken to protect the dunes.

**Ethnographic Sea Fishermen's Farmstead** MUSEUM
(Etnografinė Pajūrio Žvejo Sodyba; Smiltynės gatvė; ⏲10.30am-6.30pm Tue-Sun Jun-Aug) FREE The

## Curonian Spit National Park

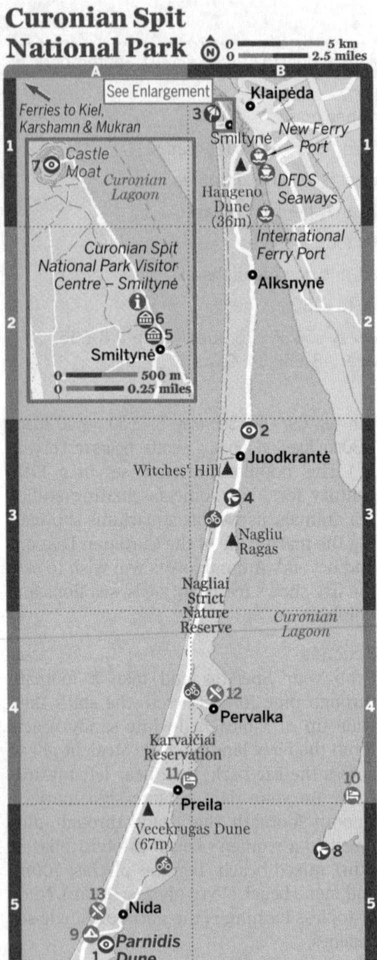


lifestyles of 19th- and 20th-century farmers are laid bare at this open-air museum, just south of Smiltynė's tourist office. Around the grassy site you can peer inside a granary, dwelling house, cellar, smokehouse, cattle shed and other outbuildings, learning about traditional bread-baking and ogling peasant costumes.

Outside are old fishing vessels to admire, including three Baltic Sea fishing trawlers built in the late 1940s and a 1935 *kurėnas* (a traditional flat-bottomed Curonian fishing boat).

## Information

**Curonian Spit National Park Visitor Centre – Smiltynė** (☎46-402 256; www.nerija.lt; Smiltynės gatvė 11; ⏲9am-noon & 1-6pm Tue-Sat Jun-Aug) The summer-only visitor centre is packed with information about the park's ecology and attractions. Guided nature tours (€31 to €36, two to eight people) can also be arranged here.

## Juodkrantė

☎469 / POP 700

Stretched along the lagoon shore, the slender village of Juodkrantė (ywad-kran-tey) – 'Black Shore', or Schwarzort to Germans – is one of the oldest settlements on Curonian Spit. Thought to date to the 15th century, shifting dunes forced the village to move from its original location. A fishing village for hundreds of years, it switched its focus to tourism in the 1860s but has retained a more sedate feel than Nida, 28km south, which attracts greater numbers of visitors.

### Sights

Contemporary stone sculptures and a smooth promenade with cycling path skirts the water's edge, while the main

### Curonian Spit National Park

**Top Sights**
1 Parnidis Dune ........ A5

**Sights**
2 Amber Bay ........ B3
3 Beaches ........ B1
4 Cormorant & Heron Colony ........ B3
5 Ethnographic Sea Fishermen's Farmstead ........ A2
6 Exposition of the National Park of the Curonian Spit ........ A2
7 Lithuania Sea Museum ........ A1
8 Ventės Ragas Ornithological Station ........ B5

**Sleeping**
9 Nidos Kempingas ........ A5
10 Šturmų Sodyba ........ B4
11 Vila Preiloja ........ A4

**Eating**
12 Marių Akis ........ B4
13 Zuikio Daržas ........ A5

road – Liudviko Rėzos gatvė – is lined with holiday homes and quaint *žuvis* (fish) outlets.

**★Witches' Hill** PUBLIC ART

(Raganų Kalnas; off Rte 167; ⌚24hr) FREE A coven of wooden sculptures is gathered on a forest-clad hill in Juodkrantė, carved by Lithuanian artists over the years since 1979. At this open-air sculpture gallery, a devil grimaces beneath an arch of wooden faces, twisted in emotion, while warty-nosed witches, dwarves and Neringa herself peep out from among the pine trees. The figures represent various characters from regional folklore, and some have an interactive quality: slide down a demon's tongue or sit on a carved throne.

The 42m-hill was a focus of pagan ritual in the centuries before Lithuania adopted Christianity. Thereafter, the midsummer festival St Jonas' Day was celebrated on the hill.

It's signposted at the southern end of the village.

**Cormorant & Heron Colony** BIRD SANCTUARY

(Rte 167; ⌚Feb-Sep) One of Europe's largest colonies of cormorants and grey herons is amassed in the forest 1km south of Juodkrantė. Wooden steps lead from the road to a viewing platform where the panorama of thousands of nests amid pine trees – not to mention the noise of the 6500-strong colony – is astonishing. Cormorants arrive in early February (herons a little later) to pick and rebuild their nests. By May chicks are screaming for food.

There has been an uneasy relationship between the two species ever since the birds migrated to this part of Curonian Spit in the early 19th century, with cormorants regarded as invaders that take over the herons' nests. Fishers blame the cormorants in particular for reduced catches, but both species are protected.

Starlings, thrushes, warblers, and grey, spotted and black woodpeckers can also be seen among the trees, many of which are blackened and broken due to the impact of the immense colony of birds.

**Amber Bay** BAY

(Gintaro įlanka) At Juodkrantė's northern end is an area around a fishing harbour known as Amber Bay (Gintaro įlanka), recalling the amber excavated in the village in three separate clusters – 2250 tonnes in all – in 1854 to 1855 and 1860. The spit is about 1.5km wide at this point and the fine stretch of forest – good for spotting elk in the early morning and evening – is among the loveliest you will find on the peninsula.

**Evangelical-Lutheran Church** CHURCH

(Liudviko Rėzos gatvė 56; ⌚hours vary) This red-brick German church at the southern end of Juodkrantė was built in 1885.

## Sleeping

**★Prie Ąžuolo** APARTMENT €€

(☎8-698 00345; www.prieazuolo.lt; L Rėzos gatvė 54b; 1-/2-/3-bedroom apt €70/120/150; 📶) These stylish, spacious, individually decorated apartments are decked out in contemporary creams and greys and come fully equipped, ideal for self-caterers and families. They're in a peaceful location at the southern end of the village, and the owner is very helpful.

**Vila Flora** GUESTHOUSE €€

(☎469-53 024; www.vilaflora.lt; Kalno gatvė 7a; s/d/tr incl breakfast €65/80/115; 📶) Open year-round, this 19th-century timber villa in the heart of Juodkrantė offers 15 comfortable rooms, many of them split-level with a separate lounge space and bedroom. Most retain a strong whiff of the 1980s, but despite the lack of contemporary flair, Vila Flora is a well-priced option. Wi-fi in reception only.

The restaurant (open 9am to 11pm) on the ground floor is among the best in town (though continents may drift before you get served). It opens daily in summer and weekends only at other times of year, serving traditional Lithuanian dishes and refined pan-European fare, such as duck breast with blueberry sauce.

**Kurėnas** HOTEL €€

(☎8-698 02711; kurenas@gmail.com; L Rėzos gatvė 10; s/d/f from €58/65/75; 📶) Named after the traditional flat-bottomed Curonian fishing boat, this busy and bright cafe-bar with street-side terrace sports large, individually decorated rooms with wooden floors and clean white walls. Reserve one with a balcony overlooking the lagoon (and pay half the price between September and May).

## Eating

**★Žuvelė** SEAFOOD €€

(☎8-684 78707; www.facebook.com/zuvele; L Rėzos gatvė 1; mains €5.50-13; ⌚10am-11pm) Near the pier, this summer-only restaurant has a menu full of crowd-pleasers, including

### SEAFARING WEATHERVANES

Nowhere are Juodkrantė's and Nida's seafaring roots better reflected than on top of the 19th-century wooden cottages that speckle these spit villages. A ruling in 1844 saw weathervanes or cocks used to identify fishing vessels in the Curonian Lagoon. They quickly became ornamentation for rooftops. Originally made from tin and later from wood, these 60cm x 30cm plaques were fastened to the boat mast so other fisherfolk could see where a *kurėnas* (Neringa boat) had sailed. Each village had its own unique symbol – a black-and-white, red-and-white or blue-and-yellow geometrical design – incorporated in the weathercock and then embellished with an eclectic assortment of mythical cut-outs; see the different designs first hand in the Neringa History Museum. Juodkrantė's Weathervane Gallery is a good place to pick one up for yourself.

*pelmeni* (meat dumplings), but what it does best is fish. Get your slab of grilled turbot, pike-perch or plaice with some fresh veggies, a squeeze of lemon, and a beer. Perfection.

**Pamario Takas** INTERNATIONAL €€
(☎8-650 97491; www.facebook.com/pamariotakas; L Rėzos gatvė 42; mains €7-12; ⊙10am-midnight daily Jun-Sep, to 10pm Fri & Sat, to 9pm Sun Oct-May; ) Though their emphasis is on healthy recipes and home cooking, the food selection at Pamario Takas is eclectic: burgers, beetroot-cured salmon salads and vegan panna cotta made with rice milk. The restaurant, in a doll's-house-like blue building, spills into a garden where rough-hewn wooden chairs and tables are arranged. With friendly service and reasonably priced wine, you're likely to linger.

## Shopping

**Weathervane Gallery** ARTS & CRAFTS
(Vetrungių Galerija; ☎8-698 27283; www.autentic.lt; L Rėzos gatvė 13; ⊙9am-7pm May-Sep, 10am-5pm Apr & Oct) Part-museum but mostly shop, this place sells smaller versions of authentic Curonian weathervanes, some wonderful amber jewellery, plus linen clothing and travel guides to Lithuania and Curonian Spit. The assistant is happy to tell you about the history of the weathervanes.

## Information

**Tourist Office** (☎469-53 490; www.visitneringa.com; L Rėzos gatvė 8; ⊙10am-1pm & 2-8pm Mon-Sat, to 3pm Sun, shorter hours Sep-May) Located opposite the bus stop inside the cultural centre. Offers more literature for sale than for free but staff give sound advice.

## Getting There & Away

Seven to 10 daily buses to/from Nida (€3, 30 minutes) and Smiltynė (€1.90, 15 to 20 minutes) stop in Juodkrantė, just opposite the tourist office. Bicycle hire (€3/12 per hour/day) can also be found in several locations, including next to the main bus stop.

# Juodkrantė to Nida

Heading south from Juodkrantė the road switches to the western side of the spit. The 16.8-sq-km **Naglių Strict Nature Reserve** (Naglių rezervatas) here protects the Dead or Grey Dunes (named after the greyish flora that covers them) that stretch 8km south and are 2km wide; a marked footpath leads into the reserve from the main road.

Shifting sands in the mid-19th century forced villagers here to flee to Pervalka and Preila on the east coast, accessible by side roads from the main road. Pine-forested **Vecekrugas Dune** (67.2m), the peninsula's highest dune, south of Preila, stands on a ridge called Old Inn Hill – named after an inn that stood at the foot of the dune before being buried by sand; view it from the Juodkrantė–Nida cycling path.

South of the dunes, there are seaside trails to ramble along and a bird hide between Pervalka and Preila for twitchers.

## Sleeping & Eating

★ **Vila Preiloja** APARTMENT €€
(☎8-613 79597; www.vilapreiloja.lt; Preilos gatvė 17-1, Preila; 2-/4-person apt from €60/70; ) If you're looking a tranquil wood-panelled cottage retreat with a sun deck overlooking the tranquil lagoon and cosy attic bedrooms, you're in the right place. Choose between the snug fisher's cottages or the more spacious and luxurious VIP options, complete with wood-burning stoves. Preila itself is the quieter alternative to Nida, yet only an 8km bike ride from the larger village.

**Marių Akis** LITHUANIAN €€

(☎8-615 36306; Pervalkos gatvė 21, Pervalka; mains €6-13; ⊙10am-10pm; 🔊) Near the pier in Pervalka and overlooking some yachts bobbing in the lagoon, the outdoor terrace of this seaside restaurant makes an excellent halfway stop if you're cycling between Nida and Juodkrantė. It serves salads and fishy and meaty mains.

## Nida

☎469 / POPULATION 1450

Old Baltic legends say it was the giantess Neringa who created Curonian Spit, and her masterpiece is surely Nida. Its hazy pine forests clasp Parnidis Dune, the largest on the peninsula. Boardwalks snake up to the height of the dune, a huge crest of wind-caressed sand that offers golden views into Russian Kaliningrad. Down in Nida village, brightly painted wooden houses and puffing fish smokeries work their magic on visitors.

As Curonian Spit's tourism hotspot, Nida is a delightful base, replete with restaurants and guesthouses. The fishing village turned artists' colony now welcomes numerous summer visitors, including Germans exploring historical East Prussia.

Nida is 48km from Klaipėda and 3km from the Russian border; the town stretches for 2km, but its centre is at the southern end, behind the harbour.

### Sights

**★Parnidis Dune** DUNES

(Parnidžio kopa) The 52m-high Parnidis Dune is simultaneously mighty and fragile. Past settlements around Nida have been engulfed by the moving sand dune but this is a delicate landscape of mountain pines, meadows and fine blonde sand speckled with purple searocket flowers. A 1700m-long path picks its way to a grand panorama at the height of the dune, where you'll find a sundial with a granite obelisk (constructed in 1995). Don't stray from the path, and take all rubbish with you.

Dunes began to move ever-closer to the lagoon after deforestation in the 16th century, which removed the natural barrier of trees. The sands continue to shift: in the space of 30 years, Parnidis Dune has decreased by 10m and it's thought that footfall on the dunes continues the erosion – all the more reason to stick to the path.

**★Nida Cemetery** CEMETERY

(Pamario gatvė; ⊙24hr) This delightful woodland cemetery features some fine examples of *krikštai* (wooden grave markers). Their origins hark back to Lithuania's pagan roots and these wooden markers with symmetrical carvings of plants, birds and more have been traditionally placed at the foot of a grave for centuries. Since the 19th century, the cross motif has been making an appearance.

**Neringa History Museum** MUSEUM

(Neringos Istorijos Muziejus; ☎469-51 162; www.neringosmuziejai.lt; Pamario gatvė 53; adult/child €1/0.50; ⊙10am-6pm Jun-Aug, to 5pm Tue-Sat Sep-May) Curonian Spit's three defining traditional crafts, fishing, crow-catching and amber collecting, are explained within this small regional museum. Look out for images of hardy fishermen sending dragnets underneath the ice of the lagoon in midwinter. Other fascinating photographs depict local hunters biting a crow's neck to kill it, then taking a shot of vodka to dull the taste.

**Amber Gallery** GALLERY

(Gintaro Galerija; ☎469-52 573; www.ambergallery.lt; Pamario gatvė 20; adult/child €2.50/1.20; ⊙10am-7pm Apr-Oct) In an old fisher's hut on the northern side of town is this museum and shop devoted to amber. Staff introduce the mythic and supposed health-boosting properties of this fossilised resin. Visitors can peer through magnifying glasses at insects trapped in amber and explore the amber-ornamented garden. The museum doubles as a boutique selling truly unusual jewellery studded with amber. Enquire ahead for hour-long amber-processing classes (€6).

Most amber jewellery ranges in hues from yellow to blood red, but the most highly prized colours are white, which occurs when the amber is aerated, and the (very rare) black and blue.

Lithuanian mythology describes amber as the frozen tears of Jūratė, a sea goddess who fell in love with a mortal fisherman.

**Ethnographic Fisherman's Museum** MUSEUM

(Žvejo Etnografinė Sodyba; ☎469-52 372; Naglių gatvė 4; adult/child €1/0.50; ⊙10am-6pm Tue-Sun) The Ethnographic Museum is a peek at Nida in the 19th century, with original weathervanes decorating the garden, and rooms inside arranged as they were a couple

## Nida

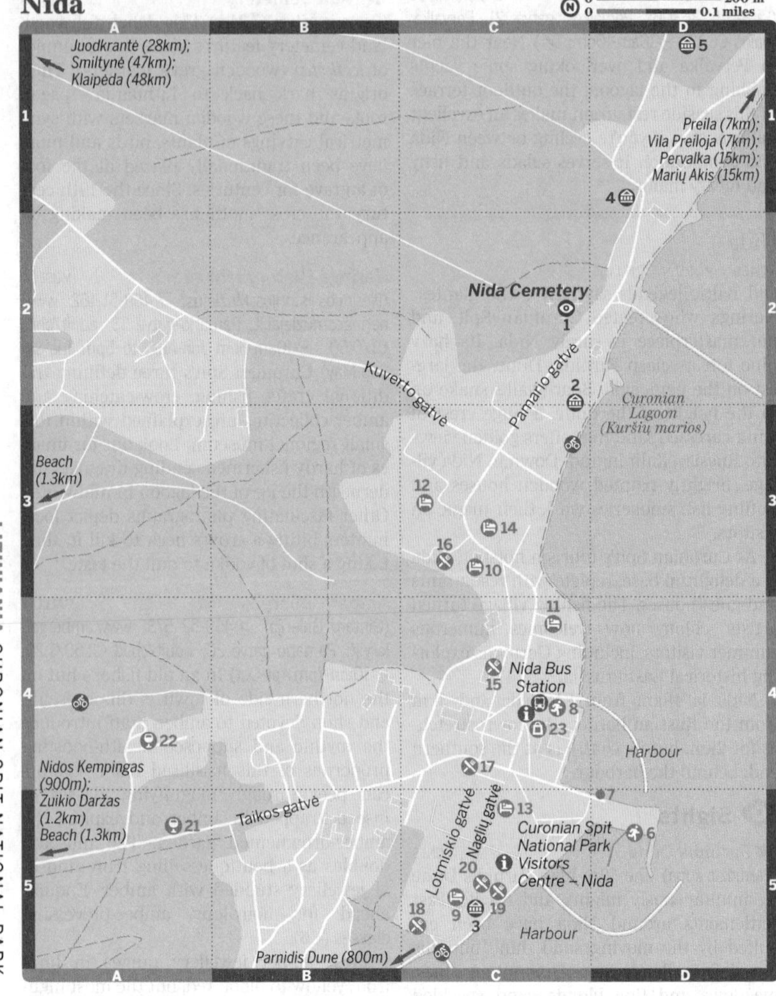




of centuries ago. Check out a traditional fishing vessel in the garden and the thicket of weathervanes.

**Thomas Mann Memorial Museum** MUSEUM

(Tomo Mano Memorialinis Muziejus; ☎469-52 260; www.mann.lt; Skruzdynės gatvė 17; adult/child €2.50/1; ⏲10am-6pm Jun-Aug, to 5pm Tue-Sat Sep-May) The German writer and Nobel laureate Thomas Mann used to own this beautifully situated villa, which is now a museum with numerous original possessions. Mann spent each summer between 1930 and 1932 here, with his wife and children, before fleeing Germany in 1933.

### Activities

You can cycle or walk the many trails that criss-cross the pine forest, take a boat tour of Curonian Lagoon or head to the beach on the opposite side of the spit. Outside high season, scour the beaches for speckles of amber washed up on the shores during the spring and autumn storms, and in the depths of winter brave the frozen lagoon and ice-fish for smelt and burbot.

## Nida



**Kuršis** BOATING

(☎8-686 65242; Nida Harbour; per hour €30) This handsome replica of a *kurėnas,* a traditional 19th-century fishing boat, takes passengers on lagoon tours between June and September and can carry up to six passengers.

**Velo Nida** CYCLING

(☎8-682 14798; www.velonida.lt; Naglių gatvė 18e; per 24hr bicycle/electric bicycle €12/30; ⏲9am-9pm May-Oct) Behind the bus station you'll find this well-run bike-hire place. You can arrange to leave your bicycle in Juodkrantė, Preila, Pervalka or Smiltynė, and luggage transport can be arranged.

**Nemunas Delta Tours** BOATING

(www.visitneringa.com; Nida Harbour; tour from €35) If you have the time, a visit to the stunning Nemunas Delta, with its waterbirds, whispering rushes and picturesque villages, is not to be missed. Operators lining the pier at Nida harbour sail across the lagoon, throwing in lunch at Mingė and an excursion to the Ventės Ragas Ornithological Station. Tours leave around 10am, and take about six hours.

### Festivals & Events

**International Folk Festival** MUSIC

(⏲late Jun) Showcasing Lithuanian and European folk music, and held on a weekend in late June, this folk fiesta swamps Nida with visitors. Book accommodation ahead.

**Nida Jazz Marathon** MUSIC

(www.nidajazz.lt; ⏲late Jul) Held over three days in late July/early August, this festival culminates in a jam session each night.

### Sleeping

There is a great spread of accommodation in Nida, including a beautifully located campground and numerous cosy guesthouses, usually decorated with handicrafts and handmade trimmings. Room prices fluctuate wildly between high season (June to August) and the rest of the year. In the 'cold season', many places close down altogether.

**Nidos Kempingas** CAMPGROUND €

(☎469-52 045; www.kempingas.lt; Taikos gatvė 45a; tent site €6, plus per adult/child €7.50/5, d/apt €75/105; ⏲May-Oct; ) Encircled by forest, Nidos Kempingas is a tranquil, well-tended campsite where the air is fragrant with pine. Beyond the tree-shaded tent sites there are trim double rooms with satellite TV and fridge, and apartments fully equipped for self-caterers. There are also bikes for hire, and basketball and tennis courts. It's at the foot of a path leading to Parnidis Dune.

★ **Miško Namas** GUESTHOUSE €€

(☎469-52 290; www.miskonamas.com; Pamario gatvė 11; d €65-85, 2-/4-person apt from €85/95; ) Overlooking a peaceful garden, this immaculately maintained guesthouse is decked out in Curonian blue-and-white and filled with elegant furnishings, ornaments and lace. Every room has a fridge and a kettle, and some have fully fledged kitchens and balconies. Guests can browse books from the small library or laze in the garden. Breakfast is an optional extra (€8.50) between April and September, and

## BY BIKE FROM NIDA TO JUODKRANTĖ

One of Lithuania's best cycling trips follows Curonian Spit end to end, connecting in the south with a path that leads into the Kaliningrad Region and to the north with another trail that heads off eventually to Palanga and onward towards Latvia. The trail forms part of Eurovelo cycling route No 10, the 'Baltic Sea Circuit'. For our money, arguably the best section of the entire trail runs the 30km from Nida to Juodkrantė.

This part of the trail passes some of the spit's greatest natural treasures, including the Vecekrugas Dune and an authentic fish smoker in Preila. Footpaths lead from the cycling path to Karvaičiai Reservation, where entire villages were buried by sand. Cycling the path also provides the perfect opportunity to spot wild boar and elk, something not so easily accomplished while seated in a car or bus.

To pick up the path in Nida, follow the red-paved cycling track north along the lagoon promenade and, after passing the Thomas Mann Memorial Museum, follow the track left around the corner onto Puvynės gatvė. On the road, turn immediately right and follow it for 3.5km until you see a dirt track forking left into pine forest: this is the start of the cycling path, complete with 0.0km marker.

Heading north, at Pervalka you can cycle through or around the village (the quicker route), arriving 4km later at the entrance to the Naglių Strict Nature Reserve. Shortly afterwards, the cycling path crosses the main road to take cyclists along the opposite (western) side of the spit for the remaining 9km to Juodkrantė.

The first 5km snake beneath pine trees alongside the main road and the final 4km skirt seaside sand dunes. Once you're out of the reserve, leap into the sea for a quick cool-down before the last leg – an uphill slog through forested dunes to arrive in Juodkrantė behind the village.

there are laundry facilities on site (€5). Prices drop by 40% in low season.

**Naglis** GUESTHOUSE €€
(☎8-699 33682; www.naglis.lt; Naglių gatvė 12; d/apt €80/110; 📶) This charming guesthouse in a wooden house near the main port is full of smiles. Doubles comprise two rooms, and some have a door opening out to the table-dotted, tree-shaded garden. There's a dining room and kitchen for guests to share; one room has a fireplace. The guesthouse hires out bikes (per hour/day €3/10).

**Vila Banga** GUESTHOUSE €€
(☎8-686 08073; www.nidosbanga.lt; Pamario gatvė 2; d/apt €98/135; 📶) Within this snug, thatched-roof cottage are seven pleasantly old-fashioned double rooms and apartments. The ambience feels traditional but services are smart: a sauna, bikes for rent (€10 per day) and the option to book yachting excursions.

**Gerda** APARTMENT €€
(☎8-682 17873; Naglių gatvė 5; 2-/4-person apt €85/100; ❄📶) In a wonderful location, literally a stone's throw from the lagoon, this traditional house offers two fully-equipped apartments for rent. The ground-floor restaurant operates well into October and serves terrific spicy bean soup and monkfish liver salad (along with Lithuanian staples).

**Inkaro Kaimas** GUESTHOUSE €€
(☎469-52 123; www.inkarokaimas.lt; Naglių gatvė 26-1; d/apt €68/90; 📶) Blue pillars prop up this beautifully maintained blue-and-red traditional wooden house on the water's edge. Accommodation is in individual apartments, each with its own entrance. The place dates from 1901 and a couple of pine-furnished rooms boast a balcony overlooking the lagoon.

**Hotel Jūratė** HOTEL €€
(☎469-52 300; www.hotel-jurate.lt; Pamario gatvė 3; s/d/tr €49/65/80; 📶) This hotel looks and feels like a sanatorium but its supremely central position and revamped, comfortable rooms with flat-screen TVs and blond wood furnishings make it a good bet. Soviet kitsch-spotters will be thrilled to know that the hotel's most recent facelift didn't get rid of the glitter cement on the corridor walls.

## Eating

Nida has several good restaurants, cafes and bakeries, and a supermarket. Smoked fish (with the smoked eel being the most prized) is a speciality of the peninsula, served at shops, casual open-air joints and full-service restaurants.

**★Tik Pas Joną** SEAFOOD €
(☎8-620 82084; www.facebook.com/rukytoszuvystikpasjona; Naglių gatvė 6-1; mains €4-8; ⏰10am-10pm Apr-Nov, Sat & Sun only Dec-Mar) Picture the scene: you select mackerel or carp or eel from a traditional smoking rack, lay it on a paper plate with a slice of rye bread, and eat with your hands while watching the lagoon glow orange at sunset. This is the best spot in Neringa to feast on the region's famous smoked fish – accompany it with cold beer or pint of *kvass*.

**Kepykla Gardumėlis** BAKERY €
(☎469-52 021; www.kepykla-gardumelis.lt; Pamario gatvė 3; snacks from €1.50; ⏰8am-6pm) Curonian Spit's best place for freshly baked goods and freshly brewed coffee, Gardumėlis makes bread only with stone-ground organic flour. Similar perfectionism is applied to the ingredients destined for their cookies, mille-feuille pastries and poppyseed rolls. Their most unusual treat is *morkų saldainiai* (carrot candy).

**Užeiga Sena Sodyba** LITHUANIAN €€
(☎8-652 12345; www.senasodyba.lt; Naglių gatvė 6; mains €4.50-12; ⏰11am-10pm Mon-Fri) The selection of fish dishes at this snug wooden cottage restaurant is impressive – and inviting – and the pike cutlets are an absolute winner. If you're here during berry season, pair them with pancakes and you'll be in gastronomic heaven.

**Zuikio Daržas** PIZZA €€
(☎8-692 06594; Nidos-Smiltynes plantas 7a; pizza €7-12; ⏰noon-midnight Sun-Wed, to 2am Thu-Sat Jun-Aug, weekends May & Sep; ☑) Right near the sea, this summer-only restaurant serves crowd-pleasing wood-fired pizzas with a plethora of toppings and high-quality ingredients. During peak meal times you're in for a long wait.

**Kavinė Kuršis** LITHUANIAN €€
(☎8-469 52804; www.facebook.com/kavinekursis; Naglių gatvė 29; mains €7-12; ⏰9am-11pm; 📶) A dependable allrounder, Kuršis pumps out omelettes and scrambled eggs at breakfast time, salads and seafood at lunch, and *cepelinai*, pork, pasta and other heavier fare in the evening. One of the very few places open outside high season.

**★Meat SteakHouse** STEAK €€€
(☎8-610 17143; www.meat.lt; Kuverto gatvė 7f; mains €13-33) The Nida branch of the stellar Vilnius steakhouse features the same pared-down decor and a menu of dry-aged rib-eyes, T-bones and filet mignons, with a supporting cast of pork ribs, duck magret and a few token fish and vegetarian dishes. It's also a stellar brunch joint, with seven different takes on eggs Benedict.

**Nidos Seklyčia** EUROPEAN €€€
(☎8-606 69000; www.facebook.com/nidosseklycia5000; Lotmiškio gatvė 1; mains €12-18; ⏰10am-11pm; 📶) Open all year, this beautifully situated restaurant, almost in the lee of the Parnidis Dune, is one of Nida's best. Prices seem steep by Lithuanian standards, but the food, from paprika-laced soups and grilled meats to fish, is really good.

## Drinking & Nightlife

**In Vino** BAR
(☎8-655 77997; www.facebook.com/invinoinnida; Taikos gatvė 32; ⏰10am-midnight May-Sep) Perched in an unlikely position above a block of flats set back from the main road is this wine bar, one of Nida's few dedicated drinking establishments serving good cocktails and a variety of beers. Inside is cosy, lit during daylight hours by picture windows, while outside the rooftop terrace overlooks the Parnidis Dune.

**Faksas** BAR
(☎8-648 53665; Taikos gatvė 32a; ⏰3pm-4am Jun-Aug) This party cabin in the pinewoods is one of the few real nightspots in Nida. Proclaiming itself 'Friendly to rockers, bikers and freaky people', Faksas puts on live acts in summer, and the beer and shots are usually flowing, while the clientele perches on wooden crates that pass for seats.

## Shopping

**Smoked Fish Outlet** FOOD
(Rūkyta žuvis; Naglių gatvė 18; ⏰10am-10pm May-Sep) Sells *ungurys* (eel), *starkis* (pikeperch), *stinta* (smelt), *ešerys* (perch) and *karšis* (bream).

## Information

**Curonian Spit National Park Visitor Centre – Nida** (Lankytojų centras; ☎469-51 256; www.nerija.lt; Naglių gatvė 8, Nida; ⏰9am-6pm Jun-Aug, 9am-noon & 12.45-6pm Mon-Sat May & Sep) A wealth of information about the park, this seasonal centre can also arrange guided nature tours (€31 to €38, two to eight people) in Lithuanian, English, Russian or German.

**Tourist Office** (☎469-52 345; www.visitneringa.com; Taikos gatvė 4; ⏰9am-1pm & 2-6

Mon-Sat; ) Sells maps, books accommodation and stocks loads of information (including photographs) of private rooms and apartments to rent. Can also advise on ferries to/from the Nemunas Delta. Operates reduced hours September to May.

**Police** (469-52 202; Taikos gatvė 5)

**Šiaulių Bankas** (www.sb.lt; Naglių gatvė 18e; 8am-12.30pm & 1.30-4pm Mon-Fri)

## Getting There & Away

The **bus station** (Nidos autobusų stotis; 469-54 859; Naglių gatvė 18e; 7.45am-8pm, to 5pm Sep–mid-Jun) has services to/from Smiltynė (€4, one hour, 10 and 12 daily), stopping en route in Juodkrantė (€3, 35 minutes). The passenger ferry to/from Klaipėda leaves from Smiltynė.

For longer trips, there is at least one daily bus to Vilnius (€27, 5¾ hours) and Kaunas (€24, 4½ hours), and a service at 8.09am to Kaliningrad on the Russian part of Curonian Spit (€8, two hours). During summer, there's an additional service to Kaliningrad at 7.10pm.



# Nemunas Delta

441

The low-lying, marsh-dotted eastern side of the Curonian Lagoon (Kursių marios) could be the end of the world. Tourism has scarcely touched this remote, rural and isolated landscape where summer skies offer magnificent views of the spit's white dunes across the lagoon. In winter ice-fishers sit on the frozen lagoon – up to 12km wide in places – waiting for a smelt to bite. In summer, the place is a haven for birdwatchers, and travellers in search of unique rural life in sleepy fishing villages.

The gateway into the extraordinary Nemunas Delta (Nemuno Delta), where the Nemunas River ends its 937km journey from its source in neighbouring Belarus, is **Šilutė** (population 20,800), a sleepy town an hours' drive south of Klaipėda. **Rusnė Island**, the largest island, covers 48 sq km and increases in size by 15cm to 20cm a year.

## Sights

Apart from a couple of rural museums, a unique waterside village and ample birding in the wetlands and the Ventės Ragas Ornithological Station, here in the delta the joy is very much in the journey and the unhurried exploration of a unique rural landscape.

**★ Nemunas Delta Regional Park** NATIONAL PARK

(Nemuno Deltos Regioninis Parkas; www.nemunodelta.lt) Where the Nemunas, Lithuania's largest river, spills into the Curonian lagoon, it splits into four distributaries: the Skirvytė, the Atmata, the Pakalnė and the Gilija. The result is a wetland delta of surpassing beauty, teeming with birds and bristling with rushes, lilies and small patches of forest. If you're in Nida, or Šilutė, or really anywhere nearby, and have the chance to visit this incredible place, take it. The park administration is on Rusnė, the delta's largest island.

The delta should have twitchers in spasms. Its 240 sq km are dotted with islands, marshes and flooded meadows, creating the perfect environment for the 294 different species of bird noted here. It's located on a migration route running from the Arctic, through Europe to Eastern Africa, so many birds stop here to breed.

**Ventės Ragas Ornithological Station** BIRD SANCTUARY

(8-638 90619; www.vros.lt; Ventės ragas; adult/child €3/2; 10am-7pm Mon-Fri, to 8pm Sat & Sun) The first bird-ringing station was established here in 1929, but it was not until 1959 to 1960 that large bird traps were installed. Today around 100,000 birds pass through the station each migratory period; zigzag, snipe, cobweb and duck traps ensnare birds to be ringed. Two exhibition rooms inside the station explain the birdlife, and an observation deck encourages visitors to spot species first-hand. The station or tourist office can put you in contact with local English-speaking ornithological guides.

**Ethnographic Farmstead Museum** MUSEUM

(Etnografine Sodyba Muziejus; 441-58 169; Skirvytėlės gatvė; admission by donation; 10am-6pm mid-May–mid-Sep) This 200-year-old homestead exhibits fisher's tools, furnishings and three venerable farm buildings, giving a sense of the harsh basics of traditional Delta life. It's signposted 1.8km from Rusnė.

**Uostadvaris Polder Museum** MUSEUM

(Uostadvario polderių muziejus; 441-62 230; Uostadvario gatvė; admission by donation; hours vary) Housed in an old water-pumping station on the Vilkinė, this museum shows the basic technology with which Nemunas farmers have tried to keep the waters at bay. It's in Uostadvaris village, on Rusnė.

## BIRDING IN THE NEMUNAS DELTA

This wetland is a birder's heaven. Some 270 of the 294 bird species found in Lithuania frequent the Nemunas Delta Regional Park and many rare birds breed in the lush marshes around Rusnė, including black storks, white-tailed eagles, black-tailed godwits, pintails, dunlin, ruff and great snipe. The common white stork breeds like there's no tomorrow in Ventė.

The Arctic–European–East African bird-migration flight path cuts through the park, making it a key spot for migratory waterfowl. But it's not just a stopover or feeding site – the park is a breeding ground for around 170 species of bird, and some, such as the pintail, don't breed anywhere else in Lithuania.

Rare aquatic warblers, corncrakes, black-headed gulls, white-winged black terns and great crested grebes have their biggest colonies in the delta. In autumn, up to 200,000 birds – 80% of which are tits and finches – fly overhead at any one time in the sky above Ventės Ragas Ornithological Station, and up to 5000 are ringed each day for research into world migration.

## Sleeping

Campers can pitch tents at designated spots in the park. Wonderful farm accommodation is spread throughout the delta and can be booked online or organised through the regional park headquarters or the tourist office in Šilutė. Some of the most atmospheric accommodation is in Minija and along Ventės Ragas.

**Šturmų Sodyba** GUESTHOUSE €
(☎8-694 53255; www.sturmusodyba.lt; Šilutės ragas/Ventės Ragas; summer house €35, 2-/4-person apt €45/80; 📶) Several kilometres from the tip of Ventės Ragas, this is your chance to disconnect from your hectic life and enjoy the proximity of the sea in one of two comfortable apartments (we particularly like the smaller one with the statement wallpaper) or the basic, cosy summer house. The cafe serves organic vegetables from the garden and homemade *kvass* (gira).

★**Mėlynasis Karpis** GUESTHOUSE €€
(☎441-69 510; www.kintai.lt; d €55, camping per person/tent €3/3.50) This hotel-restaurant offers comfort, seclusion and a plethora of water activities. All rooms come with balcony, and some, located in a house boat, literally sit on the water. The fish dishes are terrific (mains €10 to €12). Fishing trips and boating on the delta can be organised. Guest bicycles available. Find it 6km east of Kintai village on the Minija River.

**Mingės Poilsis** RENTAL HOUSE €€€
(☎8-633 72325; www.mingespoilsis.lt; Minija; apt €60-400) Several fully-equipped traditional houses for rent in the 'Venice of Lithuania'. Apart from accommodation, these folks arrange boat trips on Curonian Lagoon and even kitesfuring lessons (from €40).

## Orientation

In the heart of the Nemunas Delta is **Rusnė**, on the island of the same name, 8km southwest of **Šilutė**, where the main stream divides. There's not much to do here but picnic on the pretty riverbanks and visit two small museums.

Dike-protected polders (land reclaimed from the sea) cover the park, the first polder being built in 1840 to protect Rusnė. Many lower polders are still flooded seasonally and serve as valuable spawning grounds for various fish species (there are some 60 in the park). Close by, on the shores of **Lake Dumblė**, is Lithuania's lowest point, 1.3m below sea level.

**Ventės Ragas** (Ventė Horn) is a sparsely inhabited area on the south-pointing promontory of the delta, which, with its dramatic nature and uplifting isolation, is beautifully wild. A Teutonic Order castle was built here in the 1360s to protect shipping, only for it to collapse within a couple of hundred years due to severe storms on this isolated point. Just east of Ventės Ragas is **Minjia**, a village known as the 'Venice of Lithuania', that straddles both sides of the namesake river and is a popular day-trip destination from Nida on Curonian Spit.

## Information

**Regional Park Headquarters** (☎441-75 050; www.nemunodelta.lt; Kuršmarių gatvė 13, Rusnė; ⏰8am-noon & 12.45-5pm Mon-Thu, to 3.45pm Fri) In the tiny village of Rusnė, this office has information about the Delta, can help with organising itineraries, and even has rooms and bicycles for hire.

**Šilutė Tourist Office** (☎441-77 785; www.siluteinfo.lt; Lietuvininkų gatvė 4; ⏰8am-8pm Mon-Fri, to 4pm Sat & Sun) This immensely helpful office on Šilutė's main road should be the first port of call for those seeking information on accommodation, activities and transport. It produces a handy cycling guide to the region and the annual newspaper *Šilutės kraštas*, which covers accommodation and cultural events in the delta area.

## Getting There & Around

Getting to the area without your own wheels is possible, but exploring it without your own wheels can be tricky.

Šilutė is served by buses from Klaipėda (€4, one hour, 10 daily), Kaunas (€13, three to 3½ hours, eight daily) and Vilnius (€20, five hours, five daily). You can also rent a car in Klaipėda.

Boats are the best means of exploring the delta (it's 8km from Pakalnė to Kintai by boat but 45km by road). The main routes follow the three main delta tributaries – the Atmata (13km), Skirvytė (9km) and Pakalnė (9km) Rivers – which fan out westwards from Rusnė.

At Kintai, Ventainė and Laimutės you can hire out boats with a guide. The office in Šilutė can also help.

Given the sparse traffic around the delta, cycling is a great way to get around the villages; several guesthouses rent bicycles.



# Palanga

☎460 / POP 15,400

One of the most popular seaside resorts since Soviet times, Palanga is a chilled-out place with a split personality – peaceful pensioner paradise in winter, pounding party spot in summer. Tourists from all over Lithuania and abroad come for its idyllic 10km sandy beach backed by sand dunes and fragrant pine forest, criss-crossed by walking and cycle paths.

Despite the crowds, Palanga is charming, with wooden houses and the ting-a-ling of bicycle bells and pedal-powered taxis in the air.

## History

Palanga has often been Lithuania's only port over the centuries; however, it was destroyed by the Swedes in 1710. It was a resort in the 19th century, and a Soviet hotspot. After 1991, villas and holiday homes nationalised under the Soviets were slowly returned to their original owners, and family-run hotels and restaurants opened. In 2005 the city's main pedestrian street enjoyed a facelift befitting the sparkling reputation Palanga now enjoys.

## Sights

Nearly all of the action happens on Basanavičiaus gatvė, a long pedestrian-only concourse that runs perpendicular to the coast and is lined end to end with restaurants, cafes, bars and shops. South of here are the city's two leading non-beach attractions: the Botanical Park and the Amber Museum.

**★Amber Museum** MUSEUM

(Gintaro Muziejus; ☎460-51 319; www.ldm.lt/en/pgm; Vytauto gatvė 17; adult/student €4/2; ⏲10am-8pm Tue-Sat, to 7pm Sun) Housed in a neoclassical palace built by Count Feliksas Tiskevicius in 1897, this revamped museum showcases what is reputedly the world's sixth-largest collection of Baltic gold – 20,000-odd examples in all. The exhibits run the gamut from the formation of amber and its early use in Neolithic times to the striking, contemporary jewellery of today, with magnifying glasses allowing you to zoom in on ancient insect life in golden stasis. Terrific temporary exhibitions of leading Lithuanian jewellery designers.

There's a good selection of amber pieces for sale.

**Botanical Park** PARK

(www.pgm.lt; 15 Vytauto gatvė; ⏲sunrise-sunset) The 1-sq-km park includes a rose garden, 18km of footpaths and Birutė Hill (Birutės kalnas), once a pagan shrine. According to legend, it was tended by vestal virgins, one of whom, Birutė, was kidnapped and married by Grand Duke Kęstutis. A 19th-century chapel tops the hill. The wonderful Amber Museum is inside the park.

**Amber Processing Gallery** GALLERY

(Gintaro Dirbtuvės Galerija; ☎8-682 69139; Dariaus ir Girėno gatvė 27; ⏲10am-7pm) FREE This is the last of the dozen or so original amber shops Palanga boasted in the late 19th century, when it was one of the largest amber-processing centres in the Baltic. Run by the Palanga Guild of Amber Masters, the gallery sells beautiful amber pieces, and lets you try your hand at fashioning your own jewellery.

**Antanas Mončys House Museum** MUSEUM

(Antano Mončio Namai-Muziejus; ☎460-49 366; www.antanasmoncys.com; Daukanto gatvė 16; adult/student €2/1; ⏲11am-5pm Wed-Sun) This museum displays large wooden sculptures, collages and masks by Lithuanian émigré artist Antanas Mončys (1921–93). The sculptor was very tactile and this is one of the very few museums where you can touch the wooden exhibits.

**Exile & Resistance Museum** MUSEUM
(☎460-537 84; J Basanavičiaus gatvė 21; ⊙4-6pm Sat & Sun Jul & Aug) FREE A modest permanent exhibition detailing resistance to foreign (particularly Soviet) occupation in Lithuania's troubled 20th century with personal stories highlighted.

## Activities

A stroll along Basanavičiaus gatvė is a sight in itself – and it's the way most holidaymakers pass dusky evenings. **Stalls** (Basanavičiaus gatvė 4) selling amber straddle the eastern end and amusements dot its entire length – inflatable slides, bungee-jump simulators, merry-go-rounds, electric cars, portrait artists, buskers and street performers with monkeys.

From the end of Basanavičiaus gatvė, a boardwalk leads across the dunes to the pier. By day, street vendors sell popcorn, *ledai* (ice cream), *dešrainiai* (hot dogs), *alus* and *gira* here. At sunset (around 10pm in July), families and lovers gather here on the sea-facing benches to watch the sunset.

From the pier end of Basanavičiaus, a walking and cycling path wends north and south through pine forest. Skinny paths cut west onto the sandy beach at several points. Follow the main path (Meilės alėja) about 500m south onto Darius ir Girėno gatvė, to reach the Botanical Park, where cycling and walking tracks are plentiful.

## Festivals & Events

**Palanga Smelt Fishing Festival** FOOD & DRINK
(Palangos ruoniai; ⊙Feb) Smelts are the tiny fish delicacy that arrive on Palanga's shores for a short period in February. During this three-day festival in mid-February the smelts are prepared around town in all their glory. As an added attraction, hundreds of hardy souls brave the cold waters of the Baltic for a polar-bear swim.

**Palanga Summer Festival** CULTURAL
(www.palangatic.lt/en/event/palanga-summer-festival) The highlight of the summer season is this festival taking place on a different week each summer, closing with a massive street carnival, song festival and pop concert on the last day.

## Sleeping

In summer everything gets booked up fast; winter sees rates slashed by up to half. There's something for all budgets, from hostels to self-catering apartments, charming guesthouses and boutique hotels. In season (June to August), many locals stand on Kretingos gatvė touting 'Nuomojami kambariai' (rooms for rent) signs.

**Laguna** GUESTHOUSE €
(☎460-49 191; www.laguna-hotel.lt; Meilės alėja 12; d from €45; 📶) It's hard to better Laguna's location, nestled under pines where Palanga meets the sea. It's a lovely three-storied timber guesthouse divided into six 'apartments' equipped with fridges, orthopedic mattresses, safes and other conveniences. Great value.

**Symbiosis Hostel** HOSTEL €
(☎8-655 12260; www.symbiosishostel.com; Klaipėdos plentas 62a; dm/s/d €14/25/30; 📶) A five-minute walk from the bus station, this hostel makes up for the 15-minute walk to the sea with its friendly hosts and genuinely nice rooms – spacious, stylishly decorated, with quality furnishings and a well-equipped kitchen. Even the dorms are for two or three people, so you're not packed in like sardines.

**Ema** GUESTHOUSE €
(☎460-48 608; www.ema.lt; Jūratės gatvė 32; s/d €26/44; P📶) This sweet guesthouse is distinguished by friendliness and decor. There's also a decent cafe and tackle shop on the premises.

**Vasaros Ambasada** HOTEL €
(☎8-698 08333; www.palangosambasada.lt; Meilės alėja 16; r from €40; P📶) This attractive small hotel enjoys one of the most enviable locations in town: right on the coast, but only metres from the throngs on Basanavičiaus gatvė. Rooms are plainly furnished and there's not much English spoken here, but everything is clean and well tended. Prices jump extravagantly in high season (June to September).

★**Vila Labas Rytas** HOTEL €€
(☎8-610 07672; www.goodmorning.lt; Gintaro gatvė 41; r/apt from €85/130; 📶) This hotel is all stylish, understated luxury: oodles of living space, blond wood headboards and understated cream and greys with bright pops of crimson. A buffet breakfast is included in the price and there's a sauna and hot tub for guest use.

# Palanga

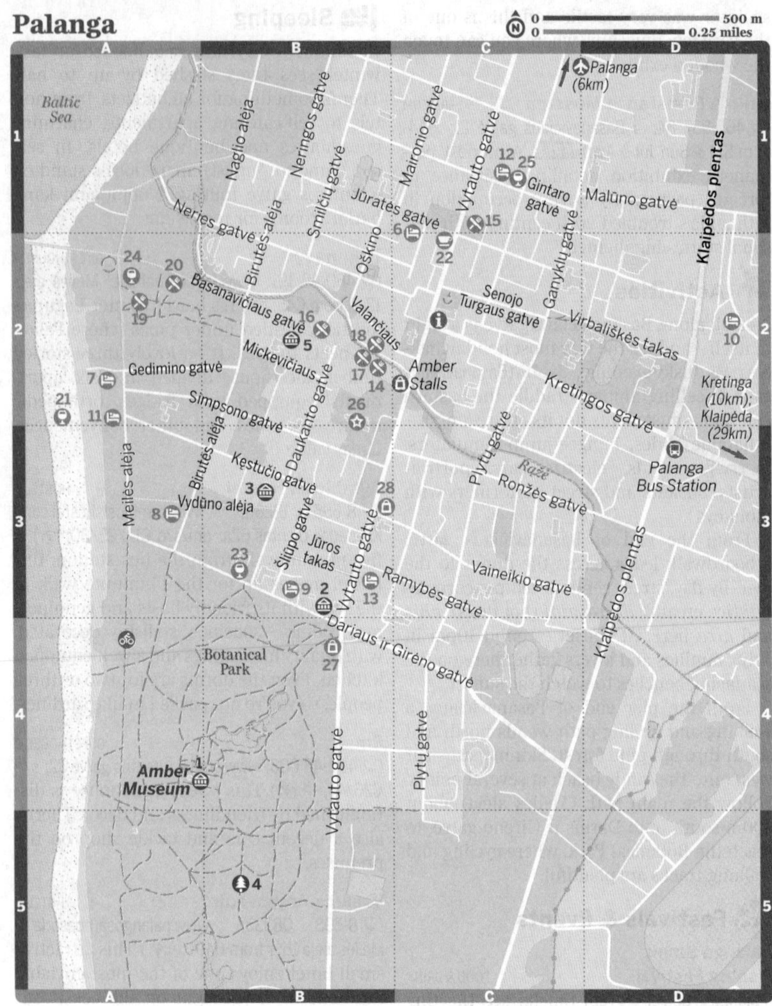


**Vila Ramybė** BOUTIQUE HOTEL €€
(☎460-54 124; www.vilaramybe.lt; Vytauto gatvė 54; s/d €60/75; 📶) It is tricky to snag a room at this stylish, unpretentious standout. Pine-clad rooms come in soothing pastel hues of blues and greens, seven of the 12 have a terrace and most have a little lounge. Apartments are also available.

**Pusų Paunksnėje** GUESTHOUSE €€
(☎460-49 080; www.pusupaunksneje.lt; Dariaus ir Girėno gatvė 2; r/d/ste €85/132/170; P 📶 🏊) We love this upscale hotel owned by Lithuanian basketball star Arvydas Sabonis, its rooms a rhapsody in pastels and creams. The suites come with fireplaces and there's a peaceful courtyard to chill out in.

★**Palanga Spa Life Balance Hotel** DESIGN HOTEL €€€
(☎460-41 414; www.palangahotel.lt; Birutės gatvė 60; d/ste from €130/295, 1-room apt from €245; P ❄ @ 📶 🏊) Wrapped in a grove of pine trees, the Palanga is a stunner. Rooms peer out at the sea and tree trunks through floor-to-ceiling glass, while furnishings are subtle and luxurious, with natural hues of amber, cream and sand predominating. Some even sport their own sauna or Jacuzzi, and there's a wellness spa for all guests.

## Palanga



## Eating

Basanavičiaus gatvė plays host to the majority of restaurants in town.

**★ A-Petit** BISTRO €

(8-602 32586; www.facebook.com/apetitpalanga; Vytauto gatvė 112; mains €4-8; 9am-10pm; ) There are many things to like about this bistro: the appealing garden setting and mismatched furniture, the friendly staff and a menu full of expertly prepared salads, decent burgers and a host of breakfast dishes, including a superlative take on *syrniki* (fried cottage-cheese fritters).

**1925 Baras** LITHUANIAN €€

(460-52 256; www.baras1925.lt; Basanavičiaus gatvė 4; mains €9-15; 10am-midnight) This handsome timbered tavern has provided relief from the main street madness since 1925. The Lithuanian cuisine is good and simple, and the restaurant's back garden as charming as you'll find in Palanga.

**Molinis ąsotis** EUROPEAN €€

(460-40 208; www.molinisasotis.lt; Basanavičiaus gatvė 8; mains €7-24; 11am-midnight; ) This handsomely timbered restaurant distinguishes itself from the plentiful competition on Palanga's main strip by selling art and jewellery as well as serving excellent food. Its broadly European menu also includes Lithuanian dishes such as meat-stuffed potato pancakes and boiled pork shank with peas and crackling.

**Čagino** RUSSIAN €€

(460-53 555; www.cagin.lt; Basanavičiaus gatvė 14a; mains €7-11; noon-midnight; ) Čagino is a slice of Russia in Palanga, offering *pirozhki* and *pelmeni* (pies and dumplings), stewed venison, veal with cherries and *holodets* (meat in aspic), plus other favourites. There's live music some nights from 8pm. Kids' menu as well.

**★ Vila Komoda** FUSION €€€

(460-20 490; www.vilakomoda.lt; Meilės alėja 5; mains €20-25, tasting menu €60; 6.30-11pm Tue-Sat) Found inside the intimate boutique hotel owned by renowned Lithuanian chef Martynas Meidus, Palanga's best restaurant is also in Lithuania's top five. Expect delicate, beautiful, contemporary Lithuanian dishes that you'll be loath to demolish, and expert pairings of local ingredients. There is a carefully chosen wine list, too.

**Restoranas Onorė** FUSION €€€

(8-618 07658; www.facebook.com/restoranas.onore; Valančiaus gatvė 1; mains €14-25; noon-11pm Mon-Sat, to 9pm Sun) Overlooking the river from a quiet location, this is Palanga's most imaginative restaurant, with a short and creative menu – tuna tartare with avocado, shellfish soup with coconut milk, octopus with lemon-peel confit. We won't tell you what the Onorė dessert consists of, but it's definitely worth your money!

**Žuvinė** SEAFOOD €€€
(☎460-48 070; www.zuvine.lt; Basanavičiaus gatvė 37a; mains €14-28; ⏲11am-midnight; 📶) It would be a crime to come to the Baltic coast and not sample some of the local fish, and Žuvinė, while more expensive than most other options in Palanga, has you covered. Try the zander with spinach and beetroot cream, or the eel smoked on Curonian Spit.

## Drinking & Nightlife

**Kablys: Jūra. Kultūra** BAR
(☎8-610 34231; www.facebook.com/kablysjura; Dariaus ir Girėno gatvė 13; ⏲10am-midnight Mon-Thu & Sun, to 3am Fri & Sat; 📶) The most off-beat and diverse venue in Palanga, Kablys ('hook') faces the Botanical Park, away from the noise and action of central Palanga. It's a bar, cafe, gallery, cinema, book exchange and event space rolled into one.

**7777** BAR
(☎8-656 23304; www.facebook.com/7777baras; ⏲noon-late) Take the wooden boardwalk across the dunes from Vasaros Ambasada to reach this beach. The drinks are pretty standard – Aperol and melon spritzes, Švyturys beers, some sparkling wine – but there are few better places for digging your toes into the sand and toasting the Baltic sunset.

**Šilelis GastroPub** PUB
(☎8-609 33601; Gintaro gatvė 43; ⏲11am-midnight Mon-Thu, to 2am Fri & Sat, noon-midnight Sun) Charming pub with an outdoor terrace peeking out of the foliage, retro '80s interior and some interesting Lithuanian craft beers on the menu. Generous portions of burgers and ribs served.

**Fotokava** COFFEE
(☎8-678 52876; www.facebook.com/fotokava; Vytauto gatvė 69; ⏲8am-9pm Mon-Sat, 9am-8pm Sun) The one independent coffee outlet among Palanga's coffee chain outlets, Fotokava is a stylish space decked out with vintage cameras. It's not a speciality coffee shop, but the brew ain't bad. Skip the cakes.

**Šachmatinė** CLUB
(☎8-604 58617; www.facebook.com/sachmatine; Basanavičiaus gatvė 45; ⏲11pm-6am Wed-Sat) One of the biggest, most raucous clubs in Palanga, playing mainly house and mainstream dance music until dawn.



## ☆ Entertainment

**Palanga Concert Hall** CONCERT VENUE
(Palangos Koncertų Salė; ☎46-241 500; www.palangosks.lt; Vytauto gatvė 43) This state-of-the-art 2200-seat auditorium stages everything from ballet to pop and rock gigs.

## Shopping

★ **Amber Cat** JEWELLERY
(☎8-633 22777; Vytauto gatvė 19; ⏲10am-7pm) An excellent choice of amber pieces made by Lithuanian master craftspeople. There's something for every price range, from small earrings in a variety of hues, to heavy necklaces, statement pendants, amber sailing-ship models and elaborate chess sets that will set you back at least €1000.

**Baltijos Auskas** JEWELLERY
(☎460-51 386; Vytauto gatvė 66; ⏲10am-2pm & 3-6pm Mon-Fri, 10am-5pm Sat) 'Baltic Gold' is among the best of Palanga's amber galleries: choose between big chunky necklaces, heavy pendants, unusual jewellery pieces involving rough-hewn amber chunks and small, delicate earrings.

## ℹ Information

**Palangos vaistinė** (Vytauto gatvė 33; ⏲9am-8pm Mon-Fri, to 6pm Sat, to 4pm Sun) Pharmacy in the former KGB headquarters (1944–51).

**Police** (☎460-53 837; Vytauto gatvė 4)

**Tourist Office** (☎460-48 811; www.palangatic.lt; Vytauto gatvė 94; ⏲9am-7pm Mon-Fri, 10am-4pm Sat & Sun) Books accommodation and sells maps and guides. Shorter hours outside July and August.

## ℹ Getting There & Away

Reach Palanga by road or air; services are substantially more frequent in summer.

### AIR

**Palanga Airport** (Palangos Oro Uostas; ☎6124 4442; www.palanga-airport.lt; Liepojos plentas 1), 6km north of the centre, has regular passenger services to Copenhagen and Oslo via SAS (www.flysas.com), as well as intermittent services to Oslo with Norwegian Air Shuttle (www.norwegian.com), Rīga via airBaltic (www.airbaltic.com) and London Luton with WizzAir (www.wizzair.com).

### BUS

Services from the **bus station** (☎460-53 333; www.naujapalangosautobusustotis.lt; Klaipėdos plentas 42; ⏲ticket office 7am-7.30pm) include Kaunas (€16.50 to €19.40, three to five hours, two to three hourly), Klaipėda (€1.40 to €2.20, 30 minutes, two to three hourly), Šiauliai (€11, three hours, seven daily) and Vilnius (€20 to €23, 4¼ to six hours, eight daily). In summer, there are daily services to Kaliningrad (€9, 5½ hours), Russia, via Klaipėda at 5pm.

### Getting Around

Bus 100 runs to/from the airport (€2.40, five or six daily) in both directions, timed to meet flights.

The main taxi stand is on Kretingos gatvė in front of the bus station; a taxi from the airport into town costs between €10 and €12.

Pedal-powered taxis are at the eastern end of Basanavičius gatvė. From May to September, stalls renting bicycles (around €8/15 per hour/day) and all manner of electric wheeled transport pepper the town. Download the **CityBee** (www.citybee.lt) app to make use of their bicycle pickup spots and electric scooters.

## Around Palanga

Brash **Šventoji**, 12km north, lacks the panache of Palanga but it entertains with its inflatable fish that spit out kids, dodgem cars and merry-go-round of restaurant entertainers and fun-fair rides. **Nemirseta**, a couple of kilometres south of Palanga, is known for its incredible sand dunes and for being the furthest east the Prussians ever got. Five buses daily run to Šventoji from Palanga, but to reach Nemirseta you'll need your own transport.

About 10km east of Palanga, the town of **Kretinga** is connected to Palanga by frequent buses (€1, 15 minutes).

### Sights

**Kretinga Museum** MUSEUM

(Kretingos Muziejus; ☎445-77 323; www.kretingosmuziejus.lt; Vilniaus gatvė 20; adult/concession €5/1.20; ⏲museum 10am-6pm Wed-Sun, winter garden 10am-6pm Tue-Sun) A crumbling winter garden attached to the Kretinga Museum houses a tropical mirage of 850 species of exotic plants. The museum itself is located in one of the many homes of the Tyszkiewicz family of Polish nobles. Find the museum west of the centre in the Kretinga city park.

★**Orvydas Garden** GARDENS

(Orvidų Sodyba; ☎613-28 624; www.orvidusodyba.lt; Gargždelė; adult/student €4/3; ⏲10am-7pm Tue-Sun) The Orvydas Garden was the work of stonemason Kazys Orvydas (1905–89) and his oldest son turned Franciscan monk, Vilius (1952–92). The carvings were originally created for the village cemetery in nearby Salantai but were brought here to the Orvydas homestead after then Soviet leader Nikita Khrushchev turned his wrath on religious objects in the 1960s. The Soviets later blocked access to the house to prevent visitors getting to the persecuted Orvydas family.

Today visitors can walk through the lovely farmstead gardens admiring literally hundreds of statues, carvings, busts and just plain oddities. Three daily buses between Kretinga and Skuodas stop in Salantai and Mosėdis. For the Orvydas Garden get off at the last stop before Salantai and walk about 1km.

## Žemaitija National Park

☎448 / POP 3500

The 200-sq-km Žemaitija National Park, a bewitching landscape of lake and forest, is as mysterious as it is beautiful. It's easy to see why it spawns fables of devils, ghosts and buried treasure.

The draw here is two-fold. You can swim, boat and bike around at your leisure, as well as pay a visit to one of the country's newest and most bizarre attractions: a museum to the Cold War, housed in what was once a Soviet nuclear missile base.

The best access point is the small town of **Plateliai**, on the western shore of the lake of the same name and home to the helpful Žemaitija National Park Visitor Centre.

### Sights

★**Cold War Museum** MUSEUM

(Šaltojo Karo Muziejus; ☎8-677 86574; www.zemaitijosnp.lt; Plokščiai; adult/child €5/2.50; ⏲tours hourly 10am-6pm May-Sep, to 4pm Oct-Apr) This museum on the site of a former Soviet nuclear missile base is situated deep in the heart of the Žemaitija National Park. The highlight is the chance to poke around inside one of the former underground bunkers, complete with multimedia displays, ominous music and displays of weaponry and mannequins in military attire.

It's about 8km from Plateliai: follow the main road to Plokštinė, then 5km along a sign-posted gravel road through the pines.

Built in the 1960s in secret from the Lithuanian people, the base had enough firepower to flatten most of Europe, and may have played a role in the Cuban missile crisis. There's a small exhibition on the history of the Cold War in the Baltic countries, and on the construction and role of the base, as well as some Soviet detritus in the gift shop.

★ **Plateliai Manor** MUSEUM
(Platelių Dvaras; ☎8-659 07918; www.zemaitijosnp.lt; Didžioji gatvė 22; adult/child €2.50/1.50; ⊙10am-5pm Tue-Sun) The old granary and stable of the former Plateliai Manor now houses a highly worthwhile museum complex. The granary holds a multistorey exhibition dedicated to the nature, history and ethnography of the area, as well as archaeological findings from Sventrokalnis and Pilies islands on the lake. The highlight is the stable housing a fascinating exhibition of local Shrove Tuesday Carnival customs, complete with around 250 elaborately carved, creepy masks.

**Žemaitija Art Museum** MUSEUM
(Žemaičių Dailės Muziejus; ☎448-52 492; www.zdm.lt; Parko gatvė 1, Plungė; adult/child €3/2; ⊙10am-6pm Tue-Sun May-Oct) The 19th-century Oginski Palace, in the nearby city of Plungė, holds an interesting collection of modern Samogitian art (carvings and metal works). The landscaped grounds surrounding the palace, criss-crossed with terraced ponds, are a sight in themselves. Shorter hours in winter.

## Activities

Most activities centre around **Lake Plateliai** (Platelių ežeras). The national park visitor centre rents bicycles and hands out cycling maps of various trails in the lake area. One of the easiest and most enjoyable rides is to remote Plokštinė (8km), the site of the former missile base and now home to the Cold War Museum.

## Festivals & Events

Many traditional Samogitian festivals are celebrated in the small town of Plateliai on the lake's western shore, including the amazingly colourful **Shrove Tuesday Carnival** (Mardi Gras; the Tuesday before Ash Wednesday in the Christian calendar).

## Sleeping & Eating

Plateliai's visitor centre has a list of B&Bs (around €20 to €25 per person) in some remote farms and private homes in the park.

**Hotel Linelis** HOTEL €
(☎8-655 77666; www.linelis.lt; Paplatelės; s/d/ste €40/45/80; ) Linelis has a fine restaurant and spa centre on the lake's eastern edge, plus a windsurfing centre. Breakfast costs an additional €5.

**Vila Runa** FARMSTAY €
(☎8-672 46572; www.poilsisplateliuose.lt; Ežero gatvė 37; d/apt €45/60; ) This delightful farmstead guesthouse is spread over several buildings, centred on a Swedish-style house. You'll find comfortable rooms, bikes for hire, swings and a grass-fringed pond for family leisure, and a welcome of real generosity from the owners. To find it, walk uphill from the town centre (not down towards the lake).

**Julija and Bronius Staponkai** FARMSTAY €
(☎8-617 03418; jbstaponkai@gmail.com; Ežero gatvė 38; r €30-45) Cosy apartments for rent, a five-minute walk from the lake. Russian and German spoken.

**Užkandinė Plate Lyn** LITHUANIAN €
(☎8-621 32194; Kalvarijos gatvė 36; mains from €3; ⊙10am-8pm Tue-Sun) The pick of a small, uninspiring bunch, this restaurant serves Lithuanian staples and quantity-over-quality set lunches (€4).

## Information

**Žemaitija National Park Visitor Centre** (Žemaitijos nacionalinio parko direkcija; ☎448-49 231; www.zemaitijosnp.lt; Didžioji gatvė 8, Plateliai; ⊙8am-5pm Mon-Thu, to 6pm Fri, 10am-5pm Sat May-Sep) rents bicycles (€10 per day), arranges guides (around €40; must be booked in advance), has information on yacht, windsurfer and boat hire, and can direct you to the workshops of local folk artists.

It also hosts a small exhibition on park flora and fauna.

## Getting There & Away

Plungė, the nearest city, is best reached by train from Klaipėda (€4 to €5, 45 minutes to 1¼ hours, six daily) and from Vilnius (€13 to €16, 3½ hours, three daily). There are several buses daily from Klaipėda (€5, 1½ hours, 12 daily), Kaunas (€12 to €14, 3¼ to four hours, five daily) and Palanga (€4, one to 1¼ hours, five daily). From Plungė, there are six buses onward to Plateliai on summer weekdays; fewer on weekends.

# UNDERSTAND LITHUANIA

## Lithuania Today

Lithuania today is in the best place it's been since Independence. Economically and culturally it's making strides: it's becoming an ever-more confident member of the EU and tourists are visiting in unprecedented numbers. It's palpably modernising, but not at the expense of its own deep-rooted, idiosyncratic culture, still widely celebrated in song, craft and cuisine.

The Lithuanian economy has grown significantly since Independence, stalling dramatically with the 2008–09 economic crisis, but picking up again in 2015. Now, it's once more one of the fastest growing economies in the EU.

Still, the recent economic growth hasn't been enough to make up for the decades of stagnation under Soviet rule. Even in the heart of Vilnius, buildings still show signs of wartime damage, and many young, educated Lithuanians are seeking work opportunities in other parts of the EU.

There's a greater sense of prosperity and optimism, especially on the streets of Vilnius, where it's evident in flashier cars and clothes, and flourishing restaurant and bar scenes. Of course, there are still plenty left behind: unemployment is at 9% and homelessness is a visible problem.

While Lithuania continues to look westwards, the spectre of Soviet occupation still hovers over the country, and there's considerable wariness of Lithuania's large, belligerent neighbour in spite of the country's EU and NATO membership.

## History

A powerful state in its own right at its peak in the 14th to 16th centuries, Lithuania subsequently disappeared from the map in the 18th century, only to reappear briefly between the wars, and ultimately regain Independence (from the Soviets) in 1991. Kaunas' Vytautas the Great War Museum and Vilnius' National Museum of Lithuania cover the whole span of Lithuania's history.

### Tribal Testosterone

Human habitation in the wedge of land that makes up present-day Lithuania goes back to at least 9000 BC. Trade in amber started during the Neolithic period (6000 to 4500 years ago), providing the Balts – the ancestors of modern Lithuanians – with a ready-made source of wealth when they arrived on the scene from the southeast some time around 2000 BC.

Two millennia on, it was this fossilised pine resin and the far-flung routes across the globe its trade had forged – all brilliantly explained in Palanga's Amber Museum – that prompted a mention of the amber-gathering *aesti* on the shores of the Baltic Sea in *Germania,* a Roman book about the Germanic tribes written in AD 98. It wasn't until AD 1009 that Litae (Latin for Lithuania) first appeared in written sources (the *Kvedlinburgh Chronicle*) as the place where an



### TOP HISTORICAL READS

**The Last Girl** (2003; Stephan Collishaw) Absolutely spellbinding, this superb historical novel set in Vilnius flits between WWII and the 1990s.

**Lithuania Awakening** (1990; Alfred Senn) From 'new winds' (the birth of the Independence movement in the 1980s) to a 'new era' (Independence), Senn's look at how the Lithuanians achieved Independence remains the best in its field.

**And Kovno Wept** (1998; Waldemar Ginsburg) Life in the Kovno ghetto is powerfully retold by one of its survivors.

**Lithuania – Independent Again: The Autobiography of Vytautas Landsbergis** (2000) The scene outside parliament on 13 January 1991 is among the dramatic moments Landsbergis brings vividly to life in his autobiography.

**Forest of the Gods** (1989; Balys Sruoga) The author's powerful account of his time spent in the Stutthof Nazi concentration camp in the early 1940s was censored, and hence not published until 1957. It was transferred onto celluloid by Algimantas Puipa in 2005.

### LATE TO THE CHURCH

While today Lithuanians are staunchly Roman Catholic (a short stroll through steeple-rich Vilnius is enough to convince any doubters), it wasn't always this way. In fact, Lithuania is considered to be the last pagan country in Europe. It wasn't fully baptised into Roman Catholicism until 1413.

There are lots of reasons for this: foremost among them was the Lithuanians' fierce independence, militating against attempts to convert them.

The country's relatively recent experience (if you can call the 15th century 'recent') with paganism explains why so much of its religious art, national culture and traditions have pagan roots.

During the Soviet years, Catholicism was persecuted and hence became a symbol of nationalistic fervour. Churches were seized, closed and turned into 'museums of atheism' or used for other secular purposes (such as a radio station in the case of Christ's Resurrection Basilica (p344) in Kaunas, open for business as usual today) by the state.

After Independence in 1991, the Catholic Church quickly began the ongoing process of reacquiring church property and reconsecrating places of worship.

These days, around 77% of Lithuanians consider themselves to be Catholics. There are small minorities of other sects and faiths, including Russian Orthodox (4%) and Protestant Christians (2%). Muslims, Jews and Karaite combined make up less than 1%.

archbishop called Brunonus was struck on the head by pagans.

By the 12th century Lithuania's peoples had split into two tribal groups: the Samogitians (lowlanders) in the west and the Aukštaitija (highlanders) in the east and southeast. Around this time, some sources say, a wooden castle was built on the top of Gediminas Hill in Vilnius.

## Medieval Mayhem

In the mid-13th century Aukštaitija leader Mindaugas unified Lithuanian tribes to create the Grand Duchy of Lithuania, of which he was crowned king in 1253 at Kernavė. Mindaugas accepted Catholicism in a bid to defuse the threat from the Teutonic Order – Germanic crusaders who conquered various Prussian territories, including Memel (present-day Klaipėda). Unfortunately, neither conversion nor unity lasted very long: Mindaugas was assassinated in 1263 by nobles keen to keep Lithuania pagan and reject Christianity.

Under Grand Duke Gediminas (1316–41), Lithuania's borders extended south and east into modern-day Belarus and Ukraine, and even included Kiev for a time. After Gediminas' death, two of his sons shared the realm: in Vilnius, Algirdas pushed the southern borders of Lithuania past Kyiv, while Kęstutis – who plumped for a pretty lake island in Trakai as a site for his castle – fought off the Teutonic Order.

Algirdas' son Jogaila took control of the country in 1382, but the rising Teutonic threat forced him to make a watershed decision in the history of Europe. In 1386 he wed Jadwiga, crown princess of Poland, to become Władysław II Jagiełło of Poland and forge a Lithuanian-Polish alliance that would last 400 years. The Aukštaitija were baptised in 1387 and the Samogitians in 1413, making Lithuania the last European country to accept Christianity.

## Glory Days

Jogaila spent most of his time in Kraków, but trouble was brewing at home. In 1390 his cousin Vytautas revolted, forcing Jogaila's hand. In 1392 he named Vytautas Grand Duke of Lithuania on condition that he and Jogaila share a common policy. The decisive defeat of the Teutonic Order by their combined armies at Grünwald (in modern-day Poland) in 1410 ushered in a golden period of prosperity, particularly for the Lithuanian capital Vilnius, which saw its legendary Old Town born.

Vytautas ('the Great') extended Lithuanian control further south and east. By 1430, when he died, Lithuania stretched beyond Kursk in the east and almost to the Black Sea in the south, creating one of Europe's largest empires. Nowhere was its grandeur and clout better reflected than in 16th-century Vilnius, which, with a population of 25,000-odd, was one of eastern Europe's biggest cities. Fine late-Gothic and Renaissance buildings sprang up, and Lithuanians such as Žygimantas I and II occupied the Polish-Lithuanian throne inside the sumptuous Royal Palace.

In 1579 Polish Jesuits founded Vilnius University and made the city a bastion of the Catholic Counter-Reformation. Under Jesuit influence, Baroque architecture also arrived.

## Polonisation & Partitions

Lithuania gradually sank into a junior role in its partnership with Poland, climaxing with the formal union of the two states (instead of just their crowns) at the Union of Lublin in 1569, during the Livonian War with Muscovy.

Under the so-called Rzeczpospolita (Commonwealth), Lithuania played second fiddle to Poland. Its gentry adopted Polish culture and language, its peasants became serfs and Warsaw usurped Vilnius as political and social hub.

A century on it was Russia's turn to play tough. In 1654 Russia invaded the Rzeczpospolita and temporarily snatched significant territory from it. By 1772 the Rzeczpospolita was so weakened that the states of Russia, Austria and Prussia simply carved it up in the Partitions of Poland (1772, 1793 and 1795). Most of Lithuania went to Russia, while a small chunk in the southwest was annexed by Prussia, but passed into Russian hands after the Napoleonic wars.

## Russification & Nationalism

While neighbouring Estonia and Latvia were governed as separate provinces, Russian rule took a different stance with rebellious Lithuania.

Vilnius had quickly become a refuge for Polish and Lithuanian gentry dispossessed by the region's new Russian rulers and a focus of the Polish national revival, in which Vilnius-bred poet Adam Mickiewicz was a leading inspiration. When Lithuanians joined a failed Polish rebellion against Russian rule in 1830, Tsarist authorities clamped down extra hard. They shut Vilnius University, closed Catholic churches and monasteries, and imposed Russian Orthodoxy. Russian law was introduced in 1840 and the Russian language was used for teaching. A year after a second rebellion in 1863, books could only be published in Lithuanian if they used the Cyrillic alphabet, while publications in Polish (spoken by the Lithuanian gentry) were banned altogether.

National revival gained some momentum in the 19th and early 20th centuries. While most Lithuanians continued to live in rural areas and villages, the rapid industrialisation of Vilnius and other towns gave nationalist drives more clout. Vilnius became an important Jewish centre during this period, with Jews making up around 75,000 of its 160,000-strong population in the early 20th century to earn it the nickname 'Jerusalem of the North'.

## Independence

Ideas of Baltic national autonomy and independence had been voiced during the 1905 Russian revolution, but it was not until 1918 that the restoration of the Independent State of Lithuania was declared. During WWI Lithuania was occupied by Germany and it was still under German occupation on 16 February 1918 when a Lithuanian national council, the Taryba, declared independence in Vilnius in the House of Signatories. In November Germany signed an armistice with the Western Allies, and the same day a Lithuanian republican government was set up.

With the re-emergence of an independent Poland eager to see Lithuania reunited with it or to cede the Vilnius area, which had a heavily Polish and/or Polonised population, things turned nasty. On 31 December 1918 the Lithuanian government fled to Kaunas, and days later the Red Army installed a communist government in Vilnius. Over the next two years the Poles and Bolsheviks played a game of tug-of-war with the city, until the Poles annexed Vilnius once and for all on 10 October 1920. Thus from 1920 until 1939 Vilnius and its surrounds formed a corner of Poland, while the rest of Lithuania was ruled from Kaunas under the authoritarian rule (1926–40) of Lithuania's first president, Antanas Smetona (1874–1944).

In 1923 Lithuania annexed Memel (present-day Klaipėda), much to the displeasure of its former ruler, a much-weakened Germany.

## WWII & Soviet Rule

With the signing of the Nazi-Soviet non-aggression pact in 1939 and the German invasion of Poland in September of that year, Lithuania fell into Soviet hands. The USSR insisted on signing a 'mutual-assistance pact' with Lithuania in October and returned Vilnius to the Lithuanian motherland as part of the inducement. But this was little consolation for the terror Lithuania experienced as a USSR republic – Soviet purges saw thousands upon thousands of people killed or deported.

Following Hitler's invasion of the USSR and the German occupation of the region in 1941, nearly all of Lithuania's Jewish population – more than 90% of the country's 200,000 Jews – was killed; most Vilnius Jews perished in its ghetto or in the nearby Paneriai Forest. Ethnic Lithuanians suffered proportionately much less, but thousands were killed, and between 1944 and 1945 some 80,000 fled West to avoid the Red Army's reconquest of the Baltic countries.

Immediate resistance to the reoccupation of Lithuania by the USSR, in the form of the partisan movement 'Forest Brothers', began in 1944. Between 1944 and 1952 under Soviet rule, a further 250,000 Lithuanians were killed, arrested or deported, as patriotic spirit and thought were savagely suppressed.



## Finally Free

A yearning for independence had simmered during the *glasnost* years of the mid-1980s, but it was with the storming success of Lithuania's popular front, Sajūdis, in the March 1989 elections for the USSR Congress of People's Deputies (Sajūdis won 36 of the 42 directly elected Lithuanian seats) that Lithuania surged ahead in the Baltic push for independence. The pan-Baltic human chain, which was formed to mark the 50th anniversary of the Nazi-Soviet nonaggression pact a few months later, confirmed public opinion and, in December that year, the Lithuanian Communist Party left the Communist Party of the Soviet Union.

Vast pro-independence crowds met then Soviet leader Mikhail Gorbachev when he visited Vilnius in January 1990. Sajūdis won a majority in the elections to Lithuania's supreme Soviet in February, and on 11 March the assembly declared Lithuania an independent republic. In response, Moscow carried out weeks of troop manoeuvres around Vilnius and clamped an economic blockade on Lithuania, cutting off fuel supplies.

Soviet hardliners gained the ascendancy in Moscow in the winter of 1990–91, and in January 1991 Soviet troops and paramilitary police stormed and occupied Vilnius' TV tower and Parliament, killing 14 people. Some of the barricades put up around the Parliament remain. On 6 September 1991 the USSR recognised the independence of Lithuania.

## Towards Europe

Lithuanians have a sense of irony: they led the Baltic push for independence then, at their first democratic parliamentary elections in 1992, raised eyebrows by voting in the ex-communist Lithuanian Democratic Labour Party (LDDP). Presidential elections followed in 1993, the year the last Soviet soldier left the country, with former Communist Party first secretary Algirdas Brazauskas winning 60% of the vote.

It was a painful time for the country. Corruption scandals dogged Brazauskas' term in office and inflation ran wild, peaking around 1000%. Thousands of jobs were lost and the country's banking system collapsed in 1995–96.

But change was under way that would eventually fuel economic growth. The litas replaced the *talonas* (coupon), the transitional currency used during the phasing out of the Soviet rouble in Lithuania, and a stock exchange opened.

Presidential elections in 1998 ushered in wild card Valdas Adamkus (b 1926), a Lithuanian émigré and US citizen who had come to the US after WWII when his parents fled the Soviet advance. Adamkus was succeeded by Rolandas Paksas, the popular Vilnius mayor and champion stunt pilot, in 2003.

Large-scale privatisation took place in 1997–98, but a deep recession struck following the 1998 economic crisis in Russia. Nevertheless, Lithuania managed to claw its way back and joined the World Trade Organization in 2000. In 2002 – in a bid to make exports competitive and show a determination to join Europe – it pegged its currency to the euro instead of the US dollar. It joined the Eurozone in 2015.

In 2004 Lithuania joined the EU and NATO and has been a staunch supporter of both ever since. In November 2004 it became the first EU member to ratify the EU constitution.

True to his Lithuanian heritage, Adamkus battled hard in the political ring and regained the presidency in 2004 following the impeachment of Paksas for granting Lithuanian citizenship to a shady Russian businessman who was a major financial supporter. Adamkus finished his five-year term in office in 2009 and was replaced by Dalia Grybauskaitė, who became the country's first female head of state, strongly critical of Putin and focused on tackling corruption, and was re-elected in 2014.

In 2019, the battle to find her successor was on as the country looked back on Soviet atrocities and convicted 67 former Soviet military and KGB officers of crimes against humanity in absentia.

## The People

The Lithuanian population is predominantly urban: two-thirds of people live in urban areas, with the five largest cities – Vilnius, Kaunas, Klaipėda, Šiauliai and Panevėžys – accounting for nearly half the population.

Lithuania is also the most ethnically homogeneous population of the three Baltic countries; indigenous Lithuanians count for 84% of the total population, making multiculturalism less of a hot potato than in Latvia or Estonia. Poles form the second-biggest grouping, making up around 7% of the population, approaching 250,000 people. Russians form around 6% of the population, while Jews make up just 0.1%.

The country's smallest ethnic community, numbering just 280, are the Karaites. An early-19th-century prayer house and ethnographic museum in Trakai provide insight into the culture and beliefs of this tiny Turkic minority.

Lithuanian Roma officially number around 3000. Vilnius' Human Rights Monitoring Institute (www.hrmi.lt) reckons some 47% are aged under 20 and many, unlike the Roma elders they live with, don't speak Lithuanian.

Net migration has been negative for the past several years, with literally hundreds of thousands of Lithuanians emigrating to countries where, even cleaning homes and tending bars, they can earn salaries two to three times higher than those available locally. Initially, Ireland and the UK were popular destinations, but Scandinavia is also now in favour.

More than three million Lithuanians live abroad, including an estimated 652,000 in the US. Other large communities exist in Canada, South America and Australia.

### DOS & DON'TS

- ➡ When visiting a Lithuanian bring an odd number of flowers: even-numbered bouquets are for dead-solemn occasions – and the dead!
- ➡ Don't shake hands across the threshold; it brings bad luck.
- ➡ Always maintain eye contact when toasting your host or they'll think you're shifty.

### Rural vs Urban

The contrast between life in Vilnius, Kaunas and the countryside is stark. Citizens of the capital enjoy a lifestyle similar to those in Western Europe, living in nice apartments, working in professional jobs and often owning a car. Many have gained a cosmopolitan view of the world and consumerism has become a way of life.

In provincial towns and rural areas poverty is still prevalent – urban dwellers have around a third more income at their disposal than their rural counterparts, and about a third of homes in farming communities are below the poverty line, compared to about 20% in built-up areas.

Life expectancy for males is relatively low compared with other European countries – around 70 years (2018 estimate). The life expectancy for women is around 80 years.

There are numerous universities, almost 90% of Lithuanians complete secondary school, and the majority of pupils go on to some form of further education. Many students work full time alongside studying and live in university dorms or with friends.

Family ties remain strong, however, and married couples often choose to live with elderly parents who are no longer able to live alone. Despite increased career prospects, especially for women, Lithuanians tend to marry relatively young – the majority of women who marry do so between the ages of 21 and 25. A high number of marriages – almost half – end in divorce, but this figure is falling. This is partly due to the fact that many couples choose cohabitation over marriage and thus don't figure in the official divorce statistics.

## Lithuania's Hoop Dreams

Though Lithuanians traditionally excel at many sports – including Olympic medals in events as disparate as the discus throw, the modern pentathlon and the decathlon – there's really only one sport that gets their blood pumping: basketball.

For Lithuanians, b-ball is more than a sport: it's a religion. During Soviet times success at basketball within the Soviet National League was one of the few acceptable ways for Lithuanians to express their national identity. Since Independence, Lithuanians have looked to basketball to help put them on the world map. The worshipped national team scooped bronze in three successive Olympic Games (1992, 1996 and 2000), only to be nosed out for bronze in both 2004 and 2008. The team also took the bronze in the FIBA World Basketball Championship in Istanbul in 2010, but failed to make the quarter-finals in China in 2019.

Lithuanians have been a global basketball power since the 1930s, but the glory years came in the mid-1980s with the unparalleled success of the leading Lithuanian team at the time, Žalgiris Kaunas. Led by star centre Arvydas Sabonis, Žalgiris won the Soviet national championship three years running in 1985, '86 and '87 – each time defeating the dreaded Red Army superpower CSKA Moscow. Lithuanians made up the core of the Soviet team that won Olympic gold in Seoul in 1988.

Lithuanian's success at the time did more than prove their dominance on the basketball court; it was part of the national revival that ultimately led to Independence in 1991.

In 2011 Lithuania hosted the FIBA Eurobasket 2011 championship, the most prestigious basketball tournament in Europe, for the first time since 1939. Though the home team didn't win, the event was deemed a big success in the main host cities of Vilnius and Kaunas, and in 2015, they won silver, prompting wild celebrations at home.

## The Arts

Lithuania is Baltic queen of contemporary jazz, theatre and the avant-garde, while its arts scene is young, fresh and dynamic.

### Contemporary Crafts

Lithuania may be striding expectantly into its new European destiny, but the old ways remain strong. Traditional crafts are enjoying a huge renaissance, with many of the younger generation becoming intrigued with skills going back centuries.

#### VILNIUS: THE JERUSALEM OF THE NORTH

One of Europe's most prominent Jewish communities flourished in pre-WWII Vilnius (Vīlne in Yiddish), but Nazi (and later Soviet) brutality virtually wiped it out.

The city's Jewish roots go back some eight centuries when 3000 Jews settled in Vilnius at the invitation of Grand Duke Gediminas (1316–41). In the 19th century Vilnius became a centre for the European Jewish language, Yiddish. Famous Jews from the city's community include rabbi and scholar Gaon Elijahu ben Shlomo Zalman (1720–97), who led opposition to the widespread Jewish mystical movement Hassidism, and landscape artist Isaak Levitan (1860–1900).

The city's Jewish population peaked on the eve of WWI at almost 100,000 (out of 240,000 in Lithuania). However, plagued by discrimination and poverty, the Jewish community diminished in the interwar years when Vilnius was an outpost of Poland.

Despite this, Vilnius blossomed into the Jewish cultural hub of Eastern Europe, and was chosen ahead of the other Yiddish centres, Warsaw and New York, as the headquarters of the Yiddish-language scientific research institute YIVO in 1925 (the institute stood on Vivulskio gatvė). Jewish schools, libraries, literature and theatre flourished. There were 100 synagogues and prayer houses, and six daily Jewish newspapers.

By the end of WWII Lithuania's Jewish community was all but destroyed and during the mid-1980s *perestroika* (restructuring) years an estimated 6000 Jews left for Israel.

There's a small but thriving Jewish community in Vilnius and a smaller one in Kaunas. An ever-present blight is the fact that Lithuania never officially came to terms with the willing participation of numerous Lithuanians in the Holocaust alongside the Nazis, and many are celebrated as heroes, as they'd fought against the Soviets.

### TOP CONTEMPORARY READS

**Silva Rerum** (2008; Kristina Sabaliauskaitė) Four-part historical novel about the Grand Duchy of Lithuania.

**The Issa Valley** (1955; Czesław Miłosz) Semi-autobiographical account of boyhood life in a valley north of Kaunas.

**Tūla** (1992; Jurgis Kunčinas) Spellbinding story of two lovers caught in the Soviet system and battling it with every step.

**Bohin Manor** (1990; Tadeusz Konwicki) Set in the aftermath of the 1863 uprising, this novel uses the past to comment on current events and evokes tensions between locals, their Russian rulers and a Jewish outsider.

**Salt to the Sea** (2016; Ruta Sepetys) Touches on painful episodes in Lithuanian history by exploring WWII and its aftermath.

**Raw Amber** (2002; ed Laima Sruoginis) Anthology of contemporary Lithuanian poetry.

One of the most visible of these is wood-carving, with many a front garden or forest trail graced by elaborately decorated totems that seem living relics of the country's pagan past. In fact, they're as likely to show Christian as pagan motifs, both common subject matter for traditional Lithuanian folk artists called *dievdirbiai*. Once blanketed in dense forests that now survive in the country's many national parks, Lithuania has long entertained a special reverence for wood. Traditionally, trees could only be cut down when 'asleep', in winter, and in pagan times some groves were designated sacred, and could never be felled.

The abundance of raw material on the Baltic coast also gave rise to a long tradition of amber craftsmanship, and many noted Lithuanian jewellers still prize the medium. Black pottery, a Neolithic craft in which pine resin (and sometimes dung) gives the finished wares their characteristic dark tint, is another age-old Lithuanian skill that has been revived in recent years. Add to that weaving, papermaking, the decoration of *margučiai* (Easter eggs) and many other traditional crafts, and today's Lithuania has a plethora of means to keep its past alive.

## Literature

The Renaissance ushered in the first book to be published in Lithuanian – a catechism by Martynas Mažvydas, whose statue stands in Klaipėda – in 1547 and the creation of Vilnius University in 1579. But it wasn't until a couple of centuries later that a true Lithuanian literature emerged.

The land was the focus of the earliest fiction: *The Seasons* (*Metai*), by Kristijonas Donelaitis, described serf life in the 18th century in poetic form, and a century later Antanas Baranauskas' poem *Anykščiai Pine Forest* (*Anykščių šilelis;* 1860–61) used the deep, dark forest around Anykščiai as a symbol of Lithuania, bemoaning its destruction by foreign landlords. The poem is mostly known for its expressive language, and Baranauskas wrote the poem, at least in part, to show that the language need not be limited to kitchen talk.

Russia's insistence on the Cyrillic alphabet for publishing from 1864 (until 1904) hindered literature's development – and inspired poet Jonas Mačiulis (1862–1932) to push for its national revival. A statue of the Kaunas priest, whose pen name was Maironis, stands in Kaunas' Old Town. The city's Maironis Lithuania Literary Museum, in Maironis' former home, tells his life story. Maironis' romantic *Voices of Spring* (*Pavasario balsai;* 1895) is deemed the start of modern Lithuanian poetry.

Several major Polish writers grew up in Lithuania and regarded themselves as partly Lithuanian, notably Adam Mickiewicz (1798–1855), the inspiration of 19th-century nationalists, whose great poem *Pan Tadeusz* begins 'Lithuania, my fatherland...' The rooms in Vilnius' Old Town, where he stayed while studying at Vilnius University, form a museum.

Winner of the 1980 Nobel Prize, Czesław Miłosz (1911–2004) was born in the central Lithuanian town of Šeteniai. While he's best known abroad for his nonfiction book *The Captive Mind* (1953), concerning the effects of Stalinism on the minds of Polish intellectuals, he was passionate about his Lithuanian roots and wrote movingly of his childhood there in books such as *The Issa Valley* (1955) and in his memoir *Native Realm* (1959).

Novelists at the fore of contemporary Lithuanian literature include Antanas Škėma (1910–61), whose modernist, semi-autobiographical novel *The White Shroud* (*Balta drobulė;* 1954) recounts a childhood in Kaunas, then emigration to Germany and New York. It pioneered stream of consciousness in Lithuanian literature. Realist novelist and short-story writer Ričardas Gavelis (1950–2002) shocked the literary world with *Vilnius Poker* (1989) and *Vilnius Jazz* (1993), which openly criticised the defunct Soviet system and mentality. Equally controversial was the story of a priest's love affair with a woman, *The Witch and the Rain (Ragana ir lietus)* by Jurga Ivanauskaitė (1961–2007). It was condemned by the Vilnius City Council on publication in 1992, which limited initial distribution of the book. Her subsequent novel *Gone with Dreams* (2000) highlighted new issues and subjects, such as religion, travel and perceptions of others' religion and cultures, that couldn't be addressed in Lithuanian literature until after 1989 and the collapse of communism throughout Eastern Europe.

Herkus Kunčius (b 1965) has gained a reputation for scandalous novels that tear at the fabric of cultural norms; his *The Tumulus of Cocks* (2004) introduced gay and lesbian scenes to Lithuanian literature. Marius Ivaškevičius (b 1973), on the other hand, has distinguished himself by looking at historical themes through a modern lens. *The Greens* (2002), detailing the partisan movement after WWII, has proven to be Ivaškevičius' best seller to date.

## Cinema & TV

Lithuania has a long cinematic history – the first short films were shot way back in 1909 – but it wasn't until the late 1980s that independent film truly began to flourish, and now Lithuanian films capture around 25% of the local box office.

The grim reality of the post-Soviet experience is the focus for talented film director Šarūnas Bartas (b 1964), whose silent black-and-white movie *Koridorius* (*The Corridor;* 1994) – set in a dilapidated apartment block in a Vilnius suburb – received international recognition. Bartas opened Lithuania's first independent film studio in 1987.

The 11 documentaries and one short film made by Audrius Stonys (b 1966) are acclaimed Europe-wide: *510 Seconds of Silence* (2000) – an angel's flight over Vilnius' Old Town, the lake-studded Aukštaitija National Park and Neringa – is awesome.

Stonys co-directed *Baltic Way* (1990) – which landed best European documentary in 1992 – with director-producer and European Film Academy member Arūnas Matelis (b 1961). Matelis won critical acclaim and a heap of awards for *Before Flying Back to the Earth* (2005), a documentary on children with leukaemia.

Algimantas Puipa became prominent with *Vilko dantu karoliai* (*The Necklace of Wolf's Teeth;* 1998) and *Elze is Gilijos* (*Elsie from Gilija;* 1999), and hit the headlines again with both *Forest of the Gods* (2005) and *Whisper of Sin* (2007).

Flying the flag for young female directors in Lithuania is Kristina Buožytė, whose film *Vanishing Waves* (2012) imagines a relationship between a comatose young woman and the scientist that manages to connect with her subconscious. Another one to look out for is Egle Vertelyte, responsible for *Stebuklas* (*Miracle;* 2017), in which struggling pig farmer Irina encounters an American benefactor.

Lithuania has been the location for a number of big-budget TV series, due to its reputation as a low-cost film location. They include *The New Adventures of Robin Hood* (1995–96), *Elizabeth I* (filmed 2005), starring Jeremy Irons and Helen Mirren, and the HBO miniseries *Chernobyl*, much of it shot in Vilnius in 2018.

The Lithuanian Film Studios (www.lfs.lt), founded in Kaunas in 1948 and now located in Vilnius, has had a hand in all major foreign productions in the country.

## Music

*Dainos* – the Lithuanian name for songs – form the basis of the country's folk music. Their lyrics deal with every aspect of life, from birth to death, and more often than not they are sung by women, alone or in a group. Instruments include the *kanklė,* a Baltic version of the zither, a variety of flutes, and reed instruments. Kaunas' Folk Music Instruments Museum (p342) has a fine collection.

Romantic folk-influenced Mikalojus Konstantinas Čiurlionis (1875–1911) is Lithuania's leading composer from earlier periods.

Two of his major works are the symphonic poems *Miske* (*In the Forest*) and *Jūra* (*The Sea;* 1900–07), but Čiurlionis also wrote many piano pieces.

Bronius Kutavičius (b 1932) is heralded as the harbinger of minimalism in Lithuanian music, while Rytis Mažulis (b 1961) represents a new generation of composers with his neo-avant-garde stance expressed in minimalist compositions for voice. Country-and-western icon Virgis Stakėnas is the larger-than-life force behind the country's cult country music festival, the Visagano Country, in the eastern city of Visaginas.

Lithuania is the Baltic jazz giant. Two noteworthy musicians are sparkling pianist Gintautas Abarius and cerebral saxophonist Petras Vysniauskas. As famed is the Ganelin Trio, whose avant-garde jazz stunned the West when discovered in the 1980s. The club Kurpiai in Klaipėda and the Birštonas and the Kaunas jazz festivals are *the* spots to catch Lithuanian jazz.

Lithuania has yet to break into the international rock and pop scene, but that doesn't mean there aren't any local heroes. Andrius Mamontovas has been a household name for almost two decades; Amberlife, Mango and Auguestė dominate the boy- and girl-band genre; Mia is a renowned pop star; and Skamp is an interesting mix of hip-hop, R & B and funk. The biggest bands to explode onto the scene in recent years are Inculto, an eclectic group whose creative output reflects diverse world influences, and Gravel, a Brit-pop-esque four-piece with talent and attitude.

## Visual Arts

Lithuania's finest painter and musician is Varėna-born Mikalojus Konstantinas Čiurlionis, who spent his childhood in Druskininkai, where his home is now a museum. He produced romantic masterpieces in gentle, lyrical tones, theatre backdrops and some exquisite stained glass. The best collection of these works is in the National Čiurlionis Art Museum in Kaunas. Depression dogged Čiurlionis, although when he died aged 35 it was of pneumonia.

Lithuania has a thriving contemporary art scene. Vilnius artists created the tongue-in-cheek Republic of Užupis, which hosts alternative art festivals, fashion shows and exhibitions in its 'breakaway' state. Some 19km north, Lithuanian sculptor Gintaras Karosas heads up a sculpture park, Europos parkas.

From Lenin to rock legend, Konstantinas Bogdanas was famed for his bronzes of communist heroes (see some in Druskininkai's Grūtas Park) and for his bust of American musician and composer Frank Zappa.

Lithuanian photography has achieved international recognition. Vytautas Stanionis (1917–66) was the leading postwar figure, while artist Antanas Sutkus (b 1939) stunned the photographic world with his legendary shots of French philosopher Jean-Paul Sartre and novelist Simone de Beauvoir cavorting in the sand on Curonian Spit. Vitalijus Butyrinas's (b 1947) famous series *Tales of the Sea* uses abstract expressionism to make powerful images. For more on these and others, visit the Union of Lithuanian Art Photographers (www.photography.lt).

## Theatre

Lithuanian theatre has become an international force, with several young experimental directors turning European heads left, right and centre.

The superstar of Lithuanian theatre directors is arguably Eimuntas Nekrošius, who has won many international awards. Another well-known name, Vilnius-based Oskaras Koršunovas (b 1969), has won a Fringe First at the Edinburgh International Theatre Festival (for *There to Be Here*; 1990), and done Europe's theatre-festival circuit with *Old Woman, Shopping and Fucking, PS Files OK* and his 2003 adaptation of *Romeo and Juliet*. In 1998 he established his own theatre company in Vilnius, the Oskaras Koršunovas Theatre (OKT), albeit one with no fixed stage.

Other big names include Gintaras Varnas (b 1961), artistic director at the Kaunas Academic Drama Theatre, voted Lithuania's best director of the year five times; and Rimas Tuminas (b 1952), who heads the Small Theatre of Vilnius. Contemporary directors include Agnius Jankevičius, who won the Fortune Award in 2017 for *Rebellion,* and Paulius Ignatavičius, whose directorial debut, *Judgment Metamorphosis*, is playing at the Vilnius City Theatre for the third year running.

# Food & Drink

Long winters and cool weather shaped Lithuanian cuisine. Potatoes are a major staple, particularly as the base for stomach-stretching dumpling dough. Smoked and fried fish reign in coastal and lake areas,

## EAT YOUR WORDS

Caught in a restaurant without a phrasebook? Here are a few useful sentences to get by.

### Useful Phrases

| | | |
|---|---|---|
| **A table for ..., please.** | *Stalą ..., prašau.* | *stah*-lah ... prah-*show* |
| **May I see the menu, please?** | *Ar galėčiau gauti meniu prašau?* | ahr gah-*leh*-chow gow-ti man-*yew* prah-*show* |
| **Do you have the menu in English?** | *Ar jūs turite meniu angliеškai?* | ahr yoos *tu*-ri-ta man-*yew* *ahn*-glish-kai |
| **I'd like to try that.** | *Aš norėčau išbandyti to.* | ahsh naw-*reh*-chow ish bahn-*dee*-ti taw |
| **I don't eat ...** | *Aš nevalgau ...* | ahsh na-*vahl*-gow |
| **meat** | *mėsiško* | *meh*-sish-kaw |

### Food Glossary

| | | |
|---|---|---|
| **beef** | *jautiena* | *yoh*-tien-a |
| **beer** | *alus* | *ah*-lus |
| **boiled potato dumplings stuffed with meat** | *cepelinai* | tsep-e-*lin*-ay |
| **breaded pork chop** | *karbonadas* | kar-bo-*na*-das |
| **butter** | *sviestas* | *svie*-stas |
| **cheese** | *sūris* | *soo*-ris |
| **chicken** | *vištiena* | vi-*shtie*-na |
| **coffee** | *kava* | ka-*va* |
| **cold beetroot soup** | *šaltibarščiai* | shal-*ti*-barshi-ay |
| **eggs** | *kiaušiniai* | (ki-o)-*shin*-i-ay |
| **Lithuanian dumplings** | *koldūnai* | kol-*doon*-ay |
| **milk** | *pienas* | *pien*-as |
| **mushrooms** | *grybai* | *gree*-bay |
| **pancakes** | *blyneliai* | blee-*nyal*-i-ay |
| **pork** | *kiauliena* | ki-ow-*lie*-na |
| **tea** | *arbata* | ar-ba-*ta* |

foraged foods like mushrooms and berries make seasonal appearances, and dairy is everywhere. Casual taverns are common, while an increasing number of restaurants offer upmarket takes on rustic Lithuanian fare, with Vilnius and Kaunas in particular hotbeds of contemporary Lithuanian restaurants that make the prestigious White Guide (www.whiteguide-nordic.com). Find the most choice (and veggie options) in Vilnius and Kaunas.

### Staples, Specialities & Zeppelins

Lithuanian food is epitomised in the formidable *cepelinai* (tsep-e-lin-ay), sometimes jokingly called zeppelins. These are rugby-ball-shaped parcels of thick potato dough stuffed with cheese, *mesa* (meat) or *grybai* (gree-bai; mushrooms). They come topped with a rich sauce made from onions, butter, sour cream and bacon bits.

Another favourite is sour cream–topped *kugelis* – a 'cannon ball' dish borrowed from German cuisine that bakes grated potatoes and carrots in the oven. *Koldūnai* (kol-doon-ay) are hearty ravioli stuffed with meat or mushrooms and *virtiniai* are stodgy dumplings.

Lithuanians tend to like the less popular bits of animals: *liežuvis* (lea-zhu-vis; cow's tongue) and *alionių skilandis* (a-lyo-nyoo ski-lan-dis; minced meat smoked in pork bladders) are delicacies, and Lithuanians pork out on *vėdarai* (fried pork innards).

Hodgepodge or *šiupinys* (shyu-pi-nees) – often mistakenly assumed to be hedgehog – is pork snout stewed with pork tail, trotter, peas and beans. Smoked pigs' ears, trotters and tails are popular beer snacks alongside *kepta duona* (kep-ta dwa-na) – sticks of black rye bread heaped with garlic and deep fried. Order them with or without a gooey cheese topping.

Wild boar, rabbit and venison are popular in the Aukštaitija National Park, where hunted birds and animals were traditionally fried in a clay coating or on a spit over an open fire in the 18th century. When perpetually drifting sands on Curonian Spit on the Baltic Sea in the 17th to 19th centuries made growing crops impossible, locals took to hunting and eating migrating crows in winter: one bite (followed by a generous slug of vodka) at the crow's neck killed the bird, after which its meat was eaten fresh, smoked or salted.

*Blyneliai* (blee-nyal-i-ay; pancakes) – a real favourite – are sweet or savoury and eaten any time of the day. *Varskečiai* (vars-ko-chyai) are stuffed with sweet curd, and *bulviniai blyneliai* are made with grated potato and stuffed with meat, *varske* (cheese curd) or fruit and chocolate.

Several foods, including the Lithuanian cheese Džiugas, have earned heritage status for their importance.

Outside influences on Lithuanian cuisine includes the popular street food *chebureki* (deep-fried, crescent-shaped pastry), courtesy of the country's small Tatar population, and *kibinai* (empanada-style filled pastries), imported by the Karaite community.

## Cold Pink Soup & Other Starters

Lithuanians love soup and no self-respecting chef would plan a meal without one, but one soup rises above all others (maybe for its shocking pink colour, or maybe simply because it's delicious). *Šaltibarščiai* (shal-ti-barshi-ay) is a cold beetroot soup popular in summer and served with dill-sprinkled boiled potatoes and sour cream.

Other soups to look out for include nettle, sorrel, cabbage and bread soup (not to mention blood soup, which does indeed have goose, duck or chicken blood in it). Eel soup is specific to Curonian Spit, where eel also comes as a main course. In Aukštaitija, fish soup served in a loaf of brown bread is the dish to try.

Popular starters include *silkė* (herring), *sprotai* (sprats) and salads. *Lietuviškos salotos* (lea-tu-vish-kos sa-lo-tos; Lithuanian salad) is a mayonnaise-coated mix of diced gherkins, boiled carrots, meat and anything else that happens to be in the fridge.

Mushrooms are popular, especially in August and September when forests are studded with dozens of different varieties – some edible, some deadly. Mushrooms are particularly abundant in the Aukštaitija and Dzūkija National Parks. In spring and early summer the same forests buzz with berry pickers; locals stand at roadsides in the region selling glass jam jars of wild strawberries, blueberries, blackberries and so on.

## Beer & Other Beverages

This is a country of beer lovers, though *alus* (beer) is far from the only thirst-quencher: cider's common and *midus* (mead) is making a comeback. *Vynas* (wine) has made inroads into urban drinking habits, while vodka and fruit liqueurs are served cold and drunk quickly. Rustic pubs are a prevailing theme – whether centuries-old vaults or faux-historic taverns lined with hunting regalia – while Vilnius' and Kaunas' craft-beer scene is gaining in breadth and popularity. Also look out for *gira* (a mildly alcoholic drink made from fermented bread) and hot fruit teas, including the popular seahawthorn.

## Festive Eating

Christmas is the major culinary feast of the year. On 24 December families sit down to dinner in the evening around a candlelit hay-covered table topped with a white linen cloth; the hay anticipates Jesus' birth and serves as a place for the souls of dead family members to rest. (Indeed, one place around the table is always laid for someone who died that year.)

The Christmas Eve feast that unfolds comprises 12 dishes – one for each month of the coming year to ensure year-long happiness and plenty. Dishes are fish and vegetable based, and often include festive *kūčiukai* (koo-chiu-kai) – small cubed poppy-seed biscuits served in a bowl of poppy-seed milk; others like herrings, pike, mushrooms and various soups are not necessarily seasonal.

### EATING PRICE RANGES

The following price ranges are based on the cost of a typical main course.

**€** less than €7

**€€** €7–14

**€€€** more than €14

*Šakotis* (sha-ko-tis) – 'egg cake' – is a large tree-shaped cake covered with long spikes (made from a rather dry, spongecake mixture of flour, margarine, sugar, sour cream and dozens and dozens of eggs), which is served at weddings and other special occasions.

## Where to Eat & Drink

Dining Lithuanian-style can mean spending anything from €7 for a three-course meal in a self-service cafe in a provincial town well off the tourist trail to €35 or more in a swish upmarket restaurant in the capital.

In Vilnius, the choice of cuisine and price range covers the whole gamut, and an English-language menu is usually available (likewise along the coast); elsewhere the choice is limited and menus are not always translated. Service is at its best in the capital – and generally average to poor everywhere else.

## Eating Habits & Customs

A traditional dose of hospitality means loosening your belt several notches and skipping breakfast. Feasting is lengthy and plentiful, punctuated by many choruses of *Išgeriam!* (ish-ge-ryam; Let's drink!) and *Iki dugno!* (Bottoms up!). Starter dishes can be deceptively generous, leading unsuspecting guests to think they're the main meal. To decline further helpings may offend and be taken to mean that you don't like the food or the hospitality.

The family meal is a ceremonious affair and one that is taken very seriously, albeit one increasingly reserved for feast days, birthdays and other occasions in urban Lithuania's quicker-paced society. Each member of the family has a set place at the table – father at the head, mother opposite. If you arrive at someone's home while the family is seated, be sure to say *skanaus* (enjoy your meal!).

# SURVIVAL GUIDE

## Directory A–Z

### ACCOMMODATION

Lithuanian accommodation prices are generally lower than in Western Europe. Unsurprisingly, capital Vilnius has the biggest spread, from five-star historic boutique hotels to lively hostels. Equally abundant are options in Baltic resorts; prices rise from June to August and drop outside the summer (and some places close). Kaunas, Klaipėda and Druskininkai are well served by hotels and guesthouses. Options are more limited in industrial towns like Šiauliai.

#### Hotels

A stay in a *viešbutis* (hotel) is the most common type of accommodation offering. The term encompasses a variety of old and new places, ranging from very basic to ultra-plush.

At the top end are the revamped historic palaces and international hotel chains that offer high-standard accommodation to a mostly business-oriented clientele, usually at prices aimed at expense accounts. Going down the line, there are plenty of smaller, privately owned boutique hotels that cater to the midrange market. While rates at these places vary, expect to pay around €45 for a single and from €60 for a double room.

#### Guesthouses & Apartments

*Svečių namai* (guesthouses) can be found all around Lithuania, particularly in the larger cities. They can run the gamut from simple rooms in private houses to near-luxury-level boutiques, but usually represent better value than hotels and are often much more atmospheric. While prices vary depending on the location and comfort level, expect to pay around €35/50 for a single/double, usually not including breakfast.

Apartment rental is super-popular in larger towns and cities and costs vary from around €35 for a studio to over €100 for luxurious digs.

#### Homestays & Farmstays

Staying on a farm or rural homestead (*sodyba*) is a popular and highly recommended way of seeing the country. Homestays and farmstays are far more common in rural areas and small towns, and in the central and eastern parts of Lithuania, particularly around national parks, it's the most popular form of accommodation.

Local tourist offices will generally keep a list of homestays on hand and can make recommendations based on your needs. Otherwise, check the helpful website of the Lithuanian Countryside Tourism Association (www.atostogoskaime.lt), which maintains a list of properties by region and has lots of good info on what to expect.

Rates vary greatly depending on the facilities and the season, but expect to pay around €40 per room in season (June to August), and half that out of season. Rates do not normally include breakfast.

### Hostels

Lithuania has an increasing number of youth hostels, many of them occupying apartment buildings in larger cities. Most hostels are located in large cities; and outside of these you're better off choosing guesthouses or farmstays. The Lithuanian Hostel Association (www.lha.lt) provides a directory of youth hostels, with links to individual properties.

Expect to pay around €12 to €15 per bed in dorm accommodation, depending on the property, location and time of year.

### Campgrounds

Lithuania is dotted with campgrounds; some are in highly scenic areas such as along the Baltic coast or occupying desirable spots in national parks. Most campgrounds are equipped to handle both tent camping and caravans. Some also offer basic accommodation in bungalows or similar.

The Lithuanian Camp Site Association (www.camping.lt) maintains a helpful website that lists campgrounds and provides contact info and photos. The association also publishes the very helpful brochure *Kempingai Lietuvoje* (Campsites in Lithuania), usually available at tourist offices or as a download from the association website.

Rates vary but expect to pay around €5 per person to camp and another €5 or so for a tent site. You will likely have to pay extra for parking a car or access to electricity. Some campgrounds operate only in season (May to September), so be sure to contact the campground in advance to ensure that it will be open during your visit.

## ACTIVITIES

Lithuanians love nature. People were still worshipping ancient oak trees a mere six centuries ago, and these days in their free time they make regular pilgrimages to their country's many luscious lakes and forests and its long, sandy coastline. Boating, berrying, mushrooming, birdwatching and ballooning are uplifting pursuits. Travellers can walk and cycle into the wilderness, sweat in traditional lakeside saunas and enjoy ice-fishing in winter.

## CUSTOMS REGULATIONS

EU customs rules apply to Lithuania. There's some information on the Lithuanian Customs Department (www.vls.lrmuitine.lt) website and a more comprehensive guide at www.iatatravelcentre.com/lt-lithuania-customs-currency-airport-tax-regulations-details.htm.

## EMBASSIES & CONSULATES

Embassies are located in Vilnius. For Lithuanian embassies abroad, see the Lithuanian Foreign Affairs Ministry (www.urm.lt) website.

**Australian Honorary Consulate** (☎5-212 3369; Vilniaus gatvė 23; ⏰10am-1pm Tue, 2-5pm Thu)

**Belarusian Embassy** (☎5-266 2200; http://lithuania.mfa.gov.by; Mindaugo gatvė 13; ⏰8.30am-noon & 1-5.30pm Mon-Fri)

**Canadian Embassy** (☎5-249 0950; www.international.gc.ca; Jogailos gatvė 4, 7th fl; ⏰8.30am-5pm Mon-Fri)

**Danish Embassy** (☎5-264 8760; http://litauen.um.dk; T Kosciuškos gatvė 36; ⏰8.30am-4.30pm Mon-Thu, to 4pm Fri)

**Estonian Embassy** (☎5-278 0200; www.estemb.lt; Mickevičiaus gatvė 4a; ⏰8.30am-5pm Mon-Fri)

**Finnish Embassy** (☎5-266 8010; www.finland.lt; Kalinausko gatvė 24, 2nd fl; ⏰8.30am-4.30pm Mon-Fri)

**French Embassy** (☎5-219 9600; www.ambafrance-lt.org; Švarco gatvė 1; ⏰9am-1pm & 2-5.30pm Mon-Fri)

**German Embassy** (☎5-210 6400; www.wilna.diplo.de; Z Sierakausko gatvė 24; ⏰8.30am-noon & 1.30-4.30pm Mon-Thu, to 4pm Fri)

**Latvian Embassy** (☎5-213 1260; www.mfa.gov.lv; MK Čiurlionio gatve 76; ⏰8.30am-5pm Mon-Fri)

**Netherlands Embassy** (☎5-211 3600; www.netherlandsandyou.nl; Kosciuškos gatvė 36; ⏰8.30am-12.30pm & 1.30-4.30pm Mon-Thu, to 4pm Fri)

**Polish Embassy** (☎5-219 7400; https://wilno.msz.gov.pl/en; Šv Jono gatvė 3)

**Russian Embassy** (☎5-272 3893; www.lithuania.mid.ru; Latvių gatvė 53; ⏰8am-noon & 1.30-4pm Mon-Fri)

**UK Embassy** (☎5-246 2900; www.gov.uk/world/organisations/british-embassy-vilnius; Antakalnio gatvė 2; ⏰8.30am-4.45pm Mon-Thu, to 1pm Fri)

**US Embassy** (☎5-214 0560; https://lt.usembassy.gov; Akmenų gatvė 6; ⏰9am-9pm Mon-Fri)

### SLEEPING PRICE RANGES

The following price ranges refer to the cost of a double room with private bathroom.

**€** less than €50

**€€** €50–100

**€€€** more than €100

### TIPPING TIPS

**Hotels** Tipping is restricted to top-end establishments with room service and porters.

**Personal services** Tip masseurs, hairdressers and others around 10%.

**Restaurants** Tip 10% to reward good service. Say *ačiū* (thank you) to show you aren't expecting change back. Even if you're paying by card, tip with cash.

**Taxis** Drivers won't expect a tip, but it's common to round up or add a couple of euros for assistance with baggage.

### INTERNET ACCESS

Lithuania has enviable internet speed, among the best in the EU. Free wi-fi is ubiquitous in pretty much all accommodation and an ever-increasing number of cafes, restaurants and bars.

With free roaming across the EU and an increasing number of countries offering free roaming in a multitude of countries, there is little need to purchase a local SIM card if you're a smartphone user.

### MONEY

Lithuania joined the Eurozone in January 2015, trading in its litas for the euro.

Multilingual ATMs are ubiquitous in cities and towns, and even small villages are likely to have at least one. The majority accept Visa and MasterCard. You can change money at banks, though the easiest way to carry money is to bring a debit card and withdraw cash as needed from an ATM.

Visa and MasterCard are widely accepted for goods and services. American Express cards may be accepted at larger hotels and restaurants, though they are not as widely recognised as other cards. It is worth carrying cash for small purchases (like museums and markets) and planning ahead if you're staying in small guesthouses, which are less likely to accept cards.

### POST

Lithuania's postal system (www.post.lt) is quick and cheap. Posting letters or postcards costs €0.75 to other EU countries, €0.71 outside the EU and €0.49 domestically. Mail to the USA takes about 10 days, to Europe about a week. State-run EMS is the cheapest express mail service; find it in Vilnius at the central post office.

### PUBLIC HOLIDAYS

**New Year's Day** 1 January

**Independence Day** (Nepriklausomybės diena) 16 February; anniversary of 1918 independence declaration

**Lithuanian Independence Restoration Day** 11 March

**Easter Sunday** March/April

**Easter Monday** March/April

**International Labour Day** 1 May

**Mothers' Day** First Sunday in May

**Fathers' Day** First Sunday in June

**Feast of St John** (Midsummer) 24 June

**Statehood Day** 6 July; commemoration of coronation of Grand Duke Mindaugas in the 13th century

**Assumption of Blessed Virgin** 15 August

**All Saints' Day** 1 November

**Christmas** (Kalėdos) 25 and 26 December

### TELEPHONE

To call other cities from a landline within Lithuania, dial 8, wait for the tone, then dial the area code and telephone number. To make an international call from Lithuania, dial 00 followed by the country code.

When calling Lithuania from abroad, the country code is 370; next dial the area code and telephone number.

Mobile numbers comprise a three-digit code and a five-digit number. Many hotels and restaurants – especially in more rural parts – list a mobile telephone as their main number. To call a mobile within Lithuania, dial 8 followed by the eight-digit mobile number. To call a mobile from abroad, dial 370 followed by the eight-digit mobile number.

### TOURIST INFORMATION

The country's official tourism website (www.lithuania.travel/en) is packed with up-to-date info. Most towns have a tourist office with staff who usually speak at least some English. Among the best tourist offices in the country are those in Vilnius, Kaunas (p350), Klaipėda (p371) and Trakai (p323).

Vilnius Old Town Tourist Office (p318) is the head office of the capital's tourist information service.

## Getting There & Away

### AIR

Vilnius and Kaunas both have good air connections within Europe. From the US and beyond, you're likely to change planes in a hub airport such as Amsterdam, Warsaw or Frankfurt.

AirBaltic (www.airbaltic.com) flies to Vilnius from Rīga several times daily and from Tallinn on most days, and also offers scheduled if sporadic service from Rīga to Palanga. These flights are more frequent in summer (May to September). Many travellers arrive via low-cost carrier Ryanair, which operates routes to Vilnius and Kaunas from several European cities.

### BUS

Long-distance bus routes link Vilnius to neighbouring countries Poland, Belarus and the Baltics. Browse routes on Eurolines (www.eurolines.lt) and Lux Express (www.luxexpress.eu), whose coaches link Vilnius with Rīga, Tallinn, St Petersburg, Warsaw and Helsinki.

### CAR & MOTORCYCLE

Lithuania shares its border with four countries. Two of them – Poland and Latvia – are part of the EU's common-border Schengen Agreement, so there are no border checks when driving between them and Lithuania. Most car-rental companies allow you to drive within the three Baltic countries but not to Poland or beyond.

It's a different story for neighbouring Belarus and Russian region Kaliningrad (where most visitors require a visa to enter). Checks are stricter and cross-border car rental is unlikely to be possible. Driving your own vehicle from Lithuania into Belarus, you're likely to be stopped and asked to show insurance documents.

### TRAIN

The ease of travelling to Vilnius by train depends very much on the departure point. Direct trains link Kaunas and Vilnius to Warsaw, departing on Saturday, Sunday and Monday; browse schedules on www.intercity.pl. There are also regular services linking Minsk and Vilnius (see www.rw.by). By 2026, Lithuania will be linked to Poland via the brand new Rail Baltica railway.

However, travelling by train to/from the Baltic States isn't as smooth a ride as it should be. At the time of writing, train travel between Vilnius and Rīga required a few hours' stop in Daugavpils. Worse, train service from Vilnius to Tallinn involves a circuitous route. In both cases, buses are quicker and more direct.

## ℹ Getting Around

### BICYCLE

Touring cyclists will find Lithuania pleasantly flat. In rural areas, some roads are unsealed but they're usually kept in good condition. Bike hire is offered in all major cities, and often in small villages along the coast. Curonian Spit, the Baltic coast and Šiauliai's surrounds are scenic, unchallenging destinations for cyclists.

Bike-friendly services are increasing. Ferries to Curonian Spit allow passengers to bring their bicycle for free, while some Kautra (www.kautra.lt) intercity buses have bike racks (no extra charge); look for the bicycle symbol next to routes when booking a ticket on Autobusų Bilietai (www.autobusubilietai.lt).

### BUS

The national bus network is extensive, linking all major cities to each other and smaller towns to their regional hubs. Most services are summarised on the extremely handy bus tickets website Autobusų Bilietai (www.autobusubilietai.lt). Larger cities and towns are well covered by public transport networks.

### CAR & MOTORCYCLE

Car hire is offered in all the major cities and Lithuanian roads are generally very good. Driving in Lithuania is easy; parking in labyrinthine old towns is less so. Four-lane highways link the main cities of Vilnius, Kaunas and Klaipėda and the drive from Vilnius all the way to the Baltic coast is a fairly straight 330km, generally taking three to four hours.

To cope with snowy conditions, winter tyres are compulsory from mid-November through March; rental vehicles should have them. Major thoroughfares are well cleared of snow and ice but authorities are slower to clear rural roads.

### TRAIN

Local services are operated by Lithuanian Rail (www.litrail.lt), with regional hubs in Vilnius, Kaunas and Klaipėda. The Lithuanian Rail website is a model of user-friendliness. Whether you take the bus or train depends very much on the route. For common train journeys like Vilnius to Kaunas or Klaipėda, the train is often cheaper than the bus. For other routes, such as Klaipėda to Kaunas or Šiauliai to Kaunas, bussing is quicker and more comfortable.

# Kaliningrad Excursion

☎4012 / POP 471,000

## Includes ➡



## Best Places to Stay

➡ Very Center Hostel (p409)

➡ Hotel Kaiserhof (p410)

➡ Crystal House Suite Hotel & Spa (p411)

## Best Places to Eat

➡ Port O Coffee (p411)

➡ Plyushkin (p411)

➡ Ugli (p412)

## Why Go?

An intriguing and obscure destination, Kaliningrad is one of the grandest could-have-beens on the map of Europe. Having emerged, matured and indeed grown old as the grandiose German city of Königsberg, it is now the capital of a Russian exclave, surrounded on all sides by EU countries, and bearing the name of a Stalin-era Communist bigwig.

But the legacy left by the Germans, deported from East Prussia (as the region was known for centuries) at the end of WWII, shines through the Soviet architectural brutality. It has a curious effect on local Russians, who have developed a peculiar Westernised identity, living in isolation from their mainland.

The free e-visa available to many visitors, still valid at the time of writing, gives access to this fascinating region of medieval German ruins, wide sandy beaches and amber-filled dunes, as well as a glimpse of Russia at yet another poignant moment in its history.

## When to Go

➡ Kaliningrad can be visited year-round, though the peak tourist season is from May to September, when the weather is best for sightseeing.

➡ If you want to catch a truly Russian spectacle, visit on 9 May when troops and tanks parade through central streets to celebrate the Soviet victory during WWII. Russian Navy Day at the end of July offers a rare chance to visit the nearby naval port of Baltiysk, which is usually off limits to tourists.

➡ Hotel prices drop considerably during the autumn/winter low season, but travellers may have to brave rain and minus temperatures (the latter from November to February).

## Kaliningrad Highlights

❶ **Amber Museum** (p408) Admiring beautiful pieces of jewellery and art made from petrified pine resin.

❷ **Kaliningrad Cathedral** (p408) Visiting the grave of philosopher Immanuel Kant and listening to an organ concert.

❸ **Museum of the World Ocean** (p408) Learning about Russian maritime history and clambering aboard ships.

❹ **Plyushkin** (p411) Savouring the best of Russian cuisine in atmospheric surroundings.

❺ **Friedland Gate** (p409) Being transported back to old Königsberg.

❻ **Yeltsin** (p412) Spending the evening sampling Russian craft beers with local hipsters.

## Sights & Activities

### Kant Island & Around

This once densely populated island – now consisting of parkland dotted with sculptures – is dominated by its reconstructed Gothic cathedral. The neo-traditional row of shops, restaurants and hotels known as **Fish Village** (Рыбная Деревня) hints at what this riverside area looked like pre-WWII, and the west side of the island hosts the lively **European Street Food Awards** (http://streetfood-festival.ru) festival in late August.

★ **Museum of the World Ocean** MUSEUM
(Музей Мирового Океана; ☎4012-538 915; www.world-ocean.ru; nab Petra Velikogo 1; adult/student R300/150, individual vessels R200-300; ⏲10am-6pm Wed-Mon; 🚌40) Strung along the banks of the Pregolya River are several ships, a submarine, maritime machinery and exhibition halls that together make up this excellent museum. The highlight is the handsome former scientific expedition vessel *Vityaz,* moored alongside the *Viktor Patsaev,* with its exhibits relating to space research; visits to this are by guided tour (included in the admission price; every 45 minutes). The pre-atomic B-413 submarine gives a taste of what life was like for its 300 former inhabitants.

**Kaliningrad Cathedral** CHURCH
(Кафедральный собор Калининграда; ☎4012-631 705; www.sobor-kaliningrad.ru; Kant Island; adult/student R200/100, concerts from R150; ⏲10am-6pm Mon-Thu, to 7pm Fri-Sun) Photos displayed inside this Unesco World Heritage site attest to how dilapidated the cathedral was until the early 1990s – the original dates back to 1333. The lofty interior is dominated by an ornate organ used for regular concerts, which are well worth attending. Upstairs, the carved-wood **Wallenrodt Library** has interesting displays of old Königsberg.

**KALININGRAD AT A GLANCE**

**Area** 15,100 sq km (region)

**Departure tax** none

**Money** rouble; €1 = R70.89; US$1 = R64.41; UK£1 = R81.43

**Official language** Russian

**Visa** You need a Russian visa to enter Kaliningrad. Citizens of 53 countries, including Schengen states, as well as Japan, can visit with a free e-visa obtained online several days in advance. Citizens of the UK, USA and Canada require a tourist visa, arranged in advance via local private travel agencies.

**Kaliningrad Art Gallery** GALLERY
(Калининградский областной музей изобразительных искусств; ☎4012-467 143; www.kaliningradartmuseum.ru; Leninsky pr 83; adult/student R250/200; ⏲10am-6pm Tue-Sun; 🚌1, 3, 5) Housed inside a neoclassical former stock exchange building from the 1870s, this art gallery has a permanent photo exhibition of the wartime ruins of Kaliningrad and its rebuilding after the war. It also showcases etchings, sketches and oil paintings of Königsberg and nearby Nida life in the late 19th century and first half of the 20th, by the likes of Heinrich Wolf, Lovis Corinth and Hans Preuss. Post-1950s Soviet art is also on exhibition.

**Yunona** TOURS
(Юнона; ☎4012-307 003; www.kldtur.ru; ul Oktyabrskaya 4; ⏲9am-7pm Mon-Fri, to 5pm Sat & Sun; 🚌40, 🚎5) Next to the Jubilee Bridge, this long-running tour company offers historical tours of Kaliningrad (R950 to R2300), as well as full-day trips to the Curonian Spit (R1300) and the town of Yantarny, home to the world's largest amber mine, for those with an interest in the stone. Contact them in advance to arrange an English-speaking guide.

### City Fortifications & Gates

Scattered around the city are the remains of Königsberg's red-brick fortification walls, bastions and gates, built in stages between the 17th and 19th centuries. Sections have been rescued from ruin and turned into museums.

★ **Amber Museum** MUSEUM
(Музей Янтаря; ☎4012-466 888; www.amber-museum.ru; pl Marshala Vasilyevskogo 1; adult/student R460/360; ⏲10am-7pm, closed Mon Oct-Apr; 🚌29, 40, 🚎5) Housed in the 19th-century **Dohna Tower** (Башня Дона) on the southern shore of the Upper Pond (Верхний пруд), this is a terrific introduction to the 'sunstone' – detailing how amber is formed, how it defined prehistoric trade routes, as well as how to differentiate imitations from the real deal. There are more than 6000 amber exhibits, including marvellous works of art by contemporary Kaliningrad craftspeople, plus reconstructed centuries-old goblets and caskets, a whopping 4.28kg amber nugget and ancient specimens of prehistoric insects and plants fossilised in resin.

**Friedland Gate** MUSEUM
(Фридландские ворота; ☎4012-644 020; www.fvmuseum.ru; ul Dzerzhinskogo 30; adult/child R200/100; ⏲10am-7pm May-Aug, to 6pm Sep-Apr, closed 1st Fri of month; 🚌1, 3, 40) This history museum is housed in the 19th-century Friedland Gate, which was for years one of the main entry points into the fortified city. Admission includes permanent exhibitions on the Teutonic Knights and the history of the city through eight centuries; some of the exhibition is in English. The highlight is a 15-minute multimedia show made up of projections of photos taken in the city between 1908 and 1913, and grainy footage shot around the castle in 1937.

## Amalienau & Central Kaliningrad

Amalienau (to the city's west along pr Mira) is Kaliningrad's most beautiful neighbourhood and offers visitors a glimpse of the city's prosperous pre-WWII past. Stroll along ul Kutuzova to find an eclectic range of villas. The streets connecting pl Pobedy and pr Mira are filled with beautiful pre-war townhouses.

**History & Arts Museum** MUSEUM
(Историко-Художественный музей; ☎4012-994 900; www.westrussia.org; ul Klinicheskaya 21; adult/student R300/150; ⏲10am-7pm Tue-Sun; 🚋5) Housed in a reconstructed 1912 concert hall built on the banks of the pretty Lower Pond (Нижний пруд), this museum features an impressive diorama upstairs, depicting the final Soviet assault on Königsberg in April 1945 that left the city in ruins. There are also exhibits showcasing the history of the city pre- and post-WWII, including fin-de-siècle Königsberg fashions, venerable 19th-century pianos and details of the Romanov legacy in East Prussia.

**Bunker Museum** MUSEUM
(Музей Бункер; ul Universitetskaya 3; adult/student R150/100; ⏲9am-6pm) The city's last German commander, Otto Lasch, capitulated to the Soviets from this subterranean command post on 9 April 1945, following the bloody Battle of Königsberg. Exhibits include wartime photographs, films, detailed dioramas of the battle in various parts of the city and a peek into the cell where Lasch surrendered. There's decent English and German signage. Find it in a small park just east of Leninsky pr.

**Altes Haus** MUSEUM
(Альтес Хаус; ☎tours 4012-335 060; www.alteshaus.ru; ul Krasnaya 11, Amalienau; R400; ⏲tours 11am, 1pm, 3pm Mon-Sat; 🚌3, 9, 12) This unique museum is housed in a 1912-era apartment house, which has been restored to its former state of early-20th-century Königsberg glory and stuffed with genteel period pieces and gorgeous antique furniture. Entry is by guided tour in Russian, although the tourist office (p414) can locate an English-speaking guide for you. Visitors are given more or less free rein to sit on the furniture and generally carry on – politely – as if they owned the joint.

**Ploshchad Pobedy** SQUARE
(Площадь победы; 🚌8, 49, 🚋5) The city's central square has come a long way since 1934, when it was known as Adolf-Hitler Platz. Today it's surrounded by shopping malls and the rather tacky-looking, gold-domed **Cathedral of Christ the Saviour** (Кафедральный Собор Христа Спасителя; ⏲8am-7pm), built in 2006 in the Russo-Byzantine style.

### KALININGRAD IN...

**One Day**

If your time is limited to a day, see **Kaliningrad Cathedral**, the **Museum of the World Ocean** and the **Amber Museum**, and stroll around Kaliningrad's leafy parks. End the day with a meal at **Plyushkin** (p411).

**Two Days**

With more time, check out Soviet art at **Kaliningrad Art Gallery** and stroll through the leafy old German suburb of **Amalienau**. Get a feel for the local craft-beer scene at **Yeltsin** (p412) and **Krany i Stakany** (p412).

## Sleeping

Kaliningrad is well served with midrange and top-end hotels, and is experiencing a hostel mini-boom. Many rates include breakfast.

★ **Very Center Hostel** HOSTEL €
(Хостел Самый центр; ☎8-901-390 9900; ul Generala Galitskogo 1-3; dm/s €7/16; @📶; 🚌5, 8, 49, 🚋5) This hostel is just a couple of minutes' walk from pl Pobedy. Bilingual staff are friendly and welcoming, and it has a sociable feel without being a party hostel (no alcohol allowed). Nice touches include cool hangout spaces, privacy curtains for the bunk beds and a massive kitchen.

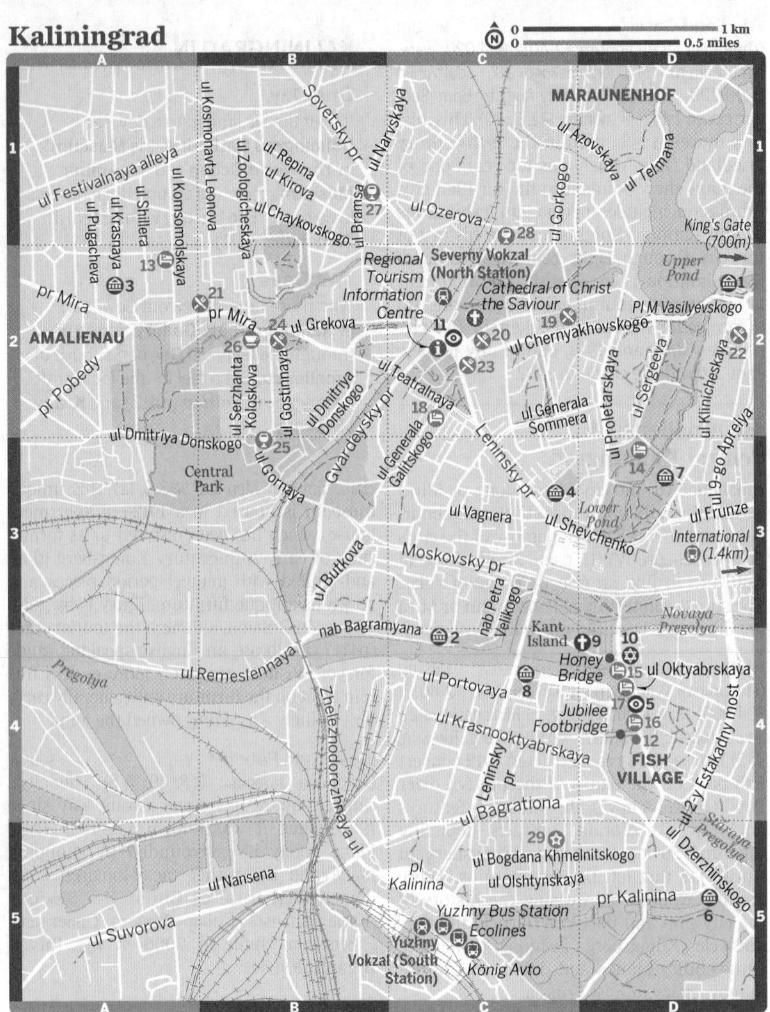


**Art-Hostel Tolstoy** HOSTEL €
(Арт - Хостел Толстой; ☎8-902-037 3301; www.tolstoy-kaliningrad.ru; ul Komsomolskaya 17; dm/d/f R650/2500/3100; 📶; 🚌8, 36) Don't be put off by the somewhat unkempt appearance of the residential building: inside hides a homey, Tolstoy-themed hostel, decorated with murals of the iconic writer, and arty, individually painted rooms and dorms. There's friendly, bilingual service, a guest kitchen and relaxed vibes.

★**Hotel Kaiserhof** HOTEL €€
(Отель Кайзерхоф; ☎4012-592 222; www.kaiserhof-hotel.com/en; ul Oktyabrskaya 6a; d/ste R5400/13700; ❄@📶🏊; 🚌40, 🚋5) Part of the Fish Village development, this stately hotel overlooking the river offers spacious, light-filled rooms, friendly and gracious service and a terrific, full-service spa with whirlpool, saunas and steam rooms. It's worth paying extra for river views.

**Honey Bridge Hotel** BOUTIQUE HOTEL €€
(Отель У Медового моста; ☎8-906-230 2620; https://u-medovogo-mosta.navse360.ru; ul Oktyabrskaya 2; d/tr from R4260/5270; 🚭📶; 🚌40, 🚋5) Sunny rooms and minimalist decor – all greys and creams and heavy wooden beams – plus its proximity to Kant Island are just

## Kaliningrad



some of the boons of this early-20th-century-style Fish Village hotel. An excellent buffet breakfast is included.

**Skipper Hotel** HOTEL €€
(Гостиница Шкиперская; 4012-307 237; www.skipperhotel.ru; ul Oktyabrskaya 4a; r from R4500; ; 40, 5) Location, ahoy! In a quaint period building with a superb riverside position in Fish Village, the Skipper is within stumbling distance of many of Kaliningrad's main attractions, cafes and bars. Rooms feature a vague nautical theme. Breakfast costs an additional R650. Ask for a room overlooking the river.

★ **Crystal House Suite Hotel & Spa** LUXURY HOTEL €€€
(4012-692 600; www.crystalhousehotel.ru; ul Sergeyeva 4; ste R6900-93,400; ) Sitting on a quiet slice of parkland overlooking the Lower Pond, Kaliningrad's first five-star, all-suite hotel is minimalist luxury at its best, with oodles of living space. The penthouse suites are remarkable; both have their own winter gardens and terraces, and floor-to-ceiling windows flood the pool area with natural light. An excellent restaurant and spa seal the deal.

## Eating

Head to the lively **Central Market** (Центральный рынок; ul Chernyakhovskogo; 8am-6pm; 5) for self-catering meals and engrossing people watching.

**Port-O-Coffee** CAFE €
(4012-379 828; ul Chernyakhovskogo 6a; mains R140-399; 7am-11pm Mon-Fri, from 9am Sat & Sun; ; 1, 3, 49, 5) Right off pl Pobedy, this branch of an excellent local mini-chain is filled with mellow background beats, a rhythmic clacking of laptops and quality coffee. It also serves hipster chow: quinoa porridge, raw banana cheesecake and avocado with baked cheese, alongside more standard burgers and egg-themed breakfasts.

**Madame Boucher** FRENCH €€
(Мадам Буше; 8-921-619 2595; ul Oktyabrskaya 2a; mains R400-650; 10am-11pm Mon-Sat, 11am-8pm Sun; 40, 5) The menu strays towards international at this restaurant that advertises its French 'home cooking', but the sweet and savoury crêpes are good, and the menu runs the gamut from fish and meat dishes to crispy *lavash* (flat bread) with spicy tomato relish.

★ **Plyushkin** RUSSIAN €€
(Плюшкинъ; 4012-355 245; pl Marshala Vasilyevskogo 2; mains R300-569; noon-midnight; ; 9, 19, 5) Named after the character from Gogol's *Dead Souls* who's an obsessive collector, this cellar restaurant resembles your friends' living room, with no space on the walls left uncluttered. Come with company to feast on authentic Russian classics: assortments of pickled vegetables and smoked meats, baked cod and dumplings. Knock back some *khrenovukha* (horseradish-based vodka) and toast the motherland.

**Borsch & Salo** UKRAINIAN €€
(Борщ и Сало; ☎4012-357 676; www.borshsalo.ru; pl Pobedy 10; mains R250-450; ⏲noon-midnight Sun-Thu, to 2am Fri & Sat; ; 1, 3, 49, 5) With a Ukrainian peasant-hut theme and a firm commitment to carbs and *salo* (smoked lard), this place does borsch really well (get the chef special with all the trimmings). *Vareniki* (filled dumplings), *draniki* (potato fritters) and a supporting cast of pickled vegetables are all present. Friendly staff treat you to a complimentary shot of sour cherry liqueur.

**Khmel** RUSSIAN €€
(Хмель; ☎4012-593 377; pl Pobedy 10; mains R400-650; ⏲noon-1am; ; 1, 3, 49, 5) Khmel is the pick of Kaliningrad's beer restaurants with a brewery-like interior featuring exposed pipes and brick walls. The ambitious menu draws on Russian staples and features game dishes as well as pies and pickles. There are four types of home-brewed beer, plus an excellent dark and slightly alcoholic *kvas* (fermented rye-bread water).

★**Ugli** INTERNATIONAL €€€
(Ресторан Угли; ☎4012-605 499; www.facebook.com/ugli.rest.kld; pr Mira 19-21; mains R300-1200; ⏲noon-midnight; ; 3, 5, 9) This restaurant, whose name means 'coals', is all about things cooked over the eponymous *ugli*, with steaks being the speciality. The chef does other meaty things very well, too, from home-smoked duck breast and salmon to baked bone marrow on rye toast, paired with some well-chosen wines.

## Drinking & Nightlife

Craft beer and speciality coffee are both now a feature of Kaliningrad nightlife. Major DJs from Russia and Western Europe jet in for gigs at Kaliningrad's clubs, which typically don't get going until well after midnight.

★**Yeltsin** CRAFT BEER
(Ельцин; ☎4012-766 420; ul Garazhnaya 2-2a; ⏲4.30pm-midnight Sun-Thu, to 2am Fri & Sat; 1, 40) Industrial-themed Yeltsin paved the way for the city's craft-beer revolution and is a favourite gathering spot for students and arty, beer-loving types in general. There's a rotating selection of 16 brews from small Russian craft breweries on tap, plus numerous bottled beers from further afield.

**Krany i Stakany** CRAFT BEER
(Краны и Стаканы; ☎8-996-521 3491; ul Bramsa 40; ⏲4pm-midnight Sun-Thu, to 2am Fri & Sat; 10, 23, 5) Even those who don't consider themselves beer fans will find something to their taste at this craft pub, with knowledgeable bar staff who can help you choose from a large selection of Russian and imported craft brews. Decor's on the spartan side, but there's a nice outdoor terrace as well.

**Club Platinum** CLUB
(Клуб 'Platinum'; ☎4012-384 848; www.club-platinum.ru; ul Dmitriya Donskogo 19; concerts R400-500; ⏲11pm-5.30am Fri & Sat; 3, 5, 9) There are regular appearances by popular rock, indie and pop acts at this heaving, upscale dance club. Dress up to get through the front door as 'face control' is strictly enforced. It's a 10-minute walk from the nearest bus stop, so consider taking a cab.

**Verf** WINE BAR
(Верфь; ☎4012-307 130; www.facebook.com/verfwinebar; ul Oktyabrskaya 4a; ⏲11am-midnight; ; 40, 5) This relaxed wine bar, with outdoor tables overlooking Kaliningrad Cathedral, has an extensive selection of wines from Europe; while the menu is heavy on Spanish and Italian vintages, there are a few from further afield. The summer terrace is among the best in the city and the bar occasionally screens movies.

### KALININGRAD'S COFFEE CULTURE

The Soyuz coffee roastery in the Kaliningrad region is the largest in Russia, but although it exports to all corners of the motherland, you won't find their coffee in Kaliningrad cafes. However, you will find quality beans at the following places:

**Port-O-Coffee** (p411) Industrial-chic coffee shops with their own roastery and an extensive menu of brunch and lunch items, with burgers sitting alongside quinoa porridge.

**GS Coffeeshop** (Кофейня N3; ☎8-962-255 4400; www.vk.com/gscoffeeshop; pr Mira 31; ⏲8am-9pm Mon-Fri, from 9am Sat, from 10am Sun; 3, 5, 9) The N3 branch is the largest of three, with a full brunch menu. The cafe sources its beans from micro-roasteries in Moscow and Stockholm, and the branch on ul Prachechnaya features Russia's top Aeropress barista.

**May Cafe** (☎8-911-495 53 70; www.facebook.com/cafemaykgd; pr Mira 66; mains R150-350; ⏲10am-8pm; ; 3, 12) Minimalist cafe with quality coffee. The short-and-sweet food menu consists of creative vegan dishes – still a rarity in Russia.

WORTH A TRIP

### KURSHSKAYA KOSA NATIONAL PARK & YANTARNY AMBER MINE

Over half of the 98km-long Curonian Spit lies in Russian territory and is protected within the **Kurshskaya Kosa National Park** (Национальный парк Куршская коса; ☎4012-310 056; www.park-kosa.ru; per person/car R100/400). Easily accessible in a day from Kaliningrad city, it's a fascinating place to explore, go wildlife- and bird-spotting or simply relax on pristine beaches. Highlights include the spectacular views of the dunes from raised platforms at **Vistota Efa**, and the **Dancing Forest** (Танцующий лес; km36) where wind-sculpted pines do indeed appear to be frozen mid-boogie.

Buses from Kaliningrad head up the spit (R101, two hours, four daily); all stop in the coastal resort of Zelenogradsk on the way there and back. Kaliningrad's Regional Tourism Information Centre (p414) has the current timetable.

Also on the coast, and easily reachable from Kaliningrad is **Yantarny** (R270, one hour, hourly), a town that's home to the world's largest amber deposit. If you're interested in seeing how the 'Baltic gold' is extracted from a viewing platform overlooking the open-cast mine, arrange a tour (R1400) with Yunona (p408) in Kaliningrad.

## ☆ Entertainment

Classical music concerts are occasionally held at Kaliningrad Cathedral (p408). Apart from a solid selection of classical-music offerings and the theatre (performances usually in Russian), Kaliningrad has several live music venues.

**★Vagonka** LIVE MUSIC
(Вагонка; ☎4012-956 677; www.vagonka.net; ul Stanochnaya 12; ⏲hours vary; 🚌5, 9, 48) Housed in a former German church about 3km from the city centre, Vagonka is one of the city's oldest and most popular venues for live rock, DJ parties and general carousing. Check the website for the current schedule.

**Philharmonic Hall** CLASSICAL MUSIC
(Филармония; ☎tickets 4012-647 890; www.kenigfil.ru; ul Bogdana Khmelnitskogo 61a; tickets from R300; ⏲box office 10.30am-7pm; 🚌1, 5, 40) This beautifully restored neo-Gothic church has excellent acoustics, and is perfect for organ concerts, chamber-music recitals and the occasional symphony orchestra performance.

# UNDERSTAND KALININGRAD

## Kaliningrad Today

Russia's latest fallout with the West has resulted in a bit of a siege complex in Kaliningrad, surrounded on all sides by NATO countries. This is especially visible during the pompous Victory Day parades on 9 May. But for most people, the annoyance of poor relations with the neighbours is gradually turning into a headache. Much of the region's economy, after all, is dependent on cross-border trade with Poland and Lithuania. With a huge devaluation of the rouble, caused by the oil price slump and Western sanctions against Russia, people's ability to buy goods in the EU has diminished. That, on the other hand, means the region has become much cheaper for foreign visitors, whose visits are made easier by free e-visas.

## History

Founded in 1255, Königsberg joined the Hanseatic League in 1340, and from 1457 to 1618 was the residence of the grand masters of the Teutonic Order and their successors, the dukes of Prussia. Prussia's first king, Frederick I, was crowned in 1701 in the city's castle. For the next couple of centuries Königsberg flourished, producing citizens such as the 18th-century philosopher Immanuel Kant.

The city centre was flattened by British air raids in August 1944 and the Red Army assault from 6 to 9 April 1945. The Soviet authorities deported all the remaining Germans and repopulated the area, mostly with Russians. Renamed Kaliningrad on 4 July 1946, the city was rebuilt in grand Soviet concrete style, albeit tempered by parks, a network of ponds and waterways and Kaliningrad Lagoon. The remains of the castle were destroyed and replaced by the outstandingly ugly Dom Sovetov (House of Soviets) in the 1960s. During the eyesore's construction it was discovered that the land below it was hollow, with a (now flooded) four-level underground passage connecting it to the cathedral. The decaying half-finished building has never been used.

# SURVIVAL GUIDE

## Directory A–Z

### TOURIST INFORMATION

**Kaliningrad Regional Hospital** (Областная Клиническая Больница; 4012-578 451; www.kokb.ru; ul Klinicheskaya 74; 24hr; 11, 29, 40, 5) Emergency services.

**Regional Tourism Information Centre** (Региональный информационный центр туризма; 4012-555 200; www.visit-kaliningrad.ru; pl Pobedy 1; 9am-8pm Mon-Fri, 11am-6pm Sat May-Aug, 10am-7pm Mon-Fri, 11am-4pm Sat Sep-Apr; 49, 5) Helpful English- and German-speaking staff with lots of information on the region. Can arrange an English-speaking guide for you or organise an excursion to suit your interests.

### VISAS

As of 1 July 2019, nationals of 53 countries may enter Kaliningrad on a free e-visa, issued online at https://electronic-visa.kdmid.ru once you complete the application form. The visa, valid for up to eight days, is issued within four calendar days and doesn't require invitations or confirmations. Once you've received it, you can either print it out or save the digital version to show at border crossings. You may use it to enter the Kaliningrad region by air, train, ship or bus, but it is not valid for any other part of Russia.

The 53 countries that may take advantage of the e-visa system (see website for details) include: Austria, Belgium, China, Estonia, France, Finland, Germany, Greece, Denmark, Ireland, Iceland, Japan, Italy, Latvia, Lithuania, Liechtenstein, Luxembourg, the Netherlands, Norway, Poland, Portugal, Spain, Switzerland, Sweden and Singapore.

Those *not* eligible for e-visas include the citizens of Australia, Canada, New Zealand, UK and the USA, who must apply for a regular Russian tourist visa (€35) well in advance of their trip at their nearest Russian consulate. Check www.visit-kaliningrad.ru for exact requirements, which are subject to change.

> **PRICE RANGES**
>
> **Sleeping**
>
> The following price ranges are for the cheapest double room per night.
>
> **€** less than R3000
>
> **€€** R3000 to R6000
>
> **€€€** more than R6000
>
> **Eating**
>
> The following price ranges refer to the price of a main meal.
>
> **€** less than R300
>
> **€€** R300 to R800
>
> **€€€** more than R800

## Getting There & Away

### AIR

**Khrabrovo airport** (Аэропорт Храброво/KGD; 4012-610 620; www.kgd.aero; 244E) is 24km north of the city. There are daily flights to Moscow, St Petersburg and Berlin; see the website for other connections.

### BUS

Most local buses depart from the **Yuzhny bus station** (Автовокзал Южный, South Bus Station; ul Zheleznodorozhnaya 7; 5am-11pm), as do international bus services run by **Ecolines** (4012-758 733; www.ecolines.net; ul Zheleznodorozhnaya 7; 9.30am-10pm) to Warsaw and several German cities. **König Avto** (4012-999 199; www.kenigauto.com) offers international services to the Baltic countries, with services to Germany, Poland, Lithuania, Latvia, Belarus and Ukraine.

There are fewer departures to Klaipėda and Palanga outside summer. The minibus to Palanga is the fastest way to reach Klaipėda.

| DESTINATION | COST (R) | TIME (HR) | FREQUENCY |
|---|---|---|---|
| Kaunas | 950 | 7 | daily |
| Klaipėda | 400-600 | 5½ | 2-3 daily |
| Nida | 400 | 4½ | 2 daily |
| Palanga | 490 | 5 | daily |
| Rīga | 1200 | 10 | 2-3 daily |
| Vilnius | 1000 | 9 | daily |

### TRAIN

All long-distance and most local trains go from **Yuzhny Vokzal** (Южный вокзал, South Train Station; www.eng.rzd.ru; Zheleznodorozhnaya ul 15/23; 5am-11pm), some passing through, but not always stopping at, **Severny Vokzal** (Северный вокзал, North Train Station; pl Pobedy 4a).

## Getting Around

Download the invaluable 2GIS app (www.2gis.ru/kaliningrad) to help you get around the city. It can be used offline and shows all the available transport routes when you click on a bus or tram stop.

Trams, trolleybuses, buses (R24 per ride) and minibuses (R30 to R35) will get you most places. For the airport, take bus 244E from the bus station (R80, 30 minutes). A taxi to/from the airport is around R700 with **Taxi Kaliningrad** (4012-585 858; www.taxi-kaliningrad.ru).

Car hire is available from **City-Rent** (4012-509 191; www.city-rent39.com; pr Mira 26; 9am-9pm), which has a branch at the airport.

# Survival Guide

# Directory A–Z

## Accessible Travel

With its cobbled streets, rickety pavements and old buildings (often without elevators), the Baltic region presents challenges for travellers with disabilities. That said, many city hotels have rooms equipped for disabled travellers; your first port of call for this information should be the tourist information centres of the capitals. Some beaches on the western Lithuanian coast in Nida and Palanga have ramps to allow wheelchair access to the sand.

Download Lonely Planet's free Accessible Travel guides from http://lptravel.to/AccessibleTravel.

Other useful resources:

**Apeirons** (www.apeirons.lv) This organisation of people with disabilities and their friends is a good first contact in Latvia.

**Freedom of Movement** (www.liikumisvabadus.invainfo.ee) This fantastic resource provides detailed information (in English) about accessibility in Estonia for wheelchair-users and those with limited movement, split into regions, towns and places of interest.

**Smarter Travel** (www.smartertravel.com/disabled-travel) Excellent resource with a number of specialised websites for disabled travellers.

## Accommodation

In the Baltic, the Eastern Bloc bedtime blues are a thing of the past. Many hotels have been renovated, and though there are still a few grey Soviet monsters lurking about, nowadays plenty of other options are available. The capitals tend to have the best range – from hostels and room-sharing services to international hotel chains – but things can get tight on summer weekends.

Generally speaking, hostels, camp sites and cheaper guesthouses fall into the budget category; most of the guesthouses and the less expensive hotels are rated midrange; and top-end places include the ritzier hotels and boutique properties. In the capitals, especially Tallinn, it's hard to come by a decent double in the budget category, but competition is fierce, so in most cases you should be able to find something after a bit of online research.

The peak tourist season is from June to August (the ski resorts have a second peak in winter, from December to March); if you're travelling then, you should book well in advance. This is essential in Tallinn, Vilnius and Rīga, as well as in popular summer-lovin' destinations, including the Estonian islands and all the coastal resorts. In winter, most rural and seaside lodgings close down altogether.

From October to April (and to a lesser extent September and May), room prices typically drop by about 30% – sometimes substantially more, depending on your powers of persuasion. Also keep in mind that popular seaside spots and other weekend getaway destinations (including Tallinn) are pricier on Friday and Saturday than during the week.

### BOOK YOUR STAY ONLINE

For more accommodation reviews by Lonely Planet authors, check out http://lonelyplanet.com/hotels/. You'll find independent reviews, as well as recommendations on the best places to stay. Best of all, you can book online.

### Camping

Many Baltic camping grounds are beautifully located by lakes or within forests, but most are difficult to reach unless you have a private vehicle. Some have permanent wooden cottages or, occasionally, brick bungalows. Cabins vary in shape and size but are usually small, one-room affairs with three or four beds. Showers and toilets are nearly always communal and vary dramatically in cleanliness.

Camping grounds usually open in May or June and close in mid-to-late September. A night in a wooden cottage typically costs €15 to €35 per person, while tent sites range from €5 to €10 per person.

Estonia has an extremely well-organised outfit overseeing camping. RMK (www.loodusegakoos.ee) maintains dozens of free, basic camp sites in forests all over the country. In Lithuania, check www.camping.lt for the camp site nearest to you, while in Latvia, www.camping.lv is a particularly useful website.

## Farmstays

The term 'farmstay' can vary widely – and isn't always the farm-based homestay experience you might be expecting. Many 'tourist farms' are set up as small guesthouses, while others offer self-contained apartments or whole cottages. Regardless, farmstays can prove to be a memorable choice. For a fee, host families will often provide home-cooked meals and arrange fishing, boating, horse riding, mushrooming, berry-gathering and other activities.

**Baltic Country Holidays** (Lauku Ceļotājs; ☎6761 7600; www.celotajs.lv) Latvia-based but books accommodation in rural settings all over the Baltic. Options include B&B and guesthouse rooms, whole cottages and camp sites.

**Countryside Tourism Association of Lithuania** (☎37-400 354; www.countryside.lt) Arranges accommodation in farmhouses and rural cottages throughout Lithuania.

**Estonian Rural Tourism** (☎600 9999; www.maaturism.ee) A broad range of accommodation – from camping and farm-based B&B to palaces and castle hotels – can be booked through this umbrella organisation.

## Guesthouses

Somewhat bigger than B&Bs but smaller than hotels, private guesthouses are a good bet for affordable travel in the Baltic and often offer a cosy, informal setting. Typically they have fewer than a dozen rooms, but beyond that there are no hard and fast rules. Some have en-suite bathrooms and others have shared bathrooms; some offer breakfast and others don't. Free wi-fi is ubiquitous. Standards of cleanliness can also vary, but generally the quality is high. Prices range from around €30 to €90 per room.

## Hostels

There are a growing number of hostels scattered throughout the Baltic, mostly concentrated in the capitals and larger cities. Dorm beds in the capital cities in high season range from about €12 to €18. Book your bed well in advance if you come in the summer.

You'll find **Hostelling International** (www.hihostels.com) hostels in all of the Baltic countries. For backpacker recommendations, check out **Hostelworld** (www.hostelworld.com). Websites with a (not comprehensive) list of hostels in each country:

**Estonia** www.hostels.ee

**Latvia** www.hostellinglatvia.com

**Lithuania** www.lha.lt

## Hotels

The Baltics have hotels to suit every price range, although budget doubles and singles in the increasingly glam capitals are fairly scarce. (The hostel and room-share scene, on the other hand, is thriving.) As more cheap hotels make the effort to brighten up their image, nightly rates are being yanked up, too. Delightfully horrible relics from the Soviet era still exist – but though they may retain their blocky exteriors, the interiors will have generally been modernised.

The midrange option, both in and outside the capitals, includes small, family-run hotels and stylish boutique hotels, whose only downside is that they have few rooms and get booked up quickly.

Top hotels are a dime a dozen. Many are under Western management or are part of a recognised international hotel chain, while others – such as Dome Hotel in Rīga, the Hotel Pacai in Vilnius and the Three Sisters in Tallinn – are housed in exquisitely renovated, historic buildings dating from the 13th to 19th centuries.

## Spa Hotels

Spa hotels are both an excellent place to be pampered and – for those with water parks attached – to take the

### COTTAGE & APARTMENT RENTALS

**Cottage Rental Estonia** (www.cottage-estonia.eu) An Estonian company with dozens of cottages on its books, throughout the country. Scour its website for a log cabin in Lahemaa National Park, a farmstead on Saaremaa, a beachside apartment in Pärnu or a city base in Tallinn.

**Lauku Celotajs** (www.celotajs.lv) This Latvian tourism company catalogues dozens of rural hotels and farmsteads in Latvia and beyond on its excellent website, though its offerings are rather dated.

**Airbnb** (www.airbnb.com) Very popular across major cities and town in the Baltics and often a good way to interact with locals.

**Booking** (www.booking.com) Short-term and long-term apartment rental is very popular and widely available on this site and others.

### WHICH FLOOR?

Before you start traipsing up the stairs, note that in the Baltic countries the ground floor is referred to as the 1st floor.

kids. Even if you don't stay overnight, you can pop in for treatments: mud baths, massages, herbal baths and dozens of other options.

The selection of spa hotels is pretty evenly spread throughout the Baltics, with Jūrmala in Latvia known as the spa centre of the Baltic. Druskininkai is Lithuania's premier spa connection; Birštonas is also popular. Kuressaare on Saaremaa is known as the spa capital of Estonia.

## Customs Regulations

If you think that a painting or other cultural object you'd like to buy in one of the Baltic countries might attract customs duty or require special permission to export, check with the seller before purchasing – you may have to get permission from a government office before it can be exported.

## Discount Cards

### City Discount Cards

All three capitals offer discount cards to visitors. Ventspils has its own virtual currency that can be earned by and spent on visiting its sights.

### Hostel Cards

A Hostelling International (HI) card yields discounts of up to 20% at affiliated hostels (though there are many non-HI hostels throughout the Baltic). You can buy one at participating hostels en route, or purchase one before you go via your national **Youth Hostel Association** (YHA; www.hihostels.com).

### Seniors' Cards

There are some discounts available to older people – museums often reduce the entrance fee, and concert and performance tickets may also be reduced, so it's always worth asking. Ferries and long-distance buses will often have seniors' fares (discounts of around 10%). To take advantage of discounts, be sure to carry ID providing proof of your age.

### Student & Youth Cards

Carrying a student card entitles you to a wide variety of discounts throughout the Baltics. The most common card is the **International Student Identity Card** (ISIC; www.isic.org), which is issued to full-time students aged 12 years and over, and gives the bearer discounts on accommodation, transport and admission to some attractions. It's available from student unions, hostelling organisations and some travel agencies.

The ISIC is also the body behind the **International Youth Travel Card** (IYTC), which is issued to people who are between 12 and 30 years of age and not full-time students, and gives equivalent benefits to the ISIC. A similar ISTC brainchild is the **International Teacher Identity Card** (ITIC), available to teaching professionals.

## Climate

### Rīga

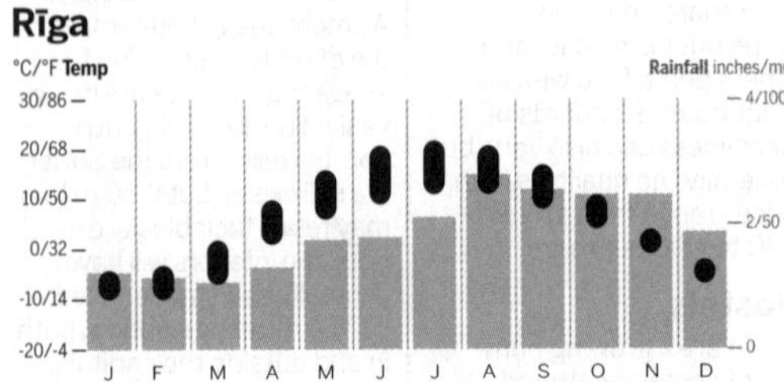


### Tallinn

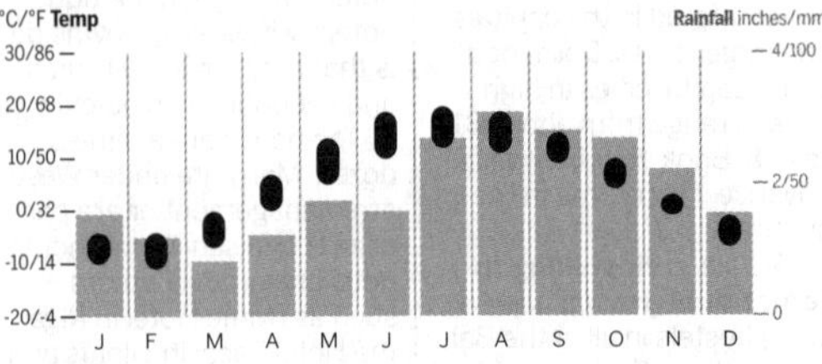


### Vilnius

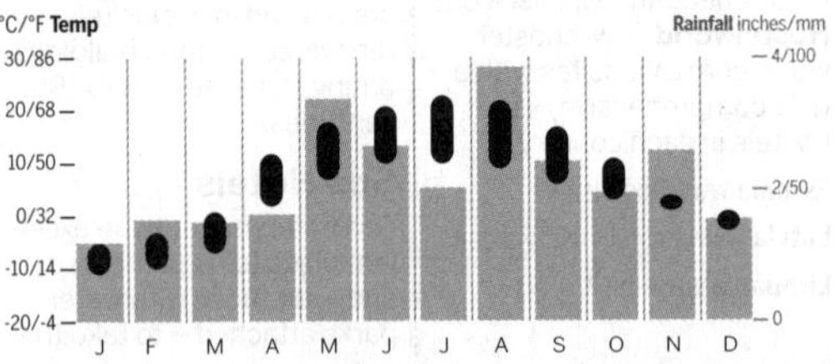

## Electricity

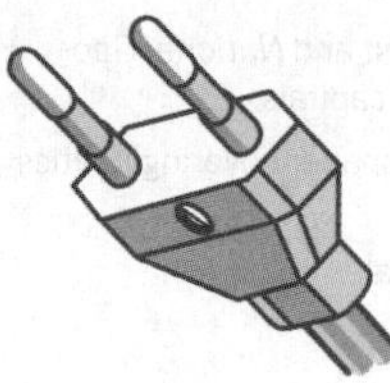

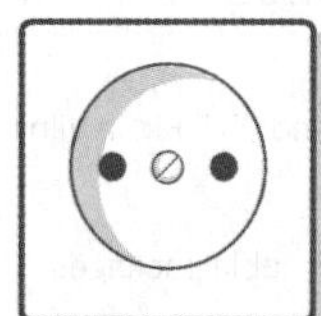

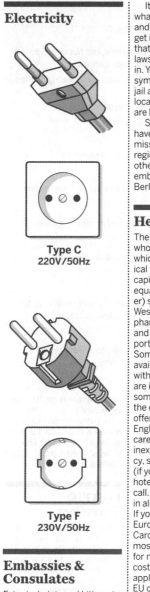

Type C
220V/50Hz

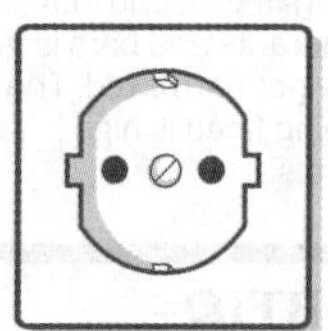

Type F
230V/50Hz

## Embassies & Consulates

Estonia, Latvia and Lithuania each have numerous diplomatic missions overseas. Likewise, many countries have their own embassies or missions in Tallinn (p178), Rīga (p285) and Vilnius (p403).

It's important to realise what your own embassy can and can't do for you if you get into trouble. Remember that you are bound by the laws of the country you are in. Your embassy will not be sympathetic if you end up in jail after committing a crime locally, even if such actions are legal in your own country.

Some countries opt to have only one diplomatic mission for the entire Baltic region (usually in Rīga), while others may be served out of embassies in Stockholm or Berlin.

## Health

The Baltic region is, on the whole, a healthy place in which to travel, and medical facilities outside the capital cities are often of equal (or sometimes higher) standards than their Western counterparts. All pharmacies in the capitals and larger towns stock imported Western medicines. Some of these medicines are available over the counter without a prescription and are inexpensive compared to some Western countries. In the capitals, private clinics offer Western-standard, English-speaking medical care, and can be relatively inexpensive. In an emergency, seek your hotel's help first (if you're in one); the bigger hotels may have doctors on call. Emergency care is free in all three countries.
If you're an EU citizen, a European Health Insurance Card (EHIC) covers you for most medical care, but not for non-emergencies or the cost of repatriation. You can apply for one online in many EU countries via your government health department's website.

### Insect Bites & Stings

Spread by tick bites, tick-borne encephalitis is a serious infection of the brain. If you intend to spend a lot of time in forested areas, including by the coast where pine forest prevails, vaccination is advised. Two doses of vaccine will give a year's protection; three doses are good for up to three years. You should always check all over your body if you have been walking through a potentially tick-infested area; signs along the Lithuanian coast alert walkers and beachgoers to areas where ticks are particularly rampant. If you find an attached tick, press down around its head with tweezers, grab the head and gently pull upwards. Avoid pulling the rear of the body as this may squeeze the tick's gut contents through the attached mouth parts into the skin, increasing the risk of infection and disease.

Mosquitoes are a voracious pest in the summer, and can cause irritation and infected bites. Use a DEET-based insect repellent.

### Water

Tap water is safe to drink all over the Baltics. Do not drink water from rivers or lakes – it may contain bacteria or viruses that can cause diarrhoea or vomiting.

## Insurance

A travel insurance policy to cover theft, loss of property and medical problems is a good idea. Worldwide travel insurance is available at www.lonelyplanet.com/travel-insurance. You can buy, extend and claim online anytime – even if you're already on the road.

Some policies offer lower and higher medical expense options. Policies can vary widely, so be sure to check the fine print. Some insurance policies will specifically exclude 'dangerous activities', which can include hiking.

You may prefer a policy that pays doctors or hospitals rather than requiring you to pay on the spot and claim later. If you do have to claim later make sure you

## PRACTICALITIES

### Print & Digital Press

Major global English-language publications, such as the *Economist* and *National Geographic*, are available at centrally located press kiosks in all three capitals.

**Baltic Times** (www.baltictimes.com) Rīga-based pan-Baltic newspaper covering politics and life in all three countries.

**news.err.ee** Estonian public broadcaster's English-language portal.

**lsm.lv/en** Latvian public broadcaster's English-language portal.

**en.delfi.lt** Lithuanian news in English.

**rebaltica.lv/en** Long reads on Latvian and international politics translated into English.

### Radio

The BBC World Service airs on 100.5 FM in Rīga, 103.5 FM in Tallinn and 95.5 FM in Vilnius.

### Television

Global English-language channels are available in most hotels and in cable packages.

### Weights & Measures

All three countries use the metric system for length (metres), weight (kilograms) and temperature (Celsius).

### Smoking

In all three countries, smoking is banned in restaurants, bars and night clubs (except for on open-air terraces). Additional restrictions on smoking near schools apply in Latvia.

### Marijuana

In Lithuania, medical marijuana has been legalised and is strictly controlled; the same applies in Estonia. In Latvia, marijuana remains illegal in all its forms.

keep all documentation. Some policies ask you to call (reverse charges) a centre in your home country, where an immediate assessment of your problem is made. Check that your policy covers ambulances and an emergency flight home.

## Internet Access

The Baltics are wired countries, with the availability and quality of wi-fi connections outstripping much of Western Europe. With the spread of wireless technology, internet cafes have become obsolete. Pretty much all accommodation in all price ranges offers free wi-fi, which is also widely available in cafes, bars, restaurants and public spaces.

Most smartphone users needn't even procure a local SIM card, since roaming charges have been abolished between many countries.

## Legal Matters

If you are arrested in the Baltic, you have the same basic legal rights as anywhere else in Europe, including the right to be informed of the reason for your arrest (before being taken to the police station); to inform a family member of your misfortune (once you are there); and to have your lawyer present during questioning. You cannot be detained for more than 72 hours without being charged with an offence.

Smoking is not permitted in restaurants, bars, nightclubs and cafes in all three countries, although it is permitted on outdoor terraces or in closed-off smoking rooms (with proper ventilation).

Drinking alcohol outside restaurants and bars is generally not permitted. The risk of being fined is high in larger capitals.

## LGBTIQ+ Travellers

Following independence, all three Baltic States decriminalised homosexual acts, and today there is an equal age of consent for sexual acts for all citizens. Yet not all is as rosy as it seems. Of the three, secular Estonia is the most tolerant, while life is considerably harder for gays and lesbians in Catholic Lithuania, and arguably worse still in Latvia. On the 2019 Rainbow Europe Map website, which ranks each nation according to the legal protection offered to its lesbian, gay, bisexual and transgender (LGBT) citizens, Estonia scored 35%, Lithuania 23%, and Latvia 16%. (By comparison, Britain is at 66%, while nearby Finland scores 69%.)

In all three countries, being 'out' creates multiple risks, as small displays of public affection can provoke some nasty responses. While there is a small gay scene in Tallinn, Rīga and Vilnius, there's almost nothing elsewhere.

That said, Baltic Pride became an annual festival in 2005, with successful, largely problem-free celebrations hosted by one of the three capitals each year. In 2015, Rīga was the first Baltic capital to host EuroPride; the march proceeded without any incidents.

### Resources

**Estonian LGBT portal** (www.lgbt.ee)

**ILGA Europe** (www.ilga-europe.org) Excellent, country-by-country information on gay life and acceptance in all of Europe, including the Baltic countries.

**Latvian LGBT portal** (www.gay.lv)

**Lithuanian LGBT portal** (www.lgl.lt)

## Maps

Decent regional and country maps are widely available outside the region, as are quality city maps in each country. A map covering the region is useful for planning: *Estonia, Latvia, Lithuania* from **Cartographia** (www.cartographia.hu) has a 1:700,000-scale map of the three countries, and many publishers produce something similar. Insight Travel Maps has a useful 1:800,000 *Baltic States* map, with city plans of Tallinn and Rīga.

Good maps to look for in the region include *Eesti Latvija Lietuva* (1:700,000) published by Vilnius-based **Briedis** (www.briedis.lt). In Estonia, **EO Map** (www.eomap.ee) does a pretty mean *Baltimaad* (Baltic States, 1:800,000), which is widely available in Estonian bookshops.

In Latvia, map publisher **Jāņa Sēta** (www.kartes.lv) is the market leader, with its pocket-sized, spiral-bound, 152-page *Baltic Countries & Kaliningrad Region* (1:500,000), which contains 72 city and town plans as well as road maps covering the entire region. Its *Baltic Countries* (1:700,000) road map is equally good.

For digital users, **Google Maps** is best if you're online, and **Maps.me** is a useful app for finding your way around while offline. For Kaliningrad, **2GIS** is a particularly useful app that works offline.

## Money

### ATMs

ATMs accepting Cirrus, Visa and MasterCard are widespread in cities and larger towns, enabling you to get cash 24 hours a day. ATMs are multilingual, using the main European languages.

### Bargaining

Some bargaining (but not a lot) goes on at flea markets; you're not likely to get more than 10% to 20% off the initial asking price.

### Credit Cards

Credit cards are widely accepted in hotels, restaurants and shops, especially at the upper end of the market. Visa and MasterCard are the most commonly accepted, but Diners Club and American Express also crop up. They are essential for hiring a car. It's generally easiest to use an ATM for a Visa or MasterCard cash advance.

### Moneychangers

Every town has somewhere you can change cash: usually a bank, exchange office or currency exchange kiosk. The latter crop up in all sorts of places, particularly transport terminals, airports, bus stations and train stations. Rates vary from one outlet to another. Exchange places are generally open during usual business hours.

### Tipping

It's fairly common, though not compulsory, to tip waiters 5% to 10% by rounding up the bill. Top restaurants in Baltic capitals may add a discretionary 10% gratuity to the bill.

## Opening Hours

Hours vary widely depending on the season and the size of the town, but the following are fairly standard:

**Banks** 9am–4pm or 5pm Monday to Friday

**Bars** noon–midnight Sunday to Thursday, to 2am or 3am Friday and Saturday

**Cafes** 9am–10pm

**Post offices** 8am–6pm Monday to Friday, 9am–2pm Saturday

**Restaurants** noon–11pm or midnight

**Shops** 10am–6pm Monday to Friday, to 3pm Saturday

**Supermarkets** 8am–10pm

## Post

Letters and postcards from any of the three countries take about two to four days to Western Europe, seven to 10 days to North America, and two weeks to Australia, New Zealand and South Africa. Occasionally, as in any other country, a letter or parcel might go astray for a couple of weeks, but generally everything arrives.

You can buy your stamps at a post office (Estonian: *postkontor;* Latvian: *pasts;* Lithuanian: *paštas*) and post your mail there. In Estonia, you can bypass the post office, buy stamps in shops and slip the envelope in any post box.

## WHICH DOOR IS WHICH?

We hope you're not busting for a pee, as working out which toilet door to enter may require some thinking time. Men's toilets are marked by the letter 'M' in Estonia and 'V' in Latvia or Lithuania; women's toilets are indicated by 'N' in Estonia, 'S' in Latvia and 'M' in Lithuania. Some doors sport the triangle system: a skirt-like triangle for women and a broad-shouldered, upside-down triangle for men. To add even more confusion, in Lithuania (as in neighbouring Poland), male toilets may be indicated by a triangle and female toilets by a circle.

For postal rates and other information, take a look at the websites of the postal companies.

**Eesti Post** (www.omniva.ee) Estonia.

**Latvijas Pasts** (www.pasts.lv/en) Latvia.

**Lietuvos Paštas** (www.post.lt) Lithuania.

Expensive international express-mail services are available in the capital cities.

Written address format conforms to Western norms, for example:

Kazimiera Jones
Veidenbauma iela 35-17
LV-5432 Ventspils
Latvia

Veidenbauma iela 35-17 means Veidenbaum St, building No 35, flat No 17. Postcodes in Estonia are the letters 'EE' plus five digits; in Latvia 'LV-' plus four digits; and in Lithuania 'LT-' plus five digits (although the LT isn't essential).

# Telephone

City codes are a thing of the past in little Estonia and Latvia – if you're calling from abroad, dial just the country code then the listed number. In Lithuania (p404) things are a little more complicated.

For smartphone users, there is little need to buy a local SIM these days, given free roaming across Europe and most phone companies in the West adding more and more countries to their free roaming list.

# Time

Estonia, Latvia and Lithuania are on Eastern European Time (GMT/UTC +2). All three countries adhere to daylight savings, which runs from the last Sunday in March to the last Sunday in October (at this time it's GMT +3).

The 24-hour clock is used for train, bus and flight timetables, while letters (the initial letter of each day) or Roman numerals (I or 1 = Monday; VII or 7 = Sunday) may indicate the days of the week in posted opening hours or timetables. Dates are listed in European style: date, then month, then year – 01.06.1974 stands for 1 June 1974.

# Toilets

Public toilets in the Baltic countries are wondrous things compared to the apocalyptic black holes of the past: today you'll find mostly clean, modern systems (though a few still can't cope with you flushing your toilet paper and provide baskets in the corner). Public restrooms of train and bus stations are usually relatively clean and cost around €0.40 to €0.50 to use. Although there are public toilets in some places, you can also stroll into large hotels in major cities and use the toilets without upsetting the staff too much (or else just pop into the nearest McDonald's).

# Tourist Information

All three capitals, plus most cities, towns and seaside resorts, sport an efficient tourist office of sorts that doles out accommodation lists and information brochures, often in English and usually delivered with a smile. These tourist offices are coordinated by each country's national tourist board. Most towns and areas covered in this book have their own tourist-focused websites.

# Visas

Your number-one document is your passport; make sure it's valid for at least six months after the end of your Baltic travels. Only some nationalities need visas. Citizens from the EU, Australia, Canada, Japan, New Zealand and the US do not require visas for entry into Estonia, Latvia or Lithuania.

Other nationalities should check the websites of the relevant Ministries of Foreign Affairs.

**Estonia** www.vm.ee

**Latvia** www.pmlp.gov.lv

**Lithuania** www.migracija.lt

## Belarusian Visas

Citizens of 74 countries, including EU states, USA, Canada, Australia and New Zealand are eligible for 30-day visa-free entry to Belarus, provided they arrive via Minsk International Airport. For a full list of countries, check www.belarus.by. Travellers must show proof of comprehensive medical insurance and may be asked to demonstrate that they have sufficient funds for the duration of their stay. Visa-free entry does not apply to land borders. For the low-down, see the Ministry of Foreign Affairs of the Republic of Belarus (www.mfa.gov.by).

### Finnish Visas

Citizens from the EU, Australia, Canada, Japan, New Zealand and the US do not require visas for entry into Finland. Other nationalities may wish to check the website for the Finnish Ministry of Foreign Affairs: www.um.fi/frontpage.

### Russian Visas

As of 1 July 2019, nationals of 53 countries may enter Kaliningrad on a free e-visa, issued online at https://electronic-visa.kdmid.ru. The visa, valid for up to eight days, is issued within four calendar days and doesn't require invitations or confirmations. Once you've received it, you can either print it out or save the digital version to show at border crossings. You may use it to enter the Kaliningrad region via air, train, ship or bus, but *it is not valid for any other part of Russia*.

The 53 countries that may take advantage of the e-visa system (see website for details) include Austria, Andorra, Belgium, China, Estonia, France, Finland, Germany, Greece, Denmark, Ireland, Iceland, Japan, Italy, Latvia, Lithuania, Liechtenstein, Luxembourg, Malta, Monaco, Netherlands, Norway, Poland, Portugal, Spain, Switzerland, Sweden and Singapore.

Those not eligible for e-visas include the citizens of Australia, Canada, New Zealand, UK and USA. Travellers from these countries must apply for a regular Russian tourist visa (€35) well in advance of their trip at their nearest Russian consulate. Check www.visit-kaliningrad.ru for exact requirements, which are subject to change.

## Volunteering

Estonia has an established WWOOF (World Wide Opportunities on Organic Farms) organisation, facilitating volunteer work on organic farms in exchange for accommodation and meals. Lithuania's branch is just starting out and Latvia has only a couple of farms listed with WWOOF Independents (www.wwoofindependents.org). Volunteer opportunities for English speakers are occasionally advertised locally in the *Baltic Times* (www.baltictimes.com) newspaper.

## Women Travellers

The Balts have some fairly traditional ideas about gender roles, but on the other hand they're pretty reserved and rarely impose themselves upon other people in an annoying way. Women are not likely to receive more aggravation from men in the Baltics than in the West, although unaccompanied women may want to avoid the sleazier bars. Local women travel on overnight buses and trains alone, but if you're travelling on a train at night, you may wish to play safe and use the hefty metal lock on the inside of the carriage door.

## Work

The Baltic region has enough difficulty keeping its own people employed, meaning there's little temporary work for visitors. Most non-locals working here have been posted by companies back home. However, these are times of change, and there is some scope for people who want to stay a while and carve themselves a new niche – though, in Western terms, you shouldn't expect to get rich doing so. The English language is certainly in demand, and you might be able to earn your keep (or part of it) teaching it in one of the main cities. For teaching and other postings, try www.goabroad.com.

# Transport

## GETTING THERE & AWAY

There are numerous ways to enter the Baltic countries, either directly or via a close neighbour. For example, it's feasible to fly or take a bus to Warsaw and then enter Lithuania by train, or fly to Helsinki and sail from there to Estonia. Within the Baltics, distances are relatively small.

This section focuses on getting to Estonia, Latvia and Lithuania from outside the region. Flights, tours and rail tickets can be booked online at www.lonelyplanet.com/bookings.

## Entering Estonia, Latvia & Lithuania

Whether you arrive by bus, boat, plane or train, entry procedures are quick and painless. If you're travelling from within the Schengen zone (ie most countries of the EU, excluding the UK and Ireland), there are no arrival formalities.

### Passport

Travellers arriving from outside the Schengen border zone need a passport, valid for six months beyond the planned stay. Citizens of EU countries, the US, Canada, Australia, New Zealand and Japan are among those who don't need a visa for entering Estonia, Latvia or Lithuania.

## Air

### Airports & Airlines

Estonia's national carrier is Nordica (www.nordica.ee), while Latvia's is airBaltic (www.airbaltic.com). Lithuania's former national carrier is defunct. International airports within the region:

**Kaunas International Airport** (Map p330; ☎8-612 44442; www.kaunas-airport.lt; Oro uosto gatvė, Karmėlava; ⏲6am-midnight; 🚌29, 29E)

**Palanga Airport** (Palangos Oro Uostas; Map p363; ☎6124 4442; www.palanga-airport.lt; Liepojos plentas 1)

**Rīga International Airport** (Starptautiskā Lidosta Rīga; Map p228; ☎1817; www.riga-airport.com; Mārupe District; 🚌22)

**Tallinn Airport** (Tallinna Lennujaam; Map p54; ☎605 8888; www.tallinn-airport.ee; Tartu mnt 101; 📶)

**Tartu Airport** (Ulenurme Airport; Map p103; ☎605 8888; www.tartu-airport.ee; Lennu tn 44, Reola)

**Vilnius International Airport** (Tarptautinis Vilniaus Oro Uostas; Map p330; ☎6-124 4442; www.vno.lt; Rodūnios kelias 10a; 📶; 🚌1, 2)

### Australia & New Zealand

If you're coming from Australasia, a trip to the Baltic will necessitate at least three

**CLIMATE CHANGE & TRAVEL**

Every form of transport that relies on carbon-based fuel generates $CO_2$, the main cause of human-induced climate change. Modern travel is dependent on aeroplanes, which might use less fuel per kilometre per person than most cars but travel much greater distances. The altitude at which aircraft emit gases (including $CO_2$) and particles also contributes to their climate change impact. Many websites offer 'carbon calculators' that allow people to estimate the carbon emissions generated by their journey and, for those who wish to do so, to offset the impact of the greenhouse gases emitted with contributions to portfolios of climate-friendly initiatives throughout the world. Lonely Planet offsets the carbon footprint of all staff and author travel.

separate flights; there's no one airline that services the entire route. Star Alliance (www.staralliance.com) has the most partner airlines serving the Baltic states – Austrian Airlines, Brussels Airlines, LOT, Lufthansa, SAS and Turkish Airlines – making an Air New Zealand or Thai Airways code-share the most flexible choice. Qantas is a member of One World (www.oneworld.com), but Finnair (www.finnair.com) is the only One World member that flies directly to the Baltic.

The cheapest fares to Europe tend to be for routes through Asia, although you can sometimes get a good deal through the USA from New Zealand. If you're considering a route via London, note that no Baltic flights leave from Heathrow, which is where most Australian and New Zealand flights land.

### Caucasus & Central Asia

AirBaltic flies from Rīga to Tbilisi (Georgia) and Baku (Azerbaijan). Uzbekistan Airways (www.uzairways.com) operates flights from Rīga to Tashkent (Uzbekistan).

### Continental Europe

Budget airlines have revolutionised European air transport in the past decade, so you are spoilt for choice when it comes to getting from Baltic airports to European Union countries. Rīga-based airBaltic alone flies to a few dozen cities all over the EU. Ryanair (www.ryanair.com) serves Vilnius, Wizz Air (www.wizzair.com) serves all three Baltic capitals, while easyJet (www.easyjet.com) operates in Tallinn and Vilnius, the three of them connecting Baltic capitals with a host of destinations, notably in Germany.

AirBaltic also flies to Ukraine, Belarus and Moldova, code-sharing with these countries' national carriers. In addition, Ukrainian International Airlines (www.flyuia.com) flies from Kyiv and Odessa to Vilnius, while Nordica (www.nordica.ee) connects Tallinn with Kyiv, Odessa and Warsaw, and Belavia (www.en.belavia.by) from Minsk serves all three Baltic capitals.

### Middle East

Turkish Airlines (www.turkishairlines.com) connects Tallinn, Rīga and Vilnius with Istanbul. AirBaltic flies to Tel Aviv.

### Nordic Countries

AirBaltic, along with SAS (www.scandinavian.net), Finnair, Norwegian (www.norwegian.no) and Wizz Air connect all Baltic airports to any Scandinavian city of note, while Nordica flies from Tallinn to Copenhagen, Stockholm and Trondheim.

### North America

From North America, the easiest way to reach the Baltics is to catch a direct flight to a European hub, such as London, Frankfurt or Amsterdam and then catch a connecting flight to one of the Baltic capitals. Check Skyscanner (www.skyscanner.net) for the most convenient connections.

### Russia

Russia's Aeroflot (www.aeroflot.com) operates flights from Moscow to all three Baltic capitals. AirBaltic also flies to Moscow and St Petersburg from Rīga.

### UK & Ireland

Budget airlines Ryanair, easyJet and Wizz Air fly numerous routes from Ireland and the UK to the Baltics, including departures from many small regional airports. If you're considering connecting flights via London, allow several hours to travel between airports, as 'London airports' are a long way from the city and from each other.

## Land

### Bicycle

Bicycles can be carried cheaply (or free) on ferries from the Nordic countries and Germany to the Baltics. Pedallers through Poland face the same choice of routes as drivers.

### Border Crossings

Travelling from north to south, Estonia shares borders with Russia and Latvia; Latvia shares borders with Estonia, Russia, Belarus and Lithuania; and Lithuania borders Latvia, Belarus, Poland and the Kaliningrad Region (part of Russia).

Now that the Baltic countries are in the EU and part of the Schengen Agreement, border checkpoints between Estonia, Lithuania, Latvia and Poland are non-existent, though it pays to carry at least an identity card with you as random border checks are sometimes performed at the Estonian border.

Travel to Belarus and Russia is another matter entirely. These borders continue to be rigorously controlled, and you'll need to get a visa in advance for both. Expect to spend at least an hour at the border regardless. It's possible to enter Belarus visa-free, but only if flying into Minsk.

Private cars queue for hours to get in and out of Russia and Belarus at major checkpoints. In Estonia, however, you can avoid the wait by booking a time slot for the border crossing at www.estonianborder.eu (unfortunately it doesn't work for cars coming back into Estonia). International buses bypass the queue.

The Kaliningrad region enjoys quieter road borders with Lithuania at Panemunė–Sovietsk, between Kybartai (Lithuania) and Nesterov, and on Curonian Spit along the Klaipėda–Zelenogradsk road. Nationals of 53 countries may enter Kaliningrad on a free e-visa (p423), valid at land borders, but it must be arranged in advance.

## Bus

With a few exceptions, buses are the cheapest but least comfortable method of reaching the Baltic from within Europe. Direct buses arrive from as far north as St Petersburg, as far west as Paris, as far south as Sofia and as far east as Moscow. From much of the rest of Europe you can reach the Baltic with a single change of bus in Warsaw. Pan-European bus companies run services from Baltic capitals to a multitude of destinations in the EU, as well as Russia and Belarus.

See bus company websites for route maps, prices, schedules, ticketing agents and more; you can also purchase tickets online. There are 10% discounts for passengers under 26 or over 60. Return tickets cost about 20% less than two one-way tickets.

**Eurolines** www.eurolines.com

**Ecolines** www.ecolines.net

**Lux Express** www.luxexpress.eu

## Car & Motorcycle

If you take your own vehicle to the Baltic, make sure it's in good condition before you leave home.

It's worth contacting motoring clubs, as well as Estonian, Latvian and Lithuanian embassies, for information on regulations, border crossing and so on.

**AA** (www.aa.co.nz) New Zealand.

**AA** (www.theaa.com) UK.

**AAA** (www.aaa.asn.au) Australia.

**AAA** (www.aaa.com) USA.

**RAC** (www.rac.co.uk) UK.

### DOCUMENTS

Bring your vehicle's registration document, preferably in the form of an international motor vehicle certificate, which is a translation of the basic registration document. Motoring associations should be able to provide one. An International Driving Permit (IDP; also obtainable from motoring associations) is recommended, but your own licence will suffice in most situations. All three Baltic countries demand compulsory accident insurance for drivers.

Insurance policies with limited compensation rates can be bought at the Estonian, Latvian and Lithuanian borders. Remember that you'll also need appropriate documentation for all the countries you pass through on the way to or from the Baltics; motoring associations can advise you.

### BELARUS

There is no particular reason to venture into Belarus, unless it is your destination, or you are transiting into Ukraine, having acquired a Belarusian transit visa in advance.

Do not attempt to approach the border or set foot in the country without a Belarusian transit visa – available only at Belarusian embassies. No visas are sold at any Belarus border. Even with a visa, expect to wait several hours at the border.

Note that although Belarus and Russia are united in a customs union and there are no checks on the border between them, you still can't enter Belarus on a Russian visa.

### FINLAND

The quickest and best-served car-ferry connection is from Helsinki to Tallinn. Alternatively, from Finland you can drive through Russia; from the Finnish–Russian border at Vaalimaa–Torfyanovka it's 360km to Narva (Estonia). You could do it in a day, but there's little point coming this way unless you want to look at St Petersburg on the way through.

### GERMANY

Bringing a vehicle into the Baltics usually entails a ferry trip from the German ports of Kiel or Lübeck to Klaipėda (Lithuania) or to Ventspils or Liepāja (Latvia). But you can also drive into Lithuania through Poland.

### POLAND

It will take some minutes before you notice you've crossed the border as it's neither guarded nor really marked; due to the Schengen agreement, border formalities are minimal to nonexistent. Brace for a painstaking drive on the truck-ridden, single-lane roads in eastern Poland. It gets better once you get into Lithuania or once you reach Warsaw on the way back.

### RUSSIA

From St Petersburg the drive to the Estonian border at Ivangorod–Narva is only 140km. Driving from all three Baltic countries into Moscow, the Rīga–Moscow highway is the most straightforward route, and both its Russian and Latvian sections are in good shape. Coming from Estonia, you can cross the border at Lütä (book your crossing time slot at www.estonianborder.eu to avoid queues) and then drive south to the Rīga–Moscow highway.

Coming from Lithuania, note that you'll need a Belarusian transit visa to use the convenient Minsk–Moscow highway. Unless you manage to get it, you'll have to drive via Zilupe checkpoint on the Rīga–Moscow highway, where the waiting time is often half a day.

### SWEDEN

Vehicle ferries run from Stockholm to Tallinn or Rīga, from Nynäshamn to Venstpils and Liepāja (Latvia) and from Karlshamn to Klaipėda.

## Train

Train travel is not really much of an option for Baltic countries, unless you are coming from Russia or Belarus. There is also a weak link connecting the region to the rest of the EU via Poland, but this is all due to change with the completion of Rail Baltica.

### POLAND

There is currently no direct train route operating between Warsaw and Vilnius. You can make a daytime journey on local trains from Warsaw to Kaunas or Vilnius, changing trains in Šeštokai, in Lithuania (close to the Poland–Lithuania border). Timetables are designed to give a 15-minute window to transfer. Total journey time is about 9½ hours. Note, too, that this option doesn't pass through Belarus.

### RUSSIA & BELARUS

The old Soviet rail network still functions over most of the former USSR. Trains linking Moscow with all the main Baltic cities enable you to combine the Baltics with a Trans-Siberian trip or other Russian or Central Asian travels. Check the Russian railways website http://pass.rzd.ru for details.

The English version of www.poezda.net allows you to search timetables for trains within the former USSR. Alternatively, you can use http://bahn.hafas.de for European train schedules (although prices aren't given).

Overnight trains connect Rīga and Tallinn with both Moscow and St Petersburg. Note that the latter is connected by fast train services with Helsinki in Finland, which allows you to make a neat circle, coming back to Tallinn by ferry. (That's provided you have a Russian visa.)

From Vilnius, there are three daily trains to Moscow's Belarus train station. These pass through Belarus, however, so you'll need a Belarusian visa. From Vilnius, three daily trains travel west to Kaliningrad (a journey of about six hours).

### RAIL BALTICA

Full steam ahead with Rail Baltica (www.railbaltica.org)! Well, OK, not steam, exactly, given how this ambitious railway network – the largest Baltic region infrastructure project of all time – will utilise the most up-to-date railway technology and be fully electrified. The project, due to be completed in 2026, includes Poland, Lithuania, Latvia, Estonia and, indirectly, Finland. Once completed, the railway will connect Helsinki, Tallinn, Pärnu, Riga, Panevežys, Kaunas, Vilnius and Warsaw. The railway will adopt the use of the 1435mm gauge, marking a symbolic return to Europe (following WWII, Eastern Europe has been using the Russian 1520mm gauge).

## Sea

Numerous seafaring options offer a slower but more relaxed journey.

From Latvia, regular car and passenger ferry services include Rīga–Stockholm, Liepāja–Travemünde (Germany) and Ventspils–Nynäshamin (Sweden).

From Klaipėda in Lithuania, passenger and car ferries serve Kiel (Germany) and Karlshamn (Sweden).

From Estonia, numerous daily ferries connect Tallinn to Helsinki. There is also an overnight ferry to Stockholm via the Åland Islands (Finland) and services to St Petersburg and Mariehamn (Finland).

For daily services to Helsinki you don't need to reserve ahead, but some of the other ferries – notably Stockholm to Tallinn and the cargo ferries to Denmark – can get booked up far in advance.

Schedules and fares change frequently – double-check both when you are planning your trip. Ferry and hydrofoil operators' websites have up-to-date schedules and fares.

### Denmark

The shipping company DFDS Seaways (www.freight.dfdsseaways.com) operates a cargo service connecting Fredericia (Denmark) and Klaipėda (Lithuania) via Copenhagen, twice a week. There is limited cabin capacity for passengers – book ahead.

### Finland

A fleet of ferries now carries well over two million people each year across the 85km Gulf of Finland separating Helsinki and Tallinn. There are dozens of crossings each way every day (ships take two to 3½ hours; hydrofoils take approximately 1½ hours). Note that in high winds or bad weather, hydrofoils are often cancelled; they operate only when the sea is free from ice (generally around late March/April to late December); larger ferries sail year-round.

Shop around: the best deals are often for advance tickets purchased on the internet. Fares vary widely, depending on season, day and time of travel, and other factors (check if the company has a fuel surcharge that's included – or not – in the advertised price). Fares are generally higher at high-demand times such as Friday evening, Saturday morning and Sunday afternoon. On most ferry lines, students and seniors get a

## Ferry Routes

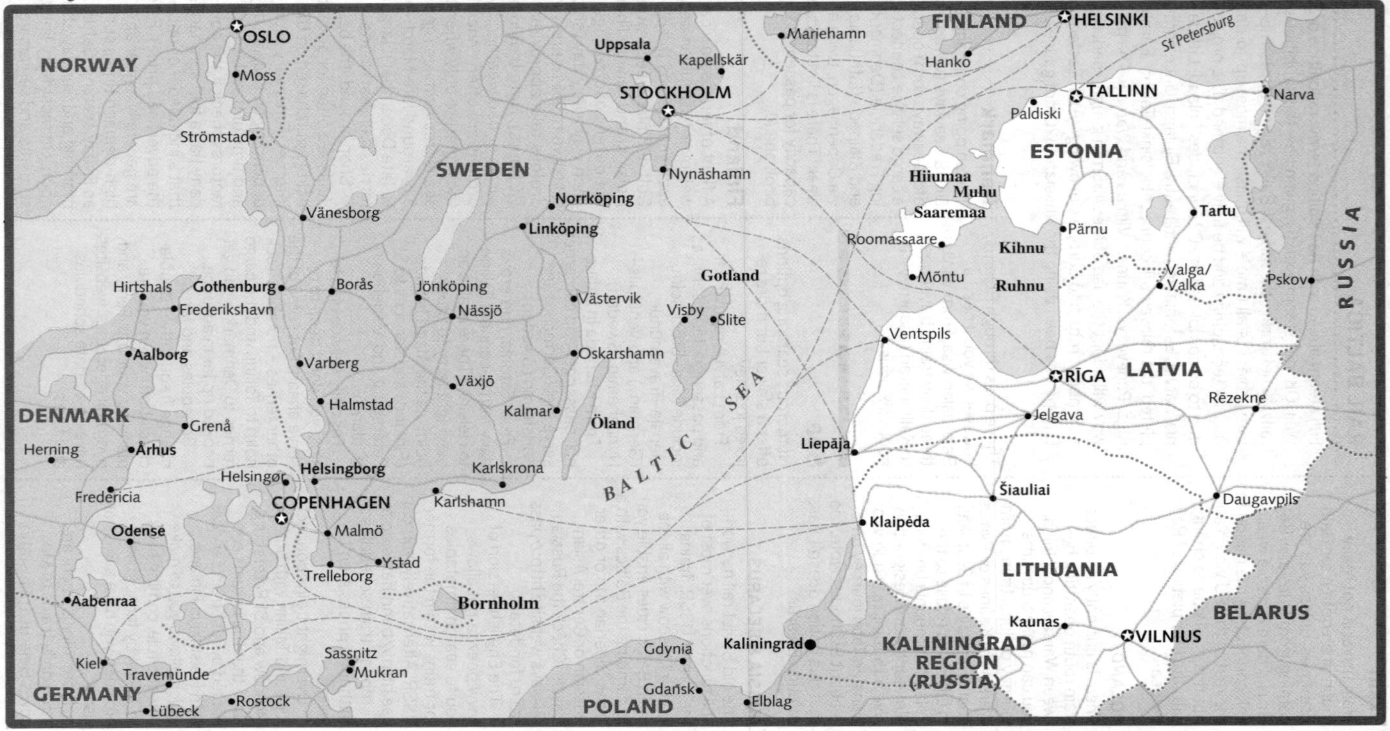

10% to 15% discount, children between ages six and 17 pay half price and those under six sail for free. Most operators offer special deals for families and serial tickets for frequent passengers.

### Germany

Scandlines (www.scandlines.lt) ferries sail twice weekly in each direction from Travemünde (Lübeck) to both Ventspils and Liepāja in Latvia. DFDS Seaways runs service between Klaipėda and Kiel.

### Sweden

#### TO/FROM ESTONIA

Tallink Silja (www.tallinksilja.com) sails every night between Tallinn and Stockholm, stopping at Mariehamn on the Aland Islands (Finland) en route. Ferries make the 17-hour crossing year-round, leaving from Terminal D in Tallinn and the Värtahamnen Terminal in Stockholm. This service gets heavily booked, so make your reservation a month or two ahead.

#### TO/FROM LATVIA

Tallink Silja operates overnight services daily between Rīga and Stockholm.

Scandlines has boats connecting the ports of Liepāja and Ventspils with Nynäshamn (about 60km from Stockholm), departing five times weekly from both ports.

#### TO/FROM LITHUANIA

DFDS Seaways (www.dfdsseaways.com) has daily ferries from Karlshamn to Klaipėda.

### Yacht

The Baltics – particularly Estonia with its islands and indented coast – attract hundreds of yachts a year, mainly from Finland and Scandinavia. Good online resources:

**www.marinas.nautilus.ee** Information on entry regulations, a database of all the local marinas, and details for ordering the *Estonian Cruising Guide*.

**http://en.seaclub.lv/ports/latvia** Offers comprehensive information on yacht ports in the entire region.

It's also possible to rent yachts throughout the region.

## Tours

Several international travel operators specialise in the Baltic region.

**Baltic Holidays** (☎in the UK 0845 070 5711; www.balticholidays.com) This UK operator offers spa or city breaks, beach, family or countryside holidays and tailor-made themed holidays. Can help with genealogy research.

**Baltics and Beyond** (☎in UK 0845 094 2125; www.balticsandbeyond.net) A UK-based company offering regular tours, self-guided options and tailor-made trips to the three Baltic countries and some of their neighbours (including Belarus, Russia and Poland).

**Regent Holidays** (☎in the UK 0117 921 1711; www.regent-holidays.co.uk) A UK company with an array of Baltic options, including fly/drive and city breaks.

**Vytis Tours** (☎in the US 718-423-6161; www.vytistours.com) A US company offering a range of tours, from an economical eight-day jaunt round the region's capitals to a more extensive 17-day 'Grand Tour'.

# GETTING AROUND

## Air

There are plenty of scheduled flights between the three Baltic capitals, but domestic flights within each country are minimal.

### Airlines Flying Within Estonia, Latvia & Lithuania

**airBaltic** (www.airbaltic.com) Flies from Rīga to Palanga, Tallinn and Vilnius; and from Vilnius to Tallinn.

**Nordica** (www.nordica.ee) Flies from Tallinn to Vilnius.

## Boat

### Ferry

At the time of writing there were no ferry links between the Baltic countries. Estonia has ferry connections to many of its islands, although smaller boats don't run in winter once the seas ice up. Ferries within Latvia are few, although you can catch a slow boat between Rīga and Jūrmala. In Lithuania, people can travel by boat from Klaipėda to Curonian Spit and from Nida to the Nemunas Delta, though the latter tends to be a day cruise.

### Yacht

Private yachting is a popular way to get around the Baltic Coast – particularly Estonia's coast, with its many islands and bays. **Sailing.ee** (Map p62; ☎5333 1117; www.sailing.ee; Sadama 25/4) rents out yachts with or without a skipper.

**www.marinas.nautilus.ee** For information and advice on Estonia's dozens of marinas.

**www.marinaslatvia.lv** Details of Latvia's marinas.

## Bus

The region is well served by buses, although services to off-the-beaten-track villages are infrequent. Direct bus services link the three capitals and there are other cross-border services between main towns.

Buses are generally faster than trains and often slightly cheaper. Those used for local journeys, up to about two hours long, offer few comforts. Avoid window seats in rainy, snowy or very cold weather; travel with someone you're prepared to snuggle up to for body warmth; and sit in the seat allocated to you.

Some shorter routes are serviced by nippier and more modern microbuses, holding about 15 passengers and officially making fewer stops than their big-bus counterparts.

By contrast, buses travelling between the Baltic countries are equal to long-distance coaches anywhere else in Europe. They are clean and have a heating system, a toilet, hot-drinks dispenser, TV and free wi-fi on board. Many scheduled buses to/from Tallinn, Rīga and Vilnius run overnight; it's a convenient and safe way of travelling.

### Buses Operating Within Estonia, Latvia & Lithuania

**Tpilet** (www.tpilet.ee) Umbrella for all Estonian services.

**Ecolines** (www.ecolines.net) Major routes include Rīga–Salacgrīva–Pärnu–Tallinn; Rīga–Valmiera–Valga–Tartu–Narva; Rīga–Panevėžys–Vilnius–Kaunas; Liepāja–Palanga–Klaipėda; Rēzekne–Daugavpils–Utena–Vilnius–Kaunas.

**Lux Express** (www.luxexpress.eu) With its associated budget line Simple Express (www.simpleexpress.eu), major routes include Tallinn–Pärnu–Rīga–Vilnius; Narva–Tartu–Valga–Rīga; Rīga–Vilnius; Rīga–Kaunas; Rīga–Šiauliai; Vilnius–Kaunas.

### Tickets & Information

Ticket offices/windows selling national and international tickets are clearly marked in the local language and occasionally in English, too. Tickets are always printed in the local language and are easy to understand once you know the words for 'seat', 'bus stop' etc. Many major bus stations across the Baltics now have multilingual electronic ticket machines.

For long-distance buses, tickets are sold in advance from the station from which you begin the journey or online from www.autobusubilietai.lt (Lithuania), www.tpilet.ee (Estonia) and www.autoosta.lv (Latvia). For local buses to nearby towns or villages, or for long-distance buses that are midroute ('in transit'), you normally pay on board. This may mean a bit of a scrum for seats if there are a lot of people waiting.

Most bus and train stations in towns and cities have information windows with staff who generally speak some English.

### Timetables & Fares

Check timetables on bus-company websites, or if for some reason you happen to be offline, check schedules at the local tourist office. The offices in Tallinn, Rīga and Vilnius in particular maintain up-to-the-minute transport schedules. The **In Your Pocket** (www.inyourpocket.com) city guides to the capitals include fairly comprehensive domestic and pan-Baltic bus schedules, updated every two months.

Comprehensive timetables are posted in bus stations' main ticket halls. A rare few need careful decoding. Most simply list the departure time and the days (using either Roman or Arabic numerals, the number 1 being Monday) on which the service runs.

Fares vary slightly between the three countries, and between bus companies, reflecting the speed of the bus, comfort levels and time of day it arrives/departs.

## Car & Motorcycle

For flexibility and access to out-of-the-way destinations, you can't beat driving.

### Fuel & Spare Parts

Petrol stations run by major companies are open 24 hours along all the major roads; many are self-service with an automated pay system accepting notes or credit cards with PINs. Western-grade fuel, including unleaded, is readily available.

### Road Rules

The whole region drives on the right. The legal maximum blood alcohol limit varies in each country (Estonia 0.02%; Latvia 0.05%; Lithuania 0.04%). Seat belts are compulsory and headlights must be on at all times while driving. The speed limit in built-up areas is 50km/h; limits outside urban areas vary from 70km/h to 110km/h – look out for signs, as these limits are often strictly enforced. Speeding seems to be a habit with locals, but don't follow their example. Fines may be collected on the spot – the amounts vary.

It is illegal to use a mobile phone while operating a vehicle (hands-free kits are allowed). Winter tyres are a legal requirement, usually from December to March every year, but if there are severe weather conditions outside these dates (likely in most years), the dates will change accordingly, so check local conditions if driving between October and April.

Traditional coin-fed parking meters are still found in some parts of the Baltics, though both Tallinn and Vilnius have moved towards electronic systems – drivers pay for parking via SMS, dialling a number and inputting the car's licence plate and location number (posted nearby).

Driving into the old towns in Rīga, Tallinn, Vilnius and Kaunas is free, but parking is pricey; multilingual parking machines usually display price per hour and applicable times. Motorists must pay a small entrance fee to drive into Latvia's prime seaside resort, Jūrmala, and to enter Curonian Spit National Park.

Take care driving near trams, trolleybuses and buses in towns: passengers may run across the road to

## ROAD DISTANCES (KM)

| | Tallin | Tartu | Pärnu | Narva | Valka/Valga | Rīga | Liepāja | Daugavpils | Ventspils | Vilnius | Kaunas | Klaipėda | Panevėžys |
|---|---|---|---|---|---|---|---|---|---|---|---|---|---|
| Tartu | 190 | | | | | | | | | | | | |
| Pärnu | 130 | 205 | | | | | | | | | | | |
| Narva | 210 | 194 | 304 | | | | | | | | | | |
| Valka/Valga | 276 | 86 | 140 | 268 | | | | | | | | | |
| Rīga | 310 | 253 | 180 | 435 | 167 | | | | | | | | |
| Liepāja | 530 | 473 | 400 | 655 | 387 | 220 | | | | | | | |
| Daugavpils | 540 | 377 | 410 | 559 | 291 | 230 | 450 | | | | | | |
| Ventspils | 510 | 453 | 380 | 635 | 367 | 200 | 119 | 430 | | | | | |
| Vilnius | 600 | 543 | 470 | 725 | 457 | 290 | 465 | 167 | 584 | | | | |
| Kaunas | 575 | 523 | 460 | 715 | 447 | 280 | 230 | 267 | 349 | 100 | | | |
| Klaipėda | 620 | 538 | 490 | 745 | 477 | 310 | 155 | 477 | 274 | 310 | 210 | | |
| Panevėžys | 460 | 403 | 330 | 585 | 317 | 150 | 270 | 168 | 350 | 140 | 110 | 235 | |
| Šiaulia | 465 | 383 | 310 | 565 | 297 | 130 | 192 | 387 | 330 | 220 | 140 | 155 | 80 |

catch a tram that's still in motion. Traffic behind a tram must stop when it opens its doors to let people in and out. Trolleybuses often swing far out into the road when leaving a stop.

# Hitching

Hitching is never entirely safe in any country in the world, and we don't recommend it. Travellers who decide to hitch should understand that they are taking a small but potentially serious risk. People who do choose to hitch will be safer if they travel in pairs and let someone know where they are planning to go.

Locally, hitching is a popular means of getting around. The **Vilnius Hitchhiking Club** (VHHC; www.autostop.lt) provides practical information and contacts for travellers hoping to hitch a ride in all three Baltic countries. Hostel noticeboards in capital cities are a good place to find or offer a ride-share.

# Local Transport

## Bicycle & Electric Scooter

The flatness and small scale of Estonia, Latvia and Lithuania, and the light traffic on most roads, make them good cycling territory. On the Estonian islands and along Lithuania's Curonian Spit especially, you'll see cyclists galore in summer. Most bring their own bicycles, but there are plenty of places where you can hire one, including each of the capitals and most major towns.

Cyclists should bring waterproof clothing, and perhaps a tent if touring: you may not find accommodation in some out-of-the-way places. Travel agencies and organisations both within and outside the region organise cycling tours.

Major cities in the Baltics are becoming more and more bicycle-friendly, with a growing number of cycle lanes and many spots where you can pick up a bicycle.

Love 'em or hate 'em, the use of electric scooters is very on-trend in the Baltic capitals as of 2019, and you can find them everywhere. Download relevant apps (such as Bolt and CityBee) to use them and ride in the cycle lanes as much as possible.

## Bus, Tram & Trolleybus

A mix of trams, buses and trolleybuses (buses run by electricity from overhead wires) provides thorough public transport around towns and cities in all three countries. All three types of transport get crowded, especially during the early-morning and early-evening rush hours.

Trams, trolleybuses and buses all run from about 5.30am to 12.30am, but services get pretty thin in outlying areas after about 7pm. In Tallinn and Vilnius, the same ticket is good for all types of transport except minibuses; Rīga has a full network of services covered by e-tickets. Tickets are sold from news kiosks displaying them in the window and by drivers (buying tickets on board costs a bit more). Multi-trip, weekly and monthly tickets are available. The system depends on honesty and lends itself to cheating, but there are regular inspections, with on-the-spot fines if you're caught riding without a valid ticket.

Travelling on all trams, trolleybuses and buses involves a particular etiquette. If you are young, fit and capable of standing for the duration of your journey, do not sit in the seats at the front – these are only for *babushkas* (senior-age women), pregnant women and small children. Secondly, plan getting off well ahead of time. It's good to know how to say 'excuse me' in the language of your Baltic country or in Russian, so people understand that you want to get to the door on a crowded bus.

All airports are served by regular city transport as well as by taxis.

### Taxi & Bolt

Taxis are plentiful and usually cheap. Night-time tariffs, which generally apply between 10pm and 6am, are higher. To avoid rip-offs, insist on the meter running. In any of the cities, it's always cheaper and safer to order a cab by phone. A reliable, cheaper alternative is Bolt (www.bolt.eu), the Baltic equivalent of Uber. Register your bank card on its app and fares are deducted automatically.

### Train

Suburban trains serve the outskirts of the main cities and some surrounding towns and villages. Most are commuter-style and are often the best option for day-trip destinations, such as Jūrmala and Cēsis from Rīga, or Trakai and Paneriai from Vilnius. Trains tend to be as fast as buses, cheaper and much more comfortable.

## Tours

A few local travel operators specialise in travel around the Baltic region and can help you organise a trip.

**City Bike** (☎in Estonia 511 1819; www.citybike.ee) Reputable and longstanding Tallinn-based company, which arranges multiday cycling tours through Estonia, Latvia and Lithuania.

**Time Travels** (☎in Finland 10 4218990; www.timetravels.fi) A backpacker-focused company offering adventure bus trips through Scandinavia and the Baltic region.

## Train

Estonia, Latvia and Lithuania have railways, and reasonably frequent intercity services, although some have been scaled back significantly in recent years and much long-distance travel within the Baltics is done by bus. However, the planned intracountry rail network, Rail Baltica (p427), will seamlessly connect the Baltics to Poland and Finland. Some sections have been built already and the project is earmarked for completion in 2026.

In the meantime, Baltic trains are slow, cheap and reasonably comfortable. You can often open the windows (but when you can't, it can be stuffy), and you stand equal chances of freezing or baking, depending on whether the heating is turned on or not. Local trains, known as suburban or electric, are substantially slower and make more frequent stops than long-distance trains.

### Routes

There are no direct train services running between the Baltic capitals, although you can travel from Tallinn to Rīga by train with a stop at Valga (on the Estonia–Latvia border).

### Tickets & Information

In Latvia and Lithuania, tickets can be purchased in advance and right before departure at train stations. In larger stations, such as Rīga, you can only buy tickets for certain types of trains or destinations at certain windows.

Except for Tallinn, Estonia's train stations are deserted places, with no ticket offices or other services of any kind. You buy your tickets on the train; don't head to the train station (which is usually quite far from the city centre) unless you know the exact departure time. You can also purchase domestic tickets online at www.elron.ee.

On long-distance trains between the Baltics and other countries, your ticket must be surrendered to the carriage attendant, who will safeguard it for the journey's duration and return it to you 15 minutes before arrival at your final destination (a handy 'alarm clock' if you're on an overnight train).

### Timetables

The following websites provide railway timetables online.

**Estonia** www.elron.ee

**Latvia** www.pv.lv

**Lithuania** www.traukinio bilietas.lt

At train stations, the timetables generally list the number of the train, departure and arrival times, and the platform from which it leaves. Some list return journey schedules, the number of minutes a train waits in your station or the time a train left the place it began its journey. Always study the small print on timetables, as many trains only run on certain days or between certain dates.

# Language

## ESTONIAN

Estonian belongs to the Baltic-Finnic branch of the Finno-Ugric languages. It's closely related to Finnish and distantly related to Hungarian. Most Estonians, especially the younger generations, understand some English and Finnish, but you'll find that people are welcoming of visitors who make an effort to speak their language.

Most Estonian consonants are the same as in English. If you read our pronunciation guides as if they were English, you'll be understood. Note that p is pronounced between the English 'p' and 'b', d between the English 't' and 'd', rr is trilled and zh sounds like the 's' in 'treasure'. As for vowels, aeh is pronounced as the 'ae' in 'aesthetic', err as the 'yrr' in 'myrrh' (rounding the lips) and ü as the 'oo' in 'too' (rounding the lips).

Stressed syllables are indicated with italics, and stress generally falls on the first syllable.

### Basics

| | | |
|---|---|---|
| **Hello.** | *Tere.* | *te*·rre |
| **Goodbye.** | *Head aega.* | head *ae*·gah |
| **Yes.** | *Jah.* | yah |
| **No.** | *Ei.* | ay |
| **Thank you.** | *Tänan.* | *ta*·nahn |
| **You're welcome.** | *Palun.* | *pah*·lun |
| **Excuse me/ Sorry.** | *Vabandage.* | *vah*·bahn·dah·ge |
| **How are you?** | *Kuidas läheb?* | *kuy*·dahs *la*·heb |
| **Fine.** | *Hästi.* | *has*·ti |

**What's your name?**
*Mis te nimi on?* — mis te *ni*·mi on

**My name is ...**
*Mu nimi on ...* — mu *ni*·mi on ...

**Do you speak English?**
*Kas te räägite inglise keelt?* — kahs te *rraa*·gi·te *ing*·li·se kehlt

**I don't understand.**
*Ma ei saa aru.* — mah ay saah *ah*·rru

> **WANT MORE?**
>
> For in-depth language information and handy phrases, check out Lonely Planet's *Baltic Phrasebook*. You'll find it at **shop.lonelyplanet.com**, or you can buy Lonely Planet's iPhone phrasebooks at the Apple App Store.

### Accommodation

| | | |
|---|---|---|
| **Where's a ...?** | *Kus asub ...?* | kus *ah*·sub ... |
| **campsite** | *kämping* | *kam*·ping |
| **hotel** | *hotell* | ho·*tell* |
| **pension** | *võõras-temaja* | *vyy*·rrahs·te·mah·yah |

**I'd like a single/double room.**
*Ma tahaksin ühe/ kahe voodiga tuba.* — mah *tah*·hak·sin *ü*·he/ *kah*·he *vaw*·di·gah *tu*·bah

**How much is it per person/night?**
*Kui palju maksab voodikoht/ööpäev?* — kui *pahl*·yu *mahk*·sab *vaw*·di·koht/*err*·paehv

### Directions

**Where is ...?**
*Kus on ...?* — kus on ...

**How far is it?**
*Kui kaugel see on?* — kuy *kau*·gel seh on

**Please show me on the map.**
*Palun näidake mulle seda kaardil.* — *pah*·lun *nai*·dah·ke *mul*·le se·dah *kaahrr*·dil

**SIGNS – ESTONIAN**

| | |
|---|---|
| **Sissepääs** | Entrance |
| **Väljapääs** | Exit |
| **Avatud/Lahti** | Open |
| **Suletud/Kinni** | Closed |
| **WC** | Toilets |
| **Meestele** | Men |
| **Naistele** | Women |

## Eating & Drinking

**Can I have a menu?**
*Kas ma saaksin menüü?* — kas mah *saahk*·sin me·*nüü*

**I'd like ...**
*Ma sooviksin ...* — ma *saw*·vik·sin ...

**I'm a vegetarian.**
*Ma olen taimetoitlane.* — mah *o*·len *tai*·me·toyt·lah·ne

**Bon appetit!**
*Head isu!* — head *i*·su

**To your health! (Cheers!)**
*Terviseks!* — *ter*·vi·seks

**The bill, please.**
*Palun arve.* — *pah*·lun *ahrr*·ve

## Emergencies

| | | |
|---|---|---|
| **Help!** | *Appi!* | *ahp*·pi |
| **Go away!** | *Minge ära!* | *min*·ge *a*·rrah |
| **Call a doctor!** | *Kutsuge arst!* | *kut*·su·ge ahrrst |
| **I'm ill.** | *Ma olen haige.* | mah o·len *hai*·ge |
| **I'm lost.** | *Ma olen eksinud.* | mah o·len *ek*·si·nud |

## Shopping & Services

**What time does it open/close?**
*Mis kell see avatakse/ suletakse?* — mis kell seh *ah*·vah·tahk·se/ *su*·le·tahk·se

**How much does it cost?**
*Kui palju see maksab?* — kui *pahl*·yu seh *mahk*·sahb

| | | |
|---|---|---|
| **bank** | *pank* | pahnk |
| **chemist/ pharmacy** | *apteek* | *ahp*·tehk |
| **market** | *turg* | turrg |
| **police** | *politsei* | po·lit·*say* |
| **post office** | *postkontor* | *post*·kon·torr |
| **toilet** | *tualett* | tua·*lett* |
| **tourist office** | *turismi-büroo* | tu·*rris*·mi·bü·*rroo* |

## Time & Numbers

| | | |
|---|---|---|
| **What time is it?** | *Mis kell on?* | mis kell on |
| **It's one o'clock.** | *Kell on üks.* | kell on üks |
| **in the morning** | *hommikul* | *hom*·mi·kul |
| **in the evening** | *õhtul* | *yh*·tul |

| | | |
|---|---|---|
| **1** | *üks* | üks |
| **2** | *kaks* | kahks |
| **3** | *kolm* | kolm |
| **4** | *neli* | *ne*·li |
| **5** | *viis* | vees |
| **6** | *kuus* | koos |
| **7** | *seitse* | *sayt*·se |
| **8** | *kaheksa* | *kah*·hek·sah |
| **9** | *üheksa* | *ü*·hek·sah |
| **10** | *kümme* | *küm*·me |

## Transport

| | | |
|---|---|---|
| **Where's the ...?** | *Kus on ...?* | kus on ... |
| **airport** | *lennujaam* | *len*·nu·yaahm |
| **bus station** | *bussijaam* | *bus*·si·yaahm |
| **ferry terminal** | *sadam* | *sah*·dahm |
| **train station** | *rongijaam* | *rron*·gi·yaahm |

| | | |
|---|---|---|
| **Which ... goes there?** | *Mis ... ma sinna saan?* | mis ... mah *sin*·nah saahn |
| **bus** | *bussiga* | *bus*·si·gah |
| **tram** | *trammiga* | *trrahm*·mi·gah |
| **trolleybus** | *trolliga* | *trrol*·li·gah |

**What time is the next bus/train?**
*Mis kell on järgmine buss/rong ?* — mis kell on *yarrg*·mi·ne buss/rrong

**Please give me a one-way/return ticket.**
*Palun üks/ edasi-tagasi pilet.* — *pah*·lun üks/ e·dah·si·*tah*·gah·si *pi*·let

# LATVIAN

Latvian belongs to the Baltic language family. Only about 55% of the population, and just over 45% of the inhabitants of Rīga speak it as their first language. Latvian and Lithuanian have a lot of vocabulary in common, but are not mutually intelligible.

In our pronunciation guides, a line above a vowel indicates that it is a long sound. Note that uh is pronounced as the 'u' in 'fund', eh as the 'ai' in 'fair', ea as in 'fear', dz as the 'ds' in 'beds', zh as the 's' in 'pleasure' and jy is similar to the 'dy' sound in British 'duty'. Word stress is indicated with italics. The markers (m) and (f) indicate the options for male and female speakers respectively.

## Basics

| | | |
|---|---|---|
| **Hello.** | *Sveiks.* (m)<br>*Sveika.* (f) | svayks<br>*svay*·kuh |
| **Goodbye.** | *Uz redzēšanos.* | uz *redz*·eh·shuhn·aws |
| **Yes.** | *Jā.* | yah |
| **No.** | *Nē.* | neh |
| **Please.** | *Lūdzu.* | *loo*·dzu |
| **Thank you.** | *Paldies.* | puhl·*deas* |
| **You're welcome.** | *Lūdzu.* | *loo*·dzu |
| **Excuse me.** | *Atvainojiet.* | *uht*·vai·naw·yeat |
| **Sorry.** | *Piedodiet.* | *pea*·doad·eat |

**How are you?**
*Kā jums klājas?* kah yums *klah*·yuhs

**Fine, thank you.**
*Labi, paldies.* *luh*·bi puhl·*deas*

**What's your name?**
*Kā jūs sauc?* kah yoos sowts

**My name is ...**
*Mani sauc ...* *muhn*·i sowts ...

**Do you speak English?**
*Vai jūs runājat angliski?* vai yoos *run*·ah·yuht *uhn*·gli·ski

**I don't understand.**
*Es nesaprotu.* es *ne*·suh·praw·tu

## Accommodation

| | | |
|---|---|---|
| **I'm looking for a ...** | *Es meklēju ...* | es *mek*·leh·yu ... |
| **hotel** | *viesnīcu* | *veas*·neets·u |
| **youth hostel** | *jauniešu mītni* | *yow*·nea·shu *meet*·ni |

**I'd like a single/double room.**
*Es vēlos vienvietīgu/ divvietīgu istabu.* es *vaa*·laws *vean*·vea·tee·gu/ *div*·vea·tee·gu *is*·tuh·bu

**How much is it per night?**
*Cik maksā diennaktī?* tsik *muhk*·sah *dean*·nuhk·tee

## Directions

**How do I get to ...?**
*Kā es tieku līdz ...?* kah es *tea*·ku leedz ...

**Is it far from here?**
*Vai tas atrodas tālu?* vai tuhs *uht*·raw·duhs *tah*·lu

### SIGNS – LATVIAN

| | |
|---|---|
| **Ieeja** | Entrance |
| **Izeja** | Exit |
| **Atvērts** | Open |
| **Slēgts** | Closed |
| **Tualetes** | Toilets |
| **Vīriešu** | Men |
| **Sieviešu** | Women |

**Could you show me (on the map), please?**
*Lūdzu parādiet man (uz kartes)?* *loo*·dzu *puhr*·ah·deat muhn (uz *kuhrt*·es)

## Eating & Drinking

**A table for ... people, please.**
*Lūdzu galdu ... personām.* *loo*·dzu *gahl*·du ... *per*·so·nahm

**Do you have a menu?**
*Vai jums ir ēdienkarte?* vai yums ir *eh*·dean·kar te

**What do you recommend?**
*Ko jūs iesakat?* kwo yoos *eah*·sah·kut

**I'm a vegetarian.**
*Es esmu veģetārietis/te.* (m/f) es *es*·mu ve·gye·tah·*reah*·tis/te

**I'd like ...**
*Es vēlos ...* es *vaa*·lwos ...

**The bill, please.**
*Lūdzu rēķinu.* *loo*·dzu *reh*·kyi·nu

## Emergencies

| | | |
|---|---|---|
| **Help!** | *Palīgā!* | *puh*·lee·gah |
| **Go away!** | *Ejiet projam!* | *ay*·eat *praw*·yam |

**Call a doctor!**
*Izsauciet ārstu!* *iz*·sowts·eat *ahr*·stu

**I'm ill.**
*Es esmu slims/ slima.* (m/f) es *as*·mu slims/ slim·uh

**I'm lost.**
*Es esmu apmaldījies/ apmaldījusies.* (m/f) es *as*·mu *uhp*·muhl·dee·yeas *uhp*·muhl·dee·yu·seas

## Shopping & Services

**What time does it open?**
*No cikiem ir atvērts?* naw *tsik*·eam ir *uht*·vaarts

**What time does it close?**
*Cikos slēdz?* *tsik*·aws slaadz

**How much is it?**
*Cik tas maksā?* tsik tuhs *muhk*·sah

**Where are the toilets?**
*Kur ir tualetes?* kur ir tu·uh·le·tes

| | | |
|---|---|---|
| **bank** | *banka* | *buhn*·kuh |
| **chemist/ pharmacy** | *aptieka* | *uhp*·tea·kuh |
| **currency exchange booth** | *valūtas maiņa* | *vuh*·loo·tuhs *mai*·nyuh |
| **market** | *tirgus* | *tir*·gus |
| **post office** | *pasts* | puhsts |

## Time & Numbers

**What time (is it)?**
*Cik (ir) pulkstenis?* tsik (ir) *pulk*·sten·is

**It's five o'clock.**
*Ir pieci.* ir *peats*·i

| | | |
|---|---|---|
| **morning** | *rīts* | reets |
| **afternoon** | *pēcpus-diena* | *pehts*·pus·dea·nuh |
| **night** | *nakts* | nuhkts |

| | | |
|---|---|---|
| **1** | *viens* | veans |
| **2** | *divi* | *di*·vi |
| **3** | *trīs* | trees |
| **4** | *četri* | *chet*·ri |
| **5** | *pieci* | *peats*·i |
| **6** | *seši* | *sesh*·i |
| **7** | *septiņi* | *sep*·ti·nyi |
| **8** | *astoņi* | *uhs*·taw·nyi |
| **9** | *deviņi* | *de*·vi·nyi |
| **10** | *desmit* | *des*·mit |

## Transport

| | | |
|---|---|---|
| **Where's the ...?** | *Kur atrodas ...?* | kur *uht*·raw·duhs ... |
| **airport** | *lidosta* | *lid*·aw·stuh |
| **bus station** | *autoosta* | *ow*·to·aws·tuh |
| **ferry terminal** | *pasažieru osta* | *puh*·suh·zhea·ru *aw*·stuh |
| **train station** | *dzelzceļa stacija* | *dzelz*·tse·lyuh *stuhts*·i·ya |
| **tram stop** | *tramvaja pietura* | *truhm*·vuh·yuh *pea*·tu·ruh |
| **I want to buy a ... ticket.** | *Es vēlos nopirkt ... biļeti.* | es vaa·laws *naw*·pirkt ... *bi*·lyet·i |
| **one-way** | *vien-virziena* | *vean*·virz·ean·uh |
| **return** | *turp-atpakaļ* | *turp*·*uht*·puh·kuhly |

# LITHUANIAN

Lithuanian belongs to the Baltic language family, along with Latvian. Low Lithuanian *(Žemaičiai)*, spoken in the west, is a separate dialect from High Lithuanian *(Aukštaičiai)*, spoken in the rest of the country and considered the standard dialect.

Note that in our pronunciation guides eah sounds as the 'ea' in 'ear', ew as in 'new', uaw as the 'wa' in 'wander', dz as the 'ds' in 'roads', zh as the 's' in 'treasure', and the r sound is trilled. Stressed syllables are in italics.

## Basics

| | | |
|---|---|---|
| **Hello.** | *Sveiki.* | *svay*·ki |
| **Goodbye.** | *Sudie.* | su·*deah* |
| **Yes./No.** | *Taip./Ne.* | tayp/na |
| **Please.** | *Prašau.* | prah·*show* |
| **Thank you.** | *Dėkoju.* | deh·*kaw*·yu |
| **You're welcome.** | *Prašau.* | prah·*show* |
| **Excuse me.** | *Atsiprašau.* | aht·si·prah·*show* |
| **Sorry.** | *Atleiskite.* | aht·*lays*·ki·ta |

**How are you?**
*Kaip gyvuojate?* kaip gee·*vuaw*·yah·ta

**What's your name?**
*Kaip jūsų vardas?* kaip *yoo*·soo *vahr*·dahs

**My name is ...**
*Mano vardas yra ...* mah·naw *vahr*·dahs ee·*rah* ...

**Do you speak English?**
*Ar kalbate angliškai?* ahr *kahl*·bah·ta *ahn*·glish·kai

**I don't understand.**
*Aš jūsų nesuprantu.* ahsh *yoo*·soo na·su·prahn·*tu*

## Accommodation

**I'm looking for a hotel.**
*Aš ieškau viešbučio.* ahsh *yeash*·kow *veash*·bu·chaw

**I'd like a single/double room.**
*Aš noriu vienviečio/ dviviečio kambario.* ahsh *nawr*·yu veahn·*veah*·chaw/ dvi·*veah*·chaw *kahm*·bahr·yaw

**How much is it per night, per person?**
*Kiek kainuoja apsistoti nakčiai asmeniui?* keahk kai·*nuaw*·yah ahp·si·staw·ti nahk·chay ahs·man·wi

## Directions

**How do I get to the ...?**
*Prašom pasakyti, kaip patekti į ...?* *prah*·shom pah·sah·*kee*·ti kaip pah·*tak*·ti i ...

**Is it far?**
*Ar toli?* — ahr taw·*li*

**Can you show me (on the map)?**
*Galėtumėt man parodyti (žemėlapyje)?* — gah·*leh*·tu·met mahn pah·*raw*·dee·ti (zham·*eh*·lah·pee·ya)

## Eating & Drinking

**A table for ..., please.**
*Stalą ..., prašau.* — *stah*·lah ... prah·*show*

**Can I see the menu, please?**
*Ar galėčiau gauti meniu prašau?* — ahr gah·*leh*·chow gow·ti man·*yew* prah·*show*

**Do you have the menu in English?**
*Ar jūs turite meniu angliškai?* — ahr yoos *tu*·ri·ta man·*yew* *ahn*·glish·kai

**I'd like to try that.**
*Aš norėčau išbandyti to.* — ahsh naw·*reh*·chow ish·bahn·*dee*·ti taw

**I don't eat (meat).**
*Aš nevalgau (mėsiško).* — ahsh na·*vahl*·gow (*meh*·sish·kaw)

## Emergencies

| | | |
|---|---|---|
| **Help!** | *Gelbėkite!* | *gal*·beh·ki·te |
| **Go away!** | *Eik šalin!* | ayk shah·*lin* |
| **I'm ill.** | *Aš sergu.* | ahsh sar·*gu* |

**Call a doctor!**
*Iššaukite gydytoją!* — ish·*show*·ki·ta gee·dee·taw·yah

**I'm lost.**
*Aš paklydusi/paklydęs. (m/f)* — ahsh pah·*klee*·du·si/ pah·*klee*·das

## Shopping & Services

**What time does it open/close?**
*Kelintą valandą atsidaro/užsidaro?* — kal·*in*·tah *vah*·lahn·dah aht·si·*dah*·raw/ uzh·si·*dah*·raw

**How much is it?**
*Kiek kainuoja?* — keahk kai·*nu* aw·yah

| | | |
|---|---|---|
| **I'm looking for the ...** | *Aš ieškau ...* | ahsh *yeahsh*·kow ... |
| **bank** | *bankas* | *ban*·kas |
| **chemist/pharmacy** | *vaistinė* | *vais*·ti·neh |
| **currency exchange** | *valiutos* | vah·*lyu*·taws |
| **market** | *turgus* | *tur*·gows |
| **police** | *policijos* | paw·*lit*·si·yaws |
| **post office** | *pašto* | *pahsh*·taw |
| **public toilet** | *tualeto* | tu ah·*lat*·aw |

**SIGNS – LITHUANIAN**

| | |
|---|---|
| **Įėjimas** | Entrance |
| **Išėjimas** | Exit |
| **Atidara** | Open |
| **Uždara** | Closed |
| **Dėmesio** | Caution |
| **Patogumai** | Public Toilets |

## Time & Numbers

**What time is it?**
*Kiek dabar laiko?* — keahk dah·bahr *lai*·kaw

**It's two o'clock.**
*Dabar antra valanda.* — dah·*bahr* ahn·*trah* vah·lahn·*dah*

| | | |
|---|---|---|
| **morning** | *rytas* | ree·tahs |
| **afternoon** | *popietė* | *paw*·peah·teh |
| **night** | *naktis* | nahk·*tis* |

| | | |
|---|---|---|
| **1** | *vienas* | *veah*·nahs |
| **2** | *du* | du |
| **3** | *trys* | trees |
| **4** | *keturi* | kat·u·*ri* |
| **5** | *penki* | pan·*ki* |
| **6** | *šeši* | shash·*i* |
| **7** | *septyni* | sap·tee·*ni* |
| **8** | *aštuoni* | ahsh·tu aw·*ni* |
| **9** | *devyni* | dav·ee·*ni* |
| **10** | *dešimt* | *dash*·imt |

## Transport

| | | |
|---|---|---|
| **Where's the ...?** | *Kur yra ...?* | kur ee·*rah* ... |
| **airport** | *oro uostas* | aw·raw u *aws*·tahs |
| **bus stop** | *autobuso stotelė* | ow·*taw*·bu·saw staw·*ta*·leh |
| **ferry terminal** | *kelto stotis* | *kal*·taw staw·*tis* |
| **train station** | *geležin-kelio stotis* | gal·azh·*in*·kal·yaw staw·*tis* |

| | | |
|---|---|---|
| **I'd like (a) ... ticket.** | *Aš norėčiau bilietą į ...* | ahsh naw·*reh*·chow *bil*·eah·tah i ... |
| **one-way** | *vieną galą* | veah·nah *gah*·lah |
| **return** | *abu galus* | ah·*bu* gah·*lus* |

# GLOSSARY

Also see the individual destination chapters for some useful words and phrases dealing with food and dining. This glossary is a list of Estonian (Est), Finnish (Fin), German (Ger), Latvian (Lat), Lithuanian (Lith) and Russian (Rus) terms you might come across during your time in the Baltic.

**aikštė** (Lith) – square
**aludė** (Lith) – beer cellar
**alus** (Lat, Lith) – beer
**apteek** (Est) – pharmacy
**aptieka** (Lat) – pharmacy
**Aukštaitija** (Lith) – Upper Lithuania
**autobusų stotis** (Lith) – bus station
**autoosta** (Lat) – bus station
**autostrāde** (Lat) – highway

**baar** (Est) – pub, bar
**babushka** (Rus) – grandmother/pensioner in headscarf
**bagāžas glabātava** (Lat) – left-luggage room
**bagažinė** (Lith) – left-luggage room
**bāka** (Lat) – lighthouse
**Baltic glint** – raised limestone bank stretching from Sweden across the north of Estonia into Russia
**baras** (Lith) – pub, bar
**baznīca** (Lat) – church
**bažnyčia** (Lith) – church
**brokastis** (Lat) – breakfast
**bulvāris** (Lat) – boulevard
**bussijaam** (Est) – bus station

**ceļš** (Lat) – railway track, road
**centras** (Lith) – town centre
**centrs** (Lat) – town centre
**Chudkoye Ozero** (Rus) – Lake Peipsi
**Courland** – Kurzeme

**daina** (Lat) – short, poetic oral song or verse
**datorsalons** (Lat) – internet cafe
**dzintars** (Lat) – amber

**ebreji** (Lat) – Jews
**Eesti** (Est) – Estonia
**ežeras** (Lith) – lake
**ezerpils** (Lat) – lake fortress
**ezers** (Lat) – lake

**gatvė** (Lith) – street
**geležinkelio stotis** (Lith) – train station
**gintarinė/gintarinis** (Lith) – amber

**hinnakiri** (Est) – price list
**hommikusöök** (Est) – breakfast

**iela** (Lat) – street
**iezis** (Lat) – rock
**informacija** (Lith) – information centre
**internetas kavinė** (Lith) – internet cafe
**interneti kohvik** (Est) – internet cafe

**järv** (Est) – lake

**kafejnīca** (Lat) – cafe
**kalnas** (Lith) – mountain, hill
**kalns** (Lat) – mountain, hill
**kämping** (Est) – campsite
**katedra** (Lith) – cathedral
**katedrāle** (Lat) – cathedral
**kauplus** (Est) – shop
**kavinė** (Lith) – cafe
**kelias** (Lith) – road
**kempingas** (Lith) – campsite
**kempings** (Lat) – campsite
**kesklinn** (Est) – town centre
**kino** (Est, Lat, Lith) – cinema
**kirik** (Est) – church
**kohvik** (Est) – cafe
**kõrts** (Est) – inn, tavern
**krogs** (Lat) – pub, bar
**Kurshskaya Kosa** (Rus) – Curonian Spit
**Kursių marios** (Lith) – Curonian Lagoon
**Kursių Nerija** (Lith) – Curonian Spit

**laht** (Est) – bay
**Latvija** (Lat) – Latvia
**laukums** (Lat) – square
**lennujaam** (Est) – airport
**lidosta** (Lat) – airport
**Lietuva** (Lith) – Lithuania
**looduskaitseala** (Est) – nature/landscape reserve
**loss** (Est) – castle, palace

**maantee** (Est) – highway
**mägi** (Est) – mountain, hill
**Metsavennad** (Est) – Forest Brothers resistance movement
**midus** (Lith) – mead
**mõis** (Est) – manor
**muuseum** (Est) – museum
**muzejs** (Lat) – museum
**muziejus** (Lith) – museum

**nacionālais parks** (Lat) – national park

**õlu** (Est) – beer
**oro uostas** (Lith) – airport
**osta** (Lat) – port/harbour

**pakihoid** (Est) – left luggage
**parkas** (Lith) – park
**parks** (Lat) – park
**paštas** (Lith) – post office
**pasts** (Lat) – post office
**Peko** (Est) – pagan god of fertility in Seto traditions
**perkėla** (Lith) – port
**piletid** (Est) – tickets
**pilies** (Lith) – castle
**pils** (Lat) – castle, palace
**pilsdrupas** (Lat) – knights' castle
**pilskalns** (Lat) – castle mound
**plats** (Est) – square
**plentas** (Lith) – highway, motorway
**pliažas** (Lith) – beach
**pludmale** (Lat) – beach
**pood** (Est) – shop
**postkontor** (Est) – post office
**prospektas** (Lith) – boulevard
**prospekts** (Lat) – boulevard

**pubi** (Est) – pub
**puhketalu** (Est) – tourist farm (ie a farm offering accommodation)
**puiestee** (Est) – boulevard
**pusryčiai** (Lith) – breakfast

**raekoda** (Est) – town/city hall
**rahvuspark** (Est) – national park
**rand** (Est) – beach
**rātsnams** (Lat) – town hall
**raudteejaam** (Est) – train station
**Reval** (Ger) – old German name for Tallinn
**rezervāts** (Lat) – reserve
**Riigikogu** (Est) – Parliament
**rotušė** (Lith) – town/city hall
**rūmai** (Lith) – palace

**saar** (Est) – island
**sadam** (Est) – harbour/port
**Saeima** (Lat) – Parliament
**Seimas** (Lith) – Parliament
**Seto** (Est) – ethnic group of mixed Estonian and Orthodox traditions
**Setomaa** (Est) – territory of the Seto people in southeastern Estonia and Russia
**sild** (Est) – bridge
**smuklė** (Lith) – tavern
**stacija** (Lat) – station
**švyturys** (Lith) – lighthouse

**Tallinna** (Fin) – Tallinn
**talu** (Est) – farm
**tänav** (Est) – street
**tee** (Est) – road
**tiltas** (Lith) – bridge
**tilts** (Lat) – bridge
**tirgus** (Lat) – market
**toomkirik** (Est) – cathedral
**trahter** (Est) – tavern
**tuletorn** (Est) – lighthouse
**turg** (Est) – market
**turgus** (Lith) – market
**turismitalu** (Est) – tourist farm (ie a farm offering accommodation)

**vanalinn** (Est) – old town
**vaistinė** (Lith) – pharmacy
**väljak** (Est) – square
**Vecrīga** (Lat) – Old Rīga
**via Baltica** – international road (the E67) linking Estonia with Poland

**žydų** (Lith) – Jews

# Behind the Scenes

## SEND US YOUR FEEDBACK

We love to hear from travellers – your comments keep us on our toes and help make our books better. Our well-travelled team reads every word on what you loved or loathed about this book. Although we cannot reply individually to your submissions, we always guarantee that your feedback goes straight to the appropriate authors, in time for the next edition. Each person who sends us information is thanked in the next edition – the most useful submissions are rewarded with a selection of digital PDF chapters.

Visit **lonelyplanet.com/contact** to submit your updates and suggestions or to ask for help. Our award-winning website also features inspirational travel stories, news and discussions.

Note: We may edit, reproduce and incorporate your comments in Lonely Planet products such as guidebooks, websites and digital products, so let us know if you don't want your comments reproduced or your name acknowledged. For a copy of our privacy policy visit lonelyplanet.com/privacy.

## OUR READERS

**Many thanks to the travellers who used the last edition and wrote to us with helpful hints, useful advice and interesting anecdotes:**

Andreas Hanzl, Bob Pearson, David Abulafia, Elisabeth Tacke, Filips Baumanis, Gilberto Falcon, Harry Kriewaldt, Hilary Hodge, Julie K Rose, Kate Walker, Katharine Ryan-Murray, Keith Ruffles, Lynne Williams, Marlies Van Hoef, Peter Calingaert, Péter Géczi, Peter Lowthian, Sabrina Wagner, Sain Alizada, Sheila Miller

## WRITER THANKS

### Anna Kaminski

Thank you to Doc and Sandie for entrusting me with Lithuania, Kaliningrad and the Baltics' top-level content, and to my fellow scribes Ryan and Hugh for their invaluable input. A huge thank you to everyone who helped me en route, including the good people of In Your Pocket, super-helpful staff in most visitor centres, Emalualis (Vilnius), Sinte (Ignalina), Gintaras and Viktor (Kaunas), Valentina (Kaliningrad), Lina and Mykolas (Curonian Spit), and Tomas in Druskininkai.

### Hugh McNaughtan

My gratitude goes out to all who made this gig possible and helped me get to grips with Estonia: my editor Sandie; Eeva, Katrin and Keneth; and most especially Tas, Maise and Willa, for allowing me to disappear for five weeks.

### Ryan Ver Berkmoes

Thanks to the extraordinary Juris Berže for his insights. Thanks also to Laila Abena and Anna Blaua as well as Elīna Pastare, Anna Burlakova, Gita Memmeņa, Kristiāna Kauliņa, Zane Krūmiņa, Kristine Štosa, Arta Celma and Dace Oberšate-Veisa. Much gratitude to Branislava Vladisavljevic, who originally pegged me for this project, which meant I could spend days lost in the wild and wonderful Latvia coast. And loving joy to Alexis Ver Berkmoes, who puts the potato in my pancakes *(kartupeļu pankūkas)*.

## ACKNOWLEDGEMENTS

Climate map data adapted from Peel MC, Finlayson BL & McMahon TA (2007) 'Updated World Map of the Köppen-Geiger Climate Classification', *Hydrology and Earth System Sciences*, 11, 1633–44.

Cover photograph: Trakai Castle, Lithuania; A Aleksandravicius/Shutterstock ©

# THIS BOOK

This 8th edition of Lonely Planet's *Estonia, Latvia & Lithuania* guidebook was researched and written by Anna Kaminski, Hugh McNaughtan and Ryan Ver Berkmoes. The previous edition was written by Peter Dragicevich, Hugh McNaughtan and Leonid Ragozin. This guidebook was produced by the following:

**Senior Product Editor** Sandie Kestell

**Regional Senior Cartographer** Valentina Kremenchutskaya

**Product Editor** Carolyn Boicos

**Book Designer** Jessica Rose

**Assisting Editors** Ronan Abayawickrema, Janet Austin, Andrea Dobbin, Karen Henderson, Gabby Innes, Kellie Langdon, Lauren O'Connell, Gabrielle Stefanos, Simon Williamson

**Cover Researcher** Brendan Dempsey-Spencer

**Thanks to** William Allen, Imogen Bannister, Liz Heynes, Catherine Naghten, Charlotte Orr, Rachel Rawling, Kira Tverskaya

# Index

## ABBREVIATIONS

Est - Estonia
Hel - Helsinki
Kal - Kaliningrad
Lat - Latvia
Lith - Lithuania

## A



## B



## C

## D

## N

Map Pages **000**
Photo Pages **000**

Map Pages **000**
Photo Pages **000**

# Map Legend

## Sights

- Beach
- Bird Sanctuary
- Buddhist
- Castle/Palace
- Christian
- Confucian
- Hindu
- Islamic
- Jain
- Jewish
- Monument
- Museum/Gallery/Historic Building
- Ruin
- Shinto
- Sikh
- Taoist
- Winery/Vineyard
- Zoo/Wildlife Sanctuary
- Other Sight

## Activities, Courses & Tours

- Bodysurfing
- Diving
- Canoeing/Kayaking
- Course/Tour
- Sento Hot Baths/Onsen
- Skiing
- Snorkelling
- Surfing
- Swimming/Pool
- Walking
- Windsurfing
- Other Activity

## Sleeping

- Sleeping
- Camping
- Hut/Shelter

## Eating

- Eating

## Drinking & Nightlife

- Drinking & Nightlife
- Cafe

## Entertainment

- Entertainment

## Shopping

- Shopping

## Information

- Bank
- Embassy/Consulate
- Hospital/Medical
- Internet
- Police
- Post Office
- Telephone
- Toilet
- Tourist Information
- Other Information

## Geographic

- Beach
- Gate
- Hut/Shelter
- Lighthouse
- Lookout
- Mountain/Volcano
- Oasis
- Park
- Pass
- Picnic Area
- Waterfall

## Population

- Capital (National)
- Capital (State/Province)
- City/Large Town
- Town/Village

## Transport

- Airport
- Border crossing
- Bus
- Cable car/Funicular
- Cycling
- Ferry
- Metro station
- Monorail
- Parking
- Petrol station
- S-Bahn/Subway station
- Taxi
- T-bane/Tunnelbana station
- Train station/Railway
- Tram
- U-Bahn/Underground station
- Other Transport

## Routes

- Tollway
- Freeway
- Primary
- Secondary
- Tertiary
- Lane
- Unsealed road
- Road under construction
- Plaza/Mall
- Steps
- Tunnel
- Pedestrian overpass
- Walking Tour
- Walking Tour detour
- Path/Walking Trail

## Boundaries

- International
- State/Province
- Disputed
- Regional/Suburb
- Marine Park
- Cliff
- Wall

## Hydrography

- River, Creek
- Intermittent River
- Canal
- Water
- Dry/Salt/Intermittent Lake
- Reef

## Areas

- Airport/Runway
- Beach/Desert
- Cemetery (Christian)
- Cemetery (Other)
- Glacier
- Mudflat
- Park/Forest
- Sight (Building)
- Sportsground
- Swamp/Mangrove

*Note: Not all symbols displayed above appear on the maps in this book*

# OUR STORY

A beat-up old car, a few dollars in the pocket and a sense of adventure. In 1972 that's all Tony and Maureen Wheeler needed for the trip of a lifetime – across Europe and Asia overland to Australia. It took several months, and at the end – broke but inspired – they sat at their kitchen table writing and stapling together their first travel guide, *Across Asia on the Cheap*. Within a week they'd sold 1500 copies. Lonely Planet was born.

Today, Lonely Planet has offices in Franklin, London, Melbourne, Oakland, Dublin, Beijing and Delhi, with more than 600 staff and writers. We share Tony's belief that 'a great guidebook should do three things: inform, educate and amuse'.

# OUR WRITERS

**Anna Kaminski**

Lithuania, Kaliningrad Excursion Originally from the Soviet Union, Anna grew up in Cambridge, UK. She graduated from the University of Warwick with a degree in Comparative American Studies, a background in the history, culture and literature of the Americas and the Caribbean, and an enduring love of Latin America. Her restless wanderings led her to settle briefly in Oaxaca and Bangkok and her flirtation with criminal law saw her volunteering as a lawyer's assistant in the courts, ghettos and prisons of Kingston, Jamaica. Anna has contributed to almost 30 Lonely Planet titles. For this guide, Anna also wrote the Plan Your Trip and Survival Guide chapters.

**Hugh McNaughtan**

Estonia, Helsinki Excursion A former lecturer and restaurant critic from Melbourne, Australia, Hugh now uses London as a launching pad for forays into the Baltics and Eastern Europe. Scouring every inch of Estonia over the endless days of midsummer was a dream assignment.

**Ryan Ver Berkmoes**

Latvia Ryan has written more than 110 guidebooks for Lonely Planet. He grew up in Santa Cruz, California, which he left at age 17 for college in the Midwest, where he first discovered snow. All joy of this novelty soon wore off. Since then he has been travelling the world, both for pleasure and for work – which are often indistinguishable. He has covered everything from wars to bars. He definitely prefers the latter. Ryan calls New York City home. Read more at ryanverberkmoes.com and at @ryanvb.

**Published by Lonely Planet Global Limited**
CRN 554153
8th edition – Jun 2020
ISBN 978 1 78657 598 2

10 9 8 7 6 5 4 3 2 1
Printed in Singapore

TEAR OUT, FOLD UP & KEEP WITH YOUR PASSPORT

# JUST LANDED
## • RĪGA •
*Easy steps from airport to city*

## Rīga International Airport

### Get Connected

**Free airport wi-fi** Connect to 'RIX Free WiFi' for unlimited access.

**Charging stations** There are outlets for charging devices around the terminal, particularly among the cafes in sector B.

**SIM card** You can purchase prepaid SIM cards at the Narvesen convenience stores (open to align with regular flight schedules) on both floors of the terminal. No ID or registration is required.

### Money

Around €180 per person should cover transport and meals for a few days.

**Credit cards** Credit cards are widely accepted.

**ATMs** There are plenty of ATMs (24hr) on both levels of the terminal.

**Currency exchange** Eurex Capital (open to align with flight schedules) is located in Arrivals sector C and E, and there is an Exchange Express counter (9am to midnight) in Arrivals sector E.

### Helpful Phrases

There are English-language signs and English is a common second language, but here are a few phrases if you get stuck.

| | | |
|---|---|---|
| **Do you speak English?** | Vai jūs runājat angliski? | vai yoos *run*·ah·yuht *uhn*·gli·ski |
| **I don't understand.** | Es nesaprotu. | es *ne*·suh·praw·tu |
| **Where are the toilets?** | Kur ir tualetes? | kur ir *tu*·uh·le·tes |
| **What time (is it)?** | Cik (ir) pulkstenis? | tsik (ir) *pulk*·sten·is |
| **Where's the bus station?** | Kur atrodas autoosta? | kur uht·*raw*·duhs *ow*·to·aws·tuh |
| **I want to buy a ... ticket.** | Es vēlos nopirkt ... biļeti. | es *vaa*·laws *naw*·pirkt ... *bi*·lyet·i |
| **one-way** | vien-virziena | *vean*·virz·ean·uh |
| **return** | turp-atpakaļ | turp·*uht*·puh·kuhly |
| **How much is it?** | Cik tas maksā? | tsik tuhs *muhk*·sah |
| **I'm lost.** | Es esmu apmaldījies/apmaldījusies. (m/f) | es *as*·mu *uhp*·muhl·dee·yeas/*uhp*·muhl·dee·yu·seas |

Find great travel tips at **www.lonelyplanet.com**

# BEST TRANSPORT FROM AIRPORT TO CITY CENTRE

Take me to this address:

..............................................................

## Bus

**25min €2**

Bus 22 and minibus 322 run to the Rīga city centre at least every 30 minutes from 5.45am to 12.10am (11.50pm on weekends), with stops at the national library, Old Town, central bus station and central railway station. Tickets can be purchased on board for €2 or for €1.15 from the 'Welcome to Rīga' information desk (in Arrivals sector E), in retail shops on level 1, or from the vending machine at the bus stop, which is 300m from the terminal exit, immediately beyond the car park (have some cash available for tickets). Follow the signs for public transport.

## Taxi

**20min around €15**

The taxi rank is immediately outside the terminal exit. Use the queue with cabs from the reliable Baltic Taxi and Red Cab. Costs vary so check with the driver before you hire. Credit cards are accepted.

## Ride-share

**20min cost varies**

The Bolt and Yandex ride-share apps are commonly used in Rīga and can be considerably cheaper than taxis. The apps will indicate where to go for pick-up.

## Getting Around Rīga

**Bicycle**

Pedal around town with Sixt Bicycle Rental (www.sixtbicycle.lv). It has self-service stands across Rīga and the first 30 minutes are free.

**Public Transport**

The centre of Rīga is too compact for most visitors to bother with public transport, but trams, buses or trolleybuses are essential if you're venturing a little further out. For routes and schedules, consult www.rigassatiksme.lv. Fares are paid by e-tickets called e-talons. You can buy and refill them at Narvessen convenience stores and vending machines on board newer trams.